D1690183

UNTOUCHABLES

ACKNOWLEDGEMENTS

The National Union of Journalists unflinchingly backed us against Scotland Yard and *The Guardian*. We would like to thank general secretary Jeremy Dear, editor Tim Gopsill, legal adviser Clare Kirby and Steve Wilkinson for their defence of press freedom.

Special thanks must also go to our astute lawyers Louis Charalambous and Robin Shaw; to our agent Leslie Gardiner for her faith and negotiating skills; to Melissa Jones for her patience and editing of early drafts, and to our publisher Bill Campbell, who stood by this difficult investigation to its natural conclusion.

Along the way a number of colleagues have given us advice, solidarity and work. Thank you Steve Boulton, David Connett, the real Michael Gillard, Jo Anne Goodwin, Dean Nelson, Mark Olden, Adam Porter, Ian Reeves, Geoff Seed, Dave Spurdens and Gibby Zobel. Thanks also to Arthur's in Kingsland Road.

Of course many people on both sides of the thin blue line have shared their files and often painful experiences. Some cannot be named. But they all deserve our appreciation and a lot more.

As does Marcello Minale for the inspired cover, Ewan and Rosanne Flynn for research and indexing, and all at Mainstream, especially Graeme, Claire and Lizzie.

Regrettably, there was a long list of individuals who refused to be interviewed. Among them are: retired Met Commissioner Lord Paul Condon; current Met Commissioner Sir John Stevens; retired DACs John Grieve and Roy Clark; Commander Brian Moore; DCSs Chris Jarratt and John Coles; D/Supt Dave Woods and reporter Graeme McLagan.

This book is dedicated to the memory of our friend Paul Foot and to the victims of police crimes and government intransigence, whom he did so much to help.

Dirty cops, bent justice and racism in Scotland Yard

by Michael Gillard and Laurie Flynn

UN TOUCH ABLES

CUTTING EDGE
EDINBURGH AND LONDON

Copyright © Michael Gillard and Laurie Flynn, 2004
All rights reserved
The moral rights of the authors have been asserted

First published in Great Britain in 2004 by
CUTTING EDGE PRESS
7 Albany Street
Edinburgh EH1 3UG

ISBN 1 903813 04 2

No part of this book may be reproduced or transmitted in any form or by any means without written permission from the publisher, except by a reviewer who wishes to quote brief passages in connection with a review written for insertion in a newspaper, magazine or broadcast

A catalogue record for this book
is available from the British Library

Typeset in Baskerville
Printed and bound in Great Britain by
Antony Rowe Ltd, Chippenham, Wiltshire

CONTENTS

Preface: Integrity is Negotiable ... 13

PART ONE: THE DARK SIDE
1   Undercover 599 – Michael's Story ... 21

PART TWO: THE GHOSTS OF THE GHOST SQUAD
2   Noble Cause Corruption ... 49
3   The Ghost Squad ... 59
4   The Ghost of Brinks Mat – A Firm Within a Firm ... 73
5   The Ghost of Brinks Mat – A *Liaison Dangereuse* ... 86
6   Death of an Expert Witness ... 99
7   The Suicide Club ... 110
8   The Ghost of David Norris ... 127
9   "What? What? Nigger!" ... 149
10 A Ragamuffin Bunch ... 165

PART THREE: THE SUPERGRASS FARCE
11 Geoff Brennan – Double Agent Supergrass ... 193
12 Hector the Selecta' – Rude Boy Supergrass ... 224
13 Ghostbusted ... 250
14 The Sleaze Machine ... 273

15	Bad Blood	284
16	Manipulating Lawrence	302
17	The Electricians Plug a Leak	310
18	The Selecta' Returns, Police Babylon Burns	319
19	Fruit of a Poisoned Tree	343
20	The Fall of the Ginger Giant	359

PART FOUR: DOUBLE STANDARDS

21	The Butcher, the Baker, the Undertaker and his Son	383
22	Secret Justice	400
23	A Lurking Doubt	415
24	W.O.G.S.	433
25	. . . and the Beating Goes On and On	442
26	In-House	455
27	"We Are Subjects Not Citizens"	485

PART FIVE: A SILENT COUP

| 28 | Watchdogged | 501 |

| Notes | 515 |
| Index | 539 |

ACRONYMS

ACC	Anti-Corruption Command (part of the DPS)
ACG	Anti-Corruption Group (formerly CIB3)
ACPO	Association of Chief Police Officers
BPA	Black Police Association
CAIU	Civil Actions Investigations Unit (part of the DPS)
CCRC	Criminal Cases Review Commission
CIB1/2	Complaints Investigation Bureau
CIB3	Complaints Investigation Bureau 3 aka The Untouchables
CIBIC	Complaints Investigation Bureau Intelligence Cell (formerly the Ghost Squad)
CO24	Racial and Violent Crimes Task Force
CPS	Crown Prosecution Service
CRA	Crime Reporters Association
DAC	Deputy Assistant Commissioner
DC	Detective Constable
DCI	Detective Chief Inspector
DCS	Detective Chief Superintendent
DEA	US Drug Enforcement Administration
DI	Detective Inspector
DPP	Director of Public Prosecutions
DPS	Directorate of Professional Standards
DS	Detective Sergeant
D/Supt	Detective Superintendent
EDM	Early Day Motion (in the House of Commons)

UNTOUCHABLES

Esda	electrostatic document analysis
FBI	US Federal Bureau of Investigation
FRU	Field Research Unit
HCDA	The Hackney Community Defence Association
HMIC	Her Majesty's Inspectorate of Constabulary
IAG	Independent Advisory Group
IDG	Intelligence Development Group (formerly CIBIC)
IIC	Internal Investigations Command (formerly CIB1/2)
IPCC	Independent Police Complaints Commission (formerly the PCA)
MPA	Metropolitan Police Authority
MPS	Metropolitan Police Service
NBPA	National Black Police Association
NCIS	National Criminal Intelligence Service
NCS	National Crime Squad (formerly the Regional Crime Squads)
PACE	Police & Criminal Evidence Act 1984
PCA	Police Complaints Authority (formerly the PCB)
PCB	Police Complaints Board
PII	Public Interest Immunity certificate
PNC	Police National Computer
QPM	Queen's Police Medal
RJW	Russell, Jones and Walker Solicitors
RUC	Royal Ulster Constabulary
SCP	Service Confidence Policy (The Yard blacklist)
SERCS	South East Regional Crime Squad
SFO	Serious Fraud Office
SIS	Special Intelligence Section (part of SO11)
SO	Special Operations (Scotland Yard)
SO10	Undercover unit
SO11	Directorate of Criminal Intelligence
SO13	Anti-Terrorist Branch
UC	Undercover officer from SO10
UDA	Ulster Defence Association
WOGS	The Walthamstow Overseas Geographical Society
WPU	Witness Protection Unit (part of ACG)

CAST OF CHARACTERS

THE UNTOUCHABLES
Paul Condon	Commissioner (1993–2000)
John Stevens	Commissioner (2000–)
	Deputy Commissioner (1998–2000)
Brian Hayes	Deputy Commissioner (1993–1998)
Ian Blair	Deputy Commissioner (1998–)
Dave Veness	Assistant Commissioner
Ian Johnston	Assistant Commissioner
Mike Todd	Assistant Commissioner
John Grieve	Deputy Assistant Commissioner
Roy Clark	Deputy Assistant Commissioner
Bill Griffiths	Deputy Assistant Commissioner
Roger Gaspar	Detective chief superintendent (Ghost Squad)
Dave Bailey	Detective superintendent (Ghost Squad)
Dave Woods	Detective chief inspector (Ghost Squad)
Andy Hayman	Commander (CIB3/CIBIC 1999–2002)
Graham James	Commander (Discipline & Complaints)
Ian Quinn	Commander (CIB2)
Ian Russell	Commander (replaced Quinn)
Dave Wood	Detective chief superintendent (CIB3, replaced Gaspar)
Chris Jarratt	Detective superintendent (CIBIC, replaced Woods)
Brian Moore	Detective superintendent (CIB3 Operation Ethiopia)
John Coles	Detective superintendent (CIB3 Operation Cornwall)
John Yates	Detective superintendent (CIB3 Operation Russia)

UNTOUCHABLES

Barry Norman	Detective superintendent (CIB3 Operation Helios)
Martin Bridger	Detective chief inspector (CIB3 Operation Ethiopia)
Bob Berger	Detective chief inspector (CIBIC)
Chris McHaffey	Detective chief inspector (CIB3)
Jill McTigue	Detective chief inspector (CIB3)
Dave Pennant	Detective chief inspector (CIB3)
Simon Cousins	Detective chief inspector (CIB3 Witness Protection Unit)
Shaun Sawyer	Detective chief Superintendent, (replaced Hayman)
Bob Quick	Detective chief superintendent (CIB3, replaced Wood)
Barbara Wilding	Deputy Assistant Commissioner (replaced Sawyer 2004)
Steve Roberts	Deputy Assistant Commissioner (replaced Wilding 2004)
David Zinzan	Detective Superintendent (IDG, formerly CIBIC)
Tony Fuller	Detective Superintendent (IDG, replaced Zinzan)
Steve Foster	Detective chief inspector (IDG)
Maxine de Brunner	Detective Superintendent (ACG, formerly CIB3)
Jack Kelly	Detective Inspector
Steve Bazzoni	Detective Inspector
Adrian Harper	Detective Inspector
Maggie Palmer	Detective Inspector
Peter Ward	Detective Inspector
Mark Holmes	Detective Inspector

CRIMINAL SUPERGRASSES
Geoff Brennan
Evelyn Fleckney
Hector Harvey
Michael Michael
Maurice O'Mahoney
Richard Price
Jason Procter
Ashley Sansom
Steve Warner

POLICE SUPERGRASSES
Kevin Garner
Duncan Hanrahan
Terry McGuinness
Neil Putnam
Kalaish Sawnhney (Customs)

CAST OF CHARACTERS

CRIMINALS
The Adams crime family (north London)
The Arif crime family (south-east London)
Henry Burgess
Kevin Cressey
John 'Goldfinger' Fleming
Ray Gray
Micky Green
Dean Henry
Jimmy Karagozlu
Bob Kean
John 'Little Legs' Lloyd
Chris McCormack
Clifford Norris
Kenny Noye
Stephen Raymond
Joey Simms
Michael Taverner
Gary Ward
Curtis Warren
'Tall' Ted Williams
Carl Wood
Brian Wright

CIVILIANS TARGETED BY THE UNTOUCHABLES
Les Brown (solicitor)
Debbie Cahill (CPS)
Jon Rees (private investigator)

EX-COPS TARGETED BY THE UNTOUCHABLES
DC Geoff Baldwin (private investigator)
DS John Davidson (private investigator)
DS Sid Fillery (private investigator)
DC Nigel Grayston (private investigator)
DS Keith Green
DS Bob Harrington (private investigator)
DC Martin King (private investigator)
DI Alec Leighton (private investigator)
DI Keith Pedder (private investigator)

COPS TARGETED BY THE UNTOUCHABLES
DS John Bull
DC Mick Carroll
DC Chris Carter
DC Michael Charman
DC Robert Clark
DC Declan Costello
D/Supt Ali Dizaei

UNTOUCHABLES

DC John Donald
DC Chris Drury
DC Colin Evans
DC Paul Goscomb
DS Len Guerard
DS Eamonn Harris
DC Dave Howells
DS Paul Kelly
DC Tom Kingston
DS Gordon Livingstone
DI Fred May
DC Jeff May
DS Denis Miller
DC John Moore
DC Martin Morgan
DI Tim Norris
DC Mark Norton
DS Terry O'Connell
DI George Raison
DI John Redgrave
DC Tom Reynolds
DC Ian Saunders
DC Paul Smith
DC Dave Thompson
DS Barry Toombs
DS Gurpal Virdi
DC Austin Warnes

Preface

INTEGRITY IS NEGOTIABLE

We pay £2 billion annually – a quarter of the entire UK police budget – for 30,000 Metropolitan police officers to serve and protect us from the bad guys outside the police station. But throughout its 175-year history, Scotland Yard has never been accountable to a fully independent body for misconduct by the bad guys inside the police station. It has always investigated itself. Police commissioner Sir John Stevens has a catchphrase – "Integrity is non-negotiable". He says it is the beacon that guides his anti-corruption squad of detectives who from time to time and on our behalf secretly pluck rotten apples from the Yard's orchard.

In late 1993 an unprecedented anti-corruption initiative was launched. A Ghost Squad of trusted undercover officers was secretly set up to examine how exposed the Yard was to corruption. The commissioner's shadowy unit operated for the first five years – spying and squirrelling away compromising information – without any legal oversight or democratic accountability.

In January 1998, Scotland Yard went public with a second five-year phase of its anti-corruption initiative. The well-spun media offensive guaranteed banner headlines and paragraphs of praise from crime correspondents, who announced the arrival of a new "elite" group of corruption-busting detectives, CIB3, also dubbed The Untouchables. The commissioner pledged that his beyond-reproach officers would leave no stone unturned in their "relentless" crusade to bring bent colleagues to justice. The Yard's soul would be "purged". No Masonic bond, no seniority in rank would protect the corrupt, dishonest and unethical from their heat. Not quite.

UNTOUCHABLES

The Untouchables had borrowed their name from a fictional American television series based on the real-life exploits of Eliot Ness and his band of dedicated men who set out to break Al Capone's corrupt stranglehold on 1930s Chicago. Ness couldn't trust the local police department because the Mob boss had bought it off. So his gangbusters came from other walks of life. In contrast, the Met's Untouchables – some 200 officers – were drawn from the very pool of detectives they were supposed to be investigating. As one insider quipped, "It's like putting Dracula in charge of the blood bank."

This book is an integrity test on Scotland Yard and its Untouchables. It is the result of a five-year investigation into how the most powerful police force in the UK claims it has tackled corruption and racism within its own ranks. Our investigation has produced an enormous amount of evidence, from witnesses and documents to transcripts of bugged conversations. We have conducted hundreds of interviews with anti-corruption officers, serving detectives, suspended ones, lawyers, community activists, judges, politicians, criminals, informants and supergrasses. You will not find any celebrity gangsters in these pages. Many of the people quoted have never spoken out before, let alone on the record.

In putting *Untouchables* together we waded beneath the paving stones of London in a sewer where robbers, fraudsters and drug dealers embrace bent cops in a lethal tango of corruption often danced with dark humour. We emerged with conclusive evidence that the anti-corruption initiative was not a no-hiding-place blitz on the bent. It is a phoney war, which by fostering the illusion of ruthless efficiency and success seeks to ensure Scotland Yard continues to police itself and protect its darkest recesses from independent scrutiny.

In 1997, the commissioner informed Parliament that there were up to 250 bent cops in his force. By 2004 some 200 corrupt officers are still unaccounted for and still dealing with an unsuspecting public. Only a handful of corrupt officers have been successfully prosecuted. A small number are on a secret blacklist of defective detectives who've lost the commissioner's trust. However they are not suspended and continue to work on full pay.

The Yard refuses to release for independent scrutiny full figures so that journalists and politicians can assess what bang the taxpayers got for their buck. Preserving the myth of a good score-sheet is essential to justifying the Untouchables' undisclosed budget. At a conservative estimate, this ten-year purge has cost the taxpayer over

PREFACE

£100 million, an enormous budget diverted from "core policing" matters, such as burglary, murder and sex crimes.

The integrity of the Met remains very much negotiable because it is judge and jury in its own cause. In such a highly politicised self-regulatory system, the onus is inevitably on corruption management, damage-limitation and cover-up – not justice, accountability and transparency.

Successive governments and Met commissioners have launched various controversial wars over the last two decades, on drugs, on crime, on anti-social behaviour and so on. But the "War on Corruption" was first and foremost a crisis management strategy to cover up and to mitigate the fall-out after the murder of black teenager Stephen Lawrence in April 1993 became a public relations disaster.

Anti-corruption chiefs secretly rehabilitated a discredited weapon in the police armoury – the supergrass. And like Frankenstein it turned on them. The Crown Prosecution Service was initially kept in the dark when this unlawful supergrass system was re-established. Its unlawfulness lay in the wilful breaches of all the legal safeguards designed to prevent such dangerous witnesses from giving coached evidence in return for favours. Government lawyers eventually acquiesced and helped steer supergrass evidence through the courts.

The entire anti-corruption crusade is based on seven key supergrasses. Four of them are crooked cops, the others an assortment of career criminals. Their reliability and effectiveness have been highly questionable. Some reaped benefits by giving perjured evidence. Others conned the Untouchables in the most humiliating ways. Worse still, some supergrasses had their evidence unlawfully tailored to ensure only those allegations the Untouchables wanted to pursue were ever recorded. This process was known as "cleansing".

The Untouchables had no interest in dismantling the long established fit-up culture of the police, referred to internally as "doing God's work". The practical effect of this "cleansing" process is that corrupt officers who should be behind bars or sacked are still serving or happily retired, and innocent people who should be free remain wrongly imprisoned or convicted.

Internal inquiries are also breeding grounds for scapegoats and private vendettas as well-connected officers direct attention away from themselves and onto colleagues they consider a threat. Powerful criminals have also manipulated the process to ensure honest policemen are targeted if they get too close.

Appalling double standards lie at the heart of the anti-corruption crusade. There is no explanation why the Untouchables targeted certain specialist police squads and not others. There is a consensus among the police supergrasses that some Untouchables are simply poachers turned gamekeepers whose own pasts would not bear independent scrutiny.

In order to tell the complex story of the Untouchables we need to name a lot of officers. Not all of them were involved in the crimes, corruption and injustices that went on. Some of the cops named in this book were unwittingly caught up in the corruption probe and not everyone in the police squads we talk about should be considered corrupt.

Research for *Untouchables* began while we worked at the *Guardian* newspaper. Since we began this journey into the dark side of the Yard, senior officers have done their best to prevent this investigation reaching you. We have been threatened, assaulted, lied to, smeared, put under intense surveillance and eventually categorised as a "threat" to the organisation. We also uncovered a plot by the Yard to derail our inquiries by making false allegations of criminal conduct in a letter to *Guardian* editor Alan Rusbridger, which was kept from us. The issue led us to resign from the newspaper in 2001 to complete our investigation and write this book.

The failure of the mainstream media to properly hold Scotland Yard to account during the biggest crisis in its history has many roots. Chief among them are the Yard's effortless exploitation of the media's crime dependency and the self-censorship of editors in this dumbed down age of low-risk, light journalism.

At the heart of the problem is the lobby arrangement where access to the Yard's casebook is negotiated at a price through the Crime Reporters Association. Selected crime correspondents have been used to talk up the Untouchables' flaccid performance.

We believe the evidence assembled in this book makes a timely case for a radical new system of police complaints with unfettered independence and accountability to the people, not the politicians.

The events of September 11 changed many things, none more so than the relationship between the government, its police and intelligence services. The current "War on Terrorism" has turned Scotland Yard into a strategic political ally of the Blair government, whereas after the Stephen Lawrence Inquiry in 1999 it was on its knees, ripe for radical reform. In this atmosphere the Home Office busily crafted a new police watchdog that reflects the new alliance and betrayed the government's commitment to implement the Lawrence

PREFACE

Inquiry recommendation for proper independent investigation of police crimes.

Meanwhile, home secretary David Blunkett is using the war on terrorism to justify rolling back vital legal safeguards. The discredited methods tested out in secret during the failed war on corruption are now being introduced in mainstream law enforcement. So much so that Blunkett wants to bring back the supergrass system.

The wars on terrorism and corruption are in fact very similar. False and misleading intelligence has been sexed up as hard evidence to justify a predetermined course of action. These hidden agendas are buried in a sea of sanctimony and hypocrisy about "just causes". Weapons of mass destruction and legions of bent cops are still missing. But critics and whistleblowers who point this out are demonised in a manufactured moral atmosphere where you are either with, or against, those who lay false claim to a higher purpose.

It is perhaps fitting that the new police watchdog for England and Wales, replacing the hopelessly captured Police Complaints Authority, was launched on April Fools Day 2004.

The first director of investigations for the new Independent Police Complaints Commission is the chief strategist and boss of the Untouchables. To justify the appointment of retired deputy assistant commissioner Roy Clark, the government and Scotland Yard continue to insist that the war on corruption has been a resounding success. The Home Office is even selling the Untouchables as the benchmark of excellence that all other UK police forces should follow and as an anti-corruption model currently being exported to unsuspecting publics in Australia, the United States, South Africa and Northern Ireland.

No doubt the families of victims of police misconduct and Home Office intransigence will continue their fight for justice and accountability, justice for loved ones who have been fitted-up, left irreparably damaged by a police truncheon or killed in police custody. The list is a long one. The number of police officers who have been prosecuted for such crimes is very low.

With the Untouchables now inside the new regulator it is likely this trend will continue.

Michael Gillard
Laurie Flynn
August 2004

PART ONE

THE DARK SIDE

1

UNDERCOVER 599 – MICHAEL'S STORY

Befriend and betray. These are the two tenets of undercover policing. At any one time there are around sixty top undercover officers in the UK trained for long-term infiltrations at home and abroad. Michael was one of them, a detective constable attached to Scotland Yard's secretive SO10 department.

On 6 December 2002 commissioner Sir John Stevens honoured him with a long service and good conduct medal. For 22 years, the Met had been Michael's surrogate family.

The award ceremony should have been one of the happiest days in any police officer's career. But for Michael it was a chance to confront a commissioner he felt had betrayed him by allowing the Untouchables to ruin his life and cut short his career. The medal was a meaningless apology, a bouquet of barbed wire he pretended to want just to get close to Stevens.

Michael is trained not to betray his emotions. An ill-timed nervous smile or furtive glance could be a matter of life or death for an undercover cop infiltrating a gang of villains. A criminal once put a gun in his mouth to see if there was a chink in his psychological armour. Michael kept his cool and because of that he kept his life.

Of late, however, he has lost the self-confidence so vital to undercover work. He is, in his own words, a broken biscuit. The Yard befriended and then betrayed him, a deceit that led to self-doubt, acute depression and, eventually, the brink of suicide.

As he stood in line waiting to be called onto the podium, his gaze remained fixed on Stevens. But in his mind's eye, Michael replayed all the horrors of the last five years of his needless suspension from the force. In his hand was a well-thumbed white envelope with a personal letter sealed inside. The undercover cop had painfully crafted it that morning.

Sir John Stevens QPM
By Hand

Whilst I am fully aware of why I am entitled to this award, the pride I ought to feel is replaced by an acute sense of despair.

As you know in January 1998 I was suspended from duty, for reasons still unclear. This lasted almost five years. During those years it became abundantly clear that my suspension was ultimately enforced because of my refusal to engage with a small group of [CIB3] officers under your command in a conspiracy to pervert the course of justice. My rejection ensured that my wife and I were subjected to the most vicious and sustained campaign of harassment and psychological torture.

This letter is not a formal complaint, we realise the futility of such action as you have remorselessly demonstrated in the past a total lack of commitment to investigating the criminal and disciplinary offences committed by these officers. I believe you should know the damage caused by those whom you allowed to act with such impunity.

I hoped my father would attend today, unfortunately he died at the age of sixty-nine three weeks ago. The last five years of his life were dominated by the spectre of abuse perpetrated by your officers. He saw his son spend the best part of a year in a psychiatric hospital, the direct result of your officers' actions. He witnessed his daughter-in-law, my wife, suffer a miscarriage so traumatic we remain childless. An incident, and I am not joking, that was celebrated by one officer within the [Untouchables].

You have blocked every attempt to bring this small group to account and allowed my career to be needlessly destroyed. I weep at the memory of the suffering you allowed my family to endure and for the damage you inflicted on a service I was once proud to serve.

Yours sincerely,
Michael

UNDERCOVER 599 – MICHAEL'S STORY

Stevens looked very nervous. The man waiting next in line for his award was a wildcard. Unpredictable. As her husband's name was announced, Beth (a pseudonym) focused her telephoto lens on the commissioner, finger poised above the shutter button ready to shoot. Stevens stretched out his hand as Michael came into the frame. The undercover cop gave him the letter.

"How are you Michael? Is this a Christmas card?" asked Stevens with nervous jocularity and false bonhomie.

Stone-faced, Michael gave no reply. Stevens slid the letter into the side pocket of his ceremonial uniform. He then grabbed the undercover officer's hand like a drowning man grabs a life-jacket and turned him towards the official photographer. Out of the corner of a gottle of geer smile on a face like a smacked arse, the most powerful policeman in the UK whispered: "Big schmile, Michael. You can do it."

"All I could think of was the miscarriage, my dad's death, the failed IVF and my time in the psychiatric hospital," recalls Michael. The photograph shows it. "Before I walked off the podium, Stevens offered to speak to us at the reception after the ceremony. I said we would like that."

The Yard had laid on a multi-cultural buffet: Jamaican patties, Indian samosas, Turkish kebabs and some ham and cheese for the more traditional palate.

While the couple waited they discussed the commissioner's welcoming speech. Like the buffet, it too had something for everyone; a quote from murdered civil rights leader Dr Martin Luther King and admiration for the devotion to duty of Confederate General Robert E. Lee. Hold up. Wasn't he an advocate of slavery and an adviser to the Ku Klux Klan? thought Michael.

As the minutes ticked by without any sign of the commissioner, Michael and Beth wondered if, having read the letter, Stevens couldn't face them. Word had spread among the guests about the commissioner's predicament. A senior officer in the anti-terrorist branch, where Michael had once worked, approached the couple and shook his hand. "It took a lot of guts to confront Stevens like that," said the well-wisher.

The chairman of the Metropolitan Police Authority, Lord Toby Harris, had also attended the award ceremony. He was the man now supposed to be holding the commissioner to account. For 171 years, Scotland Yard had been responsible to the Home Office. But in June 2000, home secretary Jack Straw told the inaugural meeting of the

MPA that it was "at long last bridging the democratic gap by making the Met locally accountable".[1] Not on this occasion though. The UK's top cop never showed. He had flown off in a helicopter with Lord Harris.

The commissioner is now struggling to defend allegations in the High Court that his Untouchables fitted up Michael and ruined his life because he rebuffed their unlawful and improper plan to use him against Flying Squad detectives. It wasn't a question of the undercover officer refusing to investigate fellow cops who'd "gone native". Michael was already successfully gathering evidence for Merseyside Police against dirty cops and their criminal paymasters.

His suspension on spurious allegations seriously undermined that entire corruption probe. And when senior Merseyside officers examined the Untouchables' case against Michael, they told Scotland Yard it was baseless.

But the Untouchables couldn't back down. Not without exposing their own anti-corruption crusade as a sham. So they kept an effective and honest detective suspended for five years and in so doing undermined Merseyside's corruption probe into a group of detectives believed to be in the pocket of the UK's biggest drug trafficker – Curtis "Cocky" Warren.

This is that story.

At 33, Curtis Warren made it onto the 1996 *Sunday Times* rich list. His identifiable assets were valued at £47 million. Not bad for a mixed-race ghetto kid whose apprenticeship in the drug trade began as a £10 dope dealer on the streets of Toxteth in Liverpool.

The Merseyside police had already been seriously on his case since 1993. Customs and the North West Regional Crime Squad, working secretly from a military installation outside Liverpool, were trying to dismantle his international drug syndicate. Warren was importing something for everyone: Pakistani and Moroccan hash, Dutch ecstasy and amphetamine, Turkish heroin and Colombian cocaine.

The police operation against him was codenamed Crayfish, which seemed appropriate when Warren decided in 1995 to re-locate his drug empire across the North Sea to the Netherlands. Merseyside Police joined forces with a specialist Dutch Task Force interested in organised South American drug syndicates, some with links to Warren.

The Dutch parliament takes a different view over the admissibility of telephone taps in criminal trials. Over there the police can rely on them as evidence, whereas British law enforcement uses them for intelligence purposes only, though there are moves to change this.

By the time the Dutch phone-tappers and buggers were finished, the Warren organisation in Holland resembled a *Big Brother* reality show. But, given their thick Scouse slang, it was necessary to bring over Operation Crayfish detectives from Merseyside to translate.

In July 1996, these secret recordings revealed for the first time evidence of something long suspected – the Warren crime syndicate's corrupt links with Merseyside cops.

Cocky and several of his lieutenants in Liverpool were intercepted discussing a thorny problem. The brother of his girlfriend had tried to shoot a bouncer at the Venue nightclub. The police gave chase and claimed he had tried to shoot one of them. The man was arrested for attempted murder. Warren wouldn't normally have cared less, but the shooter was also the son of one of his key associates, Phillip Glennon.[2]

The Warren gang turned to a well-known detective chief inspector and former deputy head of the drugs squad called Elmore 'Elly' Davies. He had served Warren's entire lifetime in the Merseyside force. Davies was identified as someone who could intervene in the nightclub case without drawing attention because the shooting had occurred on his patch.

When the Dutch tipped off Operation Crayfish that one of their own had changed sides, senior officers in Liverpool went into a secret huddle.

"Liverpool in the 1990s was arguably the principal gateway into the UK for heroin, cocaine and ecstasy smugglers. The vast profits generated made multi-millionaires out of gangsters barely able to read or write. But their wealth corrupted everything it touched, including the police and legal system," says investigative reporter Geoff Seed, who examined the problem.

"By the early nineties both Customs and the North West Regional Crime Squad were telling Merseyside police that corruption in the ranks was so bad, investigations were being compromised. Telephone taps on target criminals showed them ringing tame contacts in the drugs squad and other units. Kickbacks of three to four thousand pounds "holiday money" were regularly paid to detectives for information. In this climate of unprecedented corruption, chief constable Sir James Sharples turned to Customs to monitor taps on 31 non-office telephones used by police. He could not trust his senior detectives to do it for fear of operational leaks."

The Elly Davies corruption probe was set up in great secrecy under detective superintendent Phil Jones. The operation, codenamed Admiral, was conducted within a new Professional Standards Unit, an equivalent to the Yard's CIB3 but without the puffery and sanctimony.

Two associates of the Warren organisation were identified as friends of Elly Davies. One of them was national celebrity Mick Ahearne, aka "Warrior" from the ITV series *Gladiators*. He and Davies were once flatmates whilst the Lycra muscle man's mansion was being renovated.

Operation Admiral bugged Davies' more modest flat and his office, where the stocky, balding cop was leading a murder inquiry.

An independent TV crew were at the time shadowing Davies' team for a fly-on-the-wall documentary series for the BBC called *Mersey Blues*. He came across as witty and engaging. It was a measure of his brass balls that Davies felt his corrupt agreement with Warren could be honoured despite the scrutiny of the television cameras.

But, like Davies, the TV producers had no idea of their own walk-on part in the corruption video that detective superintendent Phil Jones was now making for an audience of 12 jurors at the Crown Court.

Still, the anti-corruption boss didn't have the luxury of the BBC's deadline for his exposé. Under Dutch law the police surveillance operation against the Warren drugs syndicate would have to be disclosed to the target after six months.

The Dutch Task Force believed they had gathered enough admissible evidence, so between September and October 1996, key members of Warren's organisation, including Cocky, were charged and held on remand in Holland.

The arrests made national news in the UK and of course Liverpool. If Davies was bothered he didn't show it. Days later he applied for promotion to superintendent, oblivious to the corruption probe. When he was rejected, the BBC cameras were there to capture a bitter rant from the Jurassic detective that was a masterpiece of hypocrisy. Davies railed against bean counters in the Merseyside force making it uneconomical to deploy underpaid detectives like him to take out rich criminals with limitless resources. "So fuck 'em," he said.[3]

Under Dutch disclosure rules it wouldn't be long before Davies discovered from Warren's associates the real reason he was rejected for promotion. Phil Jones needed to know the scope of Davies' betrayal. And whether he was working with others in his force.

The head of Merseyside's undercover unit, detective chief inspector Chris Jones, helped conceive a plan to infiltrate someone into Davies' circle. A local undercover cop would not be appropriate because of the risk of compromise. So Merseyside approached Scotland Yard's undercover unit, SO10. They asked for the best available man for a very sensitive job. The Yard recommended undercover officer 599.

Michael is a Lancastrian. He was brought up from the age of five in a small fishing town on the north-west coast. His father was a local policeman, a dog handler, and his Welsh mother an estate agent. Their marriage was a "war zone", says Michael with obvious melancholy. "It was a divorce that lasted 20 years."

He has few fond memories as a teenager. One, however, was going to the legendary Wigan Casino on a Northern Soul night – the music of black artists from small independent US record labels whose stars were sadly outshone by the more mainstream Motown galaxy. Michael likes to dress natty, something essential on the Northern Soul scene, where sharply dressed men in bowling shirts cut up the dance floor with spins and moves.

Still, the emotional scars of family life were enormous for him and his two younger brothers. It had cost him his GCSE results. "I was a good student and had a lovely teacher. If I'd stayed in education I don't think I would have gone into the police, but the situation at home was intolerable. We all left at the earliest opportunity. I didn't want to become a fisherman, like one of my brothers. Instead I joined the Navy at 16. I saw the service as a family."

At first Michael worked on minesweepers patrolling the craggy coast of Northern Ireland. But it was submarines that most interested him, going deep, running silent on long missions, surfacing only when it was safe, before diving again into an underworld. He served on *Polaris*, the nuclear submarine programme, playing cat and mouse with the Russians during the Cold War. It was the nearest, he says, to the camaraderie experienced on minesweepers. But the Navy was never a career plan and after five years he applied to join the police in 1980.

The Met and Lancashire Constabulary accepted him but, after seeking advice from friends already serving in Lancashire, he was told if he wanted to make detective there was more opportunity in London. "I also didn't want to come back home. I knew when I left that was it. The Met offered the perceived warmth of a family that was missing from my life. It was a mistaken notion, I know now."

Within three years, Michael was promoted to detective constable and working the streets of central London. He had married a Malaysian girl when he was in the Navy but they divorced around this time.

UNTOUCHABLES

Michael had his own difficulties with detective culture and its blinkered insularity and macho pack mentality. He was a rugged individual and needed the space to be creative and push personal boundaries.

When he learned of the undercover unit in the mid-eighties it was very much an informal affair, a fiefdom effectively run by the most powerful detective sergeant in the Met, Peter Holman. It wasn't until 1986 that the Yard created SO10 and placed its undercover work on a formal footing with selection and training courses using the intelligence services and Special Forces' expertise.

Michael applied in 1989. His appraisals as a detective had encouraged this progression. In the meantime he achieved another one of his goals, to join the Flying Squad. He was put on the surveillance team. In those days you were sponsored onto the squad and Michael was given a leg up by a detective chief inspector he'd served under at West Ham police station.

"In my time on the Flying Squad, from 1990 to 1994, there were five or six major robberies we never dealt with properly. Not out of corruption but because of a lack of focus. There were serious political reasons too. The commissioner then was Condon. He had little interest in organised crime and hated the elitism of the central squads. So instead of looking at serious teams of robbers we were doing things like off-licence robberies. A lot of major teams were not caught in that period and who knows what they went on to do. It was a period of unfulfilment for me."

Fate intervened, and in 1992, SO10 invited Michael to take the undercover course. His sponsor was Roy Ramm, commander of special operations. He noticed in the young man a thoughtful, loyal officer who was "slightly out of the mould because of all his outside interests".

Michael was put on one of the last SO10 courses where the candidates were "kidnapped" off the street by Special Forces trainers and put in a metal box for several hours. "The Met stopped it, I think because they feared civil claims from some of the less hardy recruits," he says.

Undercover officers have a mentoring system of 'uncles', who advise new recruits. Michael's uncle was one of the founders of SO10, detective sergeant Richard Hester. He had perfected the legend (false persona) of a money launderer, the sophisticated businessman who would be introduced somewhere along the arms or drugs sting by another undercover officer.

UNDERCOVER 599 – MICHAEL'S STORY

Hester's class act excited Michael's imagination. His grandmother and aunt had immersed him as a boy in the world of acting by frequent cinema trips. If there was one film that united his love of British *film noir* with a fascination for detective work, it was Stanley Baker's gritty portrayal of a Manchester murder detective in Val Guest's 1959 classic *Hell is a City*.

When he passed SO10 selection Michael was like a boy in a spy shop. "Would Sir like to be an arts and antiques dealer, perhaps a merchant banker?" The roles to learn and perfect were endless and he was charged by the possibilities. "UC (undercover) work is like working in a pure form of policing, constantly trying to push the parameters."

Here was a special group within a wider family where he could really belong. Undercover work was well suited to him. He was already a sponge soaking up cultures viewed with suspicion by his police colleagues. The undercover cop has to move in many worlds.

"My first undercover assignment was while I was still at the Flying Squad trying to buy illegal guns." He was spotted early as someone who could also act as a "cover man", a vital support role providing equipment, debriefing the undercover officer and acting as his psychological crutch throughout the operation.

Michael worked on some harrowing assignments. One of the worst, he says, was befriending a paedophile. Before placing a bug in the man's home he had to feign excitement while watching child porn.

In 1994, an opportunity arose for several SO10 officers to work on a long-range sting operation in the "Bermondsey Triangle", so-called because property and people simply disappear in this criminal epicentre of south-east London. The operation, codenamed Sienna, was run from Southwark police station by two detectives who would soon become leading evangelical lights in the anti-corruption crusade – Dave Wood and Chris Jarratt.

The idea was to set up a pawnshop near to the train station to recover stolen goods and break up an organised group of professional thieves. The shop was bugged and Michael worked behind the counter as someone prepared to fence almost anything.

During the eighteen months he was also deployed in two similar undercover missions. Michael played the part of a second-hand dealer in computer parts living in a squat near the Oval. The operation was a mini-sting on a gang stealing memory chips from office computers. And in Glasgow he posed as a wealthy businessman willing to buy £1 million of microchips stolen in an armed robbery.

UNTOUCHABLES

Operation Sienna ended successfully in 1996 with over £1 million recovered and over seventy prosecutions, says Michael. Before they parted company, Jarratt advised the undercover cop to hold onto his coat tails because he was going places.

Detective chief inspector Peter North beckoned undercover officer 599 into his office and shut the door. The boss of SO10 looked serious. "I'm going to say something to you, Michael, and if you don't go with it I know you'll keep your mouth shut even if things get difficult."

DCI North explained that Merseyside Police believed the Curtis Warren organisation had taken out a contract on the police constable who was a key eyewitness in the Venue Nightclub shooting. "Warren's people may have someone on the inside. It will mean infiltrating police officers up there."

On 8 October 1996 Michael was introduced to superintendent Phil Jones of Merseyside police. He was the senior detective investigating Curtis Warren's drug syndicate and corrupt links to DCI Elmore "Elly" Davies. Jones briefed Michael about a new covert operation codenamed Florida. He said it would involve infiltrating a group of business people from the Wirral "who posed a serious threat to the integrity and the safety of individual officers".[4]

Jones had concerns about two officers close to Davies. One of them was detective inspector Steve Ward.

Michael's legend was that of a rich businessman with links to organised crime. To enhance his cover a female undercover officer we shall call Gillian posed as his bit of crumpet. She would later complain of being regularly goosed by those they were trying to infiltrate, especially one dangerous businessman they dubbed "Sausage Fingers".

Michael knew this was going to be the most difficult of undercover operations – a cold infiltration with no one to reference him into the criminal group. Usually that is the role of a police informant. But Jones could not risk the possibility of a treacherous informant blowing 599's cover either to Warren's business associates or to his friends in the police.

Michael's legend had to be impenetrable, more so because he was also infiltrating cops with easy access to sensitive police databases to check for signs he was a plant.

Like all good UCs, he'd been developing several legends over the years. Michael had a love of horses, as both a rider and a punter. The undercover officer had the build of a jockey and was well-suited to the saddle. He'd also developed genuine friendships with two ex-champion jockeys. Graham Thorner was now a trainer and Richard Pitman was a respected TV commentator and pundit. Michael used to visit Graham's farm in the West Country to wind down during his break from the pawnshop undercover job in Bermondsey. As part of his legend he'd also registered at the Jockey Club as Thorner's pupil assistant trainer under the pseudonym Michael Fenwick. He decided to use this for Operation Florida.

In late October "Michael Fenwick" and his girlfriend "Gillian" arrived in Liverpool in a flashy Mercedes. They booked into the Bowler Hat Hotel. After relaxing they went downstairs to the restaurant for dinner. Sitting nearby was a group of heavies discussing the recent arrest of Curtis Warren. For a moment the two UCs thought their cover had already been blown.

Michael waited for the men to leave. He clocked their registration numbers and called Jones. The men were well-known to the superintendent and featured prominently on his wall chart of Warren's associates.

Michael was told to concentrate on Elly Davies and Steve Ward. They hung out with Warren's associates at a pub called the Bassett Hound. The first time the couple turned up there it was bingo night. It looked more like an episode of Peter Kay's *Phoenix Nights* than the haunt of a major drug syndicate. The two flashy Londoners stuck out a mile among the blue-rinse brigade.

When they next returned the clientele had more of an air of Peter Flannery's *Our Friends in the North*. To explain their local ignorance and sudden arrival Fenwick claimed he was in Liverpool looking for property to buy. The couple had been to various estate agents in the area to ensure a steady stream of calls on their mobiles over the next few months. The trick was to develop a cover story that allowed you to come back and forth without raising suspicion.

"I remember talking to one local who was a counterfeiter. He assured me that although cops drank at the pub it was okay. Jones had told me that Davies was gregarious and Ward aloof. But it worked out the other way around. I met both of them at the Bassett Hound but Davies appeared wary of me. It seemed like something was playing on his mind," recalls Michael.

The seething resentment of his promotion knock-back might have been to blame. That November, the newly installed bugs in Davies' flat and office recorded him agreeing to pass information about the Venue nightclub shooting for £10,000. The bribe was paid in cash from one of Cocky's henchmen, Tony Bray, via Gladiator Mick Ahearne.

UNTOUCHABLES

Slowly Fenwick and Gillian became accepted fixtures at the Bassett Hound. They had seen Davies and Ward on numerous occasions but never spoke. Davies once raised an eyebrow of recognition, but nothing more.

The first proper contact came from Ward in early January 1997. Davies was still aloof and Operation Florida wondered whether he was using Ward to sound out the newly arrived Michael Fenwick.

Sausage Fingers had also recently threatened the undercover cop. He was someone Michael came to realise was obsessed about infiltration. "I was round his house playing snooker in his den. It was a big house, and I noticed on the shelf a row of videos. He explained how he had a keen interest in police practice and operations.

"Sometime later Sausage Fingers turned up at my hotel with a driver. I thought we were going for a drink. We got in the car and drove further and further into the darkness. I was talking to him in the back seat when suddenly the driver pulled over at a dark spot. They threatened to kill me if I wasn't who I said I was. It was a test to see if I was an undercover officer. He was satisfied by my reaction and we then went for a drink. For the rest of the evening Sausage Fingers acted as if nothing had happened.

"It was clear then that these people connected to Ward were very dangerous. Sausage Fingers was in the shipping business. He'd offered me the services of a freighter if I needed it."

It became apparent after a few weeks that Ward was not involved in Davies' efforts to sabotage the Venue nightclub shooting case. But Phil Jones still had serious concerns.

He briefed his chief constable Sir James Sharples who agreed Jones could mount an elaborate sting on Ward.[5] Michael prepared a package that was worthy of an Oscar. The resourceful undercover cop had already set up a bogus company called Skyline Racing for Mr Michael Fenwick. He suggested using it to rent a hospitality box at Haydock Park Racecourse and throw a party for his new friends. Jones loved it.

Ward, Davies and many of their business friends from the Bassett Hound pub, including Sausage Fingers, were invited to the do on 22 February. Also present was the lead singer of a Merseyside Eighties chart-topping band, which gave Fenwick some glamour.

The hospitality box came with waiting staff. Like the guests, they didn't know it was bugged and transmitting live to a van parked nearby. The plan was for Michael to make a corrupt approach to Ward.

This centred on someone who had recently been stopped in a taxi on the motorway outside Liverpool with 60,000 ecstasy pills.[6] Fenwick explained to Ward in the kitchen area that the man owed money to criminals in the South who wanted to know whether his arrest was a set up, a lucky stop or whether he had turned informant. According to Operation Florida documents, Ward agreed to help and four days later made the checks. Michael was astounded. "I had given the impression the information would be used for a contract killing. Ward said he would do the checks but didn't want money. He told me he was disillusioned with the police and suggested I gave him a job as my chauffeur when he retired!"

Jones was happy with Michael's infiltration and Operation Florida looked like it could run for many more months. There was one snag. The Curtis Warren trial in Holland was due to start. This influenced Jones' decision to arrest Elly Davies for corruption.

Jones wondered if Ward would now run for cover. So he backed off for six weeks, by which time Warren had been jailed for twelve years.

In June, Michael called Ward again to see if he was still up for helping out. The undercover cop was surprised when Ward agreed to check the Police National Computer to see if two of his criminal associates were being looked at. The Michael Fenwick legend extended to a false entry on the PNC.

On 2 July, Michael called Ward at work and asked him if he would do another check on "an associate of Curtis Warren" called Mark Quinn. To Michael's further amazement, Ward did checks on the intelligence system there and then. He told Fenwick during the secretly recorded conversation that no one was looking at Quinn. Again he refused money.

The bond developing between Ward and Fenwick in 1997 suggested there was every possibility that Operation Florida could get into other dark corners where police corruption and organised crime in Merseyside met.

Back in London, 1997 was an important year for Scotland Yard's own fight against corruption. The Ghost Squad, the secret unit set up four years earlier to examine the Yard's exposure to corruption, was being re-organised.

Deputy assistant commissioner Roy Clark's new anti-corruption squad would operate half-in and half-out of the shadows. An intelligence cell called CIBIC replaced the Ghost Squad. It remained in the shadows but moved from a covert location in west London to Tintagel House, an ugly police building overlooking the Thames.

UNTOUCHABLES

CIBIC would secretly service a new proactive squad of detectives designed to operate largely in the twilight, slipping back into the darkness when they needed to. This was CIB3, aka the Untouchables.

The Ghost Squad was not completely dismantled. Since 1994, it had been developing its own bugging, informant running and undercover capability. This super secret unit within a secret unit was referred to in hushed tones as "the Dark Side". It remained under deep cover at the covert west London location.

Detective superintendent Dave Wood and his sidekick detective chief inspector Chris Jarratt were in day-to-day charge of CIB3 and CIBIC respectively. Michael was first aware of the recruitment drive for shadow warriors when Jarratt asked to meet him in April 1997 in a police section house in south London. Michael was immersed at the time in the Merseyside corruption probe and immediately suspected Jarratt was aware of this. The CIBIC boss asked if he would join him as an undercover operative.

"Jarratt said I should be prepared 'to go that extra mile'. He'd used the expression before during the Bermondsey job we did together. I didn't like the inference."

Still, Michael was wary of turning Jarratt down. He had experienced his volatility on previous covert operations and didn't want to make an enemy of the man, especially as he was now in such a powerful position. "I told him I wanted to finish my final assessment before becoming a full detective sergeant. I left it neither saying yes or no, just hoping the offer would fizzle out."

The following month Michael sat his exam. He was the number one candidate from his police station. His personal life was also going well, an on/off romance with Beth having been re-ignited. They had met six years earlier. The couple planned to marry in October and had invited Jarratt and his wife.

But by autumn their lives started to fall apart. In September, Michael was told he had failed in his bid to become a detective sergeant. He appealed, with the support of SO10 boss, Peter North, who had originally recommended him to Merseyside. "[This] detective constable retains a sense of direction during his [undercover] deployment, maintaining the highest standards . . . such is the esteem this officer is held in that he is always invited to assist in the training of students," wrote North.[7]

The wedding was looming so Michael put the promotion appeal to one side. Jarratt's wife wrote to say they couldn't attend owing to a family tragedy. Weeks after the wedding, Michael discovered his appeal had failed.

Michael had no idea the CIBIC boss was in the middle of executing a tightly choreographed operation against the Flying Squad using two former detectives who had turned supergrass over Christmas. The operation was used to great effect in the New Year to help the Yard neutralise potential problems from a Commons Home Affairs select committee hearing on the complaints system. There was also concern in the Yard about the forthcoming Stephen Lawrence public inquiry.

On 27 January 1998 the homes of 20 former and serving Flying Squad officers were raided. Michael's was one of them. Five Untouchables arrived at 6.30am to search the newly-weds' house. Two were men Michael had served with on the Bermondsey covert operation.[8]

The press were waiting outside Tintagel House to capture the succession of officers going in to be formally suspended and give the Yard the "get tough" headlines it desperately needed in launching its Untouchables.

"I was still deployed on several undercover missions, not least the one in Merseyside, so I asked to be suspended in private," says Michael. "This was agreed at commander level, but CIB3 overruled it." It left him staggered by their recklessness. The allegations against him appeared flimsy and riven with double standards. For example, Michael was accused of having police documents at home.

Retired commander Roy Ramm, once in charge of all covert operations at Scotland Yard, says, "If you searched almost any officer's home there would be a very high possibility you would find police related documents . . . I would often take documents home to work on them . . . Good officers always took papers home to do that extra bit of work . . . I know of one officer who was the most highly commended in the Met. At one stage his wife was single-handedly running the paperwork of the undercover unit."[9]

Another allegation concerned a small terraced house in the North that Michael had inherited from his grandmother. He registered ownership with the local council under his pseudonym Michael Fenwick. The property was used for his undercover work and by other law enforcement agencies. CIB3, by now aware of Operation Florida, nevertheless tried to claim he was seeking to avoid Council Tax. DCI Chris Jones, head of Merseyside undercover unit, had been told about the arrangement and saw "nothing wrong" with it.[10] Neither did

UNTOUCHABLES

Michael's boss at SO10. But by making an issue of the second home the Untouchables jeopardised other covert operatives who were using it as an accommodation address.

For the next ten months Michael waited for the Yard to realise its error and reinstate him. Out of the blue, he received a call on 16 November from his best man, detective inspector Tony Fuller. They had known each other for 15 years. Fuller had also introduced Michael to Beth and both wives shared a circle of friends.

Detective superintendent Brian Moore, the man in charge of the Flying Squad corruption probe, had instructed Fuller to make an "off-the-record" approach to Michael with yet another highly suspect offer to join the Untouchables. His second.

Michael secretly tape-recorded his meeting that afternoon at a pub in King's Cross. Fuller explained how Moore was about to meet with government lawyers and the deputy commissioner, who at the time was John Stevens, to discuss criminal proceedings against the suspended Flying Squad officers.

"My slate would be wiped clean if I agreed to do one of three things: make a statement and give evidence incriminating them; just make a statement; or make an intelligence report that would never be disclosed, detailing everything I knew about my time on the Flying Squad, including gossip. This would have been used to influence their bosses and judges."

Michael was desperate to return to work. Moore was showing him a way back. It could all be so easy. But to take up the offer would mean accepting there was substance to the false allegations used to justify his suspension.

Michael would not bend to his tormentors. He was innocent. And though yearning to see through all his undercover jobs, he could not work for the Untouchables. He had seen how Merseyside handled their corruption problem, and this offer just wasn't right. He told Fuller: "There is a lot I want to say but nothing that I can help them with. I'm being pilloried for something I haven't done by an organisation that isn't really interested in my welfare. They've taken everything from me and I'm not going to allow them to get away with it. [The anti-corruption drive] is a media vehicle to achieve a political objective."[11]

Fuller explained that Moore was willing to meet and personally make Michael the offer, but under one condition: no solicitor could be present. "What's he got to hide?" Michael retorted.

Moore's offer had to be deniable because it drove a coach and horses through the law and exposed the case against Michael as a sham. It is arguable that the Untouchables were actually perverting the course of justice.

"How could Moore bring me 'back into the fold' if they genuinely believed there was evidence that I was a criminal? And if the offer was so above board, why couldn't my lawyer be there to hear it? My suspension was a softening-up process. I believe the Untouchables wanted me to work undercover and spy on the suspended officers. We all had the same lawyers, Russell, Jones & Walker, and I am convinced they wanted me to report back on legally privileged conversations. This is completely unlawful. I also couldn't believe they had sent Fuller. He had also served at the Flying Squad."

In December 1998, exactly one month after turning down Moore's offer, Michael was arrested at home in front of his distraught wife. CIB3 officers took him away to be interviewed. The couple had been married just over a year. "Our relationship never had a chance," says Beth. She was two months pregnant at the time. Beth started bleeding heavily and later that day she miscarried. Since then, the couple have remained childless.

Detective superintendent Phil Jones went ballistic when he found out Michael had been suspended. Operation Florida, which had looked so promising, now appeared fatally flawed.

"There were high level calls from Merseyside to the Met accusing SO10 of selling them 'damaged goods', was the phrase," recalls Michael. "I told Phil I've done nothing wrong. I assured him I would not compromise his job. I didn't hear from him for a while but I later learned he was trying to make contact but the Yard was briefing against me, effectively saying I'd be charged and was never coming back to work."

Merseyside was led to believe over many months that Michael was a thoroughly corrupt man heroically unmasked by the Untouchables. The impact on Operation Florida was enormous. Unassailable wiretap and probe evidence of Ward's willingness to pass on sensitive police intelligence to someone he must at least have suspected was connected to organised drug and track crime was severely tainted if this was true. The mere suggestion was enough to fatally damage any chance of a criminal prosecution. Consequently, Merseyside was forced to try and sack the now suspended detective inspector through disciplinary proceedings.

Meanwhile in London, the Yard's vindictiveness against Michael was spiralling out of control, with no concern for its devastating effect on his family or Merseyside's corruption probe.

A glimmer of hope came two years later in March 2000 when the Untouchables dropped all criminal proceedings against the debilitated undercover cop because there was simply no evidence he had done anything wrong at the Flying Squad. But of course having spent so much taxpayers' money incapacitating an effective and loyal detective, the illusion of ruthless efficiency needed to be maintained. Michael was therefore told he would remain suspended on full pay and face disciplinary proceedings.

His mental health was deteriorating fast and in September he went sick with severe depression associated with post-traumatic stress disorder. But Merseyside, having learned that the criminal charges had been dropped against their undercover operative, started to suspect Scotland Yard was misleading them.

The Untouchables already knew how Merseyside felt about Michael's undercover work. After all, the chief constable, Sir James Sharples, had written to the Yard in 1997 in glowing terms: "As a consequence of your officer's motivation, effective communication and appropriate decision making whilst under pressure, significant progress has been achieved." Something the Yard could hardly say about its own anti-corruption drive. Sharples continued: "I should like to place on record my personal thanks and appreciation for the conduct of the officer throughout this difficult enquiry."[12]

DCI Chris Jones of Merseyside's undercover unit had also later made a statement to the Untouchables that Michael's "commitment, professionalism and conduct during the [Florida] enquiry was exemplary".[13] In October, Merseyside asked to see the disciplinary case against him. According to a source close to the discussions, CIB3 at first refused and then delayed.

Phil Jones had another problem closer to home. Ward had discovered that his nemesis, Michael Fenwick, was in fact a suspended undercover officer from the Met. Furthermore, both men were represented by the same firm of Police Federation retained solicitors, Russell, Jones & Walker (RJW). Ward's defence was immeasurably emboldened by the revelation.

Enquiries by Jones revealed the compromise was accidental and had apparently come from someone in Special Branch. Nevertheless, he was determined to press ahead with a disciplinary hearing against Ward and so demanded an immediate briefing from the Untouchables.

UNDERCOVER 599 – MICHAEL'S STORY

"As I understand it, the deputy chief constable of Merseyside intervened on Jones' behalf with the Yard and CIB3 was forced to give a presentation effectively justifying why I was being kept suspended," says Michael.

In November 2000, Phil Jones and Chris Jones travelled to London for the briefing. Afterwards, they met with Michael and his new solicitor Karen Todner at a café in Liverpool Street station. Michael had left RJW, as had Ward, because of the conflict of interest.

Karen Todner says: "The [Merseyside] officers were advised [by the Untouchables] that they should not rely on Michael as a witness. The two officers therefore asked to look at all the papers. They told me that they reviewed all his papers at that time and were happy to rely on him as a witness of truth. They did not consider that his integrity was in question."

Merseyside knew about Michael's mental condition and Beth's miscarriage. They approached the matter with a sensitivity so lacking in the Met. "They asked Michael to strongly consider being a witness for them, otherwise they felt the disciplinary proceedings [against Ward] would be compromised," Todner adds.

Michael told them he was willing to see the undercover job through but told Jones he was not the same sharp-eyed officer. The offer was a much-needed boost to his low self-esteem and a massive vindication of his innocence. For the first time in the history of the Untouchables, an outside force had audited its secret intelligence machine and found it seriously unconvincing.

This case exposes a secret and deniable strategy to use suspension as a tool to destroy and victimise innocent detectives who refuse to do the Untouchables' unlawful bidding or threaten them in some way.

Michael couldn't complain to the Yard about the clear victimisation. Nor could he go to the Home Office. Neither can police officers complain to the watchdog. In effect, no mechanism exists for a police officer to have the grounds for his continued suspension independently assessed to ensure malice or a hidden agenda aren't working to suppress the truth.

Directly after the meeting at Liverpool Street, Michael's lawyer noticed they were under surveillance. To make sure, Michael alighted from the cab and went for a long walk into Soho. Along the route he photographed a surveillance team of two men and a woman. He then called the two Merseyside detectives who were by now on the train heading home. "I said: 'I don't believe you would do this but I am being followed.' Chris Jones goes ballistic. He was worried I would feel they had set me up and this would stop me giving evidence. I understand that Phil Jones then spoke to CIB, who denied it was them but said they couldn't speak for another agency." It's well known that the Untouchables were occasionally using MI5 surveillance teams.

Finally, in the first week of February 2001, detective inspector Steve Ward's discipline board took place. He was still pleading not guilty. There was a certain gamble that Michael would not show. But when the undercover cop arrived at the police building in Liverpool where the hearing was held, it is understood Ward changed his plea to guilty and was sacked.[14] He had the Untouchables to thank for not having to face a criminal trial like his friend, Elly Davies, who was jailed in 1998 for five years.[15]

Surely now someone in Scotland Yard would recognise how unjust, inhumane even, was Michael's continued suspension? No criminal charges were outstanding and the discipline didn't add up to a hill of beans, an expression used by Phil Jones.

But the Untouchables had to stand firm. They could not afford to have Michael free of taint and thereby able to give evidence for the defence in the forthcoming Flying Squad trials. What would the Untouchables say if he revealed in court the unlawful attempt to use him as a live bug inside the defendant's legal meetings at RJW? All conversations and correspondence between a client and his solicitor are regarded by the courts as legally privileged and therefore should not be subject to any kind of surveillance.

The Yard seriously overestimated Michael's affinity for his suspended colleagues. Out of loyalty to SO10 he had kept his undercover involvement in Liverpool secret, even from the ones he liked.

Many of the Flying Squad defendants were already suspicious of Michael's SO10 past. His lawyer, Karen Todner, explains: "As [Michael] had previously been an undercover officer they could not understand why on earth he had been suspended as there appeared to be no evidence against him. They therefore believed he was in an undercover role to gain information against them and started to ostracise him."

This reached fever pitch when they discovered he was leaving RJW because of a conflict of interest. No one knew the details other than he was giving evidence against another officer "up North".

Michael was in no psychological condition to withstand the double isolation from his SO10 colleagues and now those he'd been suspended with for three years. He stopped going to his local pub, where other coppers drank, and bought Sky to watch the football at home instead. But when the engineer came to install the black box, Michael shadowed him as he moved around the house. In his mind he remembered a discussion at the Flying Squad to develop a secret relationship with Sky so they could plant bugs in the box. After the engineer left, Michael ruined the box looking for listening devices. The engineer had to return to fix it.

For a man so adept at losing his police identity when going undercover, Michael was now desperate to be recognised as a policeman. Like the man made redundant who can't tell his wife and leaves the house every morning for "work", he would sometimes don a sharp suit and hang around the arcade near Scotland Yard hoping to "bump into" someone who knew him.

Karen Todner realised her client was slipping into darkness. She wrote to Michael's MP, Stephen Timms, who was also junior Labour minister for education. Todner laid out the whole tragic personal cost and emphasised the cost to the taxpayer as well. This was both financial and a security cost, as her client's undercover operations in London had been withdrawn as a result of his suspension.[16]

Timms wrote the next day to home secretary Jack Straw mentioning all these matters and asked the simple question, "Why does he remain suspended?" After consulting with the Yard, Lord Bassam replied for Straw. He said Michael remained suspended because of police documents he had at home and "other associated matters".[17]

Timms was still frustrated by the injustice and wrote to commissioner Stevens arguing that his constituent's explanation for the documents was "completely plausible and proper". When will the matter end, he asked.[18]

Commander Graham James was the senior officer responsible for regularly reviewing Michael's suspension. He replied to Timms on behalf of the commissioner, claiming feebly that the police documents and the Council Tax allegation were "both serious and question [Michael's] integrity".[19]

The undercover cop felt the Yard was "deliberately misleading Parliament". If it could do that, no end to his torment appeared in sight.

Beth had known Michael for about six years before they married. Sometimes they would joke before going out about what she would say when asked what her partner did for a living. "Tell them I'm in art and antiques," he'd reply.

UNTOUCHABLES

She found the deceit more stressful than sexy. "However, I was happy to support his career and accepted his belief that the Met was at the cutting edge of undercover work and as such the support offered to those officers who volunteered would be second to none. There have been many occasions I feared for his safety and the demands placed on him put a great strain on our relationship. To find that the organisation so willingly betrayed his loyalty appals me."

Since her miscarriage the couple have undergone expensive IVF treatment, but to no avail. Michael carries the guilt of her "unexplained infertility" every day. She'd had no problems before the Untouchables ripped their lives apart. Her doctors tell her she is in "biological meltdown".

Beth works for a major blue chip company. Her boss was appalled at the Yard's treatment of the couple and agreed to help extend her medical insurance to cover Michael.

In May 2001, Michael voluntarily admitted himself to a private psychiatric clinic. His psychiatrist believed there was a real risk of suicide. "As I entered the clinic I still thought the Met would put things right, that I was going back to work, there would be a call any day now. I was contemptuous of other patients and what I felt was their inability to handle things. I was in complete denial," says Michael. He thought there were "plants" in the clinic and did surveillance on some of them. Eventually the denial gave way to tears and slowly the healing began.

After a while, he wrote to us from what he called "the Cuckoo's nest": "I still struggle to shed the skin that clings from a past life. But we can see again, darkness lifted. Each day another shell washes ashore that reminds me of my strengths and weaknesses . . . I'm afraid there wasn't much left in the tank so I guess it should come as no surprise to me that I find myself domiciled with a rather odd collection of broken biscuits. Yet I am beginning to feel a sense of understanding and warmth in their fractured gaze. For too long I've been in a darkness that became unbearable. Changes had to be made."

Michael was released in August. But there was no change in the Yard's entrenched stance. He was told he would still face a disciplinary board, but only when the Flying Squad trials finished. That meant another year or more of darkness.

Michael's psychiatrist was deeply disturbed this would lead to what he called "regrettable consequences" and urged the Yard to desist. A week later, on 13 November, the discarded undercover cop disappeared. He was due to be urgently readmitted to the clinic but never turned up. Michael knew the hope of ever regaining his career as a Level One undercover operative was gone. Suicide, he convinced himself, was the only way to break through the cover-up and expose the Untouchables.

Michael drove his distinctive Mini Coupé in a dreamlike altered state of consciousness up the M1 to the Yorkshire Moors. It was a place where he and Beth had been on walking holidays. At first he slept rough in the car for a few days, then he checked into a familiar B&B just outside Skipton.

Michael planned his death with military precision. He identified a place on the Moors to park where his asphyxiated body would be found within days. A suicide note for Beth was secreted in the car lining. There was also one for the authors. It urged us to investigate the full circumstances surrounding his suicide, which at that stage were unknown because he had remained so loyal to the police.

Michael elected to die by carbon monoxide poisoning. The next morning, after signing the Visitors' Book, he strolled purposefully around Skipton Market, stopping at an electrical stall where many pieces of hose were hanging from the metal frame like sausages. He selected one he thought would connect to his exhaust but soon realised he'd left his wallet at the B&B.

Michael was undeterred. He turned to retrieve it. "Suddenly, I could smell fresh fish. It reminded me of the town where I grew up. I followed the waft until I saw George Wilson by his fish hawkers van. He was wearing his white overalls. I hoped he hadn't seen me. He was very friendly with my dad. Suddenly I felt like a kid and my dad was beside me saying, 'What are you doing here, son?' It made me think how sad my suicide would have made him."

Michael had enough change to buy a cup of tea in a nearby café. He sat there a while and cried quietly. After retrieving his wallet from the B&B, he drove to the Lake District. Overlooking a spiritual view, he had a further intense moment of clarity and hope. He didn't need to die.

Still in a fugue, Michael headed south for Gosport in Hampshire, where he had once served as a submariner. He sat in the Naval Museum until closing time trying to recover his identity. The usher had to ask him to leave. Michael then attempted to drive to Portsmouth, but ended up dazed and confused in a building society in Brighton. The staff sat him down and found his psychiatrist's business card in his wallet. After a few calls, Met officers came to take him back to the clinic where he had failed to turn up one week earlier.

UNTOUCHABLES

Beth had imagined so many scenarios. For the first few days she clung to the belief that he was clearing his head and had "gone to ground" somewhere. Michael had left his passport and taken his walking boots and a grey V-neck sweater. But when none of his relatives or friends was contacted, it started to dawn on Beth that he was going to harm himself. In the days before he disappeared they had rowed and for the first time he spent the night on the couch.

Beth is not battle hardy like her husband used to be. She avoids confrontation. "But", she says with unusual steel in her voice, "if someone hurts the people I love, I'll go for them." After the search of their home she had complained to the PCA. They referred it back to the Untouchables who investigated themselves and found there was no substance to the complaint.

Beth fumed when she learned that the same squad that had caused her husband's breakdown was muscling in on the search for him and no doubt planning a strategy for how his suicide would be spun through the media. She was on the precipice of going public herself when the call came that Michael had been found and was on his way back to the clinic. She didn't find out the details of his suicide plans for many months to come.

After Christmas, Michael's solicitor sent an urgent letter to deputy commissioner Ian Blair seeking his immediate intervention to exonerate and let her client medically retire. The Untouchables had destroyed Michael. A well-trained, loyal and honest cop would never be fit for any kind of duty again.

Commissioner Stevens and senior Untouchables vacillated for a further three months until deciding on an exit strategy.

There was one Untouchable absent from the star chamber – detective chief superintendent Chris Jarratt, the man who Michael says originally targeted him after he refused to work for the Dark Side. In March 2002, Jarratt was removed from his new post as head of all murder inquiries in south London after allegations from colleagues about bullying, expenses fraud and domestic violence. However, the allegation most relevant to Michael's case was that Jarratt had also abused his power as an Untouchable and its intelligence system to target officers he didn't like or by whom he felt threatened.[20]

On 22 April, after four and a half years, Scotland Yard withdrew all disciplinary proceedings and lifted Michael's suspension. He was allowed to medically retire with no stain on his record.

Just to show there were no hard feelings, six months later he was invited to receive a long service and good conduct medal from Sir

UNDERCOVER 599 – MICHAEL'S STORY

John Stevens. It was then that Michael handed the commissioner his letter.

The following year, Stevens dominated the news agenda when he published his third report into corruption and collusion between Loyalist death squads and British security forces in Northern Ireland. Over 14 years, his team of Scotland Yard detectives had been investigating the activities of a secret unit called the FRU inside the British Army, which had targeted Republicans for assassination.

Stevens told journalists that his report concluded there had been unethical and unlawful handling of informants, the withholding of compromising documents, the misleading of politicians and a general culture of cover-up and hostility towards his efforts to get at the truth. The commissioner even criticised the intelligence services for obstructing his inquiry. The media portrayed him as a champion of democratic accountability.

Michael knows something of how the world of shadow warriors works. He accuses Stevens of condoning in London what he is happy to condemn in Belfast. "The Untouchables are a secret unit inside Scotland Yard that is out of control and its methods should now be examined by a parliamentary inquiry."

The suggestion is gathering pace among a cross-party group of MPs. Not least among them is Andy Burnham, Labour member for Leigh and currently the parliamentary private secretary to home secretary David Blunkett. Burnham became involved through Michael's brother, a soldier in the Army and his constituent. "He came to me and said this shouldn't be allowed to happen in the UK. And I agree."

Burnham took up the case before he was appointed PPS, a stepping-stone to minister. No other issue has frustrated him more than this one, he says. Deputy commissioner Ian Blair briefed the MP and described the Untouchables as a world leader in anti-corruption work. Burnham felt he was "complacent".

Many of the key players in this affair are now leading lights in UK policing. Ian Blair was knighted; Andy Hayman appointed chief constable of Norfolk; Brian Moore made a commander; and Tony Fuller has been promoted twice to superintendent and is the current head of the CIB intelligence cell, renamed the Intelligence Development Group.

The case of Undercover 599 is estimated to have so far cost the taxpayer over £2 million. "On a human level it is unbelievable what Michael and his family have been through," says Burnham.

Sir John Stevens has still not responded to Michael's letter.

PART TWO

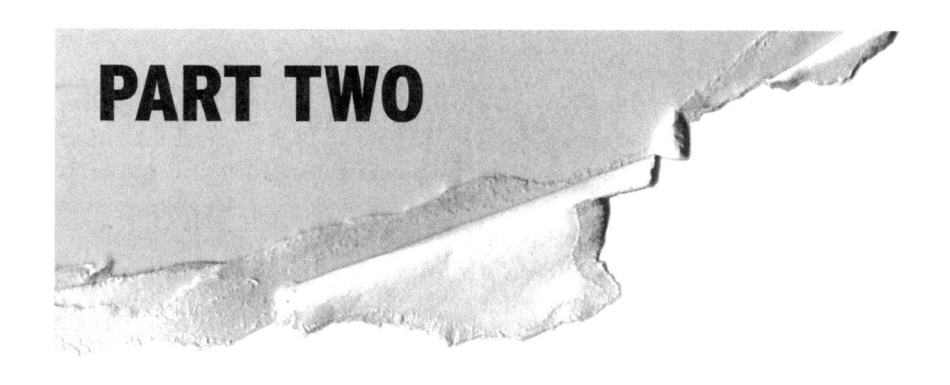

THE GHOSTS OF THE GHOST SQUAD

2

NOBLE CAUSE CORRUPTION

When it came to reinforcing the thin blue line between law and order and the descent into anarchy Margaret Thatcher was no pussy. If women like a man in uniform, during her 11-year reign, from 1979 to 1990, Maggie positively gushed over the forces of law and order. The military helped save the Conservative prime minister's political project and her bacon in 1982 with a victory thousands of miles away on the Falkland Islands. And the long-running dirty war in Northern Ireland always made the intelligence services especially welcome at Number Ten. But it was the police – Scotland Yard[1] in particular – who were singled out, above teachers and nurses, as her elite public sector workers. One political biography described them as Mrs Thatcher's "favoured class".[2]

This flirtatiousness was not just an instinctual alliance of two traditionally right-wing bodies, but a calculated union to enforce her radical vision. From the very beginning of her premiership Mrs Thatcher realised that the social and economic experiment she and her advisers planned for Britain would need the boys in blue on their side. Police pay and numbers were therefore made a priority. So much so that on the first working day of her new administration, leaders of the Police Federation, the representatives of rank and file officers, were invited to Downing Street to be informed about their large pay packet. This would be the last time anything approximating a trade union got a warm reception at Number Ten.

Inside Downing Street the political dominatrix was more than capable of handbagging any hint of a social conscience out of the remaining "wets" in her cabinet. It was outside, up and down the country, that the Iron Lady would need the police to quell rising civil disorder caused by her unfolding conviction politics.

The Greenham Common Peace Camp, made up of women opposed to Cruise missiles on British soil, was dug in outside an airbase in Berkshire – not a county known as a hotbed of radicalism. According to a secret cabinet document leaked to a newspaper, the security forces were authorised to use live ammunition if protestors tried to prevent the arrival of the nuclear warheads.

Elsewhere, the coal miners, or "the enemy within" as the prime minister called them, were striking in 1984 to save their communities from becoming ghost towns. While she swung her handbag at the Welfare State, police officers co-ordinated by Scotland Yard swung their truncheons across the coal pits of Albion. One serving detective, whose father was a miner, remembers with shame how his colleagues returned to London from duty "up North" bragging about waving wads of money at the hungry strikers. This was several years before Harry Enfield's grotesque comic creation "loads-a-money" summed up the mood.

A defining TV image of these turbulent times was the police cavalry charges at Orgreave coking plant near Sheffield. Another was the Battle of Wapping, a site in east London where press baron Rupert Murdoch had relocated his non-unionised media empire in 1986. "It was the working class pitted against the working class," recalls one recently retired detective. "But we were offered extra pay [to police the strikes] so those keen to supplement their incomes and get on in the organisation agreed to do it."

These grinding, bloody public order set-pieces, which on occasion resembled scenes from an epic movie, led to an increase in the number of assault complaints by civilians against the police. As a result, says one lawyer, the Police Federation changed the funding rules to include free legal representation for any "incident" that occurred on duty. Demonstrators responded with the satirical refrain "HELP THE POLICE – BEAT YOURSELF UP".

And what of the battle of ideas? The well-developed concerns for the erosion of civil liberties, such as freedom of association or the right to strike, were immediately dismissed by Mrs Thatcher or ridiculed by her friends in the right-wing press as the hand wringing of the bed-wetter fringe of the democratic Left.

Meanwhile, the bond between the prime minister and Scotland Yard was further cemented by three brutal police killings. The first

NOBLE CAUSE CORRUPTION

was WPC Yvonne Fletcher, shot dead by a gunman inside the Libyan embassy in April 1984. Nine months later undercover cop John Fordham died from multiple stab wounds inflicted by Kent gangster Kenny Noye, who was under surveillance for his role in the disposal of £26 million of gold bullion stolen from the Brinks Mat warehouse near Heathrow. Then, in October 1985, rioters on the Broadwater Farm Estate in Tottenham, north London, hacked to death PC Keith Blakelock.

Each death neatly identified Mrs Thatcher's three enemies – terrorism, organised crime and domestic subversion.

Despite the ideological resistance of Tory governments to restraining police powers, it was the murder of a gay man in 1972 and the inner city riots nine years later under her premiership that eventually led to the first real check on police misconduct.

Maxwell Confait, a London rent boy, was murdered in his home before it was set alight. Three suggestive boys aged between fourteen and eighteen, all with low mental ages, were jailed on confessions extracted by the police. However, the Court of Appeal quashed their convictions, saying the confessions were unreliable. A judicial inquiry was launched, followed by a Royal Commission on criminal procedure.

The main concern was police reliance on and fabrication of confession evidence, a then widespread practice known as "verballing". This criminal act involves falsely attributing incriminating comments, partial admissions or full confessions to the suspect. A good verbal has an added benefit for the police. When the defendant is giving evidence in court, the prosecution will try to rile him into accusing the officer of lying. The trap is now set because if the defendant has a criminal record and attacks the officer's character then the jury can be told of his own peccadillos.

In a recent *mea culpa* autobiography, Keith Hellawell, the former chief constable of West Yorkshire and retired Drug Tsar to the Blair government, described a corrupt culture in the detective branch from the sixties to the eighties, which the courts did their best to condone. Detectives, he wrote, were "beating confessions, fabricating evidence, doing anything at all that would help them gain the required result . . . Confessions were everything to us."[3]

On its own, the Confait case was just another *cause célèbre* that neatly exposed the institutionalised corruption of the criminal justice system, which all the key players recognised but refused to address. It took a series of inner city riots across the country, however, to make the politicians and judiciary take note.

If 1968 was the summer of love then 1981 in Thatcher's Britain was the summer of hate. Brixton, before it became ghetto fabulous, and the inner city areas of Handsworth in Birmingham, Moss Side in Manchester and Toxteth in Liverpool all burnt, as disaffected youths rioted against high unemployment, no future and overtly racist policing.

London dub poet Linton Kwesi Johnson gave lyrical expression to the "iration" in his song *Sonny's Lettah*, an attack on the police's liberal use of the "sus laws" to stop and search those in possession of afro hair and thick lips or driving while black.

> Jim start to wriggle
> The police start to giggle

The Brixton riots were followed by Lord Scarman's inquiry report in 1982. The liberal jurist called for greater accountability of the police and greater sensitivity in how they policed deprived multi-cultural inner city communities.

On the issue of accountability, Scotland Yard was way behind other regional police forces. Since its creation in 1829 the Yard had only been accountable to the Home Office, which was now in the hands of a rabidly pro-police government. However, the accumulating pressure for reform led to the introduction of unprecedented new police procedures through the 1984 Police and Criminal Evidence Act.

PACE, as it is known, now made it very risky for officers to try and obtain fabricated or coerced confessions. The act introduced due process – legal protection for the arrested person – where before there was unchecked police discretion. The right to a lawyer before questioning and the recording of all police interviews were designed to break with the corrupt past. And if officers blatantly ignored the new codes of practice then cases could now be lost at trial, no matter how pro-prosecution the judge was.

A further element of independence came from the 1985 Prosecution of Offences Act. This landmark legislation created the Crown Prosecution Service in October the following year. The CPS, instead of the police, would now prosecute and prepare all cases for trial. It was supposed to act as a check on the quality of police evidence before it was tested in front of a judge or jury.

Lord Scarman's report had also called for a fully independent

NOBLE CAUSE CORRUPTION

system of investigating complaints against the police. He criticised the existing Police Complaints Board, set up in 1976, as lacking public confidence. The police investigated themselves with no oversight and those members of the public who dared to complain feared "harassment and intimidation", he concluded.

One young detective constable from the Met succinctly summed up, without realising it, the problem of allowing the police to be judge and jury in its own cause: "I will always put loyalty [to the organisation] over honesty," he said. This rationale is as true of the officer complained about as it is of the officer carrying out the complaint investigation.

Unsurprisingly, the Thatcher government was unmoved by Scarman's arguments and opted for not even a halfway house towards independence. Out of PACE was born the Police Complaints Authority, a supervisory body with no real power and no investigative function, which Scarman rightly predicted would become "an irrelevant fifth wheel to the investigation coach".

In practice, as time passed, the PCA became complicit in many police cover-ups. Most of its government-appointed members proved themselves aloof, out of their depth, arrogant, too police friendly and susceptible to political pressure.

There was a long-held myth that British justice is the best in the world and corruption happened in other countries. But by 1988, reactionary voices in the government, the police and the judiciary were struggling to defend the *ancien régime* as the Court of Appeal began to overturn a cascade of convictions from the seventies and eighties. These miscarriages of justice exposed the true danger of politicised prosecutions where the courts connived to excuse or ignore evidence of severe police misconduct. This ranged from torture, suffocation using plastic bags, planted evidence and "lost" documents which officers knew if disclosed would clear those falsely accused.

Over the ensuing five years of Conservative rule the criminal justice system suffered its greatest crisis of public confidence as one by one prisoners wrongly incarcerated for decades emerged from the appeal court and onto the front pages. Many of these miscarriages, like the Guildford Four, the Birmingham Six, the Maguire Seven and Judith Ward, had their roots in the dirty war in Northern Ireland. They had been wrongly convicted for an IRA bombing campaign on mainland Britain that killed over 26 innocent people.

Other tragic cases, like those of Stefan Kiszko and Derek Treadaway, showed the rampant lawlessness of certain police squads when they needed "a result". Kiszko, a mentally retarded man, served 16 years after allegedly confessing to a sexual murder the prosecution knew he could not have committed. His zero sperm count did not match the semen found in the victim, but these tests weren't disclosed to his defence. Treadaway's story could easily have come out of Pinochet's Chile, but was again set in Birmingham. He maintained that detectives from the West Midlands Crime Squad suffocated him in 1982 with sealed plastic bags over his head until, fearing for his life, he confessed to four armed robberies.

For all these and other disturbing miscarriages of justice, between 1989 and 1994 no police officer accused of misconduct was ever prosecuted. Similarly, the barristers and solicitors who prosecuted these cases continued to rise within the judiciary. And Sir Peter Imbert, who had been involved in the investigation of the Guildford pub bombings, was commissioner of the Metropolitan Police at the very time the appeal was allowed.

On 31 March 1990, middle-class Conservative voters united with Labour supporters and others to march through London in protest at the introduction of the Poll Tax, a flagship Thatcherite policy which she had cynically first tested on the Scottish people one year earlier. The demonstration turned violent in Trafalgar Square, and once again her boys in blue were there to quell the riot.

No policy U-turn would be possible with Maggie at the helm, so her key cabinet colleagues and party grandees, fearing a loss at the next general election, conspired to oust her from the throne, tired as they already were with her bullying leadership style and intransigence on relations with Europe. The Iron Lady cried as she was driven out of Number Ten for the last time. Few shed a tear for her.

John Major, the incoming party leader and caretaker prime minister, was a politician whose greyness was in sharp contrast to his wounded predecessor. In April 1992 he went to the polls and beat an over-confident Labour Party to begin an unprecedented fourth term of Conservative rule. However, this time, relations with Scotland Yard and the police service would not be so cosy.

Major was desperately worried about looking weak on law and order. The early nineties was a period of economic recession with high unemployment returning and increased crime. So his ministers had to address the collapse of public confidence in the criminal justice system and the failure of a well-financed police service to deliver on crime reduction.

NOBLE CAUSE CORRUPTION

A 1992 government inquiry into police pay and conditions marked a reversal of Thatcher's financial mollycoddling. Predictably, it caused uproar among the federated ranks and senior officers. Performance-related pay, fixed-term contracts and substantial pay cuts for new recruits finally ended the immunity from the ravages of Thatcherism that the police had enjoyed for over a decade.

Senior Home Office civil servants also started to cast their net for a new Met commissioner to replace Sir Peter Imbert, whose tenure was coming to an end. In the autumn of 1992 they settled on a lanky, awkward-looking candidate, Paul Condon, who, like Major, was conspicuous for his greyness. Far more interesting was the fact that for the first time the government had decided to extend the new commissioner's period in office from five to seven years. This was a clear indication that Condon's brief from his political masters was to modernise the most powerful and recalcitrant police force in the country. He had until the new millennium.

To the crime correspondents of the national media, Condon was billed as a reformer ready to grasp the nettle on racism, perks, low professionalism and inefficiency. The *Guardian* described him as part of "a new breed of articulate, fast-track, graduate officers who emerged in the 1970s".[4] Besides his years in the Met, Paul Condon had spent two long stints at Kent Constabulary, first as an assistant chief constable and then as the top man. From there, he was plucked from relative obscurity to be appointed the most senior police officer in the UK.

When Condon took over the Met its moral authority was in tatters. It is tempting for some to buy into the spin and see him as an ethical new broom parachuted in by a cuddly, more inclusive Conservative party who'd ditched the bitch. But, as ever, the reality is murkier.

In February 1993 Paul Condon, then aged 45, took the reins of the Met. In came the management and image consultants looking for efficiencies, and fast-tracked graduate cops who were more *Brideshead Revisited* than *The Sweeney*. One crime correspondent described the commissioner as "John Birt in uniform", a reference to the director general of the BBC who was simultaneously reforming his organisation.

Later that same month, John Major gave an interview to the *Mail on Sunday* in which he expressed how strongly he felt society needed "to condemn a little more and understand a little less". The interview publicly signalled to the nation and the police service what journalist

David Rose rightly calls a period of "new authoritarianism".[5]

For the next four years, from 1993 to 1997, the Major government worked closely with Condon to win back a crime-weary public. This was done through a series of draconian measures that ignored the unresolved and awkward questions about police misconduct raised by the previous period of miscarriages of justice. What Major had taken away from the police in financial perks he was about to give back in legal powers.

In the autumn of 1993, the new home secretary, the oleaginous Michael Howard, worked closely with the Association of Chief Police Officers to develop a list of measures to bring offenders – car thieves, burglars, vandals and the like – to book. He presented his list at the October party conference to rapturous applause. Among it was an end to the right to silence. The prosecution, he said, should be able to infer to a jury a defendant's guilt if he said nothing when interviewed by the police.[6] There would also be less disclosure of police documents ahead of a trial. This, it was claimed, would prevent cunning defence lawyers picking holes in the prosecution case to acquit their "factually guilty" clients.

Howard's party piece was yet to come. What he told the conference was manna from heaven for Condon and other less enlightened senior police officers. The time had come, said the home secretary, to "rebalance" the criminal justice system in favour of protection of the public and against the criminal. The war on crime had been declared, and the police would be given the tools to recalibrate society.

The New Labour Party under Tony Blair showed in opposition how little there was between it and the Tories in their pursuit of support from Middle England. "Tough on crime and tough on the causes of crime" was Blair's pithy law and order catchphrase as shadow home secretary. That too was manna from heaven for the 44 police forces.

By contrast with his predecessor, it was clear to the new Met commissioner that the next four years would be a period of policing on the front foot. And, incredibly, the country's most powerful policeman was right to believe he would have support from the two main political parties.

The Home Office had chosen Condon to stop the slide, not stop the rot in the criminal justice system. In furtherance of this aim, Condon made two crucial appearances in 1993 to rehabilitate the authority of his officers – one in front of a parliamentary select committee and the other on BBC's *Panorama* programme.

NOBLE CAUSE CORRUPTION

On both occasions, he deployed a tidy little argument straight from the mouths of spin-doctors. It ran like this: Yes, there have been abuses. Fabricating evidence and lying on oath to convict people officers believed were "factually guilty" did occur. But those abuses are born of frustration with the excessive rights enjoyed by defendants. Pause. Solemn look. The bad days will return if the pendulum is not swung back in favour of the victims of crime and the police. Trust us. We've learned from our mistakes and moved on.

These abuses were in fact serious criminal offences – perjury and perverting the course of justice – by those in a position of public trust. And as such it should make no difference if the officer did it for money or, as Condon claimed, out of a misguided morality. Such acts are crimes and should be dealt with as such. But the image consultants at the Yard, needless to say, didn't see it that way. They told the commissioner to give such severe misconduct a more palatable name – welcome to the ignoble concept of "noble cause corruption".

This sinister phrase – which belongs among the pages of Anthony Burgess's *A Clockwork Orange* – is still used today and remains a pitiful but effective effort by the Yard at self-delusion and damage limitation. Just as politicians now call telling lies "spin", so too has the Yard substituted police crimes with "noble cause corruption".

The phrase was part of the 1993 propaganda effort to rehabilitate the police through the launching of a war on crime and on due process. One after the other, the country's top cops conspicuously failed to admit how senior management had in fact tolerated and even encouraged 'noble cause corruption'.

The fish rots from the head, but not according to Paul Condon, a Piscean. He gave typical expression to the spineless distancing exercise when he told *Panorama* about a far-off land a long, long time ago. "There was a time," he began, "when a minority of officers were prepared to bend the rules, massage the evidence, not for personal gain or not even in their own terms to tell lies about people. But I think elaborating on things that were said in a way to make sure the case had the strongest chance of going through to a conviction."[7]

Despite the Tory government's awareness of how pervasive the culture of "noble cause corruption" was, in 1993 the Home Office paved the way for a new piece of legislation which would roll back even more of the legal protections reluctantly squeezed out of the criminal justice system since PACE. The Criminal Procedures and Investigation bill was the last act in the total public rehabilitation of the police under the Major government. It put in officers' hands the power

UNTOUCHABLES

to decide which documents from the criminal inquiry should be disclosed to the defence before the trial. Any information that could help the defence's declared argument or, more crucially, that would undermine the prosecution case had to be disclosed.

But of course the system would rely entirely on the integrity of the disclosure officer and his ability to put aside his loyalty to the police and to his colleagues, and to withstand pressure from his superiors and the government. When it became law in 1996, the Act created a whole new mechanism for potential miscarriages of justice.

3

THE GHOST SQUAD

It was in the climate of "new authoritarianism" that less than one year into his post, commissioner Paul Condon took the decision to set up a covert operation to develop "a strategic intelligence picture of corruption" in Scotland Yard.[1]

The setting up in late 1993 of a Ghost Squad to develop that intelligence picture was carried out with unprecedented secrecy. The Home Office was aware of "the squad that didn't exist", and had authorised funding for it, says the Yard. But the whole affair, at first glance, appeared entirely at odds with John Major's highly public war on crime, to which a rehabilitated Scotland Yard was essential. After all, how could the government hope to restore public confidence if it ever got out that the most senior officer in the country didn't know whom he could trust in his own force?

The truth is the Ghost Squad and the intelligence it would gather over the next four years was never supposed to be made public. It was designed to operate completely in the shadows, without any legal oversight. Over a decade later Scotland Yard still won't come clean and reveal why the Ghost Squad was really set up.

Anti-corruption chiefs confirm that the strategic document to set up the covert operation was signed by the commissioner in 1993. But ask when and what underpinned it, and the shutters come down. "The decisions taken around the formation of this document and the document itself are strictly confidential," wrote one senior officer.[2]

George Orwell said in his novel *1984*, "Who controls the past controls the future. Who controls the present controls the past." In free societies, he observed, censorship is more sophisticated because "the inconvenient facts [are] kept dark without any need for an official ban". This bad news management can only be done with the help of those loyal servants of the state who pose as journalists. We are talking about many of the national media's spoon-fed crime correspondents who on command, like Pavlov's dog, scurry, fighting among themselves for a suck on the Yard's teat, where the official version is dispensed. In place of transparency about the origins of the Ghost Squad, the Yard developed a cover story disseminated by loyal crime correspondents, which portrays the Yard in a very positive light. In essence, Condon was a bold, reforming commissioner who, alerted by his concerned intelligence chiefs, decided once and for all to stop the "cycle of corruption" that had dogged Scotland Yard since the seventies.

The Ghost Squad, it is true, was the brainchild of two senior officers, commander John Grieve and his number two, detective chief superintendent Roy Clark. At the time, they ran the very secretive Directorate of Intelligence (SO11), which was at the forefront of a new type of policing. "Intelligence-led policing" was a significant departure from the past, in that targeting local and major criminals now took precedence over investigating crimes. The targeting was achieved by a greater reliance on phone-tapping and bugging criminals' premises and cars, combined with the use of informants and sting operations.

In the early nineties, SO11 was behind a series of covert intelligence-gathering operations targeting known crime families and individuals in London, especially in the East End. According to the official version, during the course of these investigations, criminals were secretly recorded talking about their corrupt links with the police. Transcripts of the secret recordings were passed to Grieve and Clark at SO11. They were already concerned, says Scotland Yard, because "a lot of their operations were being compromised . . . for no apparent reason". Consequently, they moved "to look at the state of health of the organisation and see if corruption was a problem".[3]

Retired cops are like guests at Hotel California – they might check out but they never leave. Grieve and Clark are no exception and remain very loyal to Scotland Yard. They still are the gatekeepers of its secret history. Sadly, they declined to be interviewed about their past in the Ghost Squad. Clark, however, did flesh out the official version in an academic text: "[We] analysed the information, albeit in an unconventional manner, and noticed that a small number of criminals received immunity from police attention and a degree of protection from arrest. Moreover, the criminals seemed to be confident that even if arrested they could buy their way out of trouble, and could rely on a small group of corrupt police officers for information, advice and a range of other criminal services. The analysis continued throughout 1992 and into 1993 under a cloak of secrecy."[4]

Immodestly, Clark also claimed that in "the early part of 1993" he wrote "a document that was influential in everything thereafter".[5] That document was discussed by a select group of very senior police officers before approaching their relatively new commissioner later that year. It set out the blueprint and operational ethos for what would become the Ghost Squad. It purported to outline a radical new way of dealing with police corruption in the Met, and explicitly admitted that the existing system was a failure.

At this time, the Met's internal affairs department was called the Complaints Investigation Bureau. It had two teams, CIB1 and CIB2. They overwhelmingly dealt with complaints of police misconduct generated by the public. These ranged from assault and theft to "noble cause corruption". CIB2 also investigated what they regarded as more serious offences, where for example allegations emerged during court cases that officers had taken money from criminal defendants to lose a key piece of evidence.

At the time senior Yard figures were discussing the document, CIB was engaged in Operation Jackpot, an internal inquiry led by superintendent Ian Russell into drug and noble cause corruption at Stoke Newington police station in north-east London, where Clark had been in charge from 1989 to 1992.

CIB came directly under the command of the deputy commissioner, who in 1993 was John Smith. It was natural therefore that he would be part of the small circle of very senior officers that finessed Clark's research document into a comprehensive secret strategy for the Ghost Squad. The inner circle also included assistant commissioners David Veness and Ian Johnston, commander John Grieve, detective chief superintendents Roger Gaspar and Bill Griffiths, superintendents Ian Quinn and Ian Russell, plus a newly promoted detective chief inspector called Dave Woods.

The strategy document has never been disclosed, not even to Parliament. But from well-placed police sources and listening to the court evidence of Clark and Gaspar, it is possible to identify the key elements of the plan.

Gaspar would be appointed the head of CIB. It was accepted that existing staff could not be trusted. So he would have a "cover story" to explain the arrival of a small group of detectives who only reported to him. Dave Woods would run a covert intelligence cell of between 12 and 20 officers. They would operate outside of CIB and the Met in a secret location known only to the small "high level committee" of senior officers. Gaspar said he and Clark had "buried the money" to rent premises for the intelligence cell so well that the landlord thought it might be crooked.

The intelligence cell had several functions. Firstly it would control the phone-taps and electronic bugs planted in police offices, cars and the premises of targeted criminals. After the secretly recorded conversations were transcribed and analysed, Ghost Squad officers would then decide how to further the intelligence. This, for example, could mean deploying a surveillance team – made up of retired and serving military and intelligence personnel – to follow suspect detectives and criminals.

Clark laid out the need for secrecy in these remarkable terms: "We didn't know who we could trust. The rule was there would be absolute secrecy. The fact that there was a very covert intelligence-gathering operation should not be known to anybody, irrespective of rank."[6]

Woods would also need a cover story to explain his sudden departure from normal detective duties. A fiendish plan was hatched that could have come straight from an Ian Fleming novel. Woods was going to die, then rise from the dead. First an announcement would be placed in Police Notices, the official system for appointments, commendations and retirements. It would say, "Dave Woods is retiring." The cover story was that an earlier operation to remove a lump had not been successful. It had returned as terminal cancer and Woods was therefore retiring abroad, to die.

When the plan was put into effect the tragic news spread like a bad smell through the Yard's satellite offices across London. A number of officers who had served with Woods distinctly remembered contributing to a whip-round for him in 1994. Some were a little miffed when they realised he had gone to spy on them and their colleagues.

One senior officer recalls putting £20 into the whip. But in 1997, after the Ghost Squad had been disbanded, he bumped into Woods on a superintendents' course. The Lazarus cop, he says, denied he'd been running the Ghost Squad intelligence cell and claimed instead that some dangerous criminals were after him and so the Yard had relocated him for several years. A cover story for the cover story, thought our source.

THE GHOST SQUAD

It was Roger Gaspar who presented to commissioner Paul Condon the finessed strategy document on 5 May 1994. According to Gaspar, he took 40 minutes because there was so much to explain. Again, we are not allowed to know the full details of what he told the commissioner. So we have put together a composite from well-placed sources and court evidence.

At 3.30 p.m. Gaspar arrived at the commissioner's offices at New Scotland Yard armed with a full intelligence picture. He named a number of officers whose activities he claimed were corrupt and outlined the threat they posed to the organisation. Clearly the material was "persuasive", he said, because it met with the commissioner's "full approval".[7]

Condon was told the existing system of investigating police corruption was inadequate. CIB could not be trusted and was too leaky. The argument was put this way: "An overt inquiry where officers are cautioned and asked if they are corrupt is futile. And a covert inquiry where everyone knew about it in days is ineffective."[8]

Consequently, certain officers in the Ghost Squad would become "sleepers" within their own organisation. These moles would be posted to specialist squads like the South East Regional Crime Squad (SERCS), where detectives tackling the highest levels of organised crime were thought most likely to cross the line. The sleepers would spy on suspect colleagues and report back to the intelligence cell.

The Ghost Squad's mission, Condon was told, was not to arrest bent cops and put them on trial, but to identify how exposed the Yard was to corruption. Who, in other words, among the organised criminals and the specialist detectives targeting them, were corruptly linked? The results would only be for internal purposes.

A specific type of corruption would be under the microscope. The Ghost Squad, it was made clear, wasn't interested in "noble cause corruption", or racist and violent officers who regularly abused the public: in other words the sort of general police crimes that affect Londoners most. It was only after those detectives who actively worked with organised criminals in return for money and favours.

Condon was delighted by Roger Gaspar's presentation. His approval was total. "And so began what is arguably one of the most adventurous policing operations of recent times," wrote Roy Clark. "Over the course of the next two years a secret squad of police officers gathered intelligence, which enabled a more sophisticated understanding of the corrupt relationships between criminals and a few police officers to be achieved. Whilst the numbers involved were not large it became clear that the potential damage to the reputation of the police service and the criminal justice system was immense."

For four years, Condon's Ghost Squad operated without any independent oversight. The only control was by those select senior officers who set up and ran it.

Roy Clark claimed the alarming intelligence picture he had developed between 1992 and 1993, which led to setting up the secret squad, not only identified bent cops but also "indicated there were concerns" about the integrity of certain (unnamed) members of the Crown Prosecution Service.[9] The convenience of this untested argument should not be underestimated. Who after all was in a position to challenge his self-serving assertion? Clark's unspecified "concerns" about the CPS enabled the Ghost Squad to operate as judge and jury in its own cause, without the involvement of the very agency formed seven years beforehand to prevent this.

Under such a system, anything could be said about anyone to justify the continued lack of democratic accountability or legal safeguards. It wasn't until the second, overt phase of the anti-corruption crusade began in 1998 that the CPS was formally consulted, and even then its advice was ignored on key issues around legal safeguards. Leading CPS lawyers confirm this. They also accept it would have been better if the agency had been brought in at the very beginning.[10]

Clark concedes that the covert nature of the Ghost Squad was far from ideal. However, he contends that his natural democratic tendencies were "hogtied by the need for secrecy".

This is open to question. For if the old CIB couldn't be trusted, then why weren't the public it was supposed to protect told? Instead, thousands were encouraged to continue to use the internal system when the commissioner knew it was severely compromised. If CIB was too leaky, in that officers posted there were more likely to tip off their friends under investigation than investigate the alleged misconduct, then why wasn't the commissioner seeking to reform the system? After all, just a few years before Gaspar's presentation to Condon, a 1991 Home Office study of police deviance displayed a widespread dissatisfaction from those members of the public who'd bothered to go through the internal complaints system.

Another unanswered question concerns the selection of Ghost Squad members. Who guaranteed its members weren't really poachers turned gamekeepers? Well, quite simply, the handful of detectives who made up the secret intelligence cell were selected by the bosses, and they in turn selected themselves.

There is no external or internal accounting for this selection process. On what basis were John Grieve, Roy Clark and Bill Griffiths, for example, considered any more honest or of greater integrity than the then head of SERCS, Roy Penrose, who according to Clark was not someone they felt they could bring into the Ghost Squad circle?[11] This was a strange statement for Clark to make given that his last posting at Stoke Newington had been mired in allegations of corrupt practices in the drug squad and unanswered questions about severe management failures.

The Ghost Squad was not only a self-selecting secret unit within the Yard charged with identifying pockets of corruption, it also had a second undeclared level of covertness. Some of its senior intelligence officers and those who made up the pool of detectives that eventually grew to 200 in number were active members of another secret society, Freemasonry.

No one independent existed to ask these questions or whether certain senior officers in the Ghost Squad, who had risen through the ranks during the bad old days of the seventies and eighties, were suitable to point the finger. But then as noble cause corruption was not an issue for the Ghost Squad, anyone who may have transgressed in this way was not considered unsuitable to serve on it.

The Ghost Squad gave the Yard the ability to decide for itself where the historical "cut-off point" of corruption would be. By analysing the secret intelligence it then drew a line and declared Year Zero. Gung ho officers, who now find themselves on the wrong side of that line, are understandably amazed at the sanctimony and selective amnesia of their accusers, who they claim in the past endorsed, turned a blind eye to or even participated in what is now classed as unethical or dishonest behaviour. Conveniently, their accusers' crimes and misdemeanours fall on the right side of Year Zero, and they will not be called to account for them. In a fully independent system of investigating police misconduct there would be no Year Zero. Investigators would be free to follow the evidence wherever it took them because preserving the reputation of the Yard, or a secret team within it, would not be a consideration.

The Home Office should have asked more questions when Condon presented the secret plan. But its ministers and mandarins were not interested in making the police more accountable, let alone the Ghost Squad. As the previous chapter has shown, the trend between 1993 and 1997 under the Major government was entirely in the other direction.

Asked a series of detailed questions about how the Ghost Squad operation was pitched, and what oversight function ministers fulfilled, a Home Office spokeswoman consulted with the unit in the ministry that deals with police corruption and offered this rather alarming or disingenuous reply: "There is no role for ministers and the Home Office. We haven't got the authority, therefore the Met has no need to approach the Home Office or explain what they did and why they did it . . . They don't need our authority to [launch an anti-corruption operation]. They might let us know as a matter of courtesy that they were thinking of doing it." The relevant Home Office unit would have "monitored" events, but more through parliamentary questions and press reports, she added.[12]

Former home secretary, Michael Howard, had this to say: "I'm not sure, I'm afraid, that I am going to be able to help you. And I'll explain on another occasion when I hope I'll be able to speak to you. Bye." Despite chasing him up, he never called again.[13] Six months later he became leader of the Conservative Party.

The launching of a secret undercover squad to spy on police officers was entirely at odds with and jeopardised prime minister John Major and Michael Howard's high-profile war on crime. It also ran contrary to the commissioner's public claims that the Met could be trusted.

Had Paul Condon and John Major gone public with the revelation about not knowing who could be trusted in the country's biggest police force, the political rehabilitation of Scotland Yard would have been exposed as a sham, and the government's law and order policies as unworkable, at least in the capital. The need for secrecy was not just an operational necessity, therefore, but a political one.

It should not be surprising perhaps that the Major government was willing to go along with this deception of the British public. After all, the prime minister had run his own scam on the electorate since 1992. During the Ghost Squad years, John Major launched his own sanctimonious crusade called "Back to Basics", against moral corruption in public and private life. His reassertion of "family values" was a key front in this campaign. Indeed, so concerned was John about the sanctity of the family unit, he had an affair with the former minister of rotten eggs, Edwina Currie. Other ministers followed suit, most notably heritage secretary and Spanish toe-sucker David Mellor. He achieved the impossible and appeared even oilier when he marshalled his family before the press to brazen out the allegation of adultery.

THE GHOST SQUAD

Meanwhile, in the world of big business, the prime minister's concern about probity in public life seemed to be lost on a succession of Tory ministers and MPs, who sold parliamentary favours to enrich themselves through corrupt deals and kickbacks in brown paper bags.

Some academics argue that police corruption rises when political sleaze is the order of the day. At the very least it couldn't have been much of an incentive for our boys in blue to stay straight when they saw professional lawbreakers in flash cars and lawmakers with their snouts in the trough.

Although it was not the major reason for launching the Ghost Squad, it enabled Scotland Yard to fight off the domestic security service, MI5, with whom it was locked in a fractious turf war.

MI5 already had primacy in intelligence gathering against the IRA in Europe. The intelligence agency's new director-general, Stella Rimmington, embarked on an intense lobbying campaign of the Home Office for a lead role over the Met in gathering intelligence against the IRA on the British mainland. This was fiercely, but unsuccessfully, resisted by Yard chiefs, who used their friends in the press to raise concerns about MI5, among them its lack of accountability – an argument that was advanced with a straight face. In May 1992, MI5 officially won the day.

Combating organised crime was the cause of a parallel turf war with the Yard. MI6, the overseas intelligence service, already had a role because of the global nature of the drug trade, which exploded in the eighties. MI5 made no secret to Whitehall mandarins of its desire to work on British organised crime syndicates and their international associates, an area traditionally dominated by the police and customs.[14] To advance their argument, the spooks were happy to point out police failures and the wider crisis of public confidence. Some Yard bosses retorted that MI5 was just looking for a new role after the collapse of communism. This was true. But the spooks made it plain to the Home Office that they could also investigate corruption of all kinds, including police corruption. Such a message must have sent shivers down the spine of Scotland Yard.

Concern about law enforcement corruption was a pressing issue at the Home Office, says veteran muckraker Geoff Seed. He was shown a confidential minute of a meeting attended by home secretary Michael Howard in 1994. "It dealt with the complete re-disposition of all the UK's security assets around three new threats – terrorism, money laundering and corruption," the journalist recalls. "It was a complete breakdown of the new structure and implementation." Such a re-disposition had been in the planning phase for years. The collapse of communism in 1989, the 1991 Gulf War and the dirty war in Northern Ireland were the three main factors that had led John Major to begin a radical re-alignment of Britain's security establishment.

John Grieve and Roy Clark, the Yard's intelligence chiefs, were not seen as officers who feared a closer relationship with MI5. As the architects of the Ghost Squad, they adopted a more inclusive approach. "For Grieve, it was far better to have MI5 inside the tent pissing out than outside pissing in," says a retired senior CIB officer, adding: "On the outside, the spooks could poison the well by pointing out to the Home Office where the holes in the anti-corruption strategy were." So Condon was advised to use retired and serving members of MI5 in the Ghost Squad intelligence cell. There was also an agreement to use MI5's highly experienced surveillance teams to follow target criminals and suspect detectives.

As 1993 turned into 1994, Grieve and Clark found themselves at the helm of the most politically powerful department in Scotland Yard. SO11 was the focal point of the new intelligence-led policing strategy. Meanwhile, secretly, it was also the controlling department behind the covert anti-corruption crusade.

Empire building was not unique to the Yard's intelligence chiefs. How much the Ghost Squad was used by the commissioner as a political tool over the next seven years to reduce the power base of the detective branch is an interesting question. Unfortunately, Lord Paul Condon, as he is now known, refuses to be interviewed about this.

When Roger Gaspar made his pitch, the commissioner was already skilfully implementing his Home Office brief to modernise the force. The Met's 3,000 detectives traditionally had considerable power and regarded themselves as an elite compared to their uniformed colleagues. Condon's predecessors had already reduced some of this autonomy by bringing detectives within police divisions and making them subordinate to a senior uniformed officer.

Condon, however, wanted to go further. First, he promoted more fast-tracked graduate entrants into senior positions within the "oikish" detective branch. Then he restricted the amount of time an officer could spend as a detective. And finally, he ensured that rank-and-file representatives of the detective branch no longer automatically had "the commissioner's ear".

Some senior detectives spoke of an aura of "McCarthyism" surrounding the anti-corruption crusade. The commissioner and his inner circle, it was felt, had the power to brief against their political opponents inside the Yard just with a well-timed nose tap. The fear of being told you had lost the commissioner's trust was enough to silence some of his natural critics.

The public phase of the anti-corruption crusade also gave the argument for reform a moral dimension. Those who resisted change could simply be asked whether they wanted to be on the side of the angels. One retired senior CIB officer described Condon's reforms as "a management coup".

Corruption, says Scotland Yard, is a "cyclical" phenomenon. Until the arrival of the new commissioner the force was caught up in a malignant cycle, described this way by a senior anti-corruption chief: "Every five or six years [corruption] manifested itself. We put huge resources into it to make sure it was cut out. Then back to normal duty. We felt we'd cured the problem."[15]

Other journalists were treated to a similar, cancerous excuse for why there had been no proactive approach to corruption in the eighties and early nineties. These are our favourites culled from the press clippings: "We thought it had gone away"; "We took our eye off the ball"; "We believed it was almost non-existent"; "We were not sufficiently alert or skilled to recognise the problem"; "CIB had become a sleepy hollow"; "We fell asleep at the wheel".

The idea that when it came to tackling corruption, Scotland Yard's management had collectively suffered from a special kind of narcolepsy – a rare condition characterised by sudden episodes of deep sleep – would be funny if it wasn't so intellectually dishonest. To then claim that under the new commissioner there was an ethical reawakening, with Condon in the role of Dr Oliver Sacks, followed by an unprecedented period of purge and reform, is to grossly re-write the Yard's history.

During the eighties and early nineties, the Yard wasn't complacent about corruption or lacking vigilance, as it now claims. Rather, senior officers deliberately ignored, played down or covered up the corruption allegations presented to them. And furthermore, in doing so, they allowed a number of bent detectives to thrive inside the country's biggest police force, some of whom had risen to high rank by the start of Condon's reign.

The setting up of the Ghost Squad was a defensive reaction by the Yard's senior management, its intelligence chiefs, strategic planners and spin-doctors to several pressing corruption scandals they could no longer ignore, play down or cover up. It was not, as they now maintain, an ethically proactive response. These scandals that forced Condon's hand are "the ghosts of the Ghost Squad". They arise out of three brutal and still unsolved murders in south-east London between 1987 and 1993. These restless souls have stalked the corridors of Scotland Yard for over ten years.

But it's not just the murder victims who haunt the Condon and Stevens eras, so too do the three police investigations of those murders, all of which have the same stench of corruption and cover-up.

Among all this scandal is a spate of unexplained suicides of four Scotland Yard detectives who were caught up in separate corruption inquiries.[16]

All these deaths, more than any other events, are the points of entry to the key patterns of corruption that emerged in the ten years, between 1983 and 1993, before the Ghost Squad was launched. They continue to haunt the Yard because they were deliberately ignored, played down or covered up at the time and afterwards.

In 1987, private detective Daniel Morgan was found dead in a pub car park in Sydenham, south-east London, with an axe buried in his skull. He was about to blow the whistle on local police corruption.

A few months later Morgan's friend, detective constable Alan "Taffy" Holmes, wrapped his chest around a shotgun and pulled the trigger. At the time he was under investigation for corruption, Taffy Holmes was also part of a massive investigation into the biggest robbery ever committed in the UK – the theft of gold worth £26 million from the Brinks Mat depository at Heathrow.

In 1991, Scotland Yard's most prolific informant, a man called David Norris, was gunned down as he arrived home from the pub. He had just come from a meeting with his police handler when a man, riding pillion on a motorbike, pumped him full of lead. Norris died moments later cradled by his pregnant wife.

The following year, police sergeant Gerry Carroll removed a gun from the armoury and shot himself through the head, at the height of the major corruption probe into officers at Stoke Newington police station. Scotland Yard had been forced to carry out the inquiry after a local community group exposed systematic drug corruption and police brutality that had led to at least 13 miscarriages of justice.

Then, in April 1993, black teenager Stephen Lawrence was stabbed to death by white racists with family links to organised drug crime and local cops.

THE GHOST SQUAD

Finally, in September 1993 BBC's *Panorama* broadcast a documentary exposing a corrupt South East Regional Crime Squad detective called John Donald. A south-east London drug dealer, who had been arrested by Donald and was facing trial, approached the BBC with a plan for the programme makers to secretly record him paying the bent detective for sensitive information. Police intelligence was eventually passed by Donald to a number of individuals in the criminal fraternity such as Kenny Noye. He was serving the tail end of a 14-year prison sentence for laundering the Brinks Mat gold. Donald's betrayal was even more acute because Noye had killed an undercover police officer during the Brinks Mat investigation.

This iconic heist was a watershed for organised crime and police corruption. As this book unfolds, it will become apparent just how much the ghost of Brinks Mat continues to haunt Scotland Yard today because the corruption was swept under the carpet 20 years ago, allowing a "firm within a firm" to grow inside south-east London policing. It is this corrupt firm of detectives we believe eventually contaminated the Morgan, Norris and Lawrence murder inquiries.

The Stoke Newington and Donald cases severely embarrassed Scotland Yard. Simultaneously, the families of Daniel Morgan and Stephen Lawrence were demanding justice and had voiced their concerns that the Yard was covering up police corruption. In the Morgan case Labour MP Chris Smith even suggested there was "evidence" police officers were actually involved in the murder.

It was in this climate that Yard intelligence chiefs John Grieve and Roy Clark reacted by suggesting setting up a secret Ghost Squad. Had the public known about Clark's secret role as the architect of this covert anti-corruption squad there may have been serious concerns, given his earlier stewardship of the scandal-ridden Stoke Newington police station.

The Ghost Squad was a cunning management response to all this rising pressure beyond the Yard's control, an invisible condom pulled over the Yard in late 1993 to safeguard its future reputation from bad seeds and bad publicity.

The first phase of the anti-corruption crusade was conceived as a pre-emptive strike. It allowed the intelligence chiefs to secretly "scope" the Yard's exposure to corruption, while publicly maintaining the fiction that it was still "the most honest force in the world" – something essential to the Major government's law and order policy.

The Yard's senior management was also aware that in opposition the otherwise police-friendly New Labour party had promised the parents of Stephen Lawrence it would hold a full public inquiry into the Met's handling of the murder investigation if it came to power. Sleaze and sanctimony in the Major government made that a dead certainty, as voters got weary of 18 years of Conservative hegemony. In May 1997, New Labour won the election and home secretary Jack Straw did not renege on his promise. The Yard, however, was by this stage ready for the fall-out. In late 1997 commissioner Condon announced he had been "scoping" corruption in his force for the last four years. He then revealed a new squad called the Untouchables, who he said were ready to ruthlessly arrest the bent cops his own organisation had identified during the unprecedented Ghost Squad years.

The image consultants and spin-doctors then picked up the phone to selected crime and home affairs correspondents to help create an official version. It portrayed the commissioner as a brave man driven by his conscience to grasp the nettle of corruption, and not someone who was in fact buffeted around by corrupt events the Yard had done its best for ten years to cover up.

Grieve and Clark were also given a central role in this production. They would be cast as the intelligence chiefs sitting in their office surrounded by bugging equipment who first uttered the words, "Commissioner, we have a problem."

4

THE GHOST OF BRINKS MAT
– A FIRM WITHIN A FIRM

It all starts with Brinks Mat, an audacious robbery that still casts a malevolent shadow over the most powerful police force in the UK. It is quite simply for Scotland Yard the crime that will not go away. Unsolved murders, the unexplained suicide of an alcoholic detective, corruption, Freemasonry and, most enduring of all, the grubby relationships between the criminals and their police handlers, all these elements still distort the vicious internal politics of Scotland Yard today because they were swept under the carpet 20 years ago.

On 26 November 1983, four hardened armed robbers drove out of the Brinks Mat warehouse near Heathrow Airport with 76 boxes of gold ingots worth £25,911,962. Platinum ingots, diamonds and travellers cheques raised the swag bag to a cool £26,369,778.

The Brinks Mat robbery sparked one of the longest running and most controversial investigations in British police history. Scotland Yard's Flying Squad faced one of its most important challenges. Besides recovering the bullion before it was smelted and invested across the globe, there was another compelling incentive. The 1980s saw the emergence of a new breed of organised criminal connected through a global underground network to the rapidly expanding drugs business. If the weathered criminal faces across London managed to hold on to the proceeds it would propel certain gangs into the super-league of organised drug crime.

But Brinks Mat is not just an iconic crime where the proceeds of a multi-million-pound heist were laundered through snooty offshore banks and international property deals from London's Docklands to Panama City. It is also more than just the dawn of a new era of super league drug-crime syndicates feeding off an E-generation of loved-up, jaw-grinding ravers.

For Brinks Mat was also a seedy laundry where Scotland Yard's own dirty washing went round and round, but was always guaranteed to come out clean. The top brass have known for years the benefit of washing your own dirty linen is that stubborn stains don't always have to be removed. But a closer inspection of the Yard's sheets reveals a pattern of cover-ups, corruption, shot messengers and nobbled inquiries into allegedly dirty cops that no whitewash can ever fully remove.

The previously unchallenged reputation of Scotland Yard for honesty and integrity was a distant and soiled TV myth by the time of the 1983 Brinks Mat robbery. Margaret Thatcher's government may have done much to reassert the police's powers over her subjects, but its moral authority was in tatters when masked men walked into the Heathrow warehouse.

The post Second World War *Dixon of Dock Green* consensus that the British police were fair but firm irrevocably broke down with a series of media exposés of corrupt practices that Yard chiefs had known about for years but did little to combat.

In 1969, *The Times* published a compelling exposé of police corruption. Journalists Garry Lloyd and Julian Mounter had set up a sting using a disgruntled south-east London criminal who had contacted them claiming corrupt detectives were blackmailing him. Lloyd and Mounter secretly recorded three detectives discussing bribery and corruption with their criminal. On one of the thirteen tapes later given to Scotland Yard one of the bent detectives memorably described being part of "a firm in a firm", with people in police stations across the city who, in return for money, would look the other way, water down charges or offer no evidence. But instead of investigating the newspaper's allegations of serious corruption, the journalists themselves were relentlessly interviewed as Scotland Yard tried to undermine their published story. As an extra defence the internal investigation was given to a corrupt senior detective who at the time was on the take from Soho's porn kings.[1]

Finally, Labour home secretary Jim Callaghan brought in a former provincial chief constable called Frank Williamson to conduct an inquiry. Williamson told Callaghan there should have been an immediate independent inquiry because by now the firm within a firm would have covered its tracks.[2] He was right. Important logbooks had already mysteriously disappeared. Williamson resigned in 1971 before finishing his inquiry. He claimed the Yard and the Home Office had smeared him and his key witnesses. There was no desire to properly investigate because senior Yard officers knew how high up the bribes and extras had gone. Two of the detectives identified by *The Times* were later convicted. A third, John Symonds, fled the country in mysterious circumstances.[3]

Lloyd wraps up the saga: "The trial involved legal history because this was the first time that taped evidence had been admitted in court. [Before his trial] Symonds was ordered to disappear by the corrupt element in Scotland Yard. They had a whip round to send him away to South Africa and Rhodesia. Williamson told me that Symonds was flatly ordered to go because he was threatening to blow the whistle on the whole firm. Williamson knew that it had gone right up the ranks to very, very senior officers and that's what they've always wanted to cover up."[4]

Williamson's resignation coincided with another series of newspaper exposés, this time by the *People* in 1972. Their investigations revealed top-level corruption in the Yard's Porn and Drug squads, including Chief Superintendent Bill Moody, the bent senior officer given the job of sabotaging the earlier *Times* exposé.

Soon after publication, a new commissioner, Robert Mark, set up an anti-corruption squad called A10, later renamed CIB. Mark then restructured the Flying Squad, who from then on dealt only with armed robberies. The system of payments to informants was also reformed to guard against detectives pocketing the money.

But soon the corruption merry-go-round exploded again, this time between 1978 and 1982. An inquiry, inevitably internal, called Operation Countryman was set up. One expert chronicler described it at the time as "the most famously ill-fated anti-corruption probe in British police history".[5]

The allegations centred on a firm of corrupt detectives on the take while investigating major armed robberies in the capital. Comically, the City of London Police called in Scotland Yard to investigate them. But when the Yard realised its own Flying Squad was involved, an outside force from Dorset was called in. As the years rolled by the Yard undermined Dorset Police and regained control of the damaging probe. Operation Countryman originally had a list of almost one hundred suspect officers facing allegations. In the end, after four years and millions of pounds, it achieved the successful conviction of two City of London officers. Eight Scotland Yard detectives were acquitted at the Old Bailey, three being later dismissed following disciplinary action.

Once again the outside force brought in to investigate the Yard claimed their efforts had been nobbled. Once again they pointed the finger at senior management in the Yard, Freemasonry and even the Director of Public Prosecutions.[6] Once again the firm within a firm survived and once again the public picked up the bill for a farce.

No sooner had Operation Countryman ended in failure than corruption emerged during the Brinks robbery investigation, which lasted nine years with the final trial concluding in 1992. The two senior Yard officers who led the investigation believe their efforts were constantly being undermined from within by a group of corrupt south-east London and Kent detectives working with the target criminals.

In December 1984, 13 months after the Brinks heist, an Old Bailey judge jailed armed robber Mickey "the Bully" McAvoy for 25 years. Another south-east London criminal, Brian "the Colonel" Robinson, who masterminded the robbery, got the same sentence. Tony White, the third heavyweight defendant, was acquitted, probably because he kept his mask on and could not therefore be identified by the terrified, petrol-soaked guards whom the robbers had threatened to torch if one of them didn't give up the combination to the vault.

The trial of these three top echelon villains was largely possible thanks to the evidence of the gang's "inside man", Tony Black, a guard at the Brinks Mat warehouse and Robinson's brother-in-law. In return for a reduced sentence Black "rolled over" and became a prosecution witness or supergrass in the time it takes milk to turn in the sun.

Two other notorious south-east London armed robbers are to this day widely believed to have also been "on the plot", but were never prosecuted for it. They are John "Goldfinger" Fleming and John "Little Legs" Lloyd.

Around these five Brinks Mat principals was a team of villains whose job was to smelt and launder the gold bullion through a series of convoluted financial transactions and property purchases. Among the members of what the police called the "Gold Conduit" were minicab boss Brian Perry, Kenny Noye, gold dealer John Palmer, up-and-coming north London gangster Tommy Adams and gangland lawyer Michael Relton.

It was a long and painstaking surveillance operation in late 1984

A FIRM WITHIN A FIRM

that led the Flying Squad to uncover this Gold chain. The insurers of Brinks Mat had put up a reward. And naturally it had already attracted the usual assortment of nutters, lonely people and self-publicists.

Little Legs had been linked to a major armed robbery in Kent one year before the Brinks Mat warehouse was hit. The Bluebell Hill robbery of about £1 million was at the time the biggest cash snatch from a security van. The robbers shut off the road near Maidstone, looted the van and drove off. Weeks later Lloyd was arrested and charged with Mehmet Arif, a member of the feared Turkish Cypriot family with a grip on the Old Kent Road, a main artery out of south-east London. One month later the prosecution discontinued the case for reasons that remain unclear. No money was ever recovered.

There is no doubt Lloyd was very busy in the period just before the Brinks Mat robbery. He was already diversifying into drugs, which may explain why, like many of his associates, Lloyd found it attractive to invest in a freight company. Little Legs had also diversified romantically. By 1983, the man whose mug shot bore an uncanny resemblance to white-suited war correspondent Martin Bell was living with Jeannie Savage.

The Flying Squad followed her to an address in the Kent village of West Kingsdown, near Brands Hatch. Through a Land Registry check detectives discovered that a low-profile criminal called Kenny Noye had sold Lloyd the house a few years back when he moved down the road into the large mock-Tudor splendour of Hollywood Cottage.

The Flying Squad watched in silent amazement as criminals moved heavy suitcases from Kent to Bristol in the West Country. By late January 1985 the Yard decided it was time to step up the surveillance.

Detective chief superintendent Brian Boyce was the newly promoted officer in charge of the Brinks investigation. He had served under the legendary Scotland Yard officer Leonard "Nipper" Read on the squad that busted the Krays' criminal empire. Boyce was really a soldier in a policeman's uniform. His service in Cyprus and Northern Ireland had taught him the danger of allowing donkeys to lead lions. Good intelligence, he believed, was worth its weight in gold.

Throughout most of January, Noye was observed meeting a criminal associate called Brian Reader at Hollywood Cottage. Reader regularly drove from there to London where he met with Tommy Adams.

On a number of occasions Reader was observed handing Adams heavy parcels, which he put in the boot of his white Mercedes. Adams was followed from Farringdon station near Smithfield meat market to a shop called Pussy Galore near St Pancras Station. From there he would travel to a bullion firm in Bristol called Scadlynn Limited.

Two undercover officers were inserted into the grounds of Hollywood Cottage. One was John Fordham, whom Boyce had handpicked for the job. The pair knew each other from Northern Ireland, where Boyce was an anti-terrorist officer in covert operations. Fordham was at the top of his game and had received training from the British Army's highly secret infiltration unit, 14 Intelligence Company.

The Flying Squad was already convinced Noye was moving Brinks Mat gold from his home to Scadlynn, and clean cash was coming back the same route. But it was still unclear where in Kent the stolen bullion was stashed. Boyce suspected some might be hidden in the Second World War concrete bunkers beneath Noye's house.

On 26 January 1985 Noye's Rottweilers spotted Fordham and started barking. Noye came out armed with a kitchen knife and a torch. He confronted the intruder who was dressed in military-style camouflage, wearing a balaclava. A vicious fight ensued and Noye fatally stabbed the unarmed cop.

As he sped towards Hollywood Cottage, Boyce was facing a turf war with the Kent police. Although an assistant commissioner at Scotland Yard had informed the chief constable of Kent about the 72-hour surveillance operation, no one else was supposed to know. Boyce was particularly worried because he had seen what he thought was convincing intelligence suggesting Noye was corruptly connected to some elements of the Kent police.

By the time of the robbery, Noye was part of a criminal exodus of south-east London "faces" that moved to Kent, the garden of England. Noye was a registered informant for a controversial Yard commander called Ray Adams whose name he put forward as someone who'd give him a good reference and certainly vouch that he was not a murderer. But he also worked for the Regional Crime Squad operating in Kent and was believed to be involved with a team of local villains who hijacked lorries on the A2. They would keep one load and offer up another to friendly Kent cops looking for an easy collar, and maybe a bit of the stolen gear on the side.

On the evening of Fordham's death distrust of the Kent police extended from top to bottom of the Flying Squad. The rocky relationship took a turn for the worse when within hours of the killing Boyce and his men were frozen out of the murder inquiry. Kent police

A FIRM WITHIN A FIRM

had control of Noye for the following 36 hours. The Flying Squad remained in charge of the Brinks investigation but Boyce had to fight to regain control of the murder investigation.

The turf war went Boyce's way after 11 bars of near pure gold were found in the grounds of Hollywood Cottage on Sunday afternoon. By Monday the Flying Squad were back in charge, but they didn't like what they found. During the freeze-out Boyce felt the continuity of forensic evidence had not been properly preserved. He was critical of one senior Kent officer for allowing Noye to shower, change his clothes and have a photo taken of his injuries, all without a police officer or doctor present. "A lot of forensic evidence was lost," recalls one Flying Squad detective waiting to interview Noye. Acting on a tip-off, Boyce authorised a secret assignment to target the senior Kent officer, the details of which are revealed here for the first time.

The Forge restaurant close to Hollywood Cottage in Dartford was popular with several faces from south-east London. Not long after Boyce had taken back control of the murder inquiry the restaurant's managers – a married couple – contacted detective sergeant Bob Suckling at the Flying Squad. They were concerned about earlier inquiries by Kent police because Noye was a regular diner at their restaurant with a local detective whom they could not identify by name.

Boyce gave Suckling the job of identifying the man. A second Flying Squad officer returned to The Forge with a surveillance photo of a senior Kent detective whom we shall call "Hamilton". He was identified as Noye's regular dinner guest. Hamilton, it was also discovered, had previously investigated the 1981 Bluebell Hill security van robbery for which John Lloyd and Mehmet Arif were charged but then released. Suckling decided to re-investigate. He was astonished at how little paperwork on the robbery was left at Kent Police headquarters. Undeterred, he visited some Yard detectives who were sifting intelligence on local robbers. There he made a remarkable discovery. An informant, who we shall call "Tom", had provided some unnerving information. "Tom" said there were six people on the Bluebell Hill robbery, and each one took home £130,000 cash. The total haul, however, was £900,000. He told the police that Lloyd had escaped prosecution by paying off the Kent cops.

The official police log of the debriefing session with Tom put it this way: "[The informant] describes the Arifs as powerful people – with friends in the police. [He] states that a trade was done over John Lloyd – Billy Haward [a well known armed robber and associate of Lloyd's] saw a cozzer [south-east London slang for a policeman]."

To any seasoned detective, allegations by criminals that the local police had been paid off were no surprise. The Underworld is adept at using such claims to smear an effective officer, undermine police morale or derail an investigation. Such disruption by black propaganda is a strategy deployed by both sides of the criminal divide.

While Suckling looked further into the Bluebell Hill robbery, Boyce reported the "Forge affair" to his superiors. Soon afterwards an outside police force was appointed to investigate the Kent detective and his associates. Paul Condon was number two in the Kent police at the time. He'd moved over from the Yard just a few months after the Brinks robbery.

When the detectives from the outside force visited the Forge restaurant, its owners declined to make a statement, says Suckling. Some of his Flying Squad colleagues told us they believe the criminals put the frighteners on the restaurant managers. The couple had previously run the Dolomiti restaurant on the A20, near Sidcup. It was a haunt of the Arif crime family and their associates, which of course included members of the Gold Conduit.

According to one Flying Squad detective, the outside force was unable to substantiate the allegations against Hamilton. It also concluded, unfairly he says, that Boyce had "an exaggerated view of police corruption in the Kent police" coloured by the political battle for control of the Fordham murder.

Boyce had good reason to be concerned about Noye's ability to buy cops. Soon after he was arrested for killing the undercover officer, Noye had offered Boyce a massive bribe.

Noye was concerned that Boyce and his Flying Squad team had reclaimed the murder inquiry from Kent police. Unbeknown to him the London detectives were also secretly looking into his relationship with Hamilton. At Bromley police station he asked to speak to Boyce. When they were alone in the cell Boyce claimed Noye offered to put £1 million in a bank account "anywhere in the world". Boyce politely declined and reported the "good retirement" bribe.[7]

The Brinks Mat investigation underwent a major re-organisation after the death of John Fordham. The renewed glare of the media spotlight put Scotland Yard under pressure to prove itself capable of finding the gold and dismantling the money laundering and reinvestment network. This was new territory for the police. Under Brian Boyce's guidance, a Specialist Operations Task Force, the first of its kind, was set up in early 1985 to chase the men in suits and their criminal clients around the offshore tax havens and money laundering centres of the world.

Remarkably, the officer appointed in March to handle this crucial aspect of the Brinks investigation was detective superintendent Tony Lundy, who at the time was considered the most controversial cop in Scotland Yard. Senior management were split between those who thought he was "corrupt" or lacking in integrity and others, including Lundy, who believed he was the victim of a criminal vendetta seized on by jealous colleagues threatened by his reputation as a top thief taker. Lundy had served on the Flying Squad during the seventies. There he pioneered the turning of armed robbers into supergrasses to take down some of the toughest firms in and around the capital. This strategy naturally earned him the enmity of London's top villains who decided to pay him back, with interest. Or so he would claim.

A firm of armed robbers had hijacked a lorry at Tilbury Docks and stole £3.5 million of East German-owned silver bullion in March 1980. Lundy's boys investigated the crime and managed to retrieve almost all of the silver and convict the key villains. Twelve of the 321 ingots, however, were never recovered. Someone in the Underworld had a convenient explanation. There's no prize for guessing that a criminal turned supergrass called Billy Young put Lundy's name in the frame.

The silver bullion robbery took place in the middle of Operation Countryman. The theft allegation against Lundy coincided with an anonymous note to the Yard claiming he had also conspired with his colleagues to falsely obtain a reward for an undeserving informant. Lundy would claim the note came from one of his high-ranking enemies at the Yard. But the damage was done and an internal inquiry, parallel to Countryman, got underway.

Lundy was skilled at marketing his achievements so the humiliation of being returned to divisional duties was considerable for the gruff Lancastrian. Meanwhile, a former anti-corruption chief, deputy assistant commissioner Ron Steventon, started to look into the allegations. This took a remarkable two and a half years to complete. Equally extraordinary was the decision to allow Lundy on occasion to investigate complaints against other police officers while he himself was under suspicion.

As the Steventon inquiry lumbered into 1983 a few independent journalists were hot on Lundy's trail sensing there was something endemically wrong about his relationship with a criminal informer called Roy Garner, who was also a major drug dealer. As good a criminal as he was an informant, Garner had earned handsomely from his tip-offs to Lundy's Robbery Squad. But in return was he allowed to operate his drug business with impunity?

Finally, in August 1983, a 4,000-page internal report on the Lundy affair was submitted to the Director of Public Prosecutions for a decision on whether to bring criminal charges. For roughly six months the DPP mulled over the evidence and implications of prosecuting officers like Lundy who had put away hundreds of serious criminals. Government lawyers decided the uncorroborated word of a convicted supergrass like Billy Young was good enough to convict other criminals but not police officers.[8] This perceived lack of credible evidence meant no criminal charges were brought against any of the officers under investigation. The Yard did however issue a mild admonishment to Lundy for failings in his paperwork.

In January 1985, the month John Fordham was killed, Lundy felt confident enough to publicly claim he had been fully exonerated. No one in the Yard who saw the internal inquiry report contradicted him. This was more than a little strange, as the report contained a damaging two-page memo by DAC Steventon, who wrote: "I feel bound to express a personal opinion and regrettably there is a dearth of evidence to support it, but it is my belief that Lundy is a corrupt officer who has long exploited his association with Garner." He recommended Lundy should be removed from specialist duty.

In the incongruent, bitchy world of promotion and preferment inside Scotland Yard, this would have been enough to sink the career of many detectives. Instead the total opposite occurred. On 11 March Lundy was made Brian Boyce's deputy on the Brinks Task Force. If ever there was evidence of a major split in the Yard's top hierarchy this was it. By posting him to the most high-profile and sensitive on-going inquiry, his supporters, among them four assistant commissioners, gave a two-fingered salute to Lundy's equally powerful detractors in Scotland Yard. Among those was the deputy commissioner, Albert Laugharne, the second most powerful man in the Yard and the person in overall charge of police discipline.

But what of the Steventon report and memo? It was archived – some say it was deep-sixed – but not for long. Just as Lundy thought it was safe to go back on the mean city streets, the Yard learned that two BBC journalists were almost through making a documentary called "The Untouchable" about his relationship with the drug trafficking informant Roy Garner.

A FIRM WITHIN A FIRM

Such was the concern that in April commander Phil Corbett visited a retired police officer to inquire if he had revealed the contents of the Steventon memo to the programme makers. Similarly, assistant commissioner John Dellow wrote confidentially to the BBC assistant director general, Alan Protheroe, urging restraint. The BBC executive saved Scotland Yard the trouble of any further assaults on press freedom. He pulled the documentary claiming "insoluble legal difficulties". The journalists, Andrew Jennings and Vyv Simson, consequently left the BBC. They suggest a compelling reason for why the Yard "buried its head in the sand" over the Steventon memo: "If it got out that a detective who had put so many men in jail had been labelled 'corrupt' by the Yard, the Appeal Court could be besieged for years."[9]

One faction in the Yard had certainly buried the memo, in insignificance. Had they not done so and it became public then not only would the Appeal Court be busy, but Lundy's position on the Brinks Mat Task Force would surely have been untenable.

In November 1986, after 18 months on the Brinks inquiry, Lundy's protection ran out. The refugee journalists had found a burly sponsor in Granada Television's flagship documentary series *World In Action*. An even harder version of "The Untouchable" was scheduled for broadcast in a few days.

Transmission on 6 November came at the worst possible time for the Brinks investigation. The Task Force had already failed to convict Noye for the murder of John Fordham. And even though in July he received fourteen years for handling the stolen gold, three of his associates had escaped conviction.

To make matters worse, the Yard was engaged in a Keystone Cops hunt for armed robber John "Goldfinger" Fleming whom Lundy was pursuing for dishonestly handling £480,000 of the Brinks proceeds. Fleming had bought a villa near Benidorm on Spain's Costa Blanca immediately after the robbery. He fled there when McAvoy and the others were arrested. A surveillance squad eventually found him, wired up his patio and tapped the phone. Detectives staying in a nearby hotel were entertained by some of the things they heard, like Fleming praising the wonders of anal sex.

When his passport ran out Fleming hopped from one banana republic to another looking for the best safe haven dirty money can buy. Lundy sent detective inspector Tony Brightwell after him. He left London with trepidation. The Yard feared "another Ronnie Biggs in the making" if Fleming wasn't extradited quickly, recalls Brightwell.

UNTOUCHABLES

"The Untouchable" documentary caused great damage to Scotland Yard's cherished reputation when it was broadcast. Two influential Labour MPs, Chris Smith and Clive Soley, used parliamentary privilege to call Lundy "corrupt" and to repeat the call for a full investigation of his relationship with Garner. Even his high-ranking friends could not protect Lundy now.

Fleming of course cashed in on the chaos and agreed to come back to Blighty only if Lundy was taken off his case. Boyce was furious that the Brinks investigation was back in the limelight for all the wrong reasons. Lundy had apparently ignored his order not to pursue Fleming. Boyce was under "instructions" from British intelligence to leave Fleming in Brazil or the United States.[10]

An outside force, this time from South Yorkshire, was appointed to investigate *World In Action*'s allegations. Lundy was removed from the Brinks Inquiry but still allowed to carry out sensitive drug money laundering investigations overseas, working with US law enforcement authorities, though he was not called as a witness in subsequent Brinks trials.

The whole drawn out and inconclusive affair splits Scotland Yard even today. Tony Lundy now lives in Spain. He retired as a suspended officer in December 1988 with a doctor's note diagnosing him as suffering from acute stress. His detractors made a lot of the fact that by doing so he managed to avoid six disciplinary charges arising from the outside force inquiry. His supporters say the discipline offences were "flimsy" and a justification for not having found any evidence of criminal wrongdoing.

Lundy insists his mental illness was genuine and caused by seven years of police and media persecution. He went sick after formally complaining that the South Yorkshire inquiry had acted improperly. "They got carried away and were determined to get a result," he told us. The suggestion of a Masonic conspiracy between the silver bullion robbers and his enemies in the Yard is also something Lundy genuinely believes played a part in his downfall.[11]

In some important respects Tony Lundy is a victim. He may not be a victim of jealous colleagues duped by vengeful criminals – and *World In Action* had every right to investigate the murky and uncontrolled world of the detective-informant relationship – but Lundy is a victim of a secret and undemocratic system that allows the police to investigate themselves.

Had a fully independent body of corruption investigators and prosecutors existed then the factionalism inside the Yard, the shifting

A FIRM WITHIN A FIRM

agendas and priorities, the personality politics which all did so much to obscure the facts in this case, would have been marginalised. Subordinated, if you like, to transparency, speed, public accountability and greater clarity over the verdict on Tony Lundy's guilt or innocence and the true level of corruption inside the Brinks Mat squad.

5

THE GHOST OF BRINKS MAT – A *LIAISON DANGEREUSE*

It's early spring 1986. Detective chief superintendent Brian Boyce is working in his office at Scotland Yard. The phone rings.

"Hello. My name is Professor Brian Griffiths, head of the prime minister's policy unit."

"Oh, hello," said Boyce, intrigued by why such a senior adviser to Mrs Thatcher would be calling him directly.

"Listen, would you mind coming to Downing Street? There is something we would like to discuss."

The call came at a time when the internal politics of the Yard were at their most vicious. Highly critical media coverage over Noye's acquittal for murder in December 1985 had led to recriminations. Boyce and SO11 Commander Phil Corbett were trying to raise spirits but at the same time animate the troops for Noye and Reader's second trial, due to start at the Old Bailey in May. Only 11 bars of the stolen bullion had been recovered.

Boyce agreed to meet the prime minister's adviser but decided not to tell his superiors. It was just a short walk across St James's Park to Number Ten.

Over coffee Boyce chatted with Professor Griffiths and his number two at the policy unit, Hartley Booth. Griffiths was an evangelical monetarist and economic guru of the Thatcher revolution. He came straight to the point. What, he asked, did Boyce think of the Theft Act as a weapon for tackling organised crime and terrorism? Boyce was one of a number of cops who believed the Act was outdated for the modern criminal landscape. He was confident about convicting Noye for handling, but to do so he knew he must absolutely prove the gold and the money found at Hollywood Cottage and Reader's home had come from smelting and laundering the Brinks Mat bullion.

Professor Griffiths was working on draft legislation to create a new offence of money laundering. Boyce was left under no illusion that Margaret Thatcher wanted to attack the secret financial structures of the IRA and organised crime. Until the Guinness share support scandal the following year, she had no interest in targeting Tarquin, the City dealer, and his white-collar band of pinstriped suits who were busy laundering their illegal profits from insider trading.

Until then, it was another kind of spiv entrepreneur – Kenny Noye and other members of the Gold Conduit – which was embarrassing Mrs Thatcher. They had laundered a lot of Brinks money through close-to-home offshore tax havens like the Isle of Man and the Channel Islands, and far-flung ones like the British Virgin Islands (BVI). High Street banks that asked no questions were the financial conduit to these exotic locations.

The Foreign Office had previously encouraged Caribbean colonies like the BVI to establish a welcoming offshore financial sector that would generate local employment and revenue and reduce economic dependency on the Treasury. Now the government wanted to create a legal framework to control the Frankenstein it had fostered. And the islands' politicians and business sectors didn't like it.

The irony would not have been lost on Boyce as he walked back to Scotland Yard. He supported new legislation but knew it wouldn't come soon enough to be useful to him.

After a ten-week trial, on 24 July 1986, Noye was found guilty of handling. He turned to the jury and told them he hoped they all died of cancer. The judge sentenced him to fourteen years. Brian Reader got nine. It was a success of sorts for the Task Force, in that the cop killer was finally behind bars. But Noye's business partner, Michael Lawson, was acquitted, so too was north London gangster Tommy Adams. Bristol linkman Terry Patch of Scadlynn had also walked free.[1] The Gold Conduit was far from broken. In fact there was another far more prolific gold chain that hadn't even been touched. This was the money laundering operation fronted by bent solicitor Michael Relton.

In 1984 Relton had virtually abandoned his lucrative central London criminal defence firm to become a laundryman. Selective Estates, the property company he set up with minicab boss cum gangster Brian Perry, was the vehicle for this new career.

One inspired investment they made was in London's Docklands, a boom-time development promoted by the Tory government to international property speculators. Relton and Perry certainly fitted that bill and cleverly identified a number of wharfs which they bought and sold shortly afterwards for a killing.

It seemed a case of life imitating art. The prescient British gangster film *The Long Good Friday* had developed a cult status since its release in 1981. The plot centred on an East End gangland boss, played menacingly by Bob Hoskins, who was laundering drug profits through a joint venture with the American Mafia, dirty cops and corrupt local councillors to develop London's Docklands.

Meanwhile, back in the real world, the Arif crime family was working closely with Perry. They had already secured a foothold on the capital's prime real estate by nurturing links with the London Docklands Development Corporation. The LDDC took out commercial sponsorship with crime boss Dogan Arif's beloved south London football club, Fisher Athletic, situated in a prime Docklands location on the south side of the Thames. His football stadium and the LDCC-sponsored sports ground were named after the Labour party grandee and former MP for Bermondsey, Lord Mellish.

In August 1986, the Brinks 'laundry' Mat was interrupted mid-cycle. Perry had been under surveillance ever since jailed robber Mickey McAvoy nominated him as his negotiator in the deal he hoped to strike with the Yard to return his share of the gold for a shorter sentence. By following Perry, the Task Force uncovered the other main players in this second Gold Conduit and their laundering network of offshore accounts in Switzerland, Liechtenstein, Belgium, Panama and the United States.

On 12 August, the police made their move. Perry and McAvoy's current and ex-wife – Kathy and Jackie – plus four others were charged with handling the stolen Brinks gold and laundering some of the proceeds through two large house purchases.

It was by tracing these properties that the Task Force identified Michael Relton, the sophisticated criminal defence lawyer. Detectives were surprised and concerned. Relton was known in the police as a man with rather a lot of influential friends, some of them in Scotland Yard. Now he had disappeared. Had he been tipped off before the Task Force came calling at his Buckinghamshire country home?

It would take eight eventful weeks before Relton was located and arrested on 15 October. A ginger-haired, six-foot-five detective

A *LIAISON DANGEREUSE*

sergeant called John Redgrave was the officer tasked to feel the urbane solicitor's sweaty collar. The ginger giant had been on the Flying Squad since 1982 and served throughout the Brinks Mat investigation. He was definitely not one of Relton's friends in blue.

Redgrave was put in charge of preparing the prosecution paperwork for the forthcoming trial. There were nine defendants including Relton. The files eventually ran to over 20,000 pages and took many months to compile. In October 1987, one year after Relton's arrest, Redgrave produced an alarming report. It outlined to the Yard's top brass serious concerns surrounding the approaching trial.

The concerns, revealed here for the first time, were based on secret intelligence and undisclosed evidence that painted a very different picture of the internal machinations of the Brinks investigation than the one being spun by Scotland Yard's press office. Had the media got hold of such a report, the consequences would have been devastating for the forthcoming trial and, of course, the Yard.

There were two main recommendations, firstly that the jury be given police protection and secondly that the trial should be held outside of London. Nothing unusual in that, you may think. But it was the reasoning that made this report so explosive. Examining the question of jury protection first, Redgrave reminded his bosses that Noye had tried to bribe Boyce with £1 million. He then pointed out that since Noye's two trials there'd been two failed prosecutions where juries had no protection.[2]

To support his recommendation that the trial be held outside London, Redgrave referred to the relationship between Relton and certain retired Scotland Yard detectives, some of whom had bought a bar from him. Briefs wine bar was a hostelry opposite the Inner London Crown Court, near Elephant & Castle. It was part of Relton's legitimate empire of bars and restaurants that he owned while running a highly successful criminal and conveyancing legal practice. Relton bought Briefs in 1978 with a crooked businessman. Here, the South African-born lawyer would entertain his criminal clients and journalists after work and sometimes after hours. The Underworld and its fixers mixed like gin and tonic at the bar, exchanging gossip, banter and pound notes.

Relton knew the value of such a network of criminal contacts. Cleverly, he also developed a coterie of loyal police officers, some of questionable integrity.

Throughout the Robert Mark purge and Operation Countryman, defending those officers accused of misconduct and corruption was a good sideline for Relton. It became the stuff of legend that he won thirty-five out of thirty-six criminal cases brought against police officers. Among them were three detectives who ended up buying Briefs in 1980 while facing criminal prosecution for allegedly fitting up two armed robbers and for accepting money with menaces.

Brothers John and Michael Ross and Paul Rexstrew were acquitted in 1982 at the Old Bailey. It was the third Countryman trial in a series of four that failed to secure a conviction. The Ross brothers were subsequently sacked on a police disciplinary board. Rexstrew, however, resigned and later went to work for Relton's law firm as a clerk.

Today, John Ross earns his crust using his police contacts to sell tips to the tabloids. He now operates from another wine bar, this time near the Old Bailey. "The Flying Squad and the robbers used to drink together [in Briefs]. They did the same job. There were no problems because they all earned money out of bank robberies," he recalled over a bottle of wine.

During the Brinks inquiry, the Yard had issued an order for its officers to stay away from Briefs. There was particular concern in the Task Force, which the Redgrave report reflected, about the recently disgraced Ross brothers and their loyalty to Relton. The Yard was also troubled about Rextrew's role in Relton's law firm and wondered how far he and the others would go to defend him.

Rexstrew is still a legal clerk. He originally agreed to discuss Brinks Mat and his relationship with the bent lawyer. "Unbeknownst to me at the time, I was [at the firm] when monies were going into the Bank of Ireland through the client account, monies which were later shown to be coming from the purchase of property from Docklands through Selective Estates." He subsequently cancelled our meeting and refused to answer any written questions. One of the reasons he gave was that he had represented an unnamed defendant in the Relton trial.[3]

Rexstrew also had dealings with a former business partner of Relton's, a detective turned private eye called Martin King. After Relton sold Briefs, he and King bought Docks Diner, near Tower Bridge. Rexstrew later represented King when he pleaded guilty to bribing an undercover police officer to destroy the case against two criminals.[4]

In general, the concern among senior Brinks detectives was that a "firm within a firm" was still active. And the Underworld's brokers knew exactly how to get in touch.

Former commissioner Robert Mark will for ever be remembered

A LIAISON DANGEREUSE

for his inspired comment that a good police force is one that catches more criminals than it employs. And during his nearly five-year reign in the mid-seventies he sacked or forced out over 450 detectives. But undoubtedly, and with the Yard's connivance, corrupt officers of varied ranks, some because they were Freemasons, escaped the purge.

This is why Redgrave recommended moving the trial outside the Smoke. It was thought Relton's friends in Scotland Yard and those at the Criminal Bar could and would "manipulate police organisation and the mechanics of London's legal system". And although the Yard would find it "unpalatable" to have to guard against possible traitors in its own ranks, not to do so, the report intimated, could make the difference between winning and losing the forthcoming trial.

Boyce[5] and Corbett endorsed the argument wholeheartedly in a note attached to the Redgrave report. In his supporting comments published here for the first time, Corbett gave a fascinating analysis of the calibre of British villainy in the 1980s: "We do not have crime families as recognised in Italy and the US," he wrote. "We do however have potent cliques of criminals who will variously come together in combination according to their personal criminal projects – certainly and more unfortunately, this country is recognized worldwide for what might be termed an 'invisible asset', namely prolific and expert criminal figures." Corbett added he was "convinced that serious and concerted attempts to pervert and impede the course of justice will be made" in the Relton and co. trial. But far more intriguing was his final comment – "indeed it is likely that they have already commenced".

The Yard's head of criminal intelligence was referring to an unauthorised and highly irregular *liaison dangereuse* in Paris between a Brinks detective and Michael Relton, while the bent solicitor was on the run. The detective was an inspector called Peter Atkins. In late August 1986, Atkins' friend, the disgraced detective Michael Ross, contacted him. By this stage Perry and others had been arrested. Ross said Relton was in Florida ready to deal. Atkins trusted Ross, who had been his best man, and knew he was close to Relton. So he passed on the information to the Brinks Squad.

Tony Lundy was already going to Florida, where the Task Force had opened an asset-tracing office. He waited for Relton to make contact, but the call never came. Lundy was unaware that Relton was in fact in Paris secretly meeting Atkins. He had flown there with Ross on 6 September and was picked up at the airport by the lawyer, who paid for a long lunch in Montmartre.

One month later, on 8 October, Lundy, by now back in London, told his men they must find and arrest Relton within the next two weeks. After the briefing, the team adjourned for a modest libation. What happened at the Black Dog pub is a disputed story. Lundy claims a detective came to him in a distressed state saying that a fellow detective had recently offered him a £100,000 bribe to lay off Relton. Lundy reported this to commander Corbett, but the whistle-blower subsequently refused to confirm it when he was taken to the boss's office.

According to a police source privy to the intelligence, Corbett had also just learned from a phone tap about the Paris meeting. He was furious with Atkins. Luckily, though, the Task Force had also discovered that Relton would be returning to London in 24 hours from Malaga.

John Redgrave, the ginger giant, was put in charge of the surveillance team that followed Relton on his return to London. "He was slowly getting more and more drunk and avoiding his usual [haunts]. He was making calls from a TK [telephone kiosk]. The stuff I was getting back from the surveillance team was of a man at the end of his tether. He was spooked. My judgement was that he was going to do a runner because of the way he was acting. So I requested permission to arrest him. I didn't know about the politics [over Atkins] back at the Yard but eventually I was given the green light. We were following Relton in his car near Rochester Row. I pulled him over and when I introduced myself I sensed an enormous relief on his face. I then made him open the boot. Inside were loads of documents. He must have emptied out his office."

Redgrave had stumbled on a treasure trove of documents – the Selective Estates files. Two envelopes were found in the boot of Relton's car containing highly compromising financial information about the money laundering network. Weeks earlier Relton had posted the envelopes from London to an address in Malaga province. The network had invested in a large property development there.

Further documents were seized at Relton's home. By now faced with overwhelming evidence of his corruption, he turned supergrass. During lengthy debriefs he gave vital information of the laundering network that for the first time allowed detectives behind the curtain of confidentiality that is the most attractive feature of offshore banking. Relton, who was later described in court as the "chancellor of the exchequer", effectively admitted to laundering almost £3 million.

Michael Charman, Tony Curtis and another Flying Squad detective called John Bull were Relton's bodyguards while he was in protective custody. Charman says Relton didn't take too seriously the intelligence about a contract on his life. He was allowed to meet his wife at their favourite bistro in Clapham, south London, and his bodyguards also drove him to his Buckinghamshire home for conjugal visits and dinner parties.

In late November, the Task Force's top supergrass suddenly withdrew his evidence and entered a plea of not guilty. The police wrongly assumed Relton had had the frighteners put on him by his former gangster clients. In fact it was his wife, Helena Luff, who was threatened, says Curtis.

Soon after pleading not guilty, Relton unsuccessfully applied for bail. His wife assured the court no one had threatened her husband to retract his evidence. But later she confided in Curtis that a fearsome duo had done exactly that when they visited her London flat on behalf of Brian Perry. She identified the unwanted callers as south London gangland enforcer "Mad" Frankie Fraser and Perry's son, Patrick. Fraser admits he was Brian Perry's friend and was asked by unnamed people to act as his "minder" during the Brinks trials.[6] Patrick, however, refuses to comment. But a secret intelligence report reveals that two years after the approach to Relton's wife, Patrick was linked to a separate plot to poison one of his father's co-defendants, who at the time was in a Spanish prison awaiting extradition. The alleged plot involved providing the prisoner with a specially baked cake. Although the plan never came off, according to one police source, Patrick was heard joking that he was known for a while as Mr Kipling.[7]

Boyce had also gone ballistic on learning of the Paris meeting. He recommended Atkins should be removed from the Flying Squad. He was so surprised when no disciplinary action was taken against the errant officer for what commander Corbett had described as "a flagrant breach of police protocols".[8] They wondered if Atkins had protection higher up.

Some explanation came when the detective, by then promoted to chief inspector, gave some extraordinary evidence at Relton's trial. Atkins told the court he and Ross would regularly "treat" each other to meals. On the occasion in question Ross flew him to Paris for lunch. It was only on the plane that he was told Relton would be joining them. Most of the lunch he agreed was a "highly enjoyable social occasion". But during the first half Relton apparently told Atkins he was not knowingly doing anything illegal.

Prosecution barrister Nicholas Purnell QC asked Atkins who'd paid for the flight. Atkins replied: "Well, what happened was Mr Ross paid for the flight. On the way over he told me that Mr Relton was in Paris and would meet us, and I was rather upset about that and I thought he abused our friendship, and in fact on the way back I gave him the money for the flight."

It was more than a little inconsistent that Atkins felt compelled to pay for the flight but admitted allowing Relton to pay for the meal. This wasn't the only anomaly and surprise in his evidence. Atkins also admitted to seeing Relton after Paris on three other occasions, this time in the UK. All the meetings took place in the month before he was arrested and therefore while he was on the run. On each occasion Ross organised the meeting and was present but not in earshot, Atkins was keen to stress. Once they even met in Briefs.

Remarkably, Atkins claimed he had reported back to someone in the Brinks Task Force, but didn't name the person. Certainly it wasn't Boyce, Corbett or Lundy. He also confirmed he hadn't taken any notes of these four crucial discussions with a fugitive, nor did he make a witness statement or secretly record Relton.

In one simple exchange Purnell got straight to the heart of the matter. "Detective Chief Inspector, were you going to give information to Relton or to receive information from him?"

"Receive it," replied Atkins.

In July 1988 Michael Weber Relton faced the consequences of his decision not to remain a supergrass. He was convicted and sentenced to 12 years.

After the trial, Scotland Yard did its best to quash rumours that there was a serious problem of police corruption during the Brinks Mat investigation. But Boyce and Corbett felt very differently. The SO11 commander cites the failure of the Yard to discipline errant officers as one of the reasons he chose to leave the force. Another reason, Corbett says, was the whitewash by Scotland Yard of an internal inquiry into Freemasonry.[9]

A very senior retired detective close to the Brinks investigation agreed to speak off the record about the internal machinations of Scotland Yard during this period. He was privy to important discussions. His comment is extraordinary. "It was my impression there was a concert party to undermine the Brinks [investigation] and most of it came from south-east London. There is no doubt several people wanted to undermine it. Some of those were in the police and some of those were outside of the police."

In the summer of 1993 a man in his early forties with a blond ponytail took the stand at the Old Bailey where he was on trial for armed robbery. He told the court one of those incredible defences that in journalism would be put in an imaginary tray marked "You couldn't make it up." Certainly the jury thought so, because they acquitted him.

The following account is based on allegations made in the witness box and in civil proceedings subsequently brought against the Met by Maurice O'Mahoney.

He claimed that corrupt Met detectives got him to carry out the armed robbery of a sub-post office in Shepherd's Bush, west London, in order to kill him because they suspected he was about to blow the whistle on the officers' involvement in the disposal of the Brinks money. Among the officers O'Mahoney named in court were Michael Ross and DCI Peter Atkins, who was still serving at the time of the trial.

O'Mahoney had led a life of crime, extreme violence and criminal cheek. As a west London enforcer and debt collector, he enjoyed using a hammer to persuade people to pay up. When he was arrested in June 1974 for the armed robbery of a Securicor van in Middlesex, O'Mahoney turned supergrass. He claimed he rolled over to protect his girlfriend from his accomplices on the job, who wrongly suspected he had grassed them up. Rather than wait for them to gouge his eyes out, O'Mahoney pleaded guilty and admitted 102 other offences, including another 13 armed robberies. He then named over one hundred friends and criminal associates, an act of treachery that earned him the soubriquet "Mo the grass".

In return, the court sentenced him to a lenient five years, most of which he served in very comfortable conditions with conjugal visits. At some stage though, he refused to give any more evidence against his former partners in crime so the police withdrew his protection and stopped payments from a special fund.

On his release, Mo was given a new identity. He briefly provided security for pop stars like keyboardist Rick Wakeman and claimed he once planned to kidnap Elton John.

Mo apparently recouped some criminal kudos after years of grassing by providing certain "faces" with sensitive intelligence from corrupt contacts in SO11 about whether they were being looked at.

Mo started to frequent Briefs wine bar in the early eighties and throughout the period when the Gold Conduit was at its most active. During this period he says he was involved in moving money to the United States for Relton. He travelled with a false passport to New

York on the same flight as the bent solicitor and even managed to hide two of Relton's account books from the police.

In 1990, Mo says he made contact with serving police officers at Brixton, south London, after an unnamed senior detective at the Yard refused to help him with a new identity. One of the Brixton detectives was reputedly Peter Atkins. Mo regarded him as a "friend" and claims he re-wired the detective chief inspector's house.

During his Old Bailey trial, Mo revealed that the post office robbery was proposed to him at the Brixton police station Christmas party in 1990. He then produced the winning raffle ticket from the police party – ironically the prize was a flight to Paris – when the prosecution accused him of not being there.

He spoke of his friendship with Briefs co-owner Michael Ross, whom the trial judge later described as a "rogue officer". Mo also listed from the witness box other police officers that he claimed he'd had corrupt and commercial dealings with since the seventies.

After his acquittal, Mo's lawyer wrote to home secretary Michael Howard asking him to guarantee his safety from criminals and police officers he had named in the murder plot. His lawyer later told the *Independent* that he had also asked for an inquiry into the allegations of police corruption, but, remarkably, this was refused.

In December 1994, Mo sued Peter Atkins and the commissioner for aggravated and exemplary damages, alleging malicious abuse of office and malicious prosecution. He had spent over one year in prison on remand after his arrest for the post office robbery.

The writ said the murder plot was arranged "to protect the interests of DCI Atkins and [his] friends and associates from the intended publication of details of corruption and to protect the same against possible loss of the proceeds of corruption". The writ named Michael Ross as well and alleged Mo possessed information about corrupt activities by them and senior officers known to them.

Although the claim was served on new commissioner Paul Condon, it related to a period when his predecessor Sir Peter Imbert was in charge. Nevertheless, Condon was in a very difficult position. By December 1994 he had been knighted and his Ghost Squad was secretly operating with Home Office approval.

Mo's corruption allegations in the civil claim fell into two periods – when he was a seventies supergrass and the Brinks Mat police investigation. Each one demanded a proper inquiry. Mo admitted in the writ that he'd given "perjured evidence [as a supergrass] at the direction and request of officers of the Metropolitan Police". In lieu of an independent inquiry, at the very least there should have been a separate team of officers, outside of Scotland Yard's control and supervised by the PCA, investigating this damaging allegation.

First they would have to discover which trials Mo was referring to and, if he was telling the truth, which defendants were therefore wrongly in prison. Then they would have to look at those officers Mo alleged had instructed him to give perjured evidence. This, after all, is a very serious allegation of conspiring to pervert the course of justice, and any officer successfully prosecuted not only would go to prison, but all the criminal cases he had significantly played a part in would themselves become potential miscarriages of justice. The PCA confirm they supervised no such corruption inquiry.

Mo's other more damaging allegations of police involvement in money laundering the proceeds of the Brinks robbery could not have come at a worst time for the Yard. The final Brinks trial of four key defendants in the Gold Conduit, Brian Perry, Gordon Parry, Jean Savage and Patrick Clarke, had successfully concluded in August 1992 with long prison sentences. Mo's allegations clearly challenged the safety of these convictions by attacking the police's integrity.[10]

The naming of DCI Atkins was a particular headache for the commissioner. In effect, the allegation that first emerged during Relton's trial in May 1988 that Atkins and Ross had at the very least an unethical relationship with the bent lawyer had now resurfaced six years later from someone the Yard had in the past regarded as a witness of truth.

The choice facing Scotland Yard was whether to reinvestigate the Brinks Mat robbery or settle out of court. For over four years, the Ghost Squad years, the Yard sat on the civil claim. Mo's lawyers had no idea what was going on. No one came to interview him about his allegations and take further details, he says. In the intervening period Atkins retired from the Yard in 1995. According to his friend John Ross, he slipped on some rubble outside Brixton police station and won an injury award from the force.

Then, in late 1998, commissioner Condon privately settled the case. Mo's legal costs and damages, which he estimates at £100,000, were picked up by the Yard, who in turn dipped into the public purse to save their bacon while leaving the taxpayer in the dark about what had gone on.

Such out of court settlements rarely include an admission of liability by the Yard, and this one was no exception. Although the police often try to claw back some dignity by arguing that they settled because it was too costly to continue, more often than not the reality is they have no evidence to rebut the claim or to do so would open up an even bigger scandal, in this case the secret history of corruption during Brinks Mat, something the Ghost Squad had no intention of exploring.

Asked what investigation the Yard conducted into Mo the grass's allegations, a spokesman replied: "We do not have any details of this matter on our current record system."

As far as we can establish Atkins has never been able to give his side of the story in any proceedings. Peter Atkins and Michael Ross declined to be interviewed about the *liaison dangereuse*. John Ross told us even he couldn't get the full story out of his brother or Atkins.[11]

Mo the grass is now 56 and married with grown up children. He is not worried about retribution from the criminals he put away. "There are no firms left to bash me up," he says. "They'll all be using zimmer frames."

6

DEATH OF AN EXPERT WITNESS

The elimination of private detective Daniel Morgan was planned with unusual care. At around 9pm on 10 March 1987 he left a meeting in the Golden Lion pub in Sydenham, south-east London, and walked into the rear car park. As he unlocked the door of his BMW, someone wielding a huge axe attacked him from behind.

The assailant felled Daniel with four ferocious blows to the head. He was already on his back when the crowning blow struck. It was inflicted with specially concentrated venom – in all probability to ensure that if Daniel was found before his final breath, he could speak no whisper and leave no clue. As the private detective's lifeblood drained into the tarmac, the murderer slipped away, leaving the axe in his face. Embedded. Deep.

Daniel Morgan was just thirty-seven years old and a father of two very young children.

The next day, before the pathologist began the autopsy he required considerable assistance just to extract the murder weapon. It had been fused with Danny's cheekbone. Preliminary analysis made it pretty clear this was a professional hit. The 14-inch wooden axe handle had been shrewdly modified. It was expertly wound with Elastoplast to prevent slippage and allow the killer to boost directional control.

At the inquest it was suggested that the location for the killing was specially chosen to fall within the area of Catford police station. The apparent purpose of this particular piece of strategic planning was as sinister as it was simple – to contaminate the murder investigation from the inside, restraining and frustrating the gathering of evidence while keeping well ahead of any honest cop who might be assigned to the murder inquiry. With the integrity of the investigative process subverted, the murder would become what the police call "a sticker" and conveniently remain unsolved.

Today, 17 years later, this is precisely the position. The murderer and his co-conspirators remain at large. But so does a pungent aura of police corruption. Significantly, the Daniel Morgan murder came just days after the private detective began taking steps to expose that corruption. Because of this, the killing still stalks Scotland Yard, a ghost unexorcised.

Daniel John Morgan was born on 3 November 1949, the middle of three children. The Morgan family line had its roots in Pontardawe, the Welsh valleys then renowned for coal mining. His father grew up in the interwar depression, an especially tough period in the valleys. At Arnhem during the Second World War, Daniel's father was not only badly wounded but also taken as a prisoner of war. On his liberation in 1945 he had the rank of captain and continued in service. There he met his wife Isobel who was working as an army telephonist. Later, the couple moved to Singapore where their sons Alastair and then Daniel were born, followed by Jane.

Daniel was always something of an outsider; maybe it was his clubfoot. He didn't perform well academically in his early rounds within the British education system. At grammar school he preferred wood and metal work to any other subjects. After his father died suddenly at forty-one from emphysema, Daniel went to agricultural college. He then worked on a farm in Denmark for two years learning the language while tilling the fields and chatting up the local talent.

In the late 1970s Daniel moved to London. His mother had remarried, and her new husband got him a job at a south London private detective agency called Madigans. Daniel learned the ropes in the unusual half world, half underworld of private investigation, tracing runaways and rate defaulters for local authorities and proving infidelities for other clients. In this early outpost of the information-sleaze economy, private eyes routinely gained access to confidential information supposedly held only by the state. Madigans, for example, had acquired a set of the reverse directories produced by the Post Office for state agencies, which covered all streets and phone numbers throughout Britain.

Jobs could often be accomplished even more speedily and more profitably with the help of other state assets – local police officers. They could help a private eye in a variety of ways in return for "a drink", London speak for a payoff.

By 1983 Daniel felt he had mastered the profession of a private eye. He and his Scots-born wife, Iris, were by then the parents of two young children – a daughter called Sarah and a son, also named Daniel. With these new responsibilities went a need for better pay, a pressure further compounded by Daniel's sense that Madigans cramped his style. He felt he could run a successful business himself.

Daniel first set up a small operation called DJM investigations, opening an office in Thornton Heath, south London. He had been shrewd enough to cultivate good relations with a number of key clients during his time at Madigans and lured some of them away with him when he left. Soon his client list involved tracing and bailiffing work for credit companies, banks and big law firms.

Daniel then set up Southern Investigation, recruiting a bookkeeper called Kevin Lennon as company secretary and a former Madigan employee, Jonathan Rees, as a fellow director. A tough, compact and exceptionally garrulous former merchant seaman with a Yorkshire accent in marked contrast to his Welsh family name, Rees, then 32, had some contacts in the local underworld and powerful connections in the local police, especially at Catford.

The news that her youngest son had been killed came to Isobel Morgan in the early hours of 11 March 1987 during a phone call from the police. After steadying herself, she contacted her remaining children, Alastair and Jane. When Isobel could manage to get the words out she gave them all the information she had. "Dan's dead . . . Murdered . . .That's all I've been told."

Alastair drove immediately from his home in Hampshire to London to comfort Iris, his brother's widow. On the way there he resolved to find out what he could about Daniel's last few days. Where had he been? What had he been working on? Who had he met at the Golden Lion pub before he was murdered?

Alastair's loyalty to Daniel ran deep. They'd spent fifteen years as boys sharing a room. Later as men the two became closer still. When Alastair first returned to England after separating from his Swedish wife, Daniel cheered him up and found him a temporary job working by his side at Madigans.

Alastair kept the job until he was ready to move on. But during his time there he developed a view of Jonathan Rees. He found Rees had a strong authoritarian streak and seriously enjoyed the exercise of power that went with his job as a bailiff evicting squatters and gypsies. Rees was also loud-mouthed and aggressive – with a strong rhetorical adherence to racist views that expressed his fear of the supposed swamping of the traditional British way of life.

During his drive to London, Alastair also puzzled over something his brother had told him some months earlier, concerning the disappearance of £18,280.62 in cash during a robbery outside Rees's home.

Behind Daniel's back, Rees had done a private job to protect the transit of cash for Belmont Car Auctions. The company and Daniel felt Rees's explanation for carrying so much cash strained credulity. They suspected it was a scam. Rees had claimed he took the money home because the night safe of the bank had mysteriously been super-glued. First he dropped off his brothers-in-law, Glen and Gary Vian, two ne'er-do-wells he had recruited to provide security. When he arrived home he was forced to park some distance from his house, whereupon two unidentified men apparently squirted ammonia in his eyes and robbed the money.

As he approached London, Alastair recalled his last conversation with his brother. Daniel had forcefully underlined his suspicions about the robbery and feared his company now faced ruin because Southern Investigations had no insurance for carrying cash. Furthermore, Daniel had told his brother Belmont was suing for the money. By the time Alastair arrived in London he was in a well of deep anxiety.

At the police incident room in Sydenham, Alastair learned the gruesome details of his brother's killing. Rees, he discovered, had pressed Daniel to come to the Golden Lion and then left just before the attack. Equally strange, while one of Daniel's trouser pockets had been torn open during the attack, another containing credit cards and £1,000 in cash was untouched. Yet Daniel's watch was stolen in what, Alastair suspected, was a clumsy attempt to camouflage the murder as a mugging. More intriguing still was word that his brother had been seen writing something on pieces of paper in the pub just before he died. But no notes were found.

Alastair found himself dealing with a middle-aged detective sergeant called Sid Fillery from the murder inquiry. He was a well-padded, confident man with powerful fists and a ready line in conversation. Alastair had met him briefly once before when he'd been out drinking with Daniel. At first the resumption of the relationship seemed reassuring. But very soon Alastair had cause to re-assess.

He had no idea how active Fillery had been in the immediate aftermath of the murder. Nor was he aware just how close the friendship between Fillery and Rees had become. They were the best of friends and confidants. The nature of this relationship was by then a matter of extraordinary importance, for Rees was under suspicion not only for the Belmont Car Auction robbery but also for the axe murder of his business partner.

The more Alastair learned about their relationship the more disingenuous Sid Fillery appeared. It emerged he had helped introduce Rees to Belmont.

In addition, Alastair discovered that 24 hours before the murder, Fillery and Rees were drinking at the Golden Lion. The session included a crowd of Catford cops. A row erupted, with some pushing and shoving. Those present would later claim the argument was over whether British policemen should routinely carry guns, with Daniel apparently taking a lone, dissenting view. Another theory is that the Belmont robbery and the missing £18,000 was the real cause of the row.

Rees and Fillery had been out drinking together almost every night in the days before the murder, Alastair learned. In that same period his brother was growing increasingly sceptical about the Belmont robbery and considering whether he should distance himself from Rees and file an entirely separate defence. Daniel was even thinking about bringing in someone else to replace Rees in the business.

It transpired that on the day of the murder Daniel had reluctantly agreed to return to the Golden Lion the night after the row to meet Rees, who told him a man called Paul Goodridge would meet them there to discuss lending Rees money.

Goodridge, a self-styled bodyguard, never turned up at the pub. And at around 8.45pm Rees left the Golden Lion, making him the last known person to see Daniel alive. This one fact had two immediate consequences. It made Rees an obvious suspect – a man to be carefully and neutrally questioned until he could be ruled in or out. Second, it meant that someone other than his best friend in the local police force should have been deployed to investigate and preserve all available evidence. Remarkably none of this was done.

Instead, Fillery interviewed Rees soon after the murder and took his witness statement in which no mention was made of their contact immediately before the murder. Rees was then allowed to leave the station without either his clothes or his car being forensically examined. Fillery had simply told his best friend he could bring them back later.

UNTOUCHABLES

Alastair couldn't understand how Fillery was allowed anywhere near the murder inquiry, let alone in such a direct role. He started asking awkward questions. While he waited for answers, Fillery suggested to the Morgan family that Alastair should go back home to Hampshire and not get in the way of the police investigation.

"Eventually I had to go home to get on with my own work," says Alastair, a translator. "I still made regular calls to the murder squad who could give me little assurance of any progress in the case. Like all the rest of the family I was uneasy."

Unease turned to alarm when he spoke to his brother's office manager. Peter Newby said Fillery had visited the detective agency to recover documents the morning after the murder. He claimed the detective filled a black plastic bin liner after specifically asking for at least one file by name – Belmont Car Auctions. Fillery has always denied this. Wherever the truth lies, the Belmont file has never been seen again. As Alastair puts it, "Someone had it." Significantly, Daniel's 1987 desk diary had also disappeared.

DS Sid Fillery came off the Morgan murder inquiry after four days. He says as soon as he realised there was a conflict of interest over his relationship with Rees he withdrew. But the senior officer running the murder inquiry claimed at the inquest that he had removed Fillery.

Three weeks later, Fillery was arrested in connection with the murder along with Rees and four others – Glen and Gary Vian, Rees's brothers-in-law, and two constables from Catford. They were just as suddenly released, without charge and again without anyone troubling to put the Morgan family in the picture.[1] They learned of the arrests from the media. Alastair and his mother, Isobel, kept asking questions, but the family liaison was very poor and the Morgans felt they were being deliberately kept in the dark.

Fillery's closeness to Rees was not the only flaw in the murder investigation. When Alastair went to the Golden Lion the morning after the murder he saw there was no proper crime scene cordon. This meant key evidence could have been missed or even taken away.

The Morgan family also struggled with the unexplained delay in holding an inquest into Daniel's death. One month before it opened in April 1988 Fillery was allowed to leave the force on a full medical pension. The officer complained of suffering from depression after 22 years' service.

"We were very unhappy about him leaving the force," says Alastair, "and we began telling people in high places just how seriously we viewed the situation." He wrote to the then Conservative home secretary, Douglas Hurd, asking that he authorise a substantial reward for information leading to the killer's arrest and conviction. "I stressed strongly in my letter that the inference of possible police involvement in the murder was now very serious," says Alastair. Hurd did nothing, which was somewhat ironic in that in his spare time the home secretary wrote whodunnit novels.

In a private letter to the late Paul Keel, the *Guardian* crime correspondent and one of the only journalists to take a serious interest in the background to Daniel's killing, Alastair expressed the family's growing sense of frustration: "Sometimes I get the feeling that individual coppers are so damned busy watching their own backs and guarding their precious reputations that they have little energy left to pinpoint the real villains. The really good ones get harassed out by cynical and complacent colleagues.

"An inquest is due in the fairly near future. But the police are singularly uninformative about all the ins and outs of the hearing, and reading between the lines of their almost total silence, I get the feeling that they themselves don't feel particularly comfortable about it . . . Perhaps someone is going to finish up getting egg on their face."[2]

At last, 13 months after the murder, the inquest opened. But Scotland Yard advised Iris Morgan, Daniel's widow, that there was no need for the family to be legally represented.

Alastair was appalled. "My mother was, if this is possible, even more suspicious than I was of what was going on. Despite her slender means and with a great deal of help from our solicitor at the time, she arranged for us to have a barrister present to protect our interests and cross-examine witnesses."

June Tweedie was their barrister. She arrived at the Southwark Coroner's Court direct from Gibraltar where she had been involved in another controversial inquest and one with more immediately obvious political ramifications – the "Death on the Rock" killing of three IRA members in an SAS ambush, which some argue was part of a shoot-to-kill policy exported from the dirty war in Northern Ireland.

Despite their suspicions, nothing prepared the Morgans for what came out at the inquest. An early and electrifying witness was Kevin Lennon, the bookkeeper and company secretary of Southern Investigations.

Lennon explained he had been friendlier with Rees than with the murdered man; and as a result of this friendship Rees had, he claimed, repeatedly confided in him. Rees had come to hate Daniel, repeatedly referring to him in front of other people as "the little Welsh cripple", Lennon told the inquest. The two were also rivals over a mistress they shared called Margaret Harrison, a local estate agent.

Lennon claimed Rees repeatedly discussed with him how he intended to get Daniel out of the business. Initially, Lennon told the coroner Rees had confided in him that his plan was to get Daniel breathalysed by his friends at Norbury police station while driving home late one night. This would cost Daniel his driving licence and incapacitate him in the business. Lennon added that to his certain knowledge Rees proceeded to try to make such arrangements on at least three occasions. But the plan never came off for reasons that remain unclear.

However, Lennon saved the most dramatic for last. He told the inquest Rees had asked him if he knew anyone who would kill Daniel. "I formed the opinion that Rees was determined either to kill Daniel Morgan or to have him killed," Lennon told the coroner, adding, "When he spoke to me about it Rees was calm and unemotional about planning Daniel's death."

Lennon also revealed that after Fillery left the force he went to work for Southern Investigations. The Morgan family could scarcely believe their ears. In essence, Rees's best friend who ended up playing an instrumental role in the bungled murder inquiry had effortlessly left the Yard on a full medical pension, only to resurface in Daniel's private investigation agency filling the dead man's shoes and working in partnership with the main murder suspect.

Cross-examined by Tweedie, Lennon volunteered further particulars of conversations he said he'd had with Rees. The bookkeeper testified that Rees had even discussed who would organise the murder ("Policemen from Catford") and how much it could cost ("£1,000").

Lennon again: "When questioned by me, Rees said: 'These police officers are friends of mine and will either murder Daniel or arrange for his murder . . .' He [Rees] went on to explain . . . that if they didn't do it themselves the police would arrange for some other person over whom they had some criminal charge pending to carry out Daniel's murder and in return police proceedings against that person would be dropped. Rees continued to explain to me that Daniel's murder would be carried out within the jurisdiction of Catford Police station."

At this point the Morgan family barrister interrupted him: "It was, was it not?"

Lennon: "Yes"

Tweedie: "The reason for the murder being carried out in that area was because those same Catford police officers would then be involved in the murder investigation and would suppress any information linking the murder with Jon Rees or themselves?"

Lennon: "That is right."[3]

Lennon claimed Rees had discussed murdering Daniel with his wife Sharon. She was therefore a key witness. But she never gave evidence, insisting to the coroner, Sir Montague Levine, that she wasn't mentally fit enough to attend. The coroner appeared unhappy at her absence. *Daily Mirror* reporter Sylvia Jones, however, soon tracked down Sharon Rees. She was photographed shopping the day after she lodged her sick note with the Coroner's Court.[4]

The *Mirror*'s exposé did little to bolster Rees's credibility when his turn came to give evidence. He categorically denied any involvement in the killing of Daniel Morgan.

It also emerged that the police chose Rees to identify the body to spare the family the trauma. The family felt this was completely unprofessional – if only because it gave a suspect direct access to the corpse before making a statement.

The Morgans then learned of a bizarre undercover operation run in parallel to the bodged murder inquiry. The man in charge, detective superintendent Douglas Campbell, acting alone or with CIB, was trying to sting Rees and Fillery into confessing their involvement in the murder. However, the detective constable he chose for this undercover role was entirely inappropriate. DC Duncan Hanrahan also had no undercover experience. He was, though, friendly with Rees and Fillery, and a fellow Freemason. Another disqualification was his posting at Norbury police station, where Rees had many other friends whom he was allegedly going to use ahead of the murder to fit up Morgan on a spurious drink drive offence.

Nevertheless, Hanrahan's evidence was not helpful to Rees. The detective had been the night duty officer who initially dealt with Rees's claim that he had been robbed of the car auction money. Hanrahan told the inquest he felt it was "an inside job" or "a set-up".

Turning to his undercover role, Hanrahan explained how Rees had discussed obstructing the murder inquiry. Indeed, Hanrahan told the coroner that Rees had stated that although he was in a position to give the inquiry important leads and information, he had changed his mind in retaliation for the way the murder squad was treating him after his friend Sid Fillery was reassigned.

UNTOUCHABLES

Hanrahan also claimed Rees had discussed ways of actively destabilising the inquiry by attacking its second-in-command, detective inspector Alan Jones. According to Hanrahan, Rees even contemplated planting illegal drugs in his car and having him arrested for possession. Rees denied this.

When murder inquiry boss, detective superintendent Douglas Campbell, gave evidence, he admitted that Fillery's actions had effectively sabotaged the investigation. But it was comments about Daniel Morgan's contact with the media just before his murder that really reverberated. Campbell revealed that Daniel had been talking about blowing the whistle on police corruption in south-east London. June Tweedie tried to explore with the senior officer whether this perhaps was the motive for the murder.

Tweedie: "Did you find anything relevant to the demise of Daniel Morgan?"

Campbell: "I could find no evidence at all. It was a suggestion that he had a story to sell to a newspaper. I spoke to the other persons concerned. I even went to the newspaper but if I told you what he was offered you would see it was quite ludicrous. He was alleged to have been offered £250,000 per story."

Tweedie: "I am not so interested in offers by newspapers."

Campbell: "All I will say, Madam, is that we looked in all directions to try and substantiate that and we could not."

At this point Sir Montague Levine brought the line of questioning to a halt. The name of the newspaper(s) and the persons Campbell spoke to during his murder inquiry have never been revealed. Campbell is now retired but he declined to be interviewed.

A verdict of unlawful killing was recorded at the inquest.

Daniel Morgan did have good contacts in the media. At the *Daily Mirror* he knew a number of reporters including Anton Antonowicz and the *Mirror*'s then political editor, Alastair Campbell.

Antonowicz was helpful and remembered meeting Morgan on several occasions, some of them in a pub behind the newspaper, affectionately known as The Stab in the Back. Campbell, however, was less forthcoming. He was still prime minister Tony Blair's head of spin when we approached him. He wrote back saying the name Daniel Morgan "rang a bell", but it would be "a waste of time" to meet.

Daniel had also provided information to *Private Eye*. But what was more interesting was his work in 1986, a year before the murder, for the BBC. The legal department had hired him to find witnesses to defend a crucial libel case brought by two Tory MPs who'd featured prominently in a *Panorama* documentary called "Maggie's Militant Tendency". A senior BBC source confirms Morgan was hired to locate and interview Conservative Party members who were in Berlin on an official delegation with Neil Hamilton MP. The *Panorama* exposé of right-wing extremism in the Tory ranks alleged that during the Berlin visit Hamilton goose-stepped and gave a mock Hitler salute, an illegal act in Germany at the time. Hamilton and other right-wing Tory MPs denied this and sued the BBC with the support of powerful elements in the party hierarchy and funding from the maverick billionaire, James Goldsmith.

Before caving in, the BBC had robustly defended the programme. They instructed Morgan to find any witnesses who may have been "got at" and persuaded to keep silent about that night in Berlin.

It is likely Southern Investigation's involvement with the BBC would have attracted the attention of MI5 or its freelance contractors working for the Conservative Party. Around this time, Daniel Morgan's car was burgled and his offices broken into.

But would any of this – from moonlighting cops to silenced Tory witnesses – really have attracted a media price tag of £250,000? It's unlikely. To earn that much from Fleet Street, Daniel Morgan had to have been on to something very big.

One south London detective called Derek Haslam believes he was. According to Haslam, Daniel's best contact in the south London police was detective constable Alan "Taffy" Holmes. He illegally obtained police information for Southern Investigations. But Haslam claims Taffy Holmes and Daniel were getting ready to blow the whistle just before the private detective was killed. At the time of the murder, Taffy Holmes was serving on the Brinks Mat investigation. He killed himself four months after Daniel's death. At the time of his suicide he was being investigated for corruption.

These two deaths, at first sight, appear unconnected. But Haslam says you can't understand either in isolation. "Those who kept the two deaths separate never wanted to know the truth."

7

THE SUICIDE CLUB

The ceremonial funeral of detective constable Alan 'Taffy' Holmes was a beautifully orchestrated police occasion. The coffin was draped in the force flag with a good conduct medal placed on top. His body was then carried to the chapel by a Scotland Yard guard of honour, a distinction normally reserved for officers killed on duty.

Hundreds of officers were given time off on full pay to go to the burial at Croydon cemetery in south London on 11 August 1987. Inside the chapel and down by the graveside were dozens of floral wreaths to Taffy Holmes. The dedication on one gave particular expression to the official line on his police record and tragic death. Taffy Holmes, it said, was "a shining light" to what a police officer should be.[1]

It fell to detective chief superintendent Brian Boyce to give the superbly crafted funeral oration. Taffy was one of his officers on the Brinks Task Force when he died. The oration was precision engineered to stimulate the tear ducts of everyone inside the chapel, and all those hearing the saccharine tribute outside on loudspeaker. Boyce described his departed officer as "a man who had a face as hard as granite, but a heart as soft and vulnerable as a butterfly."[2]

The following morning crime correspondents added their own moving descant to the *missa solemnis*. The funeral was no less than "a hero's send off" befitting "a man with 26 years of unblemished police service" and 16 commendations, readers were told.

But these were spray-on pieties, part of a carefully mustered bodyguard of disinformation. It looked like the deliberate intention behind this was to cast a shroud around the corrupt activities of south London detectives and distract attention from an explosive crisis growing at the highest levels in the Yard and inside the on-going Brinks Mat robbery investigation.

Taffy Holmes did not have an honourable record. Far from being a good detective with long and unblemished service, Taffy was bent. So bent that some of his police colleagues openly joked that the undertaker wouldn't be able to straighten him out long enough to nail down the coffin lid. Many believed he had killed himself rather than face up to his corrupt activities and name names. The uncomfortable fact excised from all the floral tributes was that in the four months leading up to his death Taffy Holmes was at the heart of one of the most serious – and most mismanaged – internal corruption investigations in Scotland Yard history.

"I don't wish to speak ill of the dead. But what was going on around Taffy seriously affected the Yard, and it was covered up. Taffy was no detective – he could never solve a crime. At best he was just a makeweight, someone who liked to attach himself to other detectives and make himself busy running errands, talking to informants in pubs and buying them drinks, lots of drinks, which he could then charge against expenses," says Derek Haslam, the detective who triggered the corruption probe. Taffy was "the tribe scrounger", a man always at the ready to obtain cheap booze and free food for police social occasions whether they were promotion piss-ups or a leaving do.

As the master of the Manor of Bensham Masonic Lodge in Croydon, Taffy used his position to keep in with Yard bosses, an incredible number of whom were also "on the square". But behind the funny handshakes and confused homoeroticism of Freemasonry, Taffy had a hidden agenda. He liked to earn out of these occasions by obliging people to buy tickets when the invitations were free. "His god was money and he was on the lookout for it all the time," explains Haslam. Taffy, he says, had an exaggerated need for money because he was leading several lives.

"One moment he was at home with his wife and their two adopted children. The next he was off on a lengthy assignment, which he pretended was an unavoidable part of his detective duties. In reality the assignment was often with his lover, Jean Burgess, the ex-wife of a well-known south London criminal called Henry 'Chick' Burgess – whom Taffy also knew. The two sweethearts loved nothing more than marathon drinking sessions followed by meals in places that cost serious money," recalls Haslam.

UNTOUCHABLES

The affair continued throughout Taffy's secondment from the Flying Squad to the Brinks Mat Task Force. His "scrounging" introduced him to the shallow end of 1980s police corruption to which Yard bosses turned a blind eye. Things like padding overtime, fiddling expenses, borrowing police vehicles for private use, obtaining free drink and meals. These peccadilloes are known in the lingua franca of police corruption as "eating grass". But before he died it was seeping out that Taffy had also abused his position in other meatier ways, much more than taking money off private detectives like Danny Morgan to do checks on the police national computer for a criminal record and other confidential information.

Brinks Mat detective Michael Charman was one of several who wondered how a lazy alcoholic like Taffy had managed to stay on the Brinks Task Force for so long. Charman and Taffy met infrequently but he remembers one encounter in the summer of 1987 that signified Taffy's corruption had graduated to the carnivorous big league; big enough perhaps to know of a story worth £250,000.

"He didn't usually speak to people like me," recalls Charman. "He was part of the set we christened 'The Gentlemen's Drinking Club'. As lazy as they were well connected they spent much of the morning discussing where they were going to have lunch; how long they could make it last and how much they would drink. One day I met him on the fire escape. He came straight up to me and said something strange and disturbing. 'Boyo,' he said, 'don't you ever take a penny from the likes of Kenny Noye.' From his choice of words and the look on his face there was only one way you could interpret the remark. He was speaking from experience."

Noye was already serving a 14-year sentence for laundering the gold bullion when Taffy told Charman this. The Brinks Task Force was preparing for the bigger trial of Michael Relton and other key players in the so-called Gold Conduit. The Yard was concerned about the adverse effect any internal investigations into alleged police corruption would have on this and other forthcoming Brinks trials, and indeed earlier convictions.

This concern would also affect the way the anti-corruption investigations were conducted and their results made public. This is especially true of the corruption probe into Taffy and his friend and fellow Freemason, commander Ray Adams, who was under investigation by CIB2 for an alleged improper relationship with Noye and other criminals from the southside of the Thames.

Just before he killed himself Taffy told his partner, detective sergeant John Davidson, that he planned to kill Haslam, who he believed had comprehensively betrayed him to CIB2. Davidson almost certainly passed the information on. It was one of a number of threats Haslam had received, leading him to sell the family home.

Taffy, gun in hand, did come looking for Haslam but discovered the family had suddenly moved with no forwarding address. An anxious neighbour called the police. But Taffy was never arrested for threats to kill. Nor was he offered psychiatric counselling or time off. A few of his former colleagues we spoke to believe his suicide was an outcome some in the Yard might even have welcomed.

On 28 July 1987 Alan "Taffy" Holmes could take no more. Inside his south London home he wrote a suicide note to the wife, loaded his shotgun and stepped into the garden. He turned the gun on himself and pulled the trigger. The weapon fell neatly at his feet beside the suicide note. The man with the butterfly heart was dead. He was 44 years old.

Rigor mortis had hardly set in before the cover-up began. In a flurry of hurried phone calls and crisis meetings Yard chiefs decided Taffy Holmes' death would be passed off as the poisoned outgrowth of a tangled personal life, an act of desperation born of a fear his wife would find out something the Yard was well aware she already knew – that Taffy was having an affair with gangster's moll Jean Burgess.

The Police Complaints Authority made an unusual statement the day after the suicide, which added to the Yard's woes. The PCA revealed for the first time that Commander Ray Adams was Taffy's friend and the watchdog had been for several months supervising a CIB2 inquiry into his relationship with Noye.

A few days later the *People* splashed with a headline that screamed, "YARD BOSS AND THE BULLION CROOK". It went on to detail how days after Taffy's death CIB2 investigators interviewed Noye in prison about his informant relationship with Commander Adams.

It didn't take long for Fleet Street to realise that the PCA was also supervising another corruption probe by South Yorkshire police into suspended Brinks chief superintendent Tony Lundy. Like Adams, it concerned a supposedly crooked relationship with a major criminal informant. The *News of the World* had its own exclusive, one of several scoops rooted in reporter Alex Marunchak's access to Taffy's corrupt circle of friends. "COP KILLED HIMSELF TO SAVE PALS IN THE MASONS – YARD MEN'S FURY", ran the headline. A senior officer, the reporter revealed, had made a formal complaint against

UNTOUCHABLES

CIB2, in effect accusing the anti-corruption squad of driving Taffy Holmes to his death.

It was clear then that the troubled detective had a story to tell. The newspapers were already excited by the Brinks Mat story – the robbery of the century – and the hint of corruption surrounding it. They would have paid handsomely for a confessional interview by Taffy Holmes. Was this the story he and Danny Morgan hawked around Fleet Street?

Whatever the case, the situation concerning Taffy Holmes was in danger of spiralling out of control for Scotland Yard. But a perfect opportunity presented itself to the spin-doctors. On 3 August a new commissioner, Peter Imbert, was sworn in. At the press conference he pledged to root out corruption and emphasised to the press pack that Taffy was "not in any way suspected of any wrongdoing".[3]

The lobbying for a ceremonial funeral, a powerful vehicle of both internal reassurance and external image management, followed the new commissioner's investiture. Judicious leaks to tame journalists focused on how bad it would look to the rank and file if the top man did not bestow such an honour.

Imbert had talked tough about dirty cops. Corrupt Freemason officers would also be thoroughly investigated, he pledged. The new commissioner was seen as a reformer, albeit one who had come from the shadowy counter-subversive world of Special Branch, the arresting arm of MI5. But those close to him and far from hostile believe he let himself be bounced into conceding the ceremonial burial of Taffy Holmes, thereby concealing the truth about his death.

Once the nature of the funeral had been agreed, Yard crisis managers came up with a parallel wheeze. They needed to ensure that Jean Burgess, the other woman and ex-wife of a still active south London gangster, would not attend the public occasion. Jean played along but sent an anonymous wreath. She dedicated it, "To you from me – thinking of you always".

The Yard discreetly laid on an unusual, semi-official wake immediately after the funeral in one of Taffy's favourite pubs, the Prince of Wales in Thornton Heath. The publican was an active member of the same Masonic lodge. This was Jean's turn to be the grieving "widow" while the real Mrs Holmes was kept away. It was doubles all round as 50 officers, including senior ones, came straight from the cemetery to call last orders on the dead detective.

Taffy's suicide note attacked CIB2 for driving him to wrap his guts around a shotgun, but also specifically accused Haslam of betrayal. Taffy denounced him for doing "a Serpico", a reference to the New York cop who in the 1970s exposed his corrupt colleagues to a newspaper after his bosses turned a blind eye.

Extracts of the suicide note were leaked to the press, who wrongly branded Haslam as the man who'd invited Taffy for a game of golf, got him talking about corruption and secretly taped him.

Haslam, then 40, had already been forced to relocate his family. But his situation was becoming more dangerous as police officers all over London discussed his supposed treachery. It is one of those paradoxes of police culture that an officer who develops a top quality informant to put away gangsters is a hero, but if that same officer grasses on corrupt colleagues he is, to use the vernacular, "lower than whale shit". Haslam believed his life could still be at risk either from corrupt cops or their criminal allies. CIB2 officers concurred, he says, and urged him to hide away with his wife and four children. The press even claimed there was a contract on his life.

While in hiding Haslam had plenty of time to review the situation he found himself in. What was he achieving by lying low every day while his reputation was being traduced in police canteens all over London? He resolved to break cover and attend Taffy's funeral. There was a genuine desire to pay his last respects to a friend and fellow Freemason. And since Haslam's own reputation mattered to him every bit as much as his safety, he didn't want cops to think he had anything to be ashamed of.

The Yard bosses had other ideas. Haslam knew too much and could thwart their self-serving efforts to construct a sanitised narrative of Taffy's death without any references to the internal corruption probe, Brinks Mat and commander Adams. So they made him an offer they thought he wouldn't refuse. An attractive senior woman officer he used to know and who was now working for CIB2 offered him lunch at an Italian restaurant to take his mind off the Judas rumours at work. The lunch date would by happy coincidence clash with the funeral.

The Sicilians say assassins come with smiles. Haslam knew lunch with a comely CIB officer could comprehensively finish off his reputation, especially if a newspaper photographer just happened to be passing by. A canny man who could spot an elephant trap, even when it was disguised as a free lunch, he passed on the fungi e fagioli, but also stayed away from the funeral.

A few days later, Haslam began the lengthy process of telling his side of the Taffy Holmes tragedy in a series of interviews with commander Thelma Wagstaff. She had been appointed to investigate the complaint against CIB2's handling of the internal corruption probe as well as the circumstances behind the detective's death.

It was a classic Yard farce. A new internal investigation was looking into an on-going internal corruption probe, which was looking into even older allegations against a senior officer. Commander Wagstaff was investigating a superior, the CIB2 boss, deputy assistant commissioner Peter Winship. He, in turn, was investigating commander Ray Adams, his Masonic friend Taffy Holmes and links to south-east London gangsters like Kenny Noye.

Wagstaff was certainly up to the job. She had worked her way through the male-dominated detective branch, serving on the drugs squad. She was also the highest-ranking woman officer in the country after her promotion in September 1986 to commander. As the chair of the Yard's working party on rape, Wagstaff had revolutionised the investigation of this crime and introduced so-called rape suites for victims to be debriefed in relaxed surroundings. She was highly respected by certain key male officers and tipped as a contender to become the Yard's first ever woman commissioner.

When she took up the assignment Wagstaff knew little about the background to the CIB2 corruption inquiry, its roots in the Brinks Mat robbery and the tangle of accusations and counter accusations around Kenneth Noye, his Masonic connections and friends in high places in the Kent police and Scotland Yard.

However, she was very familiar with commander Ray Adams, who just recently had mysteriously replaced her in an important post.

In February 1987, five months before the suicide, Thelma Wagstaff's police career was in the ascendant. She was given a prestigious and highly sensitive position as the head of the criminal intelligence branch, SO11. In other words, Wagstaff was to be the officer in sole charge of the Yard's entire intelligence gathering on major villains and the network of those among them who secretly double as police informers.

The previous incumbent, commander Phil Corbett, had vacated the post and later left the Yard in anger over the failure to discipline DI Peter Atkins for his unauthorised *liaison dangereuse* with Michael Relton. Corbett was also agitated by the malign influence of Freemasonry in the force and bemoaned what sources say was the internal sabotage of an earlier inquiry into the Brotherhood.

On her appointment, Wagstaff was told there were two extraordinary reasons why she got the job: one because she was beyond reproach, the other because it was essential that the head of intelligence was in no way beholden to the Masonic network. For years Freemasons had honeycombed the upper tiers of the Yard and granted favours and preferential promotion to brother officers who swore secret oaths with rolled-up trouser legs. Wagstaff's gender discounted her as a possible Mason. It was therefore highly unlikely she would do any favours for this mafia of the mediocre inside the Yard. Her sponsors knew this and appeared to push her appointment as a way of breaking with the past.

Unfortunately commander Wagstaff was not allowed to remain as head of SO11 for very long. By mid-afternoon on the very day of her appointment she had been replaced. Much to her amazement the new head of criminal intelligence was Ray Adams, a man with the most extensive and well-known Masonic connections.

Several months later, when Wagstaff was appointed to investigate the whole murky affair surrounding Taffy's suicide, she could have been forgiven for thinking her new assignment was karma.

Haslam explained to commander Wagstaff how he met Taffy in south London when they were both relatively young recruits, how they'd often gone drinking together and how Taffy had introduced him to the Freemasons early in 1987. Repeatedly Haslam underlined his co-operation with the CIB2 corruption probe, but pointed out he had never secretly taped Taffy for them.

Initially, Wagstaff's view of Derek Haslam was highly coloured by the "Serpico" taunt. It seemed at first glance that Haslam was an unhelpful troublemaker who had deliberately, and with tragic consequences, set out to stir the pot. But when the cross checking began and Haslam repeatedly offered to take a lie detector test, he saw her view change.

In one of the early sessions Haslam took her step-by-step through the origins of the CIB2 corruption probe into Adams.

It began in February 1987 with a middle-ranking drug dealer called Raymond Gray. He was linked to a violent south London gang led by a man called John Crittendon. Police intelligence in turn linked Crittendon, a dog track owner, to the notorious Richardson brothers who had extensive business interests in south-east London and also to crime figures in the United States.

Gray lived in Shirley, south London, very near both Taffy Holmes and commander Adams. Press attention at the time was drawn to the commander's mock-Tudor house called Wildacre. His £450,000 home was situated in what locals in Shirley call Millionaire's Row. The rising star in the police firmament had bought it in the late seventies with his wife, who it was said was independently wealthy and owned a local boutique. They also owned a £100,000 villa in Portugal, one newspaper revealed.⁴

Haslam had arrested Gray for supplying three kilos of speed. He turned informant in return for a letter to the judge mentioning his co-operation with the police. Gray provided good quality information. But over five lengthy taped interviews with Haslam, revealed here for the first time, he also discussed his experiences of police corruption.⁵

Gray alleged "that the gang he dealt with had access to police records and criminal intelligence records via a corrupt police officer of substantial rank at New Scotland Yard". He also claimed he had met the as yet unidentified senior officer who was connected to the Yard's Central Drug Squad.⁶

Haslam transferred in April 1987 to the Serious Crime Squad at Tottenham Court Road police station because they were already investigating the Crittendon gang as part of a wider investigation, called The Collection Plan, of London drug crime syndicates. Haslam's worry was that with insider knowledge from someone of substantial rank the gangsters would anticipate every move he intended to make.

Haslam and another officer agreed to tape-record a final interview with Gray on 9 April at 3pm. "[It was] a final attempt to discover the identity of the corrupt police officer he had stated he had met. During the course of this fifth interview without any prompting he mentioned Ray Adams' name in connection with corruption back in 1973."⁷

The tape was played to a senior member of the Brinks Task Force. Then CIB2 was called in to investigate commander Adams under PCA supervision. The allegations were two-fold. Firstly, that when Adams was working as a detective chief superintendent on the Regional Crime Squad in the seventies he and other south London detectives were on the take from local criminals. The second allegation emanated from Adams' relationship with his one-time registered informant Kenny Noye. One newspaper suggested that Adams cultivated Noye in 1977 when he was arrested for receiving stolen goods.⁸

Commander Adams was not on the Brinks Task Force but he had featured in an intriguing way. When Boyce was cross-examined in the Noye murder trial he revealed that the Kent gangster had offered him a £1 million bribe. Boyce also told the jury that Noye mentioned Ray Adams as someone who would give him a good reference. His actual words were, "You ask Ray Adams. He will tell you that I am not a violent man or a killer."

As the allegations against Adams in the Gray tapes were imprecise, the informant was re-interviewed by CIB2 at Tintagel House. Meanwhile Adams, by now the head of SO11, suffered the indignity of having to present himself to CIB2 to be served with official notification that he was subject to an investigation.

The *Daily Express* later revealed this was not the first time Adams had been quizzed by anti-corruption investigators – the Porn Squad inquiry in the seventies had spoken to him, it claimed. The *People* brought things right up to date, informing its readers how CIB2 investigators were speaking to two judges concerning "mercy plea" letters Adams had written on behalf of two unnamed defendants.

Haslam told Wagstaff he had been meeting Taffy Holmes and Jean Burgess for drinks throughout the initial stages of the CIB2 investigation. He was trying to keep Taffy out of the firing line after his friend had told him he was "good friends" with Adams. But when Taffy asked for copies of the Gray tapes for Adams, and made "veiled threats", Haslam says he decided to tell CIB2, without naming Taffy. He was unaware they had already identified him after a tip-off from another officer.

When CIB2 looked into Taffy's background they discovered he had started his affair with Jean Burgess, a local barmaid, in 1979. His marriage was sexless and he was sleeping downstairs. During one meeting, Haslam says Taffy asked if he would meet with Adams. Instead Haslam reported the approach to CIB2 and offered to go in to the commander wearing a wire. Haslam takes up the story.

"I continued to meet Taffy socially and through work. On one occasion I was having a meal with him in an Indian restaurant along with Jean Burgess. Taffy stated that if I did not co-operate with Adams harm might befall me, or a member of my family. He told me Adams had powerful friends. He went on to tell me Adams knew everything the inquiry was doing. He even knew that CIB2 officers had had his house photographed from the air by police helicopter.

"Jean Burgess then told Taffy that if any harm came to me or my family because of Adams she would go to CIB2 and tell them about the money she had paid to Adams over the years on behalf of her husband. She went on to say that she had even paid him out on his own doorstep on behalf of her ex-husband. She made other comments about Adams which left me in no doubt that she knew Adams was corrupt."[9]

UNTOUCHABLES

The CIB officers were aghast at what Haslam told them and in early June asked him to deliver a message to Taffy that it was time for him to come clean if he wanted to avoid arrest. "When I told him he seemed shocked and depressed but said he had been expecting something to happen. He told me that he believed he had been photographed meeting with Henry Burgess and Ray Adams in Jean Burgess's back garden a few weeks before."[10]

After he passed on the message Haslam had a secret rendezvous with CIB2 that evening and made a statement of what had happened. He advised that CIB2 go easy on Taffy. "I told them beneath his tough exterior he was in fact a weak man and could not cope with stress." Haslam also considered Jean Burgess the key. "I said if you play it right, Jean will give you all the evidence you need. I stressed that if Jean thought she was helping Taffy, she would give them Adams."

Haslam believes CIB2 ignored his warnings and steamed into Taffy. He feels that Taffy was deliberately encouraged to believe that he had been secretly tape-recorded by Haslam, when CIB2 knew this to be untrue.

Similarly, in place of the softly, softly approach to Jean, like butchers performing heart surgery, the anti-corruption squad arrested her on suspicion of corruption. The arrest was used to put pressure on Taffy to talk and Haslam believes his friend did start to tell CIB2 about his corrupt dealings and associates inside and outside the police.

According to Haslam's affidavit, CIB2 told him that as a result of things Taffy had told them about Adams they were in the position to obtain a warrant for the commander's arrest.

CIB2 would also need the evidence of Taffy's lover. But for Jean Burgess it was too much. When her solicitor arrived she refused to make a statement. Her ex-husband, Chick Burgess, apparently threatened to blow her head off if she opened her mouth. Haslam already suspected the anti-corruption squad was a very leaky ship but now he started to sense "a cover-up at the highest level".

This, then, is the story Derek Haslam told commander Thelma Wagstaff over the late summer and autumn of 1987. She recommended he take time off work.

In early 1988, with the Holmes inquest approaching, Haslam returned to work. He was told that for his own safety he should not return to detective duties but to a prosecution support unit at Norbury Police Station. There he worked with detectives like Duncan Hanrahan, who says he was feeding information back to Adams. One morning Haslam found an anonymous hand-written message on his desk. "You Judas rat. You're fucking dead."

In British police culture in the 1980s it was unthinkable that a police officer could talk directly and honestly to the press about corruption without fear of recrimination. Police regulations and canteen culture saw to that, concerns for their pensions and the Official Secrets Act took care of any floaters. Also, there was no independent system a courageous officer could go to. This was not an oversight but part of an arrangement between the police and the Home Office that for Scotland Yard at least, self-regulation was best all round.

Accordingly, in March 1988 Derek Haslam's best chance for the truth to emerge was the long postponed inquest into the death of Taffy Holmes. "Although I did not like the idea of having to call fellow officers liars in a courtroom full of press, I would do so if needed. The public were entitled to know the truth and politics should not come into it," Haslam wrote in a statement taken before the Holmes inquest.

As ever, the Yard had other ideas. Commander Thelma Wagstaff's responsibilities extended to preparing the inquest into Taffy Holmes' death. As one of the last people to see him alive, Haslam had vital information about the dead man's state of mind and the factors that had really brought about his death. Furthermore, he had also been named and blamed in the suicide note.

All this should have secured Haslam's presence at the inquest – his last hope of finding a forum to clear his name. "I asked when her enquiry was finished if my name would be cleared. She replied that the resulting report would be forwarded to commissioner Imbert for him to take what action he saw fit. She assured me there would not be any cover-up on her part; however, she said that I had to be realistic as regards what he decided to do having received her report. She intimated that politics might well come into it, but that would be beyond her control."[11]

As the Yard was hogtied to the lie that Taffy Holmes was not under investigation at the time of his death, Haslam says Wagstaff told him that "domestic reasons" for the suicide would be put forward at the inquest. His appearance would therefore "make things awkward" and he wouldn't be called. "I decided that if commander Wagstaff was prepared to make reference [in the inquest] to the fact that I had not tape-recorded or tricked Taffy into confessing things I would be partly satisfied," says Haslam.

While he kept his part of the deal and stayed away from the inquest, the Yard cynically broke its promise to him. The management of mendacity also extended to ensuring that the full suicide note never saw the light of day. The coroner said it would "upset too many people".

With the suicide note buried and Haslam out of the way, the inquest heard evidence of DC Alan Holmes' years of unblemished service, but that he had been having an affair he feared was about to be disclosed to his wife.

This was nonsense, says Haslam. "I knew the real reason [for his suicide] was that it was the only way out for him not to have to give evidence as regards commander Adams, a fellow Mason."[12] Not only was the inquest "a total whitewash", it was "stage-managed", says Haslam. "No denial was ever made by commander Wagstaff that I had tricked Taffy into confessing and tape-recorded the conversation."

On 14 March 1988 the coroner recorded a verdict of suicide. He suggested Taffy Holmes' mind must have been in "turmoil" over his family and future in the police.[13]

Commander Thelma Wagstaff finished her investigation into the death of Taffy Holmes and wrote a scorching report, which was ready for publication soon after the inquest. Holmes, she felt, had been thrown to the wolves and Haslam was also treated very shabbily. The corruption inquiry into commander Adams, she had come to believe, was pitiful. The investigative resources were spread too thin; the will and skill levels were too low. There was widespread leaking. The Wagstaff report also recommended that because of the poor management of the CIB2 inquiry, its head, deputy assistant commissioner Peter Winship, should be moved sideways, while his number two, deputy chief superintendent David Banks, should be denied a promotion for which he had only just been selected.

Certainly CIB2's behaviour towards Haslam was very strange. First they tried to keep him away from the funeral with a honeytrap lunch invitation. Then, Haslam reveals, the anti-corruption squad undermined Gray's credibility by speaking to his doctor, who subsequently wrote a report saying his patient was "deranged" and a drug user. Finally, when Wagstaff interviewed CIB2 officers for her inquiry, one denied asking Haslam to pass any ultimatum to Taffy Holmes.[14]

When Wagstaff interviewed detectives from the Brinks Mat Task Force they too closed ranks "to avoid adverse publicity which might lead to acquittals in subsequent trials", says Haslam. The trial of

THE SUICIDE CLUB

Brinks Mat money launderer Michael Relton, a man who had acted as an interface between criminals and crooked cops, was due to start one month after the inquest, and at the same time as the Daniel Morgan inquest. The Morgan family wouldn't discover until much later the links between the two deaths.

The temptation or pressure on those who carry out internal investigations to delay and downplay the results until the timing suits the many other priorities of the police should not be underestimated. The repercussions of an ill-timed internal inquiry can cost a multi-million pound prosecution and lead to negative headlines and a loss of public confidence.

It was not surprising, therefore, that soon after submitting her report commander Wagstaff was ordered to re-write it. Two very senior retired Scotland Yard detectives close to the Brinks inquiry confirm this. It was not the first and would certainly not be the last time that the Yard nobbled a problematic report that exposed the shortcomings of self-regulation.

Wagstaff complied with the order to re-draft her report, to a degree. But it galled her. She left the police a few years later.

In January 1990, Scotland Yard told commander Adams he would be cleared of the Noye bribery allegations and those made by drug dealer and police informant Raymond Gray.

The PCA-supervised CIB2 inquiry had produced 44 volumes of documents including 125 statements. However, neither the public nor parliament could know the contents of the report and therefore had to rely on the Yard's word that no evidence was found to justify a criminal prosecution.

No one stopped to ask how the CIB2 inquiry could ever be relied on when the two senior officers running it had been severely criticised for their stewardship and competence, at least in the early draft of the Wagstaff review. Commander Adams, however, told the *Sunday Times* that CIB2's efforts were "very thorough and rigorous" but it was time to get on with his career.[15]

Adams had not been suspended during the 30 months it took the internal investigation to conclude. He was eventually moved sideways from his highly sensitive and operational role as head of criminal intelligence to a non-operational post. By the time he was cleared, Adams had for some time been working in the Yard's own inspectorate, the force's quality assurance division. It was an odd appointment for someone under investigation for serious corruption allegations. But then Adams had a different take. He told reporters that the very fact he was still in such "an important job" meant he would not face any disciplinary action either. He didn't.[16]

Adams claimed to us that Haslam had a vendetta against him and was "on a mission to bring about [his] downfall". He added that the root of all this was a fatal car accident back in 1977.[17]

Continuing his vendetta theory, Adams claimed Haslam befriended Taffy Holmes to get dirt on him. "I told Taffy to tell CIB2 everything. Taffy knew nothing about me. Taffy could say nothing about me."

Adams denied having an unauthorised secret meeting with Holmes on a golf course that backed onto his home. He said he was walking his dog and bumped into Taffy who used to go shooting on the golf course. The conversation was limited to warning Taffy to be careful because the dog was off its lead.

Adams admitted he had considerable influence over Taffy and regrets he was unable to counsel the troubled detective and fellow Mason into not killing himself. Adams was on holiday in the immediate period leading up to Taffy Holmes' death. He revealed that Taffy had tried to contact him and believes that if they had spoken he could have prevented the suicide.

The CIB2 inquiry had investigated claims that Adams had once gone on an earlier holiday with armed robber Chick Burgess and his then wife Jean. Adams told us it was a coincidence that he and Burgess were booked into the same Spanish resort. "I approached Burgess [on the beach] and said, 'Fuck off, you've embarrassed me.'" When he returned to work Adams said he told his boss and wrote a report. "My relationship with Burgess was entirely professional," he insisted.

Adams also talked about his relationship with his informant Kenny Noye. Enigmatically, he referred to being "asked to do something [during the Brinks investigation] at a senior level" soon after Noye had been arrested for the Fordham murder. Adams said it was an assistant commissioner at the Yard who had asked him and he now "regrets" doing it because it led to his aggravation with CIB2.

Adams is more than likely referring to his secret meeting with Noye sanctioned by the Home Office and said to have taken place in the cells at Lambeth Magistrates Court. Noye was asked to help locate the gold bullion. What the *quid pro quo* was is not clear. At the very least, presumably Noye was offered some deal with regard to the murder charge he was facing.

It was during this secret meeting that the bribery allegations emerged. Noye, it was suggested, had offered Adams a large payment if he helped corrupt the Brinks investigation. When CIB2 later interviewed Noye in prison, Adams said his informant gave him "a clean bill of health". And although both men were Masons, Adams said he was not in the same lodge as Noye and had left the Brotherhood before he even knew Noye was "on the square".

Although Ray Adams was never suspended, charged or disciplined over any of these allegations the rising star would never be promoted beyond commander. Nor did he ever again hold as sensitive a post as head of criminal intelligence. Adams remained a controversial figure in and outside the Yard. Not least because he was soon back in the limelight over, among other things, his professional relationship with informant David Norris and with south-east London criminals linked to the murder of Stephen Lawrence in 1993. Adams left the police that year with a bad back after 31 years' service.

Scotland Yard fixed the Taffy Holmes inquest and rather than protect their whistle-blower cop, Derek Haslam, they allowed him to be portrayed as a hate figure, an unhinged traitor and malcontent. Yard bosses rallied to the defence of a man, Taffy Holmes, who they knew or ought to have known was corrupt. Meanwhile the signal sent out to other officers thinking of blowing the whistle was – DON'T.

As a result of his treatment by the Yard, by CIB2 and his own colleagues, Haslam lost faith in the integrity of the police service to investigate itself. He also lost his own place in the world. Depressed and ill, Haslam was right to believe he had no further prospects in the police. Senior officers suggested he should seek medical retirement. He left in October 1989 on his 42nd birthday.

Today he is still chain-smoking and very neatly dressed with his leather shoes shining to drill-ground specification. Haslam still hopes that someday soon Scotland Yard will own up to the extent of mid-eighties police corruption. "I strongly believe that a grave chapter in Scotland Yard's history needs to be opened up to public scrutiny in order that lessons be learned and certain persons who once held high rank and abused their power be subject to public examination."

His experience gives the lie to the Yard's recent claim that it took its eye off the ball about corruption in the 1980s. The handling of the Taffy Holmes saga shows quite clearly the Yard turned a blind eye to corruption while pretending to do something about it.

Alan "Taffy" Holmes was part of a corrupt network, a firm within a firm in south London, which Scotland Yard, for a variety of reasons, chose to ignore. It was the activities of this network we strongly suspect that Danny Morgan and Taffy Holmes were considering blowing the whistle on when they died within months of each other.

8

THE GHOST OF DAVID NORRIS

In Miami, the cocaine capital of America, the orgy of drug violence gripping Latin America in the late eighties was spilling onto the city's art deco streets. Brian de Palma set his gangster masterpiece, *Scarface*, there. Cuban assassin Tony Montana, played by Al Pacino, had enough of washing dishes in a greasy diner across the road from the *narcos*' favourite nightclub, so he decided to strike out on his own. After a few contract killings for the local drug boss, Montana made his own moves on the street. "Watch out," he swaggers, "there's a new bad guy in town."

A new breed of bad guy was also taking over in London and throughout the UK. These new faces were young and tuned in to drug culture. They moved seamlessly in the associated underground music and club scene both as users and abusers of those who didn't pay for their gear.

By the end of the eighties the criminal landscape was radically different. Kent, Essex and London were especially awash with good quality cocaine, ecstasy and skunk – a hydroponically grown powerful type of grass. It didn't take long for even the dumbest career villain to see that drug trafficking was safer and much more lucrative than armed robbery. The sentence was lighter and the time easier to do, especially if the large profits had been salted away or laundered through legitimate cash businesses.

Distribution to the growing community of weekend ravers and other recreational drug users would soon take all the hassle out of scoring, with some gangs offering a home delivery service, organised through laptops and untraceable mobile phones. Some special customers even received Christmas cards signed with just a mobile number. An alternative message might have been, "Let it snow, let it snow, let it snow".

This transformation of London's underworld was ironically eased by Scotland Yard's pursuit of the Brinks Mat robbers and their associates, which left a leadership vacuum in the east and south-east of London, traditionally the epicentre of villainy in the capital.

This hole in the criminal ozone layer was further widened in 1990 and 1991 by the fall of the Arif crime family, who'd usurped the Richardsons as the dominant gang in south-east London. Dogan Arif, the boss of the Turkish-Cypriot crime family, had gone down for nine years for his role in an £8 million cannabis importation, which he still maintains was a police fit-up. His brothers Mehmet and Denis received hefty 18 and 22-year stretches respectively after they were caught in a sting operation attempting an armed robbery of a Securicor van carrying £700,000. The Arifs were also engaged during this period in a bloody tit-for-tat gang war with the Brindle brothers, which saw one soldier from each family shot dead by masked gunmen, one in a bookies, the other in a pub.

Into this void stepped a number of organised crime syndicates and families who'd served their apprenticeships as armed robbers, enforcers and runners for the old school villainocracy of the seventies. Now they wanted to restructure the pecking order around drug trafficking.

The drug business can be likened to a privatised railway system in that the dominant syndicates or individuals control key parts of the track and therefore their own distribution network for the drugs they import. Alternatively, smaller criminals may come to them to rent out a part of the track for distributing drugs imported by others. Drug syndicates in different parts of the country also form temporary alliances to distribute one enormous importation, sometimes of several tons. Often a powerful syndicate will pay a "tribute" to another for moving drugs through its turf. Similarly, individual operators will pay a "tax" to the local dominant crime syndicate after carrying out "a bit of work" on their patch.

This is not to say the transformation of the British crime scene was without its turf wars. Crime syndicates battled for ascendancy in all four corners of the capital in the early nineties. The vast profits and greater opportunities to rip off "associates" was another cause of an increase in violence. Also, the greater ease with which the police could

THE GHOST OF DAVID NORRIS

insert undercover officers at most points along the drug distribution chain or run informants inside syndicates created a climate of suspicion. This quickly turned to paranoid violence, especially if criminals were getting high on their own supply.

There were said to be 43 murders in south-east London by the end of 1991, a 100 per cent rise on the previous year. The hit on David Norris was arguably the most significant.

A few minutes before 10 p.m. on Sunday night, 28 April 1991, David Norris turned the wheel of his Toyota into Regent Square. His young wife, Debbie, heard the jeep approach the driveway of their small home. Their two daughters were fast asleep. The square was otherwise quiet, an ideal suburban setting in Belvedere, Kent.

The previous month Norris had turned forty-six, and only two weeks earlier he and Debbie had celebrated their fifth wedding anniversary. She was also five months pregnant with twins.

The couple had known each other since the early eighties. They initially set up home in the Bermondsey area, living in a council flat overlooking Tower Bridge. David's dad was a retired coalman. His son officially described himself as a market trader. The job title was to some extent correct. But then deception and David Norris were always close bedfellows. Norris traded lorry-loads of stolen goods, some of which he thieved himself. He also traded drugs and one other valuable commodity – top quality information on the criminal Underworld. This he regularly sold to the police, making him one of Scotland Yard's most prolific informants.

As Norris parked in his drive, two men on a motorbike approached, cutting the silence with the sinister revving of their engine. The pillion rider was carrying a .38 calibre pistol. Norris knew exactly what it meant. He ran down the square away from his home, but was shot in the back. The assassins, one on the bike, the other on foot, gave chase. They caught him near a lamppost. Norris pleaded for his life and offered money. But the gunman was not moved and fired four more shots into his left forearm, chest, hand and head.

Neighbours, who heard the commotion from their window, saw the two helmeted men speed off. Debbie came rushing out of the house. She cradled her dying husband, his blood staining her floral nightie and his head lying on her pregnant stomach.

An article by Chester Stern, the former Met press officer turned *Mail on Sunday* reporter, which appeared one week after the Norris murder, revealed what looked suspiciously like damage limitation by the Yard. The *Sun* had already suggested an obvious motive, namely that the Underworld wanted Norris silenced because he was a grass. Stern, however, was briefed that a "gangland mythology" no less had developed around Norris, whom criminals mistakenly identified as one of the Yard's most important informants, when he wasn't.

The downplaying of Norris's role in the war on crime does not sit well with two of his former police handlers. They were both in contact with the prolific informant minutes before he died. Until now, they haven't spoken out.

Retired detective Chris Simpson is a giant of a man with a "hail fellow well met" demeanour. He left the Yard six years after Norris's murder, having completed 30 years' service. He now works in the insurance investigation world.

Simpson was the detective inspector in charge of a team at the South East Regional Crime Squad in East Dulwich. SERCS had various satellite offices across the greater London area and its detectives were on the front line of the fight against organised crime. The office at East Dulwich had a vast area of operation from the south and south-east inner city boroughs to the suburbs and borders of Kent, Sussex and Surrey.

Norris had been their registered informant since about 1985, says Simpson. He explained how a SERCS detective called Ron Harrison first arrested Norris over a major shoe robbery and "turned him" into an informant. Before leaving the squad for another posting a few years later, Harrison passed Norris to a colleague on the same team called Terry Pattinson. Under Scotland Yard rules, to avoid corrupt relationships forming between informant and handler the "grass" remained the Yard's property and was therefore passed to a new handler before the old one left the squad. Pattinson passed Norris to Simpson in early 1989 and Simpson was Norris's handler until his violent death in April 1991.

An informant handler normally has a controller above him, who is more senior in rank and above all should hardly ever meet the informant. This way the controller can in theory at least dispassionately evaluate the credibility of the intelligence and the informant's motive for giving it. But by the time Simpson was handling Norris, a more relaxed informant system was operating at East Dulwich SERCS. Simpson was both Norris's handler and the controller who assessed his tip-offs and planned police operations around them. If the job was successful Simpson was also the detective

THE GHOST OF DAVID NORRIS

who then recommended Norris for a reward and accompanied him to the Yard to be paid, usually thousands of pounds from a special Informants' Fund.

Norris was "the bizzo", says Simpson sipping his pint, "a top class informant. One of the top half dozen you could name over the last 20 to 30 years in London." In his time Norris provided tip-offs about lorry-loads of stolen gear, counterfeit currency, stolen artwork and drugs jobs, he adds. Their arrangement was worked out with clockwork efficiency, making Norris an indispensable member of the team.

"I was more or less the sole handler. At this time he was so prolific everyone on my team knew him. I would see him almost every day, five times a week," recalls Simpson. "I'd ring him up on Monday morning and say, 'Anything happening this week, Dave?' And he'd say, 'No, but I'm seeing someone this afternoon. I'll give you a call.'"

When an informant is registered his handler gives him a pseudonym. Norris's was "John Tracey", says Simpson. This is thereafter used in any internal police correspondence, especially the informant's log, a confidential document that detectives must fill in soon after having any contact with their source. Simpson remembers travelling with Norris to a café near Scotland Yard to meet assistant commissioner David Veness. There Norris signed a prepared receipt in his pseudonym and only then would Veness hand over the cash. Simpson says the largest amount he witnessed in one payment was about £3,000, adding: "He was so prolific it was almost as if he was up there every week."

Most of the top brass at the Yard knew of Norris. And the overall head of the East Dulwich SERCS, a respected detective called Pat Fleming, kept a copy of Norris's informant logs at the central London headquarters. He was the senior officer to whom Simpson first sent the request for a recommended reward. Simpson is candid about how it was normal to inflate the figure and try to get the best deal for "your man". But Fleming would invariably revise the amount downwards, he says, smiling.

Where possible, detectives are supposed to meet their informant only with another colleague present. Clearly Simpson felt very comfortable with Norris because he says he would sometimes meet him alone and without seeking permission from a superior. This was certainly the case on the night of the murder.

Simpson had arranged to meet at Norris's local pub, the Fox, in Belvedere, less than five minutes' drive from his house. They had said

8 p.m. but Simpson was running late and called Norris on his pager at about 7.50 to say he would be there in 40 minutes. When Simpson eventually arrived, over a few drinks they discussed the next week's business. Norris had put up some information about a robbery, Simpson recalls.

At a few minutes to ten they parted company. Norris drove home and Simpson headed for his mother's house in east Kent, where he was staying that night. "I had taken the Monday off to install a burglar alarm," he explains.

The second detective who spoke to Norris on the night he was killed was detective constable Peter Bleksley. He co-handled Norris while he was an undercover officer attached to the Central Drug Squad. Blex's forte was posing as a ponytailed south-east London drug dealer. Being born and bred on the London/Kent border, or "Kenny Noye country" as he calls it, helped his cover among the younger generation of drug dealers. Blex was very believable as one of the new bad guys in town, who could pull together a drug deal, knew good gear from bad, and if asked could build a spliff or rack up a few lines of Charlie (cocaine) to party with his prospective "business associates". But he was under no illusion how dangerous Norris could be.

In about 1986 Norris was starting to act like a "loose cannon", says Blex. "If a lorry-load was stolen, Norris would earn from selling it on. He would then earn again by grassing to the police. They would pay him a reward. If there was bent old bill involved, he would earn a commission for recycling some of the recovered proceeds for them."

But "he was putting up so much drug work" the police officers he gave it to just couldn't turn it down, says Blex. "Remember, these were the years when [US president] Ronnie Reagan was banging on about a War on Drugs."

The Home Office and Scotland Yard were slavishly following suit, refusing to see the drugs issue as anything but a supply problem. Tackle the drug dealers, problem solved. Consequently Whitehall threw millions at the police to fight this unwinnable war. And on this domestic battlefield, informants like David Norris were considered gold dust – the hidden tool that produced the drug seizures and arrests that satisfied the politicians who authorised the mandarins to release more money to the Yard.

Norris, too, knew exactly his worth to Scotland Yard and its gung-ho detectives, many of whom were in awe of the informant's bottle and too stupid to see his double-dealing ways.

"There was obviously shit about to hit the fan," says Blex, "so a protocol was drafted by the Yard to radically change the way Norris was used. It was decided that he would give all drug work to us on the Central Drug Squad based at the Yard and everything else he gave to the East Dulwich SERCS. The protocol meant that from then on we were supposed to let each other know if we were seeing Norris. But in practice this was an oft-breached protocol." Breached or not, the existence of the protocol made a mockery of the Yard's attempt immediately after Norris's murder to downplay his role as a major informant.

"At first Norris was handled at the Central Drug Squad by Tim Beer. Then because of my successes in informant handling and my UC status, I was introduced to him [as a co-handler]. Tim would see Norris a lot without me because I was busy on other undercover jobs," says Blex. In 1989, he left the drug squad for another posting. Norris was still providing quality information when Blex returned at the beginning of April 1991. Once again he co-handled Norris, this time with another officer.

Blex had a unique relationship with Norris. He was reliant on him in a way that other handlers weren't. Norris not only provided the Central Drug Squad with information, he also introduced Blex into the crime syndicate as the undercover "buyer" of drugs on offer. Consequently, Blex and Norris would spend a lot of time together developing the cover story.

Blex was surprised at how little Norris knew about the drugs business he was informing on. But then it was a sign of the times that career villains of his generation were diversifying into drug crime without having taken, handled or been around drugs previously.

UCs take a huge risk when dealing with informants – the most slippery of all the cast of characters in the crime business. Even with armed back-up from a surveillance team, Blex still had to walk into a business meeting trusting that Norris hadn't sold him out for a better deal.

Undoubtedly, informants like Norris also take huge risks but for dishonourable reasons. Norris knew the big rewards were in agreeing to be what is called "the participating informant", someone who must walk an incredibly difficult line between appearing to help other criminals carry out a crime without himself breaking the law or enticing them to do so.

Although the payoff is high for being a participating informant the risk of getting caught is commensurate. For even the criminal with one brain cell will eventually work out, with some help from an astute lawyer, who the grass was. It's just a process of working backwards. Once you've identified the undercover officer the next question is who referenced him. In the drug business, suspicion alone of being a grass can get you killed or at the very least badly bashed up. Norris had "a lot of front" and loved the thrill. That's why Blex dubbed him a "serial grass".

The undercover cop and the informant have a lot in common. Their trade is treachery and they must enjoy the buzz. But selling out your friends for a pound note was not a line Blex would cross. Norris was "scum of the earth" but also one of Blex's best informants. Thus on Sunday, 28 April, he was paging him no more than 90 minutes before his murder to set up another promising bit of work.

Norris and Blex spoke on payphones. Norris was at the Fox and Blex at another south-east London pub. After some general chitchat the informant explained that he was with Simpson. Blex was unaware and had a quick word with his police colleague. He then asked Norris if they were still on for a meet the next morning. Earlier that week Norris had offered information on what appeared to be a significant drug deal. Blex was calling to see if the deal was still on. Norris confirmed it was. He promised further details over breakfast in a nearby café.

The next morning Blex was driving to the café with his new co-handler, a detective sergeant called Phil Barrett. On the way the radio news reported that a man named as David "Morris" had been murdered outside his Belvedere home. Blex knew instantly it was their informant. Moments later his boss at the Central Drug Squad, detective inspector John Coles, called on the car phone. Coles was the controller of Norris at the time and would later become a major player in the Untouchables.

Blex knew there would be panic throughout the Yard and in various specialist police squads, including his own. And not only because one of their top grasses had been killed. Norris had deliberately tried to cultivate corrupt relationships with the large number of police officers of varying ranks he came across. It was his insurance policy. "I had nothing to be afraid of over any dealings with David Norris," says Blex. "But there were an awful lot of cops, some I liked, who [did]."

A few months after the murder of David Norris detectives from the drugs wing of the SERCS office in Surbiton, Surrey, received a tip-off. A gang of Protestants from Northern Ireland were sending hash from Margate on the Kent coast to Belfast using British Rail's Red Star parcel service. The drugs were being sent to a fishing tackle shop acting as a front.

According to a police source close to the operation, the National Drugs Intelligence Unit had either bugged up the fishing tackle shop or had an informant working inside it. The intelligence received from Belfast was passed to Surbiton to develop. Detectives travelled to Margate and set up a surveillance operation outside a house there. Inside were two young men identified as Stuart Warne, thirty-four, and Renwick Dennison, twenty-six. They had shacked up with two attractive girls, one of whom the detectives believed to be the daughter of an Irish policeman.

There were two other members of the drug gang unaccounted for. One was called Thomas McCreery and the other Steven Pollock. According to detective sergeant Alec Leighton, the SERCS officer leading Operation Bohemian, these two men were believed to be in Holland at the time organising another drug parcel.

Warne and Dennison were followed to a garage in the Margate area where they were storing the hash. They were arrested and taken to Margate police station where two SERCS detectives, John Donald and Alistair Clarke, interviewed them. After some questioning the two suspects made a momentous decision – they agreed to admit their guilt and give evidence against their associates.

The decision to turn supergrass was not a light one. It soon emerged that Warne and Dennison were frightened about another more serious matter – their involvement in the murder of David Norris. That admission came as a complete surprise to the two officers interviewing them, who rushed to notify Leighton. "Warne and Dennison also told us where the gun used to kill Norris was buried," recalls Leighton. "One of them thought they were next on the hit list when McCreery and Pollock returned from Holland." This, he speculates, was their reason for turning supergrass.

Leighton notified the officer in charge of the Norris murder inquiry, a detective superintendent he respected called Ian Crampton. They agreed to send two drug squad detectives with Dennison to London to locate the gun. "I believe it was buried under a bush, near a fence," says Leighton. Murder squad forensic specialists were then called in to dig up the weapon and also to search the Margate house where helmets, balaclavas and other evidence were recovered.

Warne and Dennison were subsequently produced in front of a Margate magistrate for their bail application, which the murder squad was naturally opposing. Leighton says Crampton gave him strict instructions. "He told me not to mention in court anything to do with terrorism or any association with paramilitary organisations. I was struggling to keep Warne and Dennison in custody, so I mentioned to the magistrate that they might be in personal danger from associates who were still at large."

McCreery, it appeared, had very murky connections to the Loyalist underworld and paramilitaries of the Ulster Defence Association. He was said to have recruited hit men in Belfast and dealt drugs there. His involvement in drugs made him a target for a failed punishment shooting, presumably by Republican groups. After the attempt on McCreery's life, in early 1991 he moved from Belfast to the Isle of Thanet in Kent with Pollock and Dennison, who was said to have been a UDA getaway driver during a petrol bomb attack on Catholics.[1]

Six months after the death of David Norris, Warne and Dennison were sentenced to life at the Old Bailey for plotting the murder. In mitigation they claimed they were in over their heads and regretted the crime.

In March the following year, four Ulstermen were arrested in connection with the Norris murder and drug trafficking offences. McCreery and Pollock, however, were still at large. Warne and Dennison, the star prosecution witnesses, had helped the police track down four of their six alleged accomplices. When the trial started in April 1993, two years after Norris's death, the murder squad felt they had put together a convincing case.

Crampton's number two was a south-east London detective inspector called Chris Jarratt, who would go on to be a leading figure in the Untouchables. Jarratt recruited several of his colleagues, like Jack Kelly from the Tower Bridge Flying Squad, onto the Norris murder inquiry.

Jarratt and Kelly had groomed the two supergrasses for the trial. The Old Bailey jury were given armed protection and armed police patrolled the courts' marble corridors. Terence McCrory, 30, from Belfast, and John Green, 32, from Falkirk, Scotland, were charged with murdering Norris and with conspiring to murder Norris with a third defendant called Patrick Doherty, 35, of Brockley, south-east London. Doherty and George McMahon, 46, from New Cross, also in south-east London, were charged with conspiracy to supply hashish.

In a nutshell the police case was a murder for cheap drugs plot. The prosecution claimed a south-east London drug trafficker called Terry Reeves[2] had put up the contracts to kill two men. One was John Dale, who ran a drinking club and a pub in east London. Dale was described in court as someone with "a murky past" who was "the object of dislike and hatred apparently because he was in the habit of ripping people off in drugs deals". The other target was David Norris, whom Reeves apparently wanted dead because he was a grass who'd told the police about a drug warehouse in Greenwich.

Reeves had two henchmen, Doherty and McMahon. They supplied drugs to Warne, who in turn supplied drugs to the Margate-based Protestant gang led by McCreery, Pollock and Dennison.

McCreery brought over from Belfast two Loyalist hit men, McCrory and Green, to do the hit on Dale. The asking price was £26,000. The plan was to cosh Dale and "carve his heart out" as a sign to others. However Green and McCrory were unsuccessful in locating their target and returned to Belfast. Dennison shot him instead at point-blank range with a sawn off single-barrelled shotgun. Incredibly Dale survived.

Three weeks later, the Loyalist hit men returned to London and killed Norris. This time the value of the contract was £35,000. Doherty had allegedly told Warne that "five or six" more hits were being planned.

After six weeks of evidence, on 24 May the trial suddenly collapsed and the defendants all walked free. The *Evening Standard*'s prolific court reporter, Paul Cheston, filed a story that screamed: "'Hitmen' cleared in £1m death plot trial".

A key discrepancy between Dennison's evidence and that of another prosecution witness forced the judge to direct the jury to acquit on one of four charges. This in turn led the prosecution to take a remarkable decision to drop the other three charges. The prosecutor argued that because the evidence of one supergrass could not be relied on, it undermined the evidence of the other. He therefore considered it "improper to proceed".

The police never managed to arrest McCreery and Pollock. Intriguingly, DS Alec Leighton remembers being told officially that after surviving the punishment shooting, UDA insider McCreery had been "relocated" to Kent by the British authorities. If this is correct then McCreery was collaborating with one of the key state agencies running the dirty war in Northern Ireland, which may explain why he was never caught. "You don't relocate criminals unless they are witnesses [which McCreery wasn't] or informants," Leighton explained.[3]

UNTOUCHABLES

There was a lot the Old Bailey jury were not told about in those six weeks during the spring of 1993 before the plug was pulled on the Norris murder prosecution.[4] Most of it however had nothing to do with Northern Ireland. It concerned the swirl of corruption allegations around three elite police squads – the East Dulwich and Surbiton offices of SERCS and the Central Drug Squad – directly associated with the life and death of Scotland Yard's star informant.

All that follows was known to the Yard as they prepared the prosecution against the men accused of conspiring to kill Norris. The prosecution counsel knew some of it and should have known a lot more, but one suspects the Yard chose not to tell them. The defence barristers certainly knew almost nothing about the police corruption allegations. If they had, the Crown most likely would have been forced to pull the prosecution completely or delay it pending a full inquiry – internal, of course.

For example, the jury never got to hear from Debbie Norris, the murder victim's widow who had cradled her bullet-ridden husband outside their home. By the time of the trial, two years later, much had changed in Debbie's life. The twins, a boy and a girl, were starting to walk and she had remarried – a policeman.

Mark Norton was not just any copper. He was a member of the Norris murder inquiry team who'd fallen in love with Debbie while acting as the family liaison officer. Norton was a 24-year-old trainee detective who had so impressed DI Chris Jarratt that he personally selected him for the murder inquiry.

The relationship with Debbie had developed slowly. Norton was there to help her through the funeral and the birth of the twins. But they began a full and secret relationship in January 1992. By August they had decided to marry. Norton didn't tell Crampton and Jarratt until months later. They went ballistic. The senior officers had only recently emphatically recommended Norton for promotion to full detective. News of the marriage spread through south-east London police pubs and canteens. Crampton was only too aware how bad it looked for the Yard with the trial looming. But as Norton had broken no police regulations there was nothing they could do. He was kept on the murder inquiry until the end of the trial in May 1993.

Naturally, Debbie discussed the tragedy with Norton, sharing her most intimate thoughts on what was behind the murder. The jury never had the opportunity to hear her story, which is revealed here for the first time. When we tracked Debbie Norris down she welcomed us as if she knew the opportunity to tell her side would one day arise.

THE GHOST OF DAVID NORRIS

Debbie confirmed something we'd heard on the grapevine. Within 48 hours of her husband's death she'd made an extraordinary allegation to the murder inquiry. Debbie had claimed that on the night of his murder, just before he left the house, David Norris counted out in front of her £15,000 in cash. He told her he was going to meet DI Chris Simpson at the Fox. She saw him put the money in a green carrier bag – "the kind you get at the local supermarket" – and leave for the pub. She believed he was going straight there. Shortly after his Toyota jeep pulled away, Simpson called and left a message on the answering machine saying he would be late.

Debbie told the police that the £15,000 was not found on his gunned-down body. There was never any suggestion that the two assassins had stolen it. The killing after all was a planned contract hit, not an opportunist crime where the killers hung around to go through belongings.

Debbie told us she had also informed Jarratt that her husband kept a black book of people who owed him money. There was a person listed as "Chris" in the book with no surname. And next to it was the figure £15,000. She believed Chris Simpson might have borrowed the money from her husband, and told Jarratt so, making two statements to the inquiry within days of the murder.

Mark Norton confirms a lot of Debbie's story. They split up acrimoniously in 1996, separated a year later and are now divorced. Nevertheless, Norton recalls taking Debbie's statements. He also saw the entries in Norris's diary of those who owed him money. The diary was a police exhibit in the murder inquiry. And he recalls going to see one of Debbie's ex-husbands named in it as one of Norris's debtors. The man confirmed he owed the money but was never a suspect in the case. Another name in the diary was Debbie's dad. The third name he remembers was an entry for "Chris".

Simpson had left East Dulwich on promotion as a detective chief inspector before the murder trial started. Like Debbie and Norton, he was never called as a witness. We spoke to him about her allegations.

Simpson says the murder squad knew from checking Norris's pager that he had met him the night he died. He was asked to brief Crampton and Jarratt. "They wanted to know who had a motive to shoot him and who he had grassed up. 'Give me a couple of weeks and I'll tell you,' I said." Simpson delivered the punchline with comic timing, followed by a hearty laugh and some co-ordinated shoulder shrugging. It was all very Tommy Cooper, an impression for which he is apparently well known in police circles.

UNTOUCHABLES

The murder squad had "every bit of paper that existed" including the informant logs and a list of operations based on information Norris had supplied and been paid for. Simpson says he identified the East Dulwich SERCS jobs for the murder inquiry.

He confirms they spoke to him about the £15,000 and the financial reference to "Chris" in Norris's diary. "Crampton said to me, 'Is this you?' I said it might be. He said, 'Has Norris ever lent you or given you any money, or the other way around?' I said no, except police money [for reward payments and expenses]. Crampton then says, 'Did [Norris] know someone else called Chris?' I said, 'Yes, he's a villain.'"

Simpson believed he was the only person Norris met the night he was killed but denies receiving a carrier bag of cash from his informant, although he said it was not unusual for Norris to carry a big wad of "two or three grand".

As soon as Debbie Norris alluded to possible corruption surrounding her husband's death, CIB should have been called in and an inquiry launched. This probe could have been conducted parallel to the murder inquiry but away from the very policing area of south-east London from which the corruption allegations were coming. Had this been done, at some stage the Norris murder inquiry would have had to disclose to the defence the existence of the CIB inquiry, despite the problems it would cause to a successful prosecution.

The Yard however confirms no such inquiry was ever conducted.[5] Crampton went further and told us Debbie Norris had refused to co-operate with CIB.[6] She strongly denies this. And Mark Norton counterclaims that the murder squad put Debbie under "pressure" not to make any corruption allegations.

Debbie was just 31 and the mother of six children when David Norris died. It is unusual for the Criminal Injuries Compensation Board to pay the family of those with active criminal records. But the Yard made representations to secure her a substantial payment in 1994. The CICB won't confirm the amount. Norton says it was £29,000 and that a lawyer had to persuade the board that Debbie and her kids were reliant on the money Norris earned as a police informant. Norton told us the murder squad had a list of those earnings totalling around £75,000. Debbie, he says, got an additional payment of about £25,000 from the Scotland Yard Informants' Fund after the murder.

Had there been in 1991 a truly independent system of investigating

THE GHOST OF DAVID NORRIS

police misconduct, DC Peter Bleksley says he would have unloaded some explosive information about police corruption that was weighing heavily on his mind soon after the murder of his informant.

Since his retirement Blex has been "warned off" ever speaking out about David Norris. We talked briefly over the phone and arranged to meet in his old stomping ground of south-east London. Blex ended the call with words no journalist easily forgets. "I have a story about Norris that will absolutely make your toes curl. It's linked into the demise of him and everything."

Blex says he immediately saw the danger of handling someone like Norris, a sociable, funny, hard-drinking shagger – the qualities that make it easier to break down the defences of the macho world London's detectives move in.

"Norris was driven by a pound note." He had propped up some terrific jobs right up to his death, says Blex. Interestingly though, like Simpson, he did not recall Norris ever providing information about Terry Reeves, Irish paramilitaries running drugs or the six men subsequently arrested in connection with his murder.

Norris was very "well connected" and in the big league as informants go. He had inserted Blex into top echelon drug traffickers like Liverpudlian Delroy Showers, who had contacts with the south-east London Richardson gang.

Blex remembers only too well another job Norris put up in the early summer of 1989 involving £1 million of funny money. Three arrests were made and the case went to trial. But Blex was held in contempt of court when he refused to name the informant who had introduced him to the defendants. They walked. Norris's identity was preserved.[7]

Blex did the honourable thing in court – protecting a source – but he was under no illusion that there came a time, well before Norris's murder, when it was "an open secret" in south-east London that he was a grass. It became increasingly difficult, he says, for the Yard to find ways of protecting Norris's identity in court. "He was so blasé, so stupid about who he propped up [informed on]. It was only a matter of time before someone killed him."

Detective constable Robert Clark, who worked on Simpson's team at East Dulwich, shares the same view. Clark was amazed that Norris lasted so long. "I don't know what made him go from being a good informant to a suicidal one. We thought he had a death wish." Norris would give information about drugs or stolen goods at houses he had just visited. During the briefing before the bust officers would shake their heads at the sheer risk he was taking, says Clark.

Blex has no doubt that Norris was a double agent informant playing both sides from the middle. He had insurance policies to protect him from the police and from the Underworld. For the criminals, he passed them information and used his informant status to grass up their rivals. To protect himself from the Yard he would corrupt or compromise their officers.

"Norris was such a slippery piece of work, I saw so many [detectives] taken in by him. He was someone who would try and get you involved in a divvy up over the jobs he had offered up," says Blex candidly. Norris once called him and two other officers to a meeting at the Prince of Wales pub in Belvedere. He told them a Kent coke dealer had stashed £70,000 in cash in his deep freeze. Norris suggested the cops use a search warrant to nick it. "He knew the drug dealer was hardly likely to have a scream up over the stolen money," recalls Blex. "I told him in no uncertain terms that I wasn't going to be a legalised burglary team for him."

Norris was a charming criminal but a ruthless grass. His modus operandi around detectives was to sweetly suck them into his corrupt world by socialising and getting drunk with them. DC Robert Clark, for example, can recall two occasions when Norris had taken the East Dulwich SERCS squad for a meal and paid in cash. During one of those meals, says Clark, Norris produced a "carrier bag stuffed with ten-pound notes". And when he paid the bill, no pun intended, some of the notes fell on the restaurant floor. The waiter who'd knelt down to help pick them up was told it was his tip.

Blex felt many of his colleagues were relieved by news of Norris's death. Dead men don't tell tales, but if Norris was ever arrested for something serious he would have had no hesitation cashing in his insurance policy and grassing up his corrupt friends in blue to get out of a tight spot.

All of which leads us to Blex's toe-curling story: "After Norris's murder I was at a police piss-up in a pub opposite the East Dulwich Regional Crime Squad. People were drinking and a detective who I knew from old approached me. He was a bit drunk and emotional, but there was genuine anxiety in his voice.

'You know Norris?'

'Yes,' I said. He knew I had been his handler.

'We've got a real big problem going on.'

THE GHOST OF DAVID NORRIS

"The officer proceeded to tell me that not long before Norris was shot he had given East Dulwich some information. There was a lot of cash found during the raid. And ten officers, including the man telling me this story, had had an almighty weed, to the tune of £200,000. They split it ten ways. That's £20,000 each. But one of them then split his share, down the middle, with another detective, his girlfriend, who wasn't in the inner sanctum.

"Now they were all shitting themselves that the people who killed Norris had done so because of the stolen £200,000. It wasn't that this inner sanctum of officers was worried they had Norris's blood on their hands, but that they would get caught if the weak link, the girlfriend, talked.

"She was not in on the theft but I was told she knew the money had been stolen. They feared that if she realised that the money represented the motive for the murder she might shit herself and come forward to the authorities. The geezer said to me the only way the inner sanctum could see was to bump her off. So they were seriously considering murdering the weak link – the girlfriend who'd got £10,000.

"The man who approached me said he did so because he didn't want the blood of a police officer on his hands. I was not being asked to get involved in the murder, to be a co-conspirator. It was a cry for help. I had a big reputation then. He genuinely thought I could stop it happening. I think he was hoping that I would be able to tell him that the reason Norris was killed had nothing to do with the weed. Then he could report that back and the murder would be called off. But I didn't know why Norris had been killed."

Debbie Norris had previously told us that soon after the hit on her husband his criminal associates had suggested there was some corrupt police involvement behind the murder.

"I was now in an invidious position. What do I do? I don't do grassing. It would have been the end of my career. But I've got to do something. So the following day I met up with my old friend Tim Beer. He was senior to me and we had co-handled Norris together [on Team C of the Central Drug Squad]. I regarded Tim highly and sought his advice. He was a very competent person.

"I told him what I'd been told but said I was not willing to come forward. I gave him the names of the three people I knew were involved – the man who approached me and the boyfriend and girlfriend. Tim knew all three detectives. He said, 'Leave it to me.' A few days later he came back to me and said, 'You'll never have any reason to speak to a living person about this. The murder isn't going to happen.' Call me shallow, but that was enough for me. It still leaves me cold.

"Tim, I don't think, went to CIB. I think he went to the murder squad to see what tack they were taking. As a former handler of Norris, Tim was someone who would have been in touch with the murder squad no matter what. He also went to see one of the persons who were plotting to kill the weak link and told him to stop because someone knew about it.

"If an independent system that was competent had existed it would have immensely altered my view about reporting it at the time," says Blex. He didn't go to CIB because they lacked integrity and professionalism. It's one load of bent cops investigating another, he thought.

CIB was also a leaky ship and he wasn't going to be a Serpico for them to use for their own agenda and then discard. It wasn't that he was so loyal he wouldn't work against other cops who had crossed the line. In 1989, for example, Blex went undercover as a hit man to entrap a West Midlands police sergeant who wanted to hire someone to kill his lover's husband. The job was successful and the officer went to prison for six years.[8]

Blex's objection to grassing was understandable given the explosiveness of the allegation. The internal affairs department wears two hats, and one of them is acting as the political police of the commissioner. As such, if in 1993 the top cop wanted to deep-six what Blex had to say, his promising thirteen-year career would have been over at the age of thirty-two.

What about Tim Beer? Had he said anything to the murder squad or senior Yard officers about the £200,000 murder plot? Beer is still serving as a detective inspector. He declined to comment.

Even if the murder squad was unaware of the £200,000 allegation, which is debatable, it is remarkable that detectives investigating Norris's death never spoke to Blex. Having checked Norris's pager on the night he was killed the murder squad would have been aware of the contact. "In any other murder inquiry somebody that spoke to a victim hours before they were killed would be a prime person to speak to, as a suspect or as a witness. But to this day I have never had one word of contact with anybody who investigated this murder."

What does he put that down to? "Maybe they didn't want me to know something. I don't know. It will always mystify me to my dying day. The sooner there is an independent body for investigating police complaints, the better for everyone."

The workings of the murder squad were also a mystery to another experienced officer, detective inspector Keith Pedder. When he visited its offices at Erith police station Pedder saw what he regarded as a very unusual practice. "The murder inquiry was running two action books, a super secret one and a general one. I am absolutely certain they were running two inquiries over the same incident," one on the murder and the other on police corruption, he told us.

An action book is a handwritten contemporaneous diary of the murder inquiry as it develops. It gets its name from the "actions" that the heads of the inquiry believe must be carried out to solve the murder, such as checking alibis and following up new leads. All those involved in the murder inquiry have access to the book so they can check their actions against others to avoid, among other things, duplication.

Pedder, an erudite Flying Squad detective with a sharp wit, had never heard of an inquiry run with two action books before, and it "troubled" him. He had gone to Erith police station to give his friend Chris Jarratt, the deputy head of the murder inquiry, some information he'd just received from an informant that the murder had a Turkish connection, possibly the Arifs. "At Erith there was this other room that we weren't allowed access to. There were two action books, a locked room, locked filing cabinets and secret files," Pedder remembers. "It could be that there was very sensitive material that the officers in charge didn't want the rest of the murder squad to know about so they put it in a secret action book."

What could this sensitive material be? Pedder says he was told it concerned Norris's informant activities. But we now know that it was through his registered informant status that Norris had effectively compromised two police squads who fed off his information in a mixture of legitimate and corrupt ways.

Given the aura of corruption that had emerged in the first few weeks of Norris's death, in all likelihood the secret action book was being used as a log for senior officers back at the Yard. But they decline to answer any questions about it.[9]

In March 1999 Blex retired from the Met suffering from a severe mental illness caused by seven intense years of undercover work in the drug sewers of south-east London and abroad.

He sued the Met for failing in their duty of care after he was forced to move homes when an international organised crime syndicate took a contract out on him after a lengthy undercover operation in 1992. To make matters worse a sensitive report with his real name had been stolen from the back seat of a police officer's car.

The Yard eventually settled the claim with a £10,000 payment. But Blex has had to fight his employers for a top-up medical pension. The Yard finally agreed, but only after a tribunal ruled that his mental illness was an industrial injury.

When he had fully recovered, Blex decided to write a sanitised book called *Gangbuster* about his exploits in the police. Tim Beer had been a good friend to Blex during his service. He thought if he could confide in him about the plot to murder a fellow detective, he could confide in him about his plans for a book. Beer's response took him by surprise. "He threatened me not to write the book. He said, 'You will not write this fucking book.' I said, 'Yes I fucking will. And I think this drink is coming to an end. Don't you?' I wasn't in the job any more and there he was trying to pull rank on me!"

When he completed the manuscript, Blex informed commissioner Sir John Stevens and submitted it to Scotland Yard's Directorate of Public Affairs for vetting some time in January 2001. He heard nothing for several months, then in spring that year a senior officer from the Untouchables asked for a meeting.

Blex's co-author, the former *Sun* journalist Mike Fielder, arrived at Sevenoaks police station where detective superintendent Barry Norman, an elfin corruption-buster with a goatee beard, was waiting. He told Fielder the Yard was not going to injunct the book, but did require all police officers' names to be changed to pseudonyms.

The manuscript CIB had vetted included a chapter on Norris. On the last few pages was a passing but unmistakeable reference to the £200,000 theft and murder plot. Yet to this day Blex has not been asked about it. The assassination may have been ten years old by the time of the Sevenoaks meeting, but the commissioner had publicly committed himself to a "no-hiding-place" corruption probe that would investigate serving and retired officers. It is hard to imagine an allegation more serious than a plot to kill a police officer to prevent her revealing the theft of £200,000 by ten other detectives.

It's also not the case that CIB had no knowledge of the squad alleged to be involved in the theft. Since at least 1998 they had been investigating the East Dulwich SERCS. The investigation, codenamed Operation Russia, was largely reliant on the evidence of two supergrasses, one a former squad detective called Neil Putnam

THE GHOST OF DAVID NORRIS

and the other Eve Fleckney, the registered informant who had replaced Norris as the squad's main earner. Her handler, DC Robert Clark, was already corruptly breaking in Fleckney at the very time Norris was killed. And Operation Russia knew that it was information provided by Norris to Simpson that led to Fleckney's arrest for drugs and her subsequent agreement to become an informant.

By the time CIB received Blex's manuscript, six members of the SERCS squad, including Clark, had been convicted for major drug corruption going back to 1991, the time of the Norris murder. Blex will only confirm that none of those six convicted detectives was the man who originally approached him or the detective couple who split one share of the £200,000. The inner sanctum of ten officers, who may not all be from East Dulwich, is therefore unaccounted for and they could still be serving.

It cannot be argued that CIB did not have officers capable of understanding the significance of this serious allegation. For eight detectives who had served on the Norris murder squad or had intimate knowledge of the informant were by 2000 senior members of the anti-corruption squad.

John Coles, the controller of Norris when he died, became a detective chief superintendent in the Untouchables. He declined to be interviewed.

Chris Jarratt, the deputy head of the Norris murder inquiry, went on to run the highly secretive CIB intelligence cell from 1997 to 2000. Was it a coincidence that he was allowed to recruit many of the Norris murder inquiry team as Untouchables? Jarratt was promoted to detective chief superintendent by the time we asked to interview him. He declined.

An industrious defence solicitor called Phil Kelly handled the appeals by supergrasses Stuart Warne and Renwick Dennison against their life sentences for involvement in the Norris murder. He recalls that Jarratt and an even more senior anti-corruption officer, Bill Griffiths, a founding member of the Ghost Squad, were both very involved.[10] Debbie Norris also told us that in 1997 Jarratt tried unsuccessfully to recruit her as an informant.

Despite all this, the Yard still maintains that the Norris murder was never a matter for CIB. But we now know that cannot be because there was nothing for it to investigate.

In the absence of a fully independent complaints system the sole arbiter of whether to launch such a sensitive investigation will remain the very organisation that stands to lose most from it. The temptation for CIB to ignore or bury such bad news was enormous. Corruption allegations surrounding an informant are inevitably highly sensitive and involve a multitude of senior officers, not just the handlers and controllers. A proper inquiry also has the potential to cross-contaminate other police operations and jeopardise ongoing and future trials.

The Yard's failure to investigate the aura of corruption around Norris's murder back in 1991 had profound consequences for the criminal justice system and the public who fund it to protect them. Through its inaction it appears the Yard allowed a corrupt firm within a firm to grow inside the East Dulwich SERCS for the next seven years. Some of these corrupt officers moved to other squads where they contaminated the work of honest detectives doing a difficult job. During this seven-year period, drugs were recycled, criminals let off, operations sold out and innocent people fitted up.

It is hard to imagine what palatable arguments can be marshalled by the Yard to explain why it wasted such an opportunity to tackle serious corruption. The unpalatable arguments are easier to determine, even in the face of the Yard's orchestral silence about the David Norris murder.

It was a Pandora's box. Any senior Yard officer who dared to look inside it would have seen Norris's ghost clasping an insurance policy listing all his corrupt dealings.

At the time of his murder, the Yard was desperately trying to rehabilitate its image as an efficient, effective and clean force capable of executing the Major government's controversial, draconian law and order policies. They couldn't afford to exorcise Norris's ghost in this climate.

But there was another compelling incentive to close the lid on David Norris. In 1993 his murder was linked to another brutal killing in south-east London that was rocking Scotland Yard to the core – the fatal stabbing of Stephen Lawrence by south-east London thugs from families connected to organised drug crime within the corrupt area of operations of various police squads, including the South East Regional Crime Squad.

9

"WHAT? WHAT? NIGGER!"

A bus stop in south-east London, an outburst of racist bile, which as it crossed the lips of an all-white gang of five young thugs became a sentence of death for a black teenager and for the integrity of Scotland Yard.

Two vicious stabbing movements accomplished the murder, each calculated to shed so much blood that the victim would know by his own drenching that death was on the way.

This is a snapshot of what happened at 10.40 p.m. on Thursday, 22 April 1993, at the request stop in Well Hall Road, Eltham; a cut-down version of events which engulfed a young man of 18 summers who, after an evening out with his friends in south-east London, was trying to return to home to his mother Doreen, his father Neville, his brother Stewart and his sister Georgina.

Despite his awesome wounds and because he was so fit, Stephen Lawrence managed to run 300 yards from the thugs who had stabbed him. With each yard covered and each footfall made he was pumping blood from two severed arteries. And then he fell. Unconscious.

Though traumatised, the other victim of the attack, Stephen's friend, Duwayne Brooks, had found a phone box. At 10.46 p.m. he dialled 999 pleading for an ambulance. In the meantime a police car arrived. The officers checked Stephen for a pulse. But they failed to examine him thoroughly or to give first-aid. The kit was never even taken from the patrol car. Instead, they questioned Duwayne as if he was a suspect rather than a victim, as if the two black boys had done something wrong.

UNTOUCHABLES

In 1977, when Stephen Lawrence was 3, there were just 199 black police officers in all of England and Wales.[1] When he died, 15 years later, the figure had scarcely improved. None of the detectives who investigated the murder was black. Stephen's parents, who came from Jamaica, still wonder whether the boys' colour shaped the police's attitude and contributed to the failure to give first aid. "None of the police officers attending the scene made any attempt to see if there was anything they could do. They just stood there while my son bled to death. None of them checked to see how serious his injuries were, they just stood there waiting for the ambulance. Maybe there was something they could have done to save him. But the fact was they never tried. That says it all. There are two questions I would like the police to answer. Are all officers trained in basic first aid? Or was it because they just did not want to get their hands dirty with a black man's blood?"[2]

Fourteen-year-old Catherine Avery was in the house just across the pavement where Stephen lay bleeding. She had no more first-aid instruction than the officers on the scene. Yet her basic Red Cross training made her realise they should have attempted to stem the flow of blood.

At 10.54 p.m. the ambulance arrived and a paramedic tried to restart Stephen's heart without success. By the time he was in the recovery room Stephen had lost too much blood and his veins had collapsed. At 11.17 p.m. the death certificate was signed.

It is strongly suspected by the police and the Lawrence family that the five murderers are: David Norris, aged 16 at the time, brothers Jamie and Neil Acourt, then aged 16 and 17 respectively, Luke Knight, 16, and Gary Dobson, 17.

Four of them lived on or very near the Brooke Estate. The five boys led a gang with a history of involvement in stabbings and racism in the area. Neil Acourt, for example, had been expelled from school for a racist attack in 1991. And five weeks before Stephen's murder, Gurdeep Bangal was stabbed in the stomach while serving in his dad's Wimpy Bar in Eltham High Street.

Nine months earlier, on the other side of the roundabout from the spot where Stephen was killed, Rohit Duggal, a young Asian boy, was stabbed to death outside the local kebab shop. Peter Thompson is currently serving life for this murder and he too was linked to the gang through information given to the Lawrence murder inquiry.

Sometimes ecumenical in their violence, the gang also attacked

"WHAT? WHAT? NIGGER!"

white kids. Lee Pearson, for example, was stabbed outside the local kebab shop in 1991. Eleven months before Stephen's murder, Jamie Acourt, David Norris and Luke Knight were suspected of stabbing the Witham brothers with a butterfly knife. David was charged with wounding and Jamie with possession of an offensive weapon. But the CPS withdrew the charges a few months before Stephen Lawrence was stabbed to death, claiming it would not be in the public interest to proceed.

The gang referred to themselves as the Eltham Krays, a sad homage to the dysfunctional, homosexual gauleiters of an earlier age and another part of London.

The apprentice boys from Eltham appeared to have developed contacts with another bunch of local hoodlums called the NTO, short for the Nutty or Nazi Turn Out, a group of boneheads involved in a range of racist incidents including killings in south-east London and Kent.

By April 1993, local people were giving the Eltham five another name for their gang – the Untouchables – as in someone was protecting them; as in they were thought to be able to get away with things and have some form of insurance from the local police. One way or another these five boys were completely out of control – a gang of *droogs* practising ever more perverted forms of *ultra-violence*.

Nick Jeffrey, an American-born teacher and community activist, knows the youth scene from 40 years of living in south-east London. Eleven years on he still recalls with horror the semi-literate announcement he saw soon after Stephen Lawrence's murder. Cycling along the south circular he passed the "Welcome to Greenwich – Millennium Borough" sign and up the hill towards the churchyard was a daubing that read: "Watch out coons, you are now entering Eltham".

"In Eltham centre, midday or midnight, you saw no black faces on the street. The Well Hall Road McDonald's opposite the churchyard has been a known hang-out for racist youth, as was the Wimpy Bar before it," says Nick.

His knowledge of the community comes from years of teaching at local schools and from scouting for Arsenal and Preston North End. Nick is a familiar face at the Millwall, Crystal Palace and Charlton Athletic grounds. He also trained local teams and met many of the youngsters who form the gangs. Eltham, he concludes, is the front line behind which Kent, white Kent, is in aggressive retreat.

"Following the 1981 Brixton riots more inner-city clubs were formed and boys in them had to travel out for competition and for pitches. The team I managed was called Tulse Hill but it was a Brixton and Peckham Club. When we travelled to Greenwich racial abuse was common – on and off the Sunday league pitches. The Acourts' club, Samuel Montague, began to attract racists. They expelled Neil in 1991 for a post-match knife threat allegedly against a black boy from Red Lion, a Peckham and Deptford club. His brother Jamie, David Norris and Luke Knight left as well.

"South from the Millennium Dome and along the edges of inner London are vast low-rise, mostly all-white council estates. Yards from the bus stop where Stephen was stabbed a mixed-race family had their home petrol-bombed. Along these routes are a string of mixed-sex comprehensive schools, including the first two purpose-built in this country for the post-war influx of tenants from slum clearance. The GCSE results published for that string of schools in Greenwich are among the lowest in the country for boys. Truancy rates are high. Bullying and gang violence have been major issues.

"Five of England's largest pubs from Downham to Thamesmead have been habitual meeting places of the British National Party and the National Front, each one closed for violence. The Yorkshire Grey at Eltham Green, once host to neo-Nazi organisations Blood and Honour and Combat 18, is now . . . [a] McDonald's. The NF logo, however, remains the graffiti of choice – it has more punch and is easier to scratch into a school textbook. In 1990, NF was painted in letters three feet high at the Orchards Youth Club next to the Kidbrooke Estate. Neil Acourt was excluded from the club for that along with David Norris."

Detectives call the first 60 minutes after any murder the "golden hour". It is the period when all forensic and other clues are fresh and the chance of solving the crime is at its highest. From then on the trail starts to go cold, like the victim.

The fall of Scotland Yard began at 11.17 p.m. on the Thursday night Stephen Lawrence died. In the following 96 hours the best chance of successfully prosecuting the murderers was frittered away.

In those four days the mind-boggling inaction of a handful of senior officers would ultimately cost the Yard what reputation it had left. For the black British population it merely re-confirmed what they already knew. But it was the loss of confidence among white middle Englanders and *Daily Mail* readers that rocked the police, and not just Scotland Yard. Chief constables across the country dreaded the

"WHAT? WHAT? NIGGER!"

Lawrence scandal would have ramifications for British policing in the same way the Scarman report had after the Brixton riots 12 years earlier. They were right.

The mistakes of such senior Yard detectives made the Lawrence family and their supporters question almost immediately whether this was not just another example of wilful racism but something just as sinister – police corruption.

Suspicions were raised when it emerged no officer at the scene had recorded how Duwayne Brooks had heard the attackers say, "What? What? Nigger!" As more officers arrived, the professional quality of the policing continued to decline. In all, fifty-five police officers came to the Well Hall roundabout between 10.50 p.m. and 3 a.m. The turnout included forty-four constables, five sergeants, one inspector, one detective inspector, one chief inspector, one detective superintendent and even, uniquely, two chief superintendents.

Despite this parade of top brass, there was a complete lack of co-ordination, with arriving senior officers barking contradictory orders at subordinates. Consequently, there was no search of the circular area around the murder scene, no house-to-house search of the Brooke Estate and no questioning in a methodical manner of the neighbours.

With good intelligence, the input of local officers who knew the area and proper direction and control, it was a realistic goal not only to identify and interview witnesses but to pinpoint suspects and try to catch the perpetrators red-handed before they could dispose of the evidence, like blood-stained clothing and the weapon, which to this day hasn't been found. But the golden hour and the golden opportunities that went with it were squandered.

In the weekend immediately after the murder things went from tragedy to farce. Within forty-eight hours a skinhead walked into Eltham police station with remarkable information. He named the gang of five. But no one properly registered the young man as an informant and there was no swift follow-through on his vital leads. He later stated he had given his real name but officers denied this.

There were other sources that came forward to confirm what the skinhead had told the police. Maureen Smith, for example, indicated that she had high-grade information, but there was a six-day delay in interviewing her. Swifter action would have led immediately to two key witnesses, her son and his girlfriend, who could place the Acourt brothers at the murder scene. No proper attempt was subsequently made to identify and trace these two witnesses.

An anonymous letter naming the same suspects was found by a

member of the public in a phone box near the murder scene and handed to the police. Nobody bothered to immediately follow up the information. This serious mistake was compounded the following day, when on Saturday morning the police received a call from an unidentified person saying an anonymous letter with important information would be left in a waste bin near a local pub. Two police officers went in separate cars, one to search the bin, the other to observe. The officer searching the bin found nothing. But while he was out of his car his colleague across the road saw a young man sticking a note on the back window of his car. Nothing was done to approach or follow the man. Once again the letter contained vital leads and named the same gang of five.

The landmark public inquiry into these matters five years later put it succinctly: "The truth is that although people were reluctant to give their names there was no 'wall of silence'. In fact information purporting to implicate the suspects was readily and repeatedly made available."

It poured into the murder inquiry almost as quickly as the lifeblood poured out of Stephen Lawrence's body.

The two senior officers responsible for the catalogue of errors in those first four days in April 1993 were also the detectives in charge of the highly sensitive David Norris murder inquiry since April 1991. The careers of detective superintendent Ian Crampton and his immediate superior, detective chief superintendent Bill Ilsley, had been dominated during the intervening two years by the contract killing of the Yard's top informant and preparing for the murder trial of the four Irish Protestant suspects.

Crampton, a wiry south Londoner in his mid-forties, was the senior investigating officer for both the Norris and Lawrence murders. The SIO makes the vital decisions on the ground at the relevant time and is the highest-ranking detective with day-to-day involvement in running the murder inquiry. However he deferred to Ilsley, a lean, tall detective of a similar age, for all the major strategic decisions. Ilsley, as the crime manager for south-east London, in turn reported to and took his orders from the Yard.

Six days before the killing of Stephen Lawrence, the Norris murder trial started at the Old Bailey. It was therefore uppermost in the minds of both senior officers. Crampton was preparing his evidence to withstand cross-examination by four formidable defence barristers; among them was Michael Mansfield QC, who ironically would soon be representing the Lawrence family.

"WHAT? WHAT? NIGGER!"

The Norris murder trial was going to be the biggest test of Crampton's detective acumen in the witness box, given the enormous sensitivities he would have to circumnavigate around police informant confidentiality, the use of supergrasses and the link between British intelligence and loyalist paramilitaries in the dirty war in Northern Ireland.

There was also a lot the Yard felt the defence didn't need to know. This, of course, concerned the swirl of corruption allegations around Norris and south-east London policing that emerged during Crampton's murder inquiry, and which it appears were kept in a secret and undisclosed action book.

Ilsley had been promoted to chief superintendent one month after the assassination of Norris. Since May 1991 he had been responsible for all criminal inquiries in 3 Area, an enormous patch of south-east London from Tower Bridge to the Kent borders. His officers liaised closely with the specialist detectives targeting organised crime in the region, namely the East Dulwich South East Regional Crime Squad and the Tower Bridge office of the Flying Squad. In fact detectives on these two elite squads often came from the very areas they were targeting and when their tour of duty was over they would return to normal detective duties under the command of Ilsley at one of the twenty-five or so police stations he managed.

Crampton was on night duty when Stephen Lawrence was stabbed to death. He attended the scene of the crime and early next morning spoke to Ilsley. They agreed Crampton would run the inquiry only until Monday. From then on he would be occupied with the Norris murder trial.

The two senior detectives say they made a "strategic decision" based on all the available information not to arrest the gang of five named suspects over the weekend. It was a fundamental mistake that led to withering criticism of their professional integrity and truthfulness during the Stephen Lawrence public inquiry in 1998.

Crampton never recorded in any policy file the decision not to make early arrests. Best practice required him to preserve a contemporaneous and accurate log of why certain lines of inquiry were preferred over others. The Lawrence inquiry report twice referred to the "alleged" strategic decision in terms that strongly implied Crampton and Ilsley had made this up.[3] Such improper record keeping had echoes of the highly irregular secret action book during the Norris murder inquiry.

Ever since Stephen's death the Yard has done its best to try and keep the two murders separate. Those who suggested a connection were simply dismissed as conspiracy theorists.

Young David Norris, the prime suspect in the Lawrence murder, had a notoriously violent criminal father called Clifford, who by the mid-eighties had become a successful player in the south-east London drug business. The local police and specialist detectives in 3 Area all knew of Clifford Norris. Police informant extraordinaire, David Norris, also knew Clifford and his circle.

Clifford Norris was born in Greenwich in 1958. He was the second son in the family. His brother, Alex, was eight years older. Both boys were teenage hoodlums who graduated to violent crime and then drug trafficking. In 1976, barely a man himself, Clifford and his then girlfriend Theresa had a baby boy. They named him David.

Clifford's propensity for violence seemed untempered by parental responsibility and in 1983, aged 25, as he was driving along the Old Kent Road, a van cut him up. Clifford gave chase, forced the van to a halt and smashed the window with a hammer. Realising the police were on their way, he stopped and threw away his wallet which, when recovered, had inside it a key to a safety deposit box. When this was opened it contained £17,000 in cash. Clifford denied all knowledge of the money and was fined just £150 for criminal damage.[4]

On another occasion he savagely attacked a woman shopkeeper who he believed was responsible for spreading gossip about the state of his marriage. Clifford shot her in the throat. She recovered because the bullet missed her spinal cord but wouldn't give evidence against him. It was this shooting in 1989 that led an informant to contact Bill Ilsley and name Clifford as the culprit. But without the victim's evidence the case died.

The Norris brothers had a number of criminal associates in southeast London who like them were the targets of the local detectives and also the East Dulwich SERCS and the Tower Bridge Flying Squad.

Alex Norris married into the French family. His new brother-in-law, Gary French, had a close escape in 1989 when he drove to a meeting with David Norris, the informant. Gary apparently spotted he was under surveillance and sped off. Details are scarce about what happened next. When the police confronted David Norris he denied knowing Gary, but told the officers he was the cousin of Clifford Norris.

At the time of Gary French's close escape, David Norris was "working" for the Central Drug Squad and East Dulwich. He was also

"WHAT? WHAT? NIGGER!"

nurturing corrupt relationships with several detectives. Clifford too had developed his own contacts in the police and there was one detective in particular with whom he was seen in highly suspicious circumstances.

In the late eighties Clifford and Alex Norris were under surveillance by a team of Customs investigators rightly convinced they were preparing a significant cannabis importation from Holland with several others. The Norris brothers had been tailed over eight months visiting a Dutchman in Switzerland and a detective from the Tower Bridge Flying Squad. Undercover Customs officers observed Clifford and Alex Norris on three occasions meeting detective sergeant Dave Coles, who was seen carrying a plastic bag with oblong slabs inside. One meeting which Customs videoed was on 20 June 1988 in the Tiger's Head pub in Chislehurst, around the corner from the mock-Tudor house Clifford had bought for his family. Coles was seen talking to Clifford, making notes and using a calculator.

To Customs it must have looked as if the two men were in business together. The next day their officers made a series of arrests as the gang unloaded a large parcel of cannabis from a lorry parked in an east London side road. Alex and Clifford were not there or at their homes when Customs arrived. They spent over a year on the run together until Alex was caught in July 1989 and received nine years. Incredibly, Clifford remained at large for another five years, unbothered, it seems, by the local police.

Customs immediately reported Coles' meetings with Clifford to the Yard. CIB began an investigation. Coles denied he was in any way corrupt and claimed he was trying to cultivate Clifford Norris as an informant, although he had no authorisation to do so. The CIB inquiry was totally unsatisfactory – a model of mixed messages and unanswered questions that left the strong impression that the whole highly suspect liaison between Coles and Clifford Norris had been swept under the carpet by the Yard.

Coles never faced disciplinary charges for those unauthorised meetings. A more senior officer just gave him a mild verbal rebuke, known in police terminology as "words of advice". Instead, Coles was formally disciplined in May 1989 for falsifying his duty state on a number of occasions when he claimed to be at court, but was in fact having sex with a girlfriend. This period of dishonesty coincided with his suspicious meetings with the Norris brothers.

In mitigation to his guilty plea, Coles produced a character reference from his old boss at Bexleyheath police station. Step forward detective superintendent Ian Crampton. Coles, he wrote, was to be commended for his work and indeed his honesty. The reference showed extraordinarily bad judgement on Crampton's part, as there was ample documentary evidence of Coles' dishonesty. If a detective can lie on his duty state then what is he likely to do when gathering evidence against a member of the public? Coles was required to resign.

The discipline farce continued when he appealed and was reinstated the following year by an assistant commissioner, although at the reduced rank of detective constable. Nevertheless, he was still allowed to operate as a frontline detective in the very area his highly suspicious activities had taken place with Clifford Norris, who was still on the run.

Since the Lawrence scandal exploded, Crampton and Ilsley have made emphatic claims about what they knew and didn't know in the immediate aftermath of Stephen's murder. Crampton insists that over those four days he was in charge he never connected the prime suspect as the son of Clifford Norris. Similarly, he says he never made any connection between David Norris, the informant, and Clifford Norris, the suspect's father. For his part, Ilsley says he never connected the two David Norrises during these early stages.

The Lawrence family and their lawyers have never accepted these claims. Some members of the public inquiry team also privately felt very uncomfortable about these and other aspects of the two senior detectives' evidence.

Clifford Norris remained at large throughout the period his son became a prime suspect for the murder of Stephen Lawrence. Ilsley should have taken him out of circulation. The chief superintendent accepts he was aware two days after the murder that Clifford was David Norris's father and was wanted by Customs. But his collar was never felt.

The Coles affair only emerged much later during the public inquiry. The Lawrence family felt it further justified their suspicions that Clifford Norris had some sort of illicit protection from the cops. The Lawrence family suspected that Clifford Norris had exercised corrupt pressure on Coles, who the family and its legal team speculated may have approached senior officers to delay the arrests of young David Norris. No proof was ever produced to support this alleged chain of events.[5] In fact, it seemed Clifford Norris was looking elsewhere, and had corruptly approached, through intermediaries, civilian witnesses who could damage his son.

"WHAT? WHAT? NIGGER!"

Young David had stabbed another youth called Stacey Benefield four weeks before Stephen was killed. Initially Benefield declined to name his attacker to the police. But on the weekend after Stephen's death he made a statement naming David as the one who stabbed him with Neil Acourt. This, combined with the intelligence from the skinhead informant and other witnesses who'd come forward, was clearly enough to arrest David and his gang for the Lawrence murder. Crampton and Ilsley thought otherwise but never recorded their momentous decision.

Young David was eventually arrested after Benefield picked him out in a line-up in May 1993. Weeks later, he was approached in the street by an intermediary and taken to meet a man who gave him £2,000 in cash to change his account of events. The man intimated he could take care of the local police, and they parted company. Benefield was left with the strong impression he had been talking to the fugitive Clifford Norris. He spent the money but also reported the approach to the police.

Nevertheless, young David was acquitted later that year in highly suspicious circumstances. According to Michael Mansfield QC, the Lawrence family barrister: ". . . the foreman of the jury had approached David Norris prior to the verdict, to reassure him of the result and then to subsequently offer [him] employment. The juror himself was on bail for serious fraud at the time of the trial and he was later convicted of this fraud. He has also admitted a substantial connection with the London criminal underworld."[6]

No one dispassionately looking at the Lawrence case can blame the family for believing the worst of Scotland Yard. In the run-up to the Lawrence murder and the crucial months that followed it was covering up three highly relevant corruption allegations in three specialist police squads operating in south-east London.

The first was the Dave Coles–Clifford Norris affair at Tower Bridge Flying Squad, followed by the relationship between David Norris and the East Dulwich SERCS. The third scandal once again involved south-east London drug dealers connected to Brinks Mat gangster Kenny Noye, who included among his circle of associates people like Clifford Norris.

On 25 May 1993, the day after the collapse of the David Norris murder trial, a man in Bournemouth made an unconnected complaint against four detectives from the Surbiton office of SERCS. Two of the officers named in the complaint, detective sergeant Alec Leighton and detective constable John Donald, had been intimately involved in the

UNTOUCHABLES

Norris case. Leighton was in charge of the operation that arrested Warne and Dennison in Margate and Donald was the officer who interviewed them when they turned supergrasses and admitted their involvement with others in the murder.

The next month CIB mounted a sting operation, codenamed Zorba, against Donald, Leighton and the two other detectives. Word however leaked to the targets and the anti-corruption squad had to pull back without any success.

Then, in September, five months after Stephen Lawrence's death, the Yard was shown compelling evidence by BBC's *Panorama* that Donald was in a corrupt relationship with a south-east London drug dealer called Kevin Cressey, whom he had registered a year earlier as an informant after arresting him with 55 kilos of cannabis.

Cressey decided to deal his way out of trouble by supplying information, including on the Norris murder.[7] But under the cover of the informant-handler relationship he also corruptly paid Donald for bail and for information to be passed to Kenny Noye, who although in prison at the time was believed to be behind a large cocaine shipment. To obtain further insurance, Cressey then went to *Panorama* and agreed to set up Donald.

CIB immediately suspended Leighton and Donald while mounting another operation codenamed Gallery into the Surbiton SERCS office and the new National Criminal Intelligence Service.

Through the BBC documentary the Lawrence family found out about corruption in Surbiton. But they knew nothing of the problems at East Dulwich, or for that matter at the Tower Bridge Flying Squad. Scotland Yard needed to keep the collapsed Norris case and the Lawrence murder inquiry separate in the family's mind. To do that they had to neutralise the growing view that corruption and collusion had taken place.

Paul Condon was only two months in the commissioner's chair when he started to cop the fall-out from the defective Lawrence and Norris murder investigations.

His maiden speech in February 1993 was a touchy-feely affair about ethics and racism in the police and society at large. At a Yard-organised conference on "Fairness, Community & Justice" seven weeks before Stephen's murder, commissioner Condon talked about the need for his officers to be "totally intolerant" of race hate crimes and those who peddled racial hatred for political ends.[8]

Perhaps he felt qualified to make this plea having spent four years,

"WHAT? WHAT? NIGGER!"

between 1978 and 1982, at the Community Relations Branch of Scotland Yard. Then in 1987, after returning from a stint at Kent Constabulary, he served two years in a senior rank at Notting Hill Gate police station in west London. His responsibilities involved the August Bank Holiday Carnival organised by the well-established Caribbean community. They had suffered terribly since the fifties from police brutality and corruption. Had things improved under Condon's watch? A now very senior CPS lawyer who prosecuted cases from Notting Hill Gate police station at the time told us racism and corruption were still rife, paperwork in bad order and leadership poor.

The Carnival had until recently a cynical place in the Yard's attempt to put a positive gloss on its bad relations with the local black community. Newspapers would oblige police spin doctors every year with the same condescending image, often on the front page, of a white officer with an embarrassed smile attempting to dance calypso with a matronly black woman.

Commissioner Condon told his maiden audience that racial issues presented the greatest challenge to the force. There would, he promised, be no compromise on demanding exemplary conduct from his officers. It was a standard, however, that the top cop and his circle of senior officers apparently felt did not apply to them. For within a few months of making that speech the commissioner authorised an internal investigation of the murder inquiry into Stephen Lawrence's death, which was later exposed as a most cynical whitewash.

The events leading to this cover-up began when the Lawrence family met Nelson Mandela during a state visit to London on 6 May, two weeks after the murder. The South African president lent his moral and political weight by likening their fight for justice to those black parents who had lost children during the struggle against apartheid. After Mandela spoke to the media, Doreen had her turn. She lambasted the police for their "patronising" treatment and the Major government for showing "no interest".

The moral authority of Nelson Mandela eventually propelled the Yard into action. Senior officers like Ilsley admit that "external pressures" forced him to take a greater interest in the case after Crampton had left to attend the Norris murder trial. But he and the Yard still deny that the hurried decision to arrest the five prime suspects the day after Mandela's visit was anything but "pure coincidence".[9]

In late July recriminations flowed when the CPS decided not to prosecute. The case was largely dependent on the identification evidence of Duwayne Brooks. However, even this became tainted following a disputed conversation with a detective who was escorting Brooks to the line-up. The detective alleged Brooks had admitted being coached by friends ahead of the identification parade about the Acourt brothers' physical appearance. Duwayne said the detective was lying.

The CPS had also relied on legal advice that although the five suspects were more than likely the culprits, there was no realistic chance of a successful prosecution on the available evidence. This of course was clearly down to the bungled police investigation.

By mid-summer, increasing dissatisfaction with the Yard's response to the killing of Stephen Lawrence had become a key community issue, with demonstrations being prepared. This annoyed Ilsley's immediate boss, deputy assistant commissioner David Osland, who wrote to Condon complaining that the patience of his detectives on 3 Area was "wearing thin" with the Lawrence family and "self-appointed public and media commentators".[10] Some of these busybodies included elected local MPs like the Tory left-winger, Peter Bottomley, and Labour backbencher Paul Boateng, who both sought reassurances from the commissioner. However, even Osland eventually realised the murder inquiry was getting nowhere, and began thinking up "a way to placate the influential people in the local community".[11]

Six officers were approached to give him the tools to make good this placation. But every one of them declined the poisoned chalice, until detective chief superintendent John Barker stepped forward. Although the last to be approached, Barker agreed to conduct a confidential internal review of the murder inquiry.

Osland commissioned the now infamous Barker Review with Condon's prior approval. The commissioner had told the Lawrence family he was keeping a close personal eye on the situation. The review began in September 1993 and took Barker ten weeks to complete. The commissioner saw it in November and signed it off. It was as short in length as it was self-serving and convenient in its conclusions. Barker concluded that the Lawrence murder inquiry had "progressed satisfactorily" with "all lines of inquiry being correctly pursued".

The cover-up mentality was so deeply ingrained in the Yard that Barker even considered creating two different versions of the report. One would be for internal consumption. The other, a phoney, much more anodyne alternative, would exist for disclosure to the Lawrence family and their legal advisers should they ever sue. But in the end Barker and Osland didn't proceed with this misleading strategy, creating instead only one flawed and unprofessional document that gave the murder investigation an entirely unwarranted clean bill of health.

Crampton, Ilsley, Osland and other senior officers had all seen the final draft of the Barker Review and failed to point out its wholesale untruthfulness. Of course they claimed that was because the murder inquiry, in their view, was not incompetent. This self-delusion would in all likelihood have persisted today had the Lawrence family not complained and triggered a PCA-supervised investigation in 1997.

The Kent detectives who examined the Barker Review on behalf of the PCA felt it was "misleading"; gave reassurance, which was "undeserving and highly damaging"; and did "nothing to re-focus the Stephen Lawrence murder investigation". Indeed, the PCA/Kent report specified 28 shortcomings in the initial investigation that had been missed or suppressed by the Barker Review.

The family's barrister, Michael Mansfield QC, would later submit to the Stephen Lawrence inquiry that the Barker Review demonstrated "the capacity and propensity of senior officers to collude with each other to manipulate and engineer a desired result". The inquiry report put it another way: "The Review provided a convenient shelter to those involved. The failure of all senior officers to detect the flaws in [it] is to be deplored."[12]

The Barker Review was a multi-layered cover-up, not just a whitewash of police incompetence during what had become a *cause célèbre* black murder. The Home Office under Michael Howard was hardly concerned about the effect of the case on Britain's race relations – which is why he consistently ignored calls for a public inquiry. The real concern was how the Lawrence case threatened to undermine the confidence of middle Englanders in the Major government's political project of a rehabilitated Scotland Yard efficaciously fighting the war on crime.

The Barker Review was the dishonest document the government and the Yard could point to over the next four years, like a fake environmental health certificate on the greasy wall of a back street kebab shop. It was also commissioner Condon's official imprimatur that corruption was not a problem, when his inner circle was telling him this was definitely not the case.

In other words the setting up of the Ghost Squad in late 1993 began with a deceit that would mark the commissioner's period of office for the next seven years.

UNTOUCHABLES

The Lawrence scandal was undoubtedly one of the chief reasons the anti-corruption initiative was launched covertly. For the next four years the secret strategy was one of containment. The Yard's corruption problem was not publicly admitted until 1997 by which time a small cabal of senior officers and spin doctors had worked out how bad it was and how the damage could be limited and the fall-out managed.

So it was that in the spring of 1994, commissioner Condon met the Lawrence family and their legal team at Scotland Yard to discuss the Barker Review. He looked Neville and Doreen Lawrence in the eyes and assured them with all the solemnity he could muster for the occasion that his officers had done everything they could. The Barker Review said so.

A few weeks later, Paul Condon was made a knight of the realm.

10

A RAGAMUFFIN BUNCH

On New Year's Day 1987, John Monerville went to Stoke Newington police station to report his 19-year-old son Trevor missing. The family had last seen him in the early hours of the morning. The streets of Hackney, a depressed north-east London borough, can be an unforgiving place, even to the most fly.

The police claimed no knowledge of Trevor's whereabouts and quite reasonably informed the worried father they could not register him as a missing person until 24 hours had elapsed. The next day, Friday, Mr Monerville returned to the police station with a photograph. Trevor was registered as missing and the police repeated that they still had no trace of him. They said the same on Saturday.

On Sunday, the family rang around the capital's prisons. Finally they located Trevor in Brixton Prison on the other side of London. A prison official said ominously he was in the hospital wing and asked Mr Monerville if Trevor was epileptic or took any regular medication. No, said his anxious father.

Soon after, Mr Monerville went to Stoke Newington police station. He sought details of how Trevor had ended up in prison. After all, there must have been an arrest. A police station must have charged him with some offence, then held him in police cells until the court remanded his son into prison custody. He felt the officer becoming abusive, almost ordering him out of the police station. He was told he'd get all the answers he needed at Highbury Magistrates Court when it opened Monday morning.

The next day, Mr Monerville visited his son in Brixton prison. He was shocked to see his bruised body. Three days later, Trevor underwent emergency surgery to remove a blood clot on his brain. Meanwhile, the police quietly dropped the minor charge of criminal damage – Stoke Newington officers had arrested Trevor at 10.40 p.m. on New Year's Day after finding him asleep in a car they believed he had broken into.

As the family made further inquiries and complained to the new PCA, several facts emerged with echoes of Pinochet's Chile: Trevor *was* in the cells at Stoke Newington police station when his father made inquiries on the Friday and Saturday. A group of officers had forcibly fingerprinted him. And before Trevor was taken to the Magistrates Court on Saturday, he had been examined four times by a police surgeon and twice taken to a nearby hospital.

Annette Monerville noticed a change in her son when he was discharged from hospital after the brain surgery. Trevor had contracted epilepsy and went through bouts of aggression and depression. The family set up a campaign to establish the truth behind his "disappearance".

Stoke Newington police did apologise for misleading Mr and Mrs Monerville, blaming it on an administrative error. But Trevor's parents and friends believe something far more sinister occurred inside the notorious police station.

That notoriety has been a persistent feature of local community relations with the police since the first immigrants arrived in the fifties. The borough is a vibrant mix of cultures from the Caribbean, Ireland and Cyprus, and more recently from West Africa. Hassidic Jews and Muslims, Kurds and Turks live side by side, although not always in harmony. The local police are almost entirely all white officers often from outside London, whose past experience of multiculturalism is limited to their local takeaway. Detective constable Paul Goscomb, for instance, joined the Met in the eighties after Gloucestershire Police rejected him. The West Country boy, then just 22, was sent to Stoke Newington on his first posting. He had no idea where it was and viewed the area as "Vietnam". Policing had very much its "own style", he suggested. These comments reflect the siege mentality that dominated the local force. Detective constable Declan Costello transferred to Stoke Newington in January 1988. "[The community] hated us and we hated them," he explained. "It wasn't a black thing. It wasn't as complex as that. If you went out in uniform or plain clothes you could feel the hatred." Costello and his colleagues believed if they were caught on their own they'd get a good hiding. This

A RAGAMUFFIN BUNCH

justified dishing one out. He recalled how people would run when they saw the Stoke Newington cops coming.

Racism, incivility, excessive force, poor training and corruption have all shaped community relations. But it is deaths in police custody or care that are a major cause for real concern and a flashpoint of civil resistance. Cases like Aseta Simms in 1971 and Colin Roach in 1983 were highly influential. Invariably, in these and other cases the police establishment circled its wagons and blamed black activists and red politicians for exploiting the inner city blues. Alternatively, Yard press officers would privately brief mainstream journalists that the victims of such police crimes were drug addicts, alcoholics or mentally ill.

The Trevor Monerville case was a key turning point for British policing. A storm was raging in the hearts and minds of a ragamuffin bunch of Hackney residents. And the "disappearance" of one of their sons became the catalyst to form a community defence organisation that drew a line in the pool of blood.

From 1988 until 1995, the Hackney Community Defence Association's approach to forensically investigating over 130 cases of police brutality led them to uncover a web of organised corruption in the local drug squad, and to overturn 13 miscarriages of justice. Their efforts exposed a force out of control, racist and in denial.

The founding members of HCDA shared a common experience beyond their political commitment to confronting racism and tackling the causes of other social injustices. Nearly all had a scarring experience of police brutality.

Graham Smith was the driving force behind HCDA. His personal journey is a tragic one that shaped the association it became. When Smith discovered the girlfriend he lived with in Manchester had been gang-raped, his life started to fall apart. He felt emotionally shut out, as she struggled with the additional trauma of an approaching trial. Smith's job as a supervisor in an outside leisure centre was no distraction. He blotted out his profound vulnerability with some heavy drinking. Then one evening in 1983 the police assaulted him. With time, he has managed to reflect on the incident with dark humour. "I got queer bashed by proxy," he now says.

Smith was out with a black gay friend who was still in drag from the night before. "It was only six or seven at night and we were drunk. Two officers in a van stopped and arrested us. We were charged with being drunk and disorderly. We were separated and I was taken to a room. One officer was walking up and down on my back. Another was punching me in the back of the head saying, 'You're a queer bastard!' I was thrown against the wall and passed out. The next thing I remember was coming to in hospital and seeing the officer. I screamed: 'You beat me up!' I wanted to get out of there. But the nurse insisted the officer left." The police, he says, blamed his injuries on a fall. "At that time it wasn't common for people to complain or seek redress for being assaulted. It happened before the PCA was set up." Smith pleaded guilty and the court fined him £25. "I didn't pay on principle," he recalls with indignation. Then with a smile he adds, "I bought a gold chain instead."

The following year, Smith moved to north London. With support from the Greater London Council and local trade unions he set up a community outreach programme, which ran for almost three years. By 1987, now sporting an alarming mullet haircut, he relocated to Stoke Newington. There he learned about Trevor Monerville's disappearance and joined the family's campaign for justice.

In June 1987, while Trevor was recovering from brain surgery, another young man, Tunay Hassan, died after being detained by Stoke Newington officers. Five months later, Gary Stretch, a young white window cleaner, was severely assaulted by seven off-duty cops inside a pub.[1]

These incidents galvanised Smith and others into action. Among them was a campaigning journalist and political activist called Martin Walker. He was a fellow Mancunian who'd recently published two books exposing the violent police tactics used during the Miners' Strike and against protesting students from Manchester University.

They wanted HCDA to concentrate on legal investigations of police malpractice while offering support to the victims. "Because of the isolationism of those victims, you didn't disbelieve people – this was one of the rules. You believed until your own investigation showed reason not to," says Smith. There was a "cold professionalism" about the way HCDA came together, he adds. "Although we had personal experience of police brutality we didn't discuss it except with a few close friends."

HCDA was launched on 23 July 1988 at Hackney Town Hall. Among the founders were two civil liberties lawyers, Louise Christian and Jane Deighton, and representatives of Anti-Fascist Action. HCDA's first real case came the following January when Trevor Monerville's 73-year-old grandmother was assaulted at home after reporting to the police a car accident in which she and a family friend were involved.[2] As more people in the community heard about HCDA its meetings filled up.

A RAGAMUFFIN BUNCH

Smith invited Celia Stubbs, a mental health social worker, to join in 1989. She was a long-time Hackney resident and co-founder of INQUEST, the organisation that campaigns for family rights following deaths in custody. Celia came to speak on the tenth anniversary of the death of her boyfriend Blair Peach. After his killing, Stubbs had fought to identify which officers from the Special Patrol Group had administered the fatal blow. The thing Celia loved most about HCDA was how it catered to the victims and the needs of the families they left behind.

Rudolf Hawkins, a local black bricklayer, is one such case. In February 1990 he was severely truncheoned when officers arrested him at home over a motoring incident. He ended up hospitalised and unconscious with a broken hand. "I went through one of the most traumatic and depressing periods in my life. Initially the psychological effects were unbearable, so much so that I had to seek psychiatric help. At times I found it hard to come to terms with my life. Worst of all was the thought of not being able to pursue my career as a bricklayer [and] provide for my family."

Hawkins resented having to expose himself to humiliating cross-examination to get redress. A jury found in his favour and the Met paid him substantial damages. Many took their awards and left the struggle to HCDA, but Hawkins carried on as one of the association's key caseworkers. He still works in Hackney but as a market trader. The whole experience makes him wary of talking about it, even now.

"In the early days HCDA was like political therapy where people, by reaching out and supporting other cases, dealt with the pain and shame of understanding what had happened to them," says local schoolteacher Tony Pryce, another HCDA ragamuffin.

It was the legal side of HCDA's mission that attracted his friend Russell Miller, a young radical lawyer. He had been studying law at Manchester when Martin Walker was conducting defence work for the student union. "I was radicalised in the late seventies and eighties by my parents and through the Campaign for Nuclear Disarmament," says Miller. "But it wasn't until I saw Martin building a legal case against the local police that I realised how effective a career as a solicitor could be.

"The good thing about HCDA was it was political activists working not for their own ends but for the community. We had very limited resources to bring accountability to a very powerful institution. HCDA was grounded in the needs of the victims. It sought to put pressure on every level: on the media for not reporting police crimes;

on lawyers for not defending clients properly; on the police for not investigating crimes committed by their own; on the CPS for not bringing prosecutions against those officers; and on the PCA for failing to supervise internal investigations properly."

From the 1970s to the 1990s, many inner city areas had a "Front Line", a street where locals and outsiders scored drugs. The dealers were relatively open about it, and hung out on the street, or in a café or pub waiting for punters. Prostitutes could be found touting for business nearby. Many of the girls on the game were also on the gear in a spiral of debasement and self-destruction.

Dealers on the Line knew one another and competed fiercely for the junkies and recreational users. An early warning system of clockers, people who watch for marked and unmarked patrols by the drug squad, operated on most Front Lines. But these sentries were the only hint of collegiality in an otherwise treacherous business riven with factionalism and police informers.

In Brixton there was Railton Road and in Notting Hill there was All Saints Road or the Mangrove. For the residents of Hackney the Front Line was a half-mile stretch of the borough called Sandringham Road. Dealing went on predominantly on its east side, in a section no more than 100 metres long. Notable landmarks included the Sandringham Arms, the Jerk Chicken Café, the Mitford Tavern and at number 150, a place known simply as "the Shop".

This was a late night convenience store but not in the conventional sense. The Shop was a small council house where a Jamaican mother called Pearl Cameron sold rocks of crack from a service hatch in her kitchen. Each rock was roughly the size of a peanut, wrapped in silver foil, which Pearl dispensed at £20 to £25 a time.

In August 1989 she became a registered informant for a young detective constable on the drugs squad called Roy Lewandowski. He was originally from Merseyside and had joined the Met eight years earlier. Most of that time was served at Stoke Newington police station. Lewandowski had a reputation among his colleagues for expensive tastes and the gift of the gab. On the street he was known as "Blondie", because of his mop of hair cut in a soul boy wedge that obscured most of his forehead.

Pearl was caught dealing, but in return for a caution she agreed to "work" for Blondie. In itself this was not corrupt. Detectives at Stoke Newington and elsewhere in the Met were encouraged to develop informants within the community to fight the wars on crime and

A RAGAMUFFIN BUNCH

drugs. "Snouts" were also a measure of detective acumen and a way of getting noticed by those who ran the informal reference system onto specialist squads, where the opportunities for overtime and skulduggery were greater. Relationships with informants were nominally governed by strict regulations, but lazy or results-driven senior officers often didn't enforce them properly.

Pearl tells an incredible story about her time as Lewandowski's snout. She maintains they went into the crack business together. He provided her with the drugs confiscated from other dealers and junkies. She sold it at the Shop and they split the profits. At one point she claimed he was taking between £1,000 and £2,000 every week. Pearl provided information on other dealers so Lewandowski could cover his back at the station. But his frequent visits to her house made those on the Line suspicious, so Lewandowski introduced a Greek Cypriot called Michael Kyriacou as his middleman.

Kyriacou was a local landlord who ran various businesses. Among them, he provided gaming machines to the scores of Cypriot social clubs that dominate the boroughs of Hackney and neighbouring Haringey to the north. Crucially, Kyriacou was also a registered informant to Lewandowski and his partner on the drugs squad, detective sergeant Graham Le Blond.

Pearl was happy with the new arrangement and the extra money coming in. She travelled frequently to Jamaica, where she had invested in a house jointly owned with her parents. Lewandowski even squared it with immigration to allow her cousin to stay with her in the UK. Then Cupid's arrow struck and Pearl fell in love with Blondie, who flirted back although she swears they never slept together.

After Lewandowski fell out with Kyriacou, the drug recycling business ran into difficulties. In the autumn of 1990, the drug squad turned up the heat and busted many people on the Line for possession of crack with intent to supply. They also set up an operation codenamed Cancer solely targeting Pearl. The Mitford Tavern was used as an observation post because it overlooked the Shop.

In January 1991 Pearl was arrested and remanded to prison. She faced a substantial sentence. Her 19-year-old son, Marlon, had been arrested too and was also on remand awaiting trial. Only then did she reveal her dealings with Lewandowski to CIB. Anti-corruption officers went to Holloway Prison and took Pearl's 11-page statement.

The officer in charge of CIB was a slight, angular superintendent called Ian Russell. Throughout his career he remained a uniform officer and was only made detective when he joined CIB in 1990.

UNTOUCHABLES

A friendly chief superintendent had sponsored Russell's move to CIB with a brief to improve the quality of investigations.

When Pearl Cameron outlined the allegations against Lewandowski, it was a name already on Russell's radar. CIB were also familiar with Kyriacou and were inquiring into the relationship with both his police handlers. DS Graham Le Blond had left Stoke Newington and was by then working at Edmonton police station.

A Customs investigation of VAT fraud in the gaming machine business in north London had reported concerns that Stoke Newington officers were tipping off targets in the Cypriot community. After his fall-out with Lewandowski, Kyriacou started naming names to Customs about his competitors. He had also claimed Lewandowski was protecting certain players. These allegations were passed to Russell weeks before Pearl made her claims about recycling crack provided by Lewandowski. By now CIB had a list of suspect officers.

Russell briefed senior officers at the Yard, including deputy commissioner John Smith. Senior management at Stoke Newington was also alerted. In April 1991, CIB were given the go-ahead to start Operation Jackpot to investigate allegations of drug dealing, theft and conspiracy to pervert the course of justice at Stoke Newington police station. Jackpot made applications to home secretary Michael Howard for taps on Lewandowski's office phone and his mobile, according to detective sergeant Barry Toombs, one of Russell's team. Toombs recalls CIB were refused authority to tap Le Blond.

Another fruitful source of information was CIB's taped interviews with Kyriacou. He revealed Lewandowski had stolen some antique books from the home of a man whose murder he was investigating. He also alleged he had paid Lewandowski a small fee to be able to clear the rest of the dead man's possessions. However the slippery Cypriot denied being the middleman between Pearl and Lewandowski but admitted buying drugs from her house when the cop was there. He also said Lewandowski and Le Blond had fallen out.

Then in early September 1991 yet another allegation of corruption reached CIB that partly confirmed Pearl's story, albeit from an equally problematic source. Nigerian-born Ida Oderinde, a 32-year-old mother of several children, wrote a series of letters from prison soon after being jailed for four years for possessing heroin with intent to supply. Ida claimed at trial and in letters to Scotland Yard and to prime minister John Major that the Stoke Newington drugs squad had planted a large bag of heroin in her kitchen freezer during a raid.

Ida was no angel. Her parents had abandoned her in the sixties

A RAGAMUFFIN BUNCH

when they left Nigeria for London. She rejoined them at 14 when they were living in Hackney. Ida's mother became very violent, so she was put into care. At first she shoplifted. Then she tried cheque fraud. All the while she was in an abusive relationship with a junkie whom she blames for getting her hooked on heroin. She robbed to feed their habits and their addicted baby. When Ida fell pregnant again she miscarried after the father battered her. She reported him to the police and confessed her own crimes, which led to a spell inside.

When Ida came out she befriended Pearl Cameron. Immediately she picked up rumours that her new friend was a grass. "It was becoming very obvious that at least four people were not arrested at any time because they worked for the police," she told CIB. Pearl had confided she was dealing for the police. And Ida claimed it was when she refused to do the same that she was set up.

Russell suspected there was a corrupt cell of detectives at Stokey Cokey, as locals were now calling it, and not a few lone wolves. After six months of secret investigation, the Yard made its move. It was no coincidence that the decision in November 1991 to arrest Lewandowski coincided with a formal and public complaint to the PCA by Pearl Cameron. The arrest was part of a joint operation with Customs, whose officers had detained several targets over the gaming machine VAT fraud, including Kyriacou, presumably to disguise his role as the informant.

When Lewandowski's home was searched CIB officers found some of the items stolen from the murder victim's home. Two days later Lewandowski was committed for trial to face a charge of theft and malfeasance.

While he was suspended and awaiting trial, a black DJ from Stoke Newington approached him for help with a case he hoped to mount against the police for malicious prosecution.

Benny Wilson used to spin a soul set at the Roxy in central London before the Punk-Reggae fusion pioneered by producer Don Letts and typified by bands like The Clash persuaded the owners to replace his slot. He later became DJ/manager of the Cotton Club, which opened in Stoke Newington in 1986. A well-known local sports promoter called Ambrose Mendy owned the club in partnership with the brother of cross over reggae star Eddie Grant.

Running the Cotton Club's door was a difficult business because it was also frequented by north London faces like the Adams brothers. One barmaid was the girlfriend of their enforcer, Gilbert Wynter, who later disappeared in mysterious circumstances. The Adams crime family owned bars and pubs in the neighbouring borough of Islington, like RaRa, where Arsenal footballers relaxed, and the Edward VII.

Mendy was a police target from an early age with convictions for burglary and fraud. He was friendly with the Adams brothers. They shared an interest in boxing. Mendy had moved from unlicensed boxing promotion to working with Islington's Frank Warren, who was breaking the hold Mickey Duff had on televised British boxing. Many of Mendy's other clients were entertained at the Cotton Club by Benny Wilson's platters.

The DJ lived with his young daughter in a nearby flat, which was owned by the slippery police informant Michael Kyriacou with whom he'd been engaged in a courtroom tussle over rent arrears. Wilson was arrested on 10 January 1991 on the way back from dropping his daughter at school. DS Graham Le Blond led the operation, which found firearms, ammunition, cannabis, amphetamine and cocaine in the flat. Wilson denied they were his. Wilson says he declined an offer to become a grass in return for dropping the charges. But the approach made him wonder if the operation was a way of getting at Mendy or even the Adams crime syndicate.

Certainly police pressure on the Mendy empire was intense in January. A week after Wilson's arrest, Terry Marsh, the former world champion boxer, was arrested for the attempted murder of Frank Warren, his one-time manager. Mendy was Marsh's agent at the time of the shooting. One week later, Mendy was himself bailed to face charges over a £1.2 million bank fraud.

Wilson remained in custody for six months protesting his innocence. Mendy supplied his top solicitor, Henri Brandman. In June, Wilson was discharged at committal because no evidence could link him to the objects found in his flat.

Word filtered back to him that Kyriacou was a grass. And when news of Lewandowski's arrest emerged, Wilson approached him for information about the Cypriot. Wilson says he paid Lewandowski £2,000 for copies of the secretly tape-recorded CIB interviews with Kyriacou. In them the Cypriot informant appears to confirm that he had set up Wilson with Le Blond.

Lewandowski's only condition for further co-operation was that Wilson made a formal complaint to Operation Jackpot. The DJ made a statement to CIB in 1992. That November Lewandowski was convicted of theft and jailed for 18 months. Towards the end of his sentence he made an explosive five-page statement for Wilson's lawyers, which was also provided to CIB. It alleged that Le Blond, acting for Kyriacou, had suggested planting a shotgun in Wilson's flat and then arresting him in return for money. Lewandowski said he declined the offer. But his statement went on to say Le Blond suggested instead he would approach a former Stoke Newington cop called Martin Morgan who was working with him at Edmonton.

The fall-out between Lewandowski and Le Blond and their informants, Cameron and Kyriacou, would lead Operation Jackpot to places some within the Yard did not want to go.

Mark Jackson was 26 when in May 1988 he landed a job as a junior lawyer with the CPS. The service was still in its infancy. Each police station in north London had a nominated CPS team to prosecute its cases. Jackson was given Stoke Newington to look after. It proved to be a baptism of fire. The relationship between the police and CPS was, he says, very poor. They didn't trust the lawyers and saw them as errand boys for prosecuting counsel. He recalls that officers used to prosecuting their own cases could be domineering and dismissive and few CPS lawyers would decide against prosecution.

After an initial 18-month stint, Jackson returned to Stoke Newington in early 1991, this time as the youngest senior prosecutor in the CPS. "The relationship with the police had broken down and my job was to repair the damage."

Jackson noticed that compared with other CPS teams in the office, Stoke Newington had an oppressive in-tray. He discreetly asked senior officers in charge of the detective branch what could explain this. "I was told there was an epidemic of crack and they were under immense pressure from the community to clean it up. It wasn't the crack problem but the burglary that went with it. The police in Stoke Newington were under pressure to make a lot of arrests."

However it soon became apparent to Jackson that the bad relationship with the CPS was down to the quality of those arrests. Concerns over poor paperwork were, with hindsight, clues to corruption, especially in the drug squad, he says.

Jackson recounted an example where someone had been fairly arrested for crack possession, but then an unexplained shotgun was added to the charge sheet, which the defendant complained was a plant. "When we asked the police to do a forensic test on the gun, something you'd assume they would have already thought of, they backed off the charge."

One of the most frequent anomalies was the "lack of continuity" in evidence following arrests for small possession of crack. These rocks should have been exhibited in sealed evidence bags and sent for analysis. But Jackson recalls reviewing cases where the forensic scientist was analysing a drug sample with a different seal number or the drugs had simply gone missing.

The police and the CPS came under another type of pressure when, in March 1991, the home secretary, Ken Clarke, announced a Royal Commission on Criminal Justice following the quashing of the Birmingham Six convictions. The Commission's remit was to prevent further miscarriages of justice, but these just kept coming.

In April, Jackson was called to meet his boss Jerry Hyde in his top-floor office at Highbury Corner. When he walked in he was surprised to see the head of all Stoke Newington detectives, Robin Scott, and his boss, detective chief superintendent Roy Clark. It was clear to Jackson the three men had been discussing something of great importance before his arrival. A list of about eleven police officers was passed over the desk. The detectives asked in a tone he didn't much care for, "What do you know about any of these names?" Hyde intervened and told DCS Clark that he would discuss the list with Jackson in private.

He was later taken aside and informed that a corruption probe called Operation Jackpot had been launched, beginning with the officers on the list. Jackson was told he was to continue his normal role but also to secretly review the integrity of old cases dealt with by those officers and pass this to the Jackpot team. "I felt I was being asked to spy on these officers and refused. There was an obvious conflict of interest." But Hyde, he says, told him the instructions came from the top of the CPS, the Director of Public Prosecutions, Barbara Mills. "I think it was our fire fight until we knew how we were going to sort it out. There was no back-up plan in place at the time. The special casework lawyer should have dealt with it from the beginning." But this wouldn't happen for many months.

Jackson therefore carried out his secret dual role but says he felt "very uncomfortable". Every so often he was passed new names of suspect officers. "I was shocked by the level of corruption that had gone on, not that it had happened. When I started to think back and marry things together, like the missing drugs, it started to make sense."

Operation Jackpot had parallels with the 1989 West Midlands Crime Squad scandal, whose tactics for securing confessions involved

A RAGAMUFFIN BUNCH

mixing straight fit-ups and verbals with torture. Although calls for an independent public inquiry were rejected, an outside force had at least done the two-year investigation.[3] Jackson was not alone in thinking that given the public concern which led to the Royal Commission, it was extraordinary that the government had allowed Scotland Yard not only to conduct an internal investigation, but one where the senior management at Stoke Newington were intimately involved.

Jackson thought DCS Roy Clark's role was conflicted. How could his involvement with Operation Jackpot hope to inspire public confidence when it was men under his command being investigated? Wasn't this prejudging where the corruption probe might lead?

The Yard defended its position at the time, claiming the internal inquiry was "entirely appropriate".[4] By then the PCA had been shut out for six months, even though Operation Jackpot's list of suspect officers clearly suggested a possible cell of corruption in the drugs squad that questioned the safety of many prosecutions.[5]

This had all the hallmarks of an organisation trying to keep a lid on the scandal until they had a grip on the handle. Operation Jackpot hadn't even contacted HCDA, who clearly possessed leads vital to any serious inquiry that put the public interest first.[6]

The community watchdog had lobbied the Royal Commission with its evidence and provided a report entitled *A Crime is a Crime is a Crime*. It campaigned for police officers who commit crimes in the exercise of their duty – such as fit-ups and assaults – to be treated like ordinary citizens rather than enjoy the "exceptional provisions" of an internal complaints system. Operation Jackpot was aware of the report because HCDA publicised in the media its case files. These files suggested a sinister trend of police officers assaulting members of the public then, to cover it up, charging them with assault on the police.

Superintendent Russell could not have missed the alarming development of successive officers being disbelieved or caught lying in court during a spate of cases between September and December 1991.[7] Notorious police constable Ronnie Palumbo – who Jackson says was on the list he saw in April – was later that year disowned by the prosecution as a credible witness of truth during the trial of Paul Noel, accused of possessing cannabis with intent to supply. The trial collapsed and the judge indicated Palumbo should be investigated. It emerged that in a previous trial the officer had taken the almost unprecedented step of invoking his right against self-incrimination and refused to answer further questions. Palumbo, known as "Nathan" on the Front Line, had also been involved in the disputed search of Ida

Oderinde's house, after which she alleged to CIB heroin had been planted in her freezer.

On 28 January eight Stoke Newington officers were told they were being transferred out of Hackney division and could go anywhere in east London but no two officers could transfer to the same police station. The following day, DCS Roy Clark accompanied his men to City Road. The atmosphere in the anteroom waiting to see the commander-in-charge of personnel was icy. Each officer was given official notification that they were subject to complaints now being investigated by Operation Jackpot. These ranged from theft to assault and perjury.

Deputy assistant commissioner Mike Taylor had taken the decision to transfer the eight officers at a meeting the previous day with assistant commissioner Peter Winship, who was overseeing Jackpot. They were briefed by Russell, who told them thirty-two officers had complaints against them and more were in the pipeline. The high-powered group considered three options: do nothing, suspend the officers or transfer them. The CPS was not consulted. Mark Jackson felt the officers should have been moved or suspended in April 1991, when he was first handed the Jackpot list.

A Met press release on 29 January made it clear the transfer was a result of complaints from "people accused of drug dealing" and that the eight officers had not been suspended and would "continue their full range of duties". But while journalists concentrated on making front-page news of the transfer, another equally explosive story was unfolding. At six o'clock that same morning, forty-six-year-old sergeant Gerry Carroll was found slumped in the toilets at Barkingside police station having shot himself in the head with a Smith and Wesson .38 revolver. Carroll had been the custody sergeant at Stoke Newington from 1982 until October 1990 when he moved to Barkingside. At the time of his suicide, Carroll and other officers were the subject of a civil action for the malicious prosecution of Glenford Lewis, a Jamaican man whose trial for possession of cocaine collapsed after the CPS withdrew. Lewis had alleged the police planted a matchbox of cocaine during a search of his car and had beaten him up.

Some news reports suggested an internal inquiry into the Lewis case, parallel to Operation Jackpot, was due to report its findings within days of Carroll's death, and that he had rung Stoke Newington police station the night before he killed himself to ask if he would be named in the Jackpot inquiry too.

A RAGAMUFFIN BUNCH

One of his police friends, DC Declan Costello, recalls that at Stoke Newington detectives were taken into the corrupt circle of fit-ups and theft on the recommendation of experienced hands that "they could do the business". He says Carroll, like him, had that recommendation. Costello told us Carroll made three calls to various officers without response the night before he died. Intriguingly, the Yard later confirmed to local Labour MP, Brian Sedgemore, that Carroll committed suicide after receiving three telephone calls from unnamed officers. This information could only have come from phone-taps.

A verdict of suicide was recorded at the inquest. His GP told the coroner Carroll had suffered from tinnitus – a constant ringing, buzzing or humming in one's ear or head – since he was punched on the cheek in 1986, and that two weeks before his death he had complained he couldn't sleep. A superintendent investigating Carroll's death also told the court he was not under investigation or suspicion and was not going to be disciplined.

The main causes of tinnitus are ageing and loud noises. Sufferers can train their mind to filter out unwanted sounds, but it is exacerbated by stress. One suggestion is that CIB was squeezing Carroll to turn informer against his colleagues, who at the same time were urging him to stay staunch. What the Yard says publicly and the truth surrounding officers who kill themselves during corruption inquiries can be canyons apart, as the Alan 'Taffy' Holmes case showed four years earlier.

The developments of 29 January led Sedgemore to table a colourful early day motion (EDM) two days later condemning the "nasty, vile and corrupt" cops at Stoke Newington. More explosively, DCS Roy Clark was accused of misleading the MP about "the true nature of the problems because [Clark] himself had been duped by his own police officers". The parliamentary intervention was followed by an invitation from assistant commissioner Winship to attend a briefing. Sedgemore told the senior officer he felt "badly let down" by the police, given his own efforts to clean up Sandringham Road. He said he also believed some police officers were allowing drug dealing to continue but he never imagined officers were "on the take". The MP gave Winship two names.

Sedgemore's note of the 6 February meeting records the following: "[Winship] told me we were dealing with the worst case of police corruption in the Met for ten years. It had come as a body blow to the commissioner and to Stoke Newington police station . . . Whether or not [the transferred officers] were charged and convicted there was no doubt that some at least were involved in serious corruption. The original tip off had come from Customs." The note continued: "By transferring them [the Yard] had of course reduced the chances of getting enough evidence to convict them, he said, but they had no alternative."

Roy Clark was angered by the EDM and told the local paper: "I am amazed that an MP who is a trained barrister can pre-judge an issue . . . on the strength of allegations alone. I do not feel I have been duped by my police officers. It is important these allegations are put in perspective. They are being made by people, on the whole, who are self-confessed drugs dealers. At the moment they are only allegations. It could well be that they are exonerated at the end of the day."

Sedgemore, who had also called for an independent judicial enquiry, slapped down Clark in a confidential reply seen by the authors: "In light of the very helpful briefing I had with [Winship] last week your comments as quoted in the *Hackney Gazette* were unfortunate and misinformed. I understand we are dealing with the worst case of corruption that the Met has faced in a decade."[8]

Hackney's other Labour MP, Diane Abbott, joined forces with a Stokey Cokey awkward squad of left-wing parliamentarians including Dennis Skinner, Bob Cryer and Terry Lewis. They tabled a second EDM asking home secretary Kenneth Clark to explain why senior Yard officers had attended Gerry Carroll's funeral when "they know or could have been told by their colleagues that evidence pointed unmistakably to Carroll being involved in organised crime, and hopes that this Sicilian practice will be discontinued."[9]

The Carroll suicide gave one Hackney resident, a baker called Hugh Prince, the security to come forward to HCDA. Prince had arrived from Jamaica in 1967, aged just 12. In the early eighties he moved to the borough. He hung around the Roots Pool Community Centre on the Front Line, where the talk over a game of cards or dominoes was of how the only black people safe from police brutality and fit-ups were dealers working for the drugs squad.

Prince had been arrested at a shebeen in August 1990 for possession of crack, allegedly found in his cigarette packet. He made an immediate complaint that officers working under Carroll had planted it. Nevertheless, he was convicted and jailed for two months. "For nearly a year after my release from prison I hardly left my home. I was frightened of being planted with drugs again. It wasn't until I heard that Carroll shot himself that I felt it was safe to go out."

Sedgemore took up his case and wrote to the home secretary about

A RAGAMUFFIN BUNCH

"the extraordinarily cavalier way" Prince's complaint had been ignored for two years. Operation Jackpot was forced to take it up. His appeal was subsequently allowed in December 1994 and he later won considerable compensation from the Met.

The transfer of officers in January 1992 was for HCDA the first official confirmation of a drug corruption inquiry into Stoke Newington. Only then, on Valentine's Day, did superintendent Russell make contact with the ragamuffin bunch seeking their information on corrupt officers.

"The problem for the Met," says Russell Miller, "was HCDA was going for three years before the drugs scandal broke so there was a well-oiled database in place." The drug corruption aspect gave the apparent randomness of the police brutality a meaning, adds Graham Smith.

HCDA was unique in its commitment to do the legal gumshoeing many solicitors ignored until Legal Aid was secured. That could take months, by which time the evidence trail was cold. But as Stokey Cokey snowballed into a national scandal, so did the number of local victims willing to come forward. Among the genuine ones were chancers, but most were soon weeded out by HCDA's para-legals.

At the time Jackpot made its approach, Miller was working at the radical solicitors, Birnberg & Co, who had recently defended the Birmingham Six and were engaged in unpicking numerous other miscarriages of justice. Frustrated that the CPS was not proactive enough when cases of police misconduct were brought to its attention, Miller set up a Lawyers' Liaison Group (LLG) in March 1992 to share information collated by HCDA around drugs and assault cases involving Stoke Newington officers. At first Miller says he was unsure it would work because many solicitors and barristers are not given to sharing information, let alone outside work hours and for no pay. Solicitor Debbie Tripley agrees but says colleagues soon saw the cross-examination potential of knowing the arresting officer had previously been disbelieved on oath in a similar trial; something the CPS and Yard were not exactly rushing to make widely known.[10]

Now a defence solicitor, Mark Jackson can understand her frustration. He was uneasy about how his CPS bosses were managing the legal fall-out and frustrated by CIB's unwillingness to share information with him, let alone defence lawyers. He also felt "under pressure" from senior officers at Stoke Newington to save cases jeopardised by the ongoing corruption probe. "There came a point defence solicitors would ring up and I looked a twat because they knew more than I did. I think the CPS had been kept very much in the dark. I was told by one detective inspector, 'You are being drip fed.' There were case conferences where prosecuting counsel would say to the senior officer from Stoke things like, 'How many rabbits are there left in the hat?'"

After many months in "this invidious position", the job of reviewing old cases dealt with by suspect officers on the Jackpot list was passed to Special Casework, a department within the CPS handling what are deemed sensitive and political cases.

Stuart Sampson took over in October 1992. He is an experienced lawyer with an uncanny resemblance to the bespectacled Mole from *Wind in the Willows*. "Going to Stoke Newington was like being back in Notting Hill Gate police station in the late eighties during the Mangrove days," he recalls. His new job got off to a difficult start, he says, because the Yard didn't want him to see superintendent Russell's interim and final report to the PCA. "That was the police view, which we soon disabused them of but it took a little while."

Keeping the CPS out of the decision to transfer the eight officers was also a mistake, which he feels had little regard for the disclosure problems it caused. It was Sampson's job to review the merits of past and current prosecutions, to decide whether the CPS should oppose appeals against convictions and what to disclose to the defence. This task was further hindered, he suggests, by the time CIB took to deliver its reports. The Yard was also relying on a discredited legal instrument called a public interest immunity certificate (PII) – in effect a gagging order – to prevent disclosure around Operation Jackpot.

Sampson says it wasn't until February 1993, almost two years after Operation Jackpot started, that "CIB disclosed details of all officers under investigation. Accordingly, with the pressure from the courts, the review of current cases had to be completed on the material available."

The situation typified the problem of internal corruption probes, which allow the police force to decide, without independent legal oversight, when and whether to release information prejudicial to its own interests. The practical effect is people remain in prison or with the stigma of being a criminal longer than they should. And suspect officers are dealt with away from the courts and in a way that suits the Yard rather than the interests of justice and the community it serves.

The Lawyers' Liaison Group tried to change that. It was made up of twelve solicitors' firms and nineteen barristers. They wrote to the DPP and the home secretary expressing profound concern about the injustice caused by the lack of disclosure from Operation Jackpot.

Brian Sedgemore and eleven other MPs tabled two further early day motions in June 1992 criticising the Yard's handling of Jackpot and asking why constable Palumbo, whom he called a "lying witness", had not been suspended. The MPs got an audience with Ken Clarke followed by a letter in August. A civil servant claimed Clarke had "no authority to intervene" in the internal investigation and made it very clear disclosure issues were a matter for the police.

As the months passed more convictions were quashed, largely because the CPS had to accept that the evidence of named Stoke Newington officers could no longer be relied on. Sampson recalls there were twelve unopposed appeals. The CPS did however oppose four cases but the Appeal Court still found for the appellants. The judges only refused one full appeal.

Always the barrister, Sedgemore inquired of the Attorney General whether the CPS had ever received representations from the Yard on which appeals to allow and which to oppose. He was told Sampson had simply consulted Russell and considered his views.[11] But Sampson reveals he also discussed these appeals with DCS Roy Clark and his replacement Nial Mulvihill.

The press turned out in full when two months later the Appeal Court quashed the drug convictions of Ida Oderinde, Rennie Kingsley, Dennis Tulloch and Everard Brown. All these unopposed appeals originated from arrests made in the autumn of 1990. Palumbo featured in each case and the convicted cop Lewandowski had a role in others. But the CPS indicated it also had "serious doubt as to the honesty" of the evidence of all other officers, some of whom were suspended.

Diane Abbott made an attacking speech in the Commons. "A number of officers have been accused of planting drugs, theft and conspiracy to pervert the course of justice. To date, twelve officers have been named: PC Mark Carroll has been mentioned in ten cases; PC Terence Chitty has been mentioned in twelve cases; PC Bruce Galbraith has been mentioned in five cases; DC Bernard [Jim] Gillan has been mentioned in six cases; DC Paul Goscomb has been mentioned in five cases; PC Christopher Hart has been mentioned in twelve cases; DS Graham Le Blond has been mentioned in one case; DC Roy Lewandowski has been mentioned in four cases; DC Barry Lyons has been mentioned in eight cases;

UNTOUCHABLES

DC Peter McCulloch has been mentioned in seven cases; DC Ronnie Palumbo has been mentioned in fourteen cases; DS Robert Watton has been mentioned in four cases." Abbott continued: "It is difficult to believe that senior officers were not aware of what was going on or that they did not condone it." She criticised them for a "siege mentality" and for downplaying the corruption scandal by attacking the complainants.

Around this time HCDA members began to worry about the security of their most visible representative, Graham Smith, the man they all agree made the association such an effective watchdog of the local police. "He dedicated his life to HCDA and it cost him his marriage," says his friend Mark Metcalf. "Countless times me and his wife would be waiting in the pub for him to arrive only to return to the house to see Graham on the phone dispensing some legal advice or just listening to a victim of police brutality."

In private, the senior management at Stoke Newington took HCDA a lot more seriously than its public jibes about them being "toy town revolutionaries" would suggest. Roy Clark was particularly energetic in supporting his men publicly and dismissing the long history of "myths" around police brutality in Hackney. It was HCDA, he said, that was using the scandal to "beat the police".

The community watchdog's files show that at the height of Operation Jackpot it received various anonymous threats and apparent random acts of intimidation. On Valentine's Day 1992, for example, an anonymous caller rang the office and said: "Yes, you fucking cunts, I'm going to blow your heads off, you fucking cunts!" then put the phone down. On 2 March Smith discovered one side of his bicycle handlebars had been "loosened deliberately". The following month the office received an offensive letter from a police officer.

Smith says when he left his house he would often have a marked police car overtly tail him. He also got calls saying he was being followed. But the most chilling incident happened one night when he was returning home alone from a meeting and found a dead white laboratory rat lying on his doorstep. His wife had arrived ten minutes before him, he says, and saw nothing there. Smith reported the incident to his local MP Diane Abbott. "It occurred shortly after a letter to the office calling me a white nigger. The whole point of this harassment is they turn it off and on, you never know when. It's a psychological tool that plays on your nerves and you don't know who is responsible. Is it high up or low down? I assumed it was low down, that we were getting close and someone was feeling the heat."

On 2 February 1994 the PCA released scant details of the final Operation Jackpot report. It revealed 45 officers at Stoke Newington, whose identities were kept secret, had been investigated over 3 years, at an undisclosed cost. 22 cases involving 134 allegations, most of which involved the planting of drugs and other "evidence", had been examined. The public was told the CPS was considering if any officer should face criminal charges. The Yard, meanwhile, were examining disciplinary matters.[12]

The PCA signed off Jackpot as an internal investigation "completed to the maximum extent possible". It then had a snide dig at the local community suggesting that complaints had "tended to follow publicity about the investigation and some officers" and that most were made over a year after the alleged incident, which along with "limited co-operation" from the complainants hampered the investigation and helped cause the delay.

In July 1994, the CPS announced that two suspended officers – Barry Lyons and Ronnie Palumbo – would be charged with perjury and conspiracy to pervert the course of justice. Both were tried in December 1995 and acquitted.[13] That month the PCA also announced the Yard was to discipline 8 of the 45 officers. Again they were unnamed and the punishment was minor – the equivalent of a slap on the wrist from one of Ken Dodd's tickle sticks. This tough display of self-regulation took another two years to execute.

HCDA, the Lawyers' Liaison Group and local MPs had every confidence that Jackpot would be a whitewash; that's why they wanted an independent judicial inquiry. Barrister Peter Hall wondered aloud how it was that a drug corruption probe hadn't charged any officer with drug offences when 13 drugs cases had been overturned on grounds including that officers had lied on oath and planted drugs?

HCDA also questioned the thoroughness of Jackpot, suggesting that 77 cases had not been investigated. In a letter to new home secretary Michael Howard it pointed out that despite Operation Jackpot, HCDA was still receiving complaints – 57 in 1993. One was from Audley Harrison, the young Hackney boxer who went on to win a gold medal in the 2000 Olympics. He complained after being acquitted with his girlfriend of obstruction and assaulting a police officer.[14]

The PCA came rushing to superintendent Russell's defence. Privately, he felt HCDA had an agenda – as if Jackpot didn't. He also doubted the motives of those who had complained about the police.

The HCDA campaign had been a model in community defence and support. Through it Smith came to realise that civil actions, not internal inquiries, were the best remedy for victims of police crimes. It was the solicitor Raju Bhatt, adds Miller, who was responsible for perfecting civil actions against the police in the way they are carried out now. The Yard had paid out over £500,000 in public money to the victims of corrupt and unethical policing in Stoke Newington.

Another legacy of this ragamuffin bunch was the setting up in 1994 of a database on dirty cops. Smith and Miller developed it to service defence solicitors like Bhatt. There was great resistance from the Association of Chief Police Officers to getting DIS – the Defendants' Information Service – Data Protection registered. HCDA successfully sued *Police Review* for an article suggesting "organised criminals" were behind DIS. Other attacks were more sinister. In December 1994, the office was broken into and ransacked. One computer was stolen, other equipment was urinated on and cash left untouched. Luckily, the database was elsewhere.

This burglary came on the eve of a demonstration outside Stoke Newington police station following the death in custody one week earlier of a 32-year-old Nigerian man called Shiji Lapite. His wife, cradling her six-week-old daughter, sat on the floor in the station foyer shouting: "They killed him! They beat him to death! Why? Why? Why?"

Operation Jackpot was a failure. Privately, superintendent Ian Russell felt his probe only netted a third of the core group of corrupt officers he believed were taking out the opposition on the Front line and recycling part of the proceeds. "Lewandowski, he wasn't a bit player by any stretch of the imagination, but there are others who are in some respects more important in the scheme of things. We got one third of it," a senior CIB officer on Jackpot told us.

Russell blamed untrustworthy elements in SO11 for the problems he apparently experienced getting authority for phone-taps on Stoke Newington officers. "If we had got those technical facilities at an early stage we would have got a different result. It may be wishful thinking, but we would have known what was going on early," a source close to Russell explained.

Senior CPS lawyers now agree Operation Jackpot was a failure. It just "scratched the surface", said one, who asked to remain anonymous. But at the time, the CPS, CIB and PCA were saying no

A RAGAMUFFIN BUNCH

such thing. Consequently, there was never a chance of a proper judicial inquiry into policing in Hackney after Operation Jackpot reported in 1994. Home secretary Michael Howard and his new commissioner, Paul Condon, were travelling on the other bus heading away from greater accountability. Howard had already rejected calls the previous year from the family of Stephen Lawrence for a judicial inquiry into the Yard's mishandling of their son's murder investigation and the stench of corruption coming from south-east London police stations. In fact, the disgraceful Barker Review cover-up was being concocted at precisely the same time the ink was drying on the Operation Jackpot report.

Commissioner Condon had enough difficulty keeping the Lawrence and David Norris murders apart. Both had already revealed serious allegations of corruption in the Central Drug Squad, the East Dulwich South East Regional Crime Squad and the Tower Bridge branch of the Flying Squad. The BBC exposé of bent cop John Donald in September 1993 had added concerns about the Surbiton branch of SERCS and the relatively new National Criminal Intelligence Service.

The last thing Scotland Yard now wanted was to add the Stoke Newington drug squad, Edmonton police station and the Rigg Approach branch of the Flying Squad to that list and then publicly air it before a high court judge. That would undermine the political pact between John Major's government and Scotland Yard to rehabilitate the office of constable with new, draconian powers. It was a time to condemn more and understand less, the prime minister had said.

The government could also point to the Royal Commission it had set up in response to the miscarriages of justice problem. That reported in July 1993 at roughly the same time superintendent Russell passed his final report to the PCA. However one key representative now claims the police establishment hijacked the Royal Commission. In a recent book Sir Roger Bunyard, a former commandant at Bramshill police training college and chief constable of Sussex, says the Major government went with the minority report, which was totally opposed to fundamental reform of the police, including a fully independent police complaints system and tackling the causes of noble cause corruption. Bunyard wrote: "It is very dangerous to accept the proposition that noble cause syndrome can lessen the culpability of police who tamper with evidence and obtain confessions by illegal means. It is such behaviour that resulted in courts and juries rejecting police evidence during the second half of the twentieth century. Illegal acts done in the name of 'justice' can extend to malpractice to improve statistics, to justify the continued existence of a specialist squad, for personal ambition or for personal greed. There is no line between malpractice for whatever reason and corruption."[15]

Diane Abbott MP was not alone in finding it difficult to believe senior officers at Stoke Newington were not aware of misconduct and did not condone it. But for Operation Jackpot, the PCA and the Home Office this was of no interest. Only a judicial inquiry stood a chance of unravelling whether the scandal was the result of junior officers implementing a secret and questionable policing policy for the borough. "Hackney was policed on an anti-community policy," says Miller. Smith adds that the area was also a "dustbin" for punchy and racist cops. In general the type of policing seen in inner city areas is not that experienced in affluent middle-class ones. What's good for Hackney is unsustainable in Hampstead. What happens in Brixton would not be acceptable in Barnes.

DCS Roy Clark admitted at the time that his command was under pressure to clear up the drug and associated burglary problems. But did this lead to a questionable policy of zero tolerance, where younger officers felt they could take the gloves off to get results? Mark Jackson believes that behind the volume of ramped-up arrests he reviewed daily was management pressure to take out dealers and nurture informants. This, he says, created the Frankenstein inside the drugs squad as certain officers saw the opportunity to make a lot of money, while others stuck to fitting up people with drugs, weapons and phoney assaults.

DC Declan Costello was one of the corrupt cell of detectives under Clark's watch. He told us the culture of violence, fit-ups and personal corruption operated in the belief that his management would do little if a complaint came in. Stuart Sampson of the CPS accepts Stoke Newington certainly had "problems of poor supervision and management". Jackson goes further. He says there was "massive incompetence at middle and senior management".

Again, this was never publicly addressed and no senior officer saw the need to fall on his sword. Indeed, Roy Clark left Stoke Newington in the middle of Operation Jackpot for a better posting as deputy to John Grieve at the Directorate of Intelligence, SO11.

Operation Jackpot didn't consider that any senior officers at Stoke Newington might end up being implicated criminally or for breaches of discipline. CIB simply weren't looking. And the CPS weren't forcing the issue either. Sampson confirms this: "We have to deal with the reality of life. [Clark and others] were the operational commanders and were not under suspicion or investigation."

Thus, while Operation Jackpot was ongoing Clark secretly started to develop a Ghost Squad strategy, with Home Office support, for the whole of Scotland Yard. Russell was brought into the planning phase of the Ghost Squad strategy while he was still directing Jackpot. In late 1993 he attended a crucial meeting at Tintagel House with commissioner Condon. Also present was Ian Blair, who at the time was in charge of Operation Gallery, the John Donald corruption inquiry. Today he is deputy commissioner.

No amount of asking will persuade Scotland Yard to provide the policy document Condon signed which laid out the reasons for setting up the Ghost Squad with Grieve and Clark at the helm.

The Stokey Cokey scandal taught Scotland Yard a lesson that would shape the approach of the Ghost Squad. It would never again make the mistake of launching a public corruption investigation with all the attendant problems HCDA and its lawyers had caused over disclosure, successful appeals, civil actions and a torrent of bad publicity. The Ghost Squad wouldn't publicly exist, and would not therefore be a hostage to community or media pressure. It would operate in the darkness of no accountability, gathering intelligence on corruption in its ranks and releasing what suited the Yard's wider managerial interests. Timing and control of the media became crucial to handling the unfolding Stephen Lawrence scandal and continued calls for an independent judicial inquiry into policing in London.

The Ghost Squad appeared not to be interested in tackling endemic noble cause corruption. The secret squad would become a political tool for the new commissioner to reshape his force – a management coup, as one CIB officer called it – and a damage limitation strategy for controlling the pace and appearance of reform.

Nor did the Ghost Squad seem interested in taking out every corrupt officer. The illusion of a no-hiding-place anti-corruption drive was fostered to cover up the simple fact that certain types of serious corruption were untouchable because they led to places the Yard didn't want to go.

Instead, the Ghost Squad gave the impression of carefully selecting its targets, manipulating the investigation and presenting the results through tame journalists as a measure of its willingness to clean its own house and consequently, the effectiveness of self-regulation.

To achieve this illusion the supergrass was resurrected.

PART THREE

THE SUPERGRASS FARCE

11

GEOFF BRENNAN – DOUBLE AGENT SUPERGRASS

Dealing with informants is a dangerous business for honest cops and a lucrative one for the corrupt. An effective informant is almost invariably an effective criminal and therefore his motive for grassing up dangerous people who could do him serious harm is very rarely honourable.

Some do it for the money – either a reward from the insurance company or a payment from the police informants' fund. Some do it to remove the criminal competition. Others are motivated by revenge. But there is one type of informant who is the most dangerous of all – the double agent. They specialise in working for the very criminals the police think they are grassing on. Alternatively, the double agent informant plays each side off against the other for money and to cover up his own crimes.

The Ghost Squad period from 1993 to 1997 was marked by its incredible mishandling of two very different supergrasses – Geoff Brennan, a white south-east London businessman, and Hector Harvey, a black west London armed robber. Their stories, and those of other supergrasses, are revealed in this part of the book from interviews and secret documents that were never supposed to see the light of day.

Brennan was the Ghost Squad's first supergrass. His allegations against two frontline detectives sparked off the longest running corruption inquiry in Scotland Yard history, which remarkably is still ongoing, and now in its eleventh year.

The two detectives – John Redgrave and Michael Charman – were suspended on full pay for seven years. For four years before that they were under secret investigation. The suspension alone has cost the taxpayer over £600,000. The entire corruption investigation easily exceeds the £10 million mark, but it has produced no evidence whatsoever of their guilt. That in large part is because Geoff Brennan made the whole thing up and in the process had over the anti-corruption squad.

The two detectives have always maintained their innocence and say with considerable justification they have been destroyed for challenging Scotland Yard's anti-corruption narrative.

On 25 June 1993, detective constable Michael Charman was a few months into his second posting to the Flying Squad, the elite armed robbery unit popularised by the seventies hit TV series *The Sweeney*. The first time he'd served there was during the Brinks Mat heist a decade earlier.

As Charman walked through the Tower Bridge office he heard an outside call being put through to his new boss, detective chief inspector Andy Cater. "It's a Mr John Brennan on the phone for you," the office secretary announced.

Had Charman fought his curiosity things could have been very different. But instead he put his head round the door and said: "Gov, I know who that is. I used to run old man Brennan as an informant."[1]

John Brennan had been handled by at least four detectives before he became Charman's grass on the £26 million Brinks Mat robbery.[2] By then he was in his early sixties and would typically meet Charman in the City wearing what he considered was the old-fashioned Scotland Yard detective's look – a sports jacket with leather patches and grey flannel trousers. As he grew to know him, Charman suspected old man Brennan was really "a frustrated copper". Certainly he seemed to enjoy the sneaky beaky side of his informant role, although he was also paid for his information and liked a drink.

After the call, Charman and another detective met John Brennan at his local pub, The George in Eynsford, Kent. He explained how his son, Geoff, was being pulled into something with two major south-east London criminals well known to Charman. One was "Tall" Ted Williams and the other was John "Goldfinger" Fleming. Both targets had skilfully evaded prosecution during the Brinks Mat inquiry.

Charman was intrigued. As the tale unfolded Geoff Brennan walked into the pub looking for his father. He was a heavy-set man with a facial tic that became more pronounced when he was nervous or scheming.

Williams wanted him to go to Margarita, an island off the Venezuelan coast, to help dispose of some property he owned with Fleming. The proceeds would then be funnelled through Geoff's bank account, he told the two detectives.

Apparently, Williams and Fleming had invested in a plastics business called Poliflexor in the UK that became a money pit into which they and other associates had sunk over £600,000. Disposing of the Margarita properties was a way of recouping some cash flow, which Geoff Brennan suggested would then be invested in a drug importation, probably cocaine.

Charman returned to the office excited. He spoke to detective inspector Bob Suckling, old man Brennan's co-handler during the Brinks inquiry. Suckling and Charman were very wary of the Brennans but at the same time didn't want to lose an opportunity to take down Williams and Fleming.

The Flying Squad didn't do drugs jobs so the information was passed to an old friend, detective John Redgrave, the ginger giant. He, Suckling and Charman had all worked together on the Brinks inquiry, earning them the nickname The Three Musketeers. In 1984 old man Brennan had given them a lead with which they eventually located armed robber John "Little Legs" Lloyd and Kenny Noye, the man behind the Gold Conduit – the Brinks robbers' smelting and money laundering network. Redgrave had also played a key role in the prosecution of a second laundering network run by bent solicitor Michael Relton.

Redgrave was by now an ambitious detective inspector about to turn 40. He was in charge of a drugs team working from SERCS's New Southgate office. He too shared a desire to get the ones that got away, but was also wary of the Brennans. The Three Musketeers believed Geoff Brennan had been a double agent informant for Williams and Lloyd during the Brinks inquiry. Back then he was registered to another detective called Chris Smith who will feature heavily as this story unfolds. Suffice to say, Geoff Brennan's value as an informant and his true intentions had split the Brinks squad down the middle.

Geoff's new information, however, had the ring of truth. Williams had indeed moved into the drugs business since Brinks. Another SERCS informant had revealed that he and Fleming were moving ecstasy pills from Holland by car to Hull.[3]

Redgrave decided to go with it. He got authority for Geoff to accompany Williams to Venezuela as a participating informant registered to Charman, who would be his new handler.[4]

Operation Nightshade was underway.

After the Second World War, Geoff Brennan's father moved to south-east London from Preston in Lancashire. "He was one of the few soldiers rescued from Dunkirk," says Geoff. It was through the army that his parents met and started a family. Denise came first, followed by another daughter, a son and finally Geoffrey Paul Brennan was born on 13 March 1953.

Denise and Geoff grew up in what was then the epicentre of London's criminality. The Old Kent Road is a south-east thoroughfare running from the foot of Tower Bridge through the tough inner city areas of Bermondsey, Rotherhithe and New Cross. Old man Brennan was well connected in the Bermondsey area, recalls Charman. But as he aged, his introduction to the rising criminal talent was made through Denise's circle of friends. He watched her grow up with little acorns that would later become top London villains, like John Lloyd.

At one stage Denise was being courted by Colin "the Duke" Osbourne, an armourer and trusted associate of the Krays. Dukey was bisexual and said to be Ronnie's special friend. In his early teens Geoff was very taken by Dukey. "He was a gent. I used to run bets for him and he would give me money to buy clothes and things." Geoff looked up to Dukey in a way he couldn't to his father – "a piss artist that shagged about and had a vicious mouth". Old man Brennan boasted to Charman about ending Dukey's relationship with Denise by grassing him to the police. He got a long prison stretch.[5]

Geoff Brennan's father used his relationship with the police to protect his family, says Charman. Another of his past handlers, who asked not to be named, remembers the old man once turned to a Flying Squad detective to get his wayward son out of trouble. Young Geoff had been arrested with some Bermondsey faces on the south coast after the police found guns in a caravan they were using.

"I took a wrong turn and got involved with the wrong people," says Geoff. His "salvation" was meeting Sylvia and getting married at 21. "I idolised her," he says with genuine affection. He would later give her a kidney.

Geoff tried his hand at the greeting cards business, then minicabbing. In the early eighties he became a court bailiff in south-east London. Through his father's police contacts and Freemasonry,

Geoff also became an informant for various old school Yard detectives.[6]

Meanwhile, his older sister, Denise, had given birth to a daughter called Debbie. Old man Brennan doted on her. As Debbie grew up, again he used his relationship with the police to protect her. He was particularly concerned about local up-and-coming criminal Tall Ted Williams, who'd fancied Debbie since her early teens.

When old man Brennan was first introduced to Charman in 1984 he explained how he wanted revenge on Williams, whom he blamed for introducing Debbie to drugs. It was only cannabis, says Charman, but being of an older generation he was worried for his granddaughter, who by then was in her early twenties. Old man Brennan also had no liking for Williams' close associate, John Lloyd, who back in the early days had used Denise as his runner in a stolen rent book scam.

The Brinks squad's intelligence unit had already established that Williams was Lloyd's representative in the early disposal of the stolen bullion. Detective inspector Tony Brightwell, the head of the intelligence unit, had developed a significant picture of Edward Paul Williams, born 31 March 1947.

The Yard already possessed intelligence that in 1981 Williams was involved with south-east London crime family boss Dogan Arif in a plot to kidnap and swindle some Iranian colonels secretly negotiating a $55 million embargo-busting arms deal in London and Antwerp.[7]

Shortly after the Brinks robbery two years later, surveillance officers watched in amazement as Williams tried to buy one of London's most notable landmarks – Battersea Power station. They secretly photographed Williams with Fleming and another Brinks suspect Patsy "Bolt Eyes" Clark, meeting the sellers of the derelict site. Needless to say, the sale didn't go through.

Williams certainly had the money. It came from the London Bullion Company, which he had set up in Hatton Garden, the centre of the legitimate and illegal precious stones and metals trade. Detectives believed that during the first half of 1984, LBC was handling almost all the stolen bullion.

Williams needed a "smokescreen", says Brightwell. So he set up another business venture in the West African state of Sierra Leone to justify the volume of gold passing through LBC's books. Sierra Leone is still a violent cove of diamond and arms smuggling. It also has plenty of alluvial gold. Scotland Yard detectives were dispatched to the troubled former British colony to check out the smokescreen. But in

UNTOUCHABLES

August 1984 Williams escaped prosecution again, this time after Customs officers raided LBC for VAT evasion.

Meanwhile, the Brinks Task Force was chasing Fleming all over the Spanish-speaking world because they believed he had handled almost £500,000 of the laundered money.

Brightwell, who led the chase for Fleming, says the villain spent a lot of money on lawyers fighting extradition. "This was funnelled through Lloyd and was part of Fleming's share of the robbery."

The apartments Williams and Fleming owned in Margarita were a well-kept secret from insurers Lloyds. They were the unfortunate lead underwriter of the Brinks Mat gold. After the robbery Lloyds retained legal firm Shaw & Croft to claw back from the Underworld the £26 million it had paid out to the Brinks Mat security company within days of the heist.

Civil actions to freeze the assets of about 50 defendants started in 1986. Lawyer Bob McCunn handled every claw back deal. "At one stage," he says, "we were looking at every villain in south-east London." The deal making was an experience he describes as "fishing in a dark, murky pond. I know what I've pulled out but I have no idea what's still in there."

In August 1992, the last Brinks money laundering trial concluded with the convictions of Williams' south-east London associates Brian Perry, Patsy Clark and Jeannie Ishmael, John Lloyd's wife. Williams had been looking after Lloyd's interests since he went on the run in 1985 to the US. McCunn credits Kenny Noye with bringing the other defendants like Perry to the table after the trial. "[Noye] was one of the first people to talk turkey. When he saw that it was a commercial transaction he talked to the others and said we were not the police, we were not after blood or to convict, we just wanted the money."

It was precisely at this time that Williams started to dispose of the Margarita properties, which McCunn had no idea existed.[8]

Fleming will always deny he was a Brinks robber but he confirmed to us that he and Williams bought one apartment each in Flamingo Bay for £80,000 in 1990. His dream was to extend his investment into a bar, restaurant and nightclub in the same island complex. "I could then slightly alter the name to Flemingo Bay," he quipped.

The Caribbean apartments were one of a number of schemes Williams had persuaded Fleming to invest in. He said he also put money into a diamond mine in Sierra Leone and the failed plastic business.

GEOFF BRENNAN

Geoff Brennan arrived in Margarita on 24 July 1993. Williams met him at the airport with a local girlfriend. They stayed at the Flamingo Bay apartment and then moved to the Hilton with adjoining rooms.

Brennan was not a good traveller. His Bermondsey skin, sensitive to even a bar room tan, burnt immediately. He also got "the galloping gourmets", while an unsympathetic Williams tucked into seafood platters. "He loved squid and all this and I'm a, you know what I mean, I'm a fucking . . . pie and mash would suit me."

Williams quickly sussed he was under surveillance. A maid let him into the adjacent hotel room where he found recording equipment. It wasn't Scotland Yard and he didn't suspect Brennan, although the informant was keeping Charman abreast of developments by phone. It was from the US Drug Enforcement Administration (DEA) working with Operation Nightshade.

As a career criminal, Williams expected regular interest from the authorities. He wasn't unduly concerned but cleverly complained to the hotel manager and left a note for his solicitor in the hotel safe alleging police harassment, says Brennan.

Williams didn't want to be arrested before selling the properties. His buyer was a Venezuelan colonel, whom the local army had identified from a surveillance video. The sale did go through and Williams and Brennan returned to London on the same flight. £60,000 had already been transferred to Brennan's NatWest account from the Banco Venezolano de Credito. Williams also smuggled a Lloyds bank draft for £29,000 through Customs by tucking it into the turn-ups of a pair of trousers in his suitcase.

Over the next few days, further money came into Brennan's account from Venezuela. He later told the police that Williams used some of it to pay off his debts, including to the Adams crime family. Brennan even accompanied Williams to their bar, Belugas, in Swiss Cottage.

But the informant was not being straight with Charman about why he was grassing on such a dangerous and violent enforcer like Williams and his associates.

Brennan had recently gone into the mobile phone business, setting up a company, Dial Communications, which operated from a rented shop in Bexley High Street. He became an authorised dealer for Vodafone's early incarnation as Talklands. When Williams turned to Brennan in the spring of 1993 because of his cash-flow problems, the pair had not done business for ten years. Williams was suggesting investing money from the Margarita apartment sale in a new phone shop Brennan was thinking of opening in nearby Eltham.

Brennan didn't want Williams muscling into his new business. He shared his family's hatred for the man and the way he treated Debbie. So they conspired to get rid of Williams once and for all.

"I was in there at the beginning to get rid of Ted . . . My first meeting with Mick [Charman] was regarding Margarita and the main aim of it was to have Ted nicked in possession of cocaine . . . we all really wanted to tie Williams up. That was the main aim, to get a fuck pig like that out of the way . . . He has been such a fuck cunt to my relations, and the way he's ruined this family. And it's always been me and my sister's intentions, if [a] possibility, to string Ted up if that could be done . . . legitimate information, not fitting him up."

But Geoff Brennan was playing an even more dangerous game that Charman also knew nothing about. While trying to get Williams arrested for drugs, Brennan was also using the enforcer to take advantage of a crooked business opportunity involving mobile phones that had mysteriously fallen into his lap.

The entrepreneurial nature of communist China is apparent in the state-owned companies set up abroad by each provincial government to trade in "commodities". The fantastically corrupt Guangxi Zhuang provincial government owned a company called GX Impex.[9] It had branches in the UK, Germany, Australia and Africa, and in April 1992 set itself up in Los Angeles.

In the summer of 1993 there was a worldwide shortage of a particular model of Motorola mobile phone. These were very popular with the Chinese community in LA and Hong Kong because they worked well with the communications system in the British colony.

GX Impex president Hu Yung Chuang thought he could shift 20,000 phones, a deal worth £13 million. He contacted two Chinese–Vietnamese brothers who'd become US citizens and settled in LA in 1980.

Tom and Sam Wang were an odd choice as suppliers because they mainly traded in luxury cars and spare parts. Nevertheless, like Hu, the Wang brothers also saw an opportunity to make money and approached a group of Texan car dealers in Houston to see if they could supply the large order.

James Sprouce and Vernon "Butch" Jones turned to the improbable sounding Billy Council Padon III, a fraudster who ran a company also in Houston called Delta Acceptance Corporation. A fourth Texan, Bill Padgett, who describes himself as a "self-employed investment banker and estate agent", was also brought into the deal.[10] This group of forty-something wheeler-dealers, to whom we shall refer as the Houston Four, assured the Wangs they could supply the phones. They couldn't. Calls were made across the US and UK and apparently in July 1993 Padgett alighted on Dial Communications, Brennan's new business.

After returning from Margarita, Brennan had accepted an invitation to Texas without telling his police handlers. Brennan believed the Houston Four were planning an advance fee fraud on the Wangs and wanted to use his banking facilities to execute it. They were unsuccessful in trying to open bank accounts in London and had been ejected from one bank that suspected they were trying to launder money.

Brennan played along with the Houston Four, giving them every indication the phone deal could be done, but it would have to be quick and the money up front. In the meantime, he discussed these strange happenings with Tall Ted Williams, who of course was blissfully unaware Brennan was also trying to get him arrested for drug trafficking.

Williams could spot easy money. He advised Brennan to invite the Houston Four to London with a £150,000 advance for the phones. Brennan would then introduce a lawyer friend of Williams who would pose as a Motorola representative. During the meeting Williams and another criminal known as "Nutty Brian" would burst into the hotel room and steal the money.

Brennan now saw the perfect opportunity to rip off the Americans with Williams' help and then get the enforcer arrested for drug trafficking before having to split any of the proceeds with him. But Brennan needed a further insurance policy, or each way bet, in case the devious plan didn't work out. So he contacted Charman in late August and told him about the Houston Four and the phone deal with the Wangs. However, he claimed it was Williams who was pressuring him to rip them off and that the money would be used to buy into 750 kilos of cocaine coming via Jamaica.

Charman passed the information to the Yard's Special Intelligence Section (SIS) and to Redgrave. Meanwhile, Brennan happily progressed the phone fraud behind their backs.

Sam Wang was uncomfortable with Jones and Padgett and had insisted on meeting Brennan in London when he learnt he was their supplier. On 24 August they all had dinner at the Thistle Hotel overlooking Tower Bridge and the badlands of Bermondsey, Brennan's old stomping ground.

For credibility, Brennan brought along serving south-east London detective constable Mark Norton and his new wife Debbie Norris. She was the woman who had cradled her dying husband David Norris, the prolific double agent informant, on the night he was murdered two years earlier. Brennan knew her from Bermondsey days and had met Norton when they came to his shop to buy a phone.

The dinner went well. Sam Wang believed Brennan was a "very handsome, serious businessman" with 3,000 Motorola phones in a bonded warehouse ready for onward transfer. He gave Brennan £11,000 in travellers cheques as an advance from GX Impex.

Weeks later, the balance of £402,300 was transferred into Brennan's NatWest account.[11] He couldn't believe how fast it had arrived, well before he had time to set up an untraceable account. The situation wasn't ideal but Brennan thought he could handle it.

Sam Wang had left London for LA via Houston, where Padgett and Jones persuaded him to set up new companies in the British Virgin Islands (BVI) and offshore accounts with the Bank of Bermuda. They would later claim these accounts were set up to deposit commissions from future phone deals with the Guangxi provincial government.[12]

Brennan was keeping Charman informed only of the barest details of his phone deal. For instance, he told Charman about the BVI accounts and companies and claimed the Houston Four were suggesting millions of pounds was waiting to be transferred into his NatWest account.

Redgrave had Scotland Yard's undercover unit SO10 provide a covert account at the Midland Bank in London to test Brennan's hypothesis that this was a money laundering scam.[13]

Brennan then extended his insurance policy by telling Charman a large sum of money (the £402,000) had already come into his NatWest account from the Wangs but that he had returned it. This was a lie. Brennan had in fact withdrawn a huge sum in cash and bought a new house called Silverlands.

Redgrave had every reason at this stage to accept Brennan was acting as a genuine informant. He had recently set up a surveillance operation in Portugal after Brennan revealed that Williams was trying to develop an amphetamine factory there with a Briton called David Shaw. According to Brennan's information, the drugs factory had UK investors and a planned distribution network including the Adams crime family and associates in Liverpool, Scotland and Ireland.

GEOFF BRENNAN

Redgrave sent detective sergeant Paul Kelly to liaise with the Portuguese Policia Judicial. Initially there was a turf fight between SERCS and Customs, says Kelly, but eventually they agreed to work together.

Williams had asked Brennan to bring a technical manual for chemical equipment to Shaw's villa near Albufeira. Kelly photographed Williams and Shaw at the villa. The phone was tapped and a bug inserted on the terrace. All this information was being fed back through Charman to SIS and the National Criminal Intelligence Service, which looks at Britain's top 200 criminals.

There was nothing therefore to suggest Brennan was acting falsely. Ironically, it was the Wangs who first suspected something. Back in LA, they had quickly tired of Brennan's excuses that he couldn't send the phones until the Inland Revenue finished a routine inspection. Another lie.

Sam Wang returned to London under pressure from GX Impex to look for Brennan. He discovered the phone shop in Bexley was abandoned. They eventually met at the Forte Crest Hotel in Gatwick on 6 October. Brennan assured Wang that 1,000 phones were on a British Airways flight to Hong Kong and showed him an airway bill as proof. It wasn't. Williams had bought the official document for £8,000 and Brennan filled in a false forwarding agent. A satisfied Sam Wang left for Hong Kong expecting his phones to be there.

Brennan used the time to clear up loose ends. He vanished, leaving a string of creditors owed over £35,000. One of them sent debt collectors to his house, which resulted in Brennan's arrest for assault. Helpfully, his friend DC Mark Norton was serving at Bexleyheath police station and dealt with the case papers. Brennan was bailed to return in November.

Brennan didn't know what the Wangs would do about the theft. If they were as dodgy as he believed them to be, they wouldn't report it. But if they did, Brennan knew Redgrave would have him arrested. So he devised a plan to muddy the waters.

The first step was to get re-registered to his close friend detective sergeant Chris Smith, whom he'd known for 20 years and who had handled Brennan during the Brinks Mat inquiry. Smith is originally from New Zealand. Not that you would know. He has a broad "sarf" London accent having spent most of his service in that part of the capital, half of it on the Tower Bridge Flying Squad, where Charman was based.

In late October, Brennan met their boss, DCI Andy Cater. He told him he was unhappy with the way he was being handled but made no mention of corruption or unethical practice. However, by engineering this phoney conflict of interest, the experienced informant knew DCI Cater would have to agree to let Smith take him over, at least for a short while.[14] Brennan's plan was to play one handler off against another. He eventually returned to Charman by which time two conflicting sets of informant logs had been generated.

In the end, Brennan did miscalculate the Wangs. They had come under increasingly menacing pressure to repay the money to the Chinese provincial government. In late October, the Wangs made formal allegations to the FBI that they were victims of an advance fee fraud by Brennan working with Padgett, Jones and Padon.[15]

The Wangs also reported Brennan to the Met. Detectives from Bexleyheath police station couldn't locate him but did discover he was due to answer bail on 12 November over the assault case. They waited and arrested Brennan for the theft of £400,000. He immediately played his informant card and asked to speak to DS Chris Smith.

Redgrave was also alerted. He asked the detectives investigating the theft to postpone their inquiries because Brennan was part of an important ongoing operation. He suggested that a financial investigator attached to SERCS be allowed to take over the theft inquiry so it could be developed without disturbing the other strands of Operation Nightshade – the drugs surveillance in Portugal and the potential money laundering scam by the Houston Four.

Redgrave had an abrasive and cocky way about him as if his operation was the most important one in the Met. The ginger giant was an imposing figure at six foot five. And when his judgement was questioned, he'd scowl and push his glasses up the bridge of his nose with a stabbing middle finger before throwing a few fucks into whoever was pissing him off.

Detective Inspector Peter Newman and his team didn't take to Redgrave's approach. Newman wouldn't relinquish the case and he had support from the local CPS to progress his inquiries in the United States. A nasty turf war was developing between Redgrave and Newman that Brennan sought to exploit.

To derail DI Newman's inquiries into the theft, Brennan concocted a diversion and like an evil shaman summoned the ghost of David Norris. Newman had worked on the Norris murder inquiry in 1991 with Brennan's friend DC Mark Norton. Both officers were now at Bexleyheath police station but had fallen out over Norton's marriage to Debbie Norris. On 26 January 1994 Brennan told Charman there was a plot by relatives of Norris to discredit Newman by placing

£15,000 in his bank account. To add authenticity Brennan had somehow obtained the account number and sorting code.

Brennan confected this plot from the stench of corruption surrounding the Norris hit and bits of information he'd picked up listening to Debbie Norris and Norton talk about the murder investigation. She had told the murder inquiry that on the night he died Norris left the house with £15,000 in cash on his way to meet one of his police handlers. Brennan hatched a plan with these ingredients and fed it to Charman knowing Newman and his superiors would be immediately alerted. This would hopefully buy Brennan more time while he further disposed of the remainder of the £400,000.

The plan worked. At a quickly convened meeting in Catford between the management of SERCS and the Met's 3 Area the plot was discussed. Present were detective chief superintendent Bill Ilsley and detective superintendent Ian Crampton, who had a special interest as they were in charge of the Norris murder inquiry and the failed prosecution just eight months earlier. They took news of a plot seriously.[16] It came at a very sensitive time for both senior officers and Scotland Yard. The whitewash Barker Review of their handling of the Lawrence murder inquiry was being confected at that very moment.

Several actions came out of the Catford meeting in early February. Firstly, Redgrave and Smith were told to meet Brennan and get further details about the plot. Brennan subsequently told them it had been called off following his intervention! Secondly, the head of SERCS, commander Roy Penrose, resolved with Ilsley that the theft allegation against Brennan would be taken off DI Newman and given to a full-time fraud investigator from SERCS. Detective constable Kevin Maul was ordered to investigate Brennan, mindful of Redgrave's ongoing Operation Nightshade, but to report only to Penrose and another senior officer.

Brennan had successfully used David Norris's ghost to buy time. He knew that Maul's fraud investigation would have to tread carefully, especially when making inquiries about the Houston Four. Why? Because Padgett and Jones were also engaged in an illegal arms deal with undercover officers whom Brennan had helped introduce.

In late September 1993 Brennan had told Charman that while he was in Houston discussing the phone deal, Padgett asked if he could connect him with anyone in the UK interested in buying arms.

Redgrave decided to set up a third limb to Operation Nightshade. He was already looking at the Houston Four over suspected money laundering. But illegal arms dealing would need something special. Commanders Penrose and John Grieve at SO11 gave authority to deploy an undercover officer called Micky Barr, a weapons expert.

Redgrave kept Barr's identity and appearance from Brennan. He simply instructed the informant to tell Butch Jones to expect a visit from a man called "Peter" when he was next in London.

On 11 October over a drink at the Forte Crest Hotel near Gatwick Airport, Jones and a man called Walter Le from Hong Kong met "Peter". Police documents suggest they were under no doubt he was fronting for Irish paramilitaries.

Walter said: "I have offices in Hong Kong, mainland China, Vietnam and Cambodia. I have very good contacts with Chinese government at all levels and with the military. Let me just say some of my friends are generals in the army and they like to increase their salary by selling some equipment they hold in reserve."

Walter tried to reassure "Peter" these were not unreliable Soviet Bloc weapons. "I can supply anything from fighter aircraft, tanks through to blankets and tents but I think for the type of people I believe you represent, I can supply you unlimited amounts of heavy machine guns, anti-tank grenades, explosives, same as Semtex but manufactured in China, fuses, detonator cord and of course assault rifles."

"Peter" asked about End User Certificates, the official documents that prove the arms are going to a legitimate company or government. Walter again said reassuringly, "You are dealing with the government of China. Documentation will be arranged through me. Certain people will require payment." When Le told "Peter" he could inspect the weapons ahead of shipment in mainland China, the undercover officer feigned concern he would end up in a re-education camp. But Le said there was no need to worry, he had "very good friends at the highest levels of police and government".

Butch Jones also offered Peter "hi-tech weaponry" like a GEC Gatling gun. Ideal for wasting "half of Belfast", he said. Jones spoke of a "middle man" he would introduce who was well connected, including with the nephew of the deposed Iranian Shah.[17]

It soon transpired this middle man was a colourful entrepreneur called Roger Dale Crooks, born 3 September 1948. Little is known about his early years other than his home town is Houston. Yet, since 1988, Crooks has operated from the capital of Sierra Leone, Freetown, the deepest port in Africa, making it a transhipment point for drugs, diamonds, gold and guns.

Crooks' partner in Sierra Leone was an intriguing Houston oil baron called Oscar Wyatt. The so-called 'King of Crude' had built up an energy company, Coastal Inc, into one that owned 5% of liquid and gas pipelines in the US. Crooks met Wyatt through another famous Texan, the former state governor, John Connally, who was in the car when President Kennedy was assassinated.[18] After Connally left politics in 1980 he went into business with Crooks and took a seat on the board of Coastal.

Crooks and Wyatt had a joint venture in Sierra Leone to renovate an oil refinery in Freetown using Nigerian and Iranian crude. They later had a diamond mine and Wyatt also invested when Crooks took control of the Mama Yoko, the country's premier hotel. In the grounds he set up a diamond-cutting factory.[19]

Wyatt had personal and business relationships with Quaddafi of Libya and Saddam Hussein of Iraq. In fact, in 1990, soon after the Iraqi dictator invaded Kuwait, Wyatt and Connally travelled to Baghdad to successfully negotiate the release of 21 American citizens and one Briton whom Saddam was holding as human shields against the expected US counter-offensive.

Wyatt opposed the first Gulf War and was very critical of President Bush senior, whose family also controlled Texas. British readers however may only recall Wyatt through the tabloid antics of his stepson Steve, who the society pages had linked to the Duchess of York, Sarah Ferguson. The couple met during an official engagement in 1989 when Fergie attended a party thrown by Steve's socialite mother in Houston. A year later photographs found by a cleaner in his London flat raised the spectre of an affair and were said to have helped put the skids under Fergie's marriage to Prince Andrew.

Of course Wyatt was not aware of everything Roger Crooks did, legitimate or otherwise. And Scotland Yard never produced evidence that he was arms dealing with the oil baron's say-so. A retired Houston Customs officer who had worked on Crooks says he traded on his relationship with Wyatt.[20]

On 21 December, Crooks met "Peter" at the Britannia Hotel in London. Another undercover officer, Richard Hester, came along wearing a body wire. Hester and Barr often worked together on arms stings and had established a long-term front company and reputation as international arms dealers. Hester was a founding father of the undercover unit and entirely believable as the financier "Richard Meades". His performance was polished and measured, whereas Barr was naturally more of a wide boy with his ponytail, estuary accent, jewellery and handlebar moustache.

UNTOUCHABLES

Police documents of the meeting suggest Crooks was told he was dealing with representatives of the Ulster Defence Association, a Loyalist paramilitary group. "Roger seemed happy to deal," Hester recorded. "[He] said he had no problems selling weapons to our organisation but he could only get it out of the USA to, say, Nigeria, Sierra Leone. However he could put us in contact with the right people who would facilitate its onward shipment to the UK by containers . . . He suggested he might be able to have everything ready by February . . . as he was going to book a ship for then as he was building an oil rig and would be shipping to Nigeria at about that time.

"We gave Roger a list of weapons, ammunition, explosives . . . He went through [it] and said he didn't have a problem supplying us. Roger again said he would not have a problem getting it from Sierra Leone as he had all the right contacts, in fact he even had a diplomatic passport for that country."[21]

Crooks told us the passport was issued by the Momo government in 1991 to allow him to represent it in Iran where he was negotiating the supply of oil for the refinery he and Wyatt were renovating.

Freetown in the nineties was a lot like the Casablanca of Michael Curtis's eponymous 1941 film. Crooks however was no Rick, but the Mama Yoko was like the Café Americain, a den of fraudsters, corrupt government officials, diamond smugglers, gun-runners, spies and mercenaries protecting the multinationals who had carved up the incredible mineral wealth of this former British colony.

On 5 May 1994, Redgrave travelled to Houston to brief US Customs about the arms deal involving Crooks. He had decided against Walter Le's Chinese military option because of anticipated jurisdiction and co-operation problems.

Customs advised that the Yard's two undercover officers should push Crooks for American weapons to make a prosecution in the US feasible. He had already mentioned a Californian weapons supplier called Condor. Customs also provided another undercover officer to handle the arms sting from Houston. Senior US Customs special agent Nigel Brooks had a fascinating past. He was British-born but went to live in the US in the mid-sixties aged eighteen. He served a five-year tour in Vietnam and then joined Customs, where he spent most of his time undercover infiltrating drug traffickers.

A preliminary background check by US Customs revealed Crooks had a criminal record for forgery and theft.[22] When Crooks had been recently stopped at Houston Airport on his way back from London, he was found to be carrying $14,000 in cash and some diamonds. Police reports suggest he tried to deal his way out of trouble by offering to become an informant for various agencies on the arms deal. In effect, Crooks was another Brennan! "We felt he was attempting to create an alibi should the arms deal be discovered. We decided to proceed with [the joint] investigation with DI Redgrave . . . [and] play [Crooks] along to see exactly what he would report," recalls Brooks.[23]

On 9 May Customs set up a covert account in a Houston bank and deposited $700,000. Brooks gave Crooks the PIN number to verify his terrorist clients were serious. Crooks, now satisfied, wanted to transfer the money straight away into an escrow account he controlled. Brooks declined. Cash on delivery or no deal, he replied.

The arms deal was progressing well. Crooks and Padgett had the fake end user certificate and encouraged the undercover officers to set up a bogus company in Sierra Leone. The arms would be transported to Freetown, but first "Peter" was assured he could inspect the container in Houston. That was when US Customs were planning to make the arrests for violations of the Arms Export Control Act. After consulting with the senior government lawyer in Texas they felt there was a very good case against the targets.[24]

In early March 1994, while the arms deal was progressing, DC Kevin Maul began examining the £400,000 theft as agreed at the Catford meeting.

Tom Wang had been in London for three months by then. He'd fled Los Angeles because representatives of the Chinese provincial government and people from Hong Kong were looking to beat him up. Back in LA his brother had been attacked over Christmas and New Year. Sam Wang's house was broken into and his two-year-old daughter assaulted. A car had also been driven at him on the motorway.

While hiding out in London, Tom Wang tried to find Brennan but ended up sending this message to his abandoned home: "PLEASE HELP US BY SENDING THE MONEY BACK TO OUR CUSTOMERS. YOU MAY SAVE SOME LIVES, WHICH MAY INCLUDE THOSE OF YOUR FAMILY. WE DON'T WANT TO SEE TERRIBLE THINGS HAPPENED . . . WE KNOW THERE ARE SOME PEOPLE ALREADY HERE IN UK TRYING TO FIND YOU."

DC Maul interviewed Brennan's bank manager and other key witnesses in the money trail. He then wrote to commander Penrose in late April stating there was a good prima facie case that Brennan had stolen the £400,000 and "disappeared". At this stage Maul didn't know about the purchase of Silverlands, which Brennan had disguised by putting it in his son's name. Nevertheless, the informant believed rightly that Maul's fraud net was closing in. He also had Ted Williams after him for his cut of the stolen money.

Out of the blue Brennan's identity as an informant was deliberately disclosed to Williams. Who by remains unclear, although crooked cops working with or independently of Brennan is a strong possibility.

A lot of detail surrounding the compromise is still very opaque. Over 12 days in June 1994 the actions of senior Ghost Squad officers ensured the truth was obscured even further and took Scotland Yard down a road that it could not turn back from without admitting wanton unlawfulness and staggering incompetence.

Geoff and Denise Brennan claim she was ordered to go to Williams' house in West Kingsdown where she saw Operation Nightshade documents about the covert efforts in Portugal and Venezuela. Only the informant's pseudonym, "John Millwall", was used in the confidential police documents. But Williams didn't accept Fleming had grassed him up and was easily able to identify Geoff's handiwork.

Denise took three days to alert her brother that Williams was going to kill him. Geoff Brennan was in the Isle of Wight with his wife and in-laws at the time. He phoned DS Chris Smith, who in turn phoned detective chief superintendent Bill Griffiths, a manager of the Flying Squad who was also in the Ghost Squad management group. The following day Smith was introduced to detective chief superintendent Roger Gaspar, the operational head of the Ghost Squad. Only a few weeks earlier Gaspar had given commissioner Condon a major briefing about the projected work of the secret anti-corruption squad he was in the process of setting up.

Gaspar met Smith and arranged a secret assignation in Hyde Park with Brennan later that afternoon. Appropriately they met by the Serpentine. The discussion lasted 30 minutes but strangely was not covertly recorded. Gaspar took the threat seriously because Brennan was given armed protection when he returned home that afternoon. He was also told he would be put, along with his wife and 19-year-old son, in a witness protection scheme with a new identity.

Two days later, on 16 June, Gaspar and Brennan met again in the conference room at the Hilton Hotel near Gatwick. DS Smith had ensured Denise was there as well. She had also been his informant during the Brinks Mat investigation. Again, the meeting wasn't recorded.

GEOFF BRENNAN

Brennan was still unwilling to make a statement, be interviewed under caution or be a witness. But something dramatic happened over the next five days to radically change his mind. Again all these contacts between Brennan, Smith and the Ghost Squad were also unrecorded.

On 21 June, Brennan made the first of two taped interviews with Gaspar. He confessed to the premeditated theft of £400,000 from the Wangs. The Houston Four, he explained, were going to rip them off so he did it first. Brennan said he planned to use Williams as a "minder", but when the enforcer talked of using violence, even murder, he decided to double-cross him. "It was a big scam all the way through."

That part was true. But Brennan then fed Gaspar a load of well-rehearsed lies about Redgrave and Charman. He claimed that part of the double-cross was to involve the two detectives in the theft instead of Williams. He claimed he had bunged them £50,000 to turn a blind eye and frustrate any inquiries. Redgrave got greedy and wanted more money, claimed Brennan. This caused a rift in the relationship. When he realised they were not protecting him as an informant, he turned to DS Chris Smith, his old handler.

What could account for Brennan's dramatic change of heart and willingness to be taped by Gaspar? The informant, and later his defence team, maintain with considerable justification that the Ghost Squad offered an incredible deal, which no criminal with half a brain would have turned down. The conditions were so favourable Brennan practically bit Gaspar's hand off. He was effectively offered secret immunity from prosecution for serious criminal offences in return for becoming the Ghost Squad's first supergrass. His friend and handler DS Chris Smith helped broker the deal.

Brennan agreed to admit and explain the theft on tape but only if he was not cautioned and arrested. He also agreed to talk on tape about corrupt activities with Redgrave and Charman, but again on the understanding he would never give evidence against them or make a statement. He calculated that by the time the Ghost Squad realised he was lying about the police corruption aspect it would be too late to prosecute him for the fraud.

Brennan was not legally represented throughout these secret negotiations and therefore no deal was ever written down. Nevertheless, the informant couldn't believe it when Smith told him the Ghost Squad had agreed to his conditions. It was a liar's charter.

The deal was also unlawful, which is presumably why the Ghost

Squad management hid it from the CPS and why all dealings with Brennan leading up to his taped admission were not properly documented.[25]

Supergrasses had fallen into disrepute in the seventies and eighties precisely because of the unethical way they were handled by the police in criminal trials and during the political prosecutions of alleged IRA members in Northern Ireland. Many trials collapsed or the convictions were subsequently overturned on appeal as details of inducements and secret deals emerged.

The Court of Appeal had poured so much judicial scorn on the supergrass system after the case of armed robber Derek "Bertie" Smalls in 1975 that the police were forced to abandon the policy. A senior judge determined that undertakings of immunity from prosecution should be given very sparingly and only then by the most senior government lawyer, never in secret and never by the police.

A decade later, the 1984 Police & Criminal Evidence Act made such secret deals unworkable. And in 1992 the Home Office issued new guidelines for dealing with "resident informants" (the new police term for supergrasses). The Courts' wishes could not have been clearer on how to preserve the integrity of supergrass evidence. In layman's terms the rule is if you really must use a supergrass there should be transparency during the crucial debriefing process. Tape-record everything, log every contact no matter how small, show no favouritism, apply no pressure and offer no deals. Instead of immunity, criminals wishing to "roll over" would be sentenced for their own admitted crimes before or soon after giving evidence against others.

Detectives fighting organised crime in the nineties, including those at Scotland Yard, had taken heed of judges' displeasure toward supergrass evidence and started using undercover officers instead. Their credibility and evidence was far less assailable in the courtroom and they were easier to protect from smart defence barristers. Very importantly, the chances of a successful conviction were also higher.

Yet here were senior officers deciding in secret and with no recourse to the CPS or the new guidelines that they were going to rehabilitate the old supergrass system and act like a star chamber above the law.

Before Gaspar interviewed Brennan on 21 June the Ghost Squad management was fully aware that the informant would be admitting at least four serious criminal offences of theft, fraud, conspiring to pervert the course of justice and corruption. However, Gaspar later explained that a secret "strategic decision" was taken in advance not to caution Brennan or treat him as a suspect but rather to use him as a "source of information".[26] The failure to caution and arrest someone who admits serious criminal acts is a severe disciplinary transgression.

Brennan knew that protection from Williams also meant protection from prosecution. So during his disingenuous taped interview with Gaspar he laid on the threat to his life with a spade. Williams, he said, would have no choice but to kill him to save face with his East End criminal associates for letting someone get so close. "I've seen the damage that man can inflict. He's a very, very fucking violent man. You know you are not talking about a mug here, you're talking about a proper named man that enforces what he says. And his business is drugs. It's always been drugs."

Suddenly, and with no evidence, the Ghost Squad was claiming internally that Redgrave was the source of the leak. The whole matter could have been cleared up immediately had the Ghost Squad moved to recover the documents from Williams and question him. That they did not is a serious failing, which again remains unexplained.

After all, in June 1994 the arms side of Operation Nightshade was still live and undercover officers were about to meet Crooks in London later that month. They could have been walking into a trap. Gaspar had no way of knowing how far Williams had disseminated the documents. The only way to be sure was to immediately raid his home and at the very least retrieve the documents. Williams could also have been arrested and questioned.

The Yard has never managed to recover these documents, but we did. The bundle leaked to Tall Ted Williams contained sensitive NCIS and SERCS reports (mainly by DS Paul Kelly) concerning the surveillance operations in Portugal and Venezuela. In addition there was secret information about phone-taps in the UK and abroad and the names of those detectives targeting Williams and Fleming. The latest report was dated 14 March 1994, which means Williams was given the bundle some time between then and early June.

Williams told us the documents came from a "bent copper". But he said it was "definitely not" Redgrave and he had told Denise this at the time. "I'm not afraid of coppers but Redgrave is a straightgoer." Williams was slightly miffed that anyone would think a career criminal of his stature would deal with a lowly detective inspector. "I get my information from commanders," he said.

In July 1994, the Brennan family officially became the Newmans. The Ghost Squad provided them with new National Insurance cards, driving licences and passports. Brennan says he chose the name Newman after the Bexleyheath detective inspector whom he had months earlier tried to discredit with a false corruption allegation to frustrate the fraud investigation.

Various options were discussed to explain Brennan's disappearance. One was to arrange a fake car crash in Spain. Another was emigration to Australia. Eventually it was agreed that Scotland Yard would buy Silverlands and with that money Brennan could purchase a new house in a safe location under his new identity.

The offer was remarkable, even by the Ghost Squad's standards, and Brennan knew it. Privately he couldn't believe his luck. If ever there was an indication he had been given immunity this was it. On top of not being prosecuted, he was also going to keep the proceeds of the fraud and now the Yard would help him launder some of it by purchasing the house he had bought with almost half the money stolen from the Wangs. All he had to do was keep on insisting Redgrave and Charman were corrupt.

When Brennan confessed to the theft he had lied extensively about the dispersal of the £400,000 proceeds and failed to tell Gaspar that he had bought Silverlands eight months earlier. Instead, Brennan claimed he had given £133,000 to Williams, £40,000 to the Houston Four and of course £50,000 to Redgrave and Charman.

The figures just didn't add up and had the Ghost Squad done a proper financial investigation of their supergrass they would have discovered this, which in turn would have seriously undermined his credibility at an early stage. The simple facts were that Brennan withdrew £250,000 of the £403,000 in his NatWest account 48 hours after it arrived from the Wangs and GX Impex in mid-September 1993. He went to his regular solicitors the Marston Partnership with £178,351 in cash and bought Silverlands. The house purchase was completed on 11 October. To protect the investment in case he was arrested, Brennan put the property in his son's name.

In July 1994, the Ghost Squad asked Scotland Yard's receivers to instruct London law firm Winkworth Pemberton & Co to purchase Silverlands for £169,500. This money was deposited in an Alliance & Leicester account, which the Ghost Squad had set up under Brennan's new identity. Gaspar also personally handed over £14,000 in cash to Brennan as compensation for damage to the furniture during the removal and for storage costs.

Having laundered the money with police help, Brennan bought a new home in Maidstone, called Roscott House. This one he purchased with his wife under their new identities. But the family grew weary of this property and four months later told Gaspar they wanted to sell. Winkworth Pemberton bought Roscott House for £143,500 on 14 December 1994 and transferred the money to another joint account Brennan held at the TSB in Ashford as Mr and Mrs Newman.

This was now the second time the Ghost Squad had laundered the money. But the police farce didn't end there. The Brennans no longer wanted to live so far away from their traditional stomping ground of Bexleyheath. So they arranged to move back to the very area where they were supposedly vulnerable to reprisals from Tall Ted Williams. In February 1995 the Ghost Squad watched Brennan buy 39 Braebourne Crescent in Bexleyheath with £108,000 of the funds they had knowingly laundered for him. This should have immediately raised serious questions that maybe the threat from Williams had been a "get up" by the Brennans. Denise and her family had also been re-housed. Like her brother and parents, she too eventually moved back to the same area from which the so-called threat came.

Brennan is very tight-lipped about how the threat on his life suddenly evaporated. Denise says implausibly she moved back to West Kingsdown because her daughter didn't like Maidstone.

The suspicion is that behind the back of the Ghost Squad Brennan made reparations to Williams by paying him some of the money he stole. Debbie, Williams' common-law wife, is also believed to have helped negotiate the truce so that her mother, Denise, could return.

As a result of Brennan's double-dealing antics the surveillance operation in Portugal against Williams folded with no arrests.[27] Roger Crooks, Butch Jones and Bill Padgett also evaded prosecution for arms dealing. In fact, Crooks managed to extricate himself from the arms sting in equally strange circumstances. The FBI tipped him off on the same day Brennan turned supergrass.

Over the years, as an American businessman working in Africa, Crooks had had a lot of dealings with the Feds and with the CIA. On this occasion, he says the FBI gave him a telephone number to ring at Scotland Yard. He spoke to a police officer and explained roughly that he was involved in an arms deal with Irish terrorists. Two detectives from the Yard's anti-terrorist branch SO13 came immediately to interview him at his hotel in Gatwick. He was about to fly to Sierra Leone. They retrieved a number of exhibits, including the arms list and returned to the Yard thinking they had a "coup", says undercover cop Richard Hester. There followed a high level meeting between the

SO13 boss, MI5 and Special Branch. "It was [the SO13 boss] I think who said, 'Those aren't Irish terrorists, that's Hester and Barr,' and everyone was suitably embarrassed."

US Customs felt Crooks had built himself enough of an insurance policy by contacting various US law enforcement agencies to run a successful entrapment defence. They felt in the end he was trying to get his hands on the $700,000 flash money without supplying any arms. "I beg to differ," Crooks told us. "I kept the FBI fully informed. It was never my intent to supply any kind of arms."

Crooks returned to Sierra Leone, where we shall catch up with him. US Customs asked SERCS to continue targeting Bill Padgett. But this too came to nothing.[28]

By August 1994, the light on Operation Nightshade was finally put out. A secret corruption probe into detectives John Redgrave and Michael Charman had usurped it. Operation Wrabness ran for the next 27 months.

In November 1994, Gaspar began a secret financial investigation of them and their two wives. Bank and building society accounts were examined and the wages of all four plotted against spending patterns. The secret probe concluded that Redgrave had an unexplained substantial increase in wealth and that Charman was making fewer withdrawals from the cash point.

The Ghost Squad had taken "a strategic rather than a tactical decision" not to arrest and question the two detectives.[29] Had they, says Redgrave, he would have explained the following.

John William Redgrave was born in November 1953 in London's East End. At five his parents moved to a grotty council estate in Deptford, south-east London. His father had astutely worked his way up in the City "from a slum to a stockbroker". But the marriage was an unhappy one and Redgrave's mother tried to run off with a man she'd met while working in a local pub.

"My father took her back because the bloke she tried to run off with didn't wanna know. She was willing to leave me, my brother and baby sister. She couldn't cope and was in and out of hospital. She'd tried to kill herself with a drug overdose and for a while we were farmed out to various aunts and uncles," he recalls with obvious melancholy and embarrassment. "My father detested the closed society of Freemasonry designed to advance the few by who they knew and not by what they do. He instilled that in me. When he eventually left my mother, he gave her everything. I've had nothing to do with her since then."

GEOFF BRENNAN

Redgrave joined the Met as a 17-year-old cadet in 1970 looking for a surrogate family and a sense of honour. It was the birth of his children in the early eighties which pushed him to reunite with his father. Their relationship became very close right up to his death from cancer two weeks before Brennan stole the Wangs' money.

The estate was sizeable. But Redgrave says that in the months leading up to his father's slow death they made a private arrangement, which has since caused him enormous problems. He received substantial funds that his father didn't want the rest of his family to know about. This included Redgrave's wife. His marriage was very strained by then because of his workload and the macho, heavy-drinking, womanising culture that went with it. "I remember seeing my young son's diary with repeated entries, 'Dad at work. Didn't see him today.'"

Redgrave accepts he handled his finances badly. But he was never given an opportunity to account for the extra money because the operation against him was covert.

The Ghost Squad however did have an opportunity to corroborate Brennan's allegations without alerting the two detectives. The supergrass, after all, was in their witness protection scheme. Yet not once during Operation Wrabness was Brennan asked to provide precise details of when and how he had made the alleged corrupt payments totalling £50,000. Similarly, no financial investigation was carried out into Brennan's accounts. Had the Ghost Squad done so, they would have discovered what Brennan really did with the stolen money – the cash purchase of Silverlands and a savings account where he had deposited the remaining £200,000.

Another extraordinary Ghost Squad failure was the decision not to send Brennan back into Redgrave and Charman wearing a hidden microphone to get some, any, corroboration of his corruption allegations.

What could explain this and all the other oversights? By his own admission Gaspar believed Brennan was "a dishonest man only focused on his own self-interest". So why did he not seek to record and corroborate every syllable?

It looked suspiciously like Brennan's value to the Ghost Squad was as a trophy supergrass. His mere existence helped justify their highly politicised anti-corruption campaign within the Yard and within certain corridors of the Home Office. Brennan's allegations were just too good to check, says Redgrave.

It was not as if Operation Wrabness was corroborating Brennan's claims by other means. For example, the Ghost Squad had secretly tapped more than 1,500 of Redgrave's conversations in over two years. During this time he had moved from SERCS to Belgravia police station with plenty of opportunity to act corruptly. According to senior CIB sources, Redgrave's office at Belgravia had a probe in it, and his work phone and pager were also monitored. But the Yard now admit that none of the secretly recorded material gathered over two years supported any of the allegations Brennan had made against either detective. Nor have they resulted in any other charges.

Perhaps the most bizarre aspect of Operation Wrabness came in June 1996, when Redgrave, still secretly under investigation, was told that commissioner Condon was honouring him with a long service and good conduct medal after twenty-five years. He brought his two children and wife to the ceremony. "It was one of the proudest moments of my life," says Redgrave, as the photograph of him shaking Condon's hand showed. "Although I was under investigation since 13 June 1994 I continued to be involved in high-profile, proactive operations against drug dealers involving orthodox and covert infiltration methods authorised at the highest level. How can any professional organisation allow me to conduct this type of work and honour me whilst being secretly investigated for the most serious of offences?" he asks.

Did the commissioner know about Operation Wrabness? And if not, then why did his Ghost Squad intelligence chiefs make such a fool out of their boss?

While Brennan was in the witness protection scheme, the Ghost Squad management group made DS Chris Smith the minder of their premier supergrass. Part of his duties was to help resettle Brennan into his new life as Mr Newman. Their relationship became so close that both men and their wives socialised together. Smith also lobbied Gaspar when Brennan wanted to sell his two homes and move back to Bexleyheath. He did police computer checks on neighbours to ensure there was no one who posed a threat and he introduced Brennan to a lot of his serving and retired friends in the police.

Smith would later claim that when Gaspar failed to find Brennan work, he stepped in with jobs for the supergrass. Private investigation work was a natural progression for an ex-repo man like Brennan. It was also a clever choice because the shadowy world of private eyes is dominated by retired police officers with close links to their serving colleagues, and therefore an opportunity for Brennan to keep his ear to the ground and make new contacts.

Smith had almost served his full 30 years and decided he would moonlight with Brennan on various private surveillance jobs. One company they worked for was Hazlebury, run by a former detective in the Yard's bugging unit.[30] Internal police documents show that between 1995 and 1996 Smith used Brennan as a "cut out" to receive payments in cash and cheques totalling £10,000 for this moonlighting work. Throughout this period, Smith was in regular contact with Clark, Gaspar and Griffiths. How much they knew about this highly suspect arrangement has never been clarified.

In early 1996, the Ghost Squad was busy with another thorny problem that threatened to unravel the whole deal they'd secretly forged with Brennan during those 12 days in June 1994.

On 16 February 1996, Gaspar met Brennan at City Airport. The supergrass was looking for reassurance that he wouldn't be prosecuted. Once again Gaspar failed to caution him after he admitted the theft for the second time. Exactly two months later, at a secret meeting in a Hammersmith hotel, the Ghost Squad management group decided their supergrass would not be prosecuted.

The Chinese government, however, had other ideas. Since May it had been applying diplomatic pressure on the British government. The Wangs had also recently launched a civil claim in the British courts against Brennan to recover the money. They had tired of Maul's fraud investigation, which was going nowhere for reasons that will soon become apparent.

The Ghost Squad knew the whole rotten and unlawful supergrass deal would be hopelessly exposed in the civil courts if they didn't act quickly to take control. It was decided they had to unpick the deal and prosecute Brennan for the theft. The CPS was not even consulted.

This action would undoubtedly incur Brennan's wrath so the Ghost Squad made a last ditch attempt to get him to make a witness statement against Redgrave and Charman.

On 5 November 1996 detective superintendent Dave Bailey arrived by prior arrangement at Brennan's house unaware that the supergrass was taping the meeting. He told Brennan he would be arrested and charged the following day for the theft. Brennan protested. He said they had known he stole the money for almost three years and did nothing, so why now?

Bailey explained it was "the Chinese". He told Brennan his legal defence to the theft "must be centred around corrupt policemen. This

UNTOUCHABLES

Redgrave has got to be arrested . . . These aren't human beings, Redgrave and Charman, they're just things that exist, that's all they are . . .". But the supergrass could see the writing on the wall. He wasn't going to add perjury to theft and fraud by falsely incriminating the two detectives. "I'm going down the pan. I'm dead, I'm fucking dead, and I'm going down fighting," he told Bailey.

After Bailey left, Brennan called Smith to see if anything could be done. It couldn't. The next day he arrived at Reigate police station with his lawyer. DC Kevin Maul was eagerly waiting to interview the man he had been chasing for 31 months. Out of the blue Maul had been told two days earlier that Brennan would be resurfacing.

The interview started at 3.50 p.m. Maul immediately cautioned Brennan and after going through the offence charged him with theft. Brennan responded with a prepared statement that sent Maul into a spin. He told the detective he was a protected witness who had not disappeared in June 1994, but had all this time been helping the Ghost Squad with a corruption inquiry into Redgrave and Charman.

Maul was seething with anger when Brennan revealed further details about the re-housing, the new identity and the bank accounts. It now dawned on him how systematically senior officers had misled his fraud inquiry. The Ghost Squad had allowed Maul in July 1994 to travel halfway around the world at taxpayers' expense, to Los Angeles and Houston, investigating a man they had all along secretly re-housed a mere 30 miles from Scotland Yard. While he was in the US, Maul had been unexpectedly transferred to a new posting, which meant the fraud inquiry "took a back seat" for the next two years, he told us.

From the items Maul seized at Brennan's home he was now able to carry out a full financial investigation of the supergrass. What he discovered appalled him even further. The Ghost Squad, he subsequently wrote, had "laundered" £170,000 of the proceeds of crime through the two houses bought from Brennan. These were later resold at a loss to the taxpayer of £36,937.18, during a property boom! Maul was also able to identify over £200,000 – the remainder of the theft – that Brennan had secreted in a Flexible Savings Account. As Brennan was penniless when he stole the Wangs' money, by accounting for the £400,000 Maul had proved Brennan was lying about the corrupt bribe to Redgrave and Charman.

Now that he had been charged, double agent supergrass Geoff Brennan had nothing to lose by speaking out about his arrangement with the Ghost Squad and DS Chris Smith, who'd retired in September 1996, a few weeks earlier.

Brennan turned up uninvited at Charman's home on 20 November. The off-duty detective was alarmed to see him, not least because he hadn't given Brennan his home address. There had been no contact between the pair for almost three years. As ever, Brennan's plan was self-preservation. He hoped to disrupt the fraud prosecution by tipping off Redgrave and Charman who had been the subjects of a corruption probe since June 1994.

Charman immediately contacted his superiors and Redgrave. Over the next few weeks leading up to Christmas, the two detectives wrote several detailed reports to DCS Roy Clark and others in the Yard hierarchy, unaware they were behind it all.

Redgrave and Charman didn't trust Brennan and merely repeated his claims and sought clarification. Their reports referred to the Bailey tape, and additional taped phone calls between Charman and Brennan in which the informant alleged he and his sister Denise had been prompted by Smith and other Ghost Squad officers to incriminate them. The reports also referred to Smith's moonlighting.

In a covering letter dated 9 December 1996 Redgrave demanded the whole matter be investigated. "Whatever the merits of the case against [Brennan] the content of the [Bailey] transcript must inevitably damage any likelihood of a successful prosecution of him. The conduct is tantamount to perverting the course of justice and forms the basis of a serious criminal libel against DC Charman and myself. In essence [Brennan] is induced to plead guilty in advance of proceedings against him, commit perjury and fabricate evidence against myself."

The Bailey debacle was almost identical to an incident in 1981 when the Director of Public Prosecutions had to withdraw a case against six armed robbers after one of them secretly recorded a police visit to his cell offering a deal in return for evidence against allegedly bent cops.[31] The parallels would not have been lost on a seasoned detective like Roy Clark, especially as Redgrave had indicated that his lawyer would shortly be taking a statement from Brennan as part of a legal action against Bailey.

Redgrave left nothing to chance and distributed his report to the undercover officers in Operation Nightshade. He also ensured the covert material they had gathered was kept in a secure police storeroom to prevent this crucial evidence going "missing".

Meanwhile, Smith had been complaining to DCS Clark about

Brennan, who he said was bad-mouthing him to all his contacts in the private detective world and threatening to expose Gaspar and Bailey. "Clark basically said to me this geezer [Brennan] is looking to do everyone and make trouble for everybody, do not worry about it . . . The last thing he said was, 'Chris, I want you to do one thing for me. I want you to get hold of him and tell him he either pleads guilty, if he's guilty [or] he comes forward with his solicitor as soon as possible and tells his side of it. We'll put it before the CPS and if what he says is true [the case will] get withdrawn.'"[32]

Smith and Brennan met for the last time at the Little Chef in Orpington. It was late December 1996. This is how Smith recalled the conversation.

Smith: "The Metropolitan Police have like spent fucking fortunes on you and done everything for you, why don't you just come through [and give evidence against Redgrave and Charman] if you're telling the truth?"

Brennan: "Everyone's going to suffer."

Brennan's version differs slightly. He agrees Smith made him an offer on Clark's behalf. But he says the Ghost Squad boss wanted him to return the stolen money, which he refused to do.

By the time the Little Chef meeting took place, Roy Clark had just assumed "full and lone responsibility for the [anti-corruption] strategy and investigations", reporting only to the deputy commissioner. He was setting up a new anti-corruption squad, CIB3, the Untouchables, to be publicly launched in late 1997. This was supposed to be a seamless transition in which the existence (and failures) of the Ghost Squad years would be kept secret. Brennan, however, was making this very difficult. He was a Catherine wheel going off in all directions.

Clark refuses to answer questions about his handling of Brennan. The secret approach Smith says he authorised raises serious questions. Under PACE, once someone is charged the police cannot try to interview them about the offence unless in controlled circumstances. This usually means in a police station, on tape and with their lawyer present. These safeguards are there to prevent any corrupt deals or inducements being offered to the defendant. Smith's approach effectively repeated the impropriety of Bailey's earlier visit to Brennan just before he was charged. Furthermore, the choice of Smith as the emissary was wholly inappropriate because by this stage Clark should have known that he was no longer a detective but a suspect alleged to be involved in a corrupt relationship with Brennan.

"The approaches to Brennan by Bailey and then Smith were

authorised at the highest level for morally bankrupt and operationally partial reasons," says Redgrave. "It goes to show the lengths certain people in the Yard were prepared to go to protect themselves and Chris Smith. The Ghost Squad had to be proved right and all its mistakes covered up."

Redgrave and Charman were immediately suspended and would remain so for an incredible seven years.

12

HECTOR THE SELECTA' – RUDE BOY SUPERGRASS

When armed robber Hector Byron Harvey turned supergrass in 1995, Scotland Yard launched its widest internal corruption probe costing tens of millions of pounds. It ended eight years later in wretched failure.

This should have been the finest hour of the Yard's anti-corruption squad, a bright, shining example of how the police can effectively investigate one of its most elite units, the Flying Squad. Instead it is a story of how another of the most manipulative and ruthless young supergrasses in recent police history ran rings around the anti-corruption squad in ever more humiliating ways.

The gallery of red faces extends from the commissioner's office through the Directorate of Criminal Intelligence to the Witness Protection Unit. Some of the officers responsible are still in senior positions at Scotland Yard; others are running new "independent" police watchdogs here and in Northern Ireland, or they are teaching anti-corruption techniques to international police forces.

The Hector Harvey story is a cautionary tale that echoes the mishandling of Geoffrey Brennan. Similarly, it unfolds over several chapters. Harvey's story is a further warning about the dangers of supergrass-led prosecutions driven by a politicised anti-corruption squad which thought it was wagging its own tail.

The key atop a corned-beef tin was the tool that set 15-year-old Harvey on a road to crime. He used it in 1979 to steal an Austin 1100, earning him his first conviction. Harvey learned to drive stolen cars in the garages underneath the estate near Shepherd's Bush in west London where he grew up. Eventually he graduated to the Corsair, cool enough, Harvey thought, to pick up his girlfriend outside school, but hot enough to still insist she wore gloves inside.

Harvey was born in Jamaica in 1964. He came to London with his parents in the early seventies when he was eight. Family problems forced him to run away at twelve. The next three years were spent in care homes, approved boarding schools and hostels. At sixteen Harvey was living in his own flat and had fathered his first child, a son.

He drifted into a life of casual and then professional crime. At the time of his first conviction he was just weeks from joining the police. He would have made a very good detective, if he could have stayed straight. Throughout his career, Harvey got on well with the white criminals with whom he robbed and the white police handlers to whom he grassed. He preferred to work with white robbers because he felt they were more professional and reliable. Some of his former black associates, he says, needed a few shots of rum or a long drag on a spliff before going on a job.

Harvey's no choc ice – white on the inside. It's more that detail and precision are very important to him. He doesn't drink or smoke, and prided himself as a career criminal on not getting chased off a robbery. In truth, Double H fancies himself in the role of the black outsider who plays the white system from within and wins.

He is good looking, physically impressive, disarming and flirtatious, but behind this silkiness is a ruthless manipulation of anyone who can advance his cause. Imagine an intellectual e-fit of John Shaft, Virgil Tibbs and Thomas Crown.

It wasn't long before Harvey graduated through various detention centres to mainstream prison after a conviction in 1985 for kidnapping and possession of a pump-action shotgun. "I got all of my qualifications in detention centres," he says. "I was good at English, okay at Maths and heavily into Social Studies."

Inside with the big boys, Harvey developed two skills that became his trademark – robbing security vans and riding motorbikes. He went in a burglar and came out a *blagger* (armed robber). When Harvey was freed in September 1988 he quickly returned to committing numerous post office, cash in transit and jewellery shop heists.

Harvey's path to supergrass status began in early 1989 when an associate offered to introduce him to a man called Laurel Blake, who was working as a security guard for Group 4 in London. Blake, it was said, wanted to rob a company van. Harvey's team obliged. In April 1989, £675,000 was stolen from Blake's security van in Ilford. Rigg Approach, the Flying Squad office based in Walthamstow and covering east London, investigated.[1] At first detectives were unable to identify Harvey or his associates. But six months later when a second Group 4 van was robbed, this time by another team also believed to be working with Blake, the criminal conspiracy unravelled.

Harvey had already moved to Luton and bought a house with his wife. Half the £15,000 deposit came from the proceeds of the Ilford robbery. Harvey had also taped £50,000 to the bottom of his wardrobe. He could have bummed around for a while, but decided to get a job. It wasn't just any job advert in the *Evening Standard* that caught Harvey's eye. This one said, "WANTED – Drivers for Group 4. Luton Office".

He felt he had all the credentials. He was certainly wanted by the security company, so he applied "for the balls of it", using his own name and national insurance number. It surprised him when the application form arrived. He swears he didn't lie filling it in. Or more accurately, he didn't tell the full truth. Another trademark. "I got the job with no aim to pull a job off. We'd just had a baby and the office was near my home," Harvey explains. Group 4 put him on three months' probation. He prayed no one tried to rob him while he was delivering cash, sometimes up to £3 million.

Meanwhile, back in London, the Flying Squad had arrested Blake and others. It wasn't long before they started grassing one another up. An informant had also told the police the man they were looking for was called Hector Selecta'. At first the detectives thought he might be a DJ on the London club scene they had noticed from flyers posted around the capital.

In the seventies and eighties the Selecta' was a crucial figure in the Jamaican and British reggae sound clashes. Rival sound systems had a Selecta', who played the tunes, and a DJ who sang over them. Being a Selecta' was very much a crucial but background role to the more colourful *toasting* of the DJ star. This suited Hector Harvey, who refers to himself with great pride as "the planner".

Eventually the Flying Squad realised Selecta' was Harvey's street name. He was put under surveillance. The detectives were amazed to discover him working for the very security company he had recently robbed. It was inconceivable to the Flying Squad that Harvey, a man used to taking home a whole payroll, was content instead to take just

HECTOR THE SELECTA'

£500 every month in wages. Group 4 was alerted to their probationer's outlaw past. In early February Harvey was called into the office and told sheepishly his references hadn't checked out. Harvey now realised he was definitely under surveillance.

The game of cat and mouse moved from the soulless industrial units of Luton to the Caribbean, as Flying Squad detectives in Bermuda shorts secretly followed Harvey to St Lucia and Barbados. They believed he'd salted money away, including the share owed to Blake and a man called Alan Lewis. It was this betrayal that had led to the domino grassing.

In February 1991, all three were tried. Harvey and Lewis were convicted. Blake however was acquitted, even though, according to a confidential police report, he had admitted his role to officers during earlier interviews.

Harvey was only twenty-six when he was sent down for fifteen years. He wouldn't be eligible for parole until the new millennium. So when two Flying Squad officers involved in his case approached him in prison to help clear up loose ends, he was desperate to trade. The detectives, chief inspector Albert Patrick and sergeant Tim Norris, made Harvey their registered informant, under the pseudonym "Marshall Cook".[2] In return they agreed to help with his appeal.

Harvey gave up two other men he claimed were involved in the Ilford job. He then named the woman to whom he had given the £50,000 hidden under his wardrobe to invest in the German stock market. There was also a trip to identify the house of an intermediary he said he paid £20,000 to split with a detective inspector from a west London police station. The cop had been willing to try and "lose" the case papers, Harvey claimed.[3] For all this information he received regular sums of money.

Harvey told us a Home Office official had also visited him in 1991 at Long Larton Prison to ask if he'd "befriend" Michael Bettaney, a former MI5 officer by then into the seventh year of a twenty-three-year sentence for betraying secrets to the Soviet Union. Bettaney was a hopeless alcoholic whose obvious mental breakdown and the risk it posed were completely missed by the Security Services' managers until one day he threw confidential documents over the wall of the Soviet Embassy in London.

Harvey claims the Home Office official asked him to spend one year with Bettaney, who was in another prison. The Flying Squad gave him no indication they were aware of the approach. Keen to reduce his sentence, Harvey agreed and waited to be relocated. But the shadowy official never made contact again.

DCI Patrick, however, kept his word and a confidential 'text' was sent to the appeal judge pointing out Harvey's assistance to the police. His sentence was reduced to 12 years.

In January 1994 Harvey moved to a new prison, the Mount, near Hemel Hempstead, where the conditions were more relaxed. As he neared the end of his sentence, he was allowed to work during the week at a special needs school as a caretaker. He had to return every evening to his cell.

One day Laurel Blake, the alleged inside agent acquitted of the Ilford job, visited him. "Blake told me he had a friend who worked for Security Express [the firm had taken over Group 4] who wanted his van robbed. In due course I learned the name of the person – Gregory Hepburn."[4] Harvey agreed to put a team together and told Blake he'd be in touch. He then contacted his old partner David Brown and asked if he would be interested in the job. Brown declined but offered to make enquiries of his own criminal associates. Brown was unaware that Harvey had grassed him up in 1991 as one of the two other men involved in the Ilford security van robbery.[5]

Brown wasn't the only person Harvey was willing to betray. His Flying Squad handlers had tasked him to "get close" to two new targets, a pair of well-respected armed robbers called Gary Ward and Joey Simms. Harvey had served time with them at Maidstone Prison and his police handlers hoped to exploit this association to find out what they were up to. Ward was still inside but Simms had recently been released. The two men were well-known "jump up" specialists, criminals who hijacked lorries and sold on their loads through moody shopkeepers, market traders, publicans and the like.

Deputy assistant commissioner John Grieve, the director of intelligence, authorised the tapping of Simms and Ward and the use of Harvey as a participating informant. His handlers took him to visit Ward at prison. To gain his trust, Harvey offered Ward a piece of the Security Express job he was planning with Hepburn. Ward expressed interest and confided that he too had an inside agent and was planning to rob a Post Office van with Simms later that year. Ward offered Harvey a piece of that action, and knowing how pleased his handlers would be, Harvey readily accepted.

On the way back to the Mount, Harvey told his handlers about Ward's Post Office job. He was content to let the two Flying Squad detectives feel chuffed their sneaky ruse had worked. Of course he kept from them the fact that he had just recruited Ward and Simms to rob a Security Express van.

That job was also moving forward. Derek Brown had arranged for Harvey to meet someone willing to do the robbery. Harvey agreed but didn't tell Brown that he now had another team of blaggers, Ward and Simms, interested in the same job.

One day while Harvey was working at the special needs school a Mercedes pulled up with Brown and two other men inside. The leader of the team was introduced as Chris McCormack, a feared gangland enforcer in his late thirties. Accompanying him was Dean Henry, his lieutenant and an experienced armed robber. McCormack naturally wanted to meet Hepburn, Harvey's inside agent. If the job came off sweetly, he promised Harvey £100,000 for the introduction. Harvey agreed and McCormack left thinking he was onto a nice little earner.

McCormack is a Bermondsey boy born in 1955. While serving in the armed forces he received his first major conviction for stabbing. Police sources say his apprenticeship was served as a private "soldier" for the south-east London Arif crime family. In October 1983, at the age of 28, Chris McCormack entered the big league after he was caught dressed as a policeman trying to kidnap and rob an Iranian airline executive at his home near the Albert Hall.

The Flying Squad had received an informant's tip-off. Detectives were waiting across the road when the armed robbers turned up in police uniforms they'd stolen from a dry cleaners. McCormack rang the doorbell and, when the Iranian executive's wife answered, he stuck a shotgun in her face. The Flying Squad made their move and among those arrested was another well-known south-east London villain, David Fraser, the son of Mad Frank.

McCormack, Fraser, Robert Davey and a fourth man received substantial jail sentences.[6] McCormack got 12 years. After his release in the late eighties he continued to freelance for the Arifs. But by 1994 McCormack was developing new contacts in north London with the Adams crime family.

Terry, Patrick and Tommy Adams are three of eleven brothers and sisters from an Irish Catholic working-class family. They grew up on a rough council estate in the Barnsbury area of Islington, a million miles from the skinny latte part of the borough where Tony and Cherie Blair plotted their path to Number Ten. Ironically, a police operation targeting the Adams would later covertly record Tommy boasting how he had donated several thousand pounds of dirty cash to the Labour Party's election coffers.[7]

In 1990, the Adams family sorted out its north London rivals, the Reillys, in a memorable shoot-out and so began its domination of the London criminal underworld. Their vast profits from drug trafficking, estimated by the police at over £50 million, have been laundered through investments in bars, restaurants, clubs, sports promotion, a West End ticket agency and horseracing. Before long the Adams family, known as the A-Team, were considered unassailable. Some suggested this was because for a long time they had "bent old Bill" on the payroll, and not just low-ranking detectives. It was rumoured by police and criminals alike that a south-east London commander managed to retire untouched by the current anti-corruption crusade.

Certainly the Adams brothers and their associates had a Teflon coat when it came to avoiding heavy prison sentences. They eschewed publicity of any kind, which is understandable when your empire is built on fear and extreme violence meted out to double-crossers, if not personally then by trusted enforcers like McCormack.

In the winter of 1994, Harvey chose McCormack's team over Ward and Simms to carry out the Security Express robbery. McCormack took control of the job unaware anyone else had been in the running. The robbery, he told Harvey, would take place sometime just before Christmas when Hepburn's Security Express van was outside the Barclays Bank in Clapham High Street, south London.

On the morning of 16 December, two of McCormack's team took over at gunpoint a tyre shop near to the bank. The plan was for the third member, Dean Henry, dressed as a guard, to hijack the security van with a handgun and drive it to the tyre shop where the proceeds would be transferred to a new vehicle. Fortunately, a customer was suspicious about the closed tyre shop and reported it to the police, who subsequently arrested the gang after a chase and shoot-out.

Over Christmas, Harvey devised a plan so duplicitous it would have made Machiavelli proud. In January 1995, Harvey contacted Ward and Simms. Ward had been released from prison by then. Harvey explained they needed to bring the Security Express job forward and rob the Post Office van later in the year, after he was paroled. Harvey explained that Hepburn, the inside agent, was worried he might be suspended from work while Security Express investigated the failed robbery of his van in Clapham.

Harvey now needed a pretext for his Flying Squad handlers to

HECTOR THE SELECTA'

release him from prison to carry out the robbery without their knowledge. Detectives Tim Norris and Paul Smith, who had taken over as co-handler, had no idea Harvey was behind the failed Clapham robbery. All police efforts were concentrated on the Post Office remittance van Harvey had told them Ward and Simms were planning to rob.

Harvey told Norris that Ward and Simms wanted him out on 20 January to do a "dry run", and that the Post Office van would be robbed for real a week later. Harvey knew the Flying Squad had no real reason to doubt him. DAC Grieve again gave permission for Harvey to be released from the Mount. He was under strict instructions about what he could say and do as a participating informant. The last thing the Flying Squad wanted was any future prosecution of Ward and Simms undermined because Harvey had acted as an *agent provocateur*. Of course, that was exactly what he was doing.

Harvey candidly laid out for us the point of his plan: he would do the robbery with Ward and Simms, skim off a large part of his share and then return the rest to the Flying Squad claiming he was bounced into doing the robbery during the dry run but on a different target and therefore had no opportunity to tip them off.

The Flying Squad might not like it, but would be reassured Harvey had returned his share, unaware it wasn't the full amount. Ward and Simms would then be arrested, oblivious that Harvey was the grass. To stymie probing defence lawyers, Harvey knew the police would seek a PII certificate or gagging order from the trial judge to prevent having to disclose his role. The Flying Squad would also put in a good word to the forthcoming Parole Board, ensuring Harvey's earliest possible release with a secret pot of money.

Thursday, 19 January was showtime. At midday, Harvey was released from the Mount Prison for the dry run. That night he contacted Ward and Simms and went over the robbery route. Afterwards he met his police handlers and showed them the *slaughter* – a criminal term for the secure place where the loot from the security van would be unloaded onto another vehicle.

Harvey took Norris and Smith to two separate locations, the first in Shoreditch, near the City, and the second a lock-up in Pages Walk, near Tower Bridge. This was the actual *slaughter* and Harvey deliberately mentioned it to the Flying Squad to add credibility to the story he planned to tell the police immediately after the robbery.

In the early hours of Friday morning Harvey finally got his head down for a short nap. The next 24 hours would change his life for ever.

At about 6.30 a.m. Harvey met Ward and Simms outside Stepney Green tube station in east London. Ward collected the inside agent, Hepburn, in a white transit van. They planned to meet Simms at the Pages Walk warehouse. While Harvey drove the transit van there, Ward fixed a dummy bomb around Hepburn's waist. It was made out of two twelve-bore shotgun cartridges attached by wires to two batteries.

At the Pages Walk lock-up, Harvey changed into his motorbike leathers. Simms joined Ward and Hepburn in the van, which Harvey followed on a stolen Yamaha to the Security Express depot. Hepburn was dropped off nearby. His job was to convince his wholly innocent co-driver they had no choice but to co-operate with the robbery. This meant picking up money from the nearby Barclays Bank Cash Centre, then following Harvey's motorbike to Pages Walk. To ensure his co-driver's co-operation, Hepburn was supposed to show him a family photograph, say his mother was being held hostage and then reveal the bomb on his body, claiming that an attached microphone allowed the robbers to hear every word.

The plan went perfectly. The robbery netted just over £1.4 million in various denominations. The three principal robbers took £400,000 each. Hepburn's share was £200,000, which Ward gave Blake to pass on when the heat was off.

Harvey took a mini-cab from the divvy house in the Isle of Dogs and made a pre-arranged stop at a girlfriend's house in east London where he hid at least £40,000. He then continued in the same cab to his mother's house in the White City Estate, in Shepherd's Bush. There, he hid the remainder of his share in her shed.

Now Harvey had to complete his plan and revert back to his "innocent" informant role. So he paged detective inspector Tim Norris leaving the message from Selecta' that Ward and Simms had "pulled a double whammy" on him and he was heading back to Luton where he would explain everything.

A furious Norris arrived in Luton with DC Paul Smith and two other Flying Squad officers in a second car. Norris suspected Harvey had duped him and ordered a search of the family home. Harvey said he'd hidden his share at his mother's. No mention was made of the money stored at his girlfriend's house.

The detectives drove Harvey to the White City Estate and recovered the money from the shed. Harvey was then arrested and taken to Edmonton police station in north London. There he was

HECTOR THE SELECTA'

grilled over the next 24 hours by an experienced detective sergeant called Eamonn Harris. On Saturday evening he was returned to the Mount prison.

What Harvey did next was truly extraordinary and triggered a shockwave that rocked Scotland Yard's headquarters.

After a shower and some prison food, Harvey sat in his cell and put two tapes in his beat box. He cleared his throat and began a devastating recording of the events of the last 48 hours. The tape was directed at his legal representative, Jeremy Newell, and started with the words: "Dear Jeremy, what I'm about to say on this tape is the assurance that I need for you to help me . . . in case anything goes wrong in my life as of this day."

Harvey weaved into the narrative a cataclysmic allegation that Flying Squad detectives had stolen nearly £250,000 of the recovered money over the last 24 hours. He described how Flying Squad detectives drove him to his mother's shed to recover his share. He claimed DI Tim Norris placed the money in the boot of the police car and removed a portion of it from one bag into a sports bag next to it. On the way to Edmonton police station, Harvey claimed Norris stopped at a service station on the motorway and transferred the sports bag into the boot of his own car.

Norris, he alleged, promised to take care of his wife with some of the stolen money. He also told him to ask for a local solicitor called Les Brown when they arrived at the police station because he would "take care of everything". Harvey knew Brown, who had acted for him on a domestic problem concerning access to his son. He says he confided in the solicitor about the £40,000 he had skimmed, and told him Norris had also helped himself to a share of the remainder. Brown, he says, just sniggered.

Harvey went on to claim that the two Flying Squad detectives who interviewed him, Eamonn Harris and Paul Smith, privately made him a deal: he could keep the money he had left at his girlfriend's (which Brown had apparently told them about) if he helped them steal the £200,000 share put aside for Hepburn, the inside agent.

Harvey explained on tape how he made various calls and discovered Hepburn's friend, Kevin Dwyer, had stashed the £200,000 in a lock-up. Two detectives were sent to pick it up.

Just past midnight, Harvey finished his explosive recording. He wrote a covering note to Newell: "Please put this tape in your safe and keep it there as there's enough on [it] that'll put a lot of people away! No matter WHO THEY ARE!" Harvey made two copies of the tape.

UNTOUCHABLES

He specifically asked Newell to contact CIB2 and pass them a copy.

A good planner has to think on his feet and must sometimes adapt a plan to changing circumstances. An important question is whether Harvey planned all along to contact CIB2, or was it a reaction to genuine and unexpected corruption he had witnessed? Harvey maintains he only decided to make the tape and send it to CIB2 after Harris threatened him in the car on the way back to the Mount prison.

If Harvey is telling the truth about why he contacted CIB2 then the theft of over £200,000 by the Flying Squad detectives at Rigg Approach was opportunistic. But Harvey had a problem. He was not in a position to be totally straight with CIB2, because it would mean admitting he had planned the whole robbery.

On 26 January, Newell's copy of the tape arrived at his office in Wembley. He listened to it with increasing amazement. Newell had for five years worked for Les Brown's firm until they fell out in 1993. Newell left with another employee, a retired Flying Squad detective called Fred Bunn. It was to Bunn that Newell turned to seek advice about the tape. He played it to him and Bunn advised that CIB be brought in.[8]

On 2 February, Newell called CIB. He explained that a client, whom he referred to only by the codename "Swallow" (one of Harvey's eight aliases[9]) wanted to provide details of "corrupt officers" involved in a recent armed robbery. A meeting was arranged at Hemel Hempstead police station for the following day.

By January 1995, the Yard had set up a Ghost Squad under John Grieve and Roy Clark's stewardship that even regular members of CIB2 knew nothing about. The squad that didn't exist had been operating for just over a year when Newell phoned. By then, senior Ghost Squad officers had already been fooled by Geoff Brennan, who had come to them in June 1994. Many of the same errors were about to be repeated with Hector Harvey.

On 3 February, Ghost Squad detective superintendent David Bailey and a female officer saw Harvey at Hemel Hempstead. He wasn't cautioned and the covert recording was of such poor quality it was decided to re-interview him five days later, this time under caution and with his lawyer present. Bailey had enough in the meantime to brief Grieve and other Ghost Squad chiefs that they had a problem with the Flying Squad office at Rigg Approach.

The story Harvey gave to the Ghost Squad on 8 February was a melange of fact and fiction that fleshed out the police corruption allegations against Norris, Harris, Smith and north London solicitor

Les Brown. Harvey knew that if he revealed his full role in the robbery he would be put back in prison and the key thrown away. With parole so close, once again he suggested Ward and Simms had duped him. His focus now was to make himself indispensable to the anti-corruption squad, in the same way he had previously made himself indispensable to the Flying Squad, and then betrayed them.

For the first time he declared his share of the robbery was £400,000 and that he had siphoned off £40,000, leaving £360,000 in his mother's shed. On the day of the robbery Security Express had recovered £313,000 from the Flying Squad. Harvey was therefore alleging that his handler, Norris, had removed £47,000 from the car boot. This plus the guard's share meant Flying Squad detectives were in the frame for stealing around £250,000.

The Ghost Squad's covert inquiry into the Flying Squad was aptly called Operation Spy. It had a secret room at Tintagel House where all its files and technical facilities were stored. "The room was alarmed to nearby Kennington police station. There was stuff inside it that was so sensitive they couldn't even trust people in Tintagel," recalls one former insider.

On Valentine's Day, at the Mount Prison Harvey received a visitor he wasn't expecting. An angry Chris McCormack told Harvey he wanted the £200,000 or threatened to wage war on his family. Harvey tried to persuade McCormack that the police had stolen the guard's share. But the hard man was insistent Harvey had sent his own people to pick up the guard's share. "He threatened me and said he had a detective inspector on the firm and would get me charged as the main organiser of the [failed robbery]."

Harvey was undoubtedly scared of McCormack. He knew he was more than capable of hurting him, permanently. Harvey claims that when they first discussed the robbery McCormack had boasted of killing the police informant David Norris, a fate he was apparently suggesting would befall Harvey if he ever double-crossed him. That time had now come.

Harvey was also worried about CIB connecting him to the earlier attempted robbery of the Security Express van in Clapham. Although he notified the Ghost Squad of McCormack's threat, Harvey said nothing about having been involved with him in setting up the Clapham job. Nor that he had played two teams of armed robbers off against each other as well as the Flying Squad.

Superintendent David Bailey was genuinely concerned about the threat to his witness. As a way of gathering further evidence of

McCormack's violent intentions, he taped Harvey calling the south London enforcer from a prison phone. According to a retired officer with access to the material, McCormack accused Harvey of "putting three of his mates away". The Ghost Squad paid little attention to this comment, says the source, which was clearly a reference to the forthcoming trial of Dean Henry and his two associates who were on remand for the failed Security Express robbery in Clapham.[10]

It relieved Harvey greatly that Bailey and his team were not quizzing him about McCormack's aside. To keep the two robberies apart, Harvey threw cold water on the McCormack threat and said he had sorted it out but didn't divulge how. Consequently, McCormack was never arrested or interviewed by the Ghost Squad.

On Monday, 29 May 1995, Harvey was on home leave from prison. It had just gone midday and he was getting ready to go into Luton town centre. His motorbike was parked on the front lawn under the kitchen window of his three-bedroom semi on an estate. This was the house he part paid for with the proceeds of the 1989 Ilford robbery. Harvey's wife and three children, then aged fifteen months, five and eleven, had lived there for just over five years while their father served his sentence for the robbery.

Harvey went to remove a green tarpaulin covering his Honda 750. The bike, he says, hadn't been driven for two months. "I stood beside the front wheel [and lifted] up the tarpaulin from the front. I then undid the rear of the tarpaulin and lifted it over the box by the seat. I gave the tarpaulin a couple of pulls to try and remove it all in one go, but it seemed to be stuck at the front.

"I looked over the front wheel to see what was catching the tarpaulin. To my horror I could see what appeared to be a hand grenade wedged into the spokes. It had a pin, which had a ring on the end. Attached to the ring was a length of wire, which appeared to be attached to the tarpaulin at the front. I could see the pin was about three-quarters out of its holder. I immediately let go of the tarpaulin and ran to my right. I went behind the porch of the house next door. I waited for about ten seconds in case the grenade went off. It didn't. My wife was in the house and I called for her to get out. I then phoned the police."

The bomb squad disarmed the live grenade. Meanwhile, Harvey asked the Ghost Squad to relocate his family and put him into protected police custody.

Harvey immediately suspected McCormack was behind the

HECTOR THE SELECTA'

grenade incident. He was unaware the Yard had secret intelligence suggesting he was right. A very secretive police operation involving MI5, codenamed Trinity, was targeting the Adams crime family at the time. There were numerous phone taps and bugging devices inserted in the Adams' premises. The family and its main associates were also subject to intense physical surveillance. This included Chris McCormack, who was followed to Ireland and while playing golf with one of the Adams brothers in Spain, says a police source on Operation Trinity. The Yard's Special Intelligence Section (SIS), which operates from a white building with blacked out windows by the cinema in Putney High Street, had "lines" (taps) on McCormack. According to another police source, SIS had picked up conversations where McCormack apparently admitted his involvement in the grenade incident.[11]

The Ghost Squad kept Harvey at the Mount Prison, but under a new regime of restricted movements. On 14 July Harvey walked out of the Mount into a witness protection programme organised by the Ghost Squad. Harvey and his family were moved to rented accommodation in north-west London. His wife carried on working and the kids went to school.

Shortly before his release on parole, Harvey recovered the £40,000 he had stashed with a girlfriend just hours after the robbery. He says he spent it periodically, paying off debts, loans and on "some fancy living".

It's remarkable that the Ghost Squad did not exert greater pressure on their supergrass to return this money. After all, Harvey had offered to give back £10,000 in February, but he admits this was just a ruse to buy more time. He had no intention of paying it back, and the offer was never enforced. Harvey played one senior Ghost Squad officer off against the other, later claiming to Bailey that Roger Gaspar had said he could "forget about the forty grand".

Like Brennan, Harvey had skilfully inverted the supergrass relationship. In effect he was running his Ghost Squad handlers when he needed to and without them realising it. He never felt the choke collar, because there wasn't one. His ability to manipulate the supergrass system was greatly aided when, according to a police report on Operation Spy, Gaspar and Bailey had indicated to him back in March 1995 that the CPS had agreed he would be given immunity from prosecution. The report goes on to say that the CPS had done no such thing and had in fact refused to give the Ghost Squad any undertaking. This was still the position after Harvey's release.

UNTOUCHABLES

Many villains would have thought they'd had a result. Not Hector Harvey. He wasn't content to lie low in the witness protection scheme. He wanted money from the Ghost Squad for the assistance he had given them on bent cops, even though he had kept back at least £40,000 from the robbery. Bailey said it couldn't be done and Harvey threatened to go elsewhere with his information. Operation Spy had now been running for over six months with the work phones of selected Flying Squad detectives tapped throughout this period. A leak would damage all this work, so Bailey implored Harvey to maintain the confidentiality. The reality was the Ghost Squad had no hold on Harvey and was dependent on his loyalty. But supergrasses have no loyalty, except to themselves.

In early November, Harvey developed a new plan to get some more money. He contacted Security Express national security manager, Mike O'Neill. The company had posted a £50,000 reward. Harvey introduced himself as "Mr Rogers" and said he wanted to "clear his conscience" and in return for the reward would tell them about the robbery of one of their vans.

A meeting was arranged at the Kentucky Fried Chicken on the Old Kent Road. O'Neill first contacted DCI Mick Fry of the Rigg Approach Flying Squad and told him about the call from "Mr Rogers". Fry thought quite sensibly this could be the inside agent wanting to come clean. There was no time to wire up O'Neill, so he organised for his Flying Squad team to cover the meeting.

On 23 November Harvey was photographed arriving at the KFC wearing a baseball cap–fake afro combo he'd bought in Jamaica, and using crutches he borrowed from an old girlfriend. The surveillance team were inside KFC eating the Colonel's tender nuggets when Harvey arrived looking for his own bargain bucket (of gold) from O'Neill.

He told the Security Express manager he was helping detective superintendent David Bailey of CIB2 because of corruption among the Flying Squad with whom he was originally working as their participating informant. He said he had returned his share of the robbery, and once again claimed the robbers had bounced him on the dry run. After the meeting O'Neill called Fry and from his summary of the conversation with "Mr Rogers", the senior officer realised it was Harvey.

The industrious supergrass had also been busy. He called Bailey and told him about the meeting with O'Neill while suggesting Security Express was going to sue Scotland Yard. The call sent the

HECTOR THE SELECTA'

Ghost Squad into panic. Had their covert operation into the Flying Squad been compromised? Was the Yard now facing a multi-million pound negligence claim?

Bailey met with O'Neill, an ex-Flying Squad detective, at Tintagel House. Security Express was annoyed at being kept in the dark. But after subsequent meetings with commissioner Condon and his deputy they decided against suing. In the end, the insurers, Lloyds, covered their loss, and co-ordination was improved between the police and the security company.

The whole embarrassing episode sent the Ghost Squad into a huddle to decide what to do about Operation Spy, the Flying Squad and the man who'd caused this problem, their finger-lickin' good supergrass.

On 13 December, after days of tense debate, John Grieve and other Ghost Squad chiefs decided to formally notify six Flying Squad detectives they were the subject of serious corruption allegations for theft of the recovered proceeds. Bailey suddenly appeared at Rigg Approach and served Regulation 163 Notices on Norris, Harris, Smith and three detective constables who were present when the money was removed from the shed. None of the officers was suspended. But Bailey took away all the paperwork on the operations against Ward and Simms and Harvey's informant logs.

The dramatic move was a desperate one forced on the Ghost Squad by the actions of another supergrass over whom they had lost control. The timing couldn't have been worse. By December 1995 Grieve was in the middle of another scandal over his department's appalling mishandling of two Yardies whom SO11 had used as participating informants in an abortive attempt to penetrate Jamaican drug gangs in Britain.

Eton Green and Delroy Denton had well-known, extremely violent pasts in Jamaica when they fled to Britain. Green had jumped bail for attempted murder.[12] While agreeing to grass up fellow Yardies in return for payment from the police, they were shielded from prosecution here and allowed to terrorise the local black communities in London and Nottingham over four years. Inexplicably, charges for drugs and firearms offences and the rape of a minor were quietly dropped.

However, the high-risk strategy blew up in Grieve's face in April 1995 when Denton raped and murdered a young Brixton mother of two. Marcia Lawes was stabbed twenty times during a frenzied sexual assault. Meanwhile, Green was facing trial for an armed robbery with other Yardie gangsters SO11 had encouraged him to invite over here. Green exploited his incredible lack of supervision to carry out the violent robbery in a Nottingham nightclub of 150 ravers, one of whom he shot in the leg and stood over saying, "Bleed pussy, bleed."

The trial judge criticised Grieve's department for "impeding" the local police force's inquiry into the crime. There were also concerns that the Yard had either colluded with or deceived the Immigration Service to allow their informant and his gangster friends to stay in this country illegally. The Yard tried to get the trial aborted rather than reveal Green's informant status. In other words, it was willing to watch dangerous men go free to save its own bacon. When that failed and SO11 was forced by the Attorney General to disclose the informant's file, a whole year's worth of documents – revealing who knew and authorised what – went missing. The Yard claimed that the sensitive documents had unfortunately been shredded during a routine clear out.

In September 1995, Grieve apologised for the consequences of what he nevertheless argued was a justified strategy. A few months later, he should have been back in the frame over the unfolding Hector Harvey scandal. But as the public and politicians knew nothing about that mess, no inquiry could be launched despite its having very similar features – poor supervision, putting the public at risk and armed robbery. There was also one important new ingredient, the stench of police corruption.

Over Christmas 1995 the Ghost Squad management committee developed an emergency strategy. John Grieve recommended a joint investigation. CIB2 would overtly re-investigate Harvey's corruption allegations. And the Rigg Approach Flying Squad office would reinvestigate the Security Express robbery and build a case against Ward, Simms and others.

Deputy commissioner Brian Hayes approved the recommendation. There is no explanation why the same Flying Squad office at the centre of the corruption allegations was thought appropriate to conduct an inquiry into itself. Nor will anyone explain why the joint investigation was not referred to the Police Complaints Authority for supervision.

The officer Grieve chose from Rigg Approach was an experienced detective inspector called George Raison. It was an appointment Raison did not want. He says he was always opposed to police investigating themselves and could see immediately in this case the

HECTOR THE SELECTA'

conflict of interest. Raison also feared rejection by his colleagues at Rigg. But in the end it was an order he couldn't refuse.

Ill health and a lengthy murder case meant Raison had been away from the Rigg office and therefore had little to do with the Hector Harvey case.

Raison was also unaware his colleagues were under investigation by Operation Spy until Bailey walked into his office in December and told him his "boys were at it".

Raison heard nothing more until 16 January 1996 when he was summoned to Tintagel House. There he was introduced to the man nominated to carry out the CIB2 limb of the joint investigation. Dave Niccol was an existing CIB2 superintendent.

Given the delicate situation he was in, Raison says he insisted all his meetings with CIB be properly minuted. In turn, Niccol promised he would be open with his new deputy. Raison then asked Grieve for three detectives from the Flying Squad to work with him. The Ghost Squad vetted the names by checking the phone-taps and other secret intelligence to see if it had captured any of the three saying or doing anything compromising. They all passed.[13]

Although his integrity was not in question and Grieve regarded him as "honest", Raison felt he was under permanent surveillance while part of Operation Spy, phase two. He suspected his office at Tintagel House was bugged. "My garden was also entered for the purposes of taking off or putting a probe in my car," says the detective who knows only too well the technical capabilities of the Yard. This could easily be dismissed as paranoia, but Niccol reveals: "It was openly accepted [from the beginning] that the two inquiries would flounder if the premise that [Raison] was honest proved wrong."[14]

Raison was soon exasperated by the non-disclosure of key documents. He complains that he was not allowed to see the policy docket detailing why and when important decisions were taken, or to compare past interview summaries with original police pocket-book notes. He felt the Ghost Squad wanted to shield Harvey from deeper questioning because, as with Brennan, they wanted to believe him.

Raison discovered CIB officers were authorised to falsify their duty states in order to carry out secret lines of inquiry. He was fed up. His Flying Squad colleagues thought he was a traitor and CIB saw him as a spy. "I was being treated like a leper at both ends, so I threatened to complain to a senior officer, but [CIB] said the deputy commissioner could trump anyone I put up."

UNTOUCHABLES

To reinvestigate the Security Express robbery Raison needed to review sensitive covert recordings made by the Ghost Squad, in particular Harvey's contacts with McCormack. It was through proper detective work that Raison was the first to discover the link between the Clapham and Pages Walk Security Express robberies, something Harvey had been desperate to keep apart and the Ghost Squad had missed.[15]

Raison had grudging respect for Harvey's "manipulation" of the supergrass system. "You've got to give him his due, he's good at what he does." But Raison was not fooled by Harvey's ever-shifting version of events. "On three or four occasions I asked Niccol or Bailey to give me a team of men, even MI5, and I'd have Harvey nicked in a month. Then we'd have something to put his arm up his back so we could get to the truth. They declined and I don't know why."

Niccol knew Raison had an "uncompromising style" and demanded high standards, but he felt his deputy's belief that Harvey was a liar "may have clouded his approach". Raison counters that the way the supergrass had been handled during phase one of Operation Spy left much to be desired and threatened any future prosecutions of dirty cops. Meetings with Harvey were often not taped, and when they were, he was not cautioned on every occasion. Also, certain obvious lines of inquiry, which would have helped evaluate Harvey's truthfulness, were simply not followed up. "I went there to test Harvey's evidence, whereas [the Ghost Squad] was trying to prove what he was saying."

What troubled Raison most was getting to the bottom of the true relationship between McCormack and Harvey and the threat to kill the supergrass. "I was not allowed to properly investigate McCormack. I wanted to nick him for the threats against Harvey and couldn't understand why this hadn't been done before. But I wasn't allowed."[16]

Raison suddenly got a very late break when around November 1996 an officer at Kennington police station told him they had an informant who knew about the Security Express robberies. Raison interviewed the informant at Charing Cross police station on tape. He was a close associate of a money launderer called Gerald Fleming.

We shall call the informant "John". Some of what he told Raison has to be left out to protect his identity. He revealed that on the Monday, two days after the January 1995 Security Express robbery,

HECTOR THE SELECTA'

McCormack came to Fleming's office with a sports bag containing £300,000. He asked Fleming to look after the cash, claiming it was from a recent robbery where the security guard had a bomb attached to him.

"John" also talked about McCormack's involvement in the failed Clapham robbery a month earlier. Fleming, he said, had prepared the moody documentation for the cars and motorbike McCormack later burnt and dumped. "John" could also tie in Harvey. The informant claimed that Harvey went to Fleming for a loan and had to put up his motorbike as collateral. "John" claimed Fleming returned the bike after the loan had been repaid.

The significance of this intelligence appeared considerable. Here was an independent informant claiming that McCormack had been involved in both robberies. And if "John" was correct about the money McCormack left with Fleming, it now put a big question mark over Harvey's maths concerning the divvy-up.

"John" was scared of McCormack beyond his violent reputation. He told Raison how McCormack boasted about having two unnamed senior corrupt officers on his payroll – a Yard commander and a chief inspector at the City of London police. This may explain why the Yard has consistently tried to bury this tape in PII certificates.

One copy of the tape was left with Kennington to be attached to the informant's docket. The other was taken to Tintagel House, where Raison spoke to Niccol about its contents. If Niccol was bothered by the implications he didn't show it.

Next Raison went to the Fraud Squad, who already had an interest in Fleming.[17] They took out a warrant to search his business, but when officers burst through the door it induced a massive heart attack and the suspected money launderer for the Underworld died. A promising lead had evaporated.

Raison had also been to see detective constable Paul Carpenter at the Yard's Special Intelligence Section.[18] He too was looking at McCormack as part of Operation Trinity, which was targeting the Adams crime syndicate. At SIS, Raison read the south London enforcer's file in which he was referred to as "Commander".

Raison also scrolled down the transcripts of the phone-taps on McCormack and his associates. This was how he first discovered he was behind the grenade attack on Harvey's motorbike. According to Raison, the Commander was overheard saying about the failed attempt: "That's what you get for using amateurs." SIS expressed interest in speaking to the informant, but Raison says it never happened because "John" was ultimately not willing to give evidence against McCormack.

Raison's inquiries had now cast significant doubt on whether Harvey had been completely truthful with his Ghost Squad handlers.

The "Fleming tape" and its implications emerged just as DI George Raison was preparing a final report for the CPS on Operation Spy. He started writing it with Niccol's agreement in November 1996. The report would end up several phone-books thick and contain some explosive criticisms of the Ghost Squad's investigation.

Raison stressed when interviews were not recorded and interviewees not cautioned. "I was trying to highlight the whole investigation [since January 1995]. Some might say it was biased against CIB but they did the initial inquiry. This was going to the CPS. They needed to know the fuck-ups."

As the report was prepared, things he felt needed greater ventilation, like the Fleming tape, were discussed during private meetings with the CPS. Raison's job was to amass all the evidence and determine whether the CPS could mount a successful prosecution of cops and robbers. He examined the interviews of Ward, Simms, Hepburn, Blake and others named by Harvey. They had been arrested and then let go.

Then Raison turned to the interviews with the accused Flying Squad officers. They had all refused to answer any of CIB's questions and instead read out a prepared statement denying the allegations.

Norris was confronted in his interview with the results of a financial investigation by CIB, which showed that after the robbery he had "deposited a total of £5,185 cash, mostly in £20 notes through various accounts. Mention was also made of a cheque for £4,400 payable to Norris from Les Brown one week after the robbery."[19] Brown was also interviewed by CIB and declined to comment.

Raison's conclusion was very downbeat. A successful prosecution was "impossible". He went on: "There still remain many unanswered questions. This is by no means a satisfactory conclusion to many months of investigation. Every effort has been made to establish the truth."[20] When the final report was ready in the New Year, Niccol called it "exceptional, albeit somewhat biased towards showing small flaws in Harvey's different versions".[21] The CPS was also very complimentary and suggested work of this quality was worthy of a commendation. They concurred with

HECTOR THE SELECTA'

Raison's downbeat opinion that no realistic prospect of a successful conviction existed.

Part of the problem was that compromising telephone intercepts on Ward and Simms were not admissible evidence; Harvey's informant status was already blown to the defence who would rightly argue he had acted as an *agent provocateur*; several key civilian witnesses refused to give evidence against Harvey, Blake and Hepburn; and Harvey was unreliable and largely uncorroborated in his allegations against the Flying Squad.[22]

Raison recalls that the CPS letter also expressed how "unhappy" they were with the CIB side of the inquiry. The mishandling of a slippery supergrass was a compelling reason alone for why no successful prosecutions were likely.[23]

The decision by the Ghost Squad to circumvent or openly flout Home Office guidelines and laws around supergrass handling was taken at a high level in Scotland Yard, and in secret.

Millions had been spent by the Yard on a Clouseauesque investigation by the Ghost Squad that left unresolved questions about whether a network of corrupt detectives existed in the Flying Squad. The public were kept totally in the dark about how obviously unfit the Yard was to carry out this internal corruption probe any longer, having allowed an intelligent supergrass to run rings around them for two years.

In January 1997, Raison returned to the Flying Squad. He says he was offered a posting anywhere in the Met, including CIB, but chose to return to Rigg Approach. He took a copy of the report, with CIB's authority, and kept it locked in the office.

Parallel to Raison's inquiry was a secret investigation into Rigg Approach about which he knew nothing. The Yard will not discuss it because this too ended in failure.

Norman McNamara was one of seven superintendents in CIB2, along with David Niccol and David Bailey, who worked under Roger Gaspar. McNamara served there for over two years. During that time he learned how the Ghost Squad functioned under the cover of CIB2 and was at times inducted into its secret ways during the parallel secret inquiry, which is revealed here for the first time.

After 25 years serving Scotland Yard, McNamara was still very loyal to the organisation when he joined CIB2 and had no problem with the idea of investigating his own. Not long after arriving in May 1995, he read Harvey's allegations about the Flying Squad with increasing disbelief. He thought Harvey was making it up. But that view evaporated as intelligence reached McNamara suggesting some of the Rigg Approach detectives really were "gangsters with warrant cards".

The intelligence, he says, was a list of names of detectives handed to McNamara by a friend who had served on the Flying Squad. The list was passed to Niccol sometime in early spring 1996. It purported to contain the names of those detectives who'd divided up the guard's share of £200,000 from the January 1995 Security Express robbery. Niccol secretly filed away the document, but Raison heard about it and demanded to know the contents. He was eventually allowed to read it because, as his name was not on the list, it "partly confirmed his own integrity", Niccol reasoned.[24]

The list, says one CIB officer who saw it, included the names of detective sergeant Eamonn Harris and a detective constable called Kevin Garner, whom Harris had taken under his wing at Rigg Approach. The joint investigation, Operation Spy, had already identified Garner as one of two officers Harris had sent the day after the robbery to collect the £200,000 from the guard's friend.

Garner left school without qualifications in 1976 and joined the army to escape a troubled family life. As a member of the Royal Guards, he served in Kenya, Germany and Northern Ireland. But after five years his young and pregnant wife wanted him to resign the commission. Garner obliged and joined the Metropolitan Police aged twenty-two in March 1982, passing out of training as the top cadet. Within seven years, he was a detective constable serving in London's East End. Garner now had two daughters and bought his mother's old house.

Ten years after joining the police, Garner was accepted into the Rigg Approach office of the Flying Squad in May 1992. His marriage was already on the rocks but this posting proved too much for his wife, especially when within seven months of joining the squad he volunteered for an undercover role in a high-profile murder inquiry.

In January 1993 a secretive businessman, Donald Urquhart, was shot dead by a man on a motorbike as he walked arm in arm with his Thai girlfriend in Central London. The police investigation soon established from an informer that this was a contract killing facilitated, they believed, by Charlie Kray, and that the man who'd taken it up for £20,000 was called Graeme West. West's downfall was that he couldn't stop boasting about his rise up the criminal ladder from debt collector – his BMW registration was UOI – to contract killer.

HECTOR THE SELECTA'

After Urquhart's brother posted a £100,000 reward, Garner told his bosses that he might be able to infiltrate the suspect's criminal circle. The husband of a family friend, Jackie Buisson, was willing to make the introductions. Garner was having an affair with Jackie at the time.

Garner was not mentally prepared or formally trained for this dangerous undercover role, but his bosses failed to spot his weaknesses and authorised his deployment. When he bothered to come home after heavy drinking and socialising with his new criminal "friends", Garner was often abusive to his wife and threatened violence. He had already ignored her ultimatum to transfer off the Flying Squad because the hours were so unforgiving to family life. But when he pulled an imitation firearm on her, she took out an injunction banning him from the home.

In June 1993, while in the middle of the undercover operation, Garner had a breakdown. He started living as a vagrant, sleeping in his leaky car, not washing and sometimes not turning up to work for days on end. He moved in and out of flats and stayed with his girlfriend Jackie for a while. His behaviour at work was getting increasingly erratic – sometimes lying dead still on the office floor wearing a balaclava. Colleagues would just step over him. Even then, his bosses didn't pull him out of the Urquhart job.

When Graeme West was arrested and charged that September, *The Sun* was invited by the Yard to record the early morning operation. It was one of those cosy arrangements where everyone, except West, looked good.

Garner's undercover role never featured in any media coverage of the Urquhart murder trial, which concluded with West's conviction in December 1994. Just as well, because the Flying Squad detective was imploding at a rate of knots. His itinerant lifestyle was in free-fall, punctuated by violent rages and heavy drinking. Garner had also crossed the line, probably while undercover, and declared himself to his criminal drinking buddies as a bad cop willing to work for a price. His new friends were into armed robbery, drugs and funny money.

One was Michael Taverner, a car ringer from Hackney who specialised in stolen Mercedes. Taverner was well connected and an associate of Joey Simms, the criminal who carried out the Security Express robbery with Gary Ward and Hector Harvey.

In April 1996, at around the time the list with Garner's name on it reached Operation Spy, Garner was planning what is known as a tiger kidnap. This involves blackmailing the driver of a security van to go along with the cash robbery because he believes his family has been kidnapped. Garner had inside knowledge because as a Flying Squad detective he had recently investigated a tiger kidnap of a Securicor van. He thought the driver was vulnerable to a copycat robbery and suggested it to Taverner, who expressed interest.

Taverner enlisted the help of a friend called "Irish" Mick. But Mick was also an informant for SERCS, a CIB source has revealed to us. In July, Irish Mick told his handler he was going to meet an unnamed cop in an Essex pub to discuss an armed robbery involving other Flying Squad detectives.

DAC Roy Clark was immediately notified. Time was pressing because the Essex pub meeting was scheduled the evening before the robbery. Clark met with his number two at SERCS, detective chief inspector Bill Brown and others. "The discussion centred on whether we should let the tiger kidnap run or disrupt it. Clark decided to disrupt it. Securicor were brought in and asked to change the driver's shift. The informant had told us that the robbery had to be done on a certain day because corrupt Flying Squad officers would be on duty in a response car. By changing the driver's roster this would get back to the robbers and they would have to call off the plan. But we would cover the Securicor van just in case they didn't," explained a CIB officer.

Authority was given for the informant Irish Mick to participate in the operation. Before he left for the pub meeting, he was told to ring Taverner claiming the police were following him and suggested that the bent cop they were about to meet ran a number plate check. The Ghost Squad was monitoring the Police National Computer (PNC) to see which officer applied that afternoon to trace the car. Unfortunately, says our CIB source, although a check was made on the vehicle, the call was not taped and the voice at the end of the phone never identified.

Later that July evening, a surveillance team sat in the Maypole pub garden in Chigwell and photographed the meeting. Acting superintendent Norman McNamara, who was waiting in an unmarked car, immediately identified the officer sitting with Irish Mick and Taverner as DC Kevin Garner.

The Ghost Squad management committee met soon afterwards and received authority from the deputy commissioner Brian Hayes to start a "covert inquiry" into named Rigg Approach detectives. Clark ran this from inside SERCS. The covert inquiry was separate but parallel to the joint investigation by Niccol and Raison. Niccol knew about the covert inquiry but Raison was kept out of the loop.

HECTOR THE SELECTA'

"The home secretary [Michael Howard] gave authority for taps on the home phones of Kevin Garner and Eamonn Harris. These taps were later extended to include at least three other Flying Squad detectives. The home secretary also gave authority for the covert inquiry to conduct cell site analysis on the officers' mobile phones [a system of mapping calls between targeted individuals]," the CIB officer recalls.

Police use a technique once a target's phones are "hooked up" to stimulate conversation by creating a pressure point that will get people talking. In Garner's case there were two pressure points.

Firstly, they spooked Taverner into thinking the police were following him. He contacted Garner telling him he wanted no part in the tiger kidnap. Garner was worried for himself, so two days later, on 27 July, he went sick with a bad back. Meanwhile, Clark created a second pressure point around a stolen Mercedes that Garner had bought from Taverner and registered in Jackie's name. The covert inquiry had discovered the car squad were looking into Taverner as part of an operation, codenamed Masterpiece, into a Mercedes ringing syndicate to Malaysia. Operation Masterpiece was "accelerated", says our CIB source, to rattle the cages of Taverner and Garner. Jackie was visited about the stolen Mercedes. And the car squad "innocently" spoke to Garner about two PNC checks he had done on cars they had traced to Taverner. Garner falsely claimed he had been trying to nurture him as an informant.

The covert inquiry ran from July 1996 for six months. By January 1997 it could no longer justify maintaining the phone-taps because nothing compromising was emerging, our source tells us. "There was also pressure from the National Criminal Intelligence Service whose technical facilities faced competing demands from other police squads. So the [phone-taps] were taken off, ending the covert inquiry."

That same month the CPS, whose lawyers were kept in the dark about this parallel secret inquiry, also closed down Operation Spy after agreeing with Raison's report that no successful prosecution of Flying Squad detectives was possible.

13

GHOSTBUSTED

1997 was to be a year of transformation for Scotland Yard. Ahead of commissioner Sir Paul Condon was an unknown road paved with political minefields that could cost him his job and personal humiliation if he put a foot wrong. His Ghost Squad was an undisclosed failure and needed reform to meet the challenges ahead, not least the possibility of a left-leaning government after 18 years of Tory rule.

Nearing the end of his five-year term, prime minister John Major had no choice but to call a general election for May while his party and government were drowning in a sea of political sleaze, sex scandals, lies and sanctimony. This electoral meltdown made it almost inconceivable for Tony Blair's remodelled New Labour Party to lose.

In opposition, Blair had fought a canny fight to appear tougher on law and order issues than the most atavistic Tories like Michael "prison works" Howard. But what worried Scotland Yard significantly was New Labour's promise to the Lawrence family of a public inquiry into the police investigation if they came to power.

A private prosecution brought by Doreen and Neville Lawrence against three of the prime suspects had failed in April 1996. The Yard was still refusing to apologise or admit mistakes. How could it when the commissioner's integrity and that of his force had been hogtied since 1993 to defending the Barker Review cover-up?

Another of the Yard's concerns was New Labour's commitment to constitutional reform. A Bill of Rights incorporating the European Convention on Human Rights into British law would seriously affect

GHOSTBUSTED

operational policing, as would a proposed Freedom of Information Act.

Such openness was anathema to the Ghost Squad. Since 1993 it had been designed to prevent any bad seeds coming to the public's attention outside of the Yard's control. But in 1996 it all went wrong. The public and the politicians didn't know about its expensive failure and the Ghost Squad's secret management group was determined to keep it that way. The mishandling of Geoffrey Brennan and Hector Harvey had allowed both supergrasses to dupe the Ghost Squad and then expose its activities to the very people it was targeting. These two cases, sold to commissioner Condon as big breakthroughs, were in fact in utter disarray.

So too was the Ghost Squad's intelligence-gathering capability, run by the colourful Dave "Lazarus" Woods. He was the detective who mysteriously developed cancer, retired to die but reappeared as a shadow warrior in the anti-corruption crusade. The intelligence cell was very much a work in progress. But according to several CIB sources, by the end of 1996 it too was in "chaos". "Woods worked on the principle that knowledge is power. He tried to recreate the IRA cell structure where only one or two people knew the entire picture. But this led to confusion," recalls one detective who worked with him. "There was a lot of back-stabbing. They thought everyone was at it," says another, adding that the intelligence amassed from phone-taps and probes had not been properly sifted. "There was a lot [of intelligence] going in but nothing going out."

John Grieve, who oversaw most of this mess, had by late 1996 moved from director of intelligence to head of the anti-terrorist squad. He was still a Ghost Squad boss, as was his deputy Roy Clark. However, their cover was now blown. Clark was recalled to the Yard in November for another special assignment: to develop a new anti-corruption strategy that would meet the emerging public relations needs of Scotland Yard.

A new intelligence cell, called CIBIC, replaced the Ghost Squad. CIBIC operated totally in the shadows. It provided intelligence to a new proactive squad called CIB3, dubbed the Untouchables. Detectives from CIB3 would use that intelligence to mount sting operations against suspect cops identified by CIBIC.

Roy Clark's new anti-corruption model was a refined continuation of the illegal supergrass system his Ghost Squad had operated since 1994. In practice, CIBIC and CIB3 would also circumvent democratic and legal checks and balances during the evidence and intelligence-gathering process. In other words, it was a system designed to allow CIB3 detectives to manage any adverse findings they came across and thereby limit the damage to Scotland Yard's reputation while protecting the reputations of its favoured sons or those it could least afford to see exposed.

James Morton, in his excellent book *Supergrasses and Informers*, makes the point that the most interesting thing about supergrasses is who they don't name. This is more so when the supergrass is part of a police corruption probe. Under the CIB3 system, supergrasses would in effect be debriefed in a way that controlled the naming process.

The Ghost Squad had been a law unto itself with no outside scrutiny. Its shadow warriors operated an illegal and ultimately disastrous policy of not cautioning its supergrasses, not taping all interviews, not taking extensive debrief notes and offering deals that could be construed as inducements. It turned out that the same would happen at CIB3, with one important difference. Unlike the Ghost Squad, this new squad hoped to produce supergrasses like Harvey as key prosecution witnesses of truth against corrupt officers.

Liberal barrister Michael Mansfield QC recalls being invited in 1997 to address a meeting of some 200 police at a secret location in Surrey. "I hadn't heard much about the anti-corruption squad. Sir Paul Condon spoke before me. I was given no brief so I assumed they wanted me to talk about how corruption in the police has occurred. It was only when I took a question from the floor that it was apparent the Yard wanted me to talk about the use of supergrasses and informants, some of whom would be cops who turned Queen's Evidence for corruption trials. I was somewhat taken aback because I had spent my entire career arguing against the use of supergrasses. If they had been upfront I would have said no to the talk. If I had been asked to give advice on the merits of a supergrass strategy for the anti-corruption squad I would have advised against it."

So too would the CPS. Martin Polaine left private practice as a defence barrister to join the CPS special casework directorate in 1994. Four years later he became the lead lawyer for the newly created CIB3.

CPS involvement in the covert Ghost Squad phase was "marginal to say the least", Polaine confirmed. Back in 1993, Roy Clark did not want any formalised CPS involvement. He had argued that the agency wasn't trustworthy.

Polaine says Clark never consulted the CPS about the merits of a supergrass system. Had he, they would have advised against it. "If one was looking pre-1998 I think just about everyone in the CPS who looked at it would have said the supergrass system and debrief have fallen into disrepute. It would have been put that highly I think."

It is ironic that until Clark became witchfinder-general and resurrected the discredited supergrass system, he and the Yard had been vocal critics during previous anti-corruption inquiries into the force. When he served at Rigg Approach during the ill-fated Operation Countryman probe into the Flying Squad back in the early eighties, the Yard complained bitterly that the outside force was being led a merry dance by investigating the self-serving allegations of criminals against cops. And during Operation Jackpot into corruption at Stoke Newington police station, Clark defended his men against the allegations of what he repeatedly told the press were "self-confessed drug dealers". It is hard to see how after Brennan and Harvey, Clark was still a convert to the discredited supergrass system.

As the new operations director of the anti-corruption squad Clark replaced many of the old Ghost Squad bosses. Roger Gaspar was promoted and soon rewarded with an appointment as deputy director general of the National Criminal Intelligence Service where he became a leading advocate of Big Brother policing.[1] Superintendent David Bailey apparently took up a job with MI5 in the vetting section.

Two south London detectives replaced Dave "Lazarus" Woods. Confusingly, one was called David Wood, a detective superintendent whose last posting had been at the corruption-troubled Surbiton office of SERCS. It is thought Wood had been placed at Surbiton as a "sleeper" after the John Donald scandal. His new job was to convert the tangled affairs of the Ghost Squad into the tidy new intelligence cell that could service CIB3 with "intelligence packages".

David Wood had left school with few qualifications. He worked as a bank clerk, but got bored and sought more excitement by joining the police. His first arrest gives an insight into his character – young Wood frogmarched an impudent street beggar to the police station when he dared ask him for money.[2] For most of his service up until joining CIB3, Wood was stationed in south-east London where he had hooked up with the equally ambitious detective chief inspector Chris Jarratt in Southwark division, running covert operations, like the pawnshop in Bermondsey with undercover cop Michael.

Clark was said to be a mentor to Wood and he in turn was a mentor figure for Jarratt. One colleague recalls how Jarratt described Wood as someone who if he felt the cause was just could smile in your face and when your back was turned put a bullet in your head, metaphorically of course. The pair became a spooky double act in the anti-corruption crusade. Wood and Jarratt spoke a very telling fundamentalist argot to accompany their crusade. They talked of "doing God's work" and once described to us how errant cops willing to "purge their souls" would be "cleansed of their criminality".

Once CIBIC was properly functioning, Jarratt took over as head of intelligence and covert operations. Jarratt was also the officer who had investigated the controversial killing of prolific informant, David Norris, back in 1991, where key questions about police corruption were never properly answered. Jarratt was allowed to bring almost the entire Norris murder inquiry team with him to the new CIB3 and CIBIC, an intriguing move that says a lot about how sensitive the Yard viewed the Norris scandal and its links to their ongoing Stephen Lawrence problem. Others Jarratt invited onto CIBIC were colleagues he had served with on the Brixton Robbery Squad and Tower Bridge Flying Squad, two units with controversial histories of racism and misconduct dating back to the seventies, some of it before Jarratt arrived there. This group of south-east London detectives would dominate this next five-year phase of the anti-corruption campaign.

Jarratt was an active Freemason as were a number of others pulled onto CIB3. Clearly, the Yard did not see Freemasonry as an impediment to anti-corruption work. They could hardly have argued it wasn't a live issue. In March 1997, one month before Jarratt joined CIBIC, the Home Affairs select committee published its report on Freemasonry in the police and judiciary. It recommended there should be a publicly available register.

Freemasons doing normal police work often argue that it is a personal intrusion to be asked if they are "on the square", and unfair to automatically assume that membership implies anything sinister. We are not a secret society but a society with secrets, is their refrain. But a Home Office report on Police Integrity summed up the obvious danger this way: "The perceived impartiality of the Police Service is fundamental to public confidence and therefore its effectiveness, and no person within the police service – regular, civilian or special – should belong to an organisation which may cause the public to mistrust his or her impartiality."[3]

CIB superintendent Norman McNamara recalls being told by a Ghost Squad superior not to make disparaging remarks about the Brotherhood. "If you are being totally objective there is a conflict of interest with having people in senior positions in the Masons running the CIB inquiry. Does Masonry affect it? It must do because it excludes so many honest people from having a voice. It is also an ethic based on looking after your own and not hurting anyone on the square." The Masonic rulebook in fact refers to "a column of mutual defence and support".

The Home Office diluted the committee's recommendation and suggested a voluntary register. Clark wrote a round robin asking detectives to return the declaration form as a "positive demonstration of our respect for public concerns". It wasn't. Voluntary registration has been a failure and that includes the anti-corruption squad.

Another surprise appointment was that of superintendent Ian Russell who led the failed Operation Jackpot into Clark's old police station. In January 1998, he was appointed to lead the new-look CIB2, working alongside the Untouchables, or CIB3. Russell's new role was "to analyse information, gather intelligence and to investigate allegations and suspicion of serious corruption and matters of corporate interest".[4]

CIB2 would end up investigating several former alumni of Stoke Newington and even one of Russell's own detective sergeants on Operation Jackpot.[5]

So, as with the Ghost Squad, Clark selected detectives for CIB3 whom he liked and felt he could trust. They in turn selected others on the same basis. The end result looked like jobs for the boys. We say boys because CIB is still a male-dominated environment, a view echoed by one of the few senior female officers up there. "The Flying Squad was once regarded as the last bastion of male chauvinism, but now it is the anti-corruption squad," she says. Our source also feels that many male detectives on CIB3 were given accelerated (over) promotion while female detectives stayed in the same rank for years.

As CIB3 developed and grew in size to two hundred detectives over the next three years, the inducement to those who received the call was very alluring. Officers earmarked as high flyers were promised promotion, by at least two ranks, and a prestigious posting afterwards – a ruse often more effective than the Official Secrets Act. Others were told there were good overtime opportunities.

The mixing of preferment, friendship and Freemasonry with the inducement of accelerated promotion and financial reward put another question mark over CIB3's objectivity from the very beginning. In addition, detectives recruited there would be required to investigate friends, former sexual partners, enemies, fellow Masons and godfathers to their children. Not only did this make the anti-corruption squad potentially very leaky, it was also a recipe for score settling, partiality and victimisation.

The setting up of CIB3 and CIBIC in the first half of 1997 took place in an increasingly charged political atmosphere. In March, one month after the inquest into Stephen Lawrence's death, the family made a formal complaint against the Yard, claiming that corruption and collusion had contaminated the murder inquiry. The PCA appointed Kent Police to investigate.

Then in July, two months after New Labour's landslide election victory, new home secretary Jack Straw announced the setting up of the public inquiry. Preliminary hearings, where the inquiry would listen to the public's criticism of the Yard, were scheduled to start in the autumn. The language of New Labour created a wide public expectation that it would dismantle the entrenched culture of official secrecy and use its massive majority to open up British society by making it less anachronistic and reverential to the titled and unelected.

But Clark and CIB3 were on a Tardis travelling the other way. Corruption management with the appearance of reform was their brief. But now there was an additional danger coming from the elected chamber of the Commons. The powerful Home Affairs select committee was under Labour control and its chairman was a former investigative reporter who knew first-hand about so-called noble cause corruption in the criminal justice system and institutional cover-up.

Chris Mullin, the MP for Sunderland South, had persuaded his select committee colleagues to look into how the police investigated and disciplined their own. The hearings were scheduled from October to December 1997 and therefore dovetailed with the Stephen Lawrence Inquiry.

In the mid-eighties, Mullin had campaigned with Granada's *World In Action* to uncover malpractice in the West Midlands Serious Crimes Squad. His tenacity, with that of others, eventually led the Appeal Court to overturn in 1991 the conviction of six Irishmen wrongly accused of the Birmingham pub bombings seventeen years earlier. For his troubles, Mullin had been smeared by the right-wing press as a "Loony Lefty" and by the police as an IRA sympathiser or at best their dupe.

Mullin's select committee threatened to reveal the failures of a system of internal investigations that was well past its sell-by date. The Yard, in response, decided to go on a charm offensive, especially targeting the luvvies of the liberal media. In the summer of 1997,

THE SUPERGRASSES

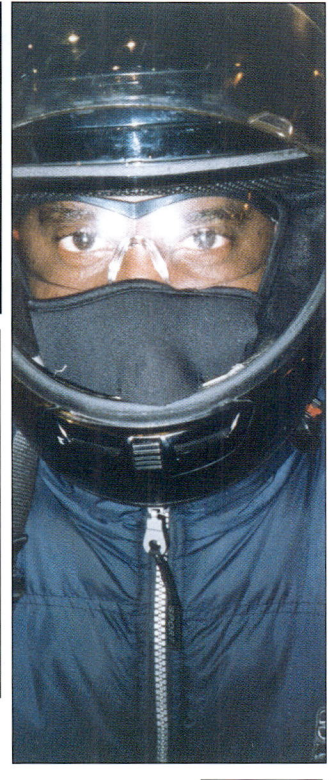

1. One of the many faces of double agent supergrass Geoff Brennan.
   (© Michael Gillard)

2. Supergrass Hector 'the Selecta' Harvey.
   (© Michael Gillard)

3. Duncan Hanrahan with one of his jailers on the supergrass wing in Basingstoke, which he says the Untouchables dubbed the Dorchester Suite.

4. Supergrass DC Neil Putnam who gave evidence against five colleagues from the East Dulwich SERCS office.

THE SUPERGRASSES

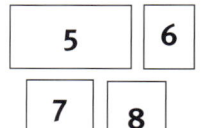

5. Flying Squad supergrass DC Terry McGuinness (right), who says the Untouchables told him they weren't interested in the police fit-up culture.

6. Supergrass DC Kevin Garner (left). His evidence helped convict three Flying Squad colleagues.

7. Evelyn Fleckney, drug dealer, lover and informant of DC Robert Clark, who later turned supergrass against him.

8. Star Yard informant David Norris. Murdered April 1991.

THE UNTOUCHABLES

Long Service Award
Presented by
Sir John Stevens QPM
6th December 2002

9. Commissioner Sir Paul Condon awards DI John Redgrave a long service and good conduct medal in June 1996. Did Condon know his Ghost Squad was investigating Redgrave at the time? After his retirement in 2000, the Labour Government made Condon a People's Peer. He now investigates corruption for the International Cricket Council.

10. 'Big schmile, Michael.' Commissioner Sir John Stevens awards Undercover 599 a long service and good conduct medal after the Untouchables ruined his life and undermined Merseyside Police's corruption probe.

THE UNTOUCHABLES

11	12
13	14

11. Deputy commissioner Sir Ian Blair, who's been directly responsible for the Untouchables since 2000. He is tipped as the Home Office's candidate to take over when Sir John Stevens retires in January 2005. (© uppa.co.uk)

12. Commander John Grieve, joint architect with Roy Clark of the Ghost Squad.

13. Stoke Newington boss Roy Clark before he left to set up the Ghost Squad and the Untouchables. He is now the director of investigations for the new Independent Police Complaints Commission.

14. Untouchables Commander Andy Hayman, who tried to undermine our investigation with a secret smear letter to *The Guardian*. He is now the chief constable of Norfolk Police.

THE UNTOUCHABLES

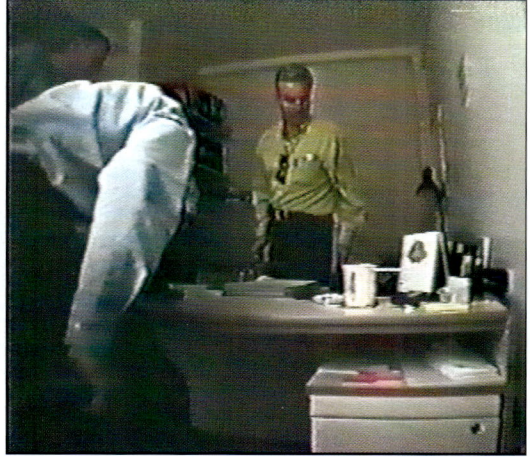

15. Ghost Squad chief D/Supt Roger Gaspar after giving evidence at Brennan's trial in 2001: 'I always suspected he thought I was a soft touch.' (© Michael Gillard)

16. DS Chris Smith, the Ghost Squad officer corruptly paid £10,000 by Brennan for moonlighting work. Smith later joined Esher Investigations and was secretly filmed in April 1997 offering his services to ret red detective Alec Leighton.

17. DCI Dave 'Cancer' Woods, whose illness was faked so he could run the Ghost Squad intelligence cell.

18. Detective Superintendent Tony Fuller, the current boss of the Untouchables' covert arm, the Intelligence Development Group.

19. D/Supt Chris Jarratt (left), with his then best friend Keith Pedder, the detective who investigated Rachel Nickell's murder and was later wrongly targeted by CIB.

20. DCS David Wood, who replaced Gaspar. Wood is now Northern Ireland Deputy Ombudsman, executive director of complaints.

THE VICTIMS

21. Ira Thomas, a victim of Stoke Newington policing. Wrongfully convicted for shooting Freddy Brett in 1988. (© Michael Gillard)

22. Erkin 'Egg' Guney, freed by the Appeal Court in May 2003 after serving seven years. Scotland Yard suppressed information on police corruption that showed his drug conviction was unsafe. (© Michael Gillard)

23. 1988 W.O.G.S. on tour to Cyprus. Brian Moore has always denied any link to W.O.G.S. Here he is in the middle with his arms around Terry McGuinness (left) and DC Yan Stivrins (right). Like Moore, Stivrins later joined the Untouchables.

24. (l to r) DS Gurpal Virdi, Superintendent Ali Dizaei, retired DI David Michael, founder of the BPA, and Inspector Leroy Logan. (© Michael Gillard)

THE VICTIMS

|25|26|
|27|28|

25. John Wilson outside the High Court in July 2001. A judge ruled he had been 'deliberately assaulted' during Euro 1996 by an officer who the Untouchables claimed they couldn't find. (© Photo News Service Limited)

26. Daniel Morgan with his children shortly before he was axed to death in March 1987.

27. Alastair Morgan, his mother Isobel, and girlfriend Kirsteen outside the House of Commons in July 2004 after the government had refused a public inquiry. (© Michael Gillard)

28. Suicide cop DC Alan 'Taffy' Holmes, who died before he could blow the whistle.

THE VILLAINS

29. Master criminal Stephen Raymond, who admits putting up £600,000 to undermine the Ecstasy case against him put together by DI John Redgrave.

30. Tall Ted Williams hailing a cab outside the Old Bailey after his dramatic appearance at Brennan's trial in March 2001. (© Sylvia Dubain)

31. Adams crime family associate Chris McCormack. He was suspected of trying to kill Hector Harvey over the 1995 Security Express robbery double cross. (© Mark St George)

GHOSTBUSTED

Condon gave interviews to the *Guardian* and the *New Statesman*, in which he called for a London Police Authority to monitor the Yard instead of the Home Office. The commissioner also claimed he was going to dedicate his last two years in office to "ethical matters". He started by calling for lowering the standard of proof required to sack dishonest officers at police disciplinary boards. The criminal test of beyond reasonable doubt should, he argued, be replaced by the civil test of determining guilt based on the balance of probabilities. Condon also told the *Guardian* there were "up to 200" bent cops in his force.[6]

In Britain's emaciated democracy, such "reformist" utterances can appear radical, especially when mouthed by the most powerful policeman in the country through a liberal newspaper. But a police authority was no more than Londoners deserved and something to which all other police forces already answered. Meanwhile, blaming tricky detectives who exploited the discipline process was hardly a clarion call for a fully independent police complaints system. It was, though, a pitiful attempt to compensate for Condon's silence over the Stephen Lawrence scandal.

Chris Webb, one of the Yard's spin-doctors, confirms that around this time a media strategy was developed that involved sending the commissioner on an extended "round of visits" to editors of national media organisations and potential troublemaking programmes and newspapers. The message was a simple one: Scotland Yard had the necessary integrity to investigate itself and put its own house in order, once and for all.

It was not a hard sell. The wholesale removal or blunting of ITV's once powerful quartet of factual programmes – *This Week*, *World in Action*, *Weekend World* and *The London Programme* – meant there was already little counter to the breathless, drive-by journalism of the Crime Reporters Association. Editors took seriously Condon's entreaties, mindful as they were of how easily the crime tap is turned off and that they could find themselves out of the loop as their competitors stole a march on the next circulation-ramping orgy of gore and sleaze.

Condon offered access to the CIB casebook in return for the media's support for his war on corruption. In the emerging low-risk, dumbed-down news age such handouts not only help assuage in-house libel lawyers but could also be repackaged with two narcissistic ingredients – a public interest claim and the pretence of independent investigation. What's in it for the police? They get to control the media access while looking serious about clearing out their stables.

UNTOUCHABLES

Subliminally or explicitly, the argument for self-regulation is also reinforced.

The Yard and CIB3 were delighted by the resulting media comparisons with 1930s Chicago federal corruption buster Eliot Ness and his Untouchables. The name evoked imagery of lilywhite crusading cops who couldn't be bought. Of course Untouchables can also mean those imbued with a sense they are above the law. And by secretly operating an illegal supergrass system, senior officers were explicitly telling their new CIB3 recruits exactly that. But with key sections of the media now firmly embedded in the war on corruption, the ill-served public had few opportunities over the next six years of getting behind the spin.

It is standard operating procedure nowadays for police and intelligence services to conjure up what is known as a media "spectacular" when a positive publicity coup is required to offset a crisis. But what happened next was police choreography that made *Lord of the Dance* seem clubfooted. The co-ordination between the commissioner's office, his press bureau and CIB3 was worthy of an Olympic opening ceremony, although more Berlin than Barcelona.

Planning for the Untouchables' spectacular began in late November 1997 with two critical events in mind, the forthcoming select committee appearance of commissioner Condon, followed shortly by the presentation to Parliament and the Stephen Lawrence public inquiry of the PCA/Kent Police report into the family's complaint of corruption, collusion and incompetence at the Yard.

Leading Untouchables David Wood and Chris Jarratt busily reassessed the failed Operation Spy into Flying Squad detectives at Rigg Approach and settled on 37-year-old DC Kevin Garner as the weak link.

Jarratt and Wood came up with a highly risky sting operation that they hoped would entrap Garner and his corrupt colleagues still serving in the Flying Squad. By doing so, CIB3 sought to corroborate Harvey's evidence that these defective detectives had stolen £250,000 of recovered proceeds from the January 1995 Security Express robbery.

This CIB3 sting operation was codenamed Brunei. On the orders of Wood and Jarratt, 80 kilos of black hash were borrowed from the Yard's confiscated drugs stash. Each one-kilo slab was wrapped in cling film and marked on its side with a varnish invisible to the human eye.

GHOSTBUSTED

In late November 1997 a flat in east London, near City Airport, was rented under a false name and a few days later, on 2 December, two days before the commissioner was due in Parliament, the drugs were put inside green bin liners and planted in a cupboard under the bathroom sink. CIB3's bugging unit had also wired up the flat for sound and pictures. Across the road from the front entrance CIB3 officers set up a 24-hour observation post.

The trick now was to persuade Garner to steal the drugs. He had retired two months earlier on an enhanced medical pension, suffering from post-traumatic stress disorder. CIB3 turned to Garner's petty criminal friend, Mick Taverner. The Untouchables "persuaded" him to work for them after Taverner had been arrested earlier in the year for car ringing and possession of a gun and ammunition. A secret deal was struck: Taverner pleaded guilty to the ringing and the weapon offences were dropped. He received a low sentence and in return agreed to help police informant Irish Mick entrap Garner.

They spun Garner a lie about a man who was looking after a parcel of drugs and wanted it robbed in a way he could pretend to the owners that the police had raided his flat. He agreed to do the job for £20,000.

Operation Brunei was not the only preparation the Untouchables were undertaking in advance of Condon's appearance in front of the Home Affairs select committee. While spin-doctors worked on the commissioner's speech, Roy Clark had put together an intelligence package for committee chairman Chris Mullin as a little taster of the difficulties the Yard faced in getting rid of its rotten apples.

The intelligence package concerned three detectives who soon after their suspension for moonlighting went sick with stress and depression then retired on ill-health pensions before they could be disciplined.[7] Mullin mentioned the case during the committee hearing which allowed the *Times* crime correspondent to oblige the Yard with a splash highlighting Condon's "frustration" that his anti-corruption efforts were "routinely curtailed by abuses of an ancient, creaking disciplinary and pensions system".[8]

On 3 December, Garner visited an old Flying Squad buddy known as Meathead. Detective constable Terry McGuinness was serving at Limehouse police station not far from the flat where the 80 kilos of dope had been planted by CIB3. McGuinness, then 39 years old, agreed to help nick the drugs the following evening when he would be on night duty. He also agreed to get a false search warrant to make it look like a police raid.

UNTOUCHABLES

The next day, at lunchtime, Garner knocked on the front door of another former Flying Squad colleague. Keith Green had been retired for 18 months when Garner unexpectedly arrived. Green was now a rugby coach to schoolchildren, a job that was slowly helping him recover from a mental breakdown brought on by a near-fatal shooting accident caused by McGuinness during their time on the Flying Squad.

Meanwhile, that same day at the Commons Sir Paul Condon was sitting in the committee room flanked by his deputy Brian Hayes and operational chief of the Untouchables, Roy Clark. They had kept him abreast of the sting operation and briefed him for his committee appearance. Primed crime reporters and television crews eagerly awaited the top cop's speech.

The committee had already heard in the past six weeks from the Police Establishment – the Association of Chief Police Officers, the Police Superintendents' Association and the Police Federation – and from the Home Office and CPS. To balance the evidence, there had also been submissions from the pressure group Liberty and the more radical Police Action Lawyers' Group, who told the committee how they advised victims of police crimes not to bother using the internal complaints system but to bring civil actions instead as a more effective remedy – a position that still holds today.

The commissioner's carefully crafted speech started by emphasising that the vast majority of his 27,000 employees were honest and hard-working. There was, however, a "minority" who were corrupt, dishonest and unethical. Their activities, said Condon, did "immense damage to public confidence". But these rotten apples in his orchard were "cunning" and wise to anti-corruption measures, like pesticide-resistant fruit flies. And in the event the Yard did catch one of them "at it", Condon bemoaned their cynical manipulation of the disciplinary process. "The nature of the problem is such that tackling and preventing serious misconduct needs to be a constant part of police strategy. The system must allow for the effective investigation and punishment of wrongdoers," he roared.

After finishing the speech the commissioner was subjected to some gentle questioning. Having neatly shifted the blame for a lack of public confidence in its entirety onto the small minority of corrupt cops, Condon was asked to quantify the size of the problem: "I would say it is less numerically than the seventies. I do not believe and I hope it is not as serious as [former commissioner] Sir Robert Mark's nearly 500 officers who left the Met under a cloud. If you want a percentage

GHOSTBUSTED

figure on it, I would hope and believe it is contained somewhere between 0.5 per cent and one per cent. There is a spurious precision to that but I would say somewhere between 100 officers and 250 officers would be the range in which we are operating."

Condon and his troupe of advisers left the Commons with the satisfaction of a job well done. The commissioner had come across as a reformer who bravely admitted his problem and requested political support to carry out a purge.

What was needed now was the media spectacular to reveal to the politicians that his Untouchables were already poised behind enemy lines. That evening, just after 9.30 p.m., two CIB3 officers watched as Garner, McGuinness and Green arrived at the flat. Garner broke in and walked up the stairs shouting, "Police, anyone in?" McGuinness followed him, pretending he had a search warrant. Green remained on the doorstep, a police truncheon in his hand.

Within seconds of entering Garner went straight for the bathroom cabinet where he found the drugs. "Here you are, it's here," he said to McGuinness, who grabbed some of the bin liners. Green had come upstairs by now and was given two sacks to take to Garner's car. In five minutes they were away. The drugs were stored in a lock-up. Green went home, McGuinness went back to the police station and Garner met Taverner and Irish Mick to hand over the keys.

The following morning, as commissioner Condon digested his shredded wheat and the favourable coverage of his select committee performance, he now had a "spectacular" up his sleeve for the second phase of the propaganda war.

Four days later, on 8 December, CIB3 officers mounted a series of co-ordinated dawn raids on the homes of Garner, McGuinness and Green. Only Garner put up a struggle. They were taken to separate police stations and interviewed over two days. Garner and McGuinness declined to comment. Green, however, waived his right to a solicitor and explained himself over six hours of careful questioning. On 9 December all three men were charged with aggravated burglary and conspiracy to supply drugs.

The next day they were taken to Bow Street Magistrates court and remanded. The media were there to record the CIB3 triumph. At 6.40 p.m., Garner and McGuinness changed the course of their lives for ever.

What suddenly persuaded them to turn supergrass is unclear, because CIB3's dealings with the two men were not tape-recorded. Maybe it was the unassailable video evidence against them.

McGuinness later told us he decided to roll over when he was told Garner had coughed and Green was talking. He wanted to make it as easy on his family as possible and thought he would get a lighter sentence. Garner later claimed he became a supergrass because he felt his life was going nowhere. But roll over they did. CIB3 now had its first police supergrasses and the timing could not have been better for their bosses at Scotland Yard.

Just before the select committee hearing closed, on 15 December Parliament was given a copy of the PCA/Kent Police inquiry report into the Lawrence family's complaint. It was highly critical of the original murder investigation and attacked as "misleading" the scandalous Barker Review, to which Condon had pinned his integrity. Had the commissioner not already pre-empted the problem, this PCA report would have been very damaging for relations between Scotland Yard and the government. After all, his boss, home secretary Jack Straw, had just a few months earlier pinned *his* credentials to a public inquiry into the Lawrence scandal.

CIB3 couldn't yet go public that it was debriefing two former Flying Squad detectives who had turned supergrass. But in the end, a political showdown was not necessary because the Yard privately briefed the Home Office about their "spectacular" success with Operation Brunei. In the run-up to Christmas, Jack Straw felt confident enough to field parliamentary questions from MPs like Chris Mullin who were concerned about what the Yard was doing to catch the 250 bent cops.

On 22 December Straw told the Commons: "No police officer should be in any doubt about the resolve of both the commissioner and I to ensure that any corruption is rooted out vigorously and firmly." Straw directed MPs to Condon's recently launched "five-year strategic plan" and commented that the commissioner had informed him he was using "proactive methods and intelligence to target suspects". CIB would have "all the resources necessary" and the detectives it needed to tackle the problem, he promised. This was music to Condon's ears given that his failed Ghost Squad had spent millions since 1993. At least that could now be lost in the new corruption budget he was authorised to spend. The Yard refuses to disclose the true cost.

Mullin asked Straw for an assurance he would not give in to "mighty vested interests", as his Tory predecessors had done, over shaking up the police disciplinary process. Straw replied that he looked forward to the select committee report and repeated his determination to ensure Britain's top cop had "the full range of powers effectively and ruthlessly to root out corruption".[9]

Over Christmas, Garner and McGuinness formally became supergrasses, a system supposedly regulated by the 1992 Home Office guidelines and PACE. But CIB3 flouted those guidelines. There was immediate pressure to get results from both corrupt cops, especially as Green had pleaded not guilty and was also rebuffing crude attempts by Wood and Jarratt to roll him over.

On 15 January, Mullin's select committee finally reported its findings. It unanimously concluded that the current police discipline and complaints procedures didn't command public confidence. The report expressed concern over the damaging influence of the "small minority" of up to 250 bent cops in the Yard, and recommended lowering the standard of proof in discipline cases, removing the right to silence and abolishing the double jeopardy rule, whereby a police officer could not be disciplined on the same facts for a crime he had been acquitted of in the criminal courts.

The report was also in some ways a radical blueprint for ending closed, internal police investigations of serious police crimes from corruption offences to deaths in custody. A key written and oral submission came from ragamuffin lawyer, and veteran of the HCDA exposé of corrupt practice at Stoke Newington, Russell Miller of Birnberg & Co.

Miller described the PCA as "an unmitigated failure", remarking that the percentage of proved complaints had steadily decreased from five per cent in 1984 to two per cent in 1990. He also accused them of smearing as greedy and uncooperative those who reject the police complaints system in favour of civil actions. "The result of trying to dispel public cynicism without actually doing anything about the substantive issues was to widen the gulf in public confidence as the façade of independence at the PCA inevitably descended into political apology for the problem it could not solve."

Miller reminded the committee that since Scarman's inquiry created the PCA, the "crisis of faith" in marginalised communities had widened. The police were widely seen as "above the law", a view supported by the failure to convict one officer associated with the miscarriage of justice cases, deaths in custody and by the exceptional legal privileges extended to officers under investigation.

Civil actions were not the solution, said Miller, but symptomatic of relevant authorities not controlling or prosecuting police crimes.

He highlighted how in 1996 commissioner Condon had successfully persuaded the High Court to put a cap on jury awards in civil actions against the police and was now seeking to create a new offence of making a malicious complaint. The Police Federation lawyers were also on the counter-attack by seeking to prevent a successful plaintiff from having a statement read out in court naming the guilty officers involved in planting evidence or acts of violence and corruption.

Mullin's committee were clearly persuaded, and concluded "independent investigation would be desirable in principle not least because of the boost this would give to public confidence". It warned the government and the police that if the recommended reforms to the current complaints and discipline system "continued to enjoy only low credibility, then independent investigation will have to be considered". Consequently, the report called for increased powers and funding for the PCA and more openness, expedited apologies and *ex gratia* payments to complainants from the police. Meanwhile, it suggested the government commission "a feasibility study for an independent complaints investigation process".

"War is declared on corrupt police," announced the *Guardian*. The commissioner was quoted endorsing the recommendations concerning the disciplinary process, which he said would make his "crack down" on corrupt cops easier. Honest officers had nothing to fear, he said. But there was total silence on the issue of independent investigation and the failures and bias of CIB.[10]

The problem for Condon was this: the parliamentary clamour for an independent investigation system now "legitimised" the long-held demands of those the police had previously dismissed as the drug-addled rantings of "toy town revolutionaries" and assorted misfits with beards and sandals. That clamour was only going to get stronger when the Stephen Lawrence Inquiry formally opened in a few weeks on 24 March and started to examine Condon's conduct over the Barker Review, among other scandals.

The success of Condon's Untouchables therefore was crucial to his own political survival. If CIB3 could be seen to be ruthlessly rooting out the 250 bent cops in the force then Scotland Yard stood a chance of convincing the Home Office it should not be stripped of its privilege to investigate itself. And in the meantime the Lawrence Inquiry would leave corruption matters to the Yard. What was needed was to accelerate the media "spectacular".

Garner and McGuinness had given CIB3 the names of various

members of the Rigg Approach Flying Squad who they said were corrupt. The secret, unrecorded debriefings of Garner were way off corroborating Hector Harvey's accounts of the January 1995 Security Express robbery. Nor did Garner and McGuinness corroborate each other on key issues. Altogether it was just a mishmash of admittedly explosive but as yet uncorroborated allegations of organised and regular criminality at Rigg Approach.

After high-level discussions at the Yard a decision was taken for CIB3 to set up a new operation codenamed Ethiopia under a new superintendent on the squad called Brian Moore, another ex-Stoke Newington officer who had served under Clark. Moore's number two was detective chief inspector Martin Bridger, a former member of the Tower Bridge Flying Squad.

On 27 January, CIB3 carried out a series of dawn raids on the homes of fourteen serving and five retired Rigg Approach Flying Squad detectives from the rank of detective constable to detective chief inspector. Undercover cop Michael, who'd rebuffed Jarratt's request to join the Untouchables, was one of them.

The serving officers were suspended and served with formal notification of the catch all allegations against them. It read: "Between 1992 and 1997, a group of police officers from the Robbery Squad at Rigg Approach were engaged in committing a series of thefts, robberies, offences of dishonestly handling stolen property, and conspiracies to pervert the course of justice. You are one of those officers."

The raids were co-ordinated with coverage on radio bulletins and in the press. The banner headlines were a gratifying propaganda coup for the Yard. "GHOST SQUAD ROOTS OUT YARD CORRUPTION" was *The Times'* take. "CLEANING UP THE FORCE" was the strap the *Sunday Telegraph* used above an interview with commissioner Condon. The top cop talked of how it was better to "wear the short term damage" rather than bury your head in the sand while the problem worsened. He stressed how London's force was the envy of most big city police chiefs because the corruption was not as widespread as in other major capitals.

With the suspensions under his belt, Condon and his spin-doctors went on a whistlestop tour of the national media shortly before the Stephen Lawrence Inquiry formally opened in March.

Three months later, on 23 June 1998, ten of the most important police officers and intelligence chiefs met secretly at the headquarters of NCIS in Vauxhall, south London.

Among the group were the chief or deputy chief constables of

UNTOUCHABLES

Manchester, Merseyside and West Midlands. Roy Penrose, formerly of the Yard, represented the new National Crime Squad, which had replaced the disbanded Regional Crime Squads. The director general of NCIS, John Abbot, was present with his deputy Roger Gaspar, the former head of the Ghost Squad. DAC Roy Clark was the most senior ranking officer representing Scotland Yard, the force Home Office mandarins were now hailing as the benchmark of excellence and success in anti-corruption work.

The meeting was called to develop a future nationwide "anti-corruption strategy". Managing the media was a prime concern. Controlling the Untouchables' image was crucial to neutralising the growing call for independent investigation of police crimes and misconduct. The Stephen Lawrence Inquiry hearings were in full swing. And the Lawrence family was demanding a public inquiry into police corruption, something the recent and high-profile launch of the Untouchables was designed to avoid.

Roger Gaspar delivered the key presentation. "Intelligence development to combat corruption should include investigation analysis of the recipients, brokers and sources of leaks to the media," he told the assembled group of securocrats. Gaspar also pointed out "many officers" in police work "don't regard contact with the media or the release of inappropriate information as corruption". Consequently, reinforcing a "culture of need to know" was essential, he proposed. With that in mind, the meeting agreed to develop a "publicity strategy" for the Association of Chief Police Officers (ACPO), the governing body for all forces in England and Wales.

The confidential minutes explained how "within the coming year or so a number of high-profile corruption cases will come within the public gaze. It was felt ACPO should develop a strategy for dealing with the adverse publicity that would accompany such a process. While benefit could be made from revealing the lengths to which the Police Service has gone to detaining and prosecuting these individuals, great care must be taken not to educate the opposition."

The NCIS meeting signalled a new phase of police-media relations. From it came a strategy for dealing with those reporters who wanted to find their own rotten apples and do their own independent health-check on the orchard. It would involve criminalising the unauthorised relationships between independent journalists and police sources, thereby internally justifying surveillance, phone-tapping and other spookery against untamed elements in the media.

It was veteran investigative reporter Geoff Seed who was leaked the

GHOSTBUSTED

19-page confidential NCIS document. When he read it he realised immediately there was a deliberate strategy to mislead the public about the true level of police corruption in the UK. Gaspar had warned the meeting that corruption was "pervasive" and may have reached "Level 2: the situation which occurs in some Third World countries". Lie detector tests were to be considered for rank and file detectives, the leaked minutes said. But not, it seems, for senior officers. One month after the NCIS meeting, ACPO put out a wholly misleading press release stating that corruption was in fact "extremely low".

When the *Sunday Telegraph* splashed Seed's story in September 1998, NCIS launched an immediate leak inquiry. Officers were sent to the newspaper to demand a return of the document. Seed says he was rung at home and asked the name of his source. He politely declined to assist.

This reaction was flatly at odds with how the then BBC home affairs correspondent, Graeme McLagan, was handled. While Seed was being attacked, McLagan was being spoon-fed. The BBC veteran of 30 years admits receiving "instructions" from an anonymous caller to go to an address in London where over 2,000 pages of confidential Operation Ethiopia documents were made available to him for future programmes. Only CIB3 or the intelligence services could legitimately have had access to these documents on the Flying Squad corruption probe. This was either an authorised leak, of the kind Chapman Pincher used to get from the intelligence services, or a massive security breach at the anti-corruption squad.

Yet there was no leak inquiry. But when Seed received a mere 19-page document that revealed a strategy to deceive the public and nobble independent journalism, the securocrats went "potty", he says. "The work of hackery and policery are very similar in that there is a search for information. It is what you do or don't do with it that matters. The police know the power they have got and can reward supplicants or cast into commercial darkness those who don't play ball." There are journalists, he says, who joined the Crime Reporters Association (CRA) waiting for the scoop that never comes.

"My worry is the master-servant relationship. You can have that. You can have this. You can't have anything at all. Metaphorically the police tell the crime correspondents, 'Here is the DO NOT CROSS tape.' Many have sold their independence and it is not a defence to say that the news desk had a gun to their ear. Crime correspondents are made privy to some material and leave the briefing with a warm glow that they are part of some elite, secret club. It's Masonic with a small M. Every so often they are thrown some red meat but in the main the lions of the press are docile."

The ACPO media strategy also focused on how to deal with potential troublemakers in the CRA, like veteran *Mirror* crime correspondent Jeff Edwards. He was marked as "too close" to certain police officers, and therefore a risk to the official version about the Untouchables, a *Mirror* source reveals. A senior executive was warned about Edwards during a party attended by the deputy head of MI5. The spook suggested how unfortunate it would be if Edwards was allowed to become "aligned" with the Rigg Approach Flying Squad, said the source. The crime reporter had built up an enviable list of contacts in different corners of the Yard over the years; some had even become good friends. "My view has always been that the police have every right to drive down hard on corruption, but their tactics in doing so have to be absolutely beyond reproach. Anything less undermines the whole ethos," says Edwards.

Among all the puffery and bum-fluffery of Scotland Yard's propaganda efforts was one story that had to be suppressed. The Untouchables' much-vaunted drug sting, Operation Brunei, had a dirty secret which if exposed would severely damage political confidence in the newly launched anti-corruption squad's competency and honesty.

Wood and Jarratt had arranged the planting of 80 kilos of hash worth £500,000 in the east London flat *against* the advice of government lawyers, who quite understandably feared the drugs would be stolen. The two Untouchables convinced their bosses at the Yard that the risks were "acceptable and legitimate". However, one week after the sting operation, only 54 kilos were recovered. Just as the CPS predicted, CIB3 had "lost" 26 kilos of dope worth a staggering £162,500.

Not only did CIB3 ignore legal advice, no surveillance team was deployed to follow Garner from the flat to the lock-up where he stored the drugs. CIB3 claim he might have spotted the tail. But this doesn't explain why the lock-up, which CIB3 knew about in advance through their informant Irish Mick, was not wired up as the flat had been. Similarly, tabs were not kept on Taverner and Irish Mick in case they decided to help themselves to the dope and pull a double whammy on CIB3.

GHOSTBUSTED

When the Untouchables finally arrested Garner, McGuinness and Green none of the hash was found in their homes. Green was never asked about the drugs and McGuinness confirms he too was never questioned about them during his debrief. Incredibly, Jarratt never asked Garner, the prime mover, one question about the missing dope in the days after his arrest or at any point during his subsequent debrief.

At 5 a.m. on 16 December the 54 kilos were "recovered" in the strangest of circumstances. Later that day, unannounced, Wood and Jarratt saw Green at the hospital wing of Brixton Prison. Green's depression had returned and he was feeling suicidal. CIB3 needed him to turn supergrass just as Garner and McGuinness had done six days earlier. That way they would not have to disclose details of the sting operation to Green's lawyers, and more importantly, they could hide their embarrassment over the missing 26 kilos of dope. In return for an admission and details of the corruption of others, Green claims Wood offered to recommend a two to four-year sentence in a secure location, a new identity for him and his family and some financial help to start a new life. He refused.

The next day Green appeared at Bow Street Magistrates Court to ask for bail. What happened in court was extraordinary. In opposing the bail application Jarratt swore on oath that Green had made a "full confession" the previous day. Green jumped up and denied it. Jarratt also told the magistrate that Green had access to the drugs, something which was untrue, given that they had been recovered the day before.

As a result of Jarratt's forceful submission, Green was denied bail and spent the next 11 months on remand until his trial in October 1998. During that time he attempted to hang himself. A fellow inmate intervened when he saw Green fixing the noose around the showerhead.

Green was transferred to a psychiatric intensive care unit in Essex. By this stage the Home Office had become involved and wrote to the hospital expressing concern that Green was a flight risk and once again repeated the canard, which could only have come from CIB3, that the drugs "have yet to be recovered".

During the six-day trial at the Old Bailey, the prosecution barrister flatly contradicted Jarratt and made it clear to the jury that Green had no control or involvement with the drugs after he helped load all 80 kilos into Garner's boot. In the witness box Green claimed he had no idea it was drugs. He was just helping a mate recover some property.

UNTOUCHABLES

The prosecution never used Garner or McGuinness, the only two people who could challenge this. Instead they relied on the video evidence. "The prosecution thought the video played to the jury would sink me," says Green.

The Yard now says it acted on CPS advice that the video evidence was ample enough to secure a conviction. But CIB3 had another more important motive for not using McGuinness and Garner: they didn't want to burn either supergrass too early. For had they, the unlawful debriefing system, damaging inconsistencies between Garner and McGuinness and the scandal of the missing 26 kilos of dope would have all been exposed under cross-examination. Instead, it made strategic sense to work out how their supergrasses, including Hector Harvey, corroborated one another before using them against the main targets – those Flying Squad detectives at Rigg Approach believed to be involved in the Security Express robbery.[11]

Just before the jury retired to deliberate on Green's fate, CIB3 tipped off the media about the dawn arrest and charging of four serving detectives and a lawyer in connection with that robbery.[12] The publicity forced the judge to sequester the jury overnight in a hotel without access to the television or newspapers. If this was an attempt to influence their decision it failed, as the next day the jury unanimously acquitted Green.

A few months later, he complained to the PCA. Green alleged that Jarratt and Wood had "lied in court" about his disputed "confession" and conspired to pervert the course of justice by covering this up. Both Untouchables, who denied this, were key prosecution witnesses in the forthcoming Flying Squad and other CIB3 trials. So the complaint investigation was going to be a real test of the PCA's independence from the police and Home Office.

However, Green was unaware that soon after his arrest in early December 1997 CIB3 had approached the PCA and asked if they wanted to supervise the Flying Squad inquiry. The clever approach coincided with the publication of the damning PCA/Kent inquiry report. However, the PCA's then chairman Peter Moorhouse and his deputy, John Cartwright, took a very strange decision. After what a spokesman called an "agonising" debate, the two PCA bosses overruled colleagues who favoured supervision. A lack of resources and manpower were the reasons the PCA couldn't offer any "meaningful" supervision, the spokesman explained. "We'd just have been onlookers." The decision, however, was highly questionable given that at the very same time the PCA/Kent inquiry concluded that the Yard had covered up during its internal Barker Review of the Lawrence murder inquiry. So how could they be trusted to get the Flying Squad corruption probe right without some supervision?

Strangely, Moorhouse did find resources for the PCA to supervise Green's very damaging complaint. The Yard's Area Complaints Unit, a very poor relation to the commissioner's Untouchables, carried out the actual investigation. Green was not alone in doubting it would go anywhere other than into the long grass.[13]

After the introduction of PACE to end the practice of verballing, confessions were so rare that they immediately attracted suspicion. This suspicion grows when best practice regulations are not followed. Jarratt, the PCA discovered, had not tape-recorded Green's alleged confession. Instead he made a pocket-book note but never got Green to sign it as an accurate account. Nor had Jarratt timed and date stamped his own notebook to show it was contemporaneous. Similarly, although Wood had countersigned Jarratt's note, he did not make his own entry in a pocket book.

Green had also complained that CIB3 officers including Jarratt had repeatedly stressed to him they were not interested in detectives who fitted people up or ramped up the evidence. In his statement to the PCA, Green recalled one CIB3 officer saying: "That's God's work, God wants you to do that, we're after people who work against God, ruin cases etc." I said, "Who's God?" He said, "The commissioner." In other words, the Untouchables were telling potential supergrasses that so-called noble cause corruption was of no interest to them. This was a very serious allegation, which the PCA inquiry failed to look into.

The months rolled by, and in December 1999 the PCA informed Green there was insufficient evidence to substantiate his complaint. He cried "cover-up at the highest level" and told the PCA the investigation had not examined all the available supporting evidence. The PCA sought a response from the Yard, who after months of silence claimed they had "lost" the file. The Home Office declined to bring in an outside force to re-investigate.[14]

So where is the 26 kilos of dope? At the time of writing, the Yard confirms the drugs are still "missing". "They're gone. Obviously sold, smoked. Gone. Not under our control. No idea where they are," said Untouchable Dave Pennant, rather defensively.

The finger of suspicion points to a small number of people. Did Garner skim off 26 kilos before he handed the keys of the lock-up over to Taverner and Irish Mick? Certainly the CPS believed this at one stage. That's why in early 2000 they served the supergrass with a statement claiming he had profited by £200,000 from the drugs he admitted stealing from the flat. But Garner's lawyer was having none of it. He wrote to the CPS that his client was considering "withdrawing his co-operation" as a supergrass willing to give evidence against the four charged Flying Squad detectives if the confiscation issue was not abandoned. He also alerted the CPS to "contradictory earlier promises" from CIB3.[15]

To its surprise, the CPS discovered that in October 1998, one day after Keith Green's acquittal, Wood had written confidentially to Garner's lawyer in the following unequivocal terms: "Your client transferred the drugs to a garage from where the drugs were removed by another. At this point your client no longer had control of the drugs and it is our view he was not responsible for the disposal of the missing 26 kilos of cannabis resin." After consulting with CIB3, the CPS wrote back to Garner saying it was all a dreadful mix-up.

Lawyers for the Flying Squad detectives suggested CIB3 discovered Garner had sold on the drugs and allowed him to escape repaying the proceeds in return for giving his evidence against their clients. Garner still denies this. Nevertheless, the Yard told us it would be looking into why he was never asked about the drugs during his entire debrief. We are still waiting for a reply.

So if Garner didn't have them, did Taverner or Irish Mick take the drugs from under the Untouchables' noses? Worse still, was one of them allowed to keep the 26 kilos as payment for their services to the anti-corruption squad?

CIB3 would have us believe that following a fortuitous and anonymous tip-off to Crimestoppers, 54 kilos of the dope was mysteriously recovered one week after Garner's arrest. Local police discovered the drugs in a flat, which CIB3 would also have us believe Taverner had rented. However the anti-corruption squad has consistently prevented any disclosure of material that would support their claim. Incredibly, they even resorted to PII certificates to prevent disclosure of the Crimestoppers docket. Furthermore, Taverner wasn't arrested until almost a year after the drugs were recovered. He refused to answer questions and the CPS decided there was insufficient evidence to prosecute. Irish Mick, the CIB3 informant, wasn't even interviewed.

A cross-party group of MPs has raised the case of the missing dope with the Attorney General, the Director of Public Prosecutions and the Home Secretary, but to no avail. The Yard told us it would examine the issue. We are still waiting for the results.

14

THE SLEAZE MACHINE

Sid Fillery is a big, jovial, Toby jug of a man. With sad spaniel's eyes and a laugh as large as the London Palladium, he seems on first impressions as if he could have stepped out of an episode of *Dixon of Dock Green*.

It's a matter of dispute when Fillery started working as an equal partner with Jon Rees in Southern Investigations. Fillery says it wasn't until he left the Met one month before the April 1988 inquest into Danny Morgan's murder. For six months before that Fillery was off sick with depression.

Clearly, he found in Rees someone who lifted his spirits. Both men genuinely felt alive in each other's company. When the routine bailiffing and warrant-serving work had been farmed out to friends and contacts, Rees and Fillery relocated around lunchtime to a tiny pub called The Victory. Tucked away behind another more salubrious boozer in Thornton Heath high street, that south London no man's land somewhere between Streatham and Croydon, The Victory had a pleasing, run-down air which betrayed definite signs that it had last been decorated sometime around the end of the Second World War when, in the view of many of its regulars, England was still England.

One day in 1989, *News of the World* reporter Alex Marunchak came to the pub by arrangement. The two private eyes had first crossed paths with him during the Morgan inquest and the suicide of detective Alan "Taffy" Holmes. This time Marunchak wanted help covering the forthcoming wedding of Princess Diana's Hooray Henry brother to a slender "commoner" with a supposed drugs habit.

UNTOUCHABLES

There was a high concept embedded in this piece of low journalism – to see if Southern Investigations could snatch a picture of the bride-to-be taking drugs in the week before her wedding. Rees and Fillery leaped at the chance and quickly rounded up a stake-out team. While no pictures were forthcoming by the wedding day, their passion for tabloid sleaze had been aroused.

Other missions for News International, Rupert Murdoch's media empire, were brought to a more successful conclusion. The target on one occasion was Tory Cabinet minister David Mellor and his affair with an unemployed actress, Antonia de Sancha. There followed a series of assignments with Mazher Mahmood, the *News of the World*'s star investigator, a smooth operator who would eventually fool Sophie, the Countess of Wessex, into destroying her entire business career by her hunger to obtain golden ducats for her domestic treasury through public relations work for Arab tyrants.

Sadly for Southern Investigations not all Mazher's early sheikh impersonations went off quite as smoothly as the destruction of Wessex Girl. The mark on this occasion was a friend of Prince Charles who the *News of the World* believed was involved in procuring what Fillery describes as "high class toms", prostitutes for wealthy businessmen and lonely foreign dignitaries from oil-rich Arab states. As part of the play, Mazher and Sid took a £2,000-a-night suite at London's Dorchester Hotel so they could secretly film both procurer and procured. Mazher dressed up in his trademark sheikh outfit while Fillery played "His Majesty's English private secretary", in blazer and bow tie.

Understandably, Fillery still relishes telling the story. The entire caper was progressing nicely. They were pretending it was his majesty's birthday – serving champagne and canapés to the girls and Arab potentates – when misfortune set in. Because they were working undercover Mazher could not settle his bills by personal or company credit card, so everything was paid in cash. But at Dorchester rates they soon ran out. Fearful that their carefully choreographed con might collapse, Mazher arranged for an emergency transfusion of cash from Wapping HQ. £10,000 was biked over and handed in to the concierge. Sadly, the money was to prove their undoing. The delivery driver left a yellow Post-It note attached to the rear of the package. It read: "Deliver to the Dorchester, Park Lane. PS. On no account identify yourself or the recipients as working for the *News of the World*." With their cover blown, a burly bouncer escorted Mazher and Fillery to the door, with the private eye retorting, "I've been thrown out of better places than this."

THE SLEAZE MACHINE

Another Southern Investigations assignment from the *News of the World* involved an eight-man team spending a week in Blackpool during the Trades Union Congress annual conference. The idea was to film union leaders and TUC delegates indulging gargantuan appetites for expensive bourgeois fare, copious drink and illicit sex, all improperly claimed on expenses, of course. At the end of the week the Southern Investigations team had been in and out of just about every hotel, bar, nightclub and knocking shop in Blackpool, without discovering Arthur Scargill or anyone else having sex with a cross-dressing midget lap dancer.

In the run up to the April 1992 general election, Rees and Fillery were once again on the job for the *News of the World* outing of a high-ranking Romeo MP. Liberal Democrat leader and former Special Boat Squadron officer, Paddy Ashdown, had been over the side with a House of Commons secretary called Tricia Howard.

Definitive proof of the affair was in the office safe of Ashdown's solicitor. It had been burgled and the documents were being hawked around Fleet Street. The *News of the World* was interested and Southern Investigations went to meet a man in the Brighton area. Fillery denies having anything to do with the actual burglary but felt his own team were under surveillance by Special Branch or MI5.

Ashdown knew the game was up once the documents – notes of his conversation with his solicitor about the affair – were on the sleaze market. He held a press conference admitting his error, which led to the inspired headline "Paddy Pantsdown". At the time of the burglary, the Liberal Democrat leader was trying to broker a coalition with New Labour in return for their commitment to proportional representation. The governing Tories feared such an alliance and Ashdown believes they had a strong interest in destabilising it. "What a terrible coincidence. That a thief should have broken in; that it should have been just before the election; that the Clinton/Gennifer Flowers saga is running at the same time; and that it should have all ended up in the hands of the *News of the World*."[1] Later, after the 1992 election defeat, Ashdown recorded in his diary his thoughts on an article he recently read about the NERDS, "a group of scandal hitmen who operate in America and are said to have been active here – for the Tories of course . . . I wonder if this is what happened to us."[2]

Southern Investigations were also hired to spy on Murdoch's own journalists at the *News of the World*, *The Sun*, *The Times* and the *Sunday Times*. The management were apparently concerned about moonlighting hacks working shifts and selling stories and commercial information to its rivals.

After New Labour came to power in May 1997, the search for Romeo MPs was renewed. According to Fillery, they had established before Robin Cook became foreign secretary that he was having an affair. The *News of the World* apparently sat on the story until one of its rivals got wind, and then splashed it. Fillery also maintains that Jack Straw, the new home secretary, had attracted their attention.[3] Other victims of drugs stings were England rugby captain Lawrence Dallaglio and *London's Burning* TV star John Alford.

Alas, thereafter it came to an end when Rees and Fillery fell out with News International over an unpaid bill. It is at this point, perhaps coincidentally, that having lost the protection of Rupert Murdoch's media empire, Southern Investigations became a target of the Untouchables. Little had been done in the previous decade since Danny Morgan's murder to tackle so obvious a network of sleaze and police corruption as the one Fillery and Rees were plugged into.

A key player in that network was south London detective constable Duncan Hanrahan, whose corruption had few limits. When the Untouchables caught him in May 1997 they had the best opportunity ever to break up the firm within a firm in south and south-east London that had continued uninterrupted at least since the Brinks Mat robbery. If handled properly, Hanrahan was also the tool that could open up the mystery of the Morgan murder.

Duncan Hanrahan is undoubtedly the most disarmingly devious of all the police supergrasses used by the Untouchables.

He joined the Met in 1977, aged 19. "I just had this thing I wanted to be a detective. I never wanted to help people or help society. I just fancied nicking people," he says with his trademark lopsided smile and lazy eye. Hanrahan insists he only became corrupt on retiring from the police after 14 years' service. What he really means is he was not personally corrupt in the police but corrupt for the police. "When I was in the job I never took a pound note. I was involved in sorting out evidence, a verbal here and a verbal there. I pulled strokes," he admits matter-of-factly.

Perversely, for a man who has done so many corrupt things, it really matters to Hanrahan that no one thinks he took backhanders for blowing out operations while he was in the police. He sees himself more as a corrupter of police officers, and less as a corrupt cop.

Throughout his police service Hanrahan had a knack for riding the

THE SLEAZE MACHINE

coat tails of influential officers and Freemasons, in particular commander Ray Adams. Becoming a Freemason was also part of Hanrahan's survival strategy. He is too clever to take seriously the world of funny handshakes and homoerotic ceremonies, but saw in Masonic membership a way to benefit from the network of professional people providing "a column of mutual support".

The death of his one-month-old baby daughter in 1985 had a profound effect on his outlook on life and his future commitment to the police. "Nothing ever again seemed that important," he says. "It's very hard to think of anything that is going to hurt you more than that, you know."

Hanrahan had started drinking heavily and his marriage was falling apart when he transferred to Norbury police station. There he identified Jonathan Rees, a fellow Freemason and pub veteran, as someone to know in south London. The private investigator, says Hanrahan, already had very good contacts in two other police stations, South Norwood and Addington.

After the Danny Morgan murder it was widely suspected that Hanrahan knew a lot more than he was letting on. To redeem himself perhaps, he agreed to approach Rees undercover and report back to the murder inquiry on their pub conversations. Nothing overly incriminating ever came of the undercover mission. But when it emerged during the Morgan inquest, Hanrahan became locally known as "double agent Dunk". It was never clear, though, which side he was really working for.

In the immediate aftermath of the Morgan murder, Hanrahan transferred to Kennington police station. The private sector was becoming far more alluring than a career in the Met. Respecting rank, taking orders and biting your tongue were not traits that came naturally to him.

Rees was willing to bury the hatchet with Hanrahan and gave him some moonlighting work watching sticky-fingered bar staff at a nightclub in Croydon – a sign, say some, that his undercover role was really a farce. According to former DS Alec Leighton, a mutual friend, Hanrahan later provided Rees with statements for his civil claim against the police at "total variance" to those he provided to the murder squad.[4]

In September 1991, Hanrahan retired from the Met. The defective detective had been on sick pay for almost a year following an injury sustained on duty. It was not so inhibiting as to curtail his desire to privatise the criminal justice system and, for the next five years,

UNTOUCHABLES

Hanrahan embraced a corrupt lifestyle like an alcoholic embraces a free bar. "I don't want my kids to think that what I did was really cool. At the time I thought it was the business. We were taking the piss out of the system. We were earning a few quid here and there. But when you look back at it, we were slags. We were the people we in the police would have called slags. We were the villains. I don't like that and I don't find it easy to live with. But that is what I was."

Hanrahan had his own relationship with Alex Marunchak of the *News of the World*, but he recalls they fell out over a story about Ms Whiplash, Lindi St Clair, the dominatrix. Her car had been found abandoned in Sussex and Hanrahan had a cop willing to sell him the details. He passed these to the *News of the World* for an agreed fee but inexplicably the story appeared in the *Mail on Sunday* instead. Hanrahan says Marunchak denied he had passed it on but was eventually persuaded to pay up.

Still aggrieved, Hanrahan scuppered the Paddy Pantsdown exposé the *News of the World* was working on with Rees and Fillery. While hanging around the office of Southern Investigations, he overheard the location of the rendezvous to buy the stolen Ashdown documents and the name of the broker who was hawking it to the tabloid. Hanrahan called commander Ray Adams who passed the information to the City of London police, presumably because they were dealing with the break-in at Ashdown's solicitors. The City Police registered Hanrahan as an informant and managed to arrest the broker before he met the tabloid representatives. Fillery suspected a leak and put up a sign in the office warning his staff and visitors, "WHAT YOU HEAR IN HERE STAYS IN HERE".

Alastair Morgan has what he called "an uneasy feeling" that Masonic influence was playing a part in the "horror story" slowly unfolding around his brother's gruesome death. This was not some fanciful construct he'd invented to compensate for the official stonewalling of the family. In fact, many of the key players in the Morgan case, from the suspects, the witnesses and even the murder squad detectives were members of the Brotherhood.

An officer at Norbury set up the Brothers in Law luncheon club in June 1988 for serving and retired members of Scotland Yard and Surrey Police who were Freemasons, says Leighton. Its emblem, a police shield with a sprig of holly in the middle, was on the invitation to the annual Christmas do at the Oakfield Road Masonic Halls in Croydon.

In December 1993, Leighton, Rees, Fillery and Hanrahan attended.

THE SLEAZE MACHINE

On a nearby table was a familiar face, detective inspector Alan Jones, the number two in the Morgan murder inquiry. "[Jones] was furious that I was there with Fillery and Rees. It gripped his shit," says Leighton, who had recently been suspended over the *Panorama* exposé of corrupt detective John Donald. One of the CIB officers investigating Leighton was also at the luncheon.

Another ex-south London cop whom Hanrahan worked with in the private sector was Martin King, a man with extensive contacts in the Underworld. King had once worked as a security consultant for bespoke tailors Austin Reed, the one place in the Metropolitan Police area where people were legally fitted up. But when he met Hanrahan, King was providing a special service to heavyweight villains, some of whom he knew through his long association with the crooked Brinks Mat lawyer, Michael Relton.

Hanrahan had something King's friends needed: an ability to identify which serving police officers were approachable to sort out a bit of bail or maybe lose some case papers. Together they were a formidable partnership. "I was impressed by the big lunches. But I was running before I could walk," recalls Hanrahan.

In 1994 Hanrahan set up his own private investigations company. At first it was run from Leighton's converted garage. But their relationship broke down so Hanrahan Associates moved to an accommodation address in Marble Arch. The corrupt opportunities kept coming his way, along with some more freelance work from Rees and Fillery.

Hanrahan says it only dawned on him how corrupt he'd really become when he lost his rag because a serving officer had refused to go along with some bent scheme. "I realised I'd lost all sense of proportion. Corrupting people was a way of life."

Most of his skulduggery was planned in one of two south London pubs, The Victory in Thornton Heath or The Prince Frederick in Bromley, where Hanrahan met corrupt detectives from the local drugs squad and the infamous East Dulwich SERCS office. The cash-for-police-favours were usually exchanged in plastic bags in the beer garden.

In May 1997, Duncan Hanrahan's greed and arrogance finally got the better of him. He and King were arrested in a sting operation trying to corrupt a CIB officer.[5] Their clients were a pair of criminals who hoped to sabotage two prosecutions they were facing for car fraud and grievous bodily harm. The arrest sent shock waves throughout south London. Hanrahan managed to get word to Fillery.

And when Leighton heard the news he felt CIB would now recruit Hanrahan as a supergrass against him. "CIB refer to me as some sort of 'godfather' orchestrating a cell of corruption from my exalted position as leader of the gang. This is absolute nonsense," he wrote to his solicitors at the time.[6]

Hanrahan admitted his corruption with King; the evidence was too damning to do otherwise. But unlike Hanrahan, King never turned supergrass.

The Untouchables secretly relocated Hanrahan to Basingstoke for extensive debriefing. He spent the next "seven months telling lies". Hanrahan was terrified of getting caught out. But when nothing happened, he settled into a routine. He loved to wind up his debriefers by using obscure words they were forced to look up, and playing one off against the other with bits of gossip he had picked up. But he resented what he regarded as the bullying and threatening manner of Dave Wood and Chris Jarratt, the two senior Untouchables in charge of the debriefing. Anyone who has spent time with Hanrahan, as the authors have, can see he will not be forced to do anything, no matter how bad his circumstances are. He also has an acute bullshit detector. The Untouchables' primitive approach to a complex and very valuable witness was counterproductive and ultimately, he says, encouraged him not to come clean.

In November, Hanrahan moved to the supergrass wing at Parkhurst Prison on the Isle of Wight. Here his deception would finally come to an end, but not for another nine months of mendacity. Hanrahan couldn't resist boasting to other supergrasses that he was having over his debriefers by pretending to purge his soul. To earn a reduced sentence he told the Untouchables what he felt they wanted to hear, but not too much that could be independently corroborated. "You've got to put yourself on offer to get the reduction. If my case continues this way I'll get a reduction without giving evidence," he told one inmate.

In August 1998, he confided in a supergrass called Bob Bown that he had taken part in a major crime CIB knew nothing about. He said it involved getting two detectives to help steal 40,000 ecstasy pills from a drug dealer.

Bown was a supergrass in a major guns and explosives trial involving serious gangsters.[7] That month he wrote to his police handler with as much detail as he could remember including the names of the two detectives. The letter was passed to the Untouchables. Wood and Jarratt went ballistic. This was the third supergrass who'd duped the anti-corruption squad. First Brennan and Harvey had over the Ghost Squad. Now Hanrahan had done the same to its supposedly more hardnosed replacement. In all likelihood the Untouchables would never have realised they were being mugged off had it not been for the duplicity of Bob Bown, whose motivation was undoubtedly to earn a further reduction of his sentence.

Hanrahan was due to be sentenced with Martin King for his original crimes.[8] He was expecting a substantial reduction. But the Untouchables had other ideas. In secret, an Old Bailey judge granted a delay while Wood and Jarratt set in motion an extraordinary plan that would only backfire and compound their humiliation.

The Untouchables gave Bown a crash course in the use of sophisticated bugging equipment worn on the body. His mission was to secretly record Hanrahan discussing the "ecstasy job" and anything else he was holding back. Between late October and early December, Bown covertly recorded hours of conversations at Parkhurst.

When the Untouchables felt they had enough, Hanrahan was arrested on 6 December and sent to a normal prison wing to contemplate how tantalisingly close he had come to getting away with the greatest gamble of his life. Eventually he pleaded guilty to a further eight corruption charges including conspiring with detectives in 1995 to steal the 40,000 ecstasy tablets. He also put his hands up to conspiring with the same officers to rob a Lebanese courier at Heathrow Airport of £1 million.[9] On 19 March 1999, Hanrahan was jailed for eight years and four months. The prosecutor revealed in court the identity of four detectives alleged to be part of his web of crime. They were named as Chris Carter, Len Guerard and Nigel Grayston, who had all since retired into the world of private investigations, and Steven Lee. He was on sick leave at the time.

Detective constable Nigel Grayston was Hanrahan's key contact in the south London police; they'd served together at Kennington. Grayston started off doing checks for him on the Police National Computer but the pair graduated to sabotaging cases for money, according to statements Hanrahan made to CIB.[10]

CIB threw money and manpower at trying to corroborate Hanrahan's allegations about Carter and Guerard's involvement in the ecstasy job. The owner of the drugs, Jason Proctor, at first denied being robbed of his stash. But when he was caught trying to sell to an undercover cop he turned supergrass.

Steve Warner was a key player in the theft of the 40,000 ecstasy pills. Hanrahan met him through a mutual friend of Rees called Barry

UNTOUCHABLES

Nash, aka Barry "the Fish". Warner then introduced Hanrahan to two other criminals, Vincent Arneil and John Walter, whom he recruited to sell the stolen ecstasy. Warner was under investigation by the National Crime Squad at the time. He had sold a kilo of cocaine to one of their undercover officers and was introduced to another posing as a hit man when he offered a £10,000 contract to kill a man called Jimmy Cook. Cook was also a friend of Barry "the Fish" and very close to Rees. In fact Nash and Cook were repo men for Southern Investigations. On his arrest Warner also turned supergrass and agreed to give evidence.

The Untouchables still had a serious problem prosecuting Carter and Guerard. How could Hanrahan be presented as a witness of truth when at his recent sentencing prosecution counsel had called him "a complete fraud"? Furthermore, a CIB assessment of Hanrahan said this of him: "He lied from the outset. He cynically manipulated the criminal justice system intending to falsely receive credit from the court that would eventually sentence him."[11] Even Hanrahan was amazed when the Untouchables told him they were going to rely on him as a witness. "I wouldn't have used me," he says. His instincts were right. The Old Bailey trial in October 2000 was a fiasco.

The Untouchables never wanted the transcripts of Bob Bown's secretly recorded conversations with Hanrahan ever to see the light of day. The CPS is tight-lipped about how they were disclosed so late in the day. But when they were, defence barristers put them to lethal effect in cross-examining Hanrahan. The first he knew of their existence, he says, was when the ring binders were produced for him to read aloud in the witness box.

Hanrahan told the jury he was just "bragging" to pass the time when he had regaled Bown with appalling stories of all the fit-ups, assaults and planted drugs he had been involved with as a cop. The effect of all this and much more was terminal for the prosecution case. Its fate was sealed when Hanrahan was asked to read out a reference he'd made to "white slags who fuck black men". The jury included three white women and two black men.

Proctor and Warner fared little better in the witness box. Just before Christmas the jury acquitted Carter and Guerard, and a third detective, Colin Evans. It was a black day for the Untouchables. Their risky decision to bug Hanrahan's cell conversations, apparently taken without CPS advice, had totally backfired.[12] Hanrahan returned to the supergrass wing where he served out the rest of his sentence.

THE SLEAZE MACHINE

Among the Parkhurst transcripts was one fascinating discussion between Hanrahan and Bown about the Danny Morgan murder:

Hanrahan: The Met's investigation of it was fucking crap.

Bown: Was it?

Hanrahan: Oh fucking terrible. Stephen Lawrence one is a professional investigation compared to that.[13]

Clearly Bown had been told to get Hanrahan talking about the Morgan murder. Other than saying he was thankful for being on the "periphery" of Rees's circle at the time and that the scandal was "a fucking nightmare" for him, it was the one subject Hanrahan appeared naturally most guarded about in an otherwise free-flowing chat where he opined about many things.

By their nature supergrasses are duplicitous. But if they feel the system 'cleansing them' is riven with double or even treble standards, there is an in-built disincentive to telling it all and telling it truthfully.

Hanrahan despised the Untouchables' hypocrisy and sanctimony. On the Bown tapes he alleged that Jarratt once tried to get him to falsely incriminate a detective. Like Keith Green, Hanrahan later separately complained to the PCA that Wood and Jarratt had also told him they weren't interested in noble cause corruption. The PCA did nothing.

No one doubts Duncan Hanrahan knew a lot. But the way the Untouchables mishandled him ensured what he knew remained buried, like Danny Morgan.

15

BAD BLOOD

Just before Christmas 1996, deputy commissioner Brian Hayes and Roy Clark handed a poisoned chalice to detective superintendent John Coles. In effect, he was asked to untangle Scotland Yard from the compromising position it had got into with Geoff Brennan. As Coles went through the case file, he felt alarm at the "chaos" he was inheriting from the Ghost Squad. Coles could foresee many problems with his new assignment, which he would subsequently refer to as "this nightmare case".

He assembled a team with detective inspector Maggie Palmer, his second in command and the first woman (one of the few) to become an Untouchable. The new operation was codenamed Cornwall.

Brennan had played a blinder. He stole £400,000 from the Chinese government and then made false corruption allegations against detectives John Redgrave and Michael Charman to earn protection from the theft inquiry and from Tall Ted Williams, the gangster he had double-crossed.

The Ghost Squad cut a sweetheart deal with Brennan in June 1994. He admitted the theft but wasn't arrested. Instead the police helped him launder the money through two house purchases and hid him away from a fraud investigator, hoping he would one day become a witness against the two cops. Brennan of course had no intention of doing so.

In 1996, the Chinese government started applying diplomatic pressure to get their money back. This forced the Ghost Squad to unpick the secret deal with Brennan and in November, charge him with theft.

BAD BLOOD

The supergrass responded by exposing the whole scandal to Redgrave and Charman, who by then had been under secret investigation for over two years. The two cops were now demanding answers from Roy Clark and threatening legal action against the Ghost Squad.

Matters escalated when on 27 January 1997 Brennan sent a lengthy letter of complaint to the PCA. In it he formally withdrew the allegation of a £50,000 bung to Redgrave and Charman. He admitted making it up to ensure the Ghost Squad took him into the witness protection scheme. He claimed he was encouraged to do this by his friend, detective sergeant Chris Smith, who he said was acting out of personal enmity towards the two detectives.

Brennan alleged to the PCA that Smith had moonlighted when he was a Ghost Squad officer supposedly looking after him in the witness protection scheme. Brennan explained how he had paid Smith, and named three other detectives also doing private surveillance work. They were Spencer Mott, Alan Moralee and Jimmy Angel.

Lastly, Brennan turned on senior Ghost Squad officers Roger Gaspar and David Bailey. The latter had been to see Brennan just before he was charged. The supergrass had secretly recorded the conversation and now complained to the PCA that Bailey had tried to make him give "false evidence" about Redgrave and Charman as part of a last ditch new "deal" over the theft.

The explosive letter addressed to PCA deputy chairman John Cartwright arrived on Wednesday, 29 January. It identified a wealth of criminal and disciplinary offences by key members of the anti-corruption squad. On Thursday, Cartwright passed it to them. But both the PCA and Coles would spend the next 18 months denying they had received it. What could explain this?

Internal police documents show that the Untouchables had already decided to suspend Redgrave and Charman and use Smith as a witness against them. So they simply pretended not to know about Brennan's formal withdrawal and fresh allegations.

On Monday, 3 February, Coles obtained search warrants against Redgrave and Charman. Very early the next morning their homes were raided and the two detectives suspended over allegations that the Untouchables knew had been withdrawn and were totally uncorroborated.

The raid caused maximum embarrassment. Outside Redgrave's home arc lights, normally used on terrorist incidents, had been erected on tripods, and his son and daughter were searched before leaving for school. The whole operation was "oppressive and excessive", says Redgrave, and designed to cower him and recover any tape recordings that compromised the Ghost Squad.

Roy Clark would later claim that the suspensions were designed to "provoke a reaction". But 30 months of covert investigation had produced nothing to substantiate the original allegations, so what was he hoping the Untouchables would now discover? As events unfolded, it became clear that the suspension of Redgrave and Charman was used to buy time and protect the Yard and its favoured sons from further embarrassment.

But the Yard couldn't simply ignore Brennan's complaint. So it asked the PCA to supervise an internal investigation. Had the watchdog not been so captured by the Yard's anti-corruption crusade it should have at least given Brennan's complaint to an outside force to investigate. Instead, Coles and others were effectively investigating their own unit and their own bosses.

The first tricky problem was how to unravel the history between Brennan and Smith. Coles was also aware of the intense distrust between Smith and detectives Redgrave and Charman. It all goes back to Brinks Mat, but this was a can of worms the Yard had no interest in reopening if it could be avoided.

Coles eventually interviewed three retired senior Brinks officers who threw very important light on the situation. Detective chief superintendent Brian Boyce was by then part of a very upmarket private security firm backed by City money and run by two former MI6 officers. Detective chief inspector Peter Mellins was enjoying his retirement, and detective inspector Bob Suckling was still chasing armed robbers, but for the firm Securitas. These interviews and other secret intelligence collated by Operation Cornwall came to be known inside the Untouchables as the "bad blood papers". They are a key part of the secret history of Brinks Mat and help explain why Redgrave and Charman had to be destroyed.

After Kenny Noye stabbed to death undercover cop John Fordham during a failed surveillance operation in January 1985, the Brinks squad trebled in size to 300 detectives.

DCS Brian Boyce, who led the investigation with SO11 commander Phil Corbett, was concerned about controlling the new informants, who had also increased dramatically from a handful to over 30. £26 million could buy a career criminal a lot of police protection, especially if negotiated through a double agent informant, thought Boyce. He therefore introduced a radical new informant-handling system. The idea was borrowed from his covert work in Northern Ireland with a secret Army unit that ran agents inside Republican and Loyalist movements. The premise behind Boyce's new system was a variant on what hostage negotiators call Stockholm syndrome. To avoid the police handler becoming too close to his informant, he introduced a third party called the controller.

Boyce had become uneasy about the appointment of a detective inspector called Ian Brown as the new head of the intelligence cell, a highly sensitive post with access to all informant logs. A few months before his promotion, Brown ran the surveillance team attached to the intelligence cell. Steve Seton, the son-in-law of Brinks target John Lloyd, had asked him to a meeting where he would hear an offer he might not want to refuse. Boyce was unaware that Lloyd had paid Geoff Brennan and his sister Denise £1,000 to set up the meeting with Brown through a mutual police friend, Chris Smith.

Boyce agreed the meeting between Brown and Seton could go ahead, but on one condition. The venue was a pub in Bromley, Kent. At the local police station Boyce personally fitted Brown with a transmitter in his shoe connected to a body mike. An SO11 surveillance team secretly covered the pub meeting. Boyce also took another extraordinary step, unknown to Brown. He told Suckling – who also had reservations about Seton's approach – to handpick a separate Flying Squad surveillance team to watch what went down.

When Brown returned he explained to Boyce that the equipment had failed to record the conversation with Seton. "The essence of the deal," recalls one well-placed source, "was if [Boyce] stopped being quite so aggressive, [Lloyd] could get some of the money returned." There was no way Boyce was going to be dictated to by criminals, although clearly the villains thought some cops might go for such a deal, maybe because it had worked in the past. The equipment failure troubled Boyce, but there was no evidence of foul play so he didn't take the matter further. But after telling Corbett about it, he privately marked Brown's card and got on with the job in hand.

Several months later Brown sought permission to recruit Smith as his number two on the intelligence cell. Boyce was told Smith had a valuable informant capable of putting away John Fleming. Boyce agreed, but he wanted to know the identity of his informant. He was more than a little taken aback to learn it was Geoff Brennan.

Smith's new posting raised some eyebrows among the original Brinks detectives like Suckling, Charman and Redgrave – "the three musketeers". Brennan's father was already their snout, one of the few before Fordham's death changed everything.

Bob Suckling is a compact man who lived and breathed the Brinks Mat investigation. His peers say of him that he couldn't remember what he had for breakfast but he could remember every detail of the Brinks investigation, even 20 years later. Certainly his statement to the Untouchables confirms this.

Suckling had first come across Smith when he was serving on the cheque squad dealing with funny money. He believed Smith had dishonestly claimed an informant's reward. So when Smith joined the Brinks squad with Geoff Brennan as his wonder informant Suckling was already short on trust. Old man Brennan also didn't trust his son's long-standing relationship with Smith and had warned Suckling not to mention they were targeting Lloyd because it would get back.

Suckling told the Untouchables about two incidents in 1985, which he felt confirmed his suspicions.

Old man Brennan had tipped them off that Tall Ted Williams had a safe house in Trinity Church Square, near London Bridge. The police placed a secret camera in a tree opposite and monitored the comings and goings of the Arif crime family and other south-east London faces. Some time later old man Brennan asked Charman how the surveillance operation was going and revealed he knew about the covert camera in the tree from his son who had got it from Smith.

Weeks later, old man Brennan gave an almost verbatim account of an informant log Charman had written of their last meeting. He said Smith had told his son and then Geoff told him to keep his mouth shut, as there was money to be earned.

Old man Brennan feared it was only a matter of time before Lloyd and Williams discovered he was a grass. Suckling was now convinced Geoff Brennan was a "double agent" informant working for the gangsters to feed disinformation into the Brinks Task Force. Smith, he suspected, was being used to direct the investigation away from Lloyd.

Tony Brightwell, whom Brown had replaced on the intelligence cell, supported Suckling's assessment. If Geoff Brennan had such golden leads on the robbers why did he wait until after the death of Fordham to approach the Brinks investigation, Brightwell wondered. "When he did start working for the squad in early 1985 his arrival coincided with the very period that Lloyd realised he was in deep shit."

Brightwell's analysis is very persuasive. First, he says, Lloyd sent Seton in to the Brinks Task Force to find out if there was a deal. There wasn't. When Fordham is killed, the heat is turned up so Lloyd flees to the United States, where he stays for almost nine years. Williams becomes Lloyd's representative in the UK and used his relationship with the Brennan family to lead the Brinks inquiry down blind alleys and away from the buried gold.

Suckling and Charman immediately told Mellins and Boyce about their concern that "Smith was leaking information".[1] They suggested he should be removed from the Brinks investigation rather than force a formal corruption inquiry.

Mellins spoke to old man Brennan and was "satisfied" there had been a leak, but he didn't know who was responsible. Smith and Brown flatly denied any compromise when Boyce confronted them.

From then on the Brinks squad split into two hostile camps. "There was an awful lot of distrust going on within the squad," remembers detective Tony Curtis, who was firmly in the Suckling camp. "Our little group tried to keep everything we had to ourselves. It was becoming a very strange place to work." Charman quipped, "You had to have wing mirrors to work in that squad from then on."

Smith and Brown had also recruited Brennan's sister, Denise, to inform for the Brinks squad. The brother and sister were a poisonous double act earning money from the criminals and the police for their selective information.[2]

Privately, Boyce felt there was a concerted attempt by south London criminals and police officers to undermine his inquiry. He supported Suckling and Charman over Smith and Brown and felt their information was invariably more substantial. Boyce was also angry that Smith and Brown were handling informants outside his new system.

It is plain to see from the bad blood papers how almost ten years later when Brennan was in trouble over the Wang theft he would use Smith to make false allegations against Redgrave and Charman, believing his former Brinks handler might even delight in passing them on.

Since the Brinks inquiry, Smith's career in the Flying Squad at Tower Bridge had advanced. According to his boss there, the Kiwi detective had "powerful protectors within the job". In 1992, they selected Smith for special attachment to the Organised Crime Group Projects Team, a new surveillance unit targeting serious criminals identified by SO11. This brought him close to John Grieve and Roy Clark, who were setting up the Ghost Squad at the same time. When Brennan turned supergrass in 1994 they took Smith even further into the inner sanctum as his minder.

UNTOUCHABLES

Brennan's serious allegations to the PCA against Smith 30 months later presented serious difficulties for superintendent John Coles. The Brinks inquiry was a place the Yard didn't want to revisit, not least because of the unfolding Stephen Lawrence scandal. Another factor was Kenny Noye. He had been on the run from a road rage murder since May 1996, and one month later featured large in the police corruption trial of SERCS detective John Donald, who had a relationship with south-east London drug dealers connected to Noye, John Fleming and Ted Williams.

Coles had clearly identified what he called a "Smith camp" on the Brinks inquiry, many of whom came from the notorious Brixton Robbery Squad. One of them was DCI Peter Atkins, another officer Boyce had serious concerns about. The Brinks inquiry chief wanted to sack Atkins for his unauthorised *liaison dangereuse* in Paris with bent lawyer Michael Relton. But Boyce came to realise that like Smith, Atkins also had protection from possibly the same very senior officers at the Yard.

Atkins' Brinks past was very much a live issue when Coles was examining the "bad blood papers". Another major supergrass we've already mentioned, Maurice O'Mahoney, was still waiting in 1997 for the Yard to resolve a civil action he'd brought in 1994 against Atkins and the commissioner. Mo the grass had claimed that Atkins and a long list of south London detectives tried to kill him because he was about to blow the whistle on their corruption during the Brinks Mat investigation. Interestingly, the Yard settled the case and paid Mo damages and costs.[3]

We discovered just how selective the Untouchables were about which allegations they investigated when we learned that a former Brinks detective had passed intelligence to the anti-corruption squad about DS Chris Smith that was obviously relevant to Coles' inquiry.

Detective constable John Bull had received information in November 1997 from a former Brinks target called Tommy Farrant, whom he was trying to develop as an informant on a drug murder in Scotland. Farrant was refusing to help because he claimed he had been stuck in an allegedly corrupt relationship with Chris Smith and Ian Brown since the Brinks inquiry. DS Bull says he put the two names on a formal report and passed it to his boss, detective chief inspector Martin Bridger, who shortly afterwards became an Untouchable. Smith and Bridger had served together at the Tower Bridge Flying Squad. We asked the Yard what Bridger had done with the names. They declined to answer. We approached Bridger at the Old Bailey with the same questions. The Untouchable became very annoyed and stormed off, repeating, "I'm not going to answer that."[4] Brown and Smith also declined to discuss these and other matters.

There was another compelling Brinks-related reason why Smith had to be protected from Brennan's allegations to the PCA. While a member of the Projects Team, he had been involved in a surveillance operation in 1995 that led to the arrest of John Lloyd for an audacious attempt to defraud the British banking system of millions of pounds.

Lloyd had returned to the UK in April 1994 after nine years of self-imposed exile in the US. The CPS had agreed to drop the case against him for handling £17.3 million of the stolen Brinks gold on the grounds of insufficient evidence. A few months later he hooked up with his old friend Kenny Noye, who had just finished serving his long sentence for handling the bullion.

In January 1995, Lloyd started plotting the bank scam. The so-called Hole in the Wall gang plotted to bug cash machine telephone lines with the help of BT insiders and then copy customers' PIN numbers by accessing the banks' mainframe computers. Other members of the gang included Lloyd's son-in-law, Steve Seton, and Martin Grant, the computer expert.[5] He eventually became a participating informant and revealed that Noye had provided some start-up capital for the scam. It appears Lloyd was a bit short because while he was planning the fraud, in June 1995 he concluded an out-of-court settlement with the Brinks Mat insurers, estimated to have been £5 million.

Smith followed the gang throughout the early part of 1995. At the same time he was acting as Brennan's minder in the witness protection scheme, having delivered him to the Ghost Squad the previous year. After Lloyd was arrested in July 1995, Smith started moonlighting with other members of the Projects Team and Brennan in preparation for his retirement the following year.

Brennan claims that in 1996 a relative of Lloyd approached his sister, Denise, to see if a deal could be done over his arrest. Brennan says there was a meeting at the Asda supermarket in Swanley, Kent, which Denise reported back to Smith.

Interestingly, Lloyd pleaded guilty with the rest of the gang on 4 November 1996.[6] Two days later Brennan was charged with his role in the Wang theft. He then went off like a Catherine wheel and revealed the Ghost Squad operation to its principal targets, Redgrave and Charman. When they demanded an inquiry into Smith's role, is it any wonder he had to be protected?

UNTOUCHABLES

Brennan was losing patience with the PCA and superintendent Coles. He felt their investigation into the moonlighting was ignoring clear evidence he'd provided of payments to Smith. Brennan had never been able to provide similar evidence against Redgrave and Charman, yet the Untouchables were still pursuing them like zombies.

Coles claims Brennan refused to co-operate with his inquiry. But this doesn't explain why by August 1997 he still hadn't interviewed Smith or any other detective named in Brennan's complaint to the PCA eight months earlier.

Brennan forced the issue by going to the *Sunday Times* Insight Team with his evidence. The newspaper published an article on 24 August naming Smith and detective constable Alan Moralee. This led Smith to contact Coles two days later and give a disjointed and partial account of his relationship with Brennan on tape and under caution. Ultimately, Smith lied to Coles, denying he had moonlighted.

Brennan kept in touch with the *Sunday Times* and a wily freelance journalist, Martin Short, co-author of the great exposé in the seventies, *The Fall of Scotland Yard*. Brennan provided further evidence of his payments to Smith for the moonlighting work. Ironically, some of the cheques were issued from a TSB account the Ghost Squad had set up for Brennan under his new identity as Geoff Newman.

The Insight Team discovered that Smith, although retired, was due to give evidence in a major trial starting on 2 February 1998 at the Old Bailey. The prosecution was a spin-off from Smith's work on the Project Team tracking an armed robber called James Phillips, known to his gang as "the Ayatollah" and linked to the Adams crime family.

The day before the trial started the *Sunday Times* published a second article – "Yard officers sold secrets to criminals" – naming Smith in the moonlighting scam and claiming that a circle of officers had been paid to access the police computer to see if criminal contacts of Brennan were under investigation. Roy Clark was quoted as denying there had been a cover-up around Smith.

However, almost immediately Coles received authority to carry out a surveillance operation on Insight editor David Leppard and Martin Short. They were videoed and photographed in various London locations over the next six weeks. Surveillance was also set up outside Short's home and while he was at the Old Bailey.

David Bate, QC for Phillips, took Smith through a devastating cross-examination over four days. By showing Smith had been dishonest over his dealings with Brennan, Bate hoped to destroy the integrity of the surveillance operation against Phillips. Smith was therefore startled when suddenly Bate asked if he knew a Mr Newman aka Brennan. Smith explained how Brennan had been a police informant for the last 20 years; that he had acted as his "social worker" during a "very secret inquiry" and then Brennan turned against him.

Smith denied encouraging Brennan to make false allegations against other officers, a reference to Redgrave and Charman although they weren't named. He refuted suggestions of any impropriety with Brennan, denied he had taken "a penny" from him, but said he was "too busy" to log all his contacts with the supergrass.

Bate turned up the heat. He accused Smith of perjury and having "a totally corrupt relationship" with Brennan. Smith denied moonlighting, misusing police equipment or fiddling his expenses. He also denied that he or detective Alan Moralee had accessed the police computer on a private surveillance job in return for payment.

When Bate persisted, Smith suddenly asked to speak to a lawyer. Witnesses giving evidence can refuse to answer questions only if they believe that to respond truthfully will incriminate them or that by giving an answer they know to be false will constitute perjury. This is called invoking your right against self-incrimination. And it is very rare indeed to see among police officers.

The following day Bate went in for the kill. He asked Smith if he or other Flying Squad officers had taken money off Brennan. Smith invoked his right and refused to answer. The defence barrister was in his stride. Suddenly, Bate produced two cheques from Brennan to Smith totalling £1,400. An embattled Smith invoked his rights again. So Bate taunted him to deny he had previously committed perjury.

Two members of Coles' team watched all one thousand cuts Bate had inflicted on Smith's integrity. Luckily there was an eleven-day break before he was back in the box. But in the meantime, Bate had examined Smith's bank accounts, which he used on 16 February to deliver the final *coup de grâce*. Once again Smith invoked his right against self-incrimination, this time when Bate produced a schedule of payments from Brennan's account to his totalling £10,851. The barrister called Smith a liar and perjurer before sitting down.

Luckily the prosecution case didn't rest on Smith. Two of Phillips' gang had turned Queen's Evidence and he was eventually given a twenty-year prison sentence. The prosecution did however recognize that moonlighting was a criminal offence even if the officer had retired, because it involved obtaining money by deception. Incredibly, Smith was never arrested by the Untouchables for this or for perjury.[7]

UNTOUCHABLES

It was another three months before Coles got round to interviewing Smith for misconduct in a public office, false accounting and perjury. Smith had been disclosed a lot of evidence to prepare for the interviews in April and May. If he had an explanation this was the time to give it. But once again he invoked his right against self-incrimination when Coles asked the odd incisive question. In the end though, Smith's replies proved he had perjured himself about the moonlighting and receiving money from Brennan. To this day he has never claimed he returned the £10,000 to Scotland Yard.

If Smith could lie at the Old Bailey about this, then what else was he lying about? What really had gone on during the Brinks Mat investigation? What really happened in those 12 days in June 1994 when Smith took Brennan and Denise to the Ghost Squad? Were the brother and sister now telling the truth when they claimed Smith had "rehearsed" them on the way to meet Gaspar? Had Smith taken other money from Brennan over the years? Did the anti-corruption squad have a corrupt officer among them? These and myriad other questions should have been a key feature of Operation Cornwall. But the Untouchables never interviewed Smith again.

"What is so frightening," says Redgrave, "is that if Bate had not brought all this out in the open, CIB3 would have continued to dry clean Smith and cover up his corrupt relationship with Brennan."

By May 1998, the Untouchables were drinking in the last chance saloon. Their case against Redgrave and Charman was in tatters. Brennan was a liar and a thief who'd had over the Ghost Squad. Smith was a busted flush and the only man who had provably taken money from the supergrass and then lied about it. For their part, senior Yard chiefs had cut an unlawful deal with Brennan and helped him launder the stolen £400,000.

To add to the humiliation, the prosecution against Brennan had to be dropped on CPS advice. The CPS, it emerged, had not been consulted when the Untouchables charged Brennan in November 1996. Lead lawyer Stuart Sampson also felt he had been "kept in the dark" about the strength of the case against Redgrave and Charman.

In March 1997, he advised that if the Untouchables continued with Brennan's prosecution then details of the failed covert operation against the two suspended detectives would have to be disclosed. This would mean disaster for the ongoing propaganda efforts to launch the Untouchables to the public and parliament.

The only hope was to undermine Operation Nightshade as a

BAD BLOOD

"smokescreen" invented by Redgrave and Charman to prevent their corruption with Brennan and the Wang theft from being discovered. There were two strands to this unsustainable theory: firstly, that Redgrave had sabotaged the theft investigation and secondly, that he invented the arms deal as a diversion.

By this stage Coles had recruited DC Kevin Maul to the Operation Cornwall team. He was the fraud detective sent halfway around the world between 1994 and 1996 looking for Brennan when the Ghost Squad had hidden their duplicitous supergrass in Kent.

"When Maul was able to carry out the long overdue financial investigation of Brennan it showed exactly what the supergrass did with the £400,000 he stole from the Wangs," says Charman's combative lawyer, Mark Lake. "It also made it clear that Brennan didn't have £50,000 before the theft to bung Michael and John."

Maul told us the ginger giant had exerted no malign influence over his investigation of the theft. And Coles had statements from five senior officers confirming this.[8]

Further blows to the smokescreen theory emerged in the US when Coles' team spoke to the Houston Four. If Operation Nightshade was bogus then they had to be innocent businessmen who in no way tried to scam the Wangs. Unfortunately, when the Untouchables met Billy Padon he was in a Texas prison serving four years for six counts of bank fraud.

CPS lawyer Stuart Sampson, who specialises in fraud cases, was not impressed when he read the remaining statements from Butch Jones, Bill Padgett and James Sprouce. He felt their involvement in the mobile phone deal was too suspicious to put them forward as witnesses of truth.

Jones, Padgett and Hong Kong broker Walter Le also tried to distance themselves from the arms deal they had negotiated back in 1993 with undercover officers posing as representatives of Loyalist terrorists. A major obstacle to the fabricated arms deal theory was the covertly taped evidence of these encounters and the statements from the very experienced undercover officers, which all confirmed the bona fides of this side of Operation Nightshade. DS Richard Hester had retired from the police when we met. "As far as I was concerned [Roger Crooks] was the genuine article. This was backed up by other phone calls I had with Padgett," he said. Hester found the Untouchables' suggestion that Redgrave had duped him fantastic and unworkable.

Remarkably, Roger Crooks, the central figure in the arms deal, was never interviewed. According to Brennan's solicitor, Phil Kelly, CIB documents he'd seen showed this decision was taken in October 1997.

Crooks told us he voluntarily visited Scotland Yard in 1998 to clear up matters but no statement was taken from him and the detectives he spoke to claimed there was no reference to Operation Nightshade in their files.[9]

Coles' trip to the US then was a disaster for those in the Yard who needed evidence of a smokescreen. If Redgrave was guilty of anything it was exaggeration in some of his reports and boastfulness. According to a close police friend of the ginger giant, Redgrave already had a reputation among senior officers of over-selling his operations to get their authority for covert infiltration. Yet it was a further measure of the Untouchables' desperation that they seized on certain inflated phrases in Redgrave's Operation Nightshade reports to continue insisting the whole arms deal was a construct, or "red herring" as the PCA called it.

"I do get the feeling there seems to be with investigations [by CIB] an attempt to prove a point not to investigate the evidence – all the worst aspects of policing . . . I believe [Redgrave and Charman] are innocent. I have very good reason to doubt the integrity of those who say otherwise. There isn't a scrap of evidence except from seriously tainted people," says retired DI Bob Suckling.

Redgrave goes further. "I didn't steal the Wangs' money, Brennan did; I didn't launder the money, Gaspar did; I didn't sabotage the theft inquiry, Clark did; I didn't take money from Brennan, Smith did. None of those officers are suspended, I was."

Michael Charman was not rank ambitious like Redgrave. He was happy being an effective detective constable. Charman had drifted from a career in hotel catering into policing. Lambeth-born, he was 18 when he joined in 1969.

Charman met Redgrave on the Brinks Mat inquiry when both men were in their early thirties and married with young kids. They became close friends but the stress of suspension was severely testing that relationship.

Charman's marriage fell apart after he was suspended in 1997. He'd already begun a relationship with a young CPS executive officer called Debbie Cahill. Their romance developed while working together preparing his Flying Squad cases for trial. The couple became closer after his suspension and the death of Debbie's mother in April 1998. When she returned to work after a month's sick leave Debbie plunged straight into a sensitive case involving one of the Arif crime family and three others in a conspiracy to supply ninety-six kilos of heroin.[10] It was sensitive because some of the key witnesses were police officers from the Projects Team who had been named in Brennan's moonlighting allegations to the PCA and in the *Sunday Times* articles. The CPS had a duty to disclose to the defence if any of the officers in the Arif case were under investigation by CIB or had been suspended. Of concern were witnesses, DC Jimmy Angel and DC Spencer Mott.[11] Debbie's boss also wanted to know the position on Chris Smith.

Detective superintendent John Coles was passed the CPS enquiry in mid-June 1998. By then Operation Cornwall was a total failure and the uncomfortable truth about Smith had recently emerged at the Old Bailey. When Coles discovered he was dealing with Charman's girlfriend he seized on the opportunity to mount a sting.

The operation was codenamed Ambleside. Coles briefed Roy Clark about bugging Debbie's work phone and placing a listening device in her house. The justification for these extremely intrusive measures was flimsy: firstly, that she was suspected of "leaking" information about Smith to Charman, and secondly, that Redgrave and Charman were in cahoots with Brennan to undermine Operation Cornwall.

To execute his sting, Coles deliberately conveyed to Debbie that there were "immense problems" around Smith and requested a case conference with the prosecuting barristers, Orlando Pownall, who was in on the sting, and his junior Mark Dennis.

Debbie says that because of her relationship with Charman she'd cleared it internally that if certain matters were mentioned she would leave the case conference, now scheduled for 15 July. Debbie had booked the following day off because she was going out that night with Mark Dennis and another barrister.

At the end of the case conference Coles' assistant handed out sealed envelopes. Debbie Cahill's one was specially marked. She didn't open it until she was on the late train home and a little sozzled. The envelope contained a transcript of the interview Coles had conducted with Smith a few months earlier. Debbie thought nothing of it. CIB3 surveillance officers watched her all the way to the front door. Another surveillance unit monitored her smoochy goodnight call to Charman. She never mentioned the contents of the envelope.

The next day Charman came over and they went shopping for fish, oblivious to the surveillance team around them. Charman wanted to invite Redgrave over for supper. He thought the ginger giant might need cheering up. He had only recently been discharged from hospital after a dramatic suicide attempt.

The search of the family home in January 1997 was the final straw for Redgrave's long-suffering wife. She had also discovered he was having an affair with a policewoman and wanted a divorce. His suspension was a bitter blow to a man who had invested his whole identity and sense of self-worth in being a successful detective. With that gone depression set in and he started drinking heavily. His mood swings at home were sometimes unbearable for his children and now estranged wife, who continued to allow him to live under the same roof. Redgrave continued the affair into 1998 and went on holiday with his lover to Spain that June. The day after returning to the marital home he took a massive overdose of anti-depressants. Redgrave then left a goodbye message on his wife's mobile phone.

Although Charman had read the Smith interview before he called Redgrave from Cahill's phone, he made no mention of it when he invited the ginger giant and his son for dinner. After much persuasion Redgrave arrived at Debbie's alone.

The ginger giant was on strong medication, but they all tucked into the wine as Debbie prepared the meal. Where they sat in the kitchen was right next to the bug. Coles was outside in a police car listening to the conversation, which moved from the TV coverage of the day's Stephen Lawrence inquiry hearings to the Smith transcript. Neither Redgrave nor Charman were overly impressed and Debbie says she then joked about burning the document.

Coles decided this was all he needed to make an arrest. His men came crashing through the front door. All three were arrested and bailed. But over the next few months Coles had difficulty finding an A-list London prosecutor who would take the case. Various Treasury Counsel turned it down because they knew Debbie Cahill professionally or personally. But the defence suspect there was another motive: the merits of the prosecution were very weak.

A prosecutor called Richard Latham QC was given the brief. Latham had the air of a frustrated Latin teacher stuck in a provincial public school. His junior was a vampish barrister called Maureen Baker.

The Yard was hoping they could extricate the Untouchables from the entire mess over Redgrave and Charman. Latham saw boxes of files before giving Coles an effusive opinion in November 1998 that both defendants and Cahill should be charged with conspiracy to pervert the course of justice and breaches of the Official Secrets Act.

Latham wrote that there were several "tactical reasons" why Redgrave and Charman should be charged immediately rather than wait for the outcome of Operation Cornwall. He didn't specify, but lawyers representing the two detectives would later assert that the Ambleside charges were rushed through because it was already known that Cornwall was going nowhere.

In May 1999, we met Redgrave and Charman for the first time at the committal hearing in Bow Street Magistrates Court. Latham was so confident the district judge would commit the case to the Old Bailey for trial that he sent his junior instead.

In a highly embarrassing ruling, district judge Lorraine Morgan discharged all three defendants. She accepted Cahill had acted in an "improper and unprofessional" way in showing the transcript to Redgrave and Charman, but added that the prosecution had failed to go beyond that and show "aiding and abetting" by the two suspended detectives. She also ruled that the mere disclosure of the Smith interview transcript (something Redgrave and Charman would have been entitled to see anyway) was unlikely to prevent the detection of crime and did not amount to a conspiracy.

The humiliation for Latham and the Untouchables was total. It is very, very unusual for a magistrate not to commit a case on its merits especially when involving such serious charges. Having failed the criminal test once, Latham and the Yard resolved to approach a High Court judge to overturn the decision. But on careful study of the papers Mr Justice Eady upheld the district judge's decision, once again questioning Latham's judgement in preferring so serious a charge with so little legal merit.

In July 1999, the game was up. Having considered the wider corruption case against Redgrave and Charman, Latham advised the Untouchables there was insufficient evidence to prosecute them. However his advice wasn't communicated to the two detectives until December.

Remarkably, Latham also advised against prosecuting Chris Smith for any criminal charges due to "insufficient evidence".[12] Smith was not the only Untouchable to conveniently escape censure. Nothing had been done about Brennan's PCA complaint against Commander Roger Gaspar, who by then had been promoted to deputy director of NCIS.

Similarly, detective superintendent David Bailey was never suspended. He retired in May 1997 while the investigation into him was ongoing. Apparently he was concerned about being made the scapegoat for all the Ghost Squad failures. A CIB source told us Bailey discreetly moved to the MI5 section dealing with positive vetting.

Redgrave, Charman and Cahill made separate complaints to the PCA against Coles for malicious prosecution and conspiring to pervert the course of justice.

Operation Ambleside ultimately had two agendas, lawyers representing Redgrave and Charman argue: to divert attention from Smith by mounting an unlawful entrapment operation in the hope that a successful prosecution would remedy the failures of Operations Wrabness and Cornwall.

The Yard successfully persuaded the PCA to allow the complaints against Coles to be investigated by his colleagues in CIB. Redgrave protested to the hopelessly captured watchdog demanding an independent inquiry. He wrote: "I have been suspended for more than two and a half years in relation to a complaint that is almost six years old. This has caused the complete destruction of every aspect of my personal and professional life. Friends, financial security, family, marriage, career, reputation, the building blocks of life have all gone, with no hope of recovery."

The PCA was unmoved. Deputy assistant commissioner Andy Trotter eventually got round to interviewing Coles a year later. The Untouchable was allowed to rant and rave for three hours about how *he* was the victim of a smear campaign by Redgrave, Charman and Brennan. Coles maintained the two detectives were guilty – he just couldn't prove it. Despite all the witness statements to the contrary, Coles repeated that the arms deal was fabricated and Redgrave had sabotaged the Wang theft investigation and "hoodwinked" everybody; although he admitted for the first time that CIB had "unfortunately" laundered the £400,000.

Coles also spoke of an elaborate plan to wreck his marriage. It concerned allegations that were flying around the media about an incident at the Hendon training school. According to the story, Coles had made an impromptu visit to see a young female recruit he was allegedly having an affair with, only to find her with a male recruit. It was further alleged he had assaulted one of them and threatened to ruin their careers if they made a fuss. When asked about this, the Yard replied: "There has been no complaint of assault (formally or informally) on Samantha Bird or any other person – therefore the suggestion of an investigation into criminal allegations against DCS Coles is without foundation."

By this time we had written a number of critical articles in the

BAD BLOOD

Guardian about the Untouchables' unlawful supergrass strategy and the mishandling of Brennan and protection of Smith. Coles took the opportunity in his interview with Trotter to join us to the "conspiracy" against him. He revealed that our "fabricated" articles had been referred unsuccessfully to the Attorney General with a view to prosecuting us for contempt of court. He also spoke of how the head of the Untouchables, Commander Andy Hayman, had on several occasions written to the *Guardian* editor. It was only later that we uncovered this attempt to smear us and derail our investigation. The strategy was complemented with surveillance officers following us to meetings.

Predictably, and after 29 months, the PCA decided not to uphold the complaint against Coles. The CPS sacked Debbie Cahill. And the Yard continued to keep Redgrave and Charman suspended.

The criminal courts were exhausted so the Yard brought the case into a pseudo-legal forum they controlled absolutely – disciplinary proceedings. In September 2000 both officers were told they would be disciplined for discreditable conduct, notwithstanding that the same ingredients of this "offence" had failed to impress two independent criminal judges.

Detectives Redgrave and Charman would remain suspended for another four years as they fought to clear their name and expose the cover-up.

16

MANIPULATING LAWRENCE

Commissioner Condon was unhappy with the televised Lawrence Inquiry hearings that ran from March to October 1998. A row of arrogant, surly detectives of all ranks had passed before the Inquiry panel, many with implausible excuses met by boos and derision from the public gallery. Condon moaned that the cross-examination was "unfair" to his men. It was also only a matter of time before the Barker Review of the first murder inquiry he had signed off back in 1993 would be publicly exposed as an appalling whitewash.

The Untouchables were a significant part of Scotland Yard's containment strategy for the Lawrence Inquiry. The corruption intelligence and evidence they had accumulated since 1993 was not freely shared, as the case of Redgrave and Charman showed.

During their bugged dinner conversation on 17 July 1998, both suspended detectives had resolved to give evidence to the Stephen Lawrence Inquiry. Redgrave was particularly riled about references to Brinks Mat and the murdered informant David Norris, which had emerged during the cross-examination of retired commander Ray Adams the previous day. Michael Mansfield QC, the Lawrence family's barrister, was lacking "raw intelligence" about corruption in south-east London, Redgrave told Charman. "It's really a shame they don't know the truth . . . Mansfield had almost got it right, he's putting the allegations to them but he doesn't know the answers."

Just weeks earlier, Doreen Lawrence had called for a separate independent investigation into the aura of police corruption around her son's murder. The Lawrence Inquiry had hoped officers would come forward. But the thick blue line was never crossed. Redgrave and Charman would have been the first. They wanted to speak about their experience of Brinks Mat, suicide cop Alan "Taffy" Holmes and the firm within a firm of corrupt detectives in south-east London who they felt were still being protected by the Yard. "I was going to talk about Brennan, Freemasonry and the allegations of corruption surrounding the Norris murder," says Redgrave.

A senior retired Kent officer who was part of the PCA-supervised investigation had already told us: "If you were to ask me is there corruption in south-east London I would say it was in the past, but that's not to say the people responsible should not be exposed and held to account. The crux of this is David Norris."

Undoubtedly, the intervention of Redgrave and Charman would have enabled the Inquiry to better probe the Yard about the Lawrence family's concerns. But it was not to be. Detective superintendent John Coles was outside listening to the bugged conversation. His ears must have pricked up when he heard the name David Norris – Coles was his controller at the time of the informant's assassination in 1991.

Not once were Redgrave and Charman asked about their secretly recorded comments, neither later that night immediately following their arrest nor in the four interviews that followed over several months. There was no investigation at all.

Lawrence Inquiry adviser John Sentamu, the Bishop of Stepney, felt it was a "serious matter" that the Yard had said nothing about Redgrave and Charman. Had he known, he said the Inquiry could have organised a private session to hear the two suspended detectives.

Even the original transcripts of the bugged dinner conversation omitted all references to Stephen Lawrence, Ray Adams and David Norris. And when the two detectives were charged in December 1998, the prosecution referred to what was left out as "inconsequential remarks".

Redgrave maintains that he was deliberately kept tainted during the final stages of the Lawrence Inquiry to ensure he could not tell what he knew about the corruption management going on in the Yard. "There are links between south-east London criminal families and policemen, senior policemen, that go way back. That's what all this was about and the Yard couldn't afford for any of this to come out during the Lawrence Inquiry."

Just before the cross-examination of retired commander Ray Adams, the Lawrence family received information about his relationship with

UNTOUCHABLES

Kenny Noye and David Norris. There was also a suggestion that the reason he'd given for retiring within days of Stephen's murder was not truthful. Did he really have a bad back or was this an excuse?

Sir William Macpherson, the retired high court judge chairing the inquiry, agreed to an adjournment while Mansfield reconsidered his cross-examination of Adams. Macpherson and his three advisers had examined the Yard's files on the controversial commander. Bishop Sentamu, Dr Richard Stone and the retired deputy chief constable of Greater Manchester Police, Tom Cook, were amazed at what they read.

We spoke to a senior police source who had clearance to read all the sensitive material, not just about Adams but also other detectives involved in the murder inquiry. He had also seen the intelligence file on south-east London drug trafficker Clifford Norris, father of the main suspect in Stephen's murder. The information left him and the Lawrence Inquiry very concerned about how the policing situation in south-east London had been allowed to develop. It "stank to high heaven", he said.

The Lawrence Inquiry was privately amazed how some of these detectives had managed to stay in the force after separate and unconnected internal investigations into their activities. In Adams' case this concerned his relationship with suicide cop Alan "Taffy" Holmes during the Brinks Mat investigation. In the case of sergeant Dave Coles, he had been investigated during the late eighties for his relationship with Clifford Norris while serving on the notorious Tower Bridge Flying Squad.[1]

Scotland Yard and Ray Adams were clearly concerned about Mansfield's cross-examination because during the adjournment DCS David Wood secretly met Adams at the Star pub in Leatherhead to discuss his forthcoming evidence. Adams had been formally notified of the allegations Mansfield would be putting to him. They concerned claims that he had inveigled his way onto the murder investigation to delay the arrest of the five suspects, and had done so because of his previous links with Noye, who knew Clifford Norris.

Adams "minced in" to the Lawrence Inquiry looking like Donald Sinden, a member of the Inquiry team recalls. Mansfield had found out about the secret tryst with Wood and asked Adams to explain. At first he said he couldn't remember whom he met, but after a discreet intervention from the Yard's barrister, Adams admitted he had discussed the "parameters" of his evidence around David Norris, the dead informant, and Clifford Norris with the Untouchable.

MANIPULATING LAWRENCE

Adams was reluctant to discuss David Norris with Mansfield but confirmed he'd dealt with him. He denied any contact with Clifford or foreknowledge that he was the father of one of the suspects in the Lawrence murder. The panel found him "defensive" and noticed "strange features" to his evidence. But in the final analysis they determined there was no evidence of collusion nor that Adams had corruptly held back the prosecution of the suspects. His back problems were also genuine.

Adams had weathered a long and hostile cross-examination. But it appears he was more affected than he publicly let on. According to a senior Lawrence Inquiry source, the beleaguered commander did not leave the building straight away. Apparently he locked himself in a toilet cubicle and later explained to the startled security guard who found him there that he was trying to avoid the press.

Supergrass Duncan Hanrahan would also have been of great interest to the Lawrence Inquiry, had the Untouchables shared what was emerging from his debriefing.

Hanrahan rolled over immediately after his arrest with Martin King in May 1997. Hanrahan later made a formal complaint to the PCA that CIB3 officers David Wood and Chris Jarratt weren't interested in him supplying information about his corrupt activities with King because they didn't want to get into commander Ray Adams and Brinks Mat.

Hanrahan says King didn't roll over because he knew too many heavy people from south-east London and the corrupt police circles they had mixed in over the last two decades. King, a former detective, was the window between the Brinks Mat era and the Lawrence scandal, which the Yard wanted to brick up, says Hanrahan. He told CIB3 that Adams had introduced him to King and was a guest at his own wedding.

Transcripts of Hanrahan's bugged cell conversations show he talked extensively about the relationship between Adams and King and gave a strong indication it was corrupt, so much so that the inmate who was secretly recording him for the Untouchables felt compelled to tell CIB3 that the retired commander "definitely should be looked at".

In particular, Hanrahan alleged that Adams had helped King get off a drink driving charge. He described Adams effectively as someone who was too clever to be caught and alleged the retired officer had tipped off King about a sting operation over the recovery of a stolen antique. We asked the Yard whether Adams had been under investigation when Wood secretly met him at the Star pub. Commander Andy Hayman of CIB3 replied: "We are not prepared to discuss whether former commander Ray Adams has been/is subject to an investigation. DCS Wood met Mr Adams to discuss the parameters of Adams' forthcoming evidence to the Lawrence Inquiry. Assistant commissioner Johnston was aware of the meeting and agreed to it taking place. We are not prepared to comment further."

Adams thankfully was. He told us he hadn't seen Norris for years before he was murdered and stressed there was "zero opportunity" for him to have acted improperly with the informant. He said he had called Johnston to find out if there was any connection between David and Clifford Norris. Johnston appointed Wood to look into it. Adams then sent Wood a copy of Mansfield's questions unaware he was from CIB3. At the pub Wood told him there was "no connection".

Adams said he liked Hanrahan and King but had no knowledge of any allegations they'd made to CIB against him. "I could tell you a few things about Hanrahan that would make your hair stand on end," he offered tantalisingly, but refused to be drawn. He too had heard he was on a list of "ten names" floating around the Yard, but said an unnamed senior officer had assured him he wasn't under investigation.[2]

A senior Untouchable once told us that in the eighties and nineties it was well known among officers, including senior ones at the Yard, which squads were bent and to be avoided. The East Dulwich SERCS office was one of them. It had been bent for years, well before the murder of its prolific informant David Norris. His execution gave the Yard a unique opportunity to tackle the corruption. But as we have established, this was ignored. As a result, a cell of corrupt cops remained or moved to other specialist squads to carry on their corrupt ways.

During the Stephen Lawrence Inquiry the opportunity once more arose. This time it was manipulated by the Untouchables to ensure the full, appalling picture never emerged.

It began with a drug dealer called Evelyn Susan Fleckney who turned supergrass in April 1998, weeks after she was sentenced to 15 years. DCS Wood persuaded her to give information on her long-time handler and lover, detective constable Robert Clark, who she felt had sold her out in court. The Untouchable promised help in reducing her sentence on appeal.

Fleckney and DC Clark had become involved professionally and personally in 1990 when he helped arrest her for drugs. David Norris had provided East Dulwich with the information that led to Fleckney's arrest and that of her then partner, an armed robber called Billy Pope. Fleckney got a suspended sentence because while on bail, and without Pope knowing, she agreed to became an informant. DC Clark became her handler and secretly wrote to the judge informing him of her fight against crime.

Fleckney's arrival at East Dulwich created a bizarre situation where the SERCS office was running two informants at the same time, one of whom had grassed up the other. As informants, Fleckney claimed, Norris dealt her drugs which she believed he was recycling on behalf of someone on the squad. Before his murder in April 1991 she had apparently discovered he was the one who grassed her up.

After Norris's death Fleckney became the squad's number one informant and earner. DC Clark gave her the pseudonym "Jack Higgins". Their relationship was crooked from the start, she told CIB3. Fleckney would identify dealers, grass them up and recycle the drugs Clark had seized. He would share the money and rewards with her and other officers. The couple even went on holiday as Mr and Mrs Simpson, but the hotel receipts would later sink Clark at his trial.

Fleckney claimed Clark twice made her pregnant. The first she aborted, the second she miscarried. At the time, Clark was also going out with the daughter of a senior officer in the Yard.[3] He always denied any affair and later claimed that Fleckney was lying because she couldn't say whether he was circumcised.

Clark transferred to the Tower Bridge Flying Squad in October 1995, leaving Fleckney behind. But the following year a drug-dealing friend of hers called "Guilford" John Cudworth made a complaint against Clark and his partner DC Chris Drury that they had shaken him down for several kilos of cannabis.

The CIB investigation got nowhere until Fleckney rolled over in March 1998, just as the Stephen Lawrence public hearings began. Four months later, and off the back of her information, detective superintendent John Yates, a fresh-faced Untouchable, arrested Neil Stanley Putnam, a detective constable at East Dulwich. He took no time to turn supergrass and went into an extensive "cleansing" process as part of an operation codenamed Russia. None of Putnam's initial debriefs – where the "parameters" of his evidence were determined – was tape-recorded. Putnam had apparently found God and become a born-again Christian like his wife. But he had stayed corrupt and unrepentant until Yates arrested him in July 1998. The Untouchable told us Putnam's conversion was genuine, but many still scoff at the cop who found Christ so late.

Putnam corroborated Fleckney against Clark. But he also named a number of his other colleagues as corrupt; in particular a key detective involved in the Lawrence murder inquiry who one year later had joined the East Dulwich SERCS. Detective sergeant John "OJ" Davidson was an experienced officer who'd served on the Brinks Mat squad, had mouthed the Yard's official line at the inquest of his friend Alan 'Taffy' Holmes and in 1993 was responsible for tracing witnesses and dealing with the crucial informant "Grant", the skinhead who had named the five suspects soon after the Lawrence murder. Ironically, a few weeks after Davidson had given robust evidence to the Lawrence Inquiry denying he was corrupt or that he had mishandled "Grant" and held back in his inquiries, Putnam made a range of allegations against Davidson involving drugs and stolen goods.

In early September 1998, when the Lawrence Inquiry was in summer recess, the Untouchables raided Davidson's home and confiscated various documents. He was released without charge. Davidson had six months earlier retired from the police while suspended for suspected moonlighting.[4] Nothing was proved against him by the time he completed 30 years' service so he left to set up a private detective agency in Croydon.

The Yard took a strategic decision to tell the Lawrence Inquiry but not the family or its lawyers. The media were also briefed that the raid was unconnected to the Lawrence matter. However, as the unrecorded briefing of Putnam continued it emerged that he had made allegations against Davidson that directly impacted on his handling of the Lawrence murder inquiry.

Putnam is said to have claimed that Davidson had a corrupt association with Clifford Norris. Davidson denies this. However, he was arrested in May 1999, after the Lawrence Inquiry report was published. Then one month later he was told there would be no further action. Davidson left the UK to run a bar with a former police colleague in Spain. He told us shortly before he left that he was innocent.

Imran Khan, the Lawrence family solicitor, feels that had the "Putnam information" been shared it would have re-shaped the type of cross-examination, not just of Davidson but other police witnesses. He now wants an independent inquiry into the corruption allegations around the Lawrence murder. But of course the strategic point of setting up the Untouchables was to prevent this and keep the

MANIPULATING LAWRENCE

corruption allegations separate from the Lawrence Inquiry. Had there been an independent system of investigating corruption the liaison with the Lawrence Inquiry would undoubtedly have provided far greater illumination and ventilation of the persistent and well-founded suspicions of police corruption in south-east London.

Evelyn Fleckney, for example, initially refused to testify against DC Robert Clark fearing she would end up like David Norris. She claimed Clark had warned her in a non-threatening way that if she ever blew the whistle she would be shot dead.[5]

The Untouchables managed to assuage Fleckney's fears. We don't know how because the cosy prison chats were unrecorded. Eventually, she and Putnam gave strong evidence against Clark and his partner DC Chris Drury, who were subsequently convicted.[6] The Old Bailey judge Mr Justice Blofeld then passed lenient sentences on both supergrasses, but not before making this comment: "It is with regret I have to say the [East Dulwich SERCS] was not well run and supervision not what it should have been, and supervisors were not themselves adequately supervised. The approach of the squad was that they could do what they wanted."[7]

No serving senior SERCS manager was ever subsequently disciplined for the monumental and systemic failures at East Dulwich. The same was true about the Flying Squad and Stoke Newington. The Untouchables did, though, put two East Dulwich detectives on a secret blacklist. One was DS Peter Blacketer and the other DC Chris Hardy, a motorbike surveillance officer who'd once sold a car to Robert Clark. Hardy was also a close friend of retired DCI Chris Simpson, the detective who ran the squad and handled David Norris. Simpson had retired in 1997 to work as a fraud investigator in the City. The Untouchables informed Hardy he was on the blacklist because of his continued friendship with Simpson, someone they regarded as "a corrupter of police officers".[8]

We later met up with Robert Clark on one of his days out of prison. He said Fleckney had continued to write to him, send him money and a Valentine's card. After a long discussion we said goodbye at the tube station opposite Scotland Yard. He turned and said: "I've protected a lot of people by keeping my mouth shut." One senior officer, he recalled, had turned up in court "to see if I was keeping quiet".

So far he has.

17

THE ELECTRICIANS PLUG A LEAK

On 21 February 1999, Tom Baldwin, political editor of the *Sunday Telegraph*, produced a mother of a scoop. Five days earlier, in utmost secrecy, a source had shown him a copy of the Stephen Lawrence Inquiry report. The home secretary, Jack Straw, had only just received it himself under tight security.

Straw had planned to extract maximum credit and impact during a carefully planned speech to Parliament on 24 February. The home secretary was also going to announce some police reforms off the back of the stinging report's 70 recommendations.

Back at his office in Canary Wharf, Baldwin laid out the story to his editors: commissioner Condon's job was on the line if he failed to accept the report's withering personal criticisms of his leadership and of his force's "institutional racism". Baldwin assumed the newspaper wanted the story. But because of the Telegraph Group's right-wing views, he set some rather unusual conditions. The newspaper, which he knew was close to the Yard, could not simply use his scoop to rubbish the Lawrence report. He must be free to write the lead stories as he saw fit or he'd take the scoop with him to *The Times*, who had recently poached him.

No sooner had the first edition hit the streets than a furious Jack Straw sought an injunction. The next day the media rounded on Straw's heavy-handedness. The home secretary backed down and allowed reprinting by other media of what was already published.

Straw appointed a retired civil servant, John Simon, to conduct the

THE ELECTRICIANS PLUG A LEAK

mole hunt. Twenty copies of the report had arrived at the Home Office two days before Baldwin was shown it. So the leak inquiry assumed the mole was someone inside the Home Office or possibly a member of the Lawrence Inquiry.

Dozens of Straw's civil servants were aggressively questioned about any contact they may have had with the journalist. But according to a well-placed source there was an unusually tight focus on the tiny handful of black officials in the Home Office, and in particular on Straw's deputy, Paul Boateng MP. This was a rich irony given the Lawrence report's wide-reaching conclusion of "institutional racism". The focus, says the source, was convenient for those reactionary elements in the Home Office and the wider political Establishment, including the Tory Party, who wanted to protect Scotland Yard and would later be at the forefront of the Lawrence backlash.

Straw and Boateng were thought to be in favour of letting Condon go early, but it is believed Tony Blair overruled them. It was therefore handy for spin-doctors representing the *ancien régime* in the Met to be able to blame Boateng for something someone else had done for quite different reasons.

The leak inquiry was unpleasant in another respect, our source told us. A number of civil servants were pointedly asked whether they had ever taken drugs with Baldwin or been given any by him. The idea of government officials sharing a bong with the Sunday Torygraph's political editor is hilarious, but sadly typical of the grubby pressures that can so badly misfire.

Tom Baldwin withstood the government pressure and never revealed his source. The mole hunt was deemed "inconclusive" but cleared the Lawrence Inquiry. There was however another possible explanation for the leak. We learned that the Lawrence Inquiry believed Scotland Yard had "bugged" and "burgled" their offices ahead of the report being sent to the home secretary. If true, this meant the *Sunday Telegraph* had seen a stolen copy.

What follows is a composite of evidence from senior government officials and Lawrence Inquiry sources. It paints a very dark picture of the weeks leading up to publication of the Stephen Lawrence report.

Stephen Wells, the secretary to the Stephen Lawrence Inquiry, knew there was something seriously wrong as soon as he sat at his desk that morning in late January 1999. A draft of the Lawrence report was in its final stages when Wells noticed the special orthopaedic chair he used because of a bad back had been significantly re-adjusted.

UNTOUCHABLES

Security measures at Hannibal House, the Inquiry headquarters in south London, were in place to guard against unauthorised entry. Inquiry staff were already on edge and had received anti-surveillance training because of a spate of nail-bombings believed to be the work of far-right groups.

No one was allowed to drift in and out of the secretariat's private rooms where the report was being written. All copies of early drafts were immediately shredded to avoid leaks. There were three computers in Wells' office. But the draft report was written and saved on the only computer with a detachable disc drive. Every night the disk drive was removed by Wells' assistant and locked in an armoured filing cabinet in the anteroom.

Wells and his small team trusted one another completely. During a discussion about the chair Wells learned that the Bishop of Stepney, John Sentamu, one of the advisers to the Inquiry, was also worried. He too had noticed a change in the position of his office chair. "It was as if a person was sitting at my computer," the Bishop told us. Documents on his desk had been rifled overnight. Other documents and office equipment had also been disturbed. But most worrying was the sudden development of an identical fault on all three unlinked computers in the secretariat's office.

Wells, who came from the Home Office Police Policy Directorate, had also received an alarming call. Someone with extensive contacts in the police warned him "the Met had a plan to bug the Inquiry". The Inquiry secretary was horrified. Did someone in the Met want to blunt the impact of the report by leaking an advance copy? Had they already stolen it from his office?

It was not just the security of the draft report that worried him. After the highly charged public hearings, chairman Sir William Macpherson and his advisers would retire to private rooms and candidly discuss over a dram the quality of the evidence they had just heard from police witnesses and lawyers. As the Inquiry moved into the final phase sensitive and passionate discussions focused on the extent of commissioner Condon's responsibility for the failure to properly investigate Stephen Lawrence's murder in April 1993.

Wells knew the Yard had the means and possibly a motive. But would they really bug the private conversations of a Home Office Inquiry chaired by a former High Court judge? The thought had a hidden touch of irony, as Sir William was also the president of the tribunal that investigates official abuses of phone-tapping and mail interception.

THE ELECTRICIANS PLUG A LEAK

After a sleepless night, Wells felt he had to do something. He decided to contact DAC John Grieve, the official interface with Scotland Yard. Grieve had just been moved from anti-terrorism to head a new squad, the Racial and Violent Crimes Task Force (CO24), set up to reinvestigate the Lawrence murder. Grieve was still a leading member of the secret anti-corruption management committee and would continue to share intelligence and staff with the Untouchables. His appointment and the launch of the new murder investigation before the Lawrence Inquiry concluded was seen by many outside the police as a cynical damage limitation exercise.

There was a long silence on 1 February when Wells informed Grieve of his concerns. The senior officer was taken aback and asked Wells to do nothing until he had spoken to commissioner Condon. About 15 minutes later Grieve phoned back and gave Wells a "specific denial" that the Yard was bugging the inquiry. Grieve also relayed that Condon was "furious" the Inquiry secretary could seriously suspect his force.

Relations between the Lawrence Inquiry and the commissioner were already strained. "After the Christmas break there was a long, hard discussion about Condon's culpability. Eventually the chairman was persuaded that there were issues about Condon that should be in the report," an Inquiry source told us. In December Macpherson had written a private letter to the commissioner outlining those criticisms, in particular Condon's "lack of vigour" when signing off the "deplorable" Barker Review. The letter was personally delivered because others had been leaked to the media. "Wells personally took the letter by taxi to Scotland Yard. He had an appointment to see the commissioner and handed him the letter. But Condon has always denied ever receiving it," the source added.

The letter came at a bad time. The commissioner had just launched a "Corruption and Dishonesty Prevention Strategy" under the motto: "INTEGRITY IS NON-NEGOTIABLE". In his foreword to the glossy launch brochure, Condon promised there would be "no hiding place for the corrupt, dishonest or unethical" and everyone in the force had "a duty" to internally report instances of it.

By this logic, failure to do so would be a neglect of that duty. However, it was harder to discern from the new moral order what offence is committed when a senior officer knowingly signs off a document that gives a false and misleading impression to a member of the public. Or when an Untouchable fails to properly investigate a corruption allegation because it would harm the reputation of the force or key individuals within it. For these and other thorny issues, the public were supposed to rest easy because a new self-appointed, self-regulated Ethics Committee would ensure the Untouchables behaved accordingly.

The Lawrence Inquiry's intended criticisms of Condon were also at odds with a gushing review he had just received from Her Majesty's Inspectorate of Constabulary (HMIC), a Home Office body stuffed with senior ex-policemen. It hailed Condon's Untouchables as the yardstick by which every other force should be measured.

Grieve informed Wells that the National Criminal Intelligence Service (NCIS) would sweep the Lawrence Inquiry offices for bugs. The following day, 2 February, he was picked up outside Lambeth North tube station and driven to NCIS headquarters.

A detective inspector and several technicians debriefed Wells. He was told a six-man team would present themselves at Hannibal House the next day posing as electricians on an emergency job. It's believed the team came from the Special Project Branch and were part of NCIS's bugging department known as the Operations Support Unit. Officers told Wells that no one other than his staff should know their real purpose.

When the "electricians" arrived on 3 February Wells and his team were drafting the final report. To avoid any undetected bugs all sensitive communication was restricted to written notes passed from hand to hand. "It was a truly amazing sight to watch," one official told us. "Until you see it for yourself you have no idea what's involved. They went through everything. Curtains, blinds, light fittings, toilet rolls, kettles, coffee tins, clothing – everything. Over two days and nights the de-buggers took the offices apart, including every item in the stationery cupboard, each and every biro, every box of Tippex or paper clips. And then picture frames." At the end of the lengthy sweep the Inquiry secretary was told no bug had been found. NCIS dismissed the identical computer faults, but provided no reasoned report. None of this reassured the Inquiry's staff. And Wells' own suspicions were heightened when he later spoke to the Bishop.

The Right Reverend John Sentamu is a former magistrate and lawyer in the Ugandan High Court. In 1976 he left Uganda to study theology at Cambridge University, rising within the Church hierarchy to become the Anglican Bishop of Stepney in 1996.

After the sweep of Hannibal House, NCIS offered to sweep the homes of all the advisers and the chairman. They all declined with the

THE ELECTRICIANS PLUG A LEAK

exception of Bishop Sentamu. At first the Bishop was unwilling to discuss the matter with us. Then out of the blue he rang to say he would. What had changed his mind? We had John Grieve to thank. The Bishop was angered that Grieve had tried to pressure him into not contributing to the story we were preparing for publication in the *Guardian*. Bishop Sentamu had stood up to security goons before in Idi Amin's Uganda. He was so outraged that he went on the record.

The Bishop's home computer had developed an inexplicable fault, he said. No server or network linked it to the three terminals at Hannibal House, but they all seized at the same time.

The Bishop had set aside two weeks in January 1999 to stay at home and write his advice to the Inquiry chairman. His report was highly sensitive. It dealt with institutional racism in the police and outlined the radical reforms he thought were necessary, among them independent investigation of complaints against the police.

During these two weeks the Bishop discussed with Wells his growing conviction that his cordless home phones were bugged. "For four days I could hear these clicks on the line when I made a call as if someone was picking up the phone and listening in," he told us. There were also problems with the lock on his front door. "Suddenly it would not close properly." That's why he asked NCIS to sweep his home.

Four men came to his house. One of them kept a lookout from outside. Those inside picked up signals on a scanner, which they said were coming from an embossed book in the Bishop's bookcase, but concluded the fault was with their equipment.

They then conducted an unusual experiment. One officer went a good distance from the house with equipment that intercepted phone conversations. Another arranged for the cordless phone in the dining-room to be rung from an outside line. The entire conversation was immediately intercepted. The officers told him his phones were "easily compromised" and replaced three of them with what they claimed were "unbuggable" cordless phones. The team also recommended he change the locks on his front door immediately. A locksmith confirmed the front door lock had been "interfered with".

Finally, the officers looked at the home computer. They could not explain the computer crash but suggested it might be a "software problem" which he should have examined. The Bishop sent his computer to a security expert who took months to retrieve data from the frozen hard disk. The expert couldn't explain the fault but said it was definitely not virus- or software-related.

When the *Guardian* put all this to Condon he claimed the Lawrence

Inquiry had "overreacted" and were "embarrassed" that the NCIS sweep had found no bugs. He said the decision to change the Bishop's home phones was a "reassurance" measure.

Bishop Sentamu reacted angrily to Condon's insinuation. "There were very clear signs that something untoward had happened both at Hannibal House and at my home – the chairs, the computers, the clicks. I ask myself why did they change my phones, tell me to change the locks, recommend that we check my computer and leave a card should the worrying signs persist," he hissed. The Bishop paused, then smiled, as if he'd had a moment of divine inspiration. "Maybe it was an act of God, but under suspicious circumstances."

A senior government official who'd been helpful throughout our investigation of this story said Condon's reaction was precisely the problem of the police investigating themselves. They may say they've found nothing, but how do you know for sure?

Other senior figures inside the Lawrence Inquiry were also adamant there had been a "burglary" at their offices. They believe it was carried out to obtain and leak a draft copy of the report to the right-wing press sympathetic to concerns that the debate about racism in the Yard had gone too far. It had not escaped their attention that along with Baldwin's balanced copy, the *Sunday Telegraph* ran a comment piece claiming institutional racism, the key conclusion, was "a flawed and dangerous concept".

The same edition also carried a report based on an authorised "leak" from the Yard of a confidential document setting out DAC John Grieve's "radical strategy", codenamed Operation Athena, to convince the public that the police were not racist. The document proposed using undercover black and Asian officers to "integrity test" fellow white officers. Undercover white and black officers would also be used against members of the public, like hotel owners, in sting operations to expose racist attitudes; offenders could be "named and shamed", it was suggested. There was also talk of a major advertising campaign backed by Asian and black celebrities to show CO24 were serious about prosecuting racist and violent crimes.

Wells and his team had done their own sleuthing after the leak. They concluded that the copy seen by Baldwin was not the final draft prepared for the home secretary. The final draft was Version 8 of the report, but the Sunday newspaper had been shown Version 7. It differed in significant respects around language and phrases.

All copies of early drafts of the report had been shredded immediately. Only the current text was retained. This was stored on a

THE ELECTRICIANS PLUG A LEAK

detachable disk drive locked every night in a two-drawer armoured filing cabinet kept in the anteroom. Only one copy of any draft of the report had been printed out and the advisers could not take it home but had to read it at the Inquiry offices under controlled circumstances. It too was locked in the cabinet with the key held in a safe inside a different room with a digital lock.

Inquiry sources told us Version 7 was what they were working on at the time of "the burglary" but the hard copy had been destroyed. Consequently, they concluded that the stolen copy was obtained by breaking into the anteroom and downloading from the detachable disk drive. It was then leaked.

During the meeting at NCIS before the sweep, Stephen Wells was asked an interesting question: "If it's not the Met, who could it be?" He named a London-based private security company with a revolving door to the Yard and MI6 called Kroll Associates. Wells had no evidence, just speculation based on his knowledge that three senior officers involved in the first Lawrence murder inquiry had joined Kroll after they left the Yard.

Kroll confirmed that a former commander of the Flying Squad called John O'Connor had brought Ray Adams into the company; Adams then recommended Bill Ilsley, who sub-contracted Ian Crampton from time to time. Kroll say references for Adams and Ilsley were taken at the highest level in the Yard and the suggestion of any involvement with the bugging and burglary of the Lawrence Inquiry was "fantasy". The firm had previously been linked to a bugging operation against the attorney general of Gibraltar on behalf of MI6. But this was a freelance venture run by Michael Oatley, a former MI6 officer, who at the time was working for Kroll.

What about MI5? Its most controversial part is A Branch, and a covert search section known as A1A. The former agent David Shayler claims MI5 has the means to "copy the entire contents of a computer hard drive".[1]

Of course the Yard's own Surveillance and Technical Support Unit, part of the Directorate of Intelligence, carries out concealed entry and bugging operations. And the Untouchables have their own covert resource known internally as the Dark Side. Neither unit requires Home Office approval for such spookery.[2]

The Lawrence Inquiry did not believe Jack Straw was in any way behind the leak to the *Sunday Telegraph*, because it blunted the impact he was trying to achieve and diverted attention into sideshow debates. We approached him at the inauguration ceremony for the

UNTOUCHABLES

Metropolitan Police Authority in June 2000. We'd heard that privately Straw was "incandescent" with NCIS for not giving his department a formal report on the sweep of the inquiry's offices. The home secretary was clearly relying on his own officials, who he said had told him "there were no bugs found" and that Baldwin more than likely saw a "government internal summary" of the final Lawrence Report. The *Sunday Telegraph* disagrees. It saw a "copy" of the report.

All of which suggests reactionary elements in the Home Office were misleading their boss.

18

THE SELECTA' RETURNS, POLICE BABYLON BURNS

By mid-1997 Hector Harvey was an angry and bitter man about to slip back into his old ways as a dandy armed robber.

After the failed grenade booby-trap two years earlier, the Yard's witness protection unit (WPU) moved Harvey's family from Luton to rented accommodation in north-west London. He joined them a few months later when he was granted parole in July 1995. There followed a stint of unemployment, then Harvey started working as a chauffeur for the chief executive of Hillsdown Holdings plc, a prestigious company with political connections. Its chairman was the former Tory defence minister, Sir John Nott.

The WPU kept an eye on the supergrass chauffeur, but from a distance. They took seriously the perceived threat from Chris McCormack, the gangland enforcer Harvey had double-crossed in January 1995 over the £1.4 million Security Express robbery. Police intelligence had linked McCormack to the grenade attack and intercepted the south London hard-nut promising to wage war on Harvey unless he paid him £200,000 from his share of the robbery.

Harvey wanted as little contact with the anti-corruption squad as possible. He figured he owed them nothing, especially after he was told in January 1997 that the CPS had decided there was insufficient evidence to prosecute any of the Flying Squad detectives or the armed robbers he had grassed-up during Operation Spy. As Harvey tells it, he'd put his life on the line to expose police corruption. The Yard had allowed the Flying Squad to investigate itself and naturally nothing came of it; except the criminals he had so handsomely double-crossed now all knew he was a grass because his name was mysteriously disclosed to defence lawyers during the joint investigation.[1]

The Selecta's recall conveniently ignores how he toyed with the Ghost Squad and spun everyone lies. In fact, two years after the Security Express robbery the anti-corruption squad still believed Harvey had been "bounced" by veteran blaggers Gary Ward and Joey Simms into carrying it out during the dry-run, when he had planned it that way all along.

Harvey had almost no contact with the Yard throughout 1997. He had no idea DAC Roy Clark had set up the Untouchables, or that this new anti-corruption squad was working secretly to trap the corrupt detective Kevin Garner, the man they believed had stolen the guard's £200,000 share and divided it with other Flying Squad colleagues.

After a row with his boss, Harvey resigned from his chauffeuring job and set up his own company, Elegant Chauffeur Services. The business was unpredictable, which exacerbated his financial pressures and marital problems. Behind the back of his long-suffering wife, Harvey hooked up with a petty criminal from west London and returned to robbing. This time it wasn't security vans but the capital's massage parlours, where businessmen drop in for executive relief before catching the 7.15 p.m. to Chalfont St Giles and a light supper with the wife.

Between June and October 1997, Harvey carried out five robberies at knifepoint, netting anything between £80 and £400 each time. "I was doing it as a favour to a bird that I knew who worked in that game. She was just telling us the layout and marking our card with the girls that were in there, letting them know that we were coming in," says Harvey with his customary gloss.

His wife eventually found out in the late autumn. "She wasn't having it, after all we had gone through with prison and with CIB. Don't forget that nothing had come out in the newspapers about all this yet. I was slipping back into criminal mode 'cos I was strapped for cash and other personal things, like arguments in front of the children. So I just packed my bags and moved out in the October/November of 1997."

Harvey lived for the next few months on the couches of his friends and in the beds of various lovers. He was unaware of the recent arrests by CIB3 of Garner, McGuinness and Green. It wasn't until January 1998 after a run of press articles that the new anti-corruption squad walked back into his life. The article that most concerned Harvey was in the *News of the World* – BENT COPS' STOOGE IS UNMASKED – naming him as the supergrass against the Flying Squad.

Harvey met with new CIB3 recruits, detective chief inspector Martin Bridger, detective sergeant Dave Pennant and detective constable Sam Miller from Operation Ethiopia. Bridger described the meeting: "I was able to tell him that as far as the police were concerned we would not be seeking his prosecution for the robbery but made it clear to him that if the CPS and/or counsel took a different view in the future he would obviously be informed immediately. He expressed his concerns. I assured him this was a new investigation team and everything would be looked at again."

By this stage Kevin Garner had formally turned supergrass and was telling his CIB3 debriefers how he stole the guard's £200,000 share and then split it ten ways with his police colleagues.

Bridger met Harvey again on 29 January and asked him if he would corroborate Garner by giving evidence. Harvey said he would think about it. They met one week later and Harvey made the first of many written statements for Operation Ethiopia. But the Selecta' had no intention of telling the real truth in any of them. That would involve coming clean that he had planned the Security Express robberies all along. It would also involve admitting he had recently embarked on an armed robbing spree across London to get money to flee the country with his family.

The first armed robbery took place on 8 January, a few weeks before he was approached by the Untouchables. But two days after making a statement for them, he robbed a CashCo van outside the Asda supermarket in Hendon, north London, on 6 February. That robbery had a touch of the Carry Ons about it. When Harvey got the cash box into his vehicle it started bleeping and then billowing red smoke. He threw it under a parked car and drove off. Most of the £20,000 inside was ruined by the dye.

Harvey didn't trust CIB3, but he could smell their desperation, unaware, as he was, how much Operation Ethiopia meant to commissioner Condon's damage limitation strategy. Once again, Harvey was manipulating the anti-corruption squad for his own ends. Over the next six months he would do to Condon's Untouchables what he had done three years earlier to his Ghost Squad.

Between 8 January and 13 July 1998 Hector Harvey and his crew secretly carried out over 70 off-licence robberies, netting some £100,000. All the while he provided his CIB3 handlers with pages of misleading witness statements and was being looked after by the WPU.

Harvey's crew included Ricky Welsh, the driver, and Darren Lewis, who entered the off-licence with Harvey carrying a gun. On occasion they used a Walter PPK, James Bond's weapon of choice, only this one was an imitation cigarette lighter bought for £5 in a market, says Harvey.

The favoured off-licence was Threshers because the time safe was less secure. The robberies had roughly the same modus operandi. Harvey and Lewis would enter shortly before closing time, close the shutters, threaten the staff with the gun, tie them up with duct tape, seize the security videotape from the machine and then help themselves to cash, cigarettes and on occasion some champagne. They would leave having taken personal details from the staff to scare them into not helping the police. The whole robbery took up to 30 minutes.

Harvey is "embarrassed" about the calibre of crime to which he was now resorting. "I'd gone from using inside agents against Security Express to knocking over Threshers!" In June, a female member joined the crew. Michelle Niles drew the single salesperson from behind the counter to help choose an expensive wine. This would be the signal for Harvey and Lewis to strike.

That month Harvey also moved into a west London bedsit in Ladbroke Grove, the heart of the capital's Caribbean community. Relations with his wife were still cool. Harvey called the single room his "robber's lair"; a place to store all the spoils of what one lawyer later described as an "undeclared war on Threshers".

Throughout this "war" Harvey carried on chauffeuring for some top business and celebrity clients. "I was Jekyll and Hyde; a chauffeur by day and a robber by night. I took a multi-millionaire client to the OXO Tower restaurant [overlooking the Thames] and I had my blagging gear in the boot of the car. I parked up, jumped into another car, went and done a Threshers, got dropped off, changed into work clothes and went and picked [the client] up."

Throughout it all Harvey kept in regular touch with the Untouchables, meeting them in a café by Putney Bridge, near to their new headquarters. In April, for example, with five robberies under his belt, he helped DS Dave Pennant do a reconstruction of the moment when he alleged DI Norris had removed £47,000 from the bag containing his share of the robbery.

Before robbing another off-licence, Harvey cheekily persuaded CIB3 to pay off £2,600 rent arrears accumulated at the family home.

THE SELECTA' RETURNS...

Then in June, days after robbing almost £4,000 from Threshers in South Norwood, he had the front to complain to CIB3 that the squad was not doing enough to relocate his wife and children to a more affordable home. Apparently the local council had started eviction proceedings.

Ironically, since January 1998 the Finchley office of the Flying Squad had been investigating the off-licence robberies unaware they were being committed by an informant who was grassing up their colleagues at Rigg Approach to the Untouchables. According to sources at Finchley Flying Squad, there was strong suspicion that CIB3 eventually pulled Harvey out when they realised the robberies he was committing threatened to severely undermine Operation Ethiopia.

The rude boy supergrass had told CIB3 on 9 June that Finchley were on his tail over "some armed robberies" but denied any involvement. Harvey says the Untouchables then gave him a "veiled warning" that if he was robbing there was nothing they could do for him. As he was only stringing CIB3 along about co-operating as a witness, he went on to commit several more armed robberies well into mid-July. He maintained contact with the Untouchables throughout. They were desperate for Harvey to make another statement. It is clear from documents we've seen that in the period leading up to Harvey's arrest on 3 August, CIB3 were aware of Finchley Flying Squad's interest in their supergrass, and that tensions between the two squads increased when it came to interview Harvey over the robberies.[2]

"We were outside the room and CIB3 debriefers would come out and ask us what to ask him and tell us his replies," recalls one Finchley detective. "Harvey was charged and then taken out of our control by CIB3. This case was being run at a high level." Do you think CIB3 tipped Harvey off? "I wouldn't say that. We might as well pack up and all go home if that was the case," replied the Finchley detective, a sardonic smile on his face.

After Harvey had confessed he was bailed into CIB3 custody and whisked away by senior detectives in charge of Operation Ethiopia. They kept him for several days at a police station in Norwich. If CIB3 bosses didn't already have a headache working out the effect of the Threshers robberies on the integrity of the corruption probe, their tricky supergrass was about to drop another bombshell that sent some senior officers racing for the executive toilets.

Harvey admitted for the first time that he had planned both the failed December 1994 Security Express robbery and the successful

UNTOUCHABLES

January 1995 one. There was no "double whammy" pulled on him by Ward and Simms, he confessed. Harvey was coming clean now because he realised that only by co-operating with the Untouchables did he stand a chance of avoiding an automatic life sentence for the Threshers armed robberies under the "three strikes" rule.

Detective superintendent Brian Moore came to see Harvey at Norwich. "He gave me this speech that I had to cleanse myself and if I lied I was out of the [supergrass] programme. He told me, 'If you ever see me again it's because you are out of the programme.'" From Norwich, Harvey was moved to a police station in Sevenoaks, Kent, where he spent six weeks being debriefed. And then he was moved to New Malden police station in south-west London.

CIB3 was now put straight that the corruption by Rigg Approach detectives was opportunistic not pre-planned. Harvey though reconfirmed his allegations against Norris and that he had helped arrange for other detectives to collect the guard's share.

However, his crucial debriefings were done off-tape and involved, he says, the use of two parallel sets of notebooks to record his answers. One, he explains, was an intelligence book, presumably never to be disclosed. The other notebook contained snippets of conversations that were later typed up and disclosed to defence lawyers. But in reality this second notebook could give no meaningful insight into how much pressure had been applied or inducements offered.

Dealing this way with a supergrass they knew had been so dishonest in the past is inexcusable, let alone unlawful, especially when CIB3 clearly hoped to use Harvey as a witness of truth in a forthcoming trial. But for the Untouchables it was more important to preserve control of the direction of the internal corruption probe than to abide by the well-defined laws regarding the use of supergrass evidence. Harvey recalls that his legal representative hardly attended any of the debriefings. Our investigation suggests this was typical of an unwritten CIB3 policy of keeping its supergrasses as far away from their lawyers as possible. Achieving this didn't require overt pressure or great bullying but subtle suggestion to the vulnerable supergrass that it would be in his best interests to go along with it.

A good example is what was happening around this time to Kevin Garner. Just before he agreed to turn supergrass, Garner's original lawyer had complained that senior CIB3 detective Chris Jarratt was "badgering" his mentally unstable client. After Garner was charged his solicitor went home. Jarratt then twice spoke to his prisoner alone and without tape-recording the conversation. The next day Garner agreed

THE SELECTA' RETURNS...

to become a supergrass and, at Jarratt's suggestion, changed his lawyer to someone the CIB3 officer recommended. This new solicitor rarely attended the subsequent and still unrecorded debriefing sessions.[3]

CIB3 had engineered it this way because as the supergrass is a prosecution witness the attendance notes of his solicitor are disclosable to the defence. But if the solicitor is not present then there is no note he can disclose. This leaves the supergrass in the debriefing process without someone to protect his rights. And as the debrief is not tape-recorded CIB3 are able to filter the allegations they want from those they don't want, so that when the supergrass is eventually interviewed on tape his "evidence" has effectively been moulded.

"There is no good reason why the solicitor couldn't be there or shouldn't be present throughout the debriefing of their supergrass client, especially when you know CIB3 are not taping," says defence lawyer Mark Lake. "The only credible answer is that CIB3 don't want them there while they are pulling strokes. However, if everything was above board, the defence team of a cop accused by the supergrass of corruption would be virtually toothless if CIB3 could wheel out in the trial a respected lawyer, who could say he was present throughout the debrief, saw no naughtiness and would not have tolerated it. This would have had the effect of adding some integrity to the supergrass system."

Harvey's legal representative, Jeremy Newall, shared his client's distrust of the anti-corruption squad and their ability to investigate themselves. While Harvey was being debriefed, in late August Newall's office in Tottenham, north London, was broken into over four consecutive nights.

A source at the firm, Purcell, Brown & Co, described the events: "The window at the back by the car park was smashed. We replaced it and it was smashed again. Each time the office was broken into, ransacked but nothing was taken. [Jeremy] didn't have any of his paperwork at the office. It was all at his home. Clearly someone wanted to know what the score was. They even broke into the barrister's car looking for paperwork. After the first break-in we reported it to Tottenham police station. [Jeremy] also spoke to CIB3 and asked them to sweep the office [for bugs], but they refused. Nothing like this had happened before or since."

Whether it was CIB3 or bent Flying Squad detectives behind the break-ins remains unresolved.

Terrence Patrick McGuinness was born in Ilford, Essex, on 31 January 1958. His dad had been an amateur boxer. And when he wasn't working as an odd job man for the council, he ran training sessions for the local boys clubs. Terry felt this made him a target for bullies, so after numerous fights he started training at the East Ham Boxing Club under the guidance of an ex-policeman. It was this that later inspired young Terry to join the Met. But first there was the prospect of a professional boxing career. McGuinness reached the ABA semis as a heavyweight. He then started training with Terry Lawless and sparring with British heavyweight champion John L Gardner. Lawless had helped legendary promoter Mickey Duff dominate British boxing in the seventies as manager of world champions John H Stracey, Charlie Magri, Jim Watt, Maurice Hope, Lloyd Honeyghan and then Frank Bruno. However, McGuinness was not a contender. He suffered from a cauliflower arse but had a lot of heart.

When he wasn't boxing, McGuinness followed West Ham around the country mixing with its notorious racist hooligans, the forerunners of what became the Inter City Firm. His money came from a job as an apprentice metal worker. At 20 he had enough to marry a local girl and moved into a council flat in Canning Town, near to where he would be videoed 18 years later stealing the planted cannabis.

In November 1979, McGuinness joined the police "for all the normal reasons: to make a difference, to fight crime, to serve the community". He was posted to a local East End station where he first met Keith Green.

When he got into the detective branch, McGuinness served with and befriended many of the officers he later met on the Flying Squad. He failed his first attempt to get up there so he transferred to Stoke Newington police station in 1988, a stepping-stone to Rigg Approach.

McGuinness made it onto the Flying Squad in January 1990 as a detective constable, aged 32. He later told CIB3 that almost immediately he noticed "bad practice" at Rigg Approach. "There were certain times that where the circumstances were right, money that itself may have been stolen by criminals or was the proceeds of crime would be stolen." The corrupt culture was perverse. McGuinness told us it was only those who sold out jobs to criminals that were regarded as "bent". Stealing some recovered proceeds was looked on as compensation for reduced overtime. And those officers who didn't go along with it had their lives made miserable until they left.

In January 1995, after five years at Rigg, McGuinness transferred to Limehouse police station. According to an anti-corruption squad officer, the old CIB2 were already looking at him – the allegation

THE SELECTA' RETURNS...

concerned conspiring with the legal representative of a fraudster to pervert the course of justice. That investigation was overtaken in December 1997 when McGuinness unexpectedly walked into the CIB3 drugs sting with Kevin Garner and then turned supergrass.

In July and September 1998, after extensive debriefs, McGuinness and Garner formally pleaded guilty at the Old Bailey to a raft of serious criminal offences beyond those involving the theft of 80 kilos of dope. Garner pleaded to 12 additional counts of corrupt activity involving other Flying Squad detectives at Rigg Approach. Like McGuinness, he maintained implausibly that his corruption only began while he was on the Flying Squad and spanned a shorter period, from December 1992 to October 1996.

Garner claimed his first, albeit minor, corrupt act was to accept £200 cash from a Flying Squad colleague after others had arrested a jewellery thief and stolen some of the recovered proceeds. The detectives, including senior officers, pissed it up in Brighton on champagne, he told CIB3. Garner explained that he took the money because he was beginning to be "accepted" after seven months on the squad. He didn't want to be a "minion", he said, and if you wanted "good work" you had to be "corrupt". McGuinness also pleaded to the same charge of handling stolen goods – he says he received a £50 note from the recovered proceeds.

McGuinness, who joined the Flying Squad two years before Garner, admitted seven additional corrupt offences. His first corrupt touch came in March 1992 when he was given £500 of so-called "soggy fivers". These were part of a £37,000 load recovered by the Flying Squad from a ditch. The bag of money had been thrown away by one of the robbers' girlfriends. She thought by washing the money it would remove the fingerprints before the police came calling. Again, he alleged this money was shared out with other colleagues.

Garner's first major act of corruption was a "weed" from £300,000 of newly minted ten pence coins the Flying Squad had recovered from some armed robbers in September 1993. He and McGuinness admitted helping themselves to about £3,000 each. They also alleged six other officers were involved.[4]

Another joint venture involved substituting cash stolen during searches for counterfeit money. Garner suggests he was the unofficial launderer for a corrupt cell of Flying Squad officers, and that he used his contacts with Hackney car ringer Michael Taverner to buy funny money. Garner also pleaded guilty to conspiring to commit a tiger kidnap with Taverner, Irish Mick and a serving officer.

UNTOUCHABLES

In many respects Garner was the Untouchables' favoured son. McGuinness could not corroborate Harvey over the January 1995 Security Express robbery. He wasn't involved in the investigation and had transferred off the Flying Squad that month. He was useful though for corroborating who was in the "cell" of bent detectives at Rigg.

Hector Harvey's debrief was also a drawn-out affair. On 9 October 1998, Harvey pleaded guilty to planning both Security Express robberies. Then, appropriately on Armistice Day, he pleaded guilty to 22 additional offences, asking for 55 others to be taken into consideration. They were. Unlike McGuinness, who was jailed in April 2000 for nine years, later reduced by two years on appeal, Harvey and Garner would not be sentenced until after they gave evidence against the four Flying Squad detectives and the north London lawyer, Les Brown.

This controversial feature of the Untouchables' supergrass system was not unlawful. But defence lawyers argue that there is an implicit inducement to the supergrass in these terms – those who help the police by naming names and giving a good show in court will get a persuasive recommendation to the judge for a reduced sentence.

CIB3 say there was no number chasing and that it was "down to the judge" to decide whether he sentenced the supergrass before or after giving evidence. But this is simply not how it worked in reality. CIB3 controlled their supergrasses and presented them to the courts when they were ready. Meanwhile, during their debriefing process word was leaked to the media that the two supergrass cops had named a large number of serving and retired officers. This was done in part to generate anxious phone calls between officers whose phones were tapped, but also to give an illusion of the steady march to the all-important figure of 250 bent detectives.

The first Flying Squad trial started at the Old Bailey six months later on 3 October 2000. It had taken two years since detectives Tim Norris, Eamonn Harris, Fred May, David Howell, Paul Smith and solicitor Les Brown were variously charged with theft, conspiracy to steal and perverting the course of justice. The delay was in part caused by the sickness of Smith and Brown, who were severed from the trial.

So deeply flawed were the two prosecution witnesses – Harvey and Garner – that prosecutor David Waters QC immediately gave strong health warnings to the jury. Harvey was described as someone they should "hesitate long and hard" about before believing his

THE SELECTA' RETURNS...

unsupported word. But "exceptionally", said Waters, a former policeman supported the repentant armed robber. Garner's motivation for giving evidence against his former colleagues was, like Harvey's, the hope of a reduced sentence. But when added with the independent financial evidence against the defendants this was a strong case, Waters argued.

Against Norris was Harvey's claim that he saw the detective steal £47,000 from his share, and a financial report by CIB3. This purported to show that a week after the robbery Norris paid off a bank loan with a cheque for £4,400 from severed co-defendant Les Brown. The detective and the solicitor were good friends and Brown had given Norris the cheque from his client account in return for cash. Against Howell, Harris and May were Garner and Harvey plus some cell site analysis of the officers' phone calls which CIB3 claimed showed a conspiracy to steal the guard's share of £200,000.

The prosecution opening amply anticipated Garner's evidence that he and Howells had personally divided this money ten ways and shared it out with Harris and Smith. May took the other six shares and the prosecution alleged they had gone to, amongst others, detective chief inspector Michael Fry and detective inspector George Raison. Waters added a caveat to explain why neither officer was in the dock. He said: "People are only brought before this court if there is sufficient admissible evidence to place them in that position." It was clear CIB3 and the prosecution wanted the jury to believe there was a cell of corrupt officers. The word "admissible" was an interesting choice because it implied there was incriminating wiretap evidence CIB3 could not put before a court.[5]

In response to this dramatic opening statement, a battery of eminent defence barristers countered that proven liars had fabricated all the allegations with axes to grind and much to gain from turning supergrass. The four defendants were detectives with untarnished reputations. Full stop.

The trial was peppered with PII certificates, which the jury knew nothing about. Like the supergrass system, these gagging orders were also discredited after the collapse of the 1992 Matrix Churchill trial, which triggered the Scott Inquiry into the Major government's secret and illegal rearming of Saddam Hussein. Four Tory government ministers, who signed PII certificates blocking disclosure of sensitive intelligence documents, were apparently prepared to see innocent businessmen go to prison rather than reveal their sanction-busting policy.

UNTOUCHABLES

The PII certificates in the Flying Squad trial concerned three areas: the role of Michael Taverner and CIB3 informant Irish Mick in the missing 26 kilos of dope, Garner's undercover activities during the Urquhart murder inquiry and the so-called Fleming tape made by Raison of an informant discussing how Chris McCormack had appeared at a money launderer's business with a suitcase of cash days after the Security Express robbery.

CIB3 had a strategy of liberally relying on this sinister weapon in the prosecution's armoury to block disclosure of information that would help unpick the unlawful supergrass system. Its practical effect meant CIB3 and CIBIC were protected by the courts from scrutiny.

The granting of PII certificates depends on the judge's discretion – he hears the application in chambers without the defence being present or even entitled to know what areas it covers. If the judge is pro-prosecution, he will almost always favour protecting the modesty of the secret state. More independent-thinking judges have been misled by sexed up intelligence from the police, dramatically presented by the prosecutor. CIB3 can sex up the intelligence picture for a recalcitrant judge to make it seem so prejudicial to the defence of the realm that he will grant the PII application immediately.

PII applications are to the police what cheap make-up is to an ageing prostitute – they cover the cracks. The more political the prosecution the more dangerous PII applications by unaccountable secret units within the police are to the principle of open justice and democratic accountability.

The set-piece of the Flying Squad trial was always going to be the cross-examination of the two supergrasses. Harvey's was described by court reporter Andrew Cunningham as "a master class in blagging". He spent five days in the box. He admitted having everyone over but was unswerving in his claim that he saw Norris steal the money. "I have admitted all my lies but I saw what I saw," he told the detective's barrister, Tony Glass QC, who, unperturbed, went on to dissect the supergrass.

Glass: You have succeeded in keeping the money you have creamed off in the 1995 robbery and the massage parlour and Threshers robberies?

Harvey: Yes.

Glass: You managed to deceive everyone since 1994?

Harvey: Yes.

Glass: Ward and Simms?

Harvey: Yes.

THE SELECTA' RETURNS...

Glass: Norris and Smith?
Harvey: Yes.
Glass: Your own solicitor?
Harvey: Yes.
Glass: CIB2?
Harvey: Yes.
Glass: Mr Bridger of CIB3 from February 1998 until August 1998?
Harvey: Yes.
Glass: And way back in 1990 when you last appeared before a jury you got your friend to lie and try and deceive the jury to save your skin?
Harvey: Yes.
Glass: . . . for which you have not faced any charge?
Harvey: No.

Garner fared better during some equally heavy cross-examination. But after 52 days of evidence the jury retired. They returned 36 hours later, on 25 January 2001, to find Norris innocent. Harris, Howell and May were all found guilty of conspiracy to steal and perverting the course of justice and sentenced to seven years each.

Amongst all the evidence, there was one witness the jury never got to hear from – detective inspector George Raison, the man repeatedly accused in the prosecution's opening as someone believed to be part of the corrupt cell in the Rigg Approach office. The jury had asked if Raison and Mick Fry were still serving. They were told both officers had been suspended since January 1998, but were medically unfit to be interviewed by CIB3. This was a serious but unwitting error by the judge.

Raison had waited for three days in the Old Bailey canteen for the defence to decide if they would call him to give evidence about what he had learned during the joint investigation with CIB2 called Operation Spy. "I was gagging to give evidence. I had answers to everything. I had proof in writing [about CIB3 reluctance to interview me]. I could have produced letters like a rabbit out of a hat to show the jury the truth of the matter and CIB3 would have been buggered and the jury would have looked at the prosecution in a different light entirely." In the end he wasn't used because the defence lawyers felt his suspension made him too tainted a witness whose cross-examination would do their case more harm than good. This, says Raison, is exactly what CIB3 had intended when they suspended him.

Raison had every reason not to be a defence witness. In the run-up to the trial a group of about 20 suspended detectives, including the defendants, had met every month at their lawyers' office. Paranoia about double agents was rife. They knew of Raison's role in Operation Spy. He started to notice an undercurrent emerging among the group that he might be "a mole" for "the funny firm" – a preferred nickname for CIB3.

The most intriguing allegation against Raison that "justified" his lengthy suspension was that his report to the CPS on Operation Spy was "a false, misleading and inaccurate written document". He was also alleged to have had a part of the guard's share. Raison was only notified of the "misleading report" allegation in August 1998, seven months after his suspension. He maintains that the Untouchables always had to discredit him because his report was so critical of how the Ghost Squad had mishandled Harvey and the original corruption probe into the Flying Squad.

This may explain why the prosecution feigned "surprise" in front of the jury about how it was Raison came to carry out a joint CIB investigation into the robbery when he was also suspected of having benefited from it. As if the Flying Squad detective had somehow inserted himself and undermined the Ghost Squad's corruption inquiry.

It must have slipped Waters' mind that the head of the Ghost Squad DAC John Grieve had authorised the appointment, CIB superintendent Dave Niccol had in a statement described the Raison report as "exceptional" and the CPS was equally convinced of its integrity. There were after all thousands of supporting documents to prove how incompetently and unlawfully the Ghost Squad had acted.

Thirteen months after his suspension, and still not interviewed about the two serious allegations against him, Raison was approached by a fellow Flying Squad detective allegedly acting on the instructions of Untouchable Brian Moore. Raison secretly taped the pub meeting with detective inspector Chris Coomber in February 1999.

Coomber was a work friend and Raison's welfare officer – someone nominated to represent a suspended detective's concerns to senior management. As a further measure of the muddle CIB3 had got itself into, Coomber had also been named by McGuinness as one of the many detectives aware of corrupt practices at Rigg.[6] Nevertheless, here he was being used by the Untouchables to make a very questionable approach to Raison. It is fair to say Coomber felt uncomfortable about this intermediary role.

"I was asked to provide CIB3 with a witness statement and be willing to give evidence in court, or provide an intelligence statement

THE SELECTA' RETURNS...

on anything I knew about Rigg Approach. In return the allegations of fabricating the report and having a share of the money would disappear," says Raison. He turned down the offer and reported the meeting to his lawyers. An internal CIB3 memo makes it clear Raison was seen as a danger to the Untouchables as the trial approached.

"CIB3 never had any intention of charging me with criminal offences," says Raison, a belief borne out by the fact that eight weeks after the Flying Squad trial ended he was interviewed about the allegations underpinning his suspension on full pay. This was now in its fourth year and had cost the taxpayer £130,000. After ten minutes CIB3 said he would not face prosecution. He was also allowed to retire in July 2001 with all disciplinary matters withdrawn. "I was never too sick to be interviewed," says Raison. "CIB3 could have done so at any time before the trial started." Correspondence we have seen bears this out.

Like that of undercover cop Michael, the case of George Raison raises a serious question. How do you stop an anti-corruption squad using suspension as a tool to prevent an officer giving damaging evidence against the force? And how often has and will this power be abused by the police when a whistle-blower officer's evidence is required by lawyers representing a member of the public who has, say, been fitted-up, beaten up or killed in custody?

Raison couldn't complain to the Yard about it. Nor could he go to the Home Office. And police officers are not allowed to make complaints to the PCA. In effect there is no mechanism for a police officer to have the grounds for his continued suspension independently assessed to ensure there is no malice or hidden agenda to suppress the truth.

Kevin Garner was sentenced in February 2001, one month after the trial. When he appeared at the Old Bailey he looked hollow. The corrupt detective had lost over six stone and much of his hair, and was now wearing glasses.

Head bowed throughout, Garner's barrister described him as the "lynchpin" in the Untouchables' crusade, without whom the corruption would have continued. The trial judge told him how "impressed" he had been with the supergrass's evidence and reaffirmed the highly debatable point that it was the Flying Squad that had made Garner bad. "It seems those that thought themselves to be the elite were all routinely engaged in corruption . . . all with the knowledge and approval, and in some cases active participation of officers much senior to yourself." Six years.

What of the two other defendants too ill to be tried with Norris, May, Howell and Harris? Detective constable Paul Smith was allowed to retire from the police on medical grounds in July 2001 with no finding against him.[7]

The incredible story of what happened to solicitor Leslie Leonard Brown was further evidence that the anti-corruption crusade in general and Operation Ethiopia specifically was a famine not a feast of clean, successful internal investigations. Fourteen months after the trial ended, Brown pleaded guilty to a money laundering offence that directly implicated Norris in the very crime he had just been acquitted of. The situation was made more bizarre because Norris was about to come off paid sick leave and return to work.

Brown faced four counts of converting and transferring the proceeds of criminal conduct and attempted handling of stolen goods. They all centred on the £4,400 company cheque he gave Norris days after the Security Express robbery in exchange for cash.

When Brown arrived at the Old Bailey on 11 March 2002 he looked pasty-faced and had a permanent snivel as if his sinuses were blocked. Drawing hard on his cigarette he gave every impression of taking the case to Europe if necessary. But by lunchtime there had been a dramatic U-turn. Brown pleaded guilty to: "Having reasonable grounds to suspect that £4,400 in cash directly or indirectly represented Norris's proceeds of criminal conduct, [he] transferred [it] for the purposes of assisting Norris avoid prosecution."

One week later, Brown returned to the Bailey to be sentenced. He looked haunted and still had that trademark snivel. The prosecution told the court Brown had made some important admissions about his close friend, Tim Norris, during an unrecorded intelligence interview with Untouchable Brian Moore in October 1998. They had met when Norris was serving at Tottenham. Their friendship developed over watching Spurs and going to boxing matches. Brown had done conveyancing for Norris, acted for his parents in a boundary dispute and lent his wife money to help start a business, the prosecution explained. Of course a lot of this was familiar to Moore who was also a close friend of Norris.

Brown had told the CIB3 officer that Norris called him to represent Harvey hours after the robbery. In a private consultation Harvey told Brown that Norris had stolen the money. Brown was "shocked and surprised" because he saw Norris as a man of "utmost

THE SELECTA' RETURNS . . .

integrity". He disbelieved Harvey. But a few days later Norris arrived unannounced at his office with a wad of cash and asked Brown for a company cheque to pay off a loan. At first, Brown was not unduly suspicious. The next day the solicitor left for Las Vegas and spent most of the cash on his holiday. When he returned to London, Brown had a drink with Norris and "half jokingly" asked him what he made of Harvey's allegation against him. Norris "hesitated" and didn't say no straight away. So Brown asked him, "Well, did you [steal the money]?" He told Moore he was shocked when Norris replied, "Yeah."

Brown's barrister, Andrew Trollope QC, said his client's crime was simply not alerting the authorities when he realised the money was stolen, thus enabling his friend Norris to "escape prosecution". He said Brown was left in the "curious and anomalous position" that he had pleaded guilty when Norris had been acquitted, "so the man who was the source of tainted funds walks away from the lengthy and tangled investigation scot-free". Norris, he added, "bears a very large measure of the blame for putting Brown in a wholly impossible position'. His client, he mitigated, acted out of "misguided loyalty and an error of judgement".

The judge was assured and gave Brown a fifteen-month sentence, suspended for two years. The three other counts were left on file. This seemed remarkably lenient. Asked outside the court how he felt about Norris returning to police work, Brown replied it was "disgusting" and walked off, no doubt to get some medication for those blocked sinuses.

A few weeks later we met the disgraced solicitor at his mansion on Forty Hill in leafy Enfield. The property was up for sale to pay his creditors, he explained. The lounge looked like the venue of a number of all-nighters, and the walled grounds were as unkempt as the 58-year-old solicitor, who still hadn't shaken off that cold. The Law Society had struck him off in July 2001 for an unrelated matter, which according to legal sources involved financial impropriety around a missing £30,000 from his client account. Brown described it as a "shortfall" after his accounts got "in a mess".

The criminal solicitor had actually started life as a social worker for the local council and then moved into law, establishing a practice opposite Edmonton police station. Over the years he had got to know many officers, including Garner and McGuinness. These loose friendships were lubricated when Brown became a licensee in 1991. Lawyers, clients and policemen frequented his wine bar, like Relton's place a decade earlier. But Brown says he was closed down in 1998 after undercover officers proved he was selling alcohol without food after hours.

Brown described how in October 1998 he agreed a deal with the Untouchables, where he would plead to one charge of laundering and give evidence against Norris. "If I had wanted to have rolled over I could have given [CIB3] allegations of clients who'd been nicked with an amount of drugs and charged with less." But Brown said he later reneged on the deal after receiving a threat from an unnamed ex-cop who "said I could get lead in my cranium if I rolled over".

There followed a period of sickness, genuine he insists, which meant he couldn't be tried with Norris and others. Brown therefore didn't have to explain the £4,400 cheque and left Harvey unsupported in front of the jury. After Norris's acquittal, he says a new deal was finally ironed out between counsel and the judge, behind CIB3's back. The Untouchables had wanted to try him. But instead the judge accepted a plea to the laundering charge in return for a non-custodial sentence.

Before we parted company, Brown claimed he had lied to Moore during the intelligence interview to get bail. He said Norris never admitted the theft to him. As the interview with Moore was deliberately not tape-recorded, it is impossible to know whether Brown is now telling the truth or just trying to avoid being labelled a grass.

With Brown's case out of the way, two months later in June 2002 it was Hector Harvey's turn to discover what reduction in sentence he would get for all the, erm, assistance he had given CIB3.

Harvey stood in the dock of Court 18 at the Old Bailey looking every bit the dapper rogue. The Selecta' wore a dark blue suit with a pale purple shirt and tie. He had piled on the pounds in the almost four years he had spent as a CIB3 supergrass. He was now 37 years old.

In the supergrass suite at HMP Woodhill Harvey was known as Bloggs 72. He had some personality clashes with the guards. Typically, the Selecta' had an explanation. "They don't know how to deal with an educated black man standing up for his rights. They can't take it. 'Where's this geezer coming from? He should be all blood claat, rass claat.' When I'm saying How Now Brown Cow!"

Prosecutor Ed Brown gave a heavily sanitised version of Harvey's amazing journey from robber to cleansed CIB3 supergrass. The mitigation speech by Harvey's barrister, Sir John Nutting QC, must have made very uncomfortable listening for Tim Norris, who was in the public gallery.

Unless he could point out some "exceptional circumstances" Nutting knew the judge would have no alternative but to pass an automatic life sentence on Harvey. His client, he said, had been willing to give evidence against all the people he named, both civilians and police officers, but in the end and "for tactical reasons" the prosecution had preserved him solely for the Flying Squad trial. If Harvey had been disbelieved in a previous trial it would have rendered him useless against the Flying Squad defendants. Serious armed robbers were therefore never prosecuted.

Les Brown's recent guilty plea in effect meant Harvey's evidence against Norris was true, Nutting maintained. "It will be a long, long time if ever that [Harvey] will rid himself of the fear of discovery," he told the judge. And with a final dramatic flourish Nutting kept a straight face while he explained how Harvey had turned to robbing the off-licences because he needed to restore his credibility with the Underworld.

The judge took all this into account, plus a glowing testimonial from a Methodist preacher who had been visiting Harvey inside, before passing a sentence of four years and four months.

Outside court we met up with Norris. His warrant card had been returned and he was waiting for a new posting. During his four-year suspension on full pay, Norris had completed a law degree and masters. He said it had allowed him to spot the "strokes pulled by CIB3 to manipulate evidence" in his case. Norris denied he had admitted the theft to his solicitor friend, Les Brown.

Harvey, meanwhile, returned to Woodhill prison very angry. The sentence meant he would have to serve another six months. The bitterness in Harvey had been building up for many months. He had written to the new commissioner, Sir John Stevens, who'd taken over from Condon in February 2000, asking him to intervene and help his wife and children with the "massive debts" they had incurred since having to move from their Luton home. "My head is full of anger and frustration. I implore you, Sir John, help me, help me, help me! I have kept to my end of the bargain, yet I now feel as if I am being shitted on from a great height, knowing that you've now got what you wanted from me. It's not right, Sir John."

It was a warning Scotland Yard ignored at great cost. The Selecta' decided it was time, in the words of James Brown, the Godfather of Soul, "for the big payback".

UNTOUCHABLES

Harvey sacked his entire legal team and appointed new solicitors who appealed his sentence on the grounds the judge had got his maths wrong. The judge had used a starting point of twenty-one years and taken two-thirds off for Harvey's guilty plea and supergrass evidence. From the remaining seven years he miscalculated the amount of time Harvey had already spent in CIB3 custody. Had he got his maths right he would have passed a sentence that meant Harvey was immediately eligible for parole, something he almost certainly would have got.

Believing CIB3 had betrayed him, Harvey pulled up something that would convince them of the error of their ways and encourage them to support his appeal and application for bail. He had "two aces in the hole" which the Untouchables didn't know about. He decided to play only one of them. It would involve grassing up someone new and very special.

On 23 August, Harvey summoned two CIB3 officers to come and see him urgently at HMP Woodhill. Even his new young solicitor, Sarah Brinklow, hadn't a clue what he wanted to tell the Untouchables. She takes up the story: "Detective chief inspector Simon Cousins, the head of the witness protection unit and a DC [from the intelligence cell] called Alan Cammidge turned up. With a deadpan face H reeled off an address. 'Do you recognise it?' he said to Cousins. 'That's my address!' Cousins replied. I was thinking to myself, 'Well done, H,' and trying not to smile."

Harvey then gave the gobsmacked CIB3 officers the home address of another Untouchable, Paul Bennett. They asked how he knew and he dropped the bomb – he claimed he'd had a mole inside the intelligence cell of Operation Ethiopia.

Harvey was referring to a sexy civilian worker he named as Lisa Cherry who had been attached to CIB from 1992 to 1997. According to her own staff appraisal she had handled "extremely sensitive information", especially when she worked in the intelligence cell at the height of Operation Ethiopia from January to August 1997.

Pandemonium followed when the CIB3 officers returned to London. Had the entire Flying Squad operation been compromised by a traitor? How safe were the three convictions if the supergrass knew what was going on in the prosecution? What other CIB3 jobs had been sold out? Once again the Selecta' had shown up the Untouchables.

Following a series of high-level meetings with commander Hayman and detective chief superintendent Shaun Sawyer, it was arranged for

THE SELECTA' RETURNS...

Cammidge and another officer to interview Harvey on tape at Milton Keynes police station on 18 September to ascertain exactly what he knew and what he wanted. The first interview was an "intelligence-only debrief". In other words it was meant for CIB3's ears only.

Harvey described over one hour how during the Threshers period he had met Lisa at a club. They had "danced the night away" and started a romance. After his arrest in August 1998 Harvey said he was allowed to retrieve his belongings from his bedsit to take with him to New Malden police station for the lengthy debriefing process. He told Cammidge he had buried a pay-as-you-go mobile phone and charger inside a four-kilo bag of American Easy Cook Rice and then sewn it up. He said he had made hundreds of calls on the phone over the last four years, including to Lisa Cherry. Friends would call through the PIN number for a phone voucher so he could constantly top up his credits.[8]

Harvey had moved to Godalming police station, near Guildford, in April 1999. Two cells in the unused custody area were converted into living accommodation and a bedroom and the corridor was made into a kitchenette. Lisa had visited him twice using a false name in November 2000, one month before the Flying Squad trial, he told Cammidge.

He had found out she used to work in CIB3 and cynically arranged for her to come and see him at this secure, covert location. Harvey had a list of people vetted by CIBIC whom he was allowed to call on the normal phone and receive visits from. He simply told Lisa to use the name of an approved friend, "Samantha Smith", who had never visited him. He also substituted her mobile telephone so he could save money calling her from the prison phone without raising suspicion.

Harvey: So that's how the contact continued and when the night got lonely and cold she'd phone me on my mobile . . . .

Cammidge: Like a chat line.

Harvey: Something like that.

He sent her flowers and she sent him a bouquet with a note that read: "I hope you will always want me like I want you. Love Lisa." Harvey manipulated that affection and claimed he asked her for the home addresses of four CIB3 officers, including Brian Moore and Martin Bridger. He wanted to have something to trade with as he awaited his sentence.

When Lisa next visited him he claimed she brought two names on a Post-it note and agreed to be photographed with Harvey. It was a test of her loyalty, should he ever need to call on her again, and also a test of the security of CIB3's intelligence system, he told Cammidge. The CIB intelligence officer admitted his colleagues couldn't work out how Harvey had beaten what they thought was a failsafe system.

Cammidge agreed that the judge dealing with Harvey's bail application would be told of the latest assistance. The CPS had already been informed. Harvey made it very clear he would never make a statement against Lisa Cherry. It was purely for intelligence and he didn't want his name released to her or anyone else. The CIB3 officer agreed.

Around this time we learned about the mole hunt inside CIB3. But when we rang Martin Polaine, the CPS lawyer in charge of the case, he went silent and then said, "That's not something I can comment on."

Next we called DCS Shaun Sawyer, the operational head of the Untouchables. He claimed there was no mole hunt. "We are still very secure. Currently I can confirm quite happily on the record I have no evidence of a leak in CIB3 or from CIB3 now or in the past. I'm not inquiring at this time."

Almost three weeks later, on 6 November, Sawyer sent Cammidge back to Milton Keynes to re-interview Harvey about the mole hunt that he wasn't conducting. Legal advice had been taken, especially in light of the fact that the three jailed Flying Squad detectives were now appealing their convictions. A decision was taken to disclose details of Harvey's mobile phone calls and visits from Lisa Cherry, contrary to the agreement with the supergrass.

During the second interview Harvey was asked if his past court evidence in the Flying Squad trial was his own or something he had put together by speaking to people on his smuggled phone. He reaffirmed it was his own. But he refused to give Cammidge the SIM card or reveal the second ace.

Cammidge: You can't tell me now? Maybe tell me later?

Harvey: When I'm free and sunning myself on the Hawaiian beach, yeah I'll tell ya.

At the end of the interview Harvey was assured he would "draw the highest credit" at his forthcoming appeal hearing on 18 November. In the meantime a CIB3 team were anxiously investigating the allegations against Lisa Cherry. She was now working in the Finance & Resource Unit at Edmonton police station, ironically the place where Harvey had been taken after the Security Express robbery.

The Appeal court corrected the trial judge's maths and Harvey was immediately released into a witness protection programme run by the

THE SELECTA' RETURNS...

very people whose security he had compromised. Government lawyers and CIB3 had gushingly supported their supergrass's appeal.

That same day Lisa Cherry was arrested at home on suspicion of misfeasance in a public office and suspended from duty. At first she thought this was revenge by her employer for having started a grievance procedure against a female civilian worker whom she accused of racism and belonging to the National Front.[9]

On legal advice Lisa said little during her interview except to deny leaking the home addresses. She wouldn't say whether she had met Harvey. But CIB3 had already developed the negatives showing her sitting on Harvey's knee. However, fingerprint testing and handwriting analysis proved it wasn't her mark on the Post-it note Harvey had given CIB3. He had lied to them once more.

Any publicity would be a disaster for CIB3, an internal report noted: "The impact to the resident informant system is far reaching in that the system is supposed to keep the informant sterile whilst being debriefed so that their evidence cannot be contaminated by any other source . . . The police have assured the courts that this sterile corridor has been maintained. Now we can't . . . the whole system will now have to be reviewed."[10]

CIB3 was still none the wiser who had leaked the home addresses. "It has not been possible to establish where the details were obtained," a secret internal report dated 19 March 2003 recorded. The mole was still out there but it wasn't Lisa Cherry. Criminal charges against her were dropped, though CIB3 still wanted to discipline her for gross misconduct.

She'd had a nervous breakdown and suffered dramatic weight loss during the investigation. Cherry explained how she had become "infatuated" with Harvey but never for one moment knew he was an armed robber. She believed he was in protective custody because he was bravely giving evidence against criminals. No checks were ever done when she came to see Harvey at Godalming. The couple were simply left to their own intimate devices.

As she prepared for her disciplinary hearing she became convinced her home phone was tapped and she was under surveillance. She knew what the CIB intelligence cell was capable of and how they abused a blanket authorisation to bug and burgle targets.

In December 2003, Lisa Cherry was found guilty at a disciplinary board of gross misconduct, fined £500 and put on restricted duties.

The mole hunt revealed there was a second visitor Harvey had not told them about. Jacqueline Vassell, a black police constable, had befriended Harvey when he was a free man. She later visited him on 11 occasions, between January 2001 and May 2002, when he was a CIB3 supergrass housed at various secret locations. Vassell had used a false name, Jacqueline Bissett (after the actress), to gain entry. According to the Yard she was disciplined for these "unauthorised visits".

The Selecta' is now living under a new identity in rented accommodation originally paid for by Scotland Yard. He says he still has an ace in the hole, just in case things come on top again. It apparently involves a senior serving detective of superintendent or above rank. Harvey says he's turned his back on crime, so there should be no reason to play this card.

But if he falls . . . Rewind Selecta'.

19

FRUIT OF A POISONED TREE

The first court ruling to formally expose serious malpractice at the heart of the Untouchables' supergrass system was read out to a packed crown court in Maidstone, Kent, on 14 February 2000. The lengthy judgement became known as the Valentine's Day Massacre because of its scathing attack on the integrity of a joint operation codenamed Nectarine between the Kent Police and CIB3. The appropriately named judge, Harvey Crush, threw out the case against eight defendants, including a serving Met detective, jointly accused of conspiracy to supply £12 million of cannabis. In delivering his reasons he remarked he had seen "nothing like it on the bench".

During the course of legal argument, Judge Crush discovered serious illegalities in the way a drug trafficker turned supergrass called Richard Price had been debriefed. Price, it emerged, was offered a "sweetening deal" worth £37,000, which the police hid from the defence and the Court. Price's assets, believed to be the proceeds of drug crime, should have been subject to a confiscation order but instead he was allowed to keep them in return for rolling over. The judge said there was a "strong suggestion" of financial inducements to implicate detective sergeant John Bull and other defendants.[1]

Crush's judgement identified "wholesale breaches" of PACE and other laws; a failure to tape-record and retain police interviews with the supergrass leading to major doubts about the veracity of his written statement; "prosecution misbehaviour" symptomatic of "a culture of non-disclosure" of 1,700 pages of "highly significant" police documents, despite court orders to do so; and "oppressive behaviour" and "pressure" by officers when debriefing Price. Operation Nectarine was quite simply the fruit of a poisoned tree.

The Director of Public Prosecutions ordered an "unprecedented" inquiry into the CPS's role. But the report remains secret, a spokeswoman tells us. Apparently it made 21 recommendations around the use of supergrasses, disclosure and confiscation proceedings. The internal inquiry also suggested that in large, complex and serious investigations the police should involve the CPS early, at the planning stage, and include them in the debriefing process too.[2]

The unjustified secrecy around the internal report's findings is in large part explained by the Untouchables' concern about the repercussion on future trials. CIB3 tried an amateurish distancing exercise from the operation as if the rotten nectarine came from Kent's orchard. Meanwhile a spokesman for the county force took a different approach. He suggested Judge Crush was more schooled in aviation than criminal law!

A year later, in April 2001, the supergrass system was again under attack, only this time at the Appeal Court. Three judges were considering the safety of the conviction of the five East Dulwich Regional Crime Squad detectives jailed in 2000 for major drug corruption. The grounds of appeal centred on CIB3's mishandling of the two supergrasses – Neil Putnam, their corrupt police colleague who'd found God after CIB3 found him, and drug dealer Evelyn Fleckney, who was serving a fifteen-year sentence at the time she rolled over against her lover and handler, detective constable Robert Clark.

The supergrass evidence of Putnam in the original trial had been far from clean and free of controversy. He had imploded under cross-examination. Putnam revealed he had told his CIB3 debriefers that one of the defendants, detective sergeant Terry O'Connell, was innocent of the charge and an honest man. Putnam also exposed how CIBIC boss Chris Jarratt had explained to him during an unrecorded prison visit that O'Connell was his friend and not corrupt. Putnam said he took this as a threat. Whatever the motivation behind Jarratt's highly controversial intervention, it exposes the real danger of police officers investigating their own.

The thrust of the appeal was to question the integrity and lawfulness of the supergrass system and to ask the Appeal Court to rule on this. If it went against them, CIB3 knew the whole anti-corruption crusade would be fatally holed beneath the waterline.

FRUIT OF A POISONED TREE

Alun Jones QC led the attack for the defendants. He told the Appeal Court it was "repugnant" that having revitalised the discredited supergrass system, none of the debriefs were tape-recorded but relied on derisory handwritten notes, sometimes just a few lines to represent a meeting lasting several hours. Jones also pointed out that had the defence not discovered Putnam kept a private diary they would never have learned about the "threats and inducements" during his debrief.

In his diary Putnam describes how his debriefers took him for hill walks, the odd pint, fish and chips on the beach and to test-drive an Alfa Romeo. He was also given a £50 note and allowed to shop alone at Tesco. Some parts of the diary read like scenes out of *The Sopranos*. In one, Putnam describes how his Italian debriefer, obviously called Vinny, carefully sliced the garlic for a slow-cooking pasta sauce. Only the onions were sweating during this interrogation.

In Italy supergrasses are called *Pentiti* – the repentant one, a phrase steeped in Catholic imagery. Putnam's dairy is not just a *Sopranos* cookbook, but also a celebration of the Holy Spirit, which the supergrass claimed was inside him as sure as last night's linguini. Very early into the debriefing process, the cop who found Christ wrote: "My soul and heart have been cleansed. I have no hidden sin. God has vanquished Satan." His language complemented the Untouchables' phoney crusade. They later videoed Putnam's fall and redemption to show young recruits around London's police stations.

Another defence barrister, Anthony Evans QC, was equally contemptuous of the supergrass system. He told the Appeal Court: "[CIB3] cloaked their investigation in an aura of propriety it did not have . . . We don't know what went on which caused [Putnam] to name A, B and C, rather than others," because none of it was taped. The defence argued there had been "gross wholesale breaches" of PACE, its codes and the 1992 Home Office guideline, which therefore made the convictions unsafe.

John Yates, the head of this CIB3 operation, had been promoted one rank to detective chief superintendent by this time. Rather implausibly, he told the Appeal Court that tape-recording everything would have been "impracticable" and too expensive.

Yates' boss, commander Andy Hayman, had defended the supergrass system by resorting to what defence barristers dismissively call "the uncharted waters" excuse. Here the argument runs that CIB had no experience of debriefing police supergrasses so it had to invent its own system. Hayman called it a "cutting edge" strategy where CIB officers were "pushing the parameters of the criminal justice system" while operating within its "constraints". Unfortunately, the argument does not bear scrutiny. The 1992 Home Office guidelines on debriefing supergrasses, whether police officers or criminals, could not have been clearer. The simple truth was that these guidelines didn't suit the Yard's agenda and were deliberately flouted.

To the great surprise of those present, senior Treasury Counsel Orlando Pownall, who originally prosecuted the case, stood up and accepted CIB3 had breached some PACE codes, the Home Office guidelines and the 1996 Criminal Procedure and Investigations Act. He also appeared to rebuke Yates by adding that his personal view was that it was "best practice" to tape-record everything because it gave "a more unassailable record". Strangely, Pownall had made none of these startling admissions at the original trial and in front of the jury.[3]

In normal circumstances, these concessions would have been enough to guarantee the appeal. But these were not normal circumstances. The Yard was prosecuting a War on Corruption and as such deliberate and wholesale breaches of key laws in pursuit of those who threatened the fabric of society apparently was not an affront to justice.

The judges adopted Pownall's admissions in their lengthy judgement but dismissed the appeal against the five convictions.[4] The ruling was a throwback to the seventies and eighties when the Appeal Court refused to accept the appalling vista that the police and security services could do wrong. Individual CIB3 officers did not deliberately act unlawfully, the ruling said. But clearly the supergrass strategy they followed was designed that way, and had been since 1993, although the Appeal Court was silent on this point.

Confirmation came from an unexpected source, the lead CPS lawyer, Martin Polaine, who had prosecuted these corruption cases. During a remarkably candid interview he revealed there was a serious split in the prosecution between the lawyers and the Untouchables.

Polaine accepts the CPS was deliberately shut out of Ghost Squad operations by the Yard. And that it was only five years later, in April 1998, that CIB3 formally invited him to advise it and CIBIC on future covert operations and any prosecution arising from them. The Untouchables, he says, still had concerns about the security of the CPS and the threat of compromise, so a new team called Visa card was set up. Polaine led it with two CPS lawyers who were also vetted.

Almost immediately, the Visa team realised the acute problems associated with CIB3's debriefing process, which was already well advanced in the cases of Brennan, Harvey, Garner, McGuinness and Fleckney. Astonishingly, and most unusually, Polaine reveals that CIB3 ignored the advice of government lawyers that if they must use supergrasses, then all future debriefs should be taped. He says there was a debate inside the Yard but those against taping, whom he didn't name, won the day. It is apparent that from then on government lawyers acquiesced to an unlawful policy. And like intellectual mercenaries, they did their best to shore up a system they had no faith in by trying to make it "more acceptable to the courts", as Polaine puts it.

He and the defence lawyers we consulted all agree that CIB3's arguments for not taping simply don't bear scrutiny. Not only does taping shorten the debrief period, it also protects the prosecution from allegations of inducement, and therefore any convictions that follow don't suffer from the "lurking doubt" syndrome of cover-up that has rightly dogged almost all CIB3 operations. The anti-corruption squad was also the best-resourced unit in the Met, and its supergrasses were debriefed in specially converted police stations with recording facilities. The decision not to tape-record had everything to do with managing corruption allegations to protect the cherished reputation of the Yard and its favoured sons and little to do with saving pennies or protecting the public interest.

The CPS and the Appeal Court were willing to condone underhand procedures designed by CIB to deceive, mislead and corrupt the administration of justice. "No light that should show red should be allowed to turn amber or green to suit the circumstances; the ends the police are seeking to achieve can never justify illegitimate means," an Old Bailey judge once said. The judicial establishment's tacit acquiescence to the corrupt supergrass system was alarming.

In late January 2003, it was the turn of the three former Flying Squad detectives convicted over the Security Express robbery to troop to the Appeal Court. Disgraced officers Fred May, Eamonn Harris and Dave Howell had served a little over a year of their seven-year sentences, mostly in Ford open prison. They hoped to capitalise on elements of the two earlier court rulings, but offered no fresh evidence of their own innocence. The Flying Squad appeals were also dismissed and the sentences upheld as "appropriate". However, the three different Appeal Court judges did adopt the earlier comments on the unlawfulness of key aspects of the supergrass system.

The judges were not moved by the defence suggestion that CIBIC boss Chris Jarratt – who at the time of the appeal was under investigation for dishonesty offences – and CIB3 case officer Martin Bridger had offered inducements and threats to get Garner to roll over and give evidence against others. Although the judges did accept that these conversations, especially those without a lawyer but with Garner's girlfriend Jackie Buisson present, should have been recorded. It was also conceded she had been paid money by CIB3. But the judges said the mysterious failure to serve a drug trafficking confiscation order on Garner over the missing 26 kilos of dope and the lack of a proper financial investigation into his or Buisson's affairs were not evidence of bad faith by the Untouchables. The point could have been clarified had they allowed the defence to subpoena and cross-examine Buisson. They wanted to explore deposits in her bank account and whether in return for not prosecuting her, Garner had agreed to roll over.

The judges also recognised there were significant discrepancies in CIB3's case about how the stolen £1,516,000 was distributed, especially the shares taken by Garner and Harvey.[5] But they upheld the PII application over the Fleming tape and said they were "wholly unpersuaded" that CIB3 had used suspension to keep DI George Raison tainted as a defence witness. It was not their job, the Appeal judges said, to conduct an inquiry into CIB3 over what the judges downplayed as "imperfections or irregularities in the intelligence process or preparation for trials".

But it was hard to see how having read two statements for the defence from former CIB3 supergrass Terry McGuinness, they didn't recommend that another agency conduct such an investigation. The judgement said:

> In a witness statement dated 29 November 2002 McGuinness describes how under what he claims was improper pressure from CIB3 he decided to give evidence for the Crown . . . He claimed the officers must have known that Garner was responsible for the disappearance of 26 kilos of cannabis, which was never recovered after the burglary in 1997. In a further witness statement of 24 January 2003 McGuinness enlarged upon his allegations. In particular he claims that suggestions were put to him in interview. He said he was a broken man to whom promises had been made but not kept. He said he had not read his de-briefing notes but had just signed them. Had the PACE Codes been observed, he would never have "put pen to paper".

FRUIT OF A POISONED TREE

Even this summary underplayed the seriousness of the allegations the former CIB3 supergrass was making. Had the three judges allowed McGuinness to give evidence in front of them in January 2003 – they ruled it was not relevant to the appeal – he would have expanded on his allegations that CIB3 had manipulated his evidence.

To understand the importance of McGuinness's statement we must go back to the latter part of 1999 when he was suddenly and unceremoniously dropped from the supergrass system before the Flying Squad trial. CIB3 still regarded him as a witness of truth, and he was willing to give evidence. But the reason why McGuinness was never used as a prosecution witness against any of the detectives he named explodes the myth of a no-hiding-place anti-corruption crusade.

A large part of CIB3's problem with McGuinness was that Garner had completely contradicted him on a very serious allegation. McGuinness had told his debriefers in May 1998 that there were bags of imitation guns, wigs and balaclavas that the Flying Squad took out on operations to plant on suspects. They were used "in case an armed officer shot a robber and he wasn't carrying a firearm" or to increase the chances of a prosecution. Everyone, he said, referred to it as a "first aid kit". The point he made, as if this mitigated anything, was that only the guilty career criminal was fitted up this way.

McGuinness says he became aware of the kits within six months of going to Rigg Approach. Their use was widespread and cavalier, to the point, he maintained, that senior officers referred to them during 50% of the pre-operation briefings he had attended over five years. "In my mind near nigh every senior officer had asked or knew about that first aid kit," McGuinness estimated. They were kept in officers' private cars or in the front foot well of a black taxi the Flying Squad used for surveillance operations.[6]

Such allegations were not unheard of in older Yard circles. One retired detective, Alec Leighton, told us: "In my day (the eighties) it was called a happy bag." But senior Untouchables, says McGuinness, did not like what he was revealing. Why? Because so-called noble cause corruption was not something in their brief.

The allegation had slipped out at the end of the long four-month debriefing. Remarkably, CIB3 waited another six months until November 1998 before asking Garner what he knew about the "first aid kits". In other words the Untouchables delayed an investigation into whether innocent people were languishing in prison. And when they did get around to asking Garner, he dismissed the claim as "a load of bollocks". Garner also denied there was a widespread fit-up culture.

These protestations however were totally at odds with evidence that emerged six months later in April 1999 when the Appeal Court quashed the conviction of a black man with a withered arm arrested by Garner for conspiracy to commit armed robbery with an imitation gun. Abraham Shakes maintained at his original trial in 1996 that the gun had been planted. Garner claimed it and a glove were tucked into the waistband of Shakes' loose-fitting tracksuit trousers when he made the armed arrest and pistol-whipped him to the ground. The Appeal Court was not convinced and quashed Shakes' conviction. He had already served almost four years of his eight-year sentence and would later receive £100,000 compensation.

Garner denied fitting up Shakes at the same time he denied to CIB3 the existence of a "first aid kit". Who were the Untouchables going to believe – the police supergrass that could corroborate Harvey and hopefully convict five cops awaiting trial, or Meathead, the police supergrass who was alleging a widespread culture of noble cause corruption?

Over 80 serving and retired officers were interviewed in early 1999 about the "first aid kits". They denied any such practice. Some might say, they would, wouldn't they? How far back the Untouchables explored the existence of this practice is unclear.

In May 1999, the CPS received the last file from CIB3 on the matter and after a month's deliberation decided there was "no corroborative evidence" to prosecute officers for conspiracy to pervert the course of justice or misfeasance in a public office. The latter charge related to those officers alleged to have turned a blind eye to the kits. In August the PCA advised that no officers would be disciplined for neglect and/or discreditable conduct regarding the allegations.

When McGuinness was sentenced in April 2000, CIB3 made a point of stressing how they still regarded him as a "witness of truth". Given what McGuinness told us later, another more appropriate description would be the canary that fell from his cage when he sang the wrong tune.

McGuinness now lives on the coast. CIB3 are still in contact with him through their witness protection unit (WPU). When we interviewed him, McGuinness stood by his statements and gave a further disturbing insight into what was really going on during his debrief. He said he offered CIB3 the opportunity to fudge how certain he was that most people in the Flying Squad office knew about the

FRUIT OF A POISONED TREE

"first aid kits". "I turned round in the interview and said if you want me to say I'm not sure I'll say I'm not sure. They said they want what you know or believe to be correct."

But after a while he noticed a change in CIB3's attitude toward his allegations of widespread noble cause corruption. "It got so big they couldn't handle it. It was things like that they really didn't want to know about . . . first aid kits and stuff like that. As soon as it was said it was just brushed over. At the end of the day, I know everybody else knew, even to along the lines of bleeding [prosecution] barristers. Suspected is probably the best word. It was more or less exactly the same every time."

McGuinness had no idea that for six months CIB3 hadn't put his allegation of the "first aid kits" to Garner. He was less surprised that Garner had denied their existence. From his own experience he says it is entirely possible Garner was told off-tape not to corroborate him.

What was CIB3's logic for not taping the debrief? "I can't give you one. I personally think they should have been taped." What's the advantage of not taping? "Well, one, they get to, it's like the old contem[poraneous] notes, you get a chance to talk about it and write down what you want to write, and leave out what you want to leave." Would you say there were things you said in your debriefs that were never recorded in the notebooks? "Without a doubt. If there were general chats, it was taken down rough and then re-written into the debrief books. And then sometime later I'd be asked to sign them. I was so used to doing it by then, I was signing stuff that was sometimes a week old if not longer. They kept saying we've got to be whiter than white, and I got sick of hearing it. I said you're breaking everything, every rule and all the rest of it. In the end I thought, get on with it. Within a week [of being in the supergrass system] I was a nodding dog . . . I knew what they were doing was wrong. All the time it was happening there was no way I could stop it. I've always said this would blow up in CIB's face. That sometime they'd catch a cold, because it does. It always catches up with you."

McGuinness told us CIB3 came to him after his release and asked for a false statement that he "could be mistaken" about the "first aid kits". Presumably such a document would have helped fight future court cases and civil claims where the planting of evidence was being alleged. McGuinness recalls his reply to the Untouchables' representative: "You must be fucking joking! You've banged my head against the wall for 21 months and now you are asking me that." He says he then informed his probation officer and his lawyer of the illegal approach.

UNTOUCHABLES

The PCA had remarked in its 1999 annual report how they were aware of whistle-blowers being asked by senior officers "to submit false statements or withdraw damaging [ones] about their colleagues' behaviour". But here was an allegation from McGuinness that the Untouchables were conspiring to pervert the course of justice in the same way. There has been no investigation into McGuinness's allegations, but the Yard says it still regards him as a witness of truth. We asked why the Untouchables had waited six months before putting the "first aid kit" allegations to Garner. We are still waiting for a reply.

McGuinness is not alone in claiming the Yard's no-hiding-place corruption crusade was a sham, uninterested in examining the fit-up culture. Keith Green and supergrass Duncan Hanrahan appear to corroborate him. Hanrahan told the PCA in November 2002 that during his debrief senior Untouchables told him they were not interested in noble cause corruption. In his complaint he wrote: "[Chris] Jarratt said in the presence of [David] Wood that he didn't want me to talk about what he called God's work. When I asked what he meant by this he said that – to do with police malpractice to get convictions basically for stitching people up, that side of things."

Hanrahan also complained that the two officers "verballed" him; that Jarratt had tried to get him to change his solicitor after he had agreed to become a supergrass, and that he had been prompted to incriminate John Bull, the detective at the centre of the Operation Nectarine scandal. In short, Hanrahan told the PCA, "CIB are a law unto themselves."

Hanrahan asked for an outside force to be brought in to investigate CIB3. But a PCA spokesman told us they had simply acted as a "post box" and passed the complaint to the Yard, which, we discovered, did nothing.

It is difficult to envisage how the public interest in getting to the bottom of these important complaints about the integrity of the supergrass system will be better served now the Independent Police Complaints Commission has replaced the PCA. Were it to take up the two supergrasses' complaints, Roy Clark, as director of investigations for the new IPCC, would have overall responsibility for the probe into the secret unit he set up and at least one of the Untouchables he appointed to the job.

Unquestionably, had the appeal of Eamonn Harris and his two colleagues been allowed, then the Untouchables would have had to abandon a second Flying Squad trial due to start three months later in

FRUIT OF A POISONED TREE

May 2003 at the Old Bailey. This case also involved Harris as a defendant, alongside detectives Michael Carroll, Dave Thompson and Ian Saunders. They were arrested in December 1998 on suspicion of involvement in a £1 million Post Office robbery four years earlier.

An Indian gang using a dummy security van, fake uniforms and an inside agent collected £1,065,678 in cash from the Post Office in Romford, Essex, and made their escape. Rigg Approach Flying Squad was given the job of catching them. Once again, it was alleged that the officers stole (£35,000) from the recovered proceeds.[7]

The chief prosecution witness was Garner. Without him there was no case. During his debrief he claimed he had helped steal the recovered money and shared it seven ways with the four defendants and two unnamed others. Without this confession the Untouchables would never have known about the alleged corruption. It was an "almost perfect crime", the prosecution would claim.

After Garner was freed in May 2001, he and Jackie Buisson moved into rented accommodation provided by the Untouchables. Slowly Garner tried to rebuild his life and was working in a menial job. But the thought of giving evidence for a second time against Harris was weighing heavily on his already addled mind. It appears he was also harbouring resentment towards CIB3 over the financial resettlement package he expected.[8]

The second trial did not start until 7 May 2003. The delay was not just down to the defence, as the Crown often maintains, but CIB3 too. Firstly, the anti-corruption squad had decided that the Security Express case was the stronger of the two, so delays in that prosecution had a knock-on effect on this one. Secondly, one of the defendants, Ian Saunders, became very ill and had to be severed from the indictment. Thirdly, Untouchable Chris Jarratt was under investigation for dishonesty offences. Suffice it to say, doubts about his integrity had a bearing on the second trial because he originally arrested Garner and had turned him into a supergrass in disputed circumstances. Finally, there was the mole hunt caused by Harvey's revelations about two lovers in the Met and the smuggled mobile phone.

CIB3 was under no illusion this second trial would be an all-out assault on the "unlawful" supergrass strategy and the integrity of leading Untouchables. Some observers thought this was not a prosecution Scotland Yard were looking forward to or even wanted any more. Over the weekend the wheel finally came off.

On Saturday, 10 May, Garner phoned his witness protection officer to say he had jacked in his job and was too ill to start his evidence next week. The call sparked a major panic at the Yard. The next day Garner produced a doctor's certificate that he was suffering from "acute anxiety and stress". At court on Monday, Treasury Counsel Jonathan Laidlaw QC explained the situation to Judge Gregory Stone, who gave the impression he was willing to disrobe there and then and drag Garner to court by the ear.

Notwithstanding the question mark over the supergrass's fitness, the judge was determined to press ahead with the prosecution case, despite defence objections. One of the Indian robbers, Jasvir Jhumat, gave inconclusive evidence. Afterwards, he told us he had been a reluctant witness and said CIB3 had "threatened" him back in 1998 that if he didn't give evidence against the Flying Squad detectives he'd face prosecution for bribery.

Meanwhile, when officers from the witness protection unit arrived at Garner's house, they discovered him hiding in the garden, very drunk. A confidential WPU report described Garner as "very emotional and constantly referring to himself as a wanker". The attending officer candidly reported how Garner had said, "Harris was a good bloke and no way could he give evidence. He has had six years of it, the pressure, and he had just had enough."

The following day Garner saw a psychologist he had previously consulted when he was going off the rails shortly before his arrest back in December 1997. He wrote a report in which it emerges that back then Dr Hacker-Hughes diagnosed Garner as suffering from "severe depression" and "chronic and severe post-traumatic stress disorder". The latter is characterised by, among other things, nightmares, behavioural avoidance and an inability to remember important aspects of traumatic incidents.

Here was the proof that when Garner entered the supergrass system he was an incredibly vulnerable and suggestible witness, whose handling had to be beyond the slightest reproach. Furthermore, the doctor revealed that once in the supergrass system, Garner "remained untreated" throughout his debriefing and detention. This ongoing mental illness, combined with the deliberate decision not to tape-record the debriefs, now put a severe question mark over Garner's reliability and CIB3's integrity and professionalism.

The psychologist re-examined Garner for ninety minutes on 13 May. He concluded his patient was still suffering from the same mental condition he had diagnosed six years earlier. Garner was also now showing signs of alcohol dependence. He told Dr Hacker-Hughes he was drinking three bottles of whisky a week, and that he had "come

FRUIT OF A POISONED TREE

to dread continued contact" with the police. But it was the following clinical assessment that ended the argument over whether to proceed with the second trial. Dr Hacker-Hughes wrote: "Mr Garner told me he is confused about exactly what he has said over the past six years and is continually haunted by persecutory dreams, often featuring footsteps down corridors, slamming car doors, court appearances and visions of being buried alive. Mr Garner now seems to be very confused about what is right and what is wrong and about what is the truth."

Nevertheless, the doctor, who now works for the Ministry of Defence, felt that with treatment his patient might recover to give evidence. So on 15 May the trial was aborted and rescheduled for September.

Privately, the Yard knew its flagship prosecutions were fatally weakened by the psychiatric reports on Garner. But as in life, in death Scotland Yard's anti-corruption crusade would have a carefully choreographed final curtain, presented as a triumph of integrity over dishonesty.

On Friday, 27 June 2003, at the Old Bailey, Laidlaw told the judge he had no confidence Garner would recover. The matter had been discussed at the top level of the CPS and the Yard, he said. The plug had been pulled, which left the judge no option but to acquit all four defendants.

DCS Shaun Sawyer swiftly walked over to Carroll, 47, and Thompson, 38, and told them to report for duty after the weekend. Sawyer appeared flustered when outside Court 18 we asked what he now thought about the decision to base an anti-corruption crusade on a discredited supergrass system. "We've moved away from that," he replied, before heading off.

Another Untouchable, Dave Pennant, was also in court. He had risen three ranks to detective superintendent during his almost six years at CIB3 and was about to join Surrey Police as head of proactive operations. Pennant let slip that secretly, before the second prosecution started, there had been a massive U-turn by the Yard concerning its supergrass system.

Pennant and other leading lights in CIB3 had now written a paper for ACPO recommending that all debriefs should be tape-recorded. Pennant claimed no knowledge of the 1992 Home Office guidelines. The whole experience had been "a learning curve", he said. Indeed. But at whose expense?

That same day, over at the High Court, a prosecution brought by

UNTOUCHABLES

the Health and Safety Executive against commissioner Stevens and his predecessor, Lord Condon, collapsed.[9] The two top cops had faced embarrassing cross-examination. But in the end Lord Condon told reporters common sense had prevailed. He said his and Sir John's legal costs (paid by the public) had reached £2 million and could have put "70 police officers on the streets for a year". Curiously, Scotland Yard is unwilling to put a figure on the cost of its failed Flying Squad probe lasting eight years and described by the press office as "one of the biggest anti-corruption investigations ever undertaken by a UK police force". A reasonable estimate would be £30 million. That's over 1,000 police officers.

In February 2004 Kevin Garner agreed to discuss his reflections on the whole supergrass experience. He was wearing a dark suit and had bulked up since we last saw him at the Old Bailey three years earlier. Gone were the glasses, the gaunt face and sunken expression. Garner looked like his old self, when the former detective and his Flying Squad chums were out of control.

Garner says his "first taste of corruption was at [police] training school in Hendon". Recruits were told that when stopping someone for running a set of traffic lights to "always give 'em ten yards". The acceptable level of corruption or unethical conduct, he explained, was greater on specialist squads. "Look at the Regional Crime Squad and their workload over Christmas. They always went for lorry-loads of booze and electrical goods. Then look at what the prizes were during the Christmas raffle!"

At Rigg Approach there was little difference. "Everyone used each other for their own attributes. Me, I was hard, didn't care to frighten people, go into them alone and nick the money. Eamonn Harris, he could do the paperwork." There was, he says, no sense among the team that stealing from criminals was wrong. But they drew the line at selling out jobs to villains.

When Garner was arrested over the cannabis theft he originally suspected Taverner had grassed him up. It wasn't until after he rolled over that he realised it was a CIB3 sting from beginning to end. It soon became apparent to the supergrass that the Untouchables were far from "whiter than white", he says. "The first question I was asked in the debrief was by Jarratt. He wanted to know what I knew about [corruption] in [the] Tower Bridge [Flying Squad office]. I said I knew nothing. If I had said 'loads' I wouldn't be in the position I am now."

Garner couldn't understand why Rigg Approach had been singled out as a corrupt office and not Tower Bridge, Barnes or Finchley. Tower Bridge, he recalled, had in some respects a worse reputation than Rigg. "What [CIB3] wanted was very clinical. They wanted certain people in the Flying Squad [at Rigg]. They didn't want me to drop any of their mates in the shit."

We then turned to why he thought the Untouchables had waited six months to ask him about the "first aid kits" and why he had denied they existed. "The second thing that was said to me [early in the debrief] was, 'We won't talk to you about God's work.' I told them I wouldn't go down that path." Garner does not deny the fit-up culture existed in the Flying Squad but in his warped morality he explained that "innocent Joe Public walking along the street" never had anything to fear.

On a more personal note, Garner can now admit that he had for some time been suffering from "mental illness" when he became a supergrass. He will not be drawn on whether his covert activities in Northern Ireland as a soldier contributed to this. Garner does however criticise CIB3 for not ensuring he had a responsible adult during his arrest and subsequent debriefs. Asked why the Untouchables did not ensure the debriefing process was all above board, Garner gave perhaps his most revealing reply: "They didn't want to get it right, in the same way my team [at Rigg] didn't want to."

Garner is unrepentant about grassing up his former colleagues over the Hector Harvey job, and he still maintains his and their guilt. But the retired supergrass says he "took the dairy [the rap] for a lot of people" and he feels there are those in the Flying Squad who know he never fully "cleansed" himself about their criminality.

There is a part of himself Garner despises for being a grass. Perhaps this is why he says he tried to be helpful to Harris and others in the first trial by leaving openings in his evidence for the defence to cross-examine him on and raise a reasonable doubt. "I left the door wide open and they never came at me," says Garner.

Clearly, something very bad went on at Rigg Approach. There must have been a corrupt cell of detectives operating with Garner and McGuinness. But given the way the Yard conducted its ten-year corruption crusade, by design and default it has obscured the truth about how far that corruption spread outwards and upwards.

The collapse of the Flying Squad prosecutions and the Geoff Brennan scandal reminds defence solicitor Mark Lake of a scene from the biopic *A Man for All Seasons*, about the life of Sir Thomas More. "He is speaking to his future son-in-law, Roper, an enthusiastic Protestant. They are debating chasing Satan. Roper is of the view you must tear down all the barriers to bring him to book. More poses the key question – but what if Satan is not nailed and comes back to bite his pursuers? Where then are the barriers? The point is that these barriers in the criminal justice system are there to protect the innocent majority in the event they are falsely accused. It is unfortunate that the guilty often profit by society's rules, but this is no justification to tear up the rulebook and act in a worse way than the suspects are alleged to have acted.

"I go a stage further. Even if one accepts the deterrent-based argument that the ends justify the means – that it is vital to convey the message to officers contemplating corruption that they will then be hounded to the ends of the earth by any means necessary – it fails as an effective strategy if trials collapse or convictions are set aside because of malpractice by CIB3. Arguably, guilty officers walk free with loads of compensation, the police has a massive amount of humble pie to eat and the public are rightly indignant about the waste of public funds.

"The Untouchables appear unable to appreciate that certain supergrasses duped them for their own ends. Instead of being able to admit they were had over, they press on regardless. This is the real scandal, not that mistakes were made. Mistakes will always be made when dealing with treacherous gits like Brennan and Harvey. Cover-ups, to improve the chances of a successful prosecution or hide corruption, are a different matter."

The anti-corruption crusade was based on seven main supergrasses. Undoubtedly, Brennan, Harvey and Hanrahan all made major fools out of the Yard's finest minds. Others like McGuinness and Garner lost trust in the integrity of the debriefing process. All of which leaves born-again Christian supergrass Neil Putnam. But in a private letter to Terry O'Connell, one of his former colleagues whom he helped convict, Putnam raised his own important concerns with the debrief process, which he described as "a political game".

"I will admit their [*sic*] were times I would sign anything just to get them away from me and get some peace." He then ends the letter sensationally: "CIB were desperate to get someone with rank to be prosecuted, you [O'Connell was just a detective sergeant] fitted the bill at the time. It [*sic*] a shame they did not look closer at their own staff, an entire crew from [the Flying Squad at] Tower Bridge for a start."

20

THE FALL OF THE GINGER GIANT

By 2000, the three covert operations set up to prove that detective inspector John Redgrave was corrupt had all failed at a great and still undisclosed public cost. He and Michael Charman were in their fourth year of suspension. Scotland Yard had abandoned bringing any criminal prosecution against the pair because there was no evidence of their guilt. It was still open to the Untouchables to bring disciplinary action, but even this was reduced to one minor charge that had already failed the criminal test twice.

When we pointed this out to anti-corruption chief, commander Andy Hayman, he tapped his nose judiciously and said there was "live stuff" – secret intelligence – he couldn't go into that convinced him the Untouchables were still right about the ginger giant. This "live stuff" we later learned was unsubstantiated, old intelligence very much designed to linger. Every so often the Untouchables would refer to it when they were under pressure to justify their actions.

In July, for example, commissioner Stevens offered Redgrave's MP, Andrew Mackinlay, a secret intelligence briefing after he had called for an independent inquiry into this "unsavoury can of worms". Mackinlay rejected Stevens' approach as "improper" and instead launched a withering attack on the Untouchables during an adjournment debate in the Commons a few months later.

There was some extraordinary serendipity at work here. Mackinlay is a combative and fiercely independent old Labour politician who believes in holding the executive and its shadow warriors to account through Parliament. He'd distinguished himself in 1998 as a member of the Foreign Affairs select committee's inquiry into Sandline. They were the British mercenary outfit given the nod and wink by the Foreign Office to help restore a friendly ruler in the former British colony of Sierra Leone. It was New Labour's first scandal and helped expose the hypocrisy of its "ethical" foreign policy.

Mackinlay first heard of Operation Nightshade during these tense committee hearings. At one point the two undercover officers who'd met Roger Crooks posing as representatives of Loyalist terrorists heard they were going to be called as witnesses. For his part, Mackinlay grilled Labour ministers and civil servants with such gusto that the then foreign secretary Robin Cook privately tried to apply a choke chain, he recalls.

Once Mackinlay had digested his constituent's complex story he posed a series of questions about Crooks to the Home Office, Foreign Office and Ministry of Defence. The MP had come to believe there might be "sensitive diplomatic and political reasons" behind Redgrave's plight.

Crooks had provided logistical support to the 1998 British government-sponsored counter coup in Sierra Leone – he leased his military helicopter. The shadowy businessman also had a close relationship with other western diplomats and spies through his hotel in the capital Freetown. When the coup leaders were ousted Crooks refurbished the Mama Yoko and signed a three-year rental agreement with the United Nations peacekeeping force, which still uses the hotel as its base.

The official response to Mackinlay's questions was plain wrong and looked like the Yard was deliberately misleading ministers. Charles Clarke, the police minister, said commissioner Stevens had assured him there were "no details" revealed by Operation Nightshade of arms dealing involving Sierra Leone. And foreign minister Peter Hain wrote there was "no reason to believe" Crooks was involved in an arms deal between Northern Ireland and Sierra Leone.[1]

Before the adjournment debate in October 2000, Mackinlay wrote to home secretary Jack Straw asking for a judicial inquiry into the Untouchables and Redgrave's case. Straw declined. He too said the commissioner had assured him issues raised by our articles in March were inaccurate and he "fully supported" the Yard's efforts to root out bent cops.[2]

Mackinlay was unimpressed. His subsequent performance in the adjournment debate dazzled parliamentary sketch writers with its

THE FALL OF THE GINGER GIANT

grasp of the twists and turns of his constituent's story. For 15 minutes he lambasted CIB for not alerting the Lawrence Inquiry to Redgrave's information about the "incestuous relationships" between bent cops and criminals in south-east London. "CIB is riddled with people who want to stop further light being shed on those relationships," he told the Commons. Again Mackinlay called for an independent inquiry into the "widespread misfeasance at the highest level in the Met" and "malevolence and corrupt practice" by certain Untouchables involved in Redgrave's case. Singled out were Hayman and Coles, whom the MP accused of acting "unprofessionally and with maximum spite and deceit" by continuing to insist Redgrave was corrupt and had fabricated the arms deal.

Mackinlay called for the suspension of Redgrave and Charman to be lifted and the "nonsense" disciplinary charge withdrawn. He heaped special scorn on the Yard's disciplinary tribunal, which he described as a "kangaroo court working to a predetermined conclusion". Charles Clarke responded briefly. He again expressed full support for the anti-corruption crusade but did remark on the "immense time" the case was taking to resolve.

As Coles walked past Redgrave and Charman on his way out of the chamber he was bright red with rage. The poisoned chalice he'd been given back in 1997 was hanging heavy round his neck.

The key secret intelligence held on Redgrave is believed to be a collection of bugged conversations recorded over 1992 and 1993 between various East End villains. We know that on the strength of these recordings and related intelligence Redgrave was placed on a list of suspect cops around whom the Ghost Squad was formed. The Untouchables will not disclose this secret intelligence to Redgrave's defence team so they can evaluate it. Yet the Yard continues to rely on it when privately briefing politicians and journalists.

By all accounts, at the time these secret recordings were made Redgrave had gained a reputation in the East End as a very effective and hard detective. A number of well established and up and coming criminal firms were prominent in the Canning Town and Barking area, among them three families, the Sabinis, the Wrights and the Hunts.[3]

"They had control and there were no-go areas for old bill. Part of my brief was to clean it up," says Redgrave. He was drafted on to an anti-protection team to stop local villains extorting money from pubs. The team set up two covert pubs staffed with undercover officers and successfully prosecuted various gangs. Redgrave and his team had a reputation for going into villains' pubs and clubs and physically confronting them. One of his former bosses described him memorably as a detective "hard as woodpecker's lips".

He was often attached to the local 2 Area drug squad, then led by John Grieve. He had recommended Redgrave for a commissioner's commendation for his part in taking down local hero Mickey Ishmael, a feared armed robber turned drug trafficker. Redgrave had a stand-up fight with Ishmael on his arrest and the ginger giant kept a photo of the prisoner in his office drawer as a memento.

In 1990, Redgrave transferred to the Regional Crime Squad in nearby Barkingside. His appraisal on leaving Plaistow was glowing: "DS Redgrave had a compulsive desire to take on and eventually take out major criminals . . . when he leaves the division many an East End criminal will breath a sigh of relief." At Barkingside he targeted several top echelon villains including the Hunts over a multi-million pound armed robbery of travellers cheques. Redgrave was badly hurt in this operation but recovered to arrest Raymond Hunt.

The ginger giant is also a flawed man. He got too close to informants; he made bad decisions about his father's will; he was intolerant of perceived weakness in others; he showed off and sometimes talked up his achievements. In the Condon era this style of policing had become very unfashionable and open to a pre-conviction that the detective was "not right". But it is ironic that John Grieve and Roy Clark, who would become Redgrave's main accusers, were fans of the ginger giant's detective skills until shortly before they turned on him. Clark was on the board that promoted Redgrave to detective inspector in 1992. But everything changed the following year when he and Grieve reinvented themselves as witchfinder-generals from their new base at SO11.

Intelligence on Redgrave came to them from detective chief inspector Dave Woods. He had served under Clark at Stoke Newington. Woods was then part of a little-known failed covert intelligence gathering operation for SO11 looking at East End criminals like the Sabinis and the Hunts. It was during this bugging operation that certain criminals are said to have mentioned Redgrave's name.

According to police sources intimately involved in the bugging operation, millions were wasted, including on setting up a covert pub in Canning Town with undercover officers as bar staff and bugs hidden in the dartboard, surrounding tables and bar. "But when the jukebox came on you couldn't make out what people were saying," revealed one detective who debriefed the undercover team.

THE FALL OF THE GINGER GIANT

This was not the only problem. It appears that the local underworld rather quickly worked out that the pub was "hooked up". "All of a sudden people stopped going there," our source recalls. Retired detective chief inspector Norman McNamara explained that this had nothing to do with corruption. "An undercover officer had inadvertently compromised the whole operation by walking into the Sabinis' portakabin. An internal inquiry questioned him and concluded he had over-enthusiastically gone beyond his brief."

This spooky debacle in the East End was effectively turned into the Ghost Squad intelligence cell with Dave Woods at the helm. Several detectives familiar with this affair suspect that the anti-corruption dimension was in part a way for SO11 to save face over the enormous amount of money – said to be in excess of £3 million – lost on these covert operations in the East End.[4]

Redgrave gave us precise details of how he and Woods fell out in the early eighties. The animosity, he says, was maintained up until Woods disappeared with "cancer" and joined the Ghost Squad in 1993. Woods, though, remains tight-lipped about his shadowy past and would not be interviewed about this or any bad blood with the ginger giant.

The Untouchables have also consistently rubbished Redgrave's claim that he was the target of various professional criminals who plotted to discredit him. At first we too were sceptical. Many officers pull this excuse out of the bag knowing how difficult it is to disprove. But slowly and independently we uncovered evidence of a plot hatched well before the Brennan allegations surfaced in June 1994.

The financier behind it is one of the UK's most sophisticated criminal minds.

If ever a British criminal deserved the sobriquet 'master criminal' it is Stephen Patrick Raymond. Born in 1945, Raymond came from an average working-class family in Stoke Newington. He is exceptionally bright, charming and without excuses. "I'm a criminal by design not default," he says. "I didn't do it because I was from fucking deprived circumstances as a child. I did it because I wanted some fucking money."

Today Raymond has lots of money. He lives in the south of France, makes Cognac and also owns an expensive Islington home and restaurant. "Now I've got the money I don't want to do [crime] any more. I'm more royal than a king." He says he is 95 per cent legitimate. Between the poetry and cooking, he likes to keep his hand in the

UNTOUCHABLES

Underworld just to show up the police. Every criminal has an Achilles Heel, and Raymond's is narcissism. He sees no point in making fools out of London's finest without leaving his calling card.[5]

Raymond's first serious sentence was the six years he received in 1964 for robbing an actress. While the 19-year-old was inside he initiated voluminous correspondence with Tom Driberg, the Labour MP and well-known prison reformer of the time. In the trendy era of criminology, Raymond learned to manipulate liberal concerns about the prison system. But Driberg's interest in helping him was also rooted in less altruistic fancies: his insatiable desire for troubled young men. Driberg, by then in his mid-sixties, had been a frequent guest at parties thrown by the Krays, where rent boys plucked from the "Meat Rack" in Piccadilly were available for some light fellatio.

Raymond, with his slight frame, rugged good looks and dark ginger hair, knew how to manipulate Driberg's desires. As he moved around the prison system he sought the MP's assistance to obtain privileges he maintained were being improperly denied to him. He also asked to be moved to a softer regime where he could continue his education.

After obtaining four A Levels, Raymond applied to Surrey University to study catering. In prison he also began writing dark poetry about the rages he experienced. His verse, he told Driberg, was "the equal of Bunting and others". On his release in August 1969 Raymond returned almost immediately to crime. After his re-arrest, Driberg wrote a letter to *The Times* pleading the case of the "scholar in prison". Raymond's psychiatric social worker took a more sceptical view, calling her patient "psychopathic, callously manipulative and [possessing a] destructive exploitation of others and readiness to bite the hand that feeds".

Raymond regularly betrayed Driberg, yet the lustful MP for Barking kept coming back for more. The unrepentant criminal once stole from Driberg's desk a draft obituary of prime minister Harold Wilson that he'd written for *The Times*, and sold it to *Private Eye*. More spectacularly, he used Driberg as an alibi for the 1970 murder of south London gang boss Eddie Coleman. Two of Raymond's associates lured Coleman to a shop in Tottenham. They shot him, wrapped him in polythene sheeting and then placed him in a huge trunk that Raymond had bought. The body was disposed of in the New Forest.

The two killers then fled to Scotland where Raymond joined them after posing as Driberg in the first-class carriage during the train journey there. Scottish shopkeepers tipped off the police when Raymond started caning the MP's stolen credit card. On his arrest, he gave up the whereabouts of his associates and all three were charged with what the tabloids were now calling "the body in the trunk murder".

Raymond looked sunk. But at the trial he caused a sensation when Driberg appeared as his chief witness. The MP told the jury that on the night of the murder Raymond had joined him at the Gay Hussar restaurant in Soho for dinner with two Labour grandees, former solicitor general Sir Dingle Foot QC and his brother, Michael. The alibi persuaded the judge to order that Raymond be cleared of murder and manslaughter. But the jury found him guilty of obstructing justice. He was jailed for three years. Raymond however absconded from prison and fled with his girlfriend to Australia where he briefly passed himself off as the features editor of *The Times*. He was re-arrested and deported to Britain to complete his sentence.

In June 1976, Raymond, now in his early thirties, carried out a particularly audacious heist at Heathrow that earned him the tabloid sobriquet "the Great Brain Robber". He'd obtained a job as a clerk with the American security company Purolator. His mother was proud that he appeared to be turning his back on crime. But seven weeks later, Raymond presented himself in a smart suit at the Heathrow strong rooms of British Airways and the Belgian airline Sabena with forged instructions to recover some money. His associate was dressed in a Purolator uniform. Raymond explained that the recently delivered money was improperly packed. The duo worked the con three times in one day making off with a staggering £2 million in foreign currency. They then fled abroad. But Raymond was finally arrested after a few days in Switzerland.

At his trial, Raymond defended himself. He'd learned law inside prison. The jury didn't accept that heavyweight criminals Roger Denhardt and Mickey Ishmael had threatened to kill him if he didn't participate in the robbery. It transpired that while he and Denhardt were on remand Raymond had helped concoct a fake defence for his chum, who was awaiting trial for an armed robbery. The conspiracy involved fabricating an elaborate paper trial of false companies and invoices to explain how Denhardt had so much money in his bank account. A bent solicitor, Peter Moore, was drawn into the scam and later jailed. Raymond was given the maximum ten years for the Purolator caper. He also admitted the conspiracy with Denhardt.

Behind bars Raymond made case law when the Appeal Court held that a prison governor was in contempt for interfering with the prisoner's mail to stop Raymond bringing a legal action against him.

UNTOUCHABLES

He also knew how to manipulate the supergrass system and internal corruption probes like Operations Carter and Countryman respectively. Raymond spoke to detectives, knowing his corruption allegations would by happy coincidence disrupt the criminal trials of his associates. And at a bankruptcy hearing in 1982, Raymond made a spectacular claim that he had given Driberg £25,000 from the Purolator robbery, knowing the MP could not contradict him. He had died six years earlier.

Three years later and a free man, Raymond was involved in a scam to steal Rolls Royce cars. He also posed as someone from the Department of Education to defraud Granada Television of £500,000 of electrical goods. For all this he was jailed for a further eight years. Raymond, though, had no intention of completing his sentence and in 1989 absconded. He phoned the local radio station and persuaded the DJ to dedicate a song to a "friend", the detective who had put him away. The song he chose was "Granada".

While on the run, in 1990 Raymond began courting Emma Blackburn Gittings, the wayward daughter of his top criminal lawyer. She was persuaded to impersonate a wealthy American student living in London so they could empty her bank account of £400,000. Emma was arrested and jailed for nine months. Raymond however evaded capture.

After his manipulation of the randy Driberg, it made perfect sense that three decades later Stephen Raymond would use an old Labour Party meeting hall in north London to house an ecstasy factory capable of producing one million tablets of the love drug.

In 1992, Raymond recruited criminal chemist Geoff Couzens to run the factory. It wasn't Couzens' first venture into producing large quantities of the drug. He had started experimenting as a chemistry graduate at Imperial College in the seventies. Couzens made his first batch of methylenedioxymethylamphetamine (MDMA), the chemical name for ecstasy, in 1979. But it appears he was ahead of his time. In the late eighties, Couzens flew to Yugoslavia to set up an E factory for distribution in the UK and Europe. By then the Acid House scene in London was going nationwide and mutating into an army of ravers dropping millions of Es every weekend. The manufacture of MDMA wasn't a crime in the Balkans republic, and some enterprising local politicians and civil servants were involved with the factory. But on his return to London in July 1989 the British police arrested and jailed Couzens and his accomplice, Sidney Frankel.

THE FALL OF THE GINGER GIANT

In early 1992, Couzens escaped from prison on the very day he learned his appeal against the six-year sentence had been rejected. While on the run, he hooked up with Terry "the Pig" Sansom, a south London criminal. Apparently, there was a fall-out because Sansom was selling amphetamine as ecstasy. Couzens took pride in his work, so he split, taking the tableting machine with him.[6] Couzens joined forces with Raymond, who was also still on the run. They had previously crossed paths in prison, according to a police source.

Following a tip-off, in December 1992 Redgrave's Team 13 at New Southgate SERCS began surveillance that linked Couzens to Ray Virciglio, someone of interest to Italian anti-mafia police, and Alex King. Redgrave began Operation Naples. His men watched the tableting machine arrive at The Barnhall in Ponders End. Over two months, Virciglio, a man called James Day and Couzens were filmed coming and going. Couzens was the least visible because he lived inside the drug factory on a makeshift camp bed. Redgrave recalls how one night, while Couzens was away, he accompanied the Yard's bugging unit when they broke into the premises. The ginger giant marvelled at the industrial scale of the set-up as the Technical Support Unit wired up the laboratory.

At 6.15 p.m. on 2 June, Redgrave called the attack. The Yard had extended a facility to *ITN News* to cover the arrest because of the propaganda value of dismantling such a large ecstasy factory. At this stage they knew nothing of Raymond's involvement. Detectives rushed Virciglio as he left The Barnhall with a box. The car he was heading towards was found to contain 170,000 ecstasy tablets. Couzens was arrested inside the factory and James Day was arrested trying to drive away from the scene with 11 kilos of MDMA powder in his boot.

Minutes earlier Day had dropped off Raymond, who on this occasion decided to walk the last few hundred yards to the factory. Raymond maintains that when he saw the raid develop he casually strolled away. But not before he gave a cheeky wave to Virciglio, who was being driven off in a police car.

At Edmonton police station, Couzens gave a full and frank confession. The evidence against him was overwhelming. Couzens revealed the plan was to produce three million ecstasy tablets called "White Lightning" every month. Dealers could sell them at around £10 to £15 each. The factory had been going for two months.

Virciglio was not for turning. The bent local solicitor Les Brown, who was friendly with local officers, got him bail. Raymond and

UNTOUCHABLES

Martin Onstead were soon identified from surveillance photographs and warrants were issued for their arrest.

By then Raymond had fled to Luxembourg. He revealed to us that the E factory was a joint enterprise with two silent partners, Steven Donavan and Brian Wright. Donavan, from the East End, had featured in the Brinks Mat inquiry. Before he was tried and acquitted in 1988 for laundering the proceeds through Dockland acquisitions, Donavan had resisted Redgrave's efforts to turn him into an informant. Brian Wright is an Irishman born in north London who by the early nineties was developing extensive interests in horse racing as a way to make clean money fixing races, and to launder dirty money from the drug trade. His nickname among those jockeys close to him is "The Milkman", because he always delivers.

Raymond also confirmed police suspicions at the time that the Adams organisation was distributing the ecstasy. The north London crime family had interests in a number of regular raves within the M25. Terry and Tommy Adams were Wright's "minders" in the factory.

Wright apparently brought another asset to the table – dirty cops. Raymond recalls how six weeks before the raid on the factory he conned a Chinaman from Switzerland out of 100 kilos of MDMA powder using cops in Wright's pocket. At the piano bar of a hotel in Gloucester Road, just as Raymond handed over a fake banker's draft for £2.5 million, the bent cops arrived and "arrested" everyone. Only the Chinaman thought it was real. He seized the option of returning to Switzerland without the MDMA or any criminal charge.

Raymond says police corruption of this nature is endemic and thankfully so because it made his life a lot easier. "Like genius verges on insanity, so it is with them. There's so much money flying around you can't expect them not to. There are exceptions obviously. But if you get 100 cozzers you've got to expect at least five to ten per cent will take money." In the old days you could simply try your luck and offer money to the arresting officer, he says. But now you need "a point of entry". This, he explains, is someone trusted by police officers. Who would fit such a profile? A lawyer, he replies.

In his interview with us Raymond made a startling admission that puts the intelligence on Redgrave in a very different light. While he was on the run in Luxembourg and France, Raymond says he left £600,000 of his own money with a trusted associate in London to undermine the prosecution and nobble the jury in the event he was

THE FALL OF THE GINGER GIANT

arrested. The amount seems high, but then Raymond claims to have earned £20 million out of the ecstasy factory.

The first evidence Redgrave received of such a plot came from former detective Duncan Hanrahan. He had been out of the police since 1991 and was working as a private investigator.

In January 1994, Hanrahan met Redgrave at a pub near Scotland Yard. Also present was detective sergeant Alec Leighton. He was suspended at the time over the BBC *Panorama* investigation into corruption at the Surbiton office of SERCS.

Hanrahan and Leighton were now working together. An informant, who we shall refer to by his pseudonym "Monty Weeks", had told Leighton there was a £50,000 contract on offer to discredit Redgrave. The people behind the contract were looking to transfer money from Spain into Redgrave's bank account, says Hanrahan. He told Redgrave that Raymond or those associated with him were said to be behind the contract and it concerned a drugs factory and a forthcoming trial.

Redgrave reported the meeting to his superiors, not least because DS Leighton was on bail at the time. As a security measure, he then split the Operation Naples team, sending a handful of detectives to a secret location in Hertfordshire to prepare for the trial in May and liaise with the CPS. "I wanted a sterile corridor between myself and my team because of the Hanrahan information. It was an insurance policy for me and for the job because Raymond was still at large. My plan was to relinquish day-to-day control so it could never be said at a later stage that I had the opportunity to influence the case," Redgrave explains. A CIB source confirms this.

Meanwhile, Redgrave and the rest of the team concentrated on Operation Nightshade, which had started in July 1993, one month after the raid on the ecstasy factory.

On 7 April 1994, Raymond was finally arrested in a London hotel for conspiring to supply and manufacture ecstasy and for absconding from HMP Oxford. He told us he'd returned from France for a funeral. His wife had paid by cheque for the tickets from Bordeaux, which he assumed was how he was caught.[7]

In his pockets, alongside £3,000 and 6,000 francs, officers found a Customs pass in a false name but with Raymond's photograph. In two separate bags the police found another £50,000 in cash. In the wardrobe was a strange array of recently bought cleaning items and biscuit tins. Detectives also found a false Irish passport in the name of

Noel Allen Fagan, a fake driving licence and business cards in the name of Simon Noel Alick Price-Fagan. Raymond later explained to us that he would "befriend" people who for whatever reason couldn't travel abroad but were entitled to a passport. The pseudonym "Fagan" was not a nod by the scholarly criminal to Charles Dickens, but someone he'd befriended from a Sue Ryder home.

Within days of Raymond's arrest a suspicious approach was made to a member of Redgrave's team. Detective constable Martin Morgan answered a call from former colleague Graham Le Blond with whom he'd once served at Stoke Newington and later at Edmonton. "I understand an old friend of ours has been nicked," Le Blond said down the phone. He was angling for a meeting to discuss "a big way forward," Morgan told us.

He reported the approach to Redgrave who immediately told CIB. DCS Roger Gaspar jumped at the chance to visit New Southgate. Gaspar knew that Morgan and Le Blond had been targets of the recently failed Operation Jackpot corruption probe at Stoke Newington. But Morgan had no idea he had now become a target of the Ghost Squad, who saw him as a core member of a corrupt cell of ex-Stoke Newington officers who had joined Redgrave's team.

Gaspar had reason to doubt Morgan's integrity. But the Ghost Squad had also convinced itself that Redgrave was the boss of the corrupt cell now at New Southgate SERCS. As he engendered great loyalty among those he led, it was assumed he must also be bent. Redgrave had never served at Stoke Newington and Morgan was already on the team he inherited. Redgrave protests, "By the same logic those in charge of Stoke Newington who allowed this group of detectives to escape the anti-corruption net should also be viewed with suspicion. But instead they were pursuing me to the exclusion of all exculpatory evidence."

A few weeks later in June 1994 Brennan became the Ghost Squad's first supergrass. He was unaware how little persuading Gaspar and Roy Clark really needed about the ginger giant. From then on nothing would ever disturb their fixed view that Redgrave was corrupt.

The trial of Virciglio and others had to be put back to January 1995 so Raymond could be joined as a defendant. In the intervening period, further evidence of a plot by the defendants to undermine the prosecution was presented to Gaspar.[8]

In a pre-trial hearing, Redgrave asked the judge for jury protection. Intelligence from an informant had come into Operation Naples that there was £600,000 to nobble the jury, exactly the amount Raymond

THE FALL OF THE GINGER GIANT

says he had put aside. The defence objected, Raymond in particular, who screamed across the courtroom that the ginger giant was corrupt and had taken money. This of course was all fed back to Gaspar.

When we explored the outburst with Raymond years later he admitted he had never met or paid Redgrave any money. His loaded comments in court were motivated by two factors. Firstly, jury protection would make it very difficult to buy the acquittal he wanted. Secondly, Raymond had fallen out with Brian Wright by the time of the trial. The Milkman owed him £1 million from the ecstasy factory. "It suited Wright for me not to see the light of day," says Raymond. Consequently, he assumed Wright's bent cops were now working with Redgrave to keep The Milkman out of the dock. It annoyed Raymond that the ginger giant, he assumed, would take Wright's money but not his.

Raymond freely shared his misconceived view of the ginger giant with associates in the UK like Donavan. And it is some of these conversations that the Ghost Squad intelligence cell is believed to have intercepted. No evidence has ever been produced that Redgrave was in Wright's pocket. But the suggestion made repeatedly over the phone and in court by Raymond was enough to further convince the Ghost Squad of Redgrave's guilt. After all Gaspar was already being suckered by a similar allegation from Brennan.

In any event, the judge refused jury protection but held the trial in camera. The jury's verdict was a shock given the quality of the police evidence, a senior CPS lawyer told us. Raymond was acquitted but the jury couldn't decide on Virciglio. This bemused an Italian anti-mafia judge who'd come to London to see if he would turn supergrass against people in Turin.

Gaspar spoke privately to the trial judge. It is likely the Ghost Squad chief gave the strongest impression he considered the allegations against Redgrave highly credible. These would have to be disclosed to Virciglio in the event of a retrial, which the Ghost Squad could avoid by pulling the plug on the prosecution. The judge agreed. Virciglio was also acquitted.

So Brennan's phoney allegations had ruined Operation Nightshade and now Naples. Is it any wonder when the Yard realised it had been duped the whole matter was deep-sixed?

A few years later, in 1997, the Untouchables also ignored confirmation of Raymond's plot against Redgrave from their own supergrass Duncan Hanrahan. "[My debriefers] were anxious for me to say something bad about Redgrave," Hanrahan told us. Instead he told them Redgrave had once rebuffed a corrupt offer from him and Martin King. Senior Untouchable John Coles was heavily involved in the Hanrahan case but he claims he knew nothing about the Raymond revelations. Yet Hanrahan has provided us with evidence that he was never asked to sign a statement containing references to the plot. And Raymond confirms that CIB3 never approached him.[9]

By 2001, it was clear to the ginger giant that he was never going to be fairly treated. He was living in a cycle of severe depression, excessive exercise followed by alcohol abuse as he tried to fill the days of his fifth year of suspension. His children had stopped all contact with him. This added to his sense of shame and despair and led to a further suicide bid.

Redgrave wrote to Mackinlay asking his MP to get to the bottom of his case in the event anything happened to him. "I honestly believe that a number of senior officers got their hands dirty and are determined that the truth will never come out," he wrote.

In February 2001, Geoffrey Brennan stood trial at the Old Bailey charged with stealing £400,000 from the Chinese provincial government. The Yard had given up on him ever coming to its rescue and agreeing to make a statement against Redgrave and Charman.

Brennan wanted to plead guilty and get it over with. He thought he'd only get under two years. The house he had bought with some of the stolen money was safe and in his son's name. The remaining £200,000 had been spent or salted away. But his legal team, he says, persuaded him there was a fighting chance.

Since Brennan was recharged in 1999, his solicitor Phil Kelly had been squirrelling away on the disclosure front. The Untouchables tried to hide its dark secrets behind PII certificates. But with the help of a fair-minded judge Kelly's tenacity paid off in bundles of sensitive documents never supposed to see the light of day. These laid bare the entire impropriety of Brennan's handling: from the failure to caution, the offer of immunity for evidence against Redgrave and Charman, the laundering of the Wangs' money to the misleading of the fraud inquiry and moonlighting Untouchable DS Chris Smith.

Andrew Trollope QC, Brennan's barrister, tried valiantly to get the case chucked out as an abuse of process. The delay in prosecuting a theft now seven years old was "unconscionable", he told Judge Brian Barker QC. The Untouchables had allowed the case "to collect dust on the shelf" because the mishandling of Brennan was just too embarrassing to reveal, Trollope argued. Not only that, his client had a reasonable expectation he wouldn't be prosecuted after admitting the theft and being left to his own devices.

Trollope had the unique opportunity to cross-examine the two men behind this scandal, both of whom had operated too long in the black chrysalis of the intelligence world where evidence is unnecessary to achieve a desired result.

When Roger Gaspar took the stand he had been deputy director of the National Criminal Intelligence Service since April 1998. He said he knew one day this legal reckoning would come when he had to account for his handling of Brennan.

Trollope believed that documents around the Ghost Squad's dealings with Brennan's sister Denise, who had been pivotal in getting him to turn supergrass, would unlock the offer of immunity extended by Gaspar. How else did a resolute Brennan suddenly agree to make taped admissions to the theft and falsely incriminate Redgrave and Charman? But the judge allowed all this to remain secret.

Gaspar's explanation for those 12 days in June 1994 was "wholly unconvincing", said Trollope. Still, the barrister cornered Gaspar into making a vital admission that he had "breached the rules" by not cautioning Brennan. The former Ghost Squad chief argued that the noble cause of anti-corruption justified it. As if such a consideration excused the appalling vista of police officers secretly putting themselves above parliament and the law. In the end, with neither side wishing to rehash the details, Gaspar admitted Brennan had duped him. "I always suspected he thought we were a soft touch. I always suspected he thought I was a soft touch," he told Trollope meekly.

When Roy Clark took the stand he was about to retire after 34 years of loyal service to become director of the Crimestoppers Trust. He trotted out the same line as Gaspar. The theft investigation "fell into insignificance" he said because the corruption allegations had to be pursued first. Even the simplest checks would have shown Brennan was leading them on a merry dance. But the Yard's witchfinder-general surpassed himself when explaining why they hadn't been done. He said he was "hogtied by secrecy" and a "policy" of his own making not to carry out inquiries during the Ghost Squad phase! In other words, false corruption allegations were allowed to linger while Brennan was showcased internally, a trophy supergrass whose evidential value was completely untested.

Clark tried to recover ground by blaming Redgrave for making Brennan's theft unprosecutable. He said the detective had "dressed up" Operation Nightshade as an arms, drugs and money-laundering inquiry, laying "onion skin upon onion skin of half truths". Trollope couldn't believe what he was hearing. Didn't Clark know that significant evidence, which his Untouchables had sat on for years, had now been disclosed making his "fabrication theory" wholly false? The barrister told Clark it "flew in the face" of the known facts and was "quite literally fantastic". Dragged naked and blinking into the light of public scrutiny, Clark admitted there was "no evidence" of Brennan's corruption claims and came clean that unnamed senior anti-corruption officers had displayed a "lack of control and supervision".

Newly promoted detective chief superintendent John Coles made Clark seem even more ludicrous when he said the information Brennan had provided on Tall Ted Williams' drug scheme in Portugal was genuine. He also confirmed that Brennan's allegations of moonlighting against DS Smith had been "proved" by his inquiry.

While we waited for the judge to rule, a CIB detective criticised Clark and other Ghost Squad officers for their management decisions: "The problem was there was a theft and instead of dealing with it simply, they tried to develop it as corruption, looking for links between this and that until it mushroomed out of proportion."

Judge Barker refused to chuck out the case. He was concerned about the delay but sided with prosecutor Richard Latham QC that Brennan's later actions had significantly contributed to it. Both sides were now heading towards a jury trial.

CIB felt Brennan would now plead guilty and rely on ample mitigating factors like his role as a police informant to secure a suspended sentence. Brennan says he was willing to do just that, but again his defence team persuaded him otherwise.

For any defence to succeed Trollope needed to persuade the judge that his client's admissions on the so-called Gaspar tapes should be ruled inadmissible because the confession was improperly obtained. Judge Barker agreed. He didn't criticise Gaspar but neither could he ignore *his* recent confession that PACE had been deliberately breached.

And so to trial. The jury would never know the man in the dock had already admitted the theft. The next six weeks were an expensive charade and once again the public picked up the bill. Both sides cherry-picked facts that supported their unsustainable cases. Like ballerinas Latham and Trollope tiptoed around the truth because it was as deeply unflattering to the Untouchables as it was to Brennan.

The first prosecution witnesses were the Wang brothers and Mr Hu from GX Impex, the Chinese provincial government company that had ultimately lost the £400,000 in the phone deal. The Houston Four were conspicuously absent. Latham and the CPS considered them too dodgy to call. One was in prison for fraud, and the others would struggle to explain a forged contract around the phone deal. Also, Trollope now had the Nightshade documents to directly implicate Padgett and Jones in the illegal arms deal.

Under cross-examination, the Wangs also presented credibility problems for the prosecution. Sam Wang accepted he had tried to do a "shady deal" not in accordance with company rules. The jury never heard that the CPS had warned the Untouchables that the Chinese witnesses were unreliable because the whole deal smacked of "frauds on frauds [and] fraudsters being defrauded". The jury was also unaware just how spectacularly corrupt the Guangxi Zhuang provincial government was. Beijing had been investigating official corruption among provincial communist party bosses since 1998 and discovered a black hole of a staggering $11 billion. The chairman in Guangxi province was executed five months before the Brennan trial started for taking $5 million in bribes throughout the nineties.

Sam Wang confirmed the deadly picture Trollope happily painted of those who crossed the provincial government. "If Geoff [Brennan] lived in China he dead." Wang then made a gun with his hand. "BANG. Dead long time ago." A juror gasped.

What the jury made of the prosecution case was hard to tell. However, it was clearly established that £400,000 went into Brennan's NatWest account and then he withdrew it and spent half on a house. Latham of course didn't tell the jury that the Untouchables had laundered the money for him.

The defence case was pure theatre, a one-man play with Brennan needing persuading to take the stand. He eventually got into his stride and with an ever more pronounced facial tic told the jury how he'd returned the money at a hotel to nameless men representing the Houston Four, one of whom looked like Barry from *Eastenders*. The lie was unsupported because Brennan's friend Mark Norton, the sacked detective, wasn't prepared to commit perjury by claiming he was there.

Brennan spun a totally dishonest defence to explain his cash wealth and property deals that echoed Kenny Noye during his Brinks trial 15 years earlier. "I've always dealt in cash," he told a sniggering jury. Brennan then cherry-picked the truth about his informant status to say everything he did had been authorised by Redgrave and Charman. He spoke about his help getting undercover officers into an arms deal, which he gleefully revealed involved some of the Houston Four.

UNTOUCHABLES

Brennan explained that some of his wealth came from informing on Tall Ted Williams. He regaled the jury with details of the Margarita trip and said Williams had repaid him a loan, and it was that money he then used to buy his house in cash, something he'd done many times before. The jury learned that Brennan's informant status was subsequently leaked to Williams, who had an "awesome reputation" as an enforcer and drug trafficker.

"Has he attended this trial?" asked Trollope.

"On two occasions," replied Brennan.

"Where?"

"The public gallery."

"Can you see the public gallery now?"

The judge gave Brennan permission to step out of the witness box. He looked up quickly and returned to the witness box.

"Anyone you recognise?" Trollope asked.

"Yes. That's Ted Williams."

The courtroom buzzed with much-needed excitement. The jurors discreetly glanced at a thin, bald-headed man in his late fifties sitting opposite them. He was wearing a grey suit with a black polo neck and a big grin.

Trollope later asked for Williams to be prevented from attending. Judge Barker felt that would be a dramatic step and said Brennan's role as an informant had been in the public domain for some time. Williams attended for the next few days, sometimes with his son. The Untouchables had briefed the judge that they now had considerable doubts about the threat posed by Williams.

He agreed to meet for lunch at a Chinese restaurant around the corner from the Old Bailey. Over a bottle of sake, Williams explained how as a "career criminal" who had done things that would make a bald man's hair curl it was "anathema" for him to speak to journalists. But because Brennan was talking "bollocks" he'd make an exception.

Williams said he had allowed Brennan's sister Denise to get close to him because he was impressed by the way she grieved over her young son who'd died of cancer in April 1992. He says he ignored warnings from John Lloyd's son-in-law, Steve Seaton, that she was a grass working with Smith and others since the Brinks Mat days.

He talked about the phone deal and said the plan was for him and Brennan to steal the money together. But Brennan did it himself and also nicked £90,000 from the Margarita property sales. Williams claimed he hadn't taken revenge because Brennan went into the witness protection programme one week after the gangster received the Operation Nightshade papers from bent cops. Redgrave? No, he was "a straightgoer", said Williams.

We returned to court to watch the start of Brennan's cross-examination. In Latham's plodding way he tied Brennan in knots over his finances. Every so often Brennan would complain of bowel problems – "My arsehole's alight here," he once remarked – to earn temporary respite from the questioning.

Until this point there had been no suggestion from either side of police corruption. But suddenly Latham changed the case he had originally presented to the jury. He accused Brennan of having corruptly paid Redgrave and Charman £50,000 from the stolen money. In return he claimed the detectives had created a smokescreen of arms dealing and money laundering.

Brennan denied making any corrupt payments to the two officers. Instead he turned on DS Chris Smith, the only man who the prosecution knew had taken money from the supergrass. Brennan said Smith had committed perjury and moonlighted. Latham had not called Smith as a prosecution witness for that very reason. Nevertheless, it was a pitiful sight to see the prosecutor rush to Smith's defence. Latham accepted moonlighting had taken place but not any corruption.

Latham, however, backed down when Trollope intervened to in effect warn his opponent he was dangerously close to misleading the jury by claiming the arms deal was a fabrication. Latham was also forced to admit to the jury there was "no direct evidence" of any payments from Brennan to the two detectives. Trollope went further and said there was "not a scrap of evidence".

Judge Barker summed up what he called "this highly unusual case with some highly unusual features". He said there was "perhaps little doubt" that the Houston Four had "some dishonest scheme in mind". He also supported Trollope's complaint about Latham's changed case. "I advise you to ignore suggestions that any money was taken [by Redgrave and Charman] to assist Mr Brennan."

The jury started deliberating on 2 April. It was a gloriously sunny day, the first since the trial began. Brennan was convinced he would be found guilty. DCS John Coles was in a talkative mood. He accepted the Ghost Squad had made mistakes – "They forgot they were policemen," he remarked, adding that when he took over the case it was in "chaos".

At 12.15 the next day the jury returned with a unanimous guilty verdict. Judge Barker sentenced Brennan to three and a half years for what he said was an "audacious and opportunist" theft. Brennan thought he'd had a result. He was expecting seven years. Anything under four meant he only had to serve half. As he entered the prison system, free of the need to lie, he immediately told the probation officer that he was "guilty as charged".

Meanwhile, back at the Old Bailey a CIB officer on DCS Coles' team gave an uncensored overview. "We've been had over" by Brennan and the Yard felt it would be "very embarrassing" if it ever came out and the Wangs sued, said the source. Gaspar had been a "cunt" for laundering the stolen money through two house purchases.

The CIB officer also felt there was something not quite right about the handling of Tall Ted Williams. "There were a lot of things that we weren't allowed to know about . . . it was very secret and decisions were made about people's links with others by senior officers and MI5." Like many within the Brennan family, our source felt Williams was "a protected informant for a higher authority". Even Coles told us that the Ghost Squad's failure to search Williams' home for the Nightshade documents was curious. He also said there was "no evidence" that Redgrave or Charman leaked them.[10]

The evidence of former CIB financial investigator Kevin Maul had been as explosive as his comments to us after the trial. He made a point of describing in his statement how the Ghost Squad had "laundered" the stolen money for Brennan. He was angry at the way his fraud investigation had been misled and at the attempts to claim Redgrave had tried to manipulate him. He described the ginger giant as a "grafter" who led from the front. He said there was "no whiff" around him when they both served at New Southgate SERCS. After joining CIB in 1997 Maul felt some Untouchables were "obsessional" about their targets and should have been removed from the anti-corruption squad.

Weeks after Brennan's trial ended, Charman asked to retire. He had completed 30 years' service, but because he was suspended he needed the Yard's permission to go. Redgrave would soon follow suit. Neither detective believed they would ever get a fair hearing at the planned disciplinary tribunal. They were also preparing civil actions against the commissioner.

Minutes of meetings between deputy commissioner Ian Blair, DAC Andy Hayman and DCS John Coles show just how self-serving and cynical the Yard was about covering up its failures at taxpayers' expense. All three Untouchables agreed there was "no doubt" that

THE FALL OF THE GINGER GIANT

allowing Charman and Redgrave to retire would be a "cost-effective" way forward. But it was deemed to be in the Yard's "best interests" to keep them suspended to avoid "criticism of the Met" in parliament and the press. Hayman also pointed out that a guilty finding in an internal disciplinary tribunal would "make life easier" in defending the civil actions. "A clear media strategy" was needed to "put a positive spin on events". Dick Fedorcio, chief spin-doctor for the Yard, was brought in to ensure the press did a hatchet job on Redgrave and Charman. Former BBC Home Affairs and Crime correspondent Graeme McLagan led the charge.

Unfortunately, first there was one final humiliation in the Brennan saga for the Untouchables. Latham and Coles had messed up over the confiscation proceedings. The best that could be achieved was a judge's order that Brennan pay back less than half the money he stole, or serve an extra year. He was pleading poverty having cleverly put the house he bought with the Chinese government's money in his son's name and therefore beyond the confiscation process. All this came out when Brennan appeared on 28 August 2002 at the Old Bailey.

That same day, over at the Yard, commissioner Stevens, Ian Blair and Andy Hayman held a press conference to launch the third phase of the anti-corruption drive, which they claimed had so far made the Met a "world leader" in professional standards. Stevens said he was building on the Untouchables' "successes" but "prosecutions had proved difficult". The Yard had written to the head of the CPS expressing concern that the system allowed officers to avoid going to trial.

The next day almost all the crime correspondents nosed their story with the example of Redgrave and Charman. "MET PAYS TWO DETECTIVES TO STAY AT HOME FOR FIVE YEARS" was a typical headline. Charman's solicitor Mark Lake was unconvinced by the Yard's subsequent assurances it was all coincidental, and that none of the senior officers had actually named either detective.

Redgrave and Charman were effectively kept prisoners in the police for another 20 months. The Yard was forcing them to face a disciplinary hearing but refused almost all disclosure requests, hiding behind PII.

The discipline hearing started on 19 April 2004, the eleventh year of the investigation, which the Untouchables were still refusing to cost. By then Brennan had completed his sentence and was back home. He had avoided serving an extra year by agreeing to pay the Wangs £155,000, but only in derisory monthly instalments. Brennan couldn't believe the Redgrave and Charman case was still ongoing. With no reason to lie any more, he admitted making false allegations against the two detectives to save his skin. But there was not a hint of remorse in his voice.

The detectives' barristers pulled the disciplinary case apart even with limited disclosure. Coles, the main prosecution witness, was bumptious but unconvincing on the stand, still persisting with the fabrication theory. At one point he even suggested the two Met undercover officers in the arms deal were corrupt. But the chairman of the Metropolitan Police Federation, Glen Smythe, claimed in a statement that Coles had confirmed to him that the continued pursuit of Redgrave was purely to keep him discredited.[11]

On 6 May the disciplinary board of three senior Met officers found the two detectives guilty of discreditable conduct. Strangely, though, they weren't sacked, which suggested some of the defence's points had registered. The board instead imposed a lesser sanction of requiring the two detectives to resign, something they had offered to do years earlier. A fitting end to the supergrass farce.

PART FOUR

DOUBLE STANDARDS

21

THE BUTCHER, THE BAKER, THE UNDERTAKER AND HIS SON

May 2003. It was a crisp, sunny day in London. Erkin Guney held hands with his heavily pregnant wife as they crossed the zebra opposite the Appeal Court on the Strand. It is not a London landmark like, say, the zebra crossing on Abbey Road became after the Beatles released their seminal 1969 album. But in its own way, the black and white stripes on the Strand are an important icon in the history of corruption, incompetence and cover-up in our criminal justice system.

Thirty-eight year old Erkin Guney walked through the stone portals of the Appeal Court entrance having served half of a fourteen-year sentence for possessing five kilos of heroin and a gun. He has always maintained that powerful business enemies working with corrupt cops had fitted him up.

It is usual for three appeal judges to explain to an appellant why his or her conviction is unsafe. Perhaps there was an innocent error in the prosecution case, or a forensic clue that the police "overlooked". Only rarely, as in the case of *Regina v Guney*, is it down to police corruption. But the judicial establishment was in no mood for contrition or explanation. The Untouchables had earlier made a PII application to keep the whole matter secret. The key issues of what CIB knew, when they knew it and why they didn't tell the defence have never been answered. In a matter of seconds Lord Justice Kennedy quashed Guney's conviction but refused to explain why or to apologise. He was coldly dispatched from the Appeal Court like a contestant on a tacky game show. The Justice Game.

The shadow of Stoke Newington darkened much of the prosecution papers. If it had been up to the Untouchables, Erkin Guney would have remained a convicted criminal even though their secret files held compromising information that showed his conviction was unsafe. "The process of curing any miscarriage of justice must also be to inform that person and society at large why he spent time in prison," says defence solicitor Tim Greene. He immediately wrote to the home secretary asking for an inquiry. An official replied saying it was not appropriate for the home secretary to intervene.

We've uncovered a significant part of what the Yard knew and when they knew it. This is a story of corruption in the police, Customs, MI5 and CIB; of how fugitive fraudster Asil Nadir nurtured friends in the police and the Tory Party; of the Turkish heroin trade and the Cypriot godfathers in north London who control it.

Above all it is a story of the unacceptable price someone had to pay when the interests of justice were subordinated to the interests of Scotland Yard and its anti-corruption squad.

Erkin Guney was born in north London in 1965. His Turkish Cypriot parents had a record shop in the Angel, Islington. "Jackie, the next door neighbour, could never pronounce my name. She called me Eggin. So since I was four, people started calling me Egg."

School was not something Egg enjoyed. As a teenager, he was often in trouble with the local Stoke Newington police, usually followed by a beating from his exasperated father. With maturity and reflection Egg says part of his behaviour was a craving for his dad's attention and respect as the youngest but one of three brothers and four sisters. As soon as he could, Egg dropped out of school, a decision as much to do with his dyslexia as general laddishness. By then the family had moved to the Hackney end of Green Lanes, the hub of the entrepreneurial Turkish-Cypriot community.

Egg's passion for cars led him into the moody side of the motor trade. Slowly he picked up a criminal record, though mainly for driving offences, theft of car parts and other bits of dishonesty. Porsches were his weakness. They still are.

In the mid-eighties, he set up a garage behind Green Lanes where he did legitimate and not so legitimate work. The latter involved chopping up stolen Porsches and selling the parts on. He was also fitting car stereos and phones, a new market with great opportunities to earn cash if you were willing to undercut the authorised dealers. Business grew so fast he leased a shop front with the garage behind it.

Egg made plans to set up a new telecommunications company called Intercell with Greek-Cypriot friend Andy Demitriou and a Turk called Harry Ramis. He liquidated and went bankrupt owing creditors around £700,000. The plan was that Egg would be a silent partner with an equal share in the new venture. But before Intercell took off tragedy struck. Egg's mother died on New Year's Day. Six days later, on his 27th birthday, the family buried her.

Egg found it difficult to accept his mother's death and suffered a mental breakdown, characterised by bouts of severe depression, isolation and unpredictable behaviour. "I couldn't continue the business," he says, "so I left it to Andy and Harry to run." For over a year Egg escaped into a world of anti-depressants and paranoia. What happened next is a matter of fierce dispute. In essence, Egg maintains that Demitriou sidelined him from the company. Demitriou and Ramis counter that they had built up Intercell after Egg bailed out, and therefore he is owed nothing. The feud festered over months until December 1993 when Egg was arrested in a van with two others near Demitriou's home. Also found in the van were cable wire, wigs, a knuckleduster and some hats. Egg was carrying a CS gas canister.

Egg's former partners subsequently made an allegation of blackmail to add to the charge of attempted kidnap. For several months he was held on remand, but when it came to court in April 1994, the charges were reduced to simple possession of the CS gas. For their own reasons, Ramis and Demitriou had refused to give evidence. Ramis told the police he wanted to end the feud and denied Egg's assertion that via an intermediary they'd offered him £200,000 in prison to settle his claim on the company. Either way, Egg was convicted but immediately released because of the time he'd already served.

Of course the matter didn't end there. Although Egg launched a civil claim against Intercell, through contacts in the car business he also enlisted the help of the up-and-coming Hunt brothers from Canning Town. He told them that an Ilford-based security company was on his case. Shortly thereafter, and following a visit known in the trade as "a straightener", the security company backed off.

In his defence, Egg says he sought the Hunts' protection because he believed there was a contract out on his life. His brother had secretly tape-recorded Harry Ramis allegedly admitting that Demitriou had at one time discussed taking a contract for £10,000, as Egg puts it, "to iron me out". He originally reported the matter to

UNTOUCHABLES

Stoke Newington police station, which at the time was gripped by the Operation Jackpot corruption probe. But Egg felt they had not taken him seriously.

The Pizza Pomodoro was a café near Spitalfields Market in the East End. A tall, grumpy detective inspector called Bob Skully liked to pop in on his way home. One day in July 1995 the owner asked if Skully would meet Egg.

The detective loved policing, but after 25 years he was seriously jerked off with the way the force was being run. Skully was serving on SO1, a specialist squad based at the Yard, which dealt with international, diplomatic and political cases. He had investigated some highly sensitive jobs, most recently a $4 million theft from a UN base in Somalia. However, the job he was working on in the summer of 1995 was particularly important to the Yard, because it came out of the corruption-riddled 1983 Brinks Mat gold bullion robbery. Operation Beryk was an investigation into John "Goldfinger" Palmer, the money man who in 1987 had been acquitted of handling the bullion. Since then Palmer had invested in the timeshare business operating through a crooked and ruthless company in Tenerife, Spain, where he was ripping off thousands of British pensioners in a multi-million pound fraud.

The head of SO1, Commander Roy Ramm, was particularly interested in Operation Beryk as Palmer had escaped his clutches during the original Brinks inquiry. The remnants of that squad were drafted onto SO1 to pursue the timeshare operation, which detectives believed was financed by Brinks money.

Skully still found time to research Egg's background before agreeing to meet. He brought along detective constable Dave Johnson, who had served six years at Stoke Newington and knew the value of informants in the close-knit Turkish Cypriot community. A new SO1 unit based at Chalk Farm had recently been set up to investigate Turkish crime and the activities of the Kurdish Workers' Party, or PKK, a guerrilla movement fighting since 1984 for an independent state in southern Turkey. Many unarmed Kurdish refugees, who fled persecution from the Turkish military's bloodlust, ended up in Green Lanes.

SO1 had concerns that PKK representatives in London were extorting local businesses to raise funds for the armed struggle back home. Johnson was not jaded like Skully. He was ambitious and hoped to get onto the new Turkish unit after the Palmer inquiry

THE BUTCHER, THE BAKER, THE UNDERTAKER...

ended. His chances were assured if he could bag Egg's father, Ramadan, as an informant.

As a young man Ramadan Guney served in the British Army in Cyprus, Kenya and Egypt. In 1955 he joined the Cypriot police force as a sergeant. That year, the Greek resistance launched a guerrilla campaign to wrest control from the British colonialists. Ramadan decided to take matters into his own hands to defend the Turkish minority on the island. He told us he was one of the founders of an underground and extreme right-wing paramilitary group called VOLKAN secretly set up with the help of the Turkish government. It was through this shadowy background that Ramadan Guney developed strong links with the British and Turkish intelligence communities, something he has maintained throughout his life. Nevertheless, at the end of the dirty war with the Greeks, the British deported Ramadan in 1958. He was "exiled" to London, he says, where he worked at the Soho-based Turkish Cypriot Association.

From his humble beginnings running a record shop he started to develop a property portfolio in the rundown Green Lanes area. In 1977, for example, he bought a synagogue in Hackney and converted it into a mosque. But Ramadan's most profitable investment was Brookwood Park in Surrey, Europe's largest cemetery, which he bought in 1985. He also has investments in the breakaway republic of Northern Cyprus. The current president, Rauf Denktash, is a close friend. Ramadan's sons say their father harbours his own political ambitions.[1] Certainly by the early nineties he was regarded among the Turkish Cypriot community here as a political godfather, someone they could come to for advice or who could mediate disputes.

But it was his relationship with the Turkish tycoon Asil Nadir that drew Ramadan Guney out of the shadows and into an unwelcome and probing media spotlight in 1993. Nadir's Polly Peck empire collapsed three years earlier following a dawn raid by the Serious Fraud Office (SFO). Nadir was charged with multiple counts of theft totalling £34 million. In 1992, Ramadan agreed to provide £1 million bail surety. But in May the following year, just months before a hearing at the Old Bailey, Nadir fled by private plane to the sanctuary of Northern Cyprus, which has no extradition treaty as it is not diplomatically recognised by the British government.

The Nadir affair was a further scandal for the imploding Major government. Northern Ireland secretary Michael Mates resigned from the cabinet after it was revealed he had given the fugitive a watch with the inscription "Don't let the buggers get you down". Nadir had shown his own dubious largesse to the Tories by way of a £440,000 political donation to their 1987 election war chest.²

Nadir had also developed 'friends' at Scotland Yard. Among them was said to be assistant commissioner Wyn Jones, who faced an embarrassing internal investigation for allegedly carrying out improper police work for the slippery businessman. The Yard had reportedly received allegations about this from a chief superintendent, himself under investigation. Jones denied any misconduct and the CPS decided not to prosecute. However, the findings of a disciplinary investigation into separate misconduct allegations were passed to home secretary Michael Howard in June 1993. He sacked Jones, who attempted to appeal the decision but left the force the following year.

Scotland Yard mounted a full investigation into Nadir's escape. The SFO were also gunning for Ramadan Guney. He faced two years in prison for refusing to pay them £650,000 of the surety. In February 1995 the Appeal Court ruled in his favour, but the SFO announced it was appealing to the House of Lords. Ramadan says he feared financial ruination if he lost. And Egg recalls flying to Nicosia to confront Nadir for refusing to take his father's calls. He says when he arrived at the villa he told the armed guards to tell their boss, "Ramadan's mad son is here." Nadir got in touch.

On 31 July 1995 detectives Skully and Johnson took a lengthy statement from Egg about the business feud with Harry Ramis and Andy Demitriou, now in its fourth year. To the SO1 officers, Egg seemed genuinely frightened, if not a little paranoid. He desperately wanted them to properly investigate the threats against him and to that end provided a copy of the secret tape-recording, which he said supported his claim that there had been a £10,000 contract on his life.

Egg also explained that Demitriou had sold his shares in the disputed mobile phone company Intercell to someone he described as one of London's major heroin traffickers, a Green Lanes godfather he named as Ibrahim "Jimmy" Karagozlu. If he had a piece of Intercell, even Ramadan's mad son wouldn't fuck with them, Egg said.

In 1983 Jimmy Karagozlu was jailed for 6 years for possession of 188 grams of heroin, worth £28,000, with intent to supply. Since then there was nothing to indicate his status in London's drug trade. What caught DS Johnson's eye was Jimmy's expanding business empire. It included a marble business, a new travel agents and a recently acquired airline. He'd come a long way from his roots as a family

THE BUTCHER, THE BAKER, THE UNDERTAKER...

butcher on Green Lanes. Jimmy represented a new breed of Turkish Cypriot, fully integrated and less politicised and reverential than their parents' generation. He had two brothers, Mehmet, who ran a petrol station in nearby Albion Road, and Hassan, known as Sammy, who took care of the butchers. Jimmy had originally run a minicab firm called Hit Cabs, which gave him the nickname Jimmy Hitman.

Skully is unabashed about his motives for getting involved. "We were playing Egg to get to his old man," he admits. It was cynical, certainly, but not unethical policing. Though Ramadan was no mug. He says he suspected what Skully was up to and played along so they would investigate his son's concerns. This they did. Ramis was arrested in September for suspicion of threatening to kill the undertaker's son. He told Johnson it was Demitriou's dispute although he admitted Jimmy Karagozlu was a "friend" who'd acted as a "go-between".

A few days later, with Ramis out on bail, a crucial meeting was convened between Jimmy and Egg. It was 18 September. The "sit down" was an attempt to resolve the business dispute once and for all. A special guest, Dogan Arif, head of the notorious south-east London crime syndicate, took the role of mediator.

The Arifs were another Turkish Cypriot family that had come a long way from their roots as bakers on the Old Kent Road. At the time, two of the Arif brothers were doing "heavy bird" for a failed armed robbery. Dogan meanwhile had been released in 1993 from a seven-year sentence for a massive cannabis importation.[3] The prosecutions severely affected the Arifs' power base and led to gang warfare in south-east London with the Brindles. Soldiers on both sides were killed in tit-for-tat shootings. Dogan was then perhaps best placed to mediate a financial settlement before things got further out of hand between Egg, Jimmy and the police.

He suggested Egg should be compensated with a £200,000 settlement plus a £50,000 goodwill gesture from Jimmy Karagozlu. To everyone's surprise, Egg rejected the offer, claiming Intercell was by now worth £5 million. "It wasn't about the money any more. I was doing good business. I had an exclusive contract fitting trackers for Securicor. Jimmy and that lot were trying to mug me off again. I had a hearing for my civil claim against Intercell coming up so I told them to poke it. I'd see 'em in court and let the whole thing come out."

The SO1 detectives warned Egg he could be fitted up with drugs and advised him to garage his car overnight. Meanwhile, Johnson and another SO1 officer warned Ramis to stay away.

UNTOUCHABLES

Four days later, on Friday, 29 September, Egg's life changed for ever. At 8.30 a.m. at least six officers from the 3 Area drugs squad arrived with a search warrant. It had been obtained less than 12 hours earlier.

Melanie, Egg's girlfriend, was getting their oldest daughter ready for school. The front door was open as the couple were expecting builders. They had just moved into the five-bedroom house in Clayhill, Essex. Ramadan had recently given the couple £25,000 in cash to pay for essential building work to the property.

The police swoop was not a dramatic, crash-bang-wallop affair. As soon as Egg saw "DRUGS" on the search warrant he said it was a "set-up" and urged them to call Skully at Scotland Yard.

Officers took Egg to his daughter's bedroom. In the wardrobe they found a Dr Martens shoebox containing £24,815. Egg admitted it was his, but lied about its provenance to protect his dad, claiming instead that he had earned the money. Then they found a .22 Star handgun tightly wrapped in clingfilm and three boxes of matching ammunition.

"What about the gun?"

"I don't know nothing about the gun," Egg replied. "It's a set-up."

Also in the wardrobe were five Hessian sacks of 58 per cent pure heroin inside a carrier bag.

"What's that?"

"I don't know nothing about that," said Egg.

At 9.04 a.m. he was arrested for possession of drugs with intent to supply and taken with Melanie to Barkingside police station. Meanwhile, detective sergeant Jim Gillan phoned Skully, who gave a brief rundown of Egg's dispute with the Karagozlus and warned the drug squad officer there was nothing straightforward in this case.

In his police interview, Egg explained the dispute with Karagozlu and mentioned the alleged contract against him. He spoke about the sit-down a few days earlier. Egg insisted the drugs had been planted, not by the cops, but by a mysterious gasman who had turned up the day before his arrest, supposedly on behalf of the kitchen company.

Skully told the CPS lawyer that he was nurturing Egg as an informant and thought the arrest was "too neat". The intervention was reported to the Yard as suspicious. Meanwhile, Egg was remanded to Pentonville Prison.

Ramadan Guney was at a business conference in Turkey when his son was arrested. He returned at the beginning of October and took a call from a Turkish friend, Halil "Perry" Hassan. He was described to us as the conduit, who when the Guney boys were growing up had paid off Stoke Newington cops to square up a few minor offences.

THE BUTCHER, THE BAKER, THE UNDERTAKER...

Perry arranged a meeting with a Greek Cypriot community leader from Green Lanes whom we shall call "Nico". Detectives who knew both men confirm they were well connected with many police officers, including senior ones from the Flying Squad and Scotland Yard. Nico was also friendly with Jimmy Karagozlu.

Ramadan says he was told the problem with his son could be resolved for a payment of £250,000 to unnamed police officers. The undertaker refused and the next day contacted CIB. Anti-corruption officers came to Ramadan's office in Green Lanes with some equipment to record any more approaches.

The Guney family had put it on the street that there was an unspecified reward for information that could prove Egg's innocence. The publicity around the £1 million surety for Nadir may have given an indication of how much money the undertaker would pay for his son's freedom.

It didn't take long before two men called, offering to provide the name of the informant and his police handler. In the hands of a good defence barrister, they said the prosecution would pull the plug rather than identify the informant behind the drugs swoop.

The negotiations with the anonymous pair took place between October 1995 and 1996. CIB was passed the tapes and encouraged Ramadan to keep the callers talking so they could trace them. One call was traced to a phone box near Scotland Yard, says Ramadan.

The anonymous callers tried to up the price by letting Ramadan know they had surveillance on some of his family. They also told him the informant was a close associate and was handled by a detective on the secretive National Criminal Intelligence Service (NCIS).

However, the most bizarre approach came in the middle of these phone negotiations. Ramadan and his son Onder were returning from a prison visit to see Egg. As they arrived at Green Lanes, Ramadan says a man followed him into his office. There was no time to get to the tape-recorder provided by CIB, but he later told anti-corruption detectives that his uninvited visitor claimed he was from the Home Office and had fitted up Egg to get Ramadan to work for them.

Ramadan didn't believe a word of it, especially after he was asked for £50,000, half up-front, the other half when his son was released. The man tried to suggest he was monitoring the family. To this effect he provided Ramadan with a personal letter, which he said they had intercepted, and a photograph of Egg, which he claimed was taken by a surveillance team. He also reminded Ramadan he had recently withdrawn £96,000 from the Midland Bank.

UNTOUCHABLES

The part about the money was true, but the Guneys say the letter and photograph were taken from Egg's house during the raid. Ramadan was convinced "Home Office man" was one of the two people he was already negotiating with by phone and quite possibly were part of, or working with, some officers from the drugs squad.

Whoever it was on the other end of the phone, their information was good in one key respect. A NCIS detective was handling the informant who'd fingered Ramadan Guney's son. The handler was none other than DS Keith Green. He was the man who two years later was caught in the CIB3 drug sting that also netted Terry McGuinness and Kevin Garner. Green however didn't turn supergrass and was acquitted in 1998, much to the Yard's annoyance.

During his time at NCIS Green was not under investigation. Privately, the Yard is happy to give the impression that doubts about the safety of Egg's conviction are solely down to Green's involvement. But the truth never comes in perfect packages. Green says he can see why the Yard would now want to blame him for everything. But he argues that what happened in the three months immediately after Egg's arrest reveals a far more murky and complex picture. His version of events is told here for the first time.

Green's posting at NCIS was punctuated by a long period of sickness. In mid-1994 he took six months' medical leave suffering from post-traumatic stress disorder. He'd had a delayed reaction to a near-fatal shooting accident on the Flying Squad. Green returned to NCIS early in 1995 and was given a very sensitive assignment. The stigma of depression and the need to prove himself had brought him back to work too early, he says.

Since at least 1994 the NCIS south England drug team had been collating intelligence on Turkish organised crime and the importation of heroin through the Balkans route into the UK. This operation was codenamed Centurion. It was the first multi-agency operation with NCIS officers working alongside Customs, the Benefit Agency, Immigration, SO11, MI5 and MI6.[4] The spooks were interested in information on militant organisations like Hamas and the drug trade in the UK. Centurion was also tracking lorries from the Balkans.

Green reveals that Asil Nadir was among the original targets of Operation Centurion. In the past there had been rumours that the fugitive tycoon was exporting heroin to the UK from his base in Northern Cyprus. Jimmy Karagozlu had once leased the casino in the basement of the Jasmine Court Hotel, which Nadir controlled.

THE BUTCHER, THE BAKER, THE UNDERTAKER...

Green further reveals that Ramadan Guney was also a target of NCIS. This may have been more to do with his surety for Nadir than any evidence of involvement in drug trafficking, which the undertaker denies.

While MI6 was listening to communications from the Jasmine Court Hotel complex, in London NCIS had an observation post in the Royal Oak pub on Green Lanes overlooking Ramadan Guney's office. Visitors were photographed and their licence plate numbers logged. Green's job in early 1995 was to turn this intelligence into packages of evidence for police squads to make arrests. The team he inherited lacked knowledge of the Turkish community so he recruited a Stoke Newington officer whose contacts in and around Green Lanes were enviable.

There was pressure on the Centurion team to get results and prove to the Home Office that NCIS – set up in April 1992 to improve inter-agency intelligence co-ordination – was a success. "We were spending a lot of money and to be honest achieving very little," says Green.

His team began looking at Egg as a result of the surveillance operation on his father. Centurion knew Egg was into car ringing – stripping stolen cars for parts – as a sideline to his phone business. Although some in the local community believed he was bringing in drugs using the cars, says Green. Egg fiercely denies this.

Green had an informant close to the Guneys and to the Karagozlus. One day in late September information was received at NCIS that Egg had access to a gun and was trying to buy some bullets.[5]

Green says he knew nothing at the time of the business feud with Jimmy Karagozlu. Green briefed the 3 Area drugs squad, but to protect his source he gave the false impression the intelligence had come from phone-taps, not an informant. Centurion had used the same drugs squad before for jobs as small as a few ounces of heroin, he says. But Green can't now remember whether the informant actually mentioned heroin or speculated this was why Egg needed a gun.

Within days of Egg's arrest, Green says he noticed a big change in his popularity. "Suddenly people I hadn't spoken to for years wanted to be my best friend." Officers would ring him at NCIS offering help and generally sniffing around in a way he found suspicious.

The informant, fearing Ramadan was getting close, was also making increasingly agitated calls to NCIS. Green was told the undertaker had recordings of men offering to scupper the prosecution for money and a list of names of between three and six police officers said to be on Jimmy Karagozlu's payroll.

UNTOUCHABLES

Ramadan certainly was hunting the informant and accepts he interrogated a number of people based on the information he received from his anonymous callers and his own inquiries. He told us his talks with CIB were not a secret in Green Lanes. Nico was apparently very annoyed and sent a message threatening to shoot Ramadan in the legs. We tried to contact Nico at his business in Green Lanes, but he never responded. Perry died while Egg was in prison.

Green suspected that some of the leaks were coming from inside NCIS. He says he notified his bosses after one Saturday when two Mediterranean-looking men in a red Mercedes approached him at Blackheath Rugby Club. They offered him money for information on the informant's identity. They talked about being able "to finish my career, that I was small fry and they could get to DACs". Green says it was never indicated who they worked for.

Green also supplied us with a book called *The Cyprus Triangle*, which he says was posted to his home address around this time. The paperback appeared to have a cryptic inscription from the author, president Rauf Denktash, which reads: "To him who knows or thinks he knows."

Green then dropped a bombshell. Sometime in the three months after Egg's arrest, he claims he took a call from one of the detectives on the 3 Area drugs squad who had raided Egg's home. He knew the man from their days on the Flying Squad at Rigg Approach and agreed to meet at the Met's sports club in Chigwell. When Green arrived another police officer was also there. He did all the talking and offered him a share of "a six-figure sum" to help scupper the prosecution against Egg. Strangely, he was told, the bribe money was coming from Jimmy Karagozlu. Green declined the offer and says he reported it to a CIB superintendent during a brief chat at Tintagel House. "The whole point was somebody was getting very close to identifying who the informant was. [Approaching CIB] was to try and stop that."

In December 1995, Keith Green went on sick leave. The depression had come back, he says. He never returned to work and officially retired on ill health grounds seven months later.

As Egg's trial approached in May 1996, his defence team had no idea what had emerged from CIB's investigation of Ramadan Guney's tapes. The lack of communication severely hampered their ability to rely on them in Egg's defence.

Although the family didn't know it at the time, the Ghost Squad

THE BUTCHER, THE BAKER, THE UNDERTAKER...

had decided not to refer Ramadan's complaint of police corruption to the PCA for supervision. This decision was all the more extraordinary because by then Ramadan had identified to the anti-corruption squad the man he said had come to his office posing as a Home Office official. During one of the pre-trial hearings Ramadan pointed out DS Jim Gillan, one of Egg's arresting officers. Had CIB done any analysis to compare Gillan's voice with those on the tape? Had Gillan been interviewed by CIB about the accusation? The family didn't know the answers to these and more questions by the start of the trial and felt CIB was keeping them in the dark.

Keith Green says at no point while he was at NCIS or after he retired did CIB ever ask him about the operation against Egg, or attempt to meet his informant. He points out that Operation Centurion may even have possessed photographs of the mysterious "Home Office" official who visited Ramadan's office, because of the surveillance operation from the nearby pub. But as far as he is aware no one from CIB checked the files.

Green further alleges that DS Gillan was one of the two officers who approached him at the police sports club and whom he reported to CIB. The second detective, who Green named as detective constable Martin Morgan, did all the talking, he says.

Morgan had been a major target of Operation Jackpot. He later served at Edmonton and then New Southgate SERCS. Morgan was friendly with Jimmy Karagozlu and Nico. But crucially, they were also at one time his registered informants. Mehmet Karagozlu told us his family knew Morgan before he joined the police. Morgan's father-in-law was a cutter at Smithfield meat market where the Karagozlus got their supplies. By the time of Egg's trial, Morgan had become a major target of the Ghost Squad as part of its wider investigation into New Southgate and a corrupt cell of ex-Stoke Newington detectives supposedly under DI John Redgrave's control.

The Guneys' defence team knew nothing about these goings-on. A thorough investigation of the tapes and of the Ghost Squad's secret intelligence files should have been enough to raise serious questions about continuing this prosecution. But as ever with internal investigations, there were other pressing considerations that had nothing to do with the interests of justice.

The smell of corruption around the Guney case wafted into the Ghost Squad at a very sensitive time for the Yard. One area of particular sensitivity was the ongoing prosecution of corrupt SERCS detective constable John Donald. The Ghost Squad had examined

UNTOUCHABLES

Donald's links with a major south-east drug syndicate led by Kenny Noye and suggestions of a corrupt police network that extended to detectives inside NCIS.[6] The corruption probe into NCIS coincided with Operation Centurion, some of whose senior management were embroiled in the Donald affair. This might further explain why the Ghost Squad was keeping Egg's defence team in the dark.[7]

None of Egg's fingerprints were on the gun, on the boxes of ammunition or the five hessian sacks of heroin. No drug paraphernalia, like scales or cutting agents, was found at his house, and the clingfilm the gun was wrapped in did not match that found in Egg's kitchen. The prosecution also had to concede, because of the expected evidence from SO1 detectives Skully and Johnson, that Egg feared being set up *before* his arrest and that his business enemies were well known to the police.

The judge described the defence in the following way: "The fit-up is alleged, but by the defendant's enemies and not the police witnesses in this trial. What the defence wish to explore is whether the police knew of that fit-up or perhaps, indeed, connived at it."

To be successful, Egg's defence depended on what disclosure the judge would order from the Ghost Squad's secret files. Rock Tansey QC, his barrister, wanted to explore whether Jimmy Karagozlu was the informant, or if he knew the person who was. But the prosecution asked Judge Elwen nicely to block any disclosure that would identify the sources of intelligence that led to the raid, on the grounds of PII. The judge agreed. Round one to the Ghost Squad.

Egg's lawyers had another poisoned arrow to fire into the heart of the prosecution case. They'd recently discovered that DS Gillan was one of three officers involved in the case who had been investigated by Operation Jackpot.

Gillan was one of the officers who had been transferred in January 1992 from the Stoke Newington drugs squad. Operation Jackpot investigated five serious complaints against him and he was finally cleared of any criminal or disciplinary offences by February 1995. Three months later he was posted to the 3 Area drugs squad that soon afterwards arrested Egg.

Tansey argued that in the "highly unusual circumstances of this case the evidence of the arresting officers was not reliable" because some had been "intimately involved" in Stoke Newington cases involving guns and drugs that were dropped or successfully appealed because that evidence was "tainted".

THE BUTCHER, THE BAKER, THE UNDERTAKER . . .

The defence barrister asked for the Operation Jackpot file to be disclosed. The prosecution vehemently opposed. Scotland Yard after all had neatly hidden that failure in the bowels of the Ghost Squad. The prosecution said the Jackpot inquiry report was "irrelevant" to the case and, anyway, the three officers had not been disciplined. Without reading the report, the judge agreed. Round two to the Ghost Squad.

Next, the defence asked to cross-examine DS Gillan about some of his Stoke Newington cases. One, involving Maxine Edwards, had only recently been successfully appealed following a rare referral back to the court from the home secretary, no less.

Tansey put his argument in these terms: "[My client] has said from the outset he has enemies, but there are major question marks. Are the police involved in it as well? Are they being paid, or in league with his enemies to do him down? And, therefore, that is the one reason why the whole question of honesty and dishonesty of police officers is relevant. The fact that Mr Gillan plays, in the evidence that we have, a low-key part does not mean that it was not a dishonest operation to which he was a party, and his past is, therefore, relevant. Is he a police officer on whom one can safely rely, is he a totally honest, straight policeman and may he have infected what happened on this occasion? We do not suggest that the police themselves have necessarily planted the drug."

Gillan denied on the stand that he was "Home Office" man or that he had ever been to Ramadan Guney's office let alone tried to extort money from him. But Judge Elwen wouldn't allow cross-examination of Gillan on Jackpot matters. Round three to the Ghost Squad.

The prosecution's protection of Gillan appeared entirely at odds with what was simultaneously happening in the civil courts, where the controversial detective was bringing libel proceedings against the *Guardian* over two articles written at the time of his transfer from Stoke Newington, although he wasn't named in either of them.

The former heads of Operation Jackpot, superintendent Ian Russell and deputy assistant commissioner Mike Taylor, were both prepared to undermine Gillan's libel claim by giving evidence for the *Guardian*. So too was the senior CPS lawyer involved in cleaning up the judicial fallout from the "Stokey Cokey" scandal and the PCA chairman.[8]

The prosecution position in Egg's case was all the more contradictory because after Operation Jackpot Gillan was subject to a little-known and special arrangement whereby the CPS had to assess his credibility before allowing him to give evidence in a trial.

Prosecutor David Jeremy was also concerned about the forthcoming evidence for the defence from detectives Skully and Johnson. So he called their boss, the head of SO1, commander Roy Ramm, to rubbish them. Ramm told the court he had bollocked Skully for straying from the John Palmer timeshare inquiry, even though another senior SO1 officer later gave evidence that he had given the two detectives authority to nurture Ramadan as a potential informant.

The defence asked to see the SO1 file prepared by Skully and Johnson on their dealings with Egg before his arrest. The prosecution opposed. The judge agreed. Round four to the Ghost Squad.

It was a rare sight indeed to see detectives giving evidence against their own and casting doubt on the "neatness" of the police raid. The prosecution accused Skully of moonlighting and seeking some financial benefit from the Guneys for putting "the frighteners" on Egg's former business partners and providing him with an "insurance policy while he dealt in heroin". Utter rubbish, Skully told the jury and countered that if he was corrupt he could have called Palmer's legal team at any time and named his price. "They had to rubbish me and Dave to take the spotlight away from the true story, that Egg had been fitted up," Skully told us.

He had retired from the police by the time he gave evidence, but felt there had been an underhand attempt before he left to use trumped-up disciplinary proceedings to prevent him being a credible witness for Egg. Johnson, however, was still a serving officer. He too had been served with disciplinary papers just before the trial, but these resulted in the mildest ticking off, equivalent to a set of lines – "I need to concentrate on primary operational objectives."[9] The whole exercise appeared to be another abuse of the disciplinary process to smear police witnesses who were off message.

However, the most bizarre prosecution strategy was to try and minimise the criminality of Jimmy Karagozlu by arguing that his conviction for heroin trafficking was hardly evidence he was a Green Lanes godfather. In fact, Customs believed Jimmy's syndicate was moving 1,000 kilos of heroin at that time from Pakistan through Turkey and laundering millions of pounds through his casino underneath Asil Nadir's hotel in Cyprus.

On 23 July 1996, Egg was found guilty and sentenced in all to fourteen years, ten years for the heroin, four for the gun and ammunition. The judge returned the £25,000 because the prosecution hadn't proven it was drug money.

The family immediately appealed on the grounds that the judge was wrong not to have acceded to their lawyer's disclosure requests. While they waited for the appeal to be heard, a brief letter from CIB arrived informing the solicitors that based "on the evidence available" no criminal or disciplinary action would be taken against any officer complained of by the Guneys. This was a reference to the conversations Ramadan had recorded for CIB with two anonymous callers he suspected were cops.

In February 1997, Gillan lost his libel case against the *Guardian*. The jury did not believe his reputation had been damaged and the Police Federation was left with a hefty legal bill of over £1 million.[10]

This was also the year DAC Roy Clark restructured the Ghost Squad into the Untouchables and the new intelligence cell CIBIC. The metamorphosis was part of Scotland Yard's public and political manipulation of its image as an organisation capable of reform and self-regulation before the start of the Home Affairs select committee hearings on the discredited disciplinary and internal complaint system and the Stephen Lawrence public inquiry.

Egg's case threatened to expose this confidence trick because it led to so many pockets of corruption the Yard did not want revealed to public scrutiny. However, in light of the allegation of fit-up made so prominently in Egg's trial, a second complaint inquiry began. Here was a perfect opportunity to refer it to the PCA and appoint an outside force to investigate the Yard. Instead the sensitive complaint was kept among the shadow warriors from CIBIC, led by DCI Chris Jarratt.

Jarratt sent two of his detectives[11] to re-interview the family, who repeated the allegations against Gillan but added nothing more. The missing pieces were already in the anti-corruption squad's secret files.

Throughout most of 1997, as the full appeal hearing neared, the family learned next to nothing about the progress of this new inquiry. PII was once again used to successfully persuade the Appeal Court there was no merit in the appeal. It was dismissed on 27 February 1998.

"Up until that day there was light at the end of the tunnel," says Egg's girlfriend Melanie. "But when the Appeal Court judges refused us a certificate to go to the Lords it finally hit me. I was devastated."

In his prison cell, Egg at first thought he was going mad, seeing conspiracy where there was none. But the more he replayed the events in his mind the more convinced he became that there was an almighty police "cover-up" in progress. He would spend four more years inside before it started to properly unravel.

22

SECRET JUSTICE

In June 1998, Customs charged Andy Demitriou and Jimmy Karagozlu for orchestrating a multi-million pound VAT fraud on a mobile phone business.

All was not lost. Two months earlier Demitriou had met two Asian middlemen working with a corrupt Customs officer called Kalaish Sawnhney. He was part of Operation Mamba, the Customs team behind the arrests. After his release on bail, Demitriou helped arrange a burglary to steal the Operation Mamba file. It was made easy because Customs were temporarily working from portakabins in Harmsworth near Heathrow Airport while the main office was renovated. After the files disappeared, Customs rightly suspected an inside job and the main suspect was 52-year-old Sawnhney.

In great secrecy Customs called in CIB3 to test his integrity. The job was given to Chris Jarratt at CIBIC, who set up a joint covert operation with Customs, codenamed Mongoose.

In November, a false intelligence report was created on the office computer. The report gave genuine details of Jimmy's criminality but falsely suggested there was a bug in a lamppost outside his house. Sawnhney was filmed printing out the specially marked file. He then sold it to Demitriou through middlemen Nathaniel Das and Gunsul Patel. Meanwhile, secret cameras overlooking Jimmy's house filmed private investigators he had hired to check out the lamppost. The sting was complete, and at dawn on 4 December, Jimmy and the others were arrested at different locations across London. In all, ten people were charged with conspiracy to pervert the course of justice and held on remand at Belmarsh top security prison.

Sawnhney turned supergrass and spoke about a list of corrupt Customs officers he had given Jimmy at the beginning of their relationship.[1] Jarratt mounted a dramatic search at Belmarsh but didn't recover the list.

The Karagozlu crime family's money-laundering operation was cute. It had three limbs – IMK Travel, Air Ops International and the Jasmine Court Casino. The police had also uncovered a highly embarrassing arrangement with an unwitting Thomas Cook in central London, which at one point was regularly exchanging hold-alls with £100,000 into foreign currency. Key evidence came from Athanasis Apostolopoulos, the Greek manager of IMK Travel. He told Customs how he set up the exchange deal on Jimmy's behalf in 1996.

Jimmy had negotiated payment of $1.2 million for one Tristar aeroplane plus parts through ING Barings Bank. Apostolopoulos admitted to Customs personally making a $500,000 payment for the plane which Jimmy's company, Air Ops International, flew under the licence of Holiday Air in Turkey. The travel agents would arrange flights and accommodation at the Jasmine Court Hotel. Some customers would separately give Jimmy cash in his private office above the travel agents in return for a credit note for the casino. Apostolopoulos took the cash to Thomas Cook and exchanged the sterling for US dollars and deutschmarks, which were then transferred to Northern Cyprus.

Apostolopoulos told the police he also helped run Jimmy's airline and travel agents from a new base in Sweden where the Green Lanes godfather operated as Nordic European Airlines. He said he bailed out of that venture just before the arrests in June 1998.

Co-operation between Customs and the police against the Karagozlu crime family developed from a memorandum of understanding signed that year. However, the pact obscured an even more sensitive joint enterprise: to investigate corruption in both law enforcement agencies. Before Sawnhney was unmasked, Customs told the Yard that they too appeared to have a dirty cop in a highly sensitive post.

In April 1998 Customs had arrested a major money launderer and Yard informant called Michael Michael. The Greek Cypriot accountant quickly turned supergrass. During his debrief Michael told Customs he had paid his police handler, named as detective constable Paul Carpenter, "up to £10,000 per week" for leaking intelligence to his criminal associates. Michael was the UK representative of British, Dutch and French criminals engaged in massive importations of cannabis (18 tons) and cocaine (71 kilos) into the UK. His British clients included Costa del Sol exiles Mickey Green and Patrick Adams, head of the north London crime family.

Customs estimated Michael had laundered £58 million. He had also been Carpenter's registered informant since 1991. So Customs alerted the Yard, who sent Jarratt to interview Michael. This apparent compromise was even more serious than it appeared because it threatened to undermine the carefully spun launch of the Untouchables. Carpenter was part of the Yard's Special Intelligence Section, the SO11 offshoot that collated intelligence from taps and informants on London's top-echelon criminals. He was based in the same building in Putney from which the Untouchables operated. Carpenter was part of the SIS team who had been looking at Karagozlu under the control of Terry Pattinson. Worse still, since 1997 Carpenter had been also attached to Jarratt's own intelligence cell.[2]

The Karagozlu trial began in January 2000. No sooner was the jury selected than they were discharged because of a suspicion there had been an attempt to nobble them. A new jury heard the case for six months. It had round-the-clock police protection from the Yard, but in July the jury was discharged for misconduct – according to defence solicitors, it was not taking the case seriously.

Another new jury heard the case afresh in September. But in December disaster struck once more. This time it was less a case of jury nobbling and more of jury nobbing. A member of the police witness protection team stationed at Ilford had taken his job a bit too seriously and was offering some personal close protection to one of the female jurors. CIB3 officers had received a tip-off from one of their colleagues about the sexual relationship. They discovered from his mobile phone he had texted her over 600 times, including at court. In total, 1,119 texts passed between the lovers. The trial collapsed for the second time costing many millions.

A deal was eventually worked out involving the two Karagozlu brothers. Mehmet was only involved in the corruption case, not the VAT fraud. Jimmy pleaded guilty to conspiracy to pervert the course of justice and in return the prosecution offered no evidence against his brother. Mehmet was released after twenty months on remand.

The main players in the VAT and corruption cases all pleaded guilty in 2001. Jimmy received nine years and six months. Andy Demitriou was given six years. Middleman Nathaniel Das got four years and nine months. He told us: "I found Jimmy a very nice person, a most religious person, not corrupt, a person who cared about you."[3]

In January 2000, just as the ill-fated Karagozlu trial was starting, the Untouchables began a secret operation codenamed Greyhound against DC Martin Morgan. His phones were bugged and he was put under close surveillance. The timing seemed more than coincidental. Did they suspect Jimmy would turn to his former handler for some help? Certainly by this stage the Untouchables knew the two men had an improper relationship and it is likely the targeting of Morgan was in some way a security measure to protect the Karagozlu trial. The more the anti-corruption squad listened in to the private life of the 37-year-old detective, the more they realised it was another of Morgan's informants who was looking to him for some corrupt help.

The story begins with Ashley Sansom, a money launderer for some heavy criminals involved in dope smuggling. Sansom was connected to a London drug syndicate headed by a builder called Bob Kean and one in Liverpool. With Kean's help, Sansom formed AJS Financial in Aylesbury, Buckinghamshire, in May 1997. Kean introduced a number of his criminal associates, who deposited hundreds of thousands of pounds of drug money. Kean had placed somewhere between £300,000 and £600,000 with Sansom.

But in late 1999 his launderer disappeared. At first Kean tried to track him down using the courts and a private investigator. But the pressure from one client got too much. According to friends of Kean, a violent drug dealer called Kenneth Kenny one day turned up at his Norfolk farm threatening to shoot him if he didn't get his £150,000 back.

Kean turned to his old friend and handler Martin Morgan, who had inherited the informant from a mutual police friend. Kean had been grassing since the seventies – his pseudonym was "Kevin Churchill". Morgan ran Kean when he was at New Southgate SERCS office in the early nineties. But as the relationship developed, Kean ended up running Morgan, who he knew was willing to use the cover of the informant-handler relationship to act corruptly. Morgan agreed to help locate Sansom. He recruited two of his chums from Stoke Newington days, detective constables Declan Costello and Paul Goscomb.

Morgan had no idea CIB3 were listening in March 2000 as the plot unfolded. A cool operator, Morgan had time to go on a racing holiday to Scotland with other cops, unaware CIB3 was behind him.[4] Meanwhile, in London the Untouchables came up with a plan. They took Sansom, his girlfriend and her baby into protective custody. As part of the deal, the money launderer agreed to become a supergrass.[5]

An undercover detective posing as Sansom then left a phone number for Costello at Barkingside police station, where he worked with Morgan. They traced it to a phone box at the Post House hotel in Guildford, Surrey. A receptionist said Mr Sansom was staying in room 179. Morgan spread the word and agreed to meet Kean at the hotel.

Kean arrived first with Carl Wood, an affable drug smuggler who had lost £80,000 in the Sansom laundry. Surveillance officers, it is believed from MI5, were everywhere. In addition, CIB3 placed cameras and listening devices in the television and elsewhere around Room 179. These were monitored from an adjacent room.

Morgan arrived later with Costello, who stayed in the car. In the hotel room the talk turned to what violence would be meted out to Sansom if he didn't come up with the cash. Wood had brought some ammonia. Morgan gave Kean some electric cable ties to tether Sansom, presumably during his interrogation. The cop then left. Wood and Kean stayed the night. Wood was overheard referring to a previous conversation where he claimed the "cozzers" (Morgan and Costello) had talked about putting Sansom in a "crusher". He, of course, never showed at the hotel and on the third day the criminals left.

On 6 April, the three cops and Kean were charged with conspiracy to pervert the course of justice, to falsely imprison Sansom and to cause him serious harm. Wood was on holiday in Spain at the time. He was extradited six months later.

At first Morgan said nothing to his CIB3 interviewers. Then he gave a statement that was largely invented. He tried to hide behind his informant-handler relationship, disclosing sensitive details of information Kean had given. Morgan argued that his reward for helping one informant was the opportunity to recruit another, Sansom.

In a fortuitous cock-up, Morgan's explosive statement was accidentally served by the CPS/CIB on Kean's co-accused. It had a devastating effect when Wood discovered his criminal associate had also been a high-level police informant. Kean was furious. Wood told everyone he was a grass. It was the talk of north London. Kean later confirmed to us one part of the statement where it mentions information he once gave about the IRA. A former police handler says Kean had also given information on the stolen Beit art collection, although the two things may be connected.[6] Morgan and Kean fell out as it became apparent the corrupt cop would have to expose his friend's secret past in front of a jury to stand a chance of getting off.

Slowly, snippets of their corrupt dealings emerged in whispers around the Old Bailey. CIB3 got wind that Kean's brother-in-law, a counterfeiter of funny money, had written from prison threatening to expose his alleged role in nobbling a jury if Kean didn't help him.[7] CIB3 also found witness statements in Kean's home with Morgan's fingerprints on them. The statements concerned a drugs job, Goscomb said. He and Morgan had worked the case when they were at Ilford in 1998.

The Untouchables watched with glee as Costello and Goscomb fell out with Morgan over his statement. Costello felt Morgan's version made it impossible to go along with.

Morgan's only chance was to have the probe evidence from the hotel room excluded as unlawfully obtained. The prosecution was forced to concede that the authority was lacking, but Judge Graham Boal QC did not rule it unfair. The defence also alleged CIB3 had "cooked the books" to legitimise the unlawful operation. An original page from commander Andy Hayman's diary, for example, didn't tally with the photocopy disclosed to the defence. The judge, however, was unmoved and found no bad faith by any of the CIB3 officers.

When it dawned upon the defendants that the jury would be entitled to see the hotel video in all its compromising detail it had a domino effect. Six days later, on 13 May 2002, Costello pleaded guilty to conspiracy to cause actual bodily harm. He felt his family had suffered enough. Morgan then pleaded guilty to conspiracy to falsely imprison. And one week later Kean did the same.

The sentencing on Friday, 7 July, fell on the day of a crucial World Cup match between England and Argentina. The morning session was taken up with mitigation speeches. At 12.21, with nine minutes to kick-off, the judge called half-time to reflect on what he had heard. Wood, who suffered from Crohns Disease, knew he was going down and joked, "I've got three ounces of puff up my arse."

We returned to court at three p.m. after England's victory. Morgan, just weeks away from his fortieth birthday, had spent half his life in the Met. He gritted his teeth as Judge Boal called him "a bent police officer". Seven years. Kean got the same as the co-architect of the conspiracy. Wood received four years and Costello thirty months.[8]

UNTOUCHABLES

It was rumoured that Morgan would have been charged with another matter on the steps of the Old Bailey if he had been acquitted, although CIB3 refuses to comment on this.

Morgan had been "at it" for years, former co-conspirator Declan Costello told us. He offered a solution to the riddle that hovered over the trial. Was there more than an irresistible inference that Kean had paid him and Morgan for their services? Costello admitted to us he was promised £20,000, the same as Morgan. "Martin is obsessed with money," he added.

A second riddle was why Morgan took the risk going to the hotel room when he knew for years that CIB3 considered him a target. Costello and Goscomb separately said they believed Morgan had deposited around £50,000 with Sansom before he went AWOL, although the prosecution offered no evidence of this.

Goscomb was discharged in the Morgan trial as part of the horse-trading in return for Costello's guilty plea. Senior Treasury Counsel Orlando Pownall had told the court that although there was evidence against him, a "pragmatic view" prevailed. Goscomb had little doubt he would be sacked from the police, but said he would try and string out the discipline proceedings on full pay as long as possible.[9]

He threatens to provide a prepared statement at his disciplinary interview naming Untouchables who he claims were involved in corrupt acts when they served at Stoke Newington. He talked specifically of a senior CIB3 officer who had ordered the planting of a gun on a black man. Costello also named to us another officer whose expertise was said to be planting ammunition at a crime scene.

Before he and DS Jim Gillan were transferred from Stoke Newington in January 1992, Goscomb says a senior officer tipped him off that he would not face criminal or disciplinary charges. Costello also left Stoke Newington that year. He told us a senior officer had also marked his card he wouldn't be arrested by Operation Jackpot and should quickly apply for a post coming up on the diplomatic protection squad. Costello transferred to 10 Downing Street where his duties included bodyguarding prime minister John Major.

The failure of Operation Jackpot allowed a number of officers to "bomb burst" out of Stoke Newington, says Costello, and continue their corrupt ways on proactive squads in north and east London, like the Flying Squad and SERCS, until the Yard decided it was expedient (or had its hand forced) to do something about them.

Why hadn't someone as arrogant as Morgan been taken out

earlier? Dave Pennant, the senior investigating officer in Operation Greyhound, admits there was "a certain amount of intelligence that gave serious concerns about [Morgan's] integrity".[10] However, he maintains this was not enough to bring charges, which is why in January 2000 he mounted a proactive investigation.

But this doesn't explain why the secret intelligence held by the Untouchables, which was easily good enough to undermine the safety of Egg's conviction, was never disclosed very early on.

We have pieced together what the anti-corruption squad knew about Morgan and others before Egg's appeal:

- Morgan and his partner, detective sergeant Paul Kelly, had been targets of the Ghost Squad since 1994.[11]
- The two detectives co-handled Jimmy Karagozlu and Nico between 1993 and 1995 at New Southgate SERCS.[12]
- Nico had helped the police for many years before Morgan and Kelly handled him and had friends high up in the Flying Squad and Scotland Yard.
- Kelly and Morgan were suspected of nobbling a trial in June 1997 involving a drugs syndicate connected to Bob Kean.[13]

This last bullet point is worthy of more examination. When the defence asked for the surveillance logs to be produced in court for electrostatic document analysis (Esda) testing an officer reported back to Judge Fergus Mitchell that they had gone missing. He acquitted the defendants and threatened instead to send the entire SERCS squad to prison for hatching what he called "a little conspiracy". Although the judge assumed the cops had destroyed the logs before the forensic test could reveal they had been fabricated, another explanation is that officers working with the defendants stole them to ensure the prosecution collapsed. Kelly denies any involvement, explaining he was having an operation on his varicose veins at the time. But he was later disciplined for his failure of supervision. Goscomb, however, told us Morgan was involved with Kean in the plot to steal the logs.

The Yard was forced by the judge to launch an inquiry. This was the third of four drugs trials that had collapsed or were successfully appealed between November 1996 and October 1997. Each one had attracted scathing comments from the judges.[14] Several expressed dismay at the slow reaction of the Yard in dealing with some of these officers. One judge was aghast that a particular officer, who the Appeal

Court had already branded "a liar", had not been suspended but was back on duty arresting more people.[15]

The judges had no idea this had been a deliberate strategy since the Ghost Squad years. The interests of justice were subordinated to the Yard's management needs, which were to deal secretly with its serious corruption problem at SERCS while outwardly preserving the image of the squad as an effective crime-buster. This meant presenting some detectives to the courts as witnesses of truth when the Ghost Squad and then CIBIC had disclosable intelligence to suggest they were corrupt, dishonest or unethical. By keeping the CPS out of the intelligence cell, anti-corruption chiefs were allowed to continue to mislead the courts and the public. And when all else failed the PII system could be relied on to continue the deception.

By November 1997, a few months before Egg Guney's appeal, some 23 SERCS officers were listed for interview under caution in relation to allegations ranging from missing exhibits and fabrication of evidence to perjury.

Kelly had been put on restricted duties a month earlier and sent to Bethnal Green police station because he was told SERCS had "lost confidence" in his integrity. Kelly says he was put on something called "the Townsend list" of suspect officers in north and east London. The secret blacklist was named after the area boss, deputy assistant commissioner John Townsend.[16] The Yard is still very sensitive about this because of the employment, judicial and human rights issues associated with secret blacklists. But a number of senior officers in the area confirm a list existed. One source says that in late 1997 he was asked to tell Martin Morgan he had failed his interview to join a proactive drugs squad in east London. The police source confirms it was explained to him that Morgan was on the Townsend list.

Morgan had received four complaints between 1992 and 1998. One concerned "an allegation of planted evidence". The most important is dated 6 May 1997 for "improper relationships" with informants.

Turning briefly to Keith Green, almost everything about his arrest in December 1997 as part of the 80 kilo cannabis sting was also kept from Egg's defence team in the week before the appeal. The CIB intelligence officer who arrested and interviewed Green was DI Stephen Bazzoni who had also been intimately involved in the first inquiry into the Guney tapes and whether detective DS Jim Gillan was behind any corrupt approaches.

Green says there was no attempt, throughout his 11 months on remand, or subsequently, to question him about the Guney case, either as a suspect or a witness. Intriguingly, in the same month Green was arrested, the CIB superintendent he says he told about the alleged Morgan/Gillan approach was removed from the anti-corruption squad. Detective superintendent Norman McNamara told us Roy Clark had expressed doubts about his integrity.[17]

When summarised, the way Egg Guney was treated is shocking. Since his arrest in September 1995 anti-corruption squad detectives had made repeated visits to prison to pump Egg for information, while all along allowing him to believe they were investigating his complaint.

First the Ghost Squad and then the CIB intelligence cell avoided PCA supervision and treated him as an intelligence source while they managed and manipulated the public image of the Yard's corruption problem.

Egg had given himself an insurance policy because he simply didn't trust the integrity of the anti-corruption crusade to get him out of prison. In June 1998, he wrote to the Criminal Cases Review Commission, a body set up to assume responsibilities that once rested with the Home Office for investigating "alleged and suspected miscarriages of justice" in England, Wales and Northern Ireland. The CCRC has powers to secure materials from the police and CPS.

The following year he also changed solicitors to Birnberg & Pierce, the miscarriage of justice specialists. Solicitor Tim Greene took over his case and supplied the CCRC with the limited information his client had from the police.

A lot had happened by mid-2001, but still no word from the CCRC or from Jarratt's investigation of Egg's complaint. Keith Green had been tried and acquitted and the Karagozlu crime syndicate was awaiting sentencing for the corruption and VAT fraud on a mobile phone company. "Inevitably much is hidden from us," solicitor Tim Greene wrote to the CCRC in May that year. He had also complained to the Yard about Jarratt's investigation. It was passed to CIB management, which appointed yet another detective from the Untouchables to investigate themselves.

The whole thing was absurd. This was now the third investigation since 1995, and again it wasn't being referred to the PCA. Furthermore, in March 2002, Jarratt was removed from his command pending an internal investigation into allegations of bullying, expenses fraud and assault brought by fellow officers. These remarkable events drove Tim Greene to write again to the CCRC asking what exactly was going on and what, if anything, they could disclose from their investigation, now in its fourth year.

UNTOUCHABLES

On 18 July the CCRC wrote back, 11 days after Martin Morgan was jailed for his part in the kidnap plot. Egg's case, said the CCRC, would be referred back to the Court of Appeal with a recommendation that the conviction was unsafe. By now he had served half his sentence and was almost eligible for parole. Although the CCRC had sent full reasons to the Appeal Court and CPS in a confidential annexe, Egg was told he could know almost nothing of how the decision was reached because these considerations were "sensitive". The Yard and CPS had invoked a law to keep secret all that it and NCIS had shown the CCRC.

The key phrase in the explanatory letter sent to Egg's lawyer was this: "The Commission had become aware of information which was available to neither the defence nor the prosecution at the time of Mr Guney's trial and appeal. That information amounts to evidence which substantially discredits the informant's handler . . . the information concerned might have caused the trial judge to come to a significantly different conclusion at [the PII] hearing."

Incredibly the CPS was still opposing the recommendation to quash the conviction. Tim Greene's fear of a cover-up in the making did not abate when the solicitor learned they had asked the Untouchables to make further inquiries into the case.

This tricky assignment from the CPS was given to detective inspector Adrian Harper. The Untouchable was one of Jarratt's boys who'd been brought onto the anti-corruption squad in 1998 with other members of the David Norris murder inquiry team. Harper had also debriefed supergrass Kevin Garner on Operation Ethiopia and was the number two on the recently concluded Martin Morgan investigation. He had also personally visited Egg in prison with Customs as part of the Karagozlu corruption inquiry. It could not therefore be said of Harper that he had little grasp of the uncomfortable background to Egg's case.

After four months the CPS made a remarkable volte-face. They wrote to Egg's lawyer in December 2002, saying "new sensitive material" unearthed by Harper had led them to conclude that "no sensible argument could be mounted to maintain the safety of [the] conviction". They would now not be opposing the appeal. It was a further three months before the Appeal Court was given that new material, and under very strict security conditions. The Untouchables and the CPS also notified the court of their intention to make a PII application to keep it all from Egg and the public.

On 15 May, Harper and detective constable Bill Maclean, both from

SECRET JUSTICE

the Intelligence Development Group, a re-branding of the old CIB intelligence cell, went into secret session with three Appeal Court judges.

Lord Justice Kennedy had previously indicated that "a fair amount" of what the Untouchables wanted kept secret was already in the public domain. This proved a false hope. Ten days later Egg returned, hoping to hear why his conviction was being quashed. It was a bleak day for open justice and democratic accountability of the police and the CPS.

The judgement indicated in the most guarded terms that "substantial doubt" had now been cast on the integrity of the police officers (in the plural) no longer serving, who compiled the intelligence report the day before Egg's arrest. Had the material been available at the time of the trial back in May 1996 it would inevitably have been abandoned, it said. The judgement wasn't read out. There was no apology. Egg emerged from Court 6 angry, confused and depressed. It was clear that had he not gone to the CCRC when he did, he would still be a convicted prisoner.

Why had CIB not disclosed the information that the CCRC and Court of Appeal found so persuasive? And why wasn't the highly sensitive information Harper found, which led the CPS to change its mind, disclosed earlier? Outside in the corridor Harper wouldn't be drawn on much, other than to confirm that the voices on the Ramadan Guney tapes were serving police officers. It was logical then that the Untouchables knew their names.

Media inquiries were steered away from the Flying Squad, Martin Morgan and Jimmy Karagozlu. Both the Yard and the CPS were happy to leave the impression the whole matter was to do with "unsubstantiated" allegations about Keith Green and not other corruption allegations they had sat on for over seven years.

This whole scandal is about disclosure, or to be precise, non-disclosure, from the Untouchables to the CPS; from the CPS to Egg's lawyers; and from the Courts to the public, who picked up the whole bill. The CPS is supposed to safeguard the interests of justice from those of the police. But in Egg's case it completely failed. The failure is remarkable because throughout his seven years in prison, disclosure had become the key issue for the criminal justice system.

Scotland Yard is a leading opponent of disclosure and nowhere has this been more dominant than in its dealings with the CPS during the anti-corruption crusade. The CPS had to fight to get the Operation Jackpot report into Stoke Newington released to it in 1992. The following year the Ghost Squad simply excluded the CPS from overseeing its secret activities, thereby making the issue of disclosure redundant.

UNTOUCHABLES

Ironically, Egg's appeal in 1996 led the CPS to set up something called "The Guney Group". Senior CPS lawyers and anti-corruption squad bosses debated over the next five years what should be disclosed to the defence about police officers who in effect have been disbelieved or criticised during a trial. Yet all the while they sat on intelligence that clearly cast doubt on the safety of Egg's conviction and quite possibly several other men and women wrongly imprisoned.

It was only when supergrass Terry McGuinness made allegations in May 1998 about the so called "first aid kits" that a role for the CPS in anti-corruption work was formalised. It followed a meeting in July that year between the deputy commissioner John Stevens, anti-corruption chiefs and the CPS, represented by Martin Polaine. He was already in charge of the recently created Visa Card team, which had just started advising the Untouchables on its covert operations.

Anti-corruption detectives began working with a new CPS Gold Card team to review the safety of all prosecutions by the Rigg Approach Flying Squad between 1988 and 1998. Superintendent Ian Russell represented the Yard in this endeavour. He had recently returned to the anti-corruption squad from Catford police station, where he served after being in charge of the Operation Jackpot debacle. The plan was that Russell and his men would delve into CIB's intelligence cell, and see what information should be disclosed to the CPS.

Polaine explains: "Visa Card would [then] feed the information around [suspect] officers to Gold Card in so far as they needed to know things for disclosure purposes. We would agree with them the ambit of disclosure they could give to defence solicitors. [It was a] balancing exercise of ensuring that every potential appellant had all the information they needed for appeal purposes. But equally if there were matters that remained sensitive they weren't made public."

However, according to a senior CPS source, there were concerns from prosecutors about the way CIB3 and its even more secretive sister, CIBIC, were approaching disclosure matters. Each unit had its own disclosure officer who liaised with Visa. But the CIB3 disclosure officer was not privy to CIBIC information. "This was a recipe for disaster," said the source. So the CPS insisted that there was one disclosure officer for both units. It also drafted a protocol which stated the anti-corruption squad must give Visa "at an early stage" information that allows it to address whether there is a conflict between an ongoing corruption operation and the rights of a defendant in a trial where targeted officers were giving evidence.

But Polaine was keen to stress that ultimately he and his CPS colleagues were entirely dependent on the Untouchables disclosing all that was relevant to any appeal. In other words they had to trust the integrity of the anti-corruption squad to put the interests of justice above its own and those of the Yard. The Guney case proves beyond doubt this trust was misplaced.

From the Guney Group came the formalisation of a secret blacklist of officers. It is a refinement of the so-called Townsend List. The blacklist is officially called the Service Confidence Policy and was formalised after a meeting of anti-corruption management on 28 June 2000. It is designed for those officers whose integrity is seriously doubted. These "concerns" are based on secret intelligence and information collated by the Untouchables, whether through phone-taps, surveillance, informants or public sources, like court cases.

For some, the trust of the commissioner is recoverable. For others it is an unofficial way of getting them to resign without embarrassing disciplinary hearings, court cases or employment tribunals, where the public, through the media, can get a better measure of corruption in the Yard.

Those on the secret blacklist are placed on restricted duties and are not allowed near proactive operations, sensitive databases or informants and in some cases the witness box, because the police simply don't regard them as witnesses of truth.

Every six months or so, the defective detective's case is reviewed by a senior Met civilian who is head of Workforce Deployment.[18] He assesses all the sensitive material. Some officers are taken off. Others are kept on. The entire basis of what led an officer to lose the commissioner's trust is rarely explained. Similarly, defence lawyers and members of the public are not allowed to know which of London's finest are or have been subject to the blacklist.

DS Jim Gillan, we were told by his friends and colleagues, was put on the blacklist while he was serving on the Fraud Squad. In summer 2003, he retired from the police. His friends say he was frustrated that his career in the force was stultified by the commissioner's unexplained loss of trust in his integrity.

We asked him a series of questions about the Guney case. Was he one of the anonymous callers who'd offered to sabotage the prosecution for money? Was he the mysterious "Home Office official"? Had he and Morgan corruptly approached fellow detective Keith Green? Had he tried to help Morgan and Costello onto the Fraud Squad? What relationship did he have with Jimmy Karagozlu? And in what circumstances had he left the police?

UNTOUCHABLES

Jim Gillan did not confirm or deny the corruption allegations. He simply declined to comment. Martin Morgan told us from prison: "I've got nothing to say. But it didn't happen."

The home secretary David Blunkett has refused an inquiry into this case, ludicrously suggesting Egg Guney could always make a complaint against the Yard and the CPS. Shortly after receiving this response, the Yard launched a fourth internal investigation into itself led by detective inspector Shaun Keep, formerly of the intelligence cell. At least this time there was PCA supervision by Nicola Williams.

Although sceptical of the value of making yet another formal complaint, on 11 November 2003 Egg's lawyers submitted a four-page letter to Keep and Williams in essence seeking an explanation for why "relevant information was withheld". The letter asked: "Why [was] there no disclosure at the time of the first appeal of what would form the basis five years later of the successful second appeal?" This was a reference to the arrest and prosecution of Keith Green. It went on: "There have been two substantial enquiries into complaints made by Mr Guney. We find it hard to understand why neither investigation uncovered the information which the CCRC, without the benefit of a police investigation, was able to uncover." The final paragraph was the most explosive: "There was an obvious failure to disclose information at the first reasonable opportunity and as a result Mr Guney served the whole of his sentence. We do not accept that no police officer is at fault for the fact that it took the CCRC to find out this information from police files and at no time until then had any police officer seen fit to inform Mr Guney that there was material that impacted upon the safety of his conviction."

It is telling that the Yard only sought supervision from the PCA when the "watchdog" was withering on the vine and about to be replaced by the so-called Independent Police Complaints Commission. There will be some continuity because Nicola Williams, a barrister, is now one of the twelve IPCC commissioners who guard its independence from the police. This however brings us to the heart of the paradox where the police are policing the police.

Nicola Williams' supervision of the internal inquiry into the Guney case will have to consider Roy Clark's role. But Clark is now the IPCC's director of investigation. All of which would appear to mean he will either be advising on an investigation into himself, or alternatively, Clark's former colleagues in the Met will be investigating him and other colleagues.

23

A LURKING DOUBT

In March 2000 we received an anonymous letter from someone who appeared to be a serving or retired Scotland Yard detective. Our mystery pen pal accepted that some officers under investigation were undoubtedly guilty and that corruption needed rooting out, but took issue with the double standards employed by the Yard and the suitability of some of its gamekeepers. He was also concerned with how the Untouchables were secretly setting the range on their anti-corruption radar so that certain dark corners of Scotland Yard would not be "scoped". Of special concern, he said, were those anti-corruption detectives who had once been through the revolving door between Stoke Newington police station and the Rigg Approach Flying Squad.

He directed us to one case in particular – the conviction one decade earlier of a black man called Ira Thomas. A cursory glance revealed Thomas had received 12 years for shooting a white drug dealer at point-blank range following a pub dispute.

This was a Stoke Newington case and after a few calls we discovered something rather interesting. In February 1992, the Appeal Court had wholeheartedly quashed Thomas's conviction by overturning the jury's verdict. This was almost unprecedented. The judgement was scathing of the prosecution case and stopped just short of saying Thomas had been fitted up, something the defendant had maintained all along.

More intriguingly, the cops involved in this miscarriage of justice were now on opposite sides of the war on corruption. It didn't take long to establish there was a good deal of bad blood over the perceived sanctimony of those ex-Stoke Newington cops who had donned white hats and were now singing from the anti-corruption hymn sheet.

Singled out were DAC Roy Clark and one of his protégés, detective superintendent Brian Moore. Both officers were involved with the Ira Thomas case. However, by the time we had received the anonymous note, Moore had left the Untouchables and was by then in charge of the most high-profile murder inquiry in the UK – the hunt for Jill Dando's killer. The BBC presenter had been shot at close range on her doorstep. Barry George was eventually charged after a forensic scientist found one speck of firearm residue in his coat pocket. The case split the public, the media, the legal establishment and the Yard. Critics of the prosecution argued it was based on half-baked circumstantial evidence and frenzied media and political pressure.

We then learned that a serving detective had anonymously alerted George's defence to the spooky parallels with the case of Ira Thomas. He too was charged on the basis of a few specks of firearm residue found on his coat, also seized many months after the shooting. Coincidentally, the same forensic scientist had tested both garments.

The Jill Dando case ran parallel to another high-profile prosecution led by Moore: the conviction of corrupt Flying Squad detectives from Rigg Approach. Their appeal was eventually dismissed in a turgid judgment handed down in February 2003. But buried in the dense legalese was one explosive paragraph. It referred to a recent statement by supergrass Terry McGuinness, who had worked at Stoke Newington on the Ira Thomas case alongside Moore and Clark.

During his debriefing, McGuinness had unburdened his soul of every crooked act he knew or did while in the police force. At least that is what the Yard claimed. However the supergrass was now alleging that CIB3 didn't want him to mention his time at Stoke Newington "to avoid embarrassment to one of his handlers".[1] McGuinness's soul was tortured, not purged. He felt the Untouchables were not interested in exposing the fit-up culture he and many others had been an integral part of. His allegations against the Untouchables cried out for independent investigation, but the Yard confirms none has ever been launched.

After McGuinness was released into a witness protection programme we met with the troubled supergrass and over a modest libation asked him a few clarifying questions.

A LURKING DOUBT

What were you referring to in your statement, Terry?
"The Ira Thomas case," he replied.
Whom did CIB3 want you to avoid embarrassing?
"Brian Moore."

The Anchor & Hope in Stoke Newington is a tiny pub at the bottom of a dipping cul-de-sac by the River Lea. In the summer, regulars can be found chilling on the towpath overlooking the marshes.

Thirty-five-year-old Freddy Brett was not a regular, but he liked a drink. He was a low-level drug dealer who broke the golden rule and got high, too high, on his own supply. He then committed burglaries to feed his habit. But when his shit was together Brett was considered good company. He sometimes worked as a roadie for the Mutant Waste Co, an anarcho-punk band.

The night of 30 June 1988 was one of those sticky ones where the Anchor & Hope looked more like a bar in Benidorm. Brett was at the top of the cul-de-sac when a man approached him pointing a 9mm automatic pistol. The first three shots missed, so Brett closed on the gunman, shouting cockily, "You're not much good, you can't even shoot straight." The two men fought but the gunman got the upper hand and shot Brett through the thigh at point-blank range. He could have finished him off.

Wendy Ellison was watching from her kitchen window while calling the police. And after seeing a tall black man wearing a light-coloured coat walk away, she went to Brett's aid. He was calm and lying on the pavement. "You knew who that was, didn't you?" she said to him.

"Yes," he replied. Wendy returned to her kitchen to get a tea towel for the gunshot wound. When two police officers arrived she urged Brett to identify the gunman but he told her to mind her own business and said he'd deal with it himself.

The next morning detective sergeant Gordon Livingstone, the head of the Stoke Newington crime squad, visited Brett at the local hospital. DC Terry McGuinness went with him.

Brett was already on bail for burglary and drug offences. Livingstone thought the shooting might be related. But the victim refused to name his attacker, claiming he feared for his life and that of his young daughter who lived with his estranged girlfriend.

Livingstone didn't quite believe his story so no security was put around Brett. But after eight weeks of intermittent hospital visits, the detectives eventually got a name from Brett, if still no statement.

A special bulletin was put on the Police National Computer asking

UNTOUCHABLES

officers to look out for: IRA THOMAS, CRO 11060-7BE, b HACKNEY 18-1-61, 5ft 9in, WELL BUILT. IS VIOLENT, ARMED WITH FIREARM, SHOULD BE APPROACHED WITH EXTREME CAUTION AND MAY BE IN UNLAWFUL POSSESSION OF CONTROLLED DRUGS.

"I could have taken Hackney if I wanted to but I'm not a leader of men," says Ira, sitting in his east London council flat, building a spliff. His words aren't the pathetic boasts of a wannabe hard man. As a young man, Ira Thomas was a career criminal – strong, proud, connected and staunch.

When we first met, he'd just turned 40. His criminal past was more than a decade behind him, but the demons are still in his head. The dope takes the edge off his post-traumatic stress disorder, a condition his doctor tells him developed out of his life of violence, crime and looking over his shoulder. Ira's hands are scarred and shaking. His muscular upper body is an ugly patchwork of stab wounds and crooked bones from pointless fights over respect and territory.

He fears for many of today's young inner-city black kids who've got a gun where their dick should be and dick for brains. He teaches his sons how to look after themselves, but most of all he teaches them to study. His eldest son has just got into drama school and his youngest is shaping up nicely. So too is his 18-year-old daughter, who's in the studio learning to produce some homegrown hip-hop talent.

Ira's mum would be proud of the way he brings up his kids. He never gave her much to be proud of when she was alive. When he thinks about it the tears well in his eyes. "I never told my mum I loved her before she died. She was always there for me, getting me out of trouble. I never said sorry for all the grief I caused her. She travelled all over the country to the different prisons I was in. She kept telling me to give up crime and I ignored her."

Her death in March 1999 broke Ira. He was off work and having bereavement counselling. He'd just had a new baby daughter, his fourth, with a new partner with whom he wasn't getting on. One day, one of his closest friends walked into his flat just as he was putting a shotgun in his mouth. "I had phoned the kids and said goodbye. I opened my eyes and saw Mark. I had the shotgun on a hair trigger. Somehow he snatched it away but the barrel went off. It damaged my hearing in one ear and left a hole in the roof."

The Thomas kids, all ten of them, were known around the Springfield Estate in Hackney as people who didn't take any racist shit.

A LURKING DOUBT

Ira's family were particularly close to an Irish family who lived nearby. "Old man Quigley taught me everything I know about hunting with dogs, trapping and snares. We used to go after church. Walthamstow Marshes was teeming with wildlife like pheasant and hares."

Ira became a top-class thief – of the warehouse kind – but he blew his money as soon as he got it. If there is one point when he became a serious thorn in the side of Hackney police it was after the "Battle of Springfield" in April 1986. Thirty of his mates were drinking at the Robin Hood pub before going to a party. The police turned up and insisted they left. Outside a fight erupted and Ira and some of his friends were arrested for assault and jailed for six months. But the conviction was quashed on appeal when independent witnesses, including the landlord, complained about the police's behaviour.

By the second summer of love in 1987, Ira and a friend were doing security for raves in north London backed by the Adams crime family. "They put up the money for the sound system, right down to the space cakes. Our job was to look after their ecstasy dealers and eject the others. There was hardly any trouble, which is a good thing, because everyone was so loved-up and so were we."

Around this time the Stoke Newington drugs squad was paying particular attention to the Anchor & Hope. They had an observation post in the barges opposite the pub, a detective told us.

Ira knew a lot of serious dealers but says he was not involved. He was trying to go straight in 1988. Fatherhood, the fight with the police and a near-fatal stabbing of two of his friends had caused him to re-evaluate his life. He had started working part-time with his girlfriend's brother renovating hotels and was scaling down his nights out with the boys, opting to live at her place in a neighbouring borough to Hackney. But Ira Thomas's past was about to catch up with him.

On the afternoon of 25 April 1989 two Stoke Newington officers acting on a tip-off arrested Ira in the Anchor & Hope for the attempted murder ten months earlier of Freddy Brett.

Terry McGuinness had been left with the case when Livingstone transferred to the Flying Squad at Rigg Approach one month after the shooting. McGuinness didn't show out, but privately he felt there was "little evidence" against Ira. He searched Ira's flat, in front of his prisoner, looking for a 9mm gun. Nothing was found and on the way back in the car McGuinness told Ira his inquiries were complete. Back at the station he wrote an entry in the custody record at 4.15 p.m. that the matter had been "dealt with".

This was not to everyone's liking. Brian Moore, then an acting detective inspector, had taken over the crime squad from Livingstone. He thought there was more mileage in the case. "[Moore] was up and coming," says one former colleague. "He had served at Tottenham and was considered competent. Stoke Newington was a good posting for detectives. It was a nice one to have on your CV, like Tottenham, Brixton or Harlesden. If you served successfully in any of those places, then you could work anywhere in London because of the high crime rate, the atmosphere – sometimes it was like working in Beirut."

At 7.25 p.m. Moore corrected the custody record in bold black ink in a way that looked like he was rebuking McGuinness. It read: "With reference to the entry timed at 4.15 p.m. I have now traced a number of statements, which were not available to detective constable McGuinness at the time he advised the custody officer that this matter had been dealt with. The grievous bodily harm and firearms offences have NOT been concluded and my enquiries are ongoing."

Instead of asking McGuinness to search Ira's flat again, Moore sent two less experienced PCs, Peter McCulloch and Dave Edwards. Their specific instructions were to look for any light-coloured coat of the kind seen by witness Wendy Ellison. Meanwhile, Moore and another officer visited Ira in the cells. What happened next is fiercely contested.

Moore claimed in the custody record that at 9.02 p.m. Ira refused to come out for an interview, admitted to shooting Brett but refused to sign the officers' notes recording the confession and instead demanded to see an unnamed solicitor. Moore called Les Brown & Co. The choice is interesting because ten years later Moore ended up investigating Brown for corruption offences involving one of his closest police friends.

The custody record states that at 10.48 p.m. Les Brown called the police station and said he would contact Moore in the morning. It also says Ira was checked hourly and recorded as being asleep from midnight until he was given breakfast at 8.45 a.m.

It is an abiding mystery how Ira's version of what happened on the night of 25 April was so radically different. He denies making any admission and accuses Moore of verballing him. Ira says he also specifically asked him for his usual solicitors Goodman Ray, who'd recently represented him during the "Battle of Springfield" trial and appeal. Ira also distinctly remembers three people coming into his cell on the night of 25 April. None of them is recorded on the custody sheet. The first person was Les Brown whom he says he told to "fuck off" when he realised he wasn't from Goodman Ray. Ira says a white man claiming to be a fraudster was then placed in his cell. "He kept asking me what I was in for and did I do it? I was suspicious he was

A LURKING DOUBT

undercover police so after ten or fifteen minutes I demanded that he should be removed. Then at about two a.m. they put this black guy in the cell. He had this big bag of charlie [cocaine] so we sat there and caned it." Ira recalls the black man saying he'd been done for theft. He became suspicious when after a few lines his cellmate started asking questions. "I'd seen him around the area and I just asked him, 'Are you a grass?'" The man said no and Ira stared him out until he shouted to the custody sergeant he wanted to be removed.

That night the two PCs entered Ira's flat when no one was there and returned to the station with two garments. One was a Humphrey Bogart-style beige mac, the other a camel-haired coat, which they handed to Moore. The handling of this search would become a key issue at the trial.

The next morning, 26 April, Ira was interviewed. His chosen legal representative, Anne Chiarini, was present. He gave a full account and denied knowing or shooting Brett. When the two coats were shown, Ira identified them as his flatmate's. The police released him on bail to return in six weeks.

But on 6 June Moore rang Chiarini to tell her no firearms residue had been found on the two coats. These are the microscopic particles released from the ammunition in a cloud of gas and smoke when a gun is fired. The specks attach to anything, clothing, skin and hard surfaces, in a roughly six-foot radius from the gun. Firearms residue on the outer surface of clothing is only likely to remain for up to twelve hours and then falls away.

No longer on bail, Ira started working with his dad as a wood-turner earning £124 per week in a shop on the Hackney Road. But two weeks later the police arrested him again, this time for rape.

Ira admitted having consensual sex with a young French woman he'd recently met in the pub, but felt he was being set up. He'd always been puzzled that when she left his flat in the morning two men picked her up in a car parked outside. Chiarini also thought the timing of the rape allegation was somewhat suspicious. Ira was once again bailed awaiting the rape trial. His girlfriend wasn't exactly happy about his infidelity, but she agreed to stand by him.

Then, early on 2 August, Moore arrived at Ira's front door with three other detectives. One was DC Martin Morgan, who re-arrested Ira for the attempted murder of Freddy Brett. At the police station, Moore and superintendent Roy Clark discussed the case. Clark then entered a note in the custody record at 8.43 a.m. It said he had read the file, spoken to Ira and authorised his further detention for questioning.

During the interview, Moore explained the developments that led to Ira's re-arrest. Firstly, Brett had recently made a long, detailed statement naming him as the man who shot him. Secondly, a further forensic test on the beige mac had been carried out because apparently the scientist hadn't rolled down the cuffs the first time. Having done so, firearm residue was discovered in each cuff consistent with the bullet casing found at the scene of the crime.

Moore: "Is there anything you wish to say about this evidence?"

Thomas: "Yeah. You're talking bullshit, the reason being I don't own a beige coat and you know it."

Moore: "Is there anything else you wish to say, Ira?"

Thomas: "Yes. I'd like to make a formal complaint that you, DI Moore, are trying to fit me up. I've nothing else to say."

Moore: "Your complaint is noted. You will be charged shortly with the attempted murder of Frederick Brett."

Chiarini, who was present throughout the interview, had a private consultation with her client and persuaded him not to pursue the allegation against Moore at this stage. Chiarini didn't take to Moore. She remembers him as "a stereotypical CID officer of that era. The flash suit, he looked like a City trader." Relations between Stoke Newington cops and defence lawyers (except Les Brown, of course) were "more confrontational" than nowadays, she recalls.

Ira was remanded to Pentonville Prison. Moore had opposed bail because of Ira's previous criminal record and told the magistrates he was also investigating him for rape. This, however, came to trial soon afterwards in January 1990. The jury quickly acquitted Ira after the French woman imploded on the stand. "She also admitted two men had picked her up outside my flat but didn't identify them," says Ira, which left his defence wondering if the cops had tried to fit him up.

For the forthcoming attempted murder trial, Chiarini and defence barrister David Farrer QC set about examining Brett's statement and the forensic scientist's report. It soon became apparent Moore's case didn't bear scrutiny. He had recently transferred to Bethnal Green police station to work under a new mentor, John Grieve. This left McGuinness holding the reins of a prosecution that had never impressed him.

Stoke Newington police were initially reluctant to release a full copy of the April 1989 custody report. When they relented, Chiarini passed it to Farrer with a note remarking how it differed significantly from an earlier version they'd seen. It did not have the "ring of truth", she wrote. Farrer agreed.

A LURKING DOUBT

When Ira saw the various versions of the custody record he went ballistic. The visit by Les Brown and the two cellmates were missing. Comments had been falsely attributed to him, he told his lawyers.

As the trial approached, his defence also developed suspicions about the timing of four crucial events in 1989: the second positive forensic test on 14 June, followed by Brett's lenient sentence for the drugs and burglary matter on 28 June, Ira's arrest for rape the same day and then Brett's statement naming him on 18 July.

Brett's solicitor Robert Pryce told us he strongly suspected his client felt he needed to co-operate with the police because of the burglary charges and other matters hanging over him. It emerged Brett had not been pursued over a bag of amphetamine and stolen giro cheques found on him by the police when he was shot.

Ira's trial opened on 19 March 1990 at the Old Bailey. He faced three charges of attempted murder, causing grievous bodily harm with intent and possessing a firearm with intent to endanger life.

Brett was the first prosecution witness. There follows a summary of his account.

On the night of the shooting he was taking his daughter back to her mother Jackie's house. The couple had split in 1986 after three years. During that time Brett claimed Jackie had once confided that Ira raped her when she was fourteen years old. En route to Jackie's, Brett said he stopped at the Anchor & Hope with a friend called Danny. They drank at least four pints. Ira was also there and confronted him over the way he was treating his dog. Brett told Ira to fuck off and said he raped young girls. Ira then left the pub. Brett followed shortly. At the top of the road, he spotted Ira in a distinctive green and cream Mini. Brett told Danny to take his daughter home. The car approached, Ira got out wearing a beige mac and fired a gun across the car roof. Brett thought they were blanks so ran around towards Ira brandishing a bottle of beer. A fight ensued and Ira pinned him to the pavement. He fired at close range into Brett's thigh, although he could have put one between his eyes. Ira then drove off.

David Farrer QC dismantled Brett's account, which he suggested was inherently implausible and manufactured with the police's help. For starters, Jackie had died from cancer in December 1988, six months after the shooting. So the core motivation underpinning Brett's account – the alleged rape by Ira – could not be corroborated. Also, if her safety was the reason Brett didn't initially name Ira, why did he wait seven months after her death to make a statement to the police?

UNTOUCHABLES

Danny never appeared as a witness to support Brett. No one in the pub remembered a row over a dog. And the police could not connect Ira to a green and cream Mini. In fact two eyewitnesses said the shooter walked away from the crime scene.

Brett also contradicted police witnesses. He accepted playing a bizarre "naming game" with the detectives in hospital. But he said DS Livingstone had got the name by prompting him with photographs and police files, including one with Ira Thomas's name.

Livingstone denied any prompting. However, Farrer pointed out the detective's crime report entry suggested otherwise. It read: "The victim confirms that is the suspect, Ira Thomas, but he refuses to name him in the statement." Whatever the truth, it all looked bad for the prosecution. But much worse was to come.

The defence had learned that Brett made a compensation claim while he was in hospital directly after the shooting. It was unsuccessful because he hadn't co-operated with the police. But after making his lengthy statement to Brian Moore one year later, Brett re-submitted a new claim. In evidence, Moore accepted it was "likely" he discussed with Brett how co-operation could influence the outcome of his compensation claim, but he insisted there was "no bribery, no deals, no inducements".

Moore's failure to ensure an independent witness was present during the second search for the coats also caused serious problems for PCs McCulloch and Edwards. They said they entered Ira's flat with front door keys, but couldn't recall how they came by them. Ira maintained he had given the keys to his flatmate when he was arrested. So how did they appear on the custody record?

The officers also said they were told to go straight to the bedroom where they found the beige mac and camel coat inside an enclosed wardrobe. But Ira and his flatmate produced evidence that the wardrobe was in fact a makeshift rail with no doors.

The officers said they put the coats in separate brown evidence bags with a transparent panel, but didn't have the means to seal them. Mysteriously, the journey back to the police station took three times longer. The officers claimed they had decided on the spur of the moment to speak for the first time to the landlord of the Anchor & Hope, ten months after the shooting. But this detour and interview was never recorded in any note or report.

Moore told the court he had sealed the evidence bags that night at the police station. All three officers swore the coats were never removed from these bags until the forensic scientist examined them weeks later. But Ira and Anne Chiarini said when the coats were produced in the interview the day after the search they were in clear plastic bags.

The prosecution had opened its case on the compelling basis that three specks of firearms residue were found in the left and right cuffs. But under cross-examination Robin Keeley, the forensic scientist, dropped a bombshell. Only one speck, he said, was found in the cuff and two on the outer surface of the beige mac, exactly where he'd expect it to have fallen away within twelve hours of a gun being fired. Inexplicably, it had remained there for ten months, an extraordinary feat when considering the evidence from Ira's flatmate, who owned the mac. He said he had worn, been sick on and machine-washed it weeks before the two officers seized it. This was never disputed.

Keeley told the jury he would not have accepted the mac for testing without Moore's assurance it had been seized undisturbed for a long time in the wardrobe. It is hard to understand how anyone could have given the scientist such an assurance.

Keeley had instant recall of the case when we interviewed him 11 years after the trial. The initial test for firearms residue, he told us, had been botched by his assistant and then re-done by him. But this had never been disclosed to the defence at the time of the trial.

It was Farrer's closing contention to the jury that contamination, accidental or otherwise, could have occurred the night the mac was seized. Judge Herrod QC appeared to agree in large measure, calling the scientific evidence "insubstantial" in his highly balanced summing up, which did not shy away from pointing out other major flaws in the prosecution case.[2]

Nevertheless, after four and a half hours of deliberations, the jury returned with a remarkable majority guilty verdict.[3] Ira's mum collapsed. "She was in bits. I shouted across the courtroom, 'Get up, woman! Don't let them see you like this.'" His girlfriend was also crying as the judge, reluctantly, passed a 12-year sentence.

Farrer told us: "I was absolutely stunned when he was convicted, and I think the judge was too. He wrote to me saying you will obviously be appealing. It was an extraordinary decision, we tried to get out at half-time and the judge was very concerned that he had let it go . . . there were grave doubts about the police. We felt the CPS and, I am afraid to say, prosecuting counsel unduly pressed for a prosecution . . . the whole thing certainly stank."

By the time his appeal was heard on 13 February 1992, Ira had spent two and a half years in prison. He didn't tell his mother about the hearing in case it went against him.

It was hard to believe the prosecution and police opposed the appeal. Stoke Newington police station was in the middle of the Operation Jackpot corruption crisis and a row of cases were queuing to be quashed by the Appeal Court, largely because of growing doubts around the credibility of certain police officers. One was PC Peter McCulloch, who had found the beige mac. The jury had disbelieved his evidence in a recent trial where the defendant was acquitted after alleging drugs were planted on him.[4]

The Appeal Court judgement in the Ira Thomas case was withering about the police and the forensic science. Brett's account was dismissed as "simply ludicrous" and the "so-called forensic evidence" labelled as "wholly unavailing".

It is very rare indeed for the Appeal Court to overturn the jury's verdict, but the three judges were "very uneasy" about the case and had "lurking doubts" about the way it was put together.[5]

Still, no one in the prosecution saw this stinging judicial criticism as reason enough to investigate how such a miscarriage of justice had occurred. Had there been an independent inquiry into Stoke Newington corruption, investigators would have heard from key eyewitnesses like Wendy Ellison. She told us she felt "pressured" by Moore to choose between the two coats he brought to her house weeks after Ira was charged. Neither was the coat she saw on the night of the shooting. But she was asked which one was more like it, and she selected the beige mac because it was lighter than the camel hair coat.

After the trial, Ira's solicitors began a civil action against the police. In March 1993 they took a statement from Lee Pritchard, who grew up on the same estate as Ira and was known to Stoke Newington police.

Pritchard said two constables detained him at the police station within days of Ira's arrest. He alleged they assaulted him and then offered him heroin in return for giving false evidence against Ira. The two officers wanted Pritchard to say he had seen Ira on the night of the shooting in the same road and carrying a gun. The offer, Pritchard said, was repeated on several occasions as the trial approached.[6]

At the time the civil action was being prepared, Roy Clark had left Stoke Newington and moved to SO11 on promotion to set up the Ghost Squad. Brian Moore's career similarly took off. He was identified as having the right stuff for anti-corruption work. Moore

A LURKING DOUBT

refuses to discuss claims that when he was posted to the New Southgate SERCS office he acted as a "sleeper" for the Ghost Squad.

In 1998, Roy Clark put Moore in charge of the key corruption probe into the Flying Squad – Operation Ethiopia. Though he never served at Rigg Approach, Moore knew many of the detectives he was now investigating because they had previously worked at Stoke Newington. Operation Ethiopia would reunite Moore with Terry McGuinness, albeit in very different circumstances since they last worked together on the Ira Thomas case.

The direction of the corruption probe depended in large measure on the debriefing of McGuinness and his fellow supergrass Kevin Garner. McGuinness had the strong impression the Yard wasn't interested in exposing the fit-up culture of noble cause corruption because there were too many poachers turned gamekeepers in the Untouchables.

A thorough investigation of Rigg Approach had to go back through the revolving door into Stoke Newington. But this had been successfully welded shut during Operation Jackpot. McGuinness, it appears, was willing to help prise it open but says he found little enthusiasm during the debriefing. So he decided to test the Untouchables' integrity and see how far they would go not to revisit Stoke Newington. "I said [to my debriefers]: 'If you want to speak to me about Stoke Newington, get Brian [Moore] down here to speak to me.' And of course I never saw him after that."

It was the Ira Thomas case that most troubled McGuinness, he told us. "The [beige] raincoat caused me concern because I hadn't seen it or found it [when I searched the flat]. Going on from that was the concern that I'd heard, be it from Brian [or someone else], about too much [firearms] residue [on the mac] and that it was still there after a long period of time."

These concerns were not new. McGuinness had expressed his reservations at the trial. Eight years later and now a supergrass, supposedly for a "no hiding place" anti-corruption squad, he still harboured the same concerns. But McGuinness felt the Untouchables didn't want to know what he had to say and that the man in overall charge, Brian Moore, was avoiding him.

As part of the Flying Squad corruption probe, Moore was also responsible for investigating three suspended detectives whom he had also worked with on the Ira Thomas case – Gordon Livingstone, John Moore and Colin Evans – and the lawyer, Les Brown, whom Moore had originally tried to introduce as Thomas's legal representative.

UNTOUCHABLES

In November 1999, Brian Moore eventually left the Untouchables on promotion as a detective chief superintendent. His first job was to oversee the hunt for Jill Dando's killer.

Within an hour of Dando's murder on 28 April 1999 Downing Street issued a statement of sympathy and shock. William Hague, the opposition leader, added more pathos. Finally, home secretary Jack Straw reminded the Commons how much the BBC presenter had done for the fight against crime. Dando had been the new face of *Crimewatch* since 1995. Catching her killer quickly was intimately linked to restoring Scotland Yard's reputation, which was in tatters.

The timing of the murder could not have been worse, coming just two months after publication of the excoriating Stephen Lawrence Inquiry report. Although mainly about institutional racism, the report also exposed severe problems with the way officers investigated murders, regardless of colour.

One of the post-Lawrence reforms was the creation of a new "murder" manual for senior officers and the appointment of a detective chief superintendent to oversee the inquiry. Enter Brian Moore on 6 December. Detective chief inspector Hamish Campbell had day-to-day charge of the murder hunt, codenamed Operation Oxborough, but was answerable to Moore and another shadow warrior in the anti-corruption crusade, DAC Bill Griffiths.

Despite a massive £250,000 reward from two tabloids and one anonymous businessman, when Moore took over not one of the Yard's thousands of registered informants had produced any valuable intelligence of an Underworld connection. Similarly, Oxborough had largely eliminated Dando's family, friends, lovers and colleagues from its inquiries.

The murder investigation was at an impasse. Moore's anti-corruption experience was helpful in attempting to plug unauthorised leaks. The Oxborough team were warned, says DCI Campbell, that anyone leaking to the media would be sacked.

John McVicar, the armed robber turned scribe, was working at the now defunct *Punch*, owned at the time of the Dando murder by Harrods boss Mohammed Al-Fayed. McVicar's *Punch* articles led Moore and Campbell to launch a leak inquiry.

However, CIB was already investigating allegations of a so-called "Hamper Squad" of serving officers abusing their power to arrest and harass employees whom Fayed suspected of aiding the Lonrho tycoon Tiny Rowland, his bitter rival since the battle to buy Harrods in 1985.

A LURKING DOUBT

CIB were told Fayed had a list of police officers in stations around Harrods – the Dando inquiry was run from nearby Belgravia police station – who received free hampers and also shopped without digging too deeply in their pockets. A former member of Fayed's security team, Bob Loftus, told us he gave CIB the names of serving officers who received such bribes. But no one was prosecuted.

Loftus had joined forces with Tiny Rowland after Fayed sacked him. He also told CIB about repeated break-ins of a safety deposit box held by Rowland at Harrods. Fayed and others were arrested in 1998 but not charged. The Harrods owner later paid £1.4 million in damages to Rowland's widow. But the PCA upheld his complaint over the way the security box investigation was conducted.[7]

All this was occurring while DCS Brian Moore sought to identify *Punch*'s police source. McVicar properly refuses to identify whether he was the same detective constable later disciplined for disobeying a lawful order and failing to disclose contact with the media.[8]

At the beginning of 2000, the entire suspect list in the Dando murder was revised. By March, Barry George's name was near the top. He was an obviously delusional, narcissistic suspect who suffered from petit mal epilepsy, characterised by "absences" during the day. The epilepsy had caused learning difficulties for George at school and an attention deficit he carried into adulthood.

When his flat was searched on 17 April, a three-quarter length Cecil Gee blue overcoat was seized. The flat was a mix between a magpie's nest and rat's lair. It hadn't been cleaned for months. By happy coincidence, the search was ordered days before the first anniversary of Dando's death. The press was briefed that the dominant view of the inquiry was settling on an unnamed gun nut/obsessive loner. DCI Campbell reinforced this during an anniversary appeal on *Crimewatch*.

Inexplicably, the Cecil Gee coat was not delivered to Robin Keeley at the Forensic Science Service until 2 May. Three days later he told Campbell that one speck of firearms residue found inside the left pocket was consistent with those discharged from the gun that killed Dando. The forensic scientist would later tell the court that the speck could have come from the Dando bullet or any other bullet with similar components, which were by no means uncommon.

No particle of firearms residue is unique like a fingerprint. But it was the break the Yard was looking for. No firearms residue or gun-modification tools were found during a further search of George's flat to support the one, isolated speck found in his coat twelve months after the shooting. This microscopic "nugget" was held back until the last moment of George's three-day interrogation. He told the police he had no idea how it got into his coat pocket. The Oxborough team was unmoved and on 28 May charged George with the murder of Jill Dando. The press went crazy. A weight was lifted off the Yard's shoulders.

However, the case had a fundamental flaw. Incredibly, before forensic testing the coat was first taken to a police studio where it was photographed on a tailor's dummy. Firearms had previously been photographed at the same studio – raising the issue of accidental contamination. Whose decision it was to photograph the coat has never been properly resolved. A detective sergeant, Andy Rowell, later said in court that DCI Campbell made the decision, but he denied it. DCS Moore won't discuss his role in the Dando inquiry with us.

It took another year before the trial of the new Millennium started at the Old Bailey in May 2001. In his opening speech Orlando Pownall, senior Treasury Counsel, told the jury the one speck was "compelling evidence of [George's] guilt". A defence expert, however, was produced to say the idea that one particle is evidence was a unique suggestion and in other circumstances forensic scientists would not even have reported its presence to the police. Privately, Keeley felt the police had been "stupid" not to take the Cecil Gee coat straight to his lab.[9]

During the trial a man who identified himself only as "Mr February" called the chambers of George's barrister, Michael Mansfield QC. The caller was a serving detective who had followed the Dando prosecution and wanted to make the defence aware of similarities with the Ira Thomas case. We know the identity of "Mr February" but he has asked to remain anonymous. He felt it would have been "too risky" to identify himself to Mansfield because "my life in the force would have been made hell". In truth, Mr February was motivated in large measure by his dislike for the double standards of certain senior Untouchables. But he did come up with a strong point. He suggested that Mansfield should ask the officers on the search of George's flat whether they were registered to hold firearms at home, because accidental contamination could also come from this route.

We discovered that DC Martin Morgan – awaiting trial for kidnap offences – had also ensured Barry George's defence team knew of the parallels with the Ira Thomas case. Morgan appeared to be sending a barbed signal to CIB3 ahead of his own corruption trial that there was more where that came from.

Mansfield understood the significance of the Thomas case and had serious concerns about the way it had been put together. But he couldn't use it in George's defence for some cogent reasons. Firstly, had he attacked the bona fides of the police officers, his own client's criminal record, including a sexual assault on a woman in a doorway, would have to be disclosed to the jury. Secondly, his defence around the one speck found on the Cecil Gee coat was accidental contamination, not plant. As it turned out, in the prosecution's closing speech the speck was relegated from compelling evidence to mere corroboration.

After five days of deliberations, the guilty verdict on 2 July came as a shock to Mansfield. There was no confession, no gun, highly circumstantial forensic evidence that could have been contaminated by the police, no positive ID evidence of George, no motive, no evidence of an interest or obsession with Dando and no evidence he had fired a gun of the kind that killed the TV presenter.

Grounds for appeal were drafted within weeks. The police and prosecution were accused of turning non-identifications into positive identifications. The second ground relied on the Ira Thomas case "because of similarities in relation to the actual forensic evidence and the way it had been used", George's solicitor, Marilyn Etienne, told us.

Judges called for the dusty Thomas file from storage to consider these points. But on 29 July 2002, the appeal was dismissed and George returned to complete his life sentence with no minimum tariff.

On 7 March 2003, Ira Thomas's lawyers wrote to the Home Office seeking compensation for his client under a new Miscarriages Ex Gratia Scheme. Tony Murphy of Bindman & Partners argued that Ira's wrongful conviction was due to "serious default" by the Stoke Newington police investigation, the Forensic Science Laboratory and the CPS. He wrote: "The deficiencies in the way in which this [firearms residue] evidence was presented at Court constitutes in our submission serious defaults in itself. What is more concerning however is the fact that the findings of the forensic scientist strongly suggests that the purported positioning of the residue of the fired weapon on a coat supposedly owned by Mr Thomas was fabricated by police officers involved in the investigation. There can be no other explanation as to why two of the three particles found would have remained on this garment so long after the discharge of the firearm.

"A number of key officers involved in the prosecution of Mr Thomas were subsequently discredited, and in some cases convicted at the Old Bailey. This lends a strong inference to the fact that any concerns regarding police methods in obtaining identification of Mr Thomas and/or in fabricating ballistic evidence were well founded."

McGuinness aside, the roll call of convicted, disciplined or suspect detectives associated with the Ira Thomas case is extraordinary. Equally extraordinary is that the anti-corruption detectives investigating them are ultimately responsible for this miscarriage of justice.

DS Gordon Livingstone was suspended in January 1998 as part of the Rigg Approach corruption probe, including the first aid kit allegations. He was cleared and reinstated in October 2000. But the Untouchables put him on the secret blacklist without telling him what the doubts about his integrity were. Livingstone carried out restricted duties until retiring in October 2003. He believes he was blacklisted because he continued to support many of his Flying Squad colleagues.

DC Martin Morgan pleaded guilty in July 2002 to a serious corruption offence and is now serving six years. DC John Moore was suspended in January 1998 as part of the Rigg Approach corruption probe. He was later required to resign following disciplinary proceedings concerning a separate investigation.

Detectives Peter McCulloch and Dave Edwards are still serving. Freddy Brett is dead.

Brian Moore was made a commander in October 2003. Weeks later we sent him a detailed list of questions. The Yard's Director of Legal Services, David Hamilton, replied on Moore's behalf. He informed us there would be no answer to any of our 33 questions but commander Moore refuted allegations of corruption and racism.

At the time of writing Ira Thomas is waiting for a final response from the Home Office. He would like a full investigation into those involved with his miscarriage of justice. But to whom can he complain? The new IPCC?

24

W.O.G.S.

Commander Brian Paddick is Scotland Yard's most senior openly gay policeman. He has endured the playground bullies and police canteen sniggers for most of his forty-three years.

Before coming out at work in the late eighties, Paddick first had to tell his wife of five years, whom he married while still struggling with his sexuality in an intensely homophobic profession. He has also spoken out about the malicious and baseless allegations sent anonymously and internally to his superiors. On the day of his interview to become a commander in November 2000, a letter arrived alleging he had misused a police car. Later, an anonymous call to Crimestoppers suggested he'd tipped off a gay bar about a drugs raid.

But nothing prepared the urbane cop for the betrayal and humiliation when a lurid kiss 'n' tell splash appeared in the *Mail on Sunday*. The front-page screamer on 17 March 2002 was the *coup de grâce* in a whispering campaign by reactionary voices within the Police and Tory Establishment against him.

However, Paddick's downfall was a sub-plot within a wider backlash that had begun three years earlier when the Stephen Lawrence Inquiry report was leaked to the *Sunday Telegraph* in February 1999 before being given to Parliament. There was a respectable ceasefire period after publication of the landmark report. It would have appeared crass and counter-productive for even the most atavistic Tories and antediluvian police officers to publicly attack the report and, by inference, the Lawrence family. The mutterings remained behind closed doors and in the shadows until the run-up to the June 2001 general election and the prospect of a second term for Tony Blair when the backlash could voice its venom under the guise of democratic debate.

The commissioner, Sir John Stevens, really ignited matters in a front-page interview with the *Telegraph* on 4 December 2000, one month after the fatal stabbing of ten-year-old black schoolboy Damilola Taylor in south-east London. Britain's top cop said his force was in "crisis" and attributed blame to the Lawrence report. Stevens talked of a 3,000 shortfall in cops needed to effectively police London's inner cities. Months earlier the government had launched an expensive TV campaign, drafting celebrities like footballer John Barnes and world heavyweight champion Lennox Lewis to encourage new recruits, especially "visible ethnic minorities", as the Home Office calls them.

Ten days after the Stevens interview, Tory leader William Hague launched another more odious attack on the Lawrence report, which he accused of triggering a law and order crisis. He blamed the "liberal elite" for using the report as a stick to beat the police. Columnist Simon Heffer, in the *Daily Mail*, applauded the boy leader for criticising the "stupid and meaningless" Lawrence report and its main charge of "institutional racism". The *Telegraph* said Hague deserved the "highest praise" for daring to speak the truth that the crisis of morale, recruitment and street crime was down to this "sacred text".

The pendulum had swung too far in favour of criminals and "coloured folk" and the white "liberal elite" was strangling a debate on this taboo. This, in essence, was the charge. Certainly the self-satisfaction and sanctimony of New Labourists in politics and certain sections of the media was a valid criticism of the "liberal elite".

But the Home Office under Jack Straw rivalled anything Michael Howard did during the Ghost Squad years of 1993 to 1997. And as the election approached, both parties fought ever harder to appear more illiberal than the other on law and order.

Was it coincidence, therefore, that one week after Hague's speech, Straw reinstated Met police constable Steve Hutt who had been sacked for calling a teenager a "black bastard"? Straw was also forgiving when the Yard was caught trying to massage its figures over the number of "visible ethnic minorities" recruited in the six-month period before Stevens attacked the Lawrence report in the *Telegraph*. The Yard claimed 218 black and Asian officers had joined the force between March and September 2000. The true figure was four. The others were a mix of mainly Irish, Australians, Canadians and Kiwis!

W.O.G.S.

Only when New Labour was returned with another landslide was commander Brian Paddick allowed to pilot a new project in Brixton of cautioning, not arresting, people caught with small amounts of cannabis. This, he cogently argued, would free his officers to deal with more serious drugs like crack and heroin that were rife in the inner city borough of Lambeth.

The "Brixton Experiment" had the support of the new home secretary, David Blunkett. His officials were at the time drawing up controversial plans to de-classify dope from a Class B to a Class C drug. The sound economic reasons for this shift in the drug laws would have been too politically damaging had it been mooted before the election.

Publicly, the Yard was still "wedded" to the Lawrence report and implementation of its recommendations. But internally, the organisation was seething with resentment through the ranks. Many have told us they felt fettered by political correctness, the stigma of racism and a perennial sense that criminals had too many rights and cops too much paperwork.

Blunkett's new plans to reform police pay and conditions had also sparked a rebellion by rank-and-file officers and the Police Federation, which took a full-page ad in the newspapers saying, "It's time to cut crime not costs".

It was against this backdrop that the *Mail on Sunday* plotted its attack on commander Paddick. Out came its famed chequebook and a large sum (reportedly £100,000) was handed over to French model James Renolleau. He was an ex-boyfriend from whom Paddick had acrimoniously split in 2000 after a five-year relationship. "I SMOKED POT WITH POLICE COMMANDER," roared the front page. Inside, Renolleau claimed he had smoked over one hundred spliffs with the newly dubbed "Cannabis Commander". The Yard removed Paddick from his job, much to the anger of the local community. He was given a desk to drive while an eight-month investigation was launched.

Paddick did not stay in his corner. He came out fighting, telling supporters he was the victim of a homophobic witch-hunt largely driven by political reasons. The mayor of London, Ken Livingstone, 35 MPs and the Black Police Association agreed.

Paddick says his "softly softly" drug strategy in Brixton had the prior approval of the commissioner. But Stevens, he claims, tried to distance himself, even though the Yard's own figures showed 2,000 hours of police time were saved in the experiment's first six months.

Paddick had previously attracted disproportionate and hysterical criticism when the mainstream press discovered he was a regular visitor to the radical Brixton-based Urban75 website. Comments he'd posted in a chat room as "Brian the Commander" about the attractions of anarchy were taken out of context and used to portray him as some limp-wristed, disloyal left-wing maverick.

Shortly afterwards, the *Mail on Sunday*'s "revelations" provoked a pointless PCA-supervised investigation by the deputy chief constable of Humberside. He reported to the MPA, which has responsibility for disciplining senior officers of commander and above rank, and the CPS, which would consider whether to prosecute under the Misuse of Drugs Act. Everyone knew, including the plotters, that the criminal and discipline issues were stillborn. But the damage had been done and couldn't be undone. The backlash had its scalp.

DCS Brian Moore's career had moved on swiftly since the Dando murder trial in July 2001. He was being groomed for senior rank in the Met – commander was the next one up – and was thought of as a future chief constable.

That summer Moore started to prepare for the senior command course, which would begin his ascent to the top. His studies were interrupted when the Twin Towers collapsed on 11 September. Moore was appointed silver commander for Operation Exchange, part of the UK response to President Bush's War on Terrorism. His job was to identify the Brits missing or injured in the Al-Qaeda attack.

In January 2002, Moore received a new assignment. He was posted to Brixton as commander Brian Paddick's number two. Paddick didn't relish the appointment. He had fallen out with Moore over the investigation of an incident at a Brixton nightclub involving the son of Lord Toby Harris, the chairman of the MPA.

Paddick's career was just weeks away from going into freefall. When it did, Moore took control of Lambeth borough and began stamping his authority on Brixton. The red-eyed, cotton-mouthed dope fiend would no longer find sanctuary there.

"All Change in Brixton", sighed the *Sun* with relief. Over the summer months posters went up on the walls of clubs, pubs and bars. "CANNABIS IS ILLEGAL AND WILL REMAIN ILLEGAL," they warned. Moore told a press conference there was no U-turn, just an "adjustment" of his predecessor's successful pilot project.

No Nonsense Moore had his own champion in the *Evening Standard*, the sister paper to the *Mail on Sunday*. It reported how Brixton's new police chief had single-handedly detained a man who offered him a

W.O.G.S.

draw of cannabis as he was walking to the tube station in plain clothes at the end of his shift. A report one week later in a police newspaper said the fifty-two-year-old man had been jailed for three months.[1]

Still, it must have been galling for Moore to watch Paddick, the local hero, step onto the podium of a meeting of the Lambeth Community Police Consultative Committee and take applause from a packed crowd of all colours, ages and creeds clamouring for his reinstatement.

But Moore's former boss was never coming back. The commissioner had authorised Paddick's appointment to a new intelligence unit, where the most senior openly gay officer in Scotland Yard would work under the most senior Asian officer, assistant commissioner Tarique Ghaffur, and the most senior black officer, deputy assistant commissioner Mike Fuller. Paddick called it "diversity corner", a showcase unit for the Yard to point to as a mark of its commitment to minority staff.

The MPA inquiry eventually cleared Paddick in November 2002. After a year in the wilderness he was promoted to deputy assistant commissioner overseeing criminal justice strategy in territorial policing. Another "non-job", he says. Just before Christmas 2003, Paddick received an apology and a large cheque from the *Mail on Sunday*. He would prefer his old job back.

A wry smile crossed Terry McGuinness's face the day he heard Brian Moore had taken charge of Brixton.

The furore over commander Paddick was all over the news, and McGuinness was now a free man living a new life where no one knew his past. McGuinness never did have that chat with Moore about Stoke Newington during his debriefing as a supergrass. One of the things he wanted to discuss was the Ira Thomas case. The other involved a secret that now threatened Moore's position as Lambeth police chief: Moore had been linked to a football and social club of Scotland Yard detectives collectively known as W.O.G.S.

A story we wrote in *Private Eye* about W.O.G.S. attracted an instant denial from Moore, which he sent from Brixton police station in April 2002: "I am not, nor have I ever been, a member of the Walthamstow Overseas Geographical Society (W.O.G.S.). For your information, I went on four holidays to the Mediterranean and Aegean between 1983 and 1988 as part of a group of police and non-police holidaymakers. Some of this group, myself included, played football against local people. However there was never actually a 'football team'." He demanded "an immediate retraction". We had to disappoint him.

UNTOUCHABLES

Moore's testy letter astounded former police members of W.O.G.S., our sources for the original story. The new Brixton commander may not have thought he was going abroad on a W.O.G.S. tour, but his fellow travellers were under no such illusion.

W.O.G.S. was set up in the early eighties as "a bit of a laugh" by detectives from the Flying Squad office in Walthamstow, before it was renamed Rigg Approach. W.O.G.S. was not exclusive to this one branch of the Flying Squad. The revolving door with Stoke Newington meant detectives at the north-east London police station, like Moore and McGuinness, were also involved.

Nor was W.O.G.S. a secret white supremacist cabal in the police. It was more a Bernard Manning affair that reflected the acceptable racist culture within the Met. As one former W.O.G.S. member, retired detective sergeant Chris Paddle, says: "In those days you could get away with it. Now, you'd get strung up." In 1983, Paddle went on one of the first W.O.G.S. tours to Majorca in Spain. "We upset every other person in the hotel. If they had found out who we were there would have been a hell of a complaint. How we didn't get nicked I don't know. It was just a massive piss-up. We played football. It was just a big chill-out."

Longterm member DC Yan Stivrins apparently designed the "W.O.G.S. on tour" posters announcing the forthcoming foreign beanos. These went up at Stoke Newington and Hackney police stations as well as the Flying Squad office in Walthamstow, recalls Paddle. He kept an early photograph of the Majorca trip, where all the boys are in matching blue football shirts and lined up in the goalmouth. One was fellow sergeant Graham Golder. "Golder was the mad one. He used to go and speak to all the spades down in Stoke Newington. He was the man who would walk in that pub on the Sandringham Road [on the Front Line] and come out without being stabbed. I used to drop him off down the end of the road because he told me he had an informant in there. They all thought he was possessed by the devil." Paddle jokingly calls him "the race relations guy" for Stoke Newington police station.

Golder was later suspended, tried and acquitted after the *People* splashed allegations he was taking bribes to protect a prostitution racket in Stoke Newington. The Madame, Maria Thornton, claimed to have paid Golder about £36,000 over a seven-year period as "insurance" against prosecution. She turned on him and approached the tabloid after three court appearances and a six-month stretch inside for running a brothel. The journalists set up a sting with a mini tape-recorder concealed in her bra.[2]

W.O.G.S.

Retired detective inspector Peter Wilton gave a big Sid James laugh when we strolled together down memory lane. He recalled going on a W.O.G.S. tour to Rhodes sometime in 1986 or 1987 with at least ten others. Brian Moore was there, he says. In fact there is also a photograph of the W.O.G.S. football team, again all wearing the same football shirts. Someone very like Moore is kneeling in the front row next to Wilton.[3] "The essential thing was the piss-up," says Wilton. "The football was secondary. We were half-pissed when we were playing football, that's why we lost so heavily."

Of all the W.O.G.S. associates, McGuinness was the most gobsmacked by Moore's letter to *Private Eye*. "If he was sitting here I'd say, you fucking lying cunt." McGuinness had a unique position in W.O.G.S.; he was the official keeper of the compromising photographs taken during the piss-up. He provided us with a few snaps of the W.O.G.S. tour to Cyprus in 1988. One, reproduced exclusively in this book, shows Moore and McGuinness with their arms around each other at the airport. Also on the Cyprus trip was W.O.G.S. veteran DCI Mick Lawrence. All three were serving at Stoke Newington at the time. Lawrence was later snapped wearing the group T-shirt, which McGuinness says was designed by Stivrins. The motif on the front said: "The Eagle has landed", the bird of prey being the symbol of the Flying Squad.

Returning to Moore's letter, it said: "These allegations [about W.O.G.S.] were first raised in 1999 when I was leading a major corruption inquiry. A highly respected senior officer, deputy assistant commissioner Roy Clark QPM, looked into the issues raised at the time and found no basis for a disciplinary investigation."

The "major corruption inquiry" was of course Operation Ethiopia, into Rigg Approach where Moore's old W.O.G.S. chum, Terry McGuinness, was a key supergrass. McGuinness says he told his debriefers all about W.O.G.S. But the typed statement CIB3 produced for him to sign has almost no detail, and omits any reference to Moore. It says blandly: "It was whilst I was at Stoke [Newington] that I first went on holiday with a number of my colleagues to Cyprus. There was a group of people known collectively as the Walthamstow Overseas Geographical Society, who annually went away for a jolly up." You could be forgiven for thinking this was a ramblers' association.

Until Moore's letter, we were unaware DAC Clark had "looked into" W.O.G.S. McGuinness confirms that the head of the Untouchables never spoke to him as part of his inquiries.

UNTOUCHABLES

We wanted to ask Roy Clark other questions about W.O.G.S. Was he the right man to conduct the inquiry? Hadn't he been a detective inspector at Walthamstow when W.O.G.S. started? He was later the chief superintendent at Stoke Newington, and involved with Lawrence, Moore and McGuinness in the Ira Thomas case.

The lawyers representing Thomas in his compensation claim for the miscarriage of justice incorporated these concerns in their recent letter to the Home Office: "Another worrying aspect of this case, particularly bearing in mind Mr Thomas is black, is that at least one of the officers, DC McGuinness, was a member of an organisation called 'W.O.G.S.'"

Brian Moore was not the only member of the Untouchables who had been linked to W.O.G.S. When we first contacted DC Yan Stivrins in June 2000 he refused to comment. We tried again in 2004, by which time Stivrins had been posted to the Telephone Intelligence Unit. He again declined to comment.

We had hoped Clark would enlighten us about the basis on which he decided in 1999 not to launch an official investigation or refer it to the PCA, and whether the involvement of his own men and the potential embarrassment to Scotland Yard had influenced that decision. After all, 1999 was the year the Lawrence Inquiry report was published.

It seems inconsistent that PC Steve Hutt was suspended that year for calling a teenager a "black bastard" but allegations of a police group called W.O.G.S. merited no formal investigation. The double standard was more apparent when we learned the Untouchables had in 1997 served a disciplinary notice on a serving officer for making a derogatory racist remark to his colleague in a police car.[4]

CENTREX is the centre where police recruits spend 16 weeks in basic training. They are now given race awareness courses where it is strongly emphasised that the words "Wog", "Nigger", "Coon" and "Paki" are totally unacceptable and any recruit caught using them is liable to instant dismissal.

On 21 October 2003 BBC reporter Mark Daly went undercover at CENTREX to see how prevalent racist attitudes were among raw recruits and their trainers. His admirable film, *The Secret Policeman*, caused a scandal: six recruits resigned and chief constables met hurriedly to discuss how to improve the selection process and weed out racists before they graduated.

The neo-Nazi British National Party claimed it had serving cops

W.O.G.S.

among its members. Scotland Yard's deputy commissioner Ian Blair responded by announcing he hoped to make BNP membership an instant sackable offence. Serving officers formerly involved with W.O.G.S., however, appear to be in a different league. Moore was made a commander during the fall-out over the BBC programme.

The main force in the firing line following the BBC exposé was Greater Manchester Constabulary. The chief constable, Michael Todd, was a former Scotland Yard officer and senior manager of the Untouchables. In a statement broadcast at the end of the BBC documentary, viewers were told Todd had voluntarily referred the matter to the IPCC, the new police watchdog where his former colleague Roy Clark is director of investigations.

25

... AND THE BEATING GOES ON AND ON

It was a mid-summer day in June 1996 and England was football loopy. London was hosting the European championships and the national squad had reached the semi-finals, against Germany. The *Mirror* caught the mood with no hint of jingoism. "ACHTUNG! SURRENDER!" screamed the front page. It was an update on that old favourite, "TWO WORLD WARS AND ONE WORLD CUP".

Cabbies, white-van drivers and cars criss-crossed Trafalgar Square all day, with the flag of St George flapping in the wind. Drive-time radio stations belted out the oddly tolerable *Three Lions on a Shirt*, which had become a new national anthem and number one in the charts.

A mixed Wembley crowd with warrior tones sang it during England's nail-biting path to the semis, defeating Holland, Spain and Scotland on the way. There was a real sense this was it. "Football's coming home," proclaimed the song. No more tears for Gazza; a return to the glory days of '66 when Bobby Moore's side lifted the World Cup.

Most employers suspended any pretence that this was a normal workday. As Wednesday afternoon rolled on, more and more men and women spilled out of offices and into the pub where a mass of their colleagues with moody sick notes in their back pockets and three lions on their chests were convalescing.

Chants of "Ingerland, Ingerland" soon punched the air as kick-off

... AND THE BEATING GOES ON AND ON

approached and the lager flowed. The match had an added edge because of a sudden death period called the Golden Goal.

England got off to a dream start. Shearer scored with his head from a corner in the first three minutes. Then Germany levelled. There was some consolation when the goal scorer's name, Stefan Kuntz, was announced. Plenty more action followed but no more goals after extra time, so the game went to a penalty shoot-out. The niggling, nightmare scenario every England supporter at one time had entertained was about to come true. It was five-all in penalties when Gareth Southgate stepped up to the spot, and missed. Germany didn't. They were in the final.[1]

Legendary retired German captain Franz Beckenbauer described the match afterwards as the real final. It was, he said, "the best advertisement for football". It was also one of the worst advertisements for why Scotland Yard should continue to police itself.

That night, an officer permanently disabled 16-year-old John Wilson. The anti-corruption squad claimed it could not identify the baton-wielding culprit and none of his colleagues came forward.

Most victims of a police assault do not come from a white, suburban middle-class family. There is a perception among certain inner-city communities that the internal complaints system treats such people better. But when the Wilsons fought for justice, the Yard tried everything to undermine their case, whilst proclaiming a new era of integrity in policing for Londoners. "This is an everyman case," says John Wilson's lawyer. "It could happen to anyone."

John was watching the England game with two schoolmates, Tim Gooden and Christian Marsh, in the Crown pub in Twickenham, a well-heeled south-west London suburb. School was out for summer; he'd just taken his GCSEs and was working during the holiday with a market trader selling sports shoes.

Although downhearted by England's loss, the three friends headed for Trafalgar Square, where England fans traditionally gather. Their parents weren't exactly thrilled but knew the boys could handle themselves.

When they got there, hundreds of fans were milling around. By midnight it turned ugly and the riot squad started to clear the square by forcing fans down the main road to Charing Cross tube station.

John and his two friends were corralled in the crowd when the riot cops charged. They say they were not involved in any violence or provocation of the police, but thought it wise to run. Christian and Tim were in front of John as they legged it.

At the top end of Northumberland Avenue, a group of hooligans started to attack an empty Ministry of Defence car. As the three boys ran past, John foolishly stopped to watch the frenzied vandalism. Suddenly, out of the corner of his eye he saw a riot cop carrying a shield running at quite a pace towards him with his baton raised. "I remember thinking, 'Turn to run', just to get away from him, [when] I felt a cracking blow to my head and that was it. That is my last recollection. It all happened in a split second."

A CCTV camera on the top of the National Gallery had captured the incident. As soon as the blow struck, John immediately lost consciousness and collapsed. The back of his head smashed onto the road, fracturing the skull in two places. The stocky riot cop appeared agitated as he stood astride John's prone and deadly still body. For a moment the officer paused, looked down at his victim, then ran off.

John's nose was broken and blood splattered across his face. His jaw was also fractured. Blood was pouring down the front of his sweatshirt. Tim says he asked a female riot officer to help, but she ignored him. A man, who happened to be a doctor, eventually persuaded the police to call an ambulance and did what he could for John until it arrived.

The teenager was rushed to a hospital in nearby Waterloo.

"I almost fainted when I saw him," recalls his mother, Susan. "One of the nurses had to help me to a chair." She was advised against talking to the waiting press or against accusing the police.

John regained consciousness after two days. Four days later he was discharged. At home his condition worsened and he experienced his first, major epileptic seizure. Susan rushed her son back to hospital. John had another seizure and was placed on a ventilator. In preparation for surgery, the CT scan showed bleeding on the brain. The doctors decided to postpone the operation to see if it would resolve itself. Susan was beside herself at the sight of her son among the tubes and bleeps of life support machines keeping other head injury patients alive in the High Dependency Unit.

John had developed grand mal epilepsy, the severest kind. "His life really just stopped," Susan recalls. "He tried to go to college [to start his A Levels] in September 1996 and again in 1997. But he couldn't concentrate, he couldn't keep up with the work or take notes because he was having seizures."

It took over two years to find the right dosage of medication to

...AND THE BEATING GOES ON AND ON

suppress them. "Every time I left the house I never knew if I would be coming home or ending up in a hospital," says John. The uncertainty left Susan in constant fear and today John is slightly embarrassed about his mother's concern. "I wanted to go to university with all my mates. I liked languages but to be honest I didn't really know what I would have studied. You don't really at 16, do you?" But the opportunity was lost. John watched his friends move on while his life remained stuck in a nightmare of seizures, medication, lost confidence and a lack of motivation.

Susan was 38 when John was assaulted. She'd split with his father and at the time they were living with her parents. Hers is an average middle-class family. They are not capital P political but when pressed, Susan describes herself as an old-fashioned Tory with an admiration for Margaret Thatcher. Her previous dealings with the police were minimal. She just wanted to know that if needed they'd be there with a professional response.

"She didn't want to take it to court. It was my idea. Mum was afraid to do it," says John. "I didn't want them to get away with it. I needed . . . like anyone who suffers, someone to blame. And in my case there was someone, there was a rightful reason to sue. It was more about making the officer accountable for what he'd done than suing the Met." He was never a radical student with defined politics or views about the police. "I'm pretty much apolitical. It's not that I don't care what happens, it's just that there's no one worth believing in."

Susan was reticent about "taking on the Establishment". While she too wanted to know which officer was responsible, she worried that if they sued, the local police might take revenge on her son one day. "I think what it is, is having children. I was a shy child. Going to work made me strong, because you have to stand up for yourself. Then when you have a child you want the best for them and then something happens to your son. The very last thing you expect is for your child to be injured by a policeman. When that happens you want to put things right." John brought his mother round. "When we got going, she got so into it we kept each other going."

After almost two years of legal inaction, in September 1999 a judge ordered the Met to disclose any video or photographic evidence they possessed. Two months later, recalls Susan, the Met "suddenly discovered" some CCTV footage and changed their defence to one of "accidental collision", claiming the video proved John was never hit with a baton, as he had maintained. Previously the police had suggested the injuries resulted from a drunken fall or an altercation with a member of the public.

The videotape arrived as Susan's mother was dying. She passed away on Boxing Day, never seeing Scotland Yard apologise for what it had done to her grandson.

Samantha Bird, the Met solicitor, was pushing the family for a response to the video. Meanwhile she tried to get the Legal Aid Board to withdraw funding, claiming the video showed John had "an unsustainable case". It worked. John's legal team backed out and legal aid was withdrawn just weeks before a hearing in April 2000 at the High Court.

Convinced this was the end of the road, Susan called commissioner Sir John Stevens' office. "I thought if we had to drop it I wanted him to know that a 16-year-old boy had been assaulted by one of his men and we haven't been able to do anything." A member of the commissioner's staff listened then put the phone down on her, she says.

The terse response spurred the Wilsons to appear before the High Court judge unrepresented and to plead for an adjournment. John was now 20. The judge agreed to the extra time and said they could represent themselves if necessary. "That," says Susan, "was when we knew we had a case."

Bird had sent a legal bundle with a bullish covering letter saying that if they continued their case the Met would pursue John for all costs, which would run into tens of thousands of pounds. "It's very difficult to come up against the police. You are at an immediate disadvantage. The assumptions they make about you – he's a thug, he's out for trouble – you have such a lot to prove."

The Wilsons sought help from Liberty, the legal pressure group, and were put in touch with a young solicitor called James Bell from Christian Khan, a well-known civil liberties law firm in central London with experience taking on the police and other state agencies. Bell had legal aid restored, despite a further intervention by Bird. He also instructed a young barrister who specialised in police actions. "Leslie [Thomas] was a key figure all the way through," says John with rare admiration. "He had faith in the case."

The Met tried to have it struck out on the grounds of delay. This failed and in July 2001 the case of Wilson v The Commissioner was finally ready to be heard, five years after the assault.

In that time John had tried to find work without success. His energy

...AND THE BEATING GOES ON AND ON

levels were suppressed not just by the assault but also by the medication he took twice daily to control the grand mal epilepsy. However, John knew his evidence under cross-examination would make or break the case. "For some reason I was more nervous until I got up there. The nerves just went [in the witness box]. I switched into automatic mode. Everything I was asked over three hours I'd revised for," John recalls with noticeable pride. He loathed the police barrister who was trying to trip him up.

The Met repeated its "accidental collision" claim. But Mr Justice Morland was astonished the officer hadn't come forward or filed a report on the night, unlike another colleague who'd hit a member of the public with his baton near the vandalised MoD car.

The Met had sent an email to every cop in the force just days before the hearing, asking for the officer who "inadvertently knocked a youth to the ground who it appears was attacking police vehicles" to come forward. It was made reassuringly clear that the officer was not at fault and would not face discipline. Judge Morland remarked that this email was circulated surprisingly late. He also called it "oddly worded".

The author of the email, detective inspector Ian Horrocks, gave evidence. Horrocks had discovered the CCTV footage. He then compiled a list of all units the Westminster HQ Public Order Branch believed were on duty that night in Trafalgar Square. He contacted the supervisors of each unit to see if they had been in or around the MoD car when it was attacked. Some officers were even shown the video and other material to help jog memories.

But Horrocks claimed in a statement that he was unable to identify the riot squad that charged to protect the MoD car and therefore the officer responsible for the attack on John Wilson. In court he said it was his sincere view that John was either attacking the MoD vehicle or part of the group that was. One of the many strange features of this case was that Horrocks and his boss, superintendent Hamish Campbell, were involved in the Wilson case at all. Their plate was already full running the highest profile murder case in Britain – the hunt for Jill Dando's killer.

One police constable did present himself at court in answer to the email. He said he couldn't remember who was on his squad that night. Another officer who was not part of the riot squad provided a witness statement describing the night's events and recalled seeing John lying unconscious in the road, but not how he had got there.

For Mr Justice Morland to find in John's favour it was not enough to believe he had fallen as a result of being pushed aside by a riot cop rushing towards the hooligans attacking the car. "In my judgement the facts that the officer who collided with the claimant remains unidentified and that no police documents relating to the incident have emerged are consistent with the claimant's case that he was the victim of a deliberate, unlawful assault," he ruled.

Morland had no criticism of the police strategy that night. But after repeatedly watching the video he said: "I have become more and more convinced it was not an accidental collision and was a deliberate attack on the claimant who had innocently but unwisely stopped to watch the attack on the police car . . . Considering the video in the context of the evidence as a whole I am utterly convinced he was the victim of a deliberate unlawful assault."

Morland also commented that he would have expected a serious and detailed investigation and search for documents between February 1998, when the Wilsons first notified the Met of the assault, and November 1999, when Campbell and Horrocks became involved.

His judgement on 6 July was an enormous relief to the Wilsons. "We had a High Court judge endorsing how we felt. Surely, we thought, it would now help us get answers to the question we had been asking. Surely, someone would now be held accountable," says Susan. She and John had every reason to believe all that was left was to determine the level of damages. But instead of paying up, the Met used even more public funds to appeal the ruling.

Susan thought pressure could be applied by alerting the newly created Metropolitan Police Authority. John was less convinced.

The MPA chairman was a New Labour devotee whose service to Tony Blair was rewarded in 1998 with a life peerage. Lord Toby Harris was ably assisted by an ex-Home Office civil servant from the *ancien régime* called Catherine Crawford. She is the chief clerk to the MPA, an unelected position of considerable influence, who liaises between the authority and senior figures in Scotland Yard. An MI5 officer is also secretly attached to the MPA.

During his inaugural speech in June 2000, Lord Harris hailed "a new start for the policing of London". It was, he said, time to "discard the baggage of the past" – a clear reference to the scathing 1999 Stephen Lawrence Inquiry report. He said he would personally ensure Scotland Yard treated everyone fairly and was open and honest.

But behind the noble rhetoric, the true mission of the MPA was ultimately revealed as a political one – to reduce crime. The success or failure of the MPA would be judged by this statistic alone, said the Lord. Thus, the hugely important responsibility of police oversight

... AND THE BEATING GOES ON AND ON

was, from the start, always going to be trumped by an overtly electioneering agenda – winning the war on crime.

The Wilsons were about to discover that with the MPA, preserving the integrity of the Yard's reputation in the war on crime would override holding senior officers to account for serious abuses of power.

In November 2001, Susan made a formal complaint to the MPA about commissioner Stevens' handling of the matter. She accused Britain's top cop of "misleading the High Court"; non-disclosure of documents; failing to identify the 25 riot squad officers and the officer who assaulted John; wasting public funds by appealing and interfering with their legal aid. "In conclusion, the commissioner's conduct throughout this entire case has been one of delay, undermine, frustrate rather than dealing with the merits of the case to ensure that procedures are followed and the minimum standards met," the complaint said.

After speaking privately to deputy commissioner Ian Blair and taking legal advice, a month later the MPA rejected the complaint, arguing that as it didn't concern the commissioner's personal conduct but related to his "direction and control" of the force it wasn't a matter for them. However, the MPA said it would ask commissioner Stevens to report back to them on the issues raised by the complaint and also offered the Wilsons a meeting with the MPA chairman.

Lord Harris told Susan his son was also at Trafalgar Square that night, so he too could understand how she felt. Susan wasn't convinced and replied: "If this had happened to Tony Blair's son or your son would we still not know who these officers are?" The Yard was "protecting someone", she insisted. "There's got to be a reason to defend this all the way to the High Court on the basis of an accidental collision, if you haven't even spoken to the officer involved. The justification has got to be somewhere."

According to the minutes, Lord Harris tried to assuage Susan's frustration by referring to new government proposals to make the police complaints system "more independent". He accepted the current system was "unsatisfactory". Lord Harris said he "suspected that in such cases the Met's general reaction was possibly to stonewall" and that he and his colleagues on the MPA were working with senior officers to change this "culture".[2]

But what of the unidentified riot cop? The Wilsons had no idea the assault had occurred in the middle of the most unprecedented secret intelligence gathering operation inside the Yard to identify corrupt and unethical officers. Yet for all the boasts and gadgetry of the anti-corruption crusade, the officer who assaulted John Wilson on 26 June 1996 remained the real untouchable. CIB3 couldn't even identify any of the 25 riot cops on duty in Trafalgar Square that night, or so the Wilson family were led to believe.

Deputy commissioner Ian Blair suggested Susan met CIB3 commander Andy Hayman. He explained to her what steps his Untouchables had taken to identify the officer involved. "He said that either the officer was lazy and forgot to fill in his forms or the entire riot squad was suffering from post-traumatic stress and had forgotten the incident. My jaw dropped and I just looked at him. 'Are you seriously expecting me to accept that?' I replied."

The Wilsons and their legal team had done their own sleuthing and discovered something potentially very significant. They tracked down a reporter who filmed the disturbance in Trafalgar Square for local television news. "He couldn't remember the incident with John but said he was called in to 1 Area headquarters on the Embankment the next day because several policemen were under investigation. He was asked whether his footage could assist the inquiry," says Susan.

This proved there had been an internal inquiry the Wilsons knew nothing about. Someone must have made a complaint on the night against the riot police. Perhaps it was one of the people arrested near the vandalised MoD car where John was assaulted. But when the Wilsons brought this to the attention of the Met's solicitors, they were told it was a separate matter that had been dealt with and had no bearing on their case.

John and Susan had by now developed a strong sense they were being stonewalled. When Susan went to see a campaigning organisation called INQUEST she realised they were far from alone. The visit opened her eyes to a whole world of police brutality, racism and official intransigence that challenged her white suburban, middle-class existence for ever.

INQUEST had developed out of the failure of UK police forces and coroners' courts to fully account for the hundreds of deaths in police, prison and medical custody since 1969. A disproportionate number of the victims are black or individuals with mental health problems. No police officer has ever been convicted for a death in custody. The whole internal investigation by the same force is shrouded in secrecy, as are the CPS's deliberations, giving rise to suggestions of a politicised and unhealthy cosiness between the CPS and the police.

. . . AND THE BEATING GOES ON AND ON

Susan was told about the case of Roger Sylvester, a 30-year-old black man from north London who died in January 1999 after being arrested and restrained by eight Met officers. The CPS had declined to charge the officers on the grounds of insufficient evidence.

It was Hayman's CIB that originally investigated the arresting officers from the Met. But this internal investigation was taken off them after the Sylvester family complained about its lack of integrity. The PCA subsequently supervised an investigation by Essex police into Hayman's men. They concluded that three CIB officers should face discipline for, among other things, failing to preserve potential evidence and failing to keep proper records.[3]

Before the assault on her son, Susan believed the few cases of police malpractice she had read about in the *Daily Mail* were isolated incidents. But she soon came to believe they were part of a pattern of police misconduct and an official culture of cover-up. The outpourings of mothers forced to turn off the life support systems keeping their children alive profoundly touched her. "What a disgrace," she says. "It was heartbreaking. I just sat there in tears. I couldn't believe that this goes on here. Why don't the public know about it?"

Eventually the Yard found a judge who was sympathetic to the view that the CCTV footage was not clear cut. So a full appeal hearing was set for 28 February 2002. However, when three Appeal Court judges revisited the video they upheld the original ruling that John was the victim of "a deliberate and unlawful assault".

The Yard now had no place to go, so it tried to grasp some moral high ground by telling the Press Association it had "voluntarily referred the matter to the PCA so that an independent force can be appointed to investigate". But John was unconvinced about aiding yet another internal inquiry. He was unmoved by the fiction of independence just because Northamptonshire police would now conduct a review of the Met. He couldn't see what they would find that Hayman and his Untouchables had apparently missed. "I thought, 'No, it's still the police investigating the police.'"

Over the years, as one force is called in to investigate another, a bank of favours builds up between them. Officers transfer between forces, especially with the Met. Police culture and attitudes to the public also transcend regional borders. The public know almost nothing of what goes on – the leaks and deals – when an outside force is called in, because the investigation and its report are kept from the victim's family and from the media.

"We offered to co-operate only if the PCA could guarantee we would see a copy of Northamptonshire Police's final report. The PCA said that wasn't possible," Susan explains.

Nevertheless, by the spring of 2002 Scotland Yard was facing a substantial six-figure claim for damages, aggravated because it had fought the case and never apologised. Out of the blue, on 23 April John Wilson received an "unreserved apology" from deputy commissioner Ian Blair. "It was a hollow apology that had come far too late and was hardly worth the paper it was written on," says John with undisguised contempt.

The timing could not have been more cynical, their lawyer thought. By saying sorry just weeks before the hearing on damages and costs, the Yard avoided a bigger payout. "The police had put John and Susan through six years of hell. They had every obstacle put in the way. So the apology was absolutely forced out of them. It was not genuine," says James Bell. But what about the commissioner's motto – Integrity is Non-Negotiable? "Well, that's not true. The Yard did negotiate its integrity when they agreed to pay John £500,000 in damages." They were also ordered to pay the Wilsons' substantial legal costs.

Coincidentally, that same month deputy commissioner Blair released figures for the damages the Yard had paid over the last five years. It was, he told the press, a good news story. From 1997 to 2002, Blair claimed 1,555 legal actions had cost the Met £13.6 million. As with many official statistics, this rarely told the full story. Blair's maths did not include the figure for defence costs picked up by the police and the costs incurred by its own legal department and by CIB.

Nevertheless, the deputy commissioner had this to say: "We are constantly striving to reach new levels of professionalism in the service we provide to the people of London. These figures suggest that the hard work of people across the Metropolitan Police Service is being rewarded with greater satisfaction from the public. However it would be wrong to become complacent with this success and we are determined to continue trying to reduce complaints and litigation even further. The less we spend on these matters the more of our resources go into supporting frontline policing."[4]

When added to the Yard's own legal bill the whole Wilson scandal has needlessly cost the taxpayer well in excess of £1 million. It would, of course, have been substantially less had the Yard settled back in 1997.

Lord Harris had pledged that "a major task" of the MPA was to ensure Scotland Yard delivered "value for money" and was efficiently run. The force was not subject to "the same rigorous financial regimes" as other public services, and this would change, he promised. Less than a year later the MPA chairman was admitting that financial controls inside the Met were "shambolic".[5]

The MPA confirms the payment to John Wilson was approved under the terms of a protocol with the Yard whereby sensitive cases and settlements over £100,000 had to be referred to them. This has not always been the case, Lord Harris admitted.[6] However the MPA will not discuss whether the Yard ignored independent legal advice commissioned by the watchdog, which recommended no appeal. The MPA also refuses to give the Wilsons a copy of the Yard's report on its handling of the investigation.

During their fight for justice one judge remarked that Susan had become "obsessed". She says to get anywhere she had to. "You shouldn't have to fight so hard for justice against the Metropolitan Police. And if I am obsessed I accept that. I don't think enough is being done. I think these people delude themselves into thinking things have changed, that it won't happen again."

Senior CPS lawyer Martin Polaine said getting untainted police officers without axes to grind to come forward and give evidence against their colleagues is not just a problem of top end corruption investigations, but also "just about every complaint we get", even death in custody cases. "There's a culture of loyalty and an unwillingness to put oneself out on a limb, plus a fear of ostracism," he says.

But as the Untouchables are taken from the same pool of detectives, isn't that same culture of loyalty going to permeate anti-corruption work too? "That's always an ever present concern when you've got the police investigating themselves or a police service investigating itself. The difficulty is there's not really an answer to that."

Scotland Yard deny that its inability to identify the officer who assaulted John Wilson was due to any lack of political will. But the failure of the Untouchables reflects very badly on commissioner Stevens. It is also a crushing indictment of his much-trumpeted ethical policy on integrity, which imposed a "duty" on all 45,000 employees in the Met to come forward and report bad apples in the orchard.

Stevens re-launched his ethical policy in August 2002. He told the assembled pack of crime correspondents how he was building on the good work of his anti-corruption squad: "Much of these successes are attributable to the creation of an environment where people feel able to report suspected wrong-doing, support ongoing inquiries or provide information that leads to an investigation." Clearly he was excluding the Wilson case from this backslapping homily.

"What gets me is that it's an unequal struggle. And you are fighting for justice from the very people who are supposed to provide it. And that to me seems wrong," says Susan. "I've used all the energy I had. Seven years is too high a price to pay."

A police complaints system that not only fails to inspire public confidence, but also leaves those who challenge the police with a sense of dread that one day they may suffer repercussions is deeply worrying.

Fears about the institutional vindictiveness of Scotland Yard are well founded. And it looks like those who make complaints against the Yard, which it deems "unjustified", will now be the subject of a secret investigation using a range of oppressive and intrusive methods.

John's barrister warned him he would be under police surveillance. "I always had an eye out. But I thought, if they were going to do that, fine, it's not like I was smuggling drugs."

No defence lawyer worth his salt would nowadays advise a member of the public to use the internal complaints system. Instead civil actions against the police are on the rise because the complainant has more control over the process. This is why deputy commissioner Ian Blair has set up a secretive new body called the Civil Actions Investigations Unit (CAIU), whose aim is to undermine claims through targeted investigations. This involves liaising with operational police squads "to build up a full picture of the claimant's background", surveillance, finding witnesses who can cast a negative light on the claimant's character and "sharing intelligence" for possible criminal prosecutions.

The CAIU works closely with the Untouchables and both units are part of the Directorate of Professional Standards. The well-founded fear is that the CAIU will also be used to secretly undermine legitimate and justified complaints for internal political reasons.

Today, John is twenty-three and on two types of medication twice daily. His epilepsy appears to be under control. He is still sensitive about it because people wrongly associate epilepsy with mental illness. He has now moved out of home and hopes to find a career. Despite his experience, it hasn't stopped him supporting his beloved Chelsea and England.[7]

26

IN-HOUSE

On 15 April 1998, police sergeant Gurpal Virdi reported for duty at Ealing division in west London refreshed from a short family holiday. Before starting work, he first took his young son and daughter to the dentist. As Virdi pulled out of his drive he noticed a strange car parked across the road. His suspicions were further heightened when, on turning the corner, he saw a marked police car. It too slotted in behind him. He took evasive action and returned home. The dentist would have to wait. The kids were so unhappy.

Virdi went to confront the occupants of the car, which was once again parked outside his house. Before he reached them, flustered CIB officers rushed him and he was arrested on the spot. The offence, he could scarcely believe his ears, was sending racist hate mail to himself and other ethnic officers, and perverting the course of justice.

Since late December 1997, 13 of the 15 ethnic officers on Ealing police division had been subjected to a racist hate mail campaign through the internal post. On Christmas Eve, a black officer received the first threatening letter. Below a crude computer-generated image of a black face, it stated: "NOT WANTED. KEEP THE POLICE FORCE WHITE. SO LEAVE NOW OR ELSE. NF."

Virdi had requested an independent inquiry, but senior officers at Ealing initially preferred to keep it in-house using their own officers even though some of them could have been suspects. Five days later the matter was referred to the local CIB unit. This did nothing to deter the racists inside the Met. Four weeks later a second batch of hate mail, designed to look like an official Met memo, was intercepted in the internal post. This time it was directed at eight ethnic civilian workers. Below the police crest the "memo" sinisterly stated: "YOU ARE ORDERED TO LEAVE. YOU HAVE NO RIGHT TO BE HERE. NF."

Virdi's home was searched over seven hours in a way usually reserved for anti-terrorist operations. Among items seized was his daughter's new computer, a present for her tenth birthday. Later that day Virdi was suspended after sixteen years of unblemished service.

News of the arrest of an "Asian man" was immediately leaked to two crime correspondents at the *Daily Mail*, Peter Rose and Steve Wright. Their article, published the following day, offered middle Englanders a digestible motive for the "offence" – the Asian officer had been passed over for selection to the detective branch and was laying the false ground for a racial discrimination claim. The *Mail* also described commissioner Condon as furious and speculated that the arrest of an Asian officer would "come as a shock to anti-racism campaigners who claim the police service is riddled with white bigots".

This had all the hallmarks of one of those back-scratching exercises that go on between the Yard and its trusties in the media. "As I fought to clear my name the *Daily Mail* would feature again and again as the recipient of leaked information from Scotland Yard," says Virdi. "I felt then, as I feel now, that I had lost my life, that I was now just a product on a production line. Regardless of my innocence or the feelings of myself, or my family, I was being used as a deflection device to draw public attention away from the very serious crisis the Met was embroiled in after the murder of Stephen Lawrence. They were expecting a hammering from the [public] inquiry and I firmly believe an element was looking to my case to provide a counterweight. I was picked on because I had complained persistently about racism. And I feel sure that if it hadn't been me then someone else would have been chosen as the fall-guy."

A "Restricted" Met report reveals that Virdi's arrest was authorised by John Stevens and planned well in advance with an eye on the start of the Stephen Lawrence public inquiry in March 1998. A press strategy was also developed to give Virdi's ethnicity "if asked" by journalists.

Gurpal Virdi's Sikh father, an ex-policeman in Delhi, had warned his son against joining the Met. But young Virdi was headstrong and idealistic. He believed he could "make a difference" to the poorly served black and Asian communities in west London and jacked in his career with a pharmaceutical firm. Almost immediately after joining in 1982, Virdi says he experienced a "barrage of racism", bullying by senior officers and thwarted career development. But after a stint at the Yard working in SO11, he was finally promoted to police sergeant and sent to Ealing, a borough with a large Asian community, especially in Southall, where he grew up.

Just before his arrest, Virdi had threatened to go over the head of his superiors at Ealing to Scotland Yard regarding the handling of a racist stabbing of an Iraqi and an Indian by a gang of five white boys. Virdi had arrived on the scene quickly and helped save the life of the most seriously injured victim. But the follow-up investigation had, in his view, been sloppy. The parallels with the Lawrence murder inquiry four years earlier were pointed out to his bosses. Several weeks later he was arrested.

It took almost a year after Virdi's suspension for the CPS to convince itself there was insufficient evidence to prosecute. Not least because the internal racist mailings had continued while Virdi sat at home. "There was never any chance of my being found guilty before a proper court. I had a watertight alibi. At 4 a.m. on Christmas Eve, the precise time when I was supposed to be at Hanwell Police Station printing and distributing the racist hate mail, I could prove that I was two miles away at Acton Police Station, covering for their night shift so they could attend the Christmas do."

But the Yard was determined to have a show trial of its own making. The disciplinary board was composed of three white commanders, Richard Cullen, Alan Shave and Graham James. "I told my wife Sathat that I would unquestionably be found guilty by the Met disciplinary board," says Virdi. "The board was just something we had to go through to get to the employment tribunal. I had already filed a lawsuit ahead of the disciplinary board, and I was determined to prove that the Met had racially discriminated by giving me entirely different treatment from any of the white suspects for the sending of the racist hate mail."

In March 2000, after a four-week hearing, Gurpal Virdi was sacked. Assistant commissioner Michael Todd told the press pack the verdict was an entirely fair result and described the officer's actions as "despicable". *Newsnight* senior reporter Peter Marshall recalls with considerable anger how the Yard's press office targeted him when he started to prepare an unsympathetic report. Todd was the senior Untouchable put up the day of the sacking to savage Virdi in a live studio interview after Marshall's report. "There was a deliberate plan to fuck me up," says Marshall. It included discrediting him behind his back to the producer and BBC bosses.

One month later, Virdi's father died prematurely. His mother had passed away six months earlier never having seen her son clear his name. For a brief moment, Virdi considered suicide. His life and standing among the local community – he was a school governor – was, he believed, in ruins.

However, the employment tribunal later found unanimously that he had been racially discriminated against in the way CIB conducted the investigation. Unlike his white colleagues, he had been subject to an entrapment operation, formally interviewed, his house searched, then he was arrested and suspended "without sufficient evidence to support the allegations".[1]

The Yard had relied heavily on what it claimed was incontrovertible computer evidence to sack Virdi. But the employment tribunal now concluded the computer experts for the Yard were wrong.

Virdi had been deeply unsatisfied with the attitude and service from the Police Federation and its retained solicitors, Russell, Jones & Walker (RJW), at the disciplinary hearing. Inexplicably, his legal team didn't challenge the computer evidence from a prosecution expert said to have a large software contract with the Met.

After he was sacked, an independent computer consultant, Michael Turner, contacted Virdi with an astonishing story. Turner said he had warned the Federation before the disciplinary hearing about the varying quality of computer evidence but they declined to commission him.

"It was then that I figured out the Federation were not helping me but were covering up the truth," says Virdi. His new lawyers from the Commission for Racial Equality did contact Turner, whose evidence was clearly very persuasive to the employment tribunal. Turner's report argued that the Yard's computer case was "junk science". Timings were imprecise; evidence on the internal mail system suggested that the second set of racist letters were posted two days *before* CIB claimed they were printed; there was widespread password abuse in police stations; there had also been a wholesale failure to secure and duplicate the relevant computer servers in a timely fashion; and by working on the original files it contaminated or erased a great deal of highly relevant evidence. "No criminal court would have allowed the Virdi case to proceed . . . [This was] the first miscarriage of justice that resulted directly from the interpretation and misinterpretation of computer evidence," Turner concluded.[2]

IN-HOUSE

In August 2000, the employment tribunal awarded Virdi £150,000 compensation. The majority was for the "high-handed" way the Yard had behaved towards him and manipulated the media coverage. The Independent Advisory Group, a body set up with the Yard's agreement after the Lawrence Inquiry to monitor its performance on race crime, did not mince its words. It described CIB's "disgraceful" investigation as "a high-profile character assassination".

The next month the recently inaugurated Metropolitan Police Authority moved to investigate the operation against Virdi. Meanwhile, DAC Roy Clark commissioned an incredible and strictly internal report, which still claimed there was "strong evidence" of Virdi's guilt and that the initial investigation was "thorough" even though those doing it had "little or no detective experience". There had also been no proper record for critical decisions and a failure to follow up officers with possible links to the Far Right.

After much delay and obstruction from the Yard, 15 months later the MPA produced its 170-page report. The Yard had denied the so-called watchdog timely access to its media strategy file on Virdi. But on the available evidence, the inquiry concluded there was a smear campaign against the Asian sergeant. The *Daily Mail*'s crime correspondents had been the chief recipients of the Yard's drip feed. They had even been leaked private legal correspondence during Virdi's settlement negotiations with the Yard, which resulted in the exaggerated headline, "SACKED RACE CASE POLICE OFFICER SEEKS £2M PAYOUT". The piece cast Virdi as the greedy exponent of the compensation culture, against more worthy recipients like maimed victims of crime.

The *Daily Mail* had already meted out similar treatment earlier in the year to a detective constable called Sarah Locker after the Yard settled her appalling racial and sexual discrimination case.[3]

Gurpal Virdi welcomed the MPA report but feels it had significant failings. "I gave the MPA the names of 15 officers across a range of ranks who had a part in the campaign against me or who gave false evidence. Nothing has been done and some of these officers have even been promoted. My information has never been followed up. And there has never been a proper, professional police inquiry into who sent the racist hate mail . . . elements within the Met are very frightened of a professional inquiry into this."

In February 2001, Gurpal and Sathat Virdi met commissioner Stevens to hear how after wasting millions of taxpayers' money on a discriminatory and disproportionate CIB probe it was time to let bygones be bygones and feel reassured that lessons had been learned. Virdi had recently been reinstated and received a further £200,000 settlement from the Yard and a written apology from Stevens. In return he dropped his second employment tribunal for unfair dismissal.

After months of agonising family debates on whether to return to the Met – Sathat was opposed – Virdi decided that being on the inside was the best way to fight racism and effect change. His decision to return in April 2001 meant foregoing £75,000 of the award for loss of earnings.

Gurpal Virdi is now a detective sergeant. But he is considering retiring. He says the report DAC Clark commissioned has "seriously damaged" his career. He is also still receiving hate mail.

Sathat's complaint to the PCA about the search of her home was finally concluded five years later in January 2004. Again the Yard refused to provide the PCA with its media strategy file. Sathat had previously turned down a serious financial offer from the commissioner to drop her complaint. "The PCA report was one-sided. I was promised officers would at least get words of advice, but nothing happened to them. We sent the report back to the PCA. There is no justice."

Graham James, one of the three commanders who sacked Gurpal Virdi, thereafter joined the Untouchables as Head of Discipline and Civil Actions. He later adjudicated on the cases of undercover cop Michael and of DI John Redgrave, among others.

What happened to commander James when his own integrity was called into question shows the arbitrary nature of internal investigations when they involve senior Untouchables.

After his stint in the anti-corruption squad, commander James was seconded on promotion to the Immigration & Nationality Department, part of the Home Office, where he took charge of refugee removals. However, on 27 February 2003, the Home Office relieved him of his command and sent him back to Scotland Yard after an allegation of sexual harassment brought by a senior female civil servant he'd worked closely with for many months.

The Home Office made a reported £100,000 last-minute, out-of-court settlement to Janet Stewart in return for dropping her damaging employment tribunal case. James denied the allegations and claimed not to have been involved in the negotiated settlement. However, within a few months of being back at the Yard he was suspended, this time by the MPA, on 3 June 2003 over separate allegations of false mileage claims.

James was apparently due to retire in the summer and take up a job with a private company with police links. Part of the Venson Group's business is fleet management. James was once the commander in charge of the Met's fleet of 3,500 cars, vans and motorbikes. The maintenance and repair contract was privatised and in December 1998 the Met awarded Venson a 7-year contract worth £18 million. But experts raised safety concerns. James found himself having to resolve complaints from police staff about shoddy maintenance, though he was still supportive of Venson's successful bid for a 25-year maintenance contract with Nottinghamshire Police worth £62 million.

His suspension meant James couldn't retire to Venson until the MPA-supervised inquiry by the commissioner of the City of London police was completed. However, one month into it, the MPA decided to lift his suspension without any meaningful explanation. James was reinstated, but the inquiry into him continued for another five months. Then, on 5 November, he retired. As James was no longer suspended, there was nothing to stop him going before the inquiry had concluded. And once he had gone, the inquiry ended with the allegations unresolved.

And what of Janet Stewart? She never returned to the Home Office.

Superintendent Ali Dizaei joined Scotland Yard on promotion from Thames Valley Police in March 1999, just a few weeks after the landmark Stephen Lawrence Report was published. Commissioner Sir Paul Condon was casting around for high-profile ethnic minority officers to make his force look less institutionally racist. Dizaei, with his law degree and doctorate in race and policing issues, fitted the bill. He was a vocal critic of what he perceived as racist selection processes and wasn't afraid to assert his rights through legal action.

Dizaei had come to Britain in 1973, six years before the Islamic revolution deposed the corrupt Shah regime, which his father served as a policeman.

After a stint as staff officer to assistant commissioner Ian Johnston, Dizaei was posted to the affluent west London borough of Kensington and Chelsea, where the most opulent and influential part of the Iranian community lives.

It was one of those classic contradictions that Dizaei's arrival at the Met was held up as evidence of the Yard's reformism, while elsewhere in the force Gurpal Virdi was being savaged by the same senior officers. But Dizaei's star did not shine for long. By September 1999 he too was secretly targeted by the Untouchables in a corruption probe that lasted four years and was later described in court as "Orwellian".

The Untouchables had received intelligence linking Dizaei to the recreational use of cocaine and associating with a known drug dealer and prostitutes. DAC Roy Clark gave authority to tap Dizaei's work phone. Clark also wrote on the application form that he had been "fully briefed" with "verifiable and quality information". Dizaei's barrister, Michael Mansfield QC, would later claim the Untouchables knew this was "palpably untrue".[4]

The secret operation into Dizaei was codenamed Bitten. After listening to hundreds of calls, by October CIBIC officer Stephen Wilkinson was telling his bosses there was "nothing to suggest" Dizaei used drugs or was involved in serious crime. A CIBIC report dated 11 November 1999 supports Dizaei's contention that he was being targeted because the Yard feared his new role as vice president of the National Black Police Association (NBPA). It described him as having "an influential role within the [Met]" and someone who had "the ear of many prominent and powerful figures in politics and throughout the BPA". This included home secretary Jack Straw and Tony Blair.

The Metropolitan Police chapter of the BPA was set up that autumn with an office inside the Home Office as well as the Yard. Straw attended the inauguration in October and welcomed the BPA as advisers to his department on diversity issues and ethnic recruitment. But to some senior Yard managers they were an enemy within.

Dizaei was also the NBPA's legal adviser. By bugging his work phone the Untouchables were in danger of breaking laws preventing the interception of "legally privileged" conversations between a client and lawyer. DAC Clark knew this and instructed that CIBIC should not make or pass transcripts of these intercepted calls to the Untouchables. A senior officer in the CIB intelligence cell, Bob Berger, was deputed to keep such calls to himself.

However, it later emerged that the anti-corruption officers investigating Dizaei were passed transcripts of these legal conversations, contrary to written assurances from police minister John Denham to Tory MP Peter Bottomley. He had been a vocal critic of the Met over the Virdi scandal and believed the anti-corruption squad was targeting the BPA for political reasons. It has never been revealed which Untouchables were responsible for the leak and for misleading the minister and Parliament.

IN-HOUSE

The phone-taps did reveal Dizaei had a full sex life with several lovers. But because he was married, this was described in one CIB intelligence report as "unethical". His wife knew about the lovers because they had an open marriage and were only staying together for the sake of their three young children. Unorthodox maybe, but the Untouchables were looking every bit as prurient as the Ayatollah Khomeini.

The sex and drugs allegations were augmented by unsubstantiated "concerns" that Dizaei was involved with what the Untouchables called "major criminals" carrying out a so-called advance fee fraud. The six men were all given codenames after famous composers. Dizaei was "Mozart". This part of the corruption probe, had it been made public, would have provoked a diplomatic incident because one of the five suspects was the Liberian ambassador.[5]

In January 2000, the corruption probe into Dizaei was taken over by a newly appointed Untouchable, detective superintendent Barry Norman. He was directly responsible to commander Andy Hayman and detective chief superintendent Bob Quick. The flagging Operation Bitten was renamed Helios and received a much needed boost when the mother of one of Dizaei's former lovers, Mandy Darougheh, an Iranian national, raised the spectre of espionage.

Dizaei had split acrimoniously with Mandy and left abusive and threatening calls on her answerphone. Her mother told Norman she felt Dizaei knew "exceptional details" of her husband's incarceration in Iran on suspicion of working for MI6 and had boasted of high connections – Dizaei was in fact a personal friend of the Iranian ambassador.[6] Suddenly, he was under investigation for having an "unhealthy relationship" with Iranian Intelligence. His barrister would later claim the alleged threat to national security was in effect fabricated to keep Operation Helios burning and to justify 17 months of further intrusive surveillance, as the drugs allegations were going nowhere.

Part of Dizaei's job at Kensington was to liaise with the many embassies in the borough. Had the Untouchables done their homework it would have been clear that his visits to the Iranian Embassy were reported to Special Branch.

On 25 August 2000, the Operation Helios team[7] met with Hayman and Quick to discuss what they should do about Dizaei. There was a strong hint of panic because two days earlier the employment tribunal had upheld Virdi's claim of victimisation. The Untouchables were concerned that if all its efforts resulted in disciplinary offences and nothing criminal, Operation Helios would also look like a racist witch-hunt.

Norman would later explain to the court how some secret "new intelligence" fortuitously emerged around this time, which justified continuing the intrusive surveillance against Dizaei on national security grounds. The trial judge was persuaded by the Untouchables' PII application not to disclose any details. But the so-called "fresh intelligence" can't have been very compelling, because Dizaei has never been charged with offences under the Official Secrets Act.

Norman tried on three occasions to trap Dizaei in 2000 using undercover officers, deployed at great expense. He and two Untouchables flew to Los Angeles to brief a Farsi-speaking US undercover cop. His brief was to approach Dizaei at a business conference he was speaking at, with a request for moody visas to the UK. The sting came to nothing.

In London, plans were drawn up to rent a large flat in Kensington for an undercover cop called "Billy". He was to befriend Dizaei at his gym and see if he was involved in drugs, fraud, anything. According to a report by the Untouchables' Integrity Testing Unit, the scheme "produced nothing".

The third attempt involved using a detective investigating the murder of the Adams crime syndicate's money launderer, Solly Nahome. He approached Dizaei and asked what he knew about one of the suspects, a man named in court as Jimmy Sanchez and described by CIB as an associate of the Liberian ambassador. The hope was that Dizaei would alert Sanchez. Again, the Untouchables were forced to concede there was "no evidence" of a connection between the two men.

Yet in January 2001 Ali Dizaei was suddenly suspended on full pay. The Untouchables now admit they took the decision for two extraordinary reasons: firstly, he was about to go on the senior command course, the gateway to the top tier of British policing, and secondly because it was more than likely he would also be elected the new president of the NBPA.

The decision to suspend Dizaei was taken at a very high level. Assistant commissioner Michael Todd read out the allegations to Dizaei. These included claims he had perverted the course of justice, was dishonest and lacked integrity. After over a year of no accountability, the internal operation was referred to the PCA, a body which had so frequently demonstrated its political affinity with the commissioner's anti-corruption message. The Yard tried to claim it had previously involved the Independent Advisory Group, who had recently criticised them over the Virdi affair. But a few weeks after Dizaei's suspension, four black and Asian lay members left in protest, saying this was not the case.[8] Their resignation letter on 12 February said:

> We feel that we can no longer remain members of the IAG because it is now explicitly controlled by the police [and] in the past 18 months has lost its critical distance, its capacity to challenge, its independence . . . All efforts to pull back have been sabotaged from both the police and some members of the IAG. In particular, the chair [Beverley Thompson] has, in our view, become too close to the police to be able to ask difficult questions . . . We cannot in good faith be part of a group that is supposed to be comprised of the organisation's "sternest critics", when this is clearly no longer the case. We cannot remain as nodding dogs who will not speak out for Londoners.

In December 2001, Dizaei was charged with misconduct in a public office and perverting the course of justice. These charges at first blush appeared to be the top end of corruption and left the impression Operation Helios had finally come across something that would justify all the expense and surveillance. But on further examination, Dizaei and his legal team were amazed to learn the prosecution case related to an incident in September 2000 when someone had carved cross-like shapes on the panels of his distinctive BMW. That same day, black detective constable Delroy Anglin had his car tyres slashed near his south London police station. And over at the Yard, deputy assistant commissioner Tarique Ghaffur, whom Condon had brought from Lancashire Police, received hate mail.

John Grieve's CIB spin-off, the Racial and Violent Crimes Task Force (CO24), started an investigation codenamed Operation Athena-Frieze. Grieve told the investigating officer the three attacks could be a reaction to the Virdi case and suggested she liaise with Operation Helios. Norman strained credulity when he later told the court his men didn't mention to CO24 that they had a surveillance team on Dizaei the day his car was attacked. The Untouchables knew Dizaei had lied about where the car was parked when he discovered the damage. He had claimed it was nearer Kensington police station.

There was no suggestion by the Yard that Dizaei had done this because he caused the damage to his own car. He later explained he had lied because he was on his way to a BPA meeting even though his boss at Kensington had told him not to go. The Untouchables however argued the lie was told to increase Dizaei's profile as a victim of racist police. And as a result, 56 hours of police time were wasted on inquiries and reconstructing the attack in the wrong location, they claimed.

Dizaei's behaviour did raise serious questions, but was this really a criminal matter? Or was it, as his barrister suggested, more the case that the Untouchables had seized on this to justify the covert operation? Drugs, prostitutes, major fraud and, of course, espionage had all been whittled down to wasting 56 hours of police time.

Mansfield tried unsuccessfully to get the case thrown out during a preliminary hearing in July 2002 and later in February 2003. He accused the Untouchables of acting in "bad faith", or at the very least, being grossly negligent.

Over 100 officers were deployed from CIB, SO10, CO24, MI5, Special Branch, NCIS, Forensic Science Services, Forensic Telecom Services, the Inland Revenue, the FBI, the DEA, Beverly Hills Police and Royal Canadian Mounted Police. Dizaei was kept under surveillance for 91 days using static cameras, bag cameras and old-fashioned photographers. A staggering 3,500 phone calls were monitored, his bank accounts were accessed, his friends, associates and legal team were researched and profiled, people at restaurants he frequented were interviewed and the owners questioned to see if he did anything improper and whether like a good Muslim he ate Halal meat. Every taxi driver he submitted a receipt from was traced. A woman in the public gallery at the Old Bailey started laughing when it was explained that even his dry cleaner was approached to see if he had asked for a discount. The scale of Operation Helios made a mockery of Ian Blair's claim that they had learned lessons from the Virdi affair. It is hard to imagine any of the Untouchables withstanding this level of scrutiny.

Mansfield said the Yard had faced a "proportionality dilemma": an investigation takes on a life of its own. It becomes self-justificatory, self-fulfilling and self-perpetuating, in that once you have gone so far you have to keep going, keep spending public money to justify what you've done. A focused investigation then becomes a fishing expedition to get anything. The risk, he said, was it then turns into a witch-hunt where there has to be some form of criminality. The Untouchables were "a law unto itself", and a "state within a state" that became "obsessed" with his client.

IN-HOUSE

And how much had Operation Helios cost? The Yard came up with a figure of £2.2 million. The BPA say it's nearer £7 million. Norman told Mansfield there was no costing of the operation at the time he took over. "I was never troubled by the amount of money we were spending," he said.

Under further cross-examination, Norman denied embellishing any surveillance applications or cutting and pasting tired allegations onto new surveillance applications just to keep the operation running. He also used Roy Clark's defence in the Brennan trial – simple research couldn't be done to test an allegation for fear of alerting Dizaei. Mansfield countered that these "concerns" were actually "designed to linger" and had been used to brief influential figures against Dizaei, especially Jack Straw and his number two at the Home Office, John Denham.

Norman eventually admitted there was no evidence of Dizaei misusing drugs, just intelligence. Despite the battering, Judge Michael Hyam refused to throw out the case, thereby forcing a jury trial. In his reasoning, Hyam said Operation Helios had made mistakes, but the investigation was necessary, it was by the book and with no element of bad faith or gross negligence.[9]

The jury didn't see it that way. And even though they heard Dizaei admit lying about his car's location, on 11 April 2003 he was unanimously acquitted after less than one day's deliberation. It was another humiliating blow for the Untouchables, but the media couldn't report it because, remarkably, there was the possibility of a second trial.

That prosecution was even shakier than the first. It involved allegations of inflated mileage claims totalling a whopping £270. The Yard asked for more time to consider whether to proceed with the second trial at the Old Bailey, which costs the taxpayer roughly £10,000 per day.

The play for time meant the tenth anniversary of the murder of Stephen Lawrence would not be marked with media commentary about how the Dizaei and Virdi cases showed Scotland Yard had learned nothing – a point the BPA and several MPs, including Peter Bottomley, were preparing to make at a press conference. This was cancelled and in its place London TV viewers were treated to a spoon-fed item on commissioner Stevens in riot gear and Lord Toby Harris of the MPA opening a new £5 million riot training centre in Kent.

Dizaei's solicitor, Ian Lewis, was amazed to discover two weeks later that the Yard *was* going to proceed with the second trial. Senior CIB sources told us there had been much debate inside the Yard. The new operational head of the anti-corruption squad, DCS Shaun Sawyer, was opposed to a second bite at the cherry, but had been overruled. Lewis felt the Untouchables needed to convict Dizaei to mitigate the mauling they would expect at his forthcoming employment tribunal.

Certainly the desire to prosecute Dizaei was in stark contrast to how those in charge of Operation Helios had dealt with expenses fiddles by a junior CIB3 detective.

At the time Dizaei was under investigation, DC Mark Pudney was working on a separate highly sensitive covert investigation. Pudney's line manager was Bob Quick, the senior officer who considered the operation against Dizaei was proportional.

On 5 October 1999, Pudney was informally disciplined for falsifying his duty logs and falsely claiming overtime and a meal. During an informal interview with CIB officers, Pudney admitted the offence. He then protested, "But there are other people in the office including supervisors who don't keep up to date with their duty states."[10] These are supposed to be accurately filled in to ensure a truthful record of an officer's whereabouts during an investigation. Failure to do so can lead to trials collapsing because of a lack of integrity in the evidence chain.

Nevertheless, the Untouchables decided not to bring criminal charges against Pudney for the false expense claims. The CPS and PCA weren't consulted, nor was a formal disciplinary board thought necessary. Instead, DCS David Wood decided "the most appropriate course of action was to deal with the matter immediately by official caution" and quietly kick Pudney off CIB3.

When these double standards were put to the Yard, we got a totally misleading reply. The press office claimed Pudney had never alleged routine non-compliance with duty logs. Of course, there would be no truth then in the assertion that the Untouchables didn't put DC Pudney on trial or even on a disciplinary board because he was a prosecution witness.

The Pudney and James cases pale into insignificance when compared to the double standards at work over the special treatment of senior Untouchable, detective superintendent Chris Jarratt, when he was accused of doing the same and a lot worse than Ali Dizaei.

Jarratt has served his entire career in south London, starting at Peckham, then Greenwich before his first serious detective posting on the Brixton Robbery Squad in the late eighties. By then it already had a reputation for corruption and racism that predated the riots of 1981. Detectives on the squad had a specially designed tie with five playing cards, all spades. Geddit?

Jarratt later transferred to the Tower Bridge office of the Flying Squad, where there was already a terrible stink of corruption, typified when a vital exhibit – a shotgun – went missing. In 1991, he became a detective inspector and took charge of the highly sensitive David Norris murder inquiry, working to superintendent Ian Crampton, who was godfather to one of Jarratt's young sons. After a one-year sabbatical at Exeter University, Jarratt returned in 1993 to work in Southwark on a proactive squad under his mentor David Wood. That's when they set up the pawnshop sting using undercover officer Michael. In 1996, Jarratt was appointed staff officer to assistant commissioner David Veness, a sure sign he was working his way into the Yard's inner circle. From there he was recruited the following year by Roy Clark and reunited with David Wood to run the new CIB intelligence cell. As head of intelligence and covert operations, Jarratt was intimately involved in developing stings and participated in assessing the phone-taps on Ali Dizaei.

In January 2000, Jarratt was given a new post of restructuring the anti-corruption squad. It was an odd posting for such a proactive detective and made some wonder whether it was connected to a complaint that Jarratt had made false allegations of corruption against a detective who refused to break the rules governing the bugging of prisoners.

Sergeant Dave Cross was in charge of the Yard's Prison Liaison Unit. His men were based at prisons in the greater London area and facilitated police access through the Home Office and prison governors. A part of his job was highly sensitive. The Prison Liaison Unit, attached to SO11, has responsibility for bugging cells, prison visits and, more controversially, the legally privileged conversations between inmates and their solicitors. One method used is the "talking table", so-called because it has an in-built bug and is placed in the prison waiting-rooms or the specially assigned rooms for legal conferences.

Cross was a stickler for the paperwork required to authorise this level of surveillance. He had dealt with many police squads during his seven years at the Prison Liaison Unit, but felt the Untouchables displayed an arrogance and total disregard for the rules. It wasn't just Cross. His staff had voiced their concerns since 1997. The Untouchables "were trying to pull strokes", he told us. "Breaking the rules, threatening people, staff and prisoners, trying to make unlawful visits without visiting orders – you name it, they are doing it. And we said that in the minutes of meetings."

Cross had complained directly to the Home Office Police Advisers, who promised to do something. But little had changed by 1999, when he had his own run-in with Jarratt. The cause was a rushed request from the CIB intelligence cell to video an ex-cop visiting an inmate. Cross organised the filming but refused to release the video without the paperwork.

Jarratt complained to SO11. The resulting investigation cleared Cross. But the matter didn't end there. Some time later Jarratt gave a speech as part of the CIB road show taken to various police stations to explain their work. In the audience was a friend of Dave Cross. He reported back that Jarratt had apparently referred to an operation that was compromised because of an unnamed, corrupt prison liaison officer.

Cross believed this was a reference to him and discussed his grievance with a senior officer who discouraged him from pursuing the matter. He refused and made a formal complaint about Jarratt to commander Andy Hayman. But he says Hayman refused to give Jarratt a formal reprimand. Cross's lawyer, Martin Murray, an ex-superintendent in the Met, feels the decision not to formally investigate Jarratt was almost certainly determined by the knock-on effect a more severe reprimand would have had on the anti-corruption squad.

Cross complained about Hayman, alleging he was covering up for Jarratt. Fearing reprisals from the Yard and feeling the pressure of the situation, Cross also took sick leave until retiring. He has never tried to sue the police.

Jarratt's rise was unaffected. He briefly returned to Brixton as commander Paddick's number two. In a self-assessment of his policing skills, Jarratt claimed the credit for initiating "the new cannabis debate". But he was less forthcoming about his role in the loss of 26 kilos of cannabis during the CIB3 sting that netted McGuinness and Garner. In late April 2001, Jarratt was promoted to detective chief superintendent and took responsibility for all murder squads in south London. He never lost contact with the Untouchables and kept a watching brief on Dizaei and other cases. He was also preparing for the final interview before becoming a commander. But a quiet storm was gathering among the 400 detectives and civilian staff he was now responsible for.

IN-HOUSE

On Friday, 8 March 2002, Jarratt was expecting a performance visit from the head of all of London's detectives, DAC Bill Griffiths. He arrived with commander Andre Baker and instead "removed" Jarratt from his post, pending an internal inquiry. When we contacted the press office next day they were tight-lipped, in marked contrast to the private briefings and press releases prepared for crime correspondents when Paddick, Virdi, Dizaei, Locker, Redgrave and other "targets of the Untouchables" needed to be publicly humiliated.

Jarratt didn't return our call. He wasn't being rude; he was on holiday in Antigua with his new girlfriend, Samantha Bird, the Met lawyer who was dealing at the time with the John Wilson case.

It escaped no one's attention that, unlike Dizaei, Jarratt had not been suspended. Yet the criminal and disciplinary allegations against the Untouchable were quite extraordinary: financial impropriety, oppressive conduct towards staff, abuse of power in the anti-corruption squad to target people he didn't like, and violent assaults on a former girlfriend.

While he was a serving Untouchable, complaints against Jarratt were easy to dismiss as part of a campaign by corrupt cops and their friends to undermine his work. But senior detectives and experienced administration staff with no obvious axe to grind were harder to ignore. The Yard must have considered all options before removing Jarratt, knowing what the implications for ongoing corruption cases would be. Another consideration was a front-page murder trial that the media had made a test case of how much the Yard had really learned since the Lawrence Inquiry.

In November 2000, Damilola Taylor, a ten-year-old, Nigerian-born boy, was fatally stabbed with a bottle on the North Peckham Estate. Jarratt inherited the high-profile murder inquiry. He was in overall charge when four white boys were arrested and charged. Jarratt had also overseen the debriefing of a key teenage witness known as "Bromley", who came forward after the *Daily Mail* offered a £50,000 reward.

Jarratt had boasted to his superiors how, as an "acknowledged expert on resident source debriefing", he had taken over the inquiry from detectives he described as "risk adverse and concerned that their personal credibility would be damaged". He went on to suggest that his encouragement of the use of "controversial tactics" ultimately led to Bromley becoming a prosecution witness.

But one month after Jarratt fell from grace, the Damilola case ended with all four defendants acquitted and the police on trial in the media and parliament. Bromley had been branded a liar by the judge and her evidence thrown out. The defence tore apart the way she had been debriefed and the use of financial inducements to effectively keep her sweet – a gerbil, phone calls, a promise of trainers and a holiday, a walkman, a trip to the seaside. No, this wasn't *The Generation Game* but a replica of the unlawful way the Untouchables secretly debriefed their supergrasses. No wonder that before the trial Bromley, no doubt thinking of the newspaper reward, was once recorded singing, "I'm in the money."

DAC Bill Griffiths had told the media the Damilola Taylor investigation was "by the book" and there was no comparison with the Lawrence case. Nevertheless, commissioner Stevens conceded an independent inquiry headed by an old adversary, Bishop John Sentamu, the former adviser to the Lawrence Inquiry.

While the Bishop conducted his inquiry over the summer of 2002, the internal investigation into Jarratt was producing some very compromising information about what was really going on inside the south London murder squads responsible for investigating Damilola's killing. None of what follows we understand was shared with the Bishop.

Internal documents show there had been an unprecedented mutiny by Jarratt's detectives before the Damilola trial. His "dictatorial" management style had run down staff morale so badly that senior management believed all nine murder teams had been ineffectual during the Damilola investigation. Detective chief inspector Paul McAleenan, for instance, revealed in his statement that over 100 officers had asked to transfer during the ten months of Jarratt's reign. DCI McAleenan and other senior officers suggested Jarratt was more concerned with getting promoted to commander than the core function of murder squads.

Furthermore, just before Damilola's death, all murder squads across London were being cut back because there had been serious mismanagement of the 2001–2002 budget, leading to a £20 to £30 million overspend.

The internal investigation into Chris Jarratt was headed by DAC Steve House and billed by the Yard as "independent". House, the press office told us, had come from Staffordshire Police. But he went there from the Met and had been back for some time. So the inquiry was very much in-house and wasn't referred to the PCA.

Unlike the investigation of Dizaei, Jarratt was not put under surveillance. His phones weren't tapped. He was not subject to undercover integrity tests and every facet of his past life was not scrutinised. The House inquiry was reactive and kept within a limited period of ten months when Jarratt was in charge of south London murder squads.

Although DAC House was not intending to examine Jarratt's conduct at the anti-corruption squad, there was one allegation that did spill over and was potentially very embarrassing for two other Untouchables – Brian Moore and Shaun Sawyer. In the autumn of 2001, all three were studying for the last stages of the selection process to become commanders. Jarratt was accused of misleading the head of Bramshill College to get three free rooms and facilities for five days by falsely claiming they were needed for police work. Moore and Sawyer said they were unaware of this, and had expected to pay. But they were eventually persuaded the fee had been waived.

After returning from his holiday Jarratt was moved to a desk job at human resources. This was a curious posting given that some of the allegations emerging involved severe bullying and intimidation of staff.

Just over a week before Jarratt was sent home his number two and the personnel manager challenged him about bullying, which he denied. Statements given to DAC House show Jarratt's supervisors at the Yard were aware of the problem months before they finally removed him.

Mark Benbow, the detective superintendent in charge of all informants in south London, told the internal inquiry Jarratt operated a climate of fear, was vindictive to officers he didn't like and female staff were "terrified" of him. Jarratt's staff officer, detective inspector Kevin Clingham, described how his boss's idea of feedback was to get him to tell a female member of his staff "she smelt of cigarettes and her feet stank". Julia Minton, the personnel manager with 17 years in the Met, recalled making a mistake and feeling "so frightened that Mr Jarratt would be angry that I felt physically sick and was in tears". She also spoke about a male detective inspector who had confided in her that he was so upset by Jarratt's treatment he felt like harming himself. Another experienced manager, Sally Derbyshire, gave this portrait of Jarratt: "He looks at you as though you are a complete idiot and makes you feel totally worthless. He is not at all approachable and is in fact a bully who likes to totally control people . . . He treats people like a commodity and with no respect . . . The only thing he is interested in is his [commander's exam] and he expects people to sweat blood so that he is successful. I am not afraid of anyone except Mr Jarratt and I hope I never have to meet him again."

One of the most shocking allegations was of actual bodily harm on a former girlfriend, Linda Rolfe, whom Jarratt had left in the eighties for the woman he eventually married, another police officer called Melinda. However, that marriage broke up in 2000 and Jarratt was seeing Met solicitor Samantha Bird when Rolfe made her statement.

Rolfe did not seek out the House inquiry. He approached her after collating other statements from serving officers who referred to it being "common knowledge" that Jarratt had assaulted Rolfe and his estranged wife. Rolfe's statement was not hearsay and she struck the House inquiry as very measured. She didn't want it used to charge Jarratt with actual bodily harm, but purely for a disciplinary hearing.

They had lived together from 1982 to 1985. She described Jarratt as ambitious and "very money orientated". She said on two occasions he "seriously assaulted" her at home. She gave excuses at work of having fallen down the stairs. After one assault she said Jarratt dropped her at the hospital. "Chris made threats he would use his Masonic links to ruin my father's career if I ever reported the violence."

Rolfe's best friend and fellow officer Deborah Bott made a supporting statement recalling how Linda had once sought refuge in her flat with bruises on her face. Detective sergeant Gary Flood also made a statement that Jarratt had victimised him since they served at Brixton in the mid-eighties, because he knew about the assaults on Linda Rolfe. Their paths didn't cross again until 2001, when Jarratt became Flood's boss.

Five detectives, including Jarratt's number two, superintendent Adrian Maybanks, supported Flood's account. They all made statements knowing how well connected Jarratt was at the Yard and what the consequence might be for their careers.

Flood says Jarratt smeared him to colleagues as a drunk and a gambler. From then on Flood kept timed and dated notes of every incident. This included the day he noticed a tail on his way to work. He traced the car registration to the Military Police Intelligence Section. "These were the actions of a man who appears out of control," Flood said in his statement.

The "vendetta" also had an effect on his wife who was having IVF treatment at the time. It failed. Flood saw a counsellor because he felt he was losing it. When his transfer was blocked, he went sick. Flood's solicitor unsuccessfully complained to commander Andy Hayman, who already knew about Dave Cross's concerns. The House inquiry had tried to interview Cross. But he suspected another "damage limitation exercise" and declined to be interviewed. The request by his MP, Tory John Horam, for an independent inquiry by an outside constabulary fell on deaf ears.

Finally, there was detective sergeant Steve Reeves. He claimed Jarratt had unfairly and improperly put him on the Yard's secret blacklist of corrupt and unethical cops out of personal animosity, and then had breached confidence by telling junior officers.

Intelligence documents we've seen give a rare glimpse into the sinister nature of the Yard's secret blacklist and make a compelling case that it should be abandoned immediately as failing to serve the public or the police.

Reeves and Jarratt first met at Peckham police station and then on the Tower Bridge Flying Squad. In October 2001 Jarratt notified Reeves he was subject to the Service Confidence Policy and moved him off the murder squad to a non-operational role in Streatham. After six months, Reeves exercised his right to appeal the decision by writing to the senior official who reviews the blacklist, Robert Dellegrotti. This is where the trouble began.

Reeves suspected his inclusion on the blacklist related to his past association with officers, probably from Tower Bridge and later when he served at the Swanley SERCS office. News of his appeal forced DCS Shaun Sawyer to write urging Dellegrotti to turn it down. It read: "DS Reeves was first included within the Service Confidence procedure within the first nine months of its initiation. This was based on intelligence sources spanning corrupt activity over nearly a decade. the majority of which was A1 material i.e. indisputable but not in this case discloseable. Other commitments prevented the targeting of Reeves after 1998; however, his not being dealt with overtly, on the balance of probabilities, suggests he maintained corrupt contacts as this was his modus operandi . . . There is no evidence or intelligence to indicate DS Reeves 'reformed' between 1998 and 2001 . . . The views of the CPS make clear that DS Reeves' currency as a witness of truth is untenable."

The Untouchables had briefed Martin Polaine, the head of the CPS Visa team, but didn't name Reeves or provide specific intelligence. Polaine just took it on trust that what the Untouchables were telling him was "very reliable".[11]

Dellegrotti was far less impressed and granted Reeves' appeal in April 2002, but not before saying this in his extraordinary report:

"There is clear intelligence up to early 1998 to show sufficient grounds for the inclusion of the officer . . . Nevertheless the policy allows the possibility of rehabilitation and there is nothing recorded any later than early 1998." He later told the House inquiry he was concerned that "very strong assertions [about Reeves] . . . were not fully backed up by current intelligence in the case of 'continued association' and by reliable intelligence in the case of recycling drugs. The form regarding the latter was undated, not signed, not evaluated, poorly written and extremely vague."[12]

The whole episode begs some very important questions. If Reeves is as bad as the Yard claim, what were the "other commitments" that prevented the Untouchables targeting him after 1998? Of course the main preoccupation that year was riding out the Stephen Lawrence Inquiry hearings and the family's insistence there was a corrupt association between south-east London detectives and drug dealers.

Was it a coincidence that Reeves served on the same squad as the infamous Dave Coles, known in the Lawrence Inquiry as Sergeant XX, who was once covertly videoed in highly suspicious circumstances with drug dealer Clifford Norris, the father of the main murder suspect? And how many other cases like Reeves' are there in the Met, which the Untouchables haven't got round to dealing with because of "other commitments"? Finally, it's clear from Dellegrotti's comments that the blacklist is wide open to abuse not just by individual officers using it for personal vendettas, as Reeves suggests, but also as a means of silencing the Yard's internal critics and whistle-blowers.

On 17 January 2003, DAC House finally interviewed Jarratt under caution, almost one year after he was removed from his post. An Old Bailey judge responsible for the second Flying Squad trial had warned the Yard to get a move on, but this had had little effect. Whatever decision the Yard took on Jarratt would also have an impact on the appeal of the first Flying Squad defendants.

There have been two rich seams of irony during the course of our investigation. The first is how many detectives suddenly developed a healthy respect for all the rules of evidence gathering and due process when the tables were turned and they became targets of the anti-corruption squad. Jarratt, who had been happy to operate an unlawful supergrass system, is now one of them. In his interview, he accused DAC Steve House of conducting "a less than balanced inquiry".

Jarratt denied having any longterm vendettas against junior officers. He said he had properly investigated one of the nine teams under his command because of allegations of "Spanish practices" which were never properly disclosed. However, he denied using military intelligence resources to follow DS Flood and suggested the officers who had made statements against him were in some sort of conspiracy to undermine his position.

On the bullying allegation Jarratt showed more contrition. He said he didn't set out to treat his staff unfairly but it was the consequence of having high expectations and, as he is ambitious, the performance of his command mattered to him.

He described Linda Rolfe's allegations of domestic violence as "wholly unfounded". The suggestion of threatening Rolfe's father was "preposterous", he said. "I have never concealed that I am a Freemason" but such threats would be against the tenets of the Brotherhood. Jarratt said he broke up with Rolfe because he didn't want to marry and because he was already seeing his future wife, Melinda. He said there was an "amazing fall-out" with Rolfe, who "hated" him.

DAC House didn't see it that way. Two GPs had confirmed Rolfe's account of visiting the surgery in November 1985 complaining of pain and swelling in her limbs. It was made clear to Jarratt that Rolfe didn't appear to House as desperate to "get" him. Asked his view on domestic violence, he said it was "appalling" and difficult to investigate because there are so many agendas. Jarratt also denied assaulting his ex-wife and claimed she refuted the allegations.

He then denied misusing police property and claimed he was "effectively on call permanently" and therefore entitled to the hire car and petrol. He also refuted misleading the head of the training college to get three free rooms and meals.

House did not appear impressed and accused Jarratt of acute double standards. He said: "What I would suggest is that your approach to work and your own career show that you operate with two sets of rules sometimes. A set of rules for yourself and a set of rules for other people, and they're not a consistent set of rules . . . you benefit from the set of rules and through you benefitting, others that you work with suffer."

Jarratt disagreed and then criticised the two men who had removed him, commander Andre Baker and DAC Bill Griffiths, for a failure of supervision. This was the second rich irony. No manager in Scotland Yard has ever been held to account for the failures of supervision in the specialist squads found to have rampant corruption. Roy Clark was never disciplined at Stoke Newington; the bosses of the Flying

UNTOUCHABLES

Squad also escaped any investigation, as did the men in charge of SERCS. And now Jarratt was implicitly asking why no senior Untouchable was facing any disciplinary action.

On 11 April 2003, the same day superintendent Ali Dizaei was acquitted at the Old Bailey in his first trial, the Yard published an in-house report into the humiliating collapse four months earlier of the prosecution of royal butlers Paul Burrell and Harold Brown.

Former senior Met officer Bill Taylor wrote a report that was widely regarded as a whitewash. There were no names and no blame attached to the Yard's Special Enquiry Team who had investigated the two butlers for allegedly stealing from Princess Diana's estate. Taylor told the press that commissioner Stevens had set his terms of reference. But he said there were lessons to be learned.

Burrell didn't see it that way. He told the *Mirror* – which had bought his story – the Taylor report was one "that wants the public to think Scotland Yard is full of Poirots . . . I am sick of such a fudge."[13]

The senior officer in charge of Burrell's prosecution was a former Untouchable. Commander John Yates had left anti-corruption work and in 2001 was put in charge of the Special Enquiry Team to investigate "celebrity cases". Burrell was his first real test.

But overhanging him was a serious criminal and disciplinary allegation from detective constable Jeff May that Yates and Chris Jarratt had committed perjury and conspired to pervert the course of justice during their investigation of corruption at the East Dulwich SERCS.

The anti-corruption squad had targeted May for 15 months following self-serving allegations by drug dealers turned supergrasses Diane Blanford and Eve Fleckney. They claimed that May had provided them with 8 kilos of heroin for a £140,000 payment. The detective was suspended and arrested. Eventually he was cleared and reinstated. But details started to emerge suggesting the two supergrasses had invented the claim to get a reduction in sentence. Furthermore, a CIB officer told May during a tape-recorded conversation that he had warned his superiors both women were unreliable and felt Blanford was a "fucking liar", yet the operation continued.

On 11 July 2001, May formally complained to assistant commissioner Michael Todd and commander Andy Hayman. He alleged he had been kept under investigation by the Untouchables for a simple but unlawful reason: to preserve the "integrity" of Fleckney because she was a key prosecution witness in the forthcoming prosecution of two East Dulwich detectives, Robert Clark and Chris Drury.

The timing of May's complaint could not have been worse for the Yard. Jarratt was in charge of the Damilola Taylor inquiry and Yates was in the middle of sensitive discussions with the CPS about whether to charge Paul Burrell with the theft of Princess Diana's possessions.

Before he did that, Yates and his number two, detective chief inspector Maxine de Brunner, had an important date with history. On 3 August 2001 they visited Prince Charles and Prince William at Highgrove to discuss their plans to prosecute the royal butler.

The Yard wanted the Princes' support for the prosecution because the case had large resource implications. But it was at this briefing that the two officers "grossly misled" the future Kings of England about the strength of the case against Burrell. Poorly researched intelligence around the butler's finances was presented as evidence he had sold Diana's possessions abroad and was living it up. The Princes were also told an informant had "shown the police photographs of several staff members dressing up in clothing belonging to Diana". In fact, Burrell's "unexplained increase in wealth" was easily explained had the elite Special Enquiry Team done its job properly. The butler earned good money from speaking engagements and the royalties from a recent book on etiquette.

Prince Charles knew none of this when he consented to the prosecution. Thirteen days later Burrell was charged. The Princes were also unaware of the serious complaint against Yates. How was that progressing? The Yard took five months to appoint a senior officer to take a statement from May in February 2002. By that time he had retired, aged 41, with clinical depression.

A month later Jarratt was removed from his command, but the internal inquiry by DAC House was not given May's complaint to investigate.

Fearing a cover-up, May had sought advice from pugnacious defence solicitor Mark Lake, who had plenty of experience taking on the Untouchables through his defence of DC Michael Charman and others. Over the summer of 2002, Lake wrote some searching letters to the Yard, the CPS and PCA. He complained to the CPS that Hayman's excuses for not progressing the investigation of Yates and Jarratt were "lame".[14] The solicitor told the PCA the Yard's refusal to disclose any details or update his client "only serves to cause us to believe there is a conspiracy afoot to cover up Mr May's allegations".

UNTOUCHABLES

The PCA agreed to take up the issues with Hayman, who mollified the watchdog with assurances that the investigation was serious and well advanced.

May's MP, the Liberal Democrat, Paul Burstow, followed up with a letter to the home secretary asking for an independent inquiry, but the reply, he says, was "woefully inadequate". By the beginning of October there was one question to which Burstow had still received no answer. When was Yates served with an official police notice alerting him to May's allegations? Police regulations say this should be done "as soon as is practicable" after the complaint had been made. That was in July 2001, but 14 months later no notice had been served.

The significance didn't dawn on Lake until the morning of Friday, 25 October, when he was reading the *Daily Telegraph*'s coverage of the fifth day of the Burrell trial. De Brunner had received a mauling under cross-examination by the butler's barrister, Lord Carlisle QC. She was eventually forced to concede that the Princes had been misled at Highgrove and subsequently about the butler's criminality.

Until then, Lake had no idea Yates was in charge of the Burrell case. It now made sense why the former Untouchable had not been served with official notification of May's complaint of perverting the course of justice and perjury. "If the defence knew about the investigation into Yates they would have insisted on calling him to explain about misleading the Princes. Then they could have attacked his credibility as a witness of truth," Lake explains.

The solicitor reviewed his correspondence with the Yard in the run-up to the Burrell trial. He noticed that ten days before it started the Yard had replied saying Hayman did not expect a report on the internal investigation into Yates for six weeks. How convenient, Lake thought. The Burrell trial would have been over by then.

That Friday, Lake sent Lord Carlisle a thick dossier about the May complaint. Neither lawyer was to know that this was the very day the Queen mysteriously remembered that Burrell had told her he was keeping some of Diana's letters for safekeeping. This damaging recollection was passed to Yates and the CPS the following Monday. It destroyed the prosecution case against Burrell but at least spared commander Yates the humiliation of cross-examination in front of the world's media. The trial collapsed a few days later. Paul Burstow MP told us at the time: "There is evidence Mr May was set up and now it appears [Paul Burrell] was almost sent down on a similar basis."

The Yard press office claimed, preposterously, there had been "no grounds" to serve Yates with formal notification of May's complaint.

IN-HOUSE

At best the whole affair showed how flexibly police regulations are applied. "I don't believe Yates did not know about the May complaint," says Lake. "But because the defence didn't know, de Brunner became the sacrificial lamb."

The whole affair hasn't hurt her career though. After the scandal died down, she was promoted to detective superintendent and then posted to the Untouchables. John Yates was made a deputy assistant commissioner. Meanwhile, the Yard is vigorously defending Jeff May's civil action for wrongful arrest and false imprisonment.

Superintendent Ali Dizaei's second trial for inflated mileage claims totalling £270 was scheduled for September 2003. The pressure was on because three months earlier the second Flying Squad trial had collapsed, leaving the whole anti-corruption crusade in tatters.

After high-level discussions at the Yard, on 15 September the Untouchables dropped the second prosecution of Dizaei. The CPS said there was "no realistic prospect of a conviction".

At first the Met resisted the call by MPA chairman, Lord Toby Harris, for an independent inquiry into the force's handling of high-profile cases involving ethnic minority officers. The chairman of the Met's Black Police Association, chief inspector Leroy Logan, announced the BPA was warning ethnic people not to join the police. He said the boycott would stand until there was an inquiry into who and what was really behind the Dizaei case and the wider targeting of the BPA.

The National BPA had already made a formal complaint to the MPA against deputy commissioner Ian Blair (who in the interim had been knighted), Andy Hayman (who had left the Met on promotion as chief constable of Norfolk Constabulary) and Barry Norman (who had left the Untouchables on promotion as borough commander of Islington).

Home secretary David Blunkett was especially concerned about the boycott. It came just as he was preparing to announce at the Labour Party conference that police recruitment was higher than at any time since 1921 and there were 9,000 more cops than in 1997.[15] Blunkett's officials desperately tried to broker a deal before the October party conference. Senior sections of the Yard wanted to discipline and sack Dizaei because they believed he was corrupt. But he had already started employment tribunal proceedings, which had even more chance of success given the two acquittals.

Dizaei wanted an apology, reinstatement, the dropping of all disciplinary proceedings and an assurance that he would be allowed onto the senior command course. The talks broke down in the first week of October when, according to Ray Powell, president of the National BPA, the Yard insisted on putting Dizaei on the internal blacklist. "Ali was distraught and we viewed the whole Service Confidence Policy [the blacklist] as contrary to the Human Rights Act," says Powell. "We took the unprecedented step of proactively not encouraging people to join the Met and we called for the suspension of Ian Blair, Andy Hayman and Barry Norman. This woke a few people up, including the home secretary. It wasn't all about Ali Dizaei. We wanted a national solution to a national problem."

The matter was referred to the arbitration service ACAS. The Dizaei and BPA position was greatly strengthened when the BBC broadcast its undercover exposé of racist police recruits, *The Secret Policeman*, on the first day of negotiations. At first, Blunkett tried to trash the documentary but then withdrew his attack and applied intense pressure on the Yard for a settlement.

Finally, on 30 October a deal was struck. The Yard press release described it as "groundbreaking" and designed to prevent the public purse taking a further battering. Dizaei agreed to withdraw his employment tribunal case, as did Leroy Logan.[16] The National BPA agreed to withdraw their complaint against the three Untouchables and lift the boycott on ethnic recruitment. In return, Dizaei was reinstated, assured a place on the senior command course and given a payment of around £80,000. He, in turn, expressed regret that his behaviour had fallen below the standard expected and was given words of advice, a minor sanction. But it was accepted he returned to the force "with his integrity intact". The Yard also agreed to review up to 30 other employment tribunal cases it faced from black or Asian officers concerned about the CIB operations into them or harassment at work. It also consented to the independent inquiry proposed by the MPA.

In a private letter to Dizaei's solicitors, the Met effectively agreed there would be no disciplinary proceedings and any attempt by the PCA to insist would be resisted. But this agreement was cut behind the backs of the PCA, which alone had statutory powers to decide whether to halt disciplinary proceedings. On 30 March 2004, just days before it was due to be replaced by the new Independent Police Complaints Commission (IPCC), the PCA ordered the Met to put Dizaei on a disciplinary board. The PCA was persuaded by a CIB report that claimed to have "substantiated" nine disciplinary offences against Dizaei.

IN-HOUSE

The NBPA threatened strikes, boycotts and marches if the Dizaei deal was unpicked. And immediately it took over on 1 April, the IPCC was lobbied by the Yard to withdraw the PCA's direction.

The IPCC had been set up the previous year by the Home Office, which supported the Yard's position. Furthermore, the Home Office had also ensured the founder of the Untouchables, Roy Clark, was already inside the new so-called watchdog as its director of investigations. It came as no surpise that the IPCC sided with Blunkett and commissioner Stevens.

The whole deal left a bitter taste in the mouth of those white police officers targeted unfairly by the Untouchables but who had no political capital with the Home Office. And once again showed just how arbitrary the whole discipline system is.

At the time of writing, Dizaei has just finished the senior command course, which he attended with DCS Shaun Sawyer. There was a private agreement that he and other CIB3 detectives on Operation Helios would never have to serve with Dizaei.

And what of DCS Chris Jarratt? The media, which only saw the Dizaei case as a race issue, completely missed the parallels and double standards with the Untouchables' treatment. In August 2003, exactly one month before the case against Dizaei was dropped, the CPS decided that DCS Jarratt wouldn't be charged with any criminal offences.

On 2 December the Yard told us he would face disciplinary proceedings for "five alleged breaches of the police code regarding issues of honesty and integrity around the use of police hire vehicles, overbearing conduct towards colleagues and improper disclosure of information relating to internal staff matters".

Interestingly, the domestic violence allegations were not included. Yet three days later, the Association of Chief Police Officers announced it was considering a "formal policy" to combat domestic violence by cops. This coincided with a poster campaign – "Domestic Violence abusers are losing control" – in which the Met trumpeted how it could now "pursue abusers even without evidence from the abused partner".

According to the ACPO press release its new policy would include screening for offenders and schemes to encourage relatives, partners and colleagues to report allegations. It also suggested that the current policy of arresting civilian offenders should "always" be applied to police officers – Jarratt was never arrested – and their suspension or removal from public duties should also be considered. Jarratt was never suspended. The ACPO policy also suggests that in disciplinary proceedings where for whatever reason no criminal charges have been brought, dismissal from the force should be a sanction.

The government had also commissioned a parallel study of how police forces deal with domestic violence by members of the public. Astonishingly, it reported that the police failed to record more than half the incidents reported. With this culture was it any wonder the Yard didn't see fit to discipline DCS Jarratt over Linda Rolfe's allegations?

The disciplinary board was set for June 2004, but in the months leading up to it a deal was struck. The Met dropped the charges relating to the misuse of police cars and improper disclosure because of "a lack of evidence or the receipt of a satisfactory explanation" from Jarratt. He agreed to accept a written warning for his overbearing conduct towards staff, thus negating the requirement for a potentially explosive disciplinary hearing. At the time of writing Jarratt remains at Human Resources as a chief superintendent, awaiting a management posting to front-line policing.

27

"WE ARE SUBJECTS NOT CITIZENS"

Alastair Morgan lives in a tower block in the north London constituency of Labour MP Chris Smith. One of the first things he did after moving to the capital in the mid-1990s was give Smith a detailed account of the tangled events since his brother's murder. Smith pressed the Tory Home Office and Scotland Yard, but to no avail. A senior south London detective, Bill Griffiths, a Ghost Squad boss, was also unmoved by the Morgan family's entreaties in 1996 to re-open the case.

Following the change of government in May 1997, Chris Smith entered the New Labour cabinet as minister for culture. He began to push the Yard again, this time from the inside.

Over the summer, Alastair read an article by a well-informed former Met press officer claiming that the murder inquiry would be re-opened following the arrest of Duncan Hanrahan and Martin King.[1]

Chris Smith wrote immediately to his colleague, the new home secretary Jack Straw, who'd just announced a public inquiry into the four-year-old Stephen Lawrence murder. Smith underlined the parallel plight of his own constituent.

> Mr Morgan's brother was murdered ten years ago and to date no-one has been brought to trial. His family believe that a number of police officers were involved in the murder and that not only have the murderers gone unpunished but that very serious police corruption is being covered up. This case has always caused me a great deal of unease but despite the

numerous letters I've written and various meetings I've attended, the authorities have been unwilling to re-open the investigation. I was extremely interested therefore to read the recent report in the *Mail on Sunday* . . . stating that following an anonymous tip-off Daniel Morgan's murder is now being re-investigated. I would be very grateful if you could let me know whether there is truth in this report and if so what progress has been made with the investigation. I do fear that serious police corruption may be uncovered and it is vital therefore that this case is fully investigated without delay.[2]

Commissioner Condon assured the home secretary there was no tip-off and no new investigation. Straw then wrote to Smith: "The commissioner informs me that there were some allegations that a senior officer was involved in the murder of Daniel Morgan. He has however assured me that those allegations were fully investigated at the time and proved to be incorrect." This was the first the Morgans had heard of the allegations, but they were unable to extract more details from officialdom. It was sometimes painful for the family to watch rocketing media interest in the Lawrence case, while the Fourth Estate remained largely indifferent to Danny's murder when there were so many parallels.

Alastair and his ageing mother, Isobel, felt Scotland Yard could not be trusted to investigate itself. She lived in Wales, where the media were far more receptive to the story, as was her local MP, the Liberal Democrat Richard Livesey. He and Smith arranged a meeting with commissioner Condon at the Yard on 7 November. DAC Roy Clark was also present, taking notes.

Livesey upbraided Condon for the obvious impropriety of a detective (Sid Fillery) leaving a murder inquiry, retiring from the force and then immediately filling the dead man's shoes. "He really laid into Condon, who looked extremely uncomfortable," recalls Alastair. Months passed and the family heard almost nothing unless they badgered Clark. "Even then I couldn't get any answers out of him."

A year later, in early December 1998, the Yard's witchfinder-general finally briefed the Morgans that there was a new third inquiry into Danny's murder underway. He gave no real details and Alastair and Isobel left the meeting thinking it was just more of the same lip service they had received since 1987. In fact, Clark was referring to something very unique. For at least the last six months his Untouchables had been bugging the offices of Southern Investigations. This covert operation was codenamed Nigeria.

"WE ARE SUBJECTS NOT CITIZENS"

Very early on, we saw Operation Nigeria intelligence documents, which portray the two Southern Investigations directors Jonathan Rees and Sid Fillery as "alert, cunning and devious". The documents include the bi-monthly applications the Untouchables made to senior officers at the Yard for authority to keep the bugging operation going. The 9 December application, one week after the Morgans met Clark, says: "Both Rees and Fillery have been subjects of interest to CIB for a considerable period of time. Longterm and wide ranging intelligence shows them to be deeply involved in corruption, using a network of serving and retired police officers to access sensitive intelligence for the purpose of progressing crime, frustrating the course of justice and selling sensitive information to the press. Both conduct criminality from the premises . . . Amongst their clients [they] number criminals and established media contacts. In addition, Reece [*sic*] remains a main suspect in the murder of his business partner Daniel Morgan in 1987."

It is apparent from the Operation Nigeria intelligence documents that the Morgan murder was being used as a pretext to authorise the bugging operation. Its primary purpose, it would appear, was to protect the image of Scotland Yard, whose fate by then was in the hands of the ongoing Stephen Lawrence Inquiry.

Why had Clark waited all this time to bug Southern Investigations when it had been known for over ten years that the company was at the centre of a web of corruption? The Ghost Squad was more than capable of spying on Rees and Fillery at any time between 1993 and 1997. So why wait until June 1998 to seek the first authority to insert bugs into the private detective agency? It is more than coincidence that this was precisely the month when the long history of police corruption in south-east London was becoming a politically damaging issue for the Yard as the Lawrence Inquiry public hearings progressed.

The Morgan family of course had no insight into the fascinating detail emerging from the bugging operation at Southern Investigations, which ran from June 1998 to May 1999.

What happened next showed that Rees and Fillery clearly didn't suspect they would be subject to the most intrusive surveillance, even though Hanrahan had tipped them off soon after he was arrested in May 1997 that the Untouchables were after them and their mutual friends like retired detectives Nigel Grayston and Alec Leighton.

Rees and Fillery had at least six serving police officers they used to obtain stories for the tabloids in return for what Rees euphemistically called "a few pints". He was also doing private surveillance and then tipping off friendly cops to make arrests if anything illegal was spotted.

UNTOUCHABLES

The arrangement was to be the undoing of Southern Investigations.

In May 1999, anti-corruption officers monitoring the bugs were taken aback by hard evidence of a plot Rees was developing to fit up the estranged wife of a client called Simon James, a jeweller. He was separated from Kim James, a former glamour model, and was in the middle of a nasty custody battle with her over their young son. Eventually Rees conceived a plot to plant drugs in her car and get one of his police contacts to make an arrest. This would hopefully persuade a court to turn the boy's care over to his father.

Operation Nigeria had recently been renamed Operation Two Bridges and from then on concentrated on developing a sting to catch Rees and others he had brought into the plot. This included Jimmy Cook, his repo man and someone Rees described as "a simple soul, who'd done odd jobs [for me] over many years". Another party to the conspiracy was detective constable Austin Warnes. He then engaged the bouncer turned celebrity gangster, Dave Courtney, to pretend to be the informant who tipped him off about Kim James's supposed involvement with drugs.

The sting operation to catch Rees meant letting the conspiracy run as far as the Untouchables could, which in turn meant not telling Kim James. She was arrested in June after a local police team, alerted by DC Warnes, found the cocaine Rees's people had planted in her car. The whole operation was being monitored at the highest levels of the Yard from John Stevens through Roy Clark to commander Ian Quinn to DCS Dave Wood and detective superintendent Chris Jarratt, head of the intelligence cell overseeing the bugging operation and sting.

In September 1999, Rees, Cook, Warnes and Courtney were arrested and charged with perverting the course of justice and other serious offences.

But what of the re-opened inquiry into the Morgan murder, the original justification for inserting the bugs at Southern Investigations 15 months earlier? An intelligence report at the time put it this way: "Due to the considerable manpower involved, the strategy to investigate the murder of Daniel Morgan has for the moment been curtailed."[3] In fact it had been abandoned, while the family were led to believe it was at the top of the Yard's agenda.

The firm within a firm had been ignored for a decade. It had been allowed to grow like poison ivy around the police stations of south-east London. But only when it became a serious threat to the Yard and individual officers in the inner circle did the anti-corruption squad move against it. This, however, was very much a secret pruning exercise rather than a wholesale assault on root and branch. The Yard had to steer a careful course that did nothing to undermine its unofficial policy of not sharing with the Stephen Lawrence Inquiry the evidence and intelligence it was accumulating about the endemic corruption in south-east London and how that had also contaminated the murder inquiry, as it had contaminated the earlier murders of David Norris and Daniel Morgan.

There was another compelling incentive for the Untouchables to "curtail" the Morgan inquiry. The bugging operation had caught Rees and Fillery discussing a "smear campaign to discredit" leading Untouchables, particularly Chris Jarratt, one of its most important yet vulnerable shadow warriors. He was known to many of the serving and retired cops in Southern Investigation's circle of influence.

One retired detective alleged to be part of the "smear campaign" was detective inspector Keith Pedder. He retired in December 1995 from the Met disillusioned after leading the hunt for Rachel Nickell's killer. The case ended in ignominy for the Yard when a judge threw out the prosecution evidence against Colin Stagg after lambasting the highly controversial undercover honey trap operation.

Pedder was a close family friend of Chris Jarratt and his wife. They'd served together in Brixton and Tower Bridge and were Freemasons and godfathers to each other's sons. But the pair fell out when in March 1988 the anti-corruption squad targeted Pedder in a sting operation. The corruption case against Pedder was so poor the Old Bailey judge took no time to throw it out. Pedder says he was being smeared and "set up" to prevent publication of a book he had just completed criticising senior Yard figures over their undisclosed role in the Nickell case.[4]

Jarratt's continued involvement in Operation Two Bridges was clearly not seen as inappropriate by Roy Clark. Jarratt wrote to his boss: "Product already obtained confirms that Reece [sic] at least harbours ill will against CIB3 personnel. In scanning intelligence around police corruption in London it can be stated that Reece and Fillery are a crucial link between the criminal fraternity and serving police officers. There is nothing that they do that in any way benefits the criminal justice system. I see ongoing intrusion as crucial to our efforts to control corruption within the Metropolitan Police Service. Should we be able to successfully arrest and prosecute Reece and Fillery for corruption matters it will be seen within police circles as 'untouchables' having been touched and in so saying will put off many who are currently engaged in malpractice and indeed those officers who may be contemplating committing crime."[5]

By July 1999 even the Untouchables noted that intelligence from the bug about the murder was "scarce". So that month they planted a story in the *Daily Telegraph* claiming officers had identified the driver of the getaway car used in the murder. It was hoped this would stimulate conversation in the office of Southern Investigations. It didn't. Instead it caught the attention of Alastair who immediately called Scotland Yard, forcing Clark to guardedly explain how the inquiry had been preoccupied with Rees's plot to fit up Kim James.

"I think the *Telegraph* thing was done to pretend [Clark] had done something, when in fact it appeared [in the press] when the whole James thing was almost wrapped up. It was a sop," says Alastair. He believes Clark would have said nothing until Rees's arrest in September had he not contacted the Yard. And using the murder as a pretext for a self-serving bugging operation to protect the Untouchables was a "cynical betrayal".

What emerged from the bugging operation as far as the Morgan murder was concerned were claims by the Untouchables that Rees and Fillery appeared troubled when they learned Hanrahan had been jailed for eight years on 19 March 1999. One intelligence report a few weeks later says: "Fillery is particularly concerned at what Hanrahan might have told police about the association between them, and whether Hanrahan has given information about the murder . . . implicating him and Reece [*sic*]. Clearly, Fillery is concerned and feels more vulnerable around this issue than many others discussed."

The only thing Rees and Fillery did was change the company name to Law & Commercial.

The Morgan family had first complained about the handling of the murder investigation back in July 1988. The PCA appointed Hampshire Police to investigate allegations of police involvement in the killing and the derailment of the murder inquiry. The family learned from the television news in February 1989 that Hampshire officers had re-arrested Rees and Paul Goodridge, the man Daniel Morgan thought he was going to meet with Rees at the pub on the night of his murder.

"Initially I was delighted with this development," recalls Alastair, "because something was happening at long last. But then I rang the police station and no one would talk to me. Then as I thought about the situation I became very worried indeed. No one told us, no one warned us that there would be any developments of any kind. But we were now used to this type of behaviour from the police."

Hampshire's highly publicised arrests led nowhere. The two men were released from custody and the charges of murder and conspiracy to pervert the course of justice dropped on the instructions of Treasury Counsel. The Morgan family would later learn that these charges were never referred by the police to the Director of Public Prosecutions and had only been brought in the wake of a secret meeting between top Hampshire brass and their opposite numbers at Scotland Yard. The secret meeting had also taken an extraordinary decision to alter the terms of reference of the Hampshire inquiry, thereby moving the focus away from allegations of police corruption and collusion in the murder. The whole manipulative package had been endorsed by the PCA, without a whisper to the Morgan family.

Paul Goodridge successfully sued Hampshire and the Yard for malicious prosecution. Solicitor Russell Miller represented Goodridge. He was simultaneously immersed in the battle for justice as part of the ragamuffin bunch taking on the corrupt Stoke Newington police.

As he read the Daniel Morgan case papers Miller became increasingly perturbed, and not only about the way his client had been treated. To build his client's compensation case, Miller prepared a damning analysis of the "very serious irregularities" made by Hampshire and the Yard in arresting Goodridge. He also underlined how the "truly extraordinary" Daniel Morgan case cried out for independent examination because of the "serious allegations of police corruption and criminality".

Miller also knew police forces dealing with controversial cases liked positive press coverage because it made them look busy, effective and in control. "In my view," he wrote, "Goodridge was charged simply to relieve pressure on the inquiry concerning ex-detective sergeant Fillery and other police officers close to Rees . . . It is my belief that Goodridge was charged in the certain knowledge that he would be acquitted so avoiding a trial in which embarrassing material about police corruption might emerge. But he was also charged in the equally certain knowledge that intense media coverage of the charges and sensationalist comments made by the police would distract attention from police wrongdoing."

Miller was the first to notice the secret revision of the terms of reference of the Hampshire inquiry. Unlike the Morgan family, he had obtained on disclosure and read the 80-page Hampshire report. All the Morgan family got was a summary of Hampshire's conclusions in a brusque letter from the PCA in 1990 saying there was no evidence of police impropriety or involvement in the murder. The Hampshire report and the minutes of the police meeting at which the terms of reference were changed were deemed official secrets, fit only for the eyes of state servants and their accomplices in the PCA.

For a full decade after Daniel's death the Yard had maintained that its original murder inquiry was entirely professional and uncontaminated by Fillery's presence. But the intelligence documents from Operation Nigeria showed how the Untouchables were now accepting everything the Morgan family had been saying for years about Rees and Fillery being at the heart of a network of police corruption. Roy Clark never apologised or explained how the Yard had made such a mistake. Indeed, there was still an element in the police who treated the family as if they were challenging the integrity of the world's finest police force.

In 1998, for instance, three members of the Morgan family felt that they were simultaneously under surveillance. Isobel was in Wales, Alastair in Glasgow and Jane was working for the British Army in Germany when they spotted people tailing them or taking their photographs. It occurred, says Alastair, soon after a front-page article in the local Hampshire press had quoted him calling for the chief constable to resign.

Clark was unhappy about media coverage the family generated. In July 1999, he met with the Morgans' solicitor, Raju Bhatt, another veteran of the struggle against corrupt Stoke Newington cops. Bhatt noted Clark's comments that the original murder inquiry was "good, honest and thorough" but "perhaps not innovative". Hampshire's re-investigation was also "good" and "well intentioned", Clark stressed.[6]

The following year the Morgan family met Clark again to see how he planned to progress the "curtailed" murder inquiry. He offered a formal murder review with the possibility of a fourth investigation dependent on the outcome. The family asked to see a copy of the Hampshire report. "The blood drained from his face," Alastair recalls. "I told him I wanted to see it because I thought it had been done under the old pals' act."

The Yard quickly moved to prevent disclosure. Clark's difficulty was the Lawrence Inquiry report had recommended that relevant internal reports should in most circumstances be disclosed. The Lawrence family had been given access to the Kent/PCA report into the first murder investigation. The Morgans hoped they'd be treated the same. But they were to be bitterly disappointed. Clark wrote outlining the extraordinary conditions of disclosure: "I have decided that you should not be provided with a copy but should be allowed to read it under controlled conditions. I am content for you to read it in unredacted form and assume that as is our present agreement you would do nothing to hinder the progress of ongoing inquiries."[7]

But in the run-up to Rees's trial for fitting up Kim James, the Yard suddenly moved the goalposts. In October 2000, Clark informed the family he would read them the report but they could take no notes or tape-record. There was worse to come. The Yard and Hampshire feared a massive compensation claim and all the attendant bad publicity. So Clark insisted the Morgans sign an indemnity against legal action. The family declined the invitation to sign away their right to sue and told Clark that Daniel's mother Isobel, now a frail 72 years old, needed to see the Hampshire report for her peace of mind.

In the middle of all this, Rees and Simon James were jailed in December 2000 for six years each. Warnes received four years. Unexpectedly, Jimmy Cook and Dave Courtney, who wore a jester's outfit to the Old Bailey, were acquitted. The Untouchables appealed the sentence handed down to the sacked detective Warnes. He received another year. So did Rees and James when they appealed their sentence and conviction.

Negotiations for access to the report passed to commander Andy Hayman in 2001. Alastair wrote to him on 27 March saying the "lack of openness" was having an effect on his mother's well-being. He said the "terms [were] tantamount to blackmail". In June, Hayman ruled the Hampshire report would not be disclosed in any form and if they took legal action he would no longer brief them about the continuing murder inquiry.

The family was appalled at this thinly disguised blackmail. In a letter to commissioner Stevens on 10 October Alastair expressed his loss of confidence in Hayman and questioned his fitness to be in overall stewardship of the proposed fourth murder inquiry. "We have no closure even over past inquiries. One could almost believe that the Lawrence Inquiry had never taken place."

On 25 June 2002, the Yard launched its fourth murder investigation under detective chief superintendent Dave Cook. The new investigation was codenamed Operation Abelard. However this was a cover for what was still a covert inquiry controlled by the CIB intelligence cell. As part of a general re-branding of the anti-corruption squad, the intelligence cell had been renamed the Intelligence Development Group. The detective superintendent in charge of it and the Morgan case was David Zinzan.

The new targets were Sid Fillery, Jimmy Cook and Rees's brother-in-law, Glen Vian. Zinzan had bugs and taps re-inserted at Law & Commercial and other premises.

The murder re-inquiry also had a new supergrass, Steve Warner, the criminal implicated by Duncan Hanrahan in the ecstasy job. Warner rolled over after he offered an undercover cop money to kill Jimmy Cook. Warner then made a statement alleging Cook had admitted to him he was the getaway driver in the Morgan murder. Zinzan's team had also arrested Barry Nash, who they believed was involved with Warner in the contract on Cook, although he was never prosecuted for this. According to a CPS report, Nash told the police that Cook had admitted standing over Morgan's dead body, but he refused to make a statement.

Cook was arrested for conspiracy to murder. So too was Rees, whom Zinzan had removed from Ford Open Prison and sent to a high-security jail. Fillery was also arrested, but only for offences arising out of the loss of a file in the original murder inquiry. This was eventually dropped. But in a bizarre twist, the police found child pornography on Fillery's office computer. He said he had paid to access it for research purposes but pleaded guilty in 2003 and was subsequently placed on the sex offenders register.

On the day of the 16th anniversary of the Danny Morgan murder, the Yard sent its file to the CPS recommending Cook, Rees and Vian should be charged with murder or conspiracy to murder. The CPS took five months before deciding in August 2003 there was insufficient evidence for a realistic prospect of a conviction. The reasoning suggests the CPS felt the case CIB had presented was so poor as to raise questions whether the whole exercise was a further sop to the family and evidentially doomed to failure.

Firstly, Warner, the CIB supergrass, was handled like all the others and eventually imploded. He made a serious complaint that he had been "pressured" to sign statements naming his criminal associates and Cook. He also alleged that he had received inducements like conjugal visits and a case of beer from his debriefers. He repeated these allegations to DCS Bob Quick of CIB3. But for reasons that remain unclear, and probably unrecorded, Warner decided not to proceed with the complaint. Once again the supergrass system had undermined a prosecution. Warner was already a busted flush because he had tried to kill Cook, so his value as a witness against him was limited from the start.

Secondly, Rees and others made no admissions or incriminating asides during hours of bugged conversations. The government lawyers who reviewed the case seemed to suggest that the whole bugging exercise was evidentially worthless.

DCS Dave Cook was appalled at what he'd learned during Operation Abelard. He totally contradicted Roy Clark's claim that the first murder investigation was good. At a meeting with Isobel and Raju Bhatt on 5 September 2003, Cook told them "the real mischief" had occurred during the first murder investigation, which he went on to describe as "the worst mess he had ever seen". The role of Fillery, in Cook's view, was "at the heart of the mischief" and those around Fillery, including police officers, had protected him.

With the abandonment of the prosecution, the Morgan family was now informed that the case was being referred to the Yard's Murder Review Group headed by DAC Bill Griffiths, the very man who had refused to re-open the investigation seven years earlier when he was in the Ghost Squad.

The Morgans took the Yard to the High Court over its decision not to show them the Hampshire report, which had become more important in light of DCS Cook's recent comments. The Yard folded its hand at the court door. The family, however, is prevented by a court order, sought by the Yard, from discussing the contents of the Hampshire report. Alastair Morgan says it is "a shameless whitewash".

No statement was taken from whistle-blowing cop Derek Haslam. He told us Hampshire came to see him but had no real interest in the background. "I walked out of there thinking their sole agenda was to go through the motions." The Hampshire report also says "nothing sinister should be inferred" from the relationship between Danny Morgan and detective Alan "Taffy" Holmes, who killed himself four months after the murder.[8]

Other shortcomings we've identified in the Hampshire report are:

- No assessment or investigation of police corruption in south and south-east London.
- No examination of the shocking improprieties evident in the first investigation.
- No serious evaluation of the Belmont Car Auctions robbery and moonlighting cops.
- No analysis of Morgan's readiness to expose police corruption.
- No serious effort to test Kevin Lennon's devastating allegations at Danny Morgan's inquest. They are simply dismissed as "incapable of corroboration".

UNTOUCHABLES

- No accounting of the discovery of fibres on the axe handle.
- No reference to an internal investigation into the theft of a Rolex wristwatch from Daniel Morgan's dead body. Police officers, ambulance and mortuary staff were under suspicion.

In short, the Hampshire report appears as appalling a cover-up as the Barker Review of the first Lawrence murder inquiry.

In a retrospective interview for this book Alastair Morgan underlines that the Yard's mishandling of his brother's murder is every bit as big a scandal as Stephen Lawrence and can now only be resolved by a full public inquiry.

"It makes me feel profoundly uncomfortable that the state holds all the cards. We are subjects not citizens. I feel demeaned as a human being and yet the activities of my mother and my family so far have brought to light a morass of corruption already and we still haven't got anywhere near the bottom of it yet. We've been fighting for 17 years. Let that speak for itself. That's how hard it is to get anything done in Britain. What does that tell you about the state of policing in London and the state of Britain? It's been like four people in one family trying to turn a 20,000-ton oil tanker around with their bare hands.

"We have the right to know if policemen were involved in killing my brother. Now we are at the beginning of a long battle over the disclosure of all the other documentation about the murder. We want openness and we want honesty. We're tired of groping around in a labyrinth of darkness and secrecy. I do not believe that it is a mere coincidence that my brother died in the same area as Stephen Lawrence. I believe that the way the case was handled had a profound effect on the growth of corruption in the Met. If they had stamped on them when it happened I'm certain this would have inhibited the corrupt network in south-east London. Instead it developed over the 1990s and felt it was untouchable."

A major player in that network was Duncan Hanrahan. On his release in 2001 we asked him whether he felt an independent system of investigating police corruption would have encouraged him to be more forthcoming. He said yes, noble cause corruption was routine throughout the Met. That was why he had no respect for many of the poachers turned gamekeepers at CIB. He knew there were certain areas and certain retired or serving officers they would never touch. There were also entire squads that were out of bounds.

He is also amazed how little thought had seemingly gone into the best way of approaching someone like him. The overbearing attitude was not conducive to Hanrahan coming clean. He says he would have been prepared to give more had he been debriefed in an ethical, open way with no side, no hidden agenda, no off limits areas, no craven promotion junkies and no leaks.[9]

A thorny question exercised his mind: why should he be truthful with CIB when they were not being truthful with themselves or with the public?

In May 2004, the CPS told the Lawrence family that the much-vaunted murder re-investigation started by DAC John Grieve in 1999 would not result in any criminal charges. For five years the Lawrence family had their hopes raised. Selective leaks from the Yard produced numerous articles; some of them front-page splashes heralding imminent prosecutions.

While the CPS deliberated, reporters spun the Yard's line that Grieve had produced enough evidence to charge some of the five suspects. So when the CPS dropped the case they alone were supposed to look like the bad guys. "We can't invent evidence," one exasperated CPS official told the BBC.

Imran Khan, the Lawrence family's solicitor, wanted the CPS to immediately release the reasoning behind their decision so he could consider whether to judicially review it in the High Court. But if the Morgan family's experience of the CPS is anything to go by the Lawrence family has a long wait ahead of them. The Morgans had to complain to the new Director of Public Prosecutions, Ken Macdonald QC, before the CPS gave its reasons, an incredible nine months after the decision to drop the case against Rees and others.

There had been careful triangulation between the Yard and CPS about what to tell the Morgan family. The letter finally arrived on 6 May 2004, once the storm over the Lawrence decision had subsided. Alastair Morgan called it "tripe". Only a public inquiry, he says, will let his brother's ghost rest.

PART FIVE

A SILENT COUP

28

WATCHDOGGED

The Untouchables were publicly launched to coincide with commissioner Sir Paul Condon's crucial appearance in front of the Commons Home Affairs select committee in December 1997. It was in these august and televised surroundings that Condon declared there were up to 250 bent detectives in his force.

The commissioner went to Parliament fully briefed by his intelligence chiefs about the "scale of the problem". That, after all, is what the Ghost Squad had been "scoping" for four years in unprecedented secrecy. However, the Yard now claim that Condon "made a mistake" when he spoke of 250. The real figure CIB3 was operating to back in December 1997 was 30 to 40 bent cops, DCS David Wood told us.

Let us assume Condon's "speculation" was a dreadful mistake. Why then during his well-orchestrated appearance at the committee hearing did none of his advisers jump up and correct this misleading impression? One senior officer who stayed in his chair was Roy Clark, the architect of the anti-corruption strategy since 1993 and its sole boss since 1996. He more than anyone in Scotland Yard would or should have known the commissioner was talking rubbish and that it could cost the force dearly if the "mistake" remained uncorrected. In fact, the public record wasn't corrected the following day or at any time over the next few weeks to ensure the select committee did not repeat the 250 figure in its report, which is exactly what happened when it was published in January 1998. Indeed, for the next 18 months the Yard was content to allow the 250 figure to stand uncorrected and Parliament therefore to be misled.

It was only in June 1999, during an interview with the *Evening Standard*, that John Stevens radically downsized the problem by an amazing 400%. He claimed only about 50 dirty cops involved in serious corruption would be prosecuted. Of course, by this time the Yard had weathered the select committee hearing and the Stephen Lawrence Inquiry.

On any view, Stevens' new maths said a lot about what he thought of the original intelligence given to his predecessor. But the numbers game raises another very important question that goes to the heart of why Scotland Yard conducted such an expertly choreographed anti-corruption crusade in the first place. Did the Yard exaggerate the scale of corruption and mislead Parliament in order to advance its case for an unfettered internal investigation with no independent oversight? And was this done because the Yard feared the select committee and the public inquiry into the Lawrence scandal would take away for ever the power of the police to investigate itself?

The Yard just can't seem to get its story straight over the true scale of the corruption problem at any one time. In 1993, Roy Clark, when first pitching the Ghost Squad to commissioner Condon, claimed it was "probably very few". In 1994, Roger Gaspar was said to be operating a list of 83 detectives. In 1996, Condon told the *Guardian* there were 200 bent cops in his force. In December 1997 he told Parliament it was up to 250. In June 1999 Stevens reduced that to 50. Then two months later the CIB press office told *The Job* magazine "experience and current intelligence suggest the real numbers are much closer to the 100". And in an interview with commander Andy Hayman in March 2000 we were told there were about "1,000 entries" on the CIBIC computer, of which 250 to 300 were "worth going for" and over the next three years "80 to 100 [were] real runners".

What is certain is that the anti-corruption crusade, after ten years of unfettered spending and spying, has only successfully prosecuted about twenty serving and retired officers for serious corruption. Of that figure four are their own supergrasses – Garner, McGuinness, Hanrahan and Putnam. Alternatively, around twenty serving and retired detectives have been acquitted or discharged because of question marks over the veracity of these supergrasses and the integrity of CIB3 operations.

There have been nowhere near the mass resignations by suspect officers that the public witnessed when commissioner Sir Robert

WATCHDOGGED

Mark last cleaned out the stables between 1972 and 1977. Then, some 478 officers left the force. Most jumped before they were pushed.

Condon thought criminal prosecutions were preferable, but disciplinary hearings were, he said, his "fall-back position". Yet despite new rules since April 1999 making it easier to sack an officer, under the Condon/Stevens period (1993–2004) the figure for those dismissed for serious corruption is fewer than ten.

Getting exact figures out of the Yard has proved a difficult task. When we asked for a breakdown of figures routinely spun to crime correspondents, the Yard ran into great difficulty as if they were being asked to substantiate someone else's maths.

A special case in point was 28 August 2002. Commissioner Stevens launched the third five-year phase of the anti-corruption crusade. Prevention would be the new focus, he told the assembled crime hacks. He went on to say how "prosecutions had proved difficult" and blamed tricky cops who knew how to exploit the criminal justice system. Stevens then issued a set of figures for 1998 onwards. We asked for the full figures since 1993, broken down by name and offence, of officers and civilian support staff who had been prosecuted or disciplined.

Initially, DCS Shaun Sawyer invited us in for a briefing to explain the figures, which otherwise could appear "misleading", he said candidly. At the eleventh hour the briefing was cancelled on the instructions of commissioner Stevens. He had already refused to be interviewed for this book and so it was thought no other senior officer should do so.

Seven months passed and with each one our suspicion grew that like so much with the anti-corruption crusade, the Yard's maths just don't add up. Repeated requests were met with silence or false assurances. Only when threatened with a complaint to the MPA over non-compliance with its media policy – a document peppered with commitments to "openness, honesty and flexibility" – did we finally get a response, but not an answer. We were told the figures for the Ghost Squad phase, 1993 to 1997, would not be provided because the Yard claimed a duty of confidentiality and said it was hogtied by the Data Protection Act. Laughably, it was also suggested it would not be in the public interest to make such a disclosure. This same argument was advanced to refuse us the overall discipline figures.

While the Ghost Squad period was completely shrouded in secrecy, there was some limited disclosure of figures for the Untouchables period from 1998 to April 2003. But these figures were not broken down and are impossible to decipher. Criminal convictions and disciplinary rulings for minor misdemeanours like traffic offences on and off duty were lumped in with serious cases of corruption, presumably to bump up the figures.

We also asked how many Untouchables had been removed from the anti-corruption squad for unethical, dishonest or corrupt behaviour. The Yard doesn't keep those figures, we were told.

The inescapable conclusion is that preserving the myth of a good score sheet is essential to justifying CIB3's undisclosed budget and to justifying why Scotland Yard should continue to investigate itself.

A government study has shown how an increasingly aggressive performance culture in the police force was "a major factor affecting integrity" and had led to "a trawl of the margins", "soft-targeting" and other unethical means to "drive up the figures" and therefore "portray performance in a good light".[1] The study was of course referring to normal policing and how everyday crime figures are massaged. But there is every reason to believe this deceit has simply been transferred to the war on corruption.

The true scale of the corruption problem in Scotland Yard has been deliberately obscured from the public and Parliament. When the Yard needed to appear tough on corruption and launch its Untouchables the figure was high. When the effectiveness of CIB3 became a serious embarrassment, the figure was radically downsized.

If the 250 figure is accurate, then the anti-corruption squad measured in terms of prosecutions has been a massive failure and many bent cops are still out there. If there never were 250 bent cops then the Yard misled Parliament by sexing up its intelligence to make the case for self-regulation.

Our investigation leads us to conclude that there are dirty cops who've been deliberately allowed to retire or remain in "the Job" because to do something about them would lead the Yard to places it had no intention of going, especially during the Stephen Lawrence scandal.

To mask this secret containment policy the Yard trots out the unsustainable claim that corrupt cops are more difficult to catch than organised criminals. But as one officer points out, the Untouchables can bug a police officer's work phone, his car, they know all his financial details, his circle of friends, they can monitor his movements, set integrity tests and profile him psychologically. Yet the Yard would have us believe that the corrupt cop can somehow avail himself of more loopholes in the criminal justice system than a rich career criminal.

Tales of tricky cops too slippery to catch are one of those convenient excuses senior Untouchables use to mask not just a secret containment policy but also their own inadequacies and failures as managers in charge of the best-resourced squad in Scotland Yard.

One of the ways around the low conviction rate has been the arbitrary use of suspension to falsely inflate the "success" rate and to muzzle internal critics and potential whistle-blowers. This strategy has been complemented since 2000 by the introduction of the blacklist. The Yard tells us that 35 unnamed defective detectives were put on the Service Confidence Policy between January 2000 and April 2003. These cops are not suspended, but continue to work on full pay despite doubts about their integrity. They could be dealing with your case now, whether you are the victim or witness to a crime, or even suspected of one. But you will never know. In effect, we are paying for cops who the commissioner believes are corrupt, dishonest or untrustworthy. But if he doesn't trust them, then why should we? If there is sufficient reason to blacklist an officer, why not remove him altogether? And why keep the blacklist hidden from independent scrutiny to ensure it isn't being abused?

Another totally predictable failure of the Untouchables followed the resurrection of the discredited supergrass system. Their use not only failed to secure the promised convictions, it has also led to a run of appeals and civil actions leaving the taxpayer to pick up a bill that could total several million pounds in compensation payouts.

The humiliating collapse of the second Rigg Approach trial in summer 2003 was the final nail in the rotten coffin of supergrass-driven prosecutions. Suddenly, after ten years of filtering inconvenient allegations, the Yard has finally implicitly accepted what it knew all along – the supergrass system was unlawful. But this unpublicised U-turn is too little and too late because in those ten years the Yard was able to manage its corruption problem and present the public and Parliament with a distorted and untruthful picture.

On 1 April 2004, the PCA was discarded to the dustbin of history as the "irrelevant fifth wheel to the investigation coach", just as liberal jurist Lord Scarman rightly predicted back in 1984. In its place is a new police watchdog called the Independent Police Complaints Commission. The IPCC was a seed germinated in the 1998 Home Affairs select committee report. The Blair government subsequently commissioned KPMG to do a feasibility study, although what an accountancy firm knows about the police complaints system is not readily apparent.

Liberty, the pressure group, conducted an alternative study, setting up an advisory committee that included representatives of the PCA, ACPO, the Police Federation, its retained solicitors Russell, Jones & Walker and a chief constable, alongside civil liberties lawyers and barristers with experience in representing victims of police violence and deaths in custody.

The Liberty report in May 2000 was the more progressive of the two studies. The report dismissed the protectionist mantra of the police Establishment that only cops can investigate cops and that civilian investigators don't have the necessary authority or skills to achieve effective co-operation from police witnesses or suspects. New legal powers of compulsion and good training on police procedure would overcome these objections, the report concluded. However, it recognised the usefulness of some police involvement in the investigation process, "especially in the early days of the organisation". But it felt "strict limits need to be set on the level of police involvement (25 per cent), and the roles that police officers play within the organisation so that the credibility of the IPCC is not damaged". Crucially, it went on to recommend that the "investigative teams should *always* be headed by a civilian team leader".

The Lawrence Inquiry report gave added impetus to the movement for change when the government agreed to implement its recommendation to "ensure serious complaints against police officers are independently investigated [given that] investigation by their own or another police service is widely regarded as unjust, and does not inspire public confidence".

Home Office mandarins and their police advisers used the two feasibility studies to fashion an IPCC under the 2002 Police Reform Act. There has been no appetite for the radical change championed by legal figures like Michael Mansfield QC. He wanted a European-style pool of investigating magistrates on a four-year tenure in charge of a group of civilian anti-corruption investigators who go through a well-developed training programme. Mansfield says trusted cops can be helpful but they should "never" have control of the investigation.

The main change from the PCA system has been to give the IPCC its own proactive investigative arm of so-called "civilian" investigators with powers to interview under caution, enter police premises and seize material. All cases involving deaths in custody, fatal accidents

WATCHDOGGED

and serious injuries to the public caused by the police, as well as allegations of racist conduct and certain corruption allegations, apparently, will be automatically referred to the new watchdog. The IPCC will also be able to inquire into any area, even if there has been no public complaint. But in reality over 97% of complaints will continue to be internally investigated but with IPCC supervision or direction. The hope is that internal affairs departments will raise their game.

The IPCC launch literature aims to persuade the public this is radical change. And on paper it is. But as ever the reality is a lot different.

In December 2002 the Home Office appointed Nick Hardwick as the IPCC's first chairman. By his own admission, 47-year-old Hardwick has no experience in criminal law, police procedure and investigations. He is someone who rose within the management of social work organisations dealing with prisoners, the homeless and latterly refugees.

Hardwick says his job is "to inspire public confidence" in the police complaints system, something that is at rock bottom in all communities. Crucially, he says the IPCC "will demonstrate independence by the people we appoint, scrupulously avoiding conflicts of interest". But as a measure of that public commitment, in July 2003 Hardwick rubber-stamped the appointment of the Home Office's and Scotland Yard's preferred candidate as the IPCC's first director of investigations.

For 34 years, DAC Roy Clark was the gatekeeper of the Yard's secrets. No more loyal a servant of the police's interests could one find. He is the J. Edgar Hoover of British policing, who has spent so long in the black chrysalis of intelligence work that one of his colleagues says of him: "He's trained himself not to talk in his sleep."

The justification for Clark's appointment is tied to the fiction that his stewardship of the Yard's anti-corruption crusade was a success. Secrecy and unaccountability have been at the heart of Clark's anti-corruption model so it should be of no surprise his appointment to the IPCC was achieved by stealth. Clark was one of an undisclosed number of candidates who applied for the key post through the headhunters, Veredus. They are part of the Capita group, which has numerous government contracts and also administers the Met's pension fund.

In March 2003, Mark Turner from Veredus and former senior Met officer Bill Taylor whittled the candidates down to four. At the time,

UNTOUCHABLES

Taylor was also preparing his 'no names, no blame' report for commissioner Stevens on the collapsed royal butler prosecutions led by former Untouchable John Yates.

Hardwick refuses to release the list of candidates or to name the final shortlist. So we have no idea how many were civilians. Hardwick was on the final selection panel accompanied by IPCC chief executive Sue Atkins, who had been poached from the Cabinet Office, and an assessor, Zahida Manzoor. A fourth, surprise panel member was DCS Dave Wood, one of Clark's protégés whom he handpicked in 1997 as an Untouchable.

"I asked Dave Wood to be on the interview panel because I had met him when I'd done a visit to the Northern Ireland Ombudsman office. I was impressed by what he did and the approach he'd taken," Hardwick told us in a testy interview. The Untouchables were instrumental in setting up the IPCC equivalent in Northern Ireland. In August 2000, the newly appointed Ombudsman, Nuala O'Loan, a former PCA member, visited commander Andy Hayman and Ian Russell at the Yard. She was looking for pointers on how to investigate public complaints against the new-look Royal Ulster Constabulary. The RUC, perceived as being anti-Catholic and a key player in the dirty war, was being restructured as part of the peace process. One of Sir John Stevens' key confidants, DAC Hugh Orde, was made the chief constable of the reformed RUC. Orde had worked with the commissioner on his inconclusive inquiry into state collusion with Protestant paramilitary death squads and also helped strategise over the Yard's response to the Lawrence report.

Several senior Untouchables were seconded to help O'Loan.[2] In fact, Wood was Northern Ireland Ombudsman executive director of complaints and investigations when he helped select his colleague Roy Clark for the same job covering England and Wales.

Home Office mandarins are driving this silent coup to put former Untouchables in charge of the police complaints system in the UK. Similar shadow warriors are also now overseeing other complaints mechanisms involving the criminal justice system. The former head of MI5, Stephen Lander, for example, was put in charge of public complaints at the Law Society.

As a further measure of the Labour government's betrayal of true independence, the Home Office ensured Clark was in place *before* any of the 15 IPCC commissioners were appointed. These are the men and women from different professional backgrounds – by law they cannot have served in the police – whose job it is to safeguard

WATCHDOGGED

the IPCC's independence and oversee impartial and just investigations.

But what does it tell us about the IPCC and Nick Hardwick that these commissioners, many of whom come from truly independent backgrounds, were given no say in such a key and controversial appointment as Clark's? After all, his is not a temporary post to help ease the transition, far from it. Clark has been given a fixed five-year contract at £65,000 per year, on top of his substantial police pension.

His appointment violates the spirit and letter of the philosophy underpinning the Liberty report stressing civilian control of investigations. Which is ironic because the pressure group's director, John Wadham, has now been appointed deputy chairman of the IPCC.

The IPCC commissioners have therefore inherited a system that was moulded before they took up their posts. Clark set up his department in close liaison with an ACPO Working Group and the Home Office. He has been instrumental in selecting his senior management team of five regional directors of investigation. Three of them are also senior ex-cops or Customs officers.

As with the Yard, it was hard to get the IPCC to come clean about the exact composition of the 75 so-called "civilian" investigators it has appointed. From their figures a staggering 84 per cent (63) are former government law enforcement officers: 33 are former police or Customs officers; 25 are former government investigators from agencies like the Inland Revenue and Immigration; 4 are ex-military and one from an unnamed intelligence agency. The remaining 12 are categorised as "others".

Hardwick will not name the eight ex-cops who once served in internal affairs units. We know that two of them are former Untouchables. One of them is recently retired detective superintendent Simon Cousins, the head of the Witness Protection Unit and the officer at the centre of the Hector Harvey security breach fiasco. He is now a senior IPCC investigator.

Hardwick says he has no vision of eventually phasing out the presence of former police and other law enforcement officers by creating a truly independent investigative arm drawn from the highly skilled private sector of lawyers, forensic accountants and those with no obvious conflict of interest. This does not sit well with Liberty, who told us they would like to see a plan to reduce the number of ex-cops below a ceiling limit of 25 per cent. "The further it can be reduced the better," a spokesman said.

UNTOUCHABLES

We tried to interview Clark before his IPCC appointment. He said it would be "inappropriate" because the Yard had refused to cooperate with our book. The reply showed just how close he still is to the organisation he is now supposed to hold to account. Hardwick also turned down our repeated requests to interview Clark. The watchdog chairman refused to put the matter to the IPCC commissioners – who, at least on paper, are Clark's line managers.

We wanted to ask Clark about his anti-corruption record when he served at the Flying Squad. We wanted to know why he felt his management at Stoke Newington made him suitable to set up the Ghost Squad. And how he felt his attacks on community groups that exposed the "Stokey Cokey" corruption scandal qualified him as the new people's defender. It struck us as unlikely to inspire public confidence that he had failed to spot at least 13 miscarriages of justice and rampant drug corruption, racism and brutality on his watch.

Asked about Clark's suitability as an anti-corruption crusader, leading CPS lawyer for the Untouchables, Martin Polaine, conceded, "I accept that some would raise eyebrows as to issues around Clark. I know people have raised eyebrows. Yes, he had a background that touched on those specialist squads that were being looked at. It's a difficulty. They did ensure [at the Untouchables] that those officers who were investigating former colleagues in effect made clear previous association, previous contacts. That was all documented. Yes, it is a problem if you are investigating yourself."

These comments are all the more interesting because Polaine has now been seconded to the IPCC legal department for two years. It could be argued that Polaine himself is conflicted because while at the CPS he acquiesced to Clark's unlawful supergrass strategy. He also shares a history of decision making with many senior Untouchables.

To round off the picture of independence, Polaine's boss at the IPCC is former Serious Fraud Office assistant director, John Tate, whose biggest case resulted in the failed prosecution of brothers Ian and Kevin Maxwell.

Hardwick told us he is "entirely satisfied" there are no skeletons in Clark's cupboard because the Home Office (MI5) had vetted him. And it's not just the spooks that are chuffed. Police sergeant Judy Redford, who sits on the Police Federation's National Committee, said Clark's appointment was "an absolute hoot" and had made "a lot of people in the [police] service quite happy".

"No disrespect to Roy Clark, but if you look at his career, I do have to say he's very well thought of, very popular, a well-liked bloke. But

WATCHDOGGED

I can't be the only person that noticed when you look at his career, whenever he left a location very soon after there was a major investigation. He seems to have slipped out of every single job just before it all went wrong." It wasn't for nothing that his nickname in the CPS was "non-stick Roy", recalls former CPS lawyer at Stoke Newington Mark Jackson, who is also amazed by Clark's appointment.

It's difficult to underestimate how conflicted Clark is. Many of his Untouchables are now in key positions in other specialist squads at the Yard, like commander John Coles QPM. Coles is currently head of Operation Trident, which investigates shootings within the black community, precisely the area where a truly independent watchdog is vital to restore public confidence. Many of Clark's old anti-corruption colleagues are also in senior management roles in other forces he will now be responsible for investigating. For example, Michael Todd is the chief constable of Greater Manchester, Andy Hayman QPM the chief constable of Norfolk, Barbara Wilding chief constable of South Wales Police and Bob Quick the number two at Surrey.

It could be argued the IPCC director of investigations is already a lame duck because Clark's conduct and that of the Untouchables is presently subject to several inquiries. The ongoing Sir Bill Morris inquiry, for example, was set up because of mounting internal and external criticism of the way the Untouchables pursued Asian and black officers like DS Gurpal Virdi and Superintendent Ali Dizaei.

"I do question [Clark's] suitability," says National Black Police Association president Ray Powell. "How can we have somebody who has been the head of a department whose track record speaks for itself – failures, discriminatory practice, lack of integrity and honesty – and someone who set this up is taking these horrible values to a new [watchdog]. It's fundamentally flawed."

The PCA was wholly captured by the Yard and its remodelled anti-corruption squad, now called The Directorate of Professional Standards, says Gurpal Virdi. "The DPS is well known in [ethnic] communities as Defenders of Police Suspects," he told the Morris inquiry in June 2004. Changing the PCA's name, he added, "does not bring about justice to the complainants. Promises are always being made about the future but there is no delivery. I await [a new watchdog] in a few years."

Meanwhile the Home Office department dealing with miscarriages of justice is currently assessing a compensation claim from lawyers representing Stoke Newington victim Ira Thomas, whose conviction was overturned by the Appeal Court.

Clark also faces some searching questions over the "Egg Guney affair". One of the new IPCC commissioners, Nicola Williams, is supervising a DPS investigation into why it allowed Guney to spend seven years in prison when there was credible intelligence that his conviction was unsafe. Clark's appointment puts Williams in the ridiculous position where she must investigate a senior employee of the IPCC while continuing to work with him on other cases.

Clark's record will also feature in a number of civil actions to be brought over the coming years against the Yard by former officers whose lives were unfairly savaged by the Untouchables. It remains to be seen how public confidence in the IPCC will be inspired when the Yard's legal department calls on Clark to defend his unlawful supergrass system.

Another problem will arise if the family of murdered private investigator Daniel Morgan succeed in judicially reviewing the government's decision in June 2004 not to allow a public inquiry. Clark's appointment to the IPCC has denied them the opportunity of looking to the new watchdog as an effective, alternative remedy. How many other potential complainants will feel similarly alienated?

Alastair Morgan wrote to Hardwick on the day of the IPCC inauguration stressing this point. "Given Mr Clark's aversion to full and open disclosure . . . we have grave reservations about his position in an organisation reliant on transparency for public confidence." The IPCC chairman's reply was a model of bureaucratic stonewalling. He ignored the issues and simply reaffirmed his confidence in Clark. Hardwick's unswerving support for Clark makes it hard not to feel that the IPCC chairman is something of a nodding dog in the back of a coach driven by the Home Office and Scotland Yard.

Less easy to ignore will be the group of cross-party MPs who support the call for a Home Affairs select committee inquiry into Clark's Untouchables. It's been almost seven years since Condon's 250 "bent cops" speech. Parliament is entitled to ask what bang the public got for its buck, and whether the independent police watchdog the committee envisaged is the one the government has delivered.

Labour backbencher Andrew Mackinlay MP is no stranger to dissecting sexed-up intelligence from government ministers and mandarins. He led the charge during the recent scandal over government scientist David Kelly and the Iraq war. It's not lost on Mackinlay that like the fabled weapons of mass destruction, the 250 bent coppers have also failed to materialise. He is also an opponent of Clark's appointment. "In order to demonstrate fresh thinking and a wholly independent approach, the first director of investigations for the IPCC should not have been appointed from within the existing British police fraternity," he told us. "I support the call for a select committee inquiry into the activities over the last ten years of Scotland Yard's Untouchables. It is time parliament reasserted its powers and duty to investigate difficult subjects like police corruption."

Andy Burnham MP, the parliamentary private secretary to home secretary David Blunkett, has been deeply disturbed by the treatment of undercover cop Michael and the whole fiasco in Merseyside. Burnham strongly supports a select committee inquiry and is angered by what he calls the "complacency" of Scotland Yard.

John Denham MP is the current chairman of the Labour-dominated Home Affairs select committee. He was the former police minister who resigned on principle from the government in March 2003 over its decision to go to war in Iraq. Just before he returned to the backbench, Denham had taken a personal interest in John Wilson's story. Denham wrote to the Wilsons' MP, Francis Maude, suggesting the IPCC would put a lot right when it took over. As an example, he said, under the new system the public would have a right of appeal to the new watchdog if the police refuse to record a complaint. "I had previously set my mind on introducing provisions like these and the Wilson case re-affirmed the need for them and they now form part of the Police Reform Act 2002," Denham wrote.

The Wilson case had clearly moved him. Denham told Maude he had tried to ensure in the new legislation that where an officer's identity cannot be established it wouldn't be an impediment to lodging a complaint. However, there is a significant but. In such circumstances "no criminal or discipline proceedings can be brought . . . but that should not prevent the chief officer from acknowledging to the complainant that misconduct by one of his officers has taken place".[3]

John and Susan Wilson are unconvinced by the IPCC. "We believe our case highlights how it is impossible for the police to police themselves. There must be so many people out there who have suffered at the hands of a policeman and can't do anything about it. If the Met can't identify their own officers how can they possibly be tracking down terrorists?" says Susan. John was amazed to learn that the man who created the anti-corruption squad that failed to identify the officer who disabled him for life is now at the IPCC. He calls it "a fatal flaw". The new body should be dismantled if retired cops are going to be involved, he says. Solicitor James Bell, who battled so valiantly for the Wilsons, called the IPCC "a typical New Labour re-branding".

John Denham told us that in the light of growing concern about the Untouchables he could see his select committee revisiting the issue of police corruption and self-regulation. "If the IPCC fails to inspire public confidence and raise the standard of internal investigations it will be very serious," he says.

A parliamentary inquiry would trouble the Yard. The Morris Inquiry is less of a worry. Tellingly, a police spokesman described it as "Huttonesque" in a reference to the unsatisfactory inquiry into the death of David Kelly.

Sir Bill Morris made it clear when he opened his inquiry in January 2004 that he was not going to "revisit the past", "indulge in a culture of blame" or put anyone in the dock. Critics have complained that the remit, set by the MPA, is too narrow and concentrates predominantly on race and diversity issues, when the wider issue is the massive failure of self-regulation.

Nevertheless, Bill Morris has received some powerful submissions from a range of officers and their lawyers about the wider activities of the Untouchables, which should make uncomfortable reading for Clark and his supporters at the IPCC. The recurrent themes have been: a festering mediocrity, cronyism and protectionism in the senior ranks; lip service to reform; a lack of accountability of senior officers while the public pick up the bill for their failings; and an unhealthy cosiness between the Yard and its supposed watchdogs – the CPS, the MPA, the PCA and sections of the media.

As we went to press Sir John Stevens announced his retirement in February 2005. By then the Morris Inquiry will have reported. It is likely to recommend an overhaul of the discipline and complaints system to make it quicker, fairer and more transparent. The new head of the Yard's Untouchables, DAC Steve Roberts, is a former Special Branch officer. He told the inquiry he needed even more money to recruit more qualified anti-corruption detectives. A lot of reliance is also being placed on the IPCC to raise the standard of internal investigations of public complaints. But with the Untouchables now inside the regulator, the IPCC looks less of a new dawn and more a New Labour sell-out.

NOTES

CHAPTER 1 UNDERCOVER 599 – MICHAEL'S STORY
1 The home secretary still appoints the commissioner, but must entertain the MPA's recommendations on candidates. It, in turn, is now responsible for setting targets, monitoring performance, managing the £2 billion annual budget and appointing and disciplining senior officers.
2 For a full account see *Cocky* by Tony Barnes, Richard Elias & Peter Walsh (Milo Books, 2001).
3 *Mersey Blues*: 'A Fair Cop?', BBC1, 2 February 1999 (Hart Ryan Productions).
4 Detective Superintendent Phil Jones statement, 7 June 2000.
5 *Ibid.*
6 *Ibid.*
7 Letter from DCI Peter North, 29 August 1997.
8 DS Ron Border and DC Alistair Clark also served on the David Norris murder inquiry under Jarratt.
9 Roy Ramm statement, 30 September 2001.
10 DCI Chris Jones statement.
11 Transcript of Michael's covertly taped conversation with Fuller.
12 Letter from Sir James Sharples QPM to assistant commissioner David Veness, 9 September 1997.
13 DCI Chris Jones statement.
14 Merseyside Police declined to comment on Operation Florida or Ward's case.
15 The Davies trial was held in Nottingham. His co-defendants were Mick Ahearne, Tony Bray, John Newton, John and Jo McCormack and Phil Glennon. Bray (three years) and Ahearne (fifteen months) were also found guilty. The three convicted men lost an appeal in May 2000.
16 Karen Todner letter to Stephen Timms MP, 14 February 2001.
17 Lord Bassam to Timms, 13 March 2001.
18 Timms to Stevens, 19 June 2001.

UNTOUCHABLES

19 In fact Commander James' integrity was also in question over allegations of expenses fraud and sexual harassment. See Chapter 26.
20 The case is fully explored in Chapter 26.

CHAPTER 2 NOBLE CAUSE CORRUPTION
1 In this book, "Scotland Yard" and "the Metropolitan Police" are interchangeable. We shall use "the Yard" to denote the senior management around the commissioner, and "the Met" to denote the force in general.
2 *One of Us* by Hugo Young (Pan, 1990).
3 *The Outsider* by Keith Hellawell (HarperCollins, 2002).
4 *The Guardian*, 23 October 1992.
5 *In the Name of the Law – The Collapse of Criminal Justice* by David Rose (Vintage, 1996).
6 The measure was incorporated into the 1994 Criminal Justice and Public Order Act.
7 *Panorama* 'Fair Cops', BBC1, 5 April 1993.

CHAPTER 3 THE GHOST SQUAD
1 Interview with DCS David Wood at Scotland Yard, 7 February 2000.
2 Letter from CIB Commander Andy Hayman, 10 February 2000.
3 Interview with DCS David Wood.
4 *Informers: Policing Policy Practice* edited by Roger Billingsley, Teresa Nemitz, Philip Bean (Willan Publishing, November 2000).
5 DAC Roy Clark's evidence at the Old Bailey, 6 February 2001.
6 *Ibid.*
7 DCS Roger Gaspar's evidence at the Old Bailey, 5 February 2001.
8 Clark. Old Bailey, 8 February 2001.
9 Clark. Old Bailey, 8 February 2001.
10 Interview with CPS lawyer Martin Polaine, 25 October 2002, and Stuart Sampson, 21 February 2003.
11 Clark, Old Bailey, 8 February 2001.
12 Home Office spokeswoman, 9 April 2003.
13 Telephone message from Michael Howard QC MP, 17 April 2003, in response to letter 8 March 2003.
14 MI5 eventually got a significant role in "the prevention and detection of serious crime." This arrangement was formalised by the 1996 Security Service Act.
15 Interview with DCS David Wood.
16 Detectives Alan Holmes (1987), Gerry Carroll (1992), Sidney Wink (1994), John Watt (1998).

CHAPTER 4 THE GHOST OF BRINKS MAT – A FIRM WITHIN A FIRM
1 This was chief superintendent Bill Moody. He was later sentenced to 12 years.
2 Interview by James Morton for his book *Bent Coppers* (Warner Books, 1993).
3 For a full account of this case see *The Fall of Scotland Yard* by B Cox, J Shirley and M Short (Penguin, 1977).
4 Interview, 25 July 2002.
5 *Lundy: The Destruction of Scotland Yard's Finest Detective* by Martin Short (Grafton Books, 1991).
6 Stephen Knight, in his seminal book *The Brotherhood* (1983), wrote: "It is almost

NOTES

certain that the corruption which led to Operation Countryman would never have arisen had a Masonic City of London Police commissioner in the 1970s not turned a blind eye to the activities of several desperately corrupt Freemasons under his command."

7 Details of the bribe came out later, in Noye's murder trial, when Boyce was cross-examined.
8 *Scotland Yard's Cocaine Connection* by Andrew Jennings, Paul Lashmar and Vyv Simson (Jonathan Cape, 1990).
9 *Ibid.*
10 Even with the evidence of a British money launderer called Patrick Diamond, whose other clients included a hit man for the American Mob, a London magistrate threw out the case against Fleming when he eventually returned home handcuffed to detectives in March 1987.
11 In *The Brotherhood*, Stephen Knight reveals how Scotland Yard's detective pool was stacked with Masons who were often in lodges with the very criminals they were supposed to be catching.

CHAPTER 5 THE GHOST OF BRINKS MAT – A *LIAISON DANGEREUSE*

1 Judged on convictions arising from the Brinks Mat investigation, the final tally was not great. Of 28 prosecutions there were 14 acquittals.
2 One of these involved the suspicious acquittal of Bristol linkman John Palmer. The Task Force had evidence of jury nobbling, the report said, and were investigating the Palmer jury. Palmer was brought back from Spain for the 1987 handling trial. He returned to Tenerife after his acquittal. He admitted melting the bullion but denied knowing its origins. Police believe he set up a crooked and ruthless timeshare operation in the Canary Islands using the money he earned from Brinks Mat. In May 2001, he was convicted for a massive timeshare fraud on British pensioners and given a seven-year sentence.
3 This was Stephen Donavan, the 34-year-old "Docklands investment consultant" to Selective Estates. Donavan was acquitted.
4 One year after the King trial, Rexstrew was himself tried and acquitted in 1998 of conspiring to sell rhino horn. Three others were convicted following the RSPCA–police sting. Rexstrew is a legal executive in the law firm Law Mooney Lee & Cook.
5 Soon after Relton was arrested his solicitor and friend, John Blackburn Gittings, contacted Boyce and invited him to dinner at the Carlton Club, the historic watering hole of the Conservative Party. Boyce attended with another officer. But during the meal he became uneasy and left after telling his host to stay out of his way. Boyce later got into trouble during the trial over his decision to ban some defence solicitors and clerks from the police interviews. He explained to the judge that he believed they were "bent" and would frustrate his financial inquiries by passing messages to those on the outside. Relton's senior clerk, Ted Wein, was a convicted fraudster.
6 See Fraser's autobiography *Mad Frank and Friends* (Warner Books, 1998). Frank was a criminal associate of the father of another of the Gold Conduit defendants, Gordon Parry, who got ten years.
7 A National Criminal Intelligence Service report seen by the authors said: "Believing that Parry's release to the UK would strengthen the prosecution's case against himself, Brian Perry sent his son [and two others] out to Spain [in

UNTOUCHABLES

May 1989] to murder Parry. Perry supplied his son with some stolen chemical warfare poison which when in contact with human skin would be painlessly absorbed through the tissue into the body." The alleged plan was to bake Parry a special cake to be presented during a prison visit. For unknown reasons "the plot failed", the report said. Parry was eventually extradited and stood trial with the others. He got ten years. Yard murder detectives also have old transcripts of official phone taps during the 1992 trial in which criminals discussed asking Patrick to throw a female juror off her commuter train. He declined to be interviewed.

8 *Lundy: The Destruction of Scotland Yard's Finest Detective.*
9 *Ibid.*
10 Matters were not helped when, a few months before the writ was served, a retired Met police constable called Sidney Wink blew his brains out in August 1994 shortly after the cops paid him a visit. It was suspected that Wink, who since leaving the Met had set himself up as a gunsmith and dealer, had supplied a reactivated gun to some cop killers. Crime correspondents, quoting anonymous police sources and little else, also claimed Wink may have provided the Brinks robbers with their guns.
11 John Ross was arrested on 12 July 2004 for "corrupting" detective constable David Dougal who was also arrested for malfeasance in a public office and suspended.

CHAPTER 6 DEATH OF AN EXPERT WITNESS

1 PCs Peter Foley and Alan Purvis were later compensated for wrongful arrest after they sued the Met. They received substantial damages. The Met admitted that the arrests should never have taken place.
2 Letter to Paul Keel, 23 January 1988.
3 Later in his evidence, Lennon confirmed he was awaiting trial on a fraud charge. He was subsequently convicted.
4 *The Mirror*, 16 April 1988.

CHAPTER 7: THE SUICIDE CLUB

1 *Daily Express*, 12 August 1987.
2 *Today*, 12 August 1987.
3 *Daily Telegraph*, 4 August 1987.
4 *Sunday Times*, 'Shadow Over the Yard's High Flyer', 9 August 1987.
5 Gray was not under caution when he made these tapes. They were made purely for intelligence purposes.
6 Derek Haslam affidavit, 1988.
7 *Ibid.*
8 *Sunday Times*, 2 August 1987.
9 Haslam affidavit, 1988.
10 *Ibid.*
11 *Ibid.*
12 *Ibid.*
13 *The Times*, 15 March 1988.
14 Haslam Affidavit, 1998.
15 *Sunday Times*, 21 January 1990.
16 *The Guardian*, 23 January 1990.
17 A homeless person died when hit by a police car driven by Haslam. He

NOTES

reported the incident and an independent witness confirmed he had not driven recklessly. But Haslam was fined for being over the limit and was returned to uniform duties for one year. Adams says he blocked Haslam's application to return to the detective division at Tooting police station because of the incident. Haslam says Adams used the accident to smear him to CIB2. Haslam is emphatic that he had never applied to join Tooting and was anyway returned to detective duties in another south London crime squad that Adams had no control over. Ray Adams told us on 1 August 2000 he was a member of Blackheath 1302 lodge.

CHAPTER 8 THE GHOST OF DAVID NORRIS

1 *Evening Standard*, 24 May 1993.
2 Reeves was sentenced with others in July 1997 to 18 years for his role in a 300-kilo Colombian cocaine smuggling plot. Also convicted was south-east London gangster Tony White, the so-called "King of Catford", who was previously acquitted of the Brinks Mat robbery in 1984. Reeves had his conviction quashed in 1998 on a technicality. The collapse of the case led to a major inquiry by retired judge Gerald Butler. The Norris murder squad believed Reeves had a printing business in New Cross and business interests with Doherty involving counterfeit money.
3 It cannot be overlooked that at the time of Norris's murder, the RUC and a secret British Army unit called the Field Research Unit (FRU) had penetrated the UDA. The FRU had an agent, Brian Nelson, in charge of all UDA intelligence. He was also being passed security files on Catholics by his army handlers, which Nelson then passed to Loyalist death squads. In February 1989 UDA gunmen assassinated Pat Finucane, a Belfast lawyer, in front of his family. This led to the beginning of a 14-year inquiry into collusion between state security forces and Loyalist terrorists by the current Met commissioner Sir John Stevens. The Stevens Inquiry was run by a handful of Met detectives who months before Norris's death had arrested Nelson and were debriefing him about his army handlers and involvement in the Finucane killing. Leighton confirms that Special Branch became involved in the Norris murder investigation because of the Loyalist connections. But the question still remains whether a violent drug dealer like McCreery was allowed to operate on the British mainland because of his usefulness to the intelligence services in Northern Ireland. And if so, who from the secret state was running McCreery when he was alleged to have helped plan the murder of David Norris? Did he tell them about the intended hit?
4 A few weeks after the Norris murder trial mysteriously collapsed, Maurice O'Mahoney took the stand at the Old Bailey in June 1993 to remind the Yard in the most theatrical circumstances about police corruption in south-east London. In his trial for robbery Mo specifically referred to the Norris murder and told the jury he didn't want to end up like him or several other criminal informants and weak links who'd been rubbed out between 1990 and 1992. Great Train Robber Charlie Wilson was shot in Spain in April 1990 and John Moriaty and Nick Whiting were killed two months later. In October that year Roy Atkins, said to have been behind the hit on Wilson, was himself executed.
5 Letter from commander Andy Hayman dated 10 February 2000.
6 Response from Crampton's lawyers dated 14 July 2000.
7 R v Reginald Jones, Anthony Wozny and Henry Page, 14–17 June 1990, Croydon Crown Court.

UNTOUCHABLES

8 The case of Sergeant Michael Ambizas and Anona Murphy. She pleaded guilty.
9 Letter from commander Andy Hayman, 10 February 2000.
10 Warne had his life sentence reduced on appeal and is now out on parole, believed to be living in Canada. Dennison is still appealing.

CHAPTER 9 "WHAT? WHAT? NIGGER!"

1 *The Police and Society* by lawyer and former Labour MP Ben Whittaker.
2 Press release from the Lawrence Family.
3 Stephen Lawrence Inquiry Report (SLIR) Chapter 13, paragraphs 37 and 44.
4 *The Independent*, 4 July 1998.
5 The Stephen Lawrence Inquiry concluded there was no evidence the murder investigation was contaminated over the first weekend.
6 SLIR Chapter 13, paragraph 69.
7 Donald registered Cressey under the pseudonym of "Carol West". During a meeting on 9 September 1992, Cressey told Donald and his co-handler that a consignment of 50,000 ecstasy tablets from Holland would be arriving by lorry via France to a transport company in Orpington, Kent. "The firm," Donald put in his informant's log, "is owned by the man who paid some Irishmen to kill David Norris."
8 *The Guardian*, 1 March 1993.
9 SLIR Chapter 27, paragraphs 21 and 38.
10 *The Case of Stephen Lawrence* by Brian Cathcart (Viking, 1999).
11 SLIR.
12 SLIR Chapter 27, paragraph 42.

CHAPTER 10 A RAGAMUFFIN BUNCH

1 The DPP refused to prosecute the seven officers but the PCA recommended they face a disciplinary board, where they were all dismissed from the Met in November 1990.
2 The police pounced on Mrs Burke when she went with a jug of water and some diabetes pills to give to her 79-year-old husband, who she said had been dragged out of the house in his pyjamas. She too was arrested and charged with assault on a police officer. In March 1992, a jury awarded her £50,000.
3 West Yorkshire police reported to the PCA and the DPP, Barbara Mills, in the late autumn of 1991. The DPP took a further six months before deciding not to prosecute eleven officers, to the great consternation of legal figures and the victims of twelve miscarriages of justice, who had all had their convictions overturned. Even the chief constable of West Midlands, Geoffrey Dear, who disbanded the serious crime squad, took the view that there should have been prosecutions.
4 Letter from assistant commissioner Peter Winship 24 June 1992.
5 It wasn't until November 1991 that the PCA stepped in, and only after receiving Pearl's direct complaint against Lewandowski.
6 Over 300 allegations of police brutality and planting had been received by HCDA since it was set up in 1988, of which 130 cases were taken up.
7 In September 1991 Michael Lavery and Jeff Eaton were acquitted of attacking five City Road police officers after they arrested them for being drunk and disorderly on New Year's Day. Lavery and Eaton had between them 40 injuries. They said they were assaulted in the police van, custody suite and

NOTES

cells. Independent witnesses supported their version and the jury took just 15 minutes to acquit. A month later, a court overturned the conviction of 19-year-old Clint Nelson for assault on two Stoke Newington officers in a police van, one of whom he had allegedly headbutted despite a height difference of eight inches. Nelson said he was assaulted after going to the aid of his mother.

8 Letter to Roy Clark, 10 February 1992.
9 Early Day Motion, 19 June 1992.
10 A landmark Court of Appeal ruling (R v Edwards) in January 1991 had also imposed a new disclosure obligation on the prosecution concerning an officer's discipline record and adverse judicial findings in similar cases.
11 Response, 2 March 1994, to a parliamentary question.
12 There were also 27 allegations of theft, 9 of assault and 27 of conspiring to pervert the course of justice, said the press release. The overwhelming majority of the suspect officers were constables. "One officer featured in eight cases, one in seven, three in six, two in five, two in four, four in three, and five in two. The remaining twenty-seven officers featured in only one case each."
13 Palumbo, thirty-two, was jailed for ten years on 24 February 1997 for conspiring to import cannabis from Spain in lorries with his father-in-law and two others. He had left the police in 1995.
14 Early one morning they were walking home from a party when the couple witnessed a mentally ill man being bashed up on the street by police officers. They went to Stoke Newington police station to report it, but ended up being assaulted themselves and charged.
15 *Police Leadership in the Twenty-First Century – Philosophy, Doctrine and Developments*, ed. Roger Adlam & Peter Villiers (Waterside Press, 2003).

CHAPTER 11 GEOFF BRENNAN – DOUBLE AGENT SUPERGRASS

1 John Brennan's pseudonym was "Terry Allen".
2 Detectives Bill Williamson, Frank Lovejoy and Eddy Bathgate.
3 Drug trafficker Kevin Cressey gave this information to his SERCS handlers on 2 September 1992.
4 Geoff Brennan's pseudonym was "John Millwall".
5 Osbourne's body was found on Hackney Marshes in east London in December 1980. Brennan says he was "ironed out". Others say he had a heart attack and was kept in the deep freezer until his associates decided what to do with him. But his friend, John Fleming, has another take. He told us that the Duke had committed suicide with pills because he couldn't face going back inside over a hash importation from Pakistan intercepted by Operation Wrecker in October 1979 when a Customs officer was shot dead. Customs believed the Duke was the main organiser behind the importation, along with another Kray henchman, Freddie Foreman, who later received two years on a guilty plea. George Francis was acquitted at a retrial. That verdict was dogged by suggestions of jury nobbling.
6 Detectives Jim Sutherland, Jo Cunningham and Bob Robinson.
7 According to a Special Branch document, in 1981 the Ayatollah Khomeini government dispatched three colonels to purchase 8,000 TOW anti-tank missiles for their war with Saddam Hussein's Iraq. The US embargo on Iran meant the arms deal was negotiated through a Swiss intermediary and an Iranian company in London called Metro UK Limited. Arif and Williams were believed to have helped an Iranian exile in London called Behnam

UNTOUCHABLES

Nodjoumi to kidnap the colonels and an Iranian banker, Hassam Moghaddan, and steal the money deposited in a Midland Bank account in the City. The plan was foiled and various members of the gang were arrested and stood trial. Arif and Williams were never prosecuted.

8 Between 1994 and 1996 a series of High Court judgments were made against 12 members of the Gold Conduit. Some, among them Lloyd, Noye, Clark and Perry made private settlements with Shaw & Croft in this period. By November 2001 most of the £26 million had been recovered. At the time these deals were struck police forces in the UK did not have today's asset confiscation powers. As such only one consideration dominated the settlements, recovering as much money as possible for Lloyds. McCunn is sensitive to the criticism and says on his client's instructions Scotland Yard was kept continually informed. "No deal was struck until the defendant had been dealt with by the criminal courts," he insists. Shaw & Croft recovered about £26 million for Lloyds, but this figure represents only one-half to one-third of the stolen gold, says McCunn. The robbers and their associates have benefited from the rest.

9 The Guangxi Zhuang Autonomous Region Import Export Trading Company.

10 Sprouce and Jones worked for Gallo Autos.

11 Most of the money ($479,000) came via GX Impex, but the Wangs, through their companies Lyon Aviation and Kings Automotive, got the balance ($148,000) as an upfront payment for the phones from a Hong Kong buyer called Mainperse Development Co and Nanking Hung Yin Model Company.

12 A Houston lawyer helped set up Wang Pacific Corp in the BVI. Padgett, Jones and Sprouce used the same lawyer to set up Victory Financial Group Ltd there.

13 The Switch On Enterprises company account number 113118497 was first set up in 1989 for earlier covert operations.

14 Smith re-registered Brennan under his old Brinks pseudonym "Joe Montana", the famous San Francisco 49ers quarterback. Smith was said to be a great lover of US culture.

15 The FBI in Houston had already been investigating Padon since early 1992.

16 This might explain why DC Norton was transferred from Bexleyheath shortly thereafter.

17 Statement by DC Micky Barr 7 February 1994.

18 Connally was also wounded and maintained he could have been the intended victim for refusing to overturn a disciplinary discharge on Lee Harvey Oswald's military record when he was Secretary of the Navy during the Kennedy Administration. Connally died in 1993 after bankruptcy.

19 The joint venture company was called Thames and registered in Texas, but Wyatt pulled out of Sierra Leone after the May 1997 coup. Crooks had his own company, West Africa Holdings.

20 Houston Customs had investigated and cleared Coastal of sanctions busting with Libya and Iraq in the early nineties.

21 Official summary by DS Richard Hester of the meeting. The weapons included four GEC mini guns, 2,000 kilos of C4 explosive and 100 M16 assault rifles. At one point the weapons were said to have been stolen from a military base in Miami after a hurricane. According to press reports, in September 1992 Hurricane Andrew led to looting of the National Guard armoury in south Florida.

NOTES

22 Statement from FBI agent Michael Mee, 4 June 1997.
23 Crooks recalled being stopped routinely at Customs as described. But he says he voluntarily told the FBI in Houston about the arms deal after returning from London the first time, and not as part of a trade to save his skin. He says he kept the FBI fully informed and played along with the arms dealers.
24 Memo from Special Agent in Charge, Leon Guinn, US Customs, dated 9 May 1994.
25 Senior CPS lawyer Stuart Sampson later gave evidence at the Old Bailey that he had been "kept in the dark" by the Ghost Squad management about the Brennan case and the intelligence interviews on 21 June and 28 June.
26 Statement of Roger Gaspar, 30 November 2000.
27 The *Mirror* reported on 31 January 1997 that Colombian police found 750 pounds of cocaine when searching a luxury yacht part-owned by a Mr David Shaw.
28 A Swiss-based American banker called Robert Keller was also targeted briefly. He had several inconclusive meetings with Hester and a fourth undercover officer from the City of London police as the discussion concerned bonds.
29 Evidence from Roger Gaspar at the Old Bailey, 5 February 2001.
30 DC Mark Norton also admits moonlighting with Brennan after he was suspended in May 1995 over a fight in a bar with fellow officers. Norton felt the Yard used this incident as a pretext to sack him in 1997 for the embarrassment caused by his marriage to Debbie Norris.
31 George Copley made the tape after his arrest with Frank Fraser Jnr and others for the 1976 robbery of £520,000 from Williams & Glyn Bank in the City.
32 Interview under caution with retired DS Chris Smith on 26 August 1997.

CHAPTER 12 HECTOR THE SELECTA' – RUDE BOY SUPERGRASS

1 There are four Flying Squad offices. Finchley covers north-west London, Barnes covers south-west, Tower Bridge covers south-east and Rigg Approach covers north-east.
2 Harvey says Marshall was his father's name and Cook was after a retired detective.
3 The anti-corruption squad were also told about this but Harvey is unaware of what happened to the two men.
4 Hepburn was arrested along with others allegedly involved in the robberies, but he was never charged. He denied being the inside agent.
5 The Flying Squad arrested but never charged Brown.
6 According to the informant, a fifth man, John Fleming, was also on the job, but got away. The same Flying Squad team later linked him, through the same informant, to the Brinks Mat robbery, which took place one month after the kidnap attempt on the Global Airlines executive. When Gillard visited Fleming in prison in August 2002 he maintained he wasn't involved in either job. However, Fleming's logic was somewhat askew. "How could I be in two places at once?" he said.
7 "Drug Lords Gave Labour Dirty Cash for Election Fund', by Michael Gillard and David Connett, *The Observer*, 20 September 1998.
8 Ironically, Fred Bunn's firm Bark & Co would later represent DS Harris.
9 These are Hector Selecta', Double H, Swallow, Marshall Cook, Mr Rodgers, Howard Hughes, Leroy Chadwell and Bloggs 72.
10 At first Henry offered to plead to theft and named Hepburn as the inside

agent, but he refused to give evidence against others. Hepburn denied this at trial. Henry didn't name Harvey. He was jailed for seven years. His associates Roy Page and Jo Lydon were also convicted. Harvey says McCormack wanted the £200,000 to pay the three men's families.

11 In 1998, a Customs supergrass called Michael Michael told the anti-corruption squad that McCormack had asked him to provide a safe house. McCormack told Michael he and a man called Clifford Hobbs were planning a drive-by shooting of Harvey using a motorbike. Shortly after making this request, Michael said McCormack told him the plan was off because he had sorted out Harvey by placing a grenade on his motorbike. McCormack was never charged with the attempted murder of Hector Harvey.

12 Green was a member of one of the violent street posses that terrorised Kingston, Jamaica. In the eighties, national political parties recruited these posses to kill their rivals. Green was a killer for the People's National Party, according to the *Guardian*.

13 They were Steve Cox ("my best sergeant") and constables Kevin Hooker ("because he'd just joined") and Ian Saunders ("because he didn't have a lot on"). It was an acute embarrassment for the Yard when two years later Hooker and Saunders were suspended over corruption allegations relating to their time at Rigg Approach. Hooker was required to resign. Saunders went sick and was unfit to stand trial for corruptly stealing money recovered by the Flying Squad from a Romford Post Office robbery in July 1994. He was acquitted when the trial collapsed. He now serves at Islington police station.

14 Statement by detective superintendent Dave Niccol, 13 July 1998.

15 Raison's plan was to offer Henry assistance with an appeal in return for his help on Harvey. In the end the CIB were not interested in the plan, says Raison.

16 "[McCormack] was arrested [sometime in 1998] for being suspected of putting the hand grenade on HH's bike. We thought he'd got the hump over the fact that his job [Clapham] went wrong and then Harvey's job came off and they got all the money," says detective superintendent David Pennant. "The point was we had insufficient evidence to charge him on the hand grenade job. There is still an outstanding palm print on the grenade we've never identified and we'd be very interested to know at some stage in the future."

17 The Tower Bridge Flying Squad office was also looking at McCormack and Fleming. There had been a number of armed robberies of Security Express vans in south London since 1990 with the suspected involvement of inside agents, says one detective sergeant.

18 In 1998, Customs supergrass Michael Michael told CIB that DC Paul Carpenter, his Met handler from 1991 to 1998, was a "corrupt" officer to whom he had paid "up to £10,000 per week" for leaking intelligence to his criminal associates. DC Carpenter was charged and committed for trial. But the Crown withdrew the case against him, whilst maintaining that he was "corrupt". If this is true, Carpenter was therefore in a corrupt relationship with Michael at the precise time the crooked accountant was approached by McCormack to provide a safe house after he plotted to kill Harvey. Also, Raison must have unwittingly alerted Carpenter that the Flying Squad was looking at McCormack and had an informant close to Fleming.

19 The Raison Report on Operation Spy.

20 *Ibid*.

NOTES

21 Detective superintendent Niccol statement, 13 July 1998.
22 Security Express sacked Hepburn. The company then brought a civil action against Ward and Simms. Soon after the robbery the pair had bought a house and cars and had deposited money in various banks.
23 DI Tim Norris was the only officer disciplined as a result of Operation Spy. He was given 'words of advice', a mild rebuke, for failing to ensure search records were completed, according to Niccol's statement.
24 Niccol statement.

CHAPTER 13 GHOSTBUSTED

1 In December 2000 Gaspar wrote a report on behalf of NCIS, MI5, MI6, GCHQ, Customs and ACPO advocating government access to every telephone call, email and internet connection for seven years.
2 Interview with DAC David Wood, *Police Review*, 2 August 2002.
3 *Police Integrity*, HM Inspectorate of Constabulary, June 1999.
4 *The Job*, 23 January 1998 "My Mission, by New CIB2 Head".
5 The officer was DS Barry Toombs. He was later reinstated. But while Russell was investigating Toombs, both officers were themselves being investigated following a complaint to the commissioner by an officer called Neil Abercrombie. He claimed he had been subject in the early nineties to a flawed investigation and that CIB2 then corruptly covered up the mistake.
6 *The Guardian*, 28 July 1997.
7 DS Tom Bradley, DS Ian Martin and DC Barry Porter were suspended in 1995 with others for providing bodyguarding and chauffeuring services to Reg Grundy, the producer of the Australian soap *Neighbours*. In late 1995 Grundy had reported an alleged theft to Belgravia police station. Bradley was assigned the job and privately offered to protect Grundy and his family for a fee. The Ghost Squad only discovered the moonlighting because Bradley had used the bugged work phone of DI John Redgrave to conduct his business. Bradley and the other suspended officers denied the moonlighting allegations and nothing was proved against them. In fact Bradley had been previously suspended while at NCIS after *Panorama*'s 1993 exposé of John Donald. He was reinstated in 1994. Bradley was said to be close with John Stevens who had used him as part of his special inquiry in Northern Ireland into state collusion with Loyalist death squads. After retiring in 1996 Bradley and Martin worked together in a private investigation company. Bradley now has a nightclub in central London. The Home Affairs select committee report noted: "There remains real concern that individuals who are ostensibly mentally strong before their suspension suffer severe psychiatric illness immediately afterwards and yet so quickly recover following their retirement, to the extent that they are able to function in demanding areas of employment."
8 *The Times*, 8 November 1997.
9 *Hansard*, 22 December 1997.
10 *The Guardian*, 16 January 1998.
11 McGuinness told us he was "close" to Green and he probably wouldn't have given evidence against him, although he was adamant Green knew they were collecting drugs because he claims they discussed it in the car. Green denies this.
12 The five officers were DI Tim Norris, DS Eamonn Harris, DC David Howell,

UNTOUCHABLES

DC Paul Smith and retired DI Fred May. Defence lawyer Les Brown was also charged.
13 Under a 1992 ACPO–PCA voluntary agreement these investigations should be completed within 120 days. Green's complaint of corruption in CIB3 was one of many that took years to finish.
14 *Hansard*, 18 January 2001.
15 Letter from Clarke & Co to Andrew Faires, CPS Central Case Work, 3 March 2000.

CHAPTER 14 THE SLEAZE MACHINE

1 *The Ashdown Diaries*, vol. 1.
2 *Ibid.*
3 Straw, it was alleged, had been the victim of a mugging in a park.
4 Rees was unsuccessful but he did successfully sue his solicitors.
5 DCI Peter Elcock was part of the area complaints unit at Norbury police station.
6 Leighton resigned on 31 July 1996. He was never prosecuted for any corruption associated with the John Donald case, although he says Donald made a statement implicating him as part of a deal with the CIB for accepting his guilty plea.
7 46-year-old supergrass Bob Bown was arrested in October 1997 for his part in the supply of reactivated Mac 10 machine guns to the underworld. He was due to give evidence against Brighton gun nut Tony Mitchell, who was supplying Glasgow gangster Paul Ferris.
8 King pleaded guilty and had already been sentenced on 27 March 1998 to nine years. This was reduced to six on appeal. Bown and Mahoney were jailed for five and three years respectively. Their sentences were also reduced on appeal to twenty-one months and forty-two months.
9 Detectives Carter and Guerard investigated a £1 million robbery of a Lebanese courier on 2 August 1994. Hanrahan told CIB the detectives had recommended his firm to the Shouman Exchange Company to protect future couriers who were bringing large sums of cash through Heathrow every week. Hanrahan Associates put in a bid, but Shouman didn't go with it. Hanrahan alleged he and the detectives then plotted to rob a courier. The plan was sacked when the detectives warned Hanrahan that MI5 were looking at the original robbery. Martin King was then brought in with some criminals from Grove Park. They staked out the airport but the robbery was called off at the last moment.
10 Hanrahan also named two detective constables from the East Dulwich SERCS, Tom Kingston and Tom Reynolds. Grayston was suspended for illegal PNC checks and retired in September 1997 ahead of a disciplinary hearing. He formed a company called Bridge Security. When Gillard met him he admitted he had sold information from the PNC.
11 CIB intelligence assessment of Hanrahan, 11 February 2000.
12 The following year Carter and Guerard were unanimously acquitted in a separate second trial of conspiracy to pervert the course of justice and blackmail.
13 Parkhurst Prison transcript, 3 November 1998.

NOTES

CHAPTER 15 BAD BLOOD

1 Statement of retired DCI Peter Mellins, 1 October 1998.
2 On one occasion Denise was particularly angry with Williams and she grassed him up, through her brother, to Smith, about some stolen Zhandra Rhodes dresses he had come by. It was another job, involving information about an armed robber called Danny Foye, which first brought Smith and the Brennans to the attention of John Grieve. He was present when a £1,500 reward was paid out at the Yard.
3 Another member of the "Smith camp" who also featured in O'Mahoney's civil action was the notoriously unstable Brixton-based detective Malcolm 'Basher' Howells. After Basher left the police, he worked with Smith and Brennan doing private surveillance work.
4 See Chapter 19 for more on DS John Bull.
5 Other members of the gang were brothers Steve and Graham Moore, John Maguire, Paul Kidd and Lloyd's old friend Billy Haward (see Chapter 4).
6 Lloyd eventually received a light sentence on 16 December 1996 of 5 years.
7 The judge made no order that there should be an investigation and the CPS also stayed silent even though they accept the sight of a police officer invoking his rights is very rare. Four years later, PC Phillip Davies invoked his rights at Southwark Crown Court on 27 July 2002 after a clever cross-examination by defence barrister Kyriacos Argyropolous exposed some serious police wrongdoing in the case of Roger Gilchrist. The prosecution immediately offered no evidence and Gilchrist was acquitted. Yet again no inquiry was conducted.
8 Statements by Roy Penrose, Mike McCullagh, Dave Morgan, Bill Ilsley and Ian Crampton.
9 There had been a coup in May 1997 ousting the West and multinational-friendly Kabbah government of Sierra Leone. Crooks was caught in a fire fight at his hotel, the Mama Yoko, as the RUF rebels advanced on the capital, Freetown. He had support from a former SAS trooper called Will Skully who, like many British ex-Special Forces, was working for mercenary outfits hired by British and Canadian companies to protect their diamond and gold interests. With the help of a US battleship waiting off the coast of Freetown, Crooks fled with the British High Commissioner, Peter Penfold, to neighbouring Guinea. In the capital Conakry Crooks says he had "a lot of meetings" with Penfold about restoring the Kabbah government. Crooks claims that he and Skully went on an unofficial mission to Freetown to give the RUF leaders a letter from the US State Department asking them to lay down their arms. The rebels arrested them, but he and Skully were soon released after American and British government "pressure", Crooks explained. In Conakry a secret plan to stage a counter-coup using a British mercenary company called Sandline was hatched. Sandline was run by Simon Mann and retired Falklands veteran Lt. Col Tim Spicer. A Canadian diamond company provided Kabbah with $10 million that was funnelled to Sandline for the purchase of 35 tons of Bulgarian arms. Crooks had bought a military helicopter from Sandline in 1996 to shuttle guests between the airport and his hotel. This too was used in the counter-coup, which ended successfully in February 1998 with the help of Nigerian troops. It soon emerged in the British press that the Sandline option had been given the nod and wink by the Foreign Office in contravention of UN arms sanctions. This plunged the New Labour

government into its first major scandal, not least because it had come to power promising "an ethical dimension" to its foreign policy. Tony Blair ordered a judicial inquiry parallel to the tense Commons Foreign Affairs Select Committee hearings, where an old Labour backbench terrier, Andrew Mackinlay MP, was grilling ministers and civil servants with such gusto that Foreign Secretary Robin Cook tried to apply a choke chain. Scant details had already emerged in the press about the role of Crooks and his past involvement in Operation Nightshade. According to Hester, at one stage in 1998 the select committee was going to call him and fellow undercover officer Micky Barr to give evidence. The restored Kabbah government deported Crooks from Sierra Leone in June 1998 ostensibly over his role in Operation Nightshade. However, Crooks says this was a pretext. His business rivals in Freetown wanted control of his hotel and helicopter shuttle franchise so they invented phoney charges that he had been running arms to the ousted RUF rebels. Crooks told us the US government intervened on his behalf with Kabbah and he eventually returned to Sierra Leone in October 1999.

10 R v Bekir Arif, Patrick Malloy, Les Lucas & Jo Hartfield. Arif was eventually sentenced in May 1999 to 23 years.
11 In the 18 months since Brennan's complaint to the PCA, Coles hadn't interviewed Angel (who'd retired) or Mott (who was still serving).
12 CIB also said there was insufficient evidence to prosecute detectives Mott, Moralee and Angel.

CHAPTER 16 MANIPULATING LAWRENCE

1 Dave Coles later came in for serious criticism from the Lawrence Inquiry report over his "association with Clifford Norris" and the failure to discipline him properly. He went sick in June 1998 on full pay and retired on 10 February 2000 with a pension after 28 years in the force.
2 Interview with Ray Adams, 1 August 2000.
3 Lindsay Hewitt, daughter of Commander Hewitt.
4 This was the 1995 case referred to in Chapter 13 involving Reg Grundy, the Australian TV producer of *Neighbours*.
5 On 2 February 1999, just before publication of the Lawrence Inquiry report, Hector Harvey told CIB3 that Chris McCormack had boasted about killing David Norris. McCormack had apparently claimed that crooked cops provided Norris's address, who was killed because the informant had "put a lot of people away". When CIB3 learned this McCormack was on remand in Belmarsh Prison, coincidentally in a cell next to Bob Clark. McCormack was facing trial for torturing David McKenzie, a financier who the Adams crime syndicate believed had lost £1.5 million of their money. McCormack's co-defendant was John Potter, Terry Adams' brother-in-law. Both defendants were acquitted at the Old Bailey in June 1999.
6 On 3 February 2000 Clark was sentenced to twelve years and Drury received eleven. Two other officers, DC Peter Lawson and Roger Pearce (retired), were acquitted. A third officer, DC Terry Broughton, Fleckney's co-handler, had the case against him dropped. Putnam gave evidence in a second trial in July 2000 that resulted in the conviction of DC Tom Reynolds (42 months), DC Tom Kingston (42 months) and DS Terry O'Connell (2 years).
7 Putnam, aged 42, received 3 years and 11 months for admitting 16 corrupt acts between 1991 and 1995. Fleckney, aged 43, was given 4 years and 6 months

NOTES

for 21 counts of drug trafficking, perverting the course of justice and handling stolen goods. Her sentence was to run concurrent with the 15 years she was already serving.

8 Blacketer was taken off the blacklist. Hardy was still on it at the time of writing.

CHAPTER 17 THE ELECTRICIANS PLUG A LEAK

1 *Defending the Realm: MI5 and the Shayler Affair* by Mark Hollingsworth and Nick Fielding (Andre Deutsch, 2000).
2 The *Sunday Times* reported on 9 July 2000 that in 1999 Straw personally signed 1,645 bugging warrants from the police and intelligence services to tap phones, a 60% increase since he became home secretary. A Statewatch report in January 2003 said that under Labour, phone, email and postal intercepts by the police and intelligence services had more than doubled, and were higher than at any time since the Second World War.

CHAPTER 18 THE SELECTA' RETURNS, POLICE BABYLON BURNS

1 On 23 April 1996, 13 suspects believed to have been involved with the January 1995 Security Express robbery of £1.4 million were arrested during the joint CIB/Flying Squad operation. Defence solicitors were all served with a document outlining the evidence against their clients, who included armed robbers Gary Ward and Joey Simms. This revealed that Harvey had been given authority by Scotland Yard to act as a motorbike rider during the robbery. Harvey's barrister would later claim this was a "deliberate leak" with no possible justification other than "revenge" by the Flying Squad. Much of the finger of suspicion was directed at DI George Raison. But he told the authors that the document had been prepared with CIB2 approval and it was agreed there was no longer any need to disguise Harvey's informant role because he had already disclosed it himself, firstly when he approached the Security Express manager looking for a reward in November 1995, and secondly when he brought Laurel Blake to Tintagel House shortly afterwards to back up his story. According to Raison, phone taps later revealed that Blake called Ward or Simms immediately after he left Tintagel House.
2 Darren Lewis was jailed at the Old Bailey for ten years. Ricky Welsh got six years on a guilty plea, and Michelle Niles received thirty months. She also pleaded guilty. Harvey was willing to give evidence against them.
3 The Appeal Court concluded there was "no impropriety" in Jarratt's conduct over the change of solicitors.
4 The officers – DCI Bob Brown, DS Gordon Livingstone, DS Mick Carroll, DC Colin Evans and retired DCI Mick Newstead – all denied the charges. They were later told in December 1999 that the CPS had advised CIB3 there was "insufficient evidence" to prosecute. No disciplinary action followed.
5 Raison and Fry strongly denied the allegation. They were never charged with anything but were suspended. Fry says he was never interviewed about the allegations and was subsequently allowed to retire on 16 December 2001.
6 Evidence of Terry McGuinness in the Pope and Tozer trial, 3 May 2000. Coomber was also cleared of this allegation.
7 On 12 July 2001 the judge ordered the four counts Paul Smith faced to lie on file, a CIB spokesman explained. There was no plea entered and Smith retired

immediately on medical grounds unopposed by the police. He faced no disciplinary charges.
8 In fact from October 2001 to October 2002 he'd made 4,645 calls, 94 of them to Cherry, according to telephone billing analysis.
9 The woman was named in Cherry's statement as Nicky Conway. She denied being racist and her manager moved Conway but they remained in the same office. Cherry says she was later followed when picking up her daughter from school. Two men she believed to be plain-clothes police officers called her a bitch and then sped off.
10 Report by DI Ian Sweet, 26 November 2002.

CHAPTER 19 FRUIT OF A POISONED TREE
1 The other defendants included Bull's brother, and informant "Roger Morley" (a police pseudonym) who acted as the intermediary in the affair with Tommy Farrant. See Chapter 13. Bull was later sacked. Morley received compensation for the 13 months he'd spent on remand.
2 Two months later on 10 April a trial against three Derby police officers accused of assault and perverting the course of justice collapsed because of delays laid by the judge at the door of the CPS. Then in November, the Attorney General said police officers and lawyers who fail to comply with guidelines on disclosure should face disciplinary action.
3 Pownall was later criticised by Alun Jones QC in a letter to the CCRC. The barrister lambasted Pownall and Polaine for their failure to disclose highly relevant material about the supergrasses and a "lack of control" of CIB3, whose officers he said had "suppressed" evidence damaging to the case. Jones added that CIB3 were under pressure to meet the commissioner's 250 target and in the prosecution of the five East Dulwich SERCS detectives he had never experienced so much pressure to secure a conviction.
4 Clark had his sentence reduced by two years to ten. Drury, who was not considered the prime mover, had his sentence reduced by two years to eight.
5 Security Express manager Paul Fullicks told us the total loss to his firm was £1,516,000 of which £18,500 was in unrecovered travellers cheques.
6 McGuinness also pleaded guilty to supplying a Milbrau imitation pistol for the first aid kit.
7 £941,111 is outstanding. On 27 February 1995 Jasvir Jhumat, Sudesh Kararia and Roy Ryan all pleaded guilty. Jhumat got five and a half years and the others four years. Kundan Uppal (the inside man), who fought the case, was sentenced to seven years.
8 Before he was caught, Garner had received £38,000 in a lump sum and £600 per month from his pension.
9 The HSE alleged they had failed to protect officers PC Kulwant Sidhu, who died, and PC Mark Berwick, who was seriously injured, when they fell through the roof in separate incidents while pursuing suspected burglars.

CHAPTER 20 THE FALL OF THE GINGER GIANT
1 Clarke response, 16 March 2000. Hain letter 17 April 2000.
2 Straw letter 20, March 2000. We have repeatedly asked the Yard to supply details of the "inaccuracies", but they refuse, claiming "legal and operational reasons".
3 The Hunt brothers – David, Raymond and Steven – had interests in scrap

NOTES

metal, cars, bars and a toy company in the North, according to an NCIS officer.

4 Around 1990, a well-financed operation codenamed Crocus was set up to target a number of East End villains involved in drugs and extortion rackets. DCI Norman McNamara oversaw the covert police budget. He says the origins of Operation Crocus go back to the still unsolved double murder in 1989 of Terence Gooderham and Maxine Arnold, found shot dead in their car in Epping Forest. Gooderham was a financial auditor in the clubs and pubs business. The Underworld grapevine whispered that the execution was connected to stolen drug money. Others claimed it concerned a pub protection racket. By 1991 the money ran out and Operation Crocus closed down to criticisms at division headquarters that it hadn't delivered. Supporters argued that the intelligence picture of criminality in the area was better developed. The following financial year the idea was revived under a new codename, Operation Fairway, which concentrated on the Sabini crime family. Their secretly recorded conversations were fed directly to DI Dave Woods' intelligence cell working from an old cadet centre at Wanstead. This intelligence cell was codenamed Operation Fantasy. The covert pub was codenamed Operation Frantic.

5 Interview with Raymond, 11 September 2002.

6 Interview with reporter Jo-Ann Goodwin, who interviewed Couzens for the article "Professor of Ecstasy" in the *Daily Mail*, 5 August 2000.

7 Raymond's phones in France were tapped. But according to a detective on Team 13, they had also raided the flat of a man signing on at a post office in Archway using his name. The man was found in bed with a young black boy. It was not Raymond, but among items seized were clues to his whereabouts. There was also a series of letters with homosexual overtones from a Lord.

8 The Ghost Squad had been monitoring Virciglio's efforts to corruptly nurture a police scientist and a detective from the Edmonton area. Gaspar was forced to arrest Peter Hare, the scientist, in November 1994 because a *Mirror* crime reporter had tipped him off that a private investigator working for CIB was trying to make some extra money by selling compromising videos of Hare to the newspaper. Local solicitor Les Brown, who was already representing Virciglio, took up Hare's case. The scientist was suspended from duty. Weeks later, Brown became a Ghost Squad target when Hector Harvey became its second supergrass.

9 Raymond says he and "good friend" Patrick Adams wanted to kill Wright after Adams got hold of a list of Yard informants from a corrupt CPS clerk, Mark Herbert. The Yard insisted during Herbert's trial that the list of 33 informants was intercepted before it reached the Adams crime family. But Raymond says it got there and Wright's name was on it. Unfortunately for Adams, Wright had already fled to extradition-free Northern Cyprus to avoid questioning over his role in a horse race fixing and betting scam involving high profile jockeys and trainers.

10 In his formal response to the leaking allegation Redgrave told Coles, "I am sure that Smith was the officer who took up the contract and succeeded in discrediting me."

11 Smythe statement, 3 October 2002.

UNTOUCHABLES

CHAPTER 21 THE BUTCHER, THE BAKER, THE UNDERTAKER AND HIS SON

1 Ramadan Guney fell out with Mohammed Al-Fayed over payment for the funeral of his son, Dodi, who died with Princess Diana in the Paris car crash in 1997. A woman called Diane Holiday claimed she had Dodi's love child and attempted to exploit the rivalry between Fayed and Tiny Rowland. Holiday had a past as a fraudster. She then befriended Ramadan Guney and eventually bore him a son. Egg's brother Onder says the relationship with Holiday is the reason why his father's political ambitions in Cyprus were thwarted.

2 The money was channelled through his offshore company to the Conservative Industrial Fund.

3 According to former DS Alec Leighton, who ran the operation against Arif, the cannabis came from Howard Marks, via Thailand and Australia, to Liverpool. From there it was driven by lorry to London. Dogan Arif maintained he had been fitted up. We have spoken to a drug squad detective who had concerns about the integrity of the prosecution and secretly passed information to the defence. He said there was no payment for his help. For his part, Leighton claimed Dogan planned to discredit him before the trial. "One scenario was to place drugs in [my] garage at home and a large sum of money in [my] bank account and then arrange for CIB to investigate."

4 Green claims that one of the MI5 officers on Centurion was removed after Customs intercepted heroin he was allegedly receiving through the post from one of his targets.

5 Two days before his son was arrested Ramadan had indeed bought a gun to take to Turkey – he says it was for the police. A Turkish Cypriot dry cleaner who had once owned a gun shop had recommended where to go. The gun was sent legally by the shop direct to the airport to be handed over to the captain of the plane, explained Ramadan.

6 BBC *Panorama* had secretly recorded Donald agreeing to help a major drug trafficker called Kevin Cressey, an associate of the Arifs, escape prosecution in return for £30,000. The BBC gave CIB its covert tapes in which Donald named at least ten officers. Some of these were on the drugs wing of the Surbiton office of SERCS, while others were working at NCIS. CIB arrested and suspended Donald, his boss at Surbiton, detective sergeant Alec Leighton, and detective sergeant Tom Bradley at NCIS. But in late 1995, during Donald's trial, he completely took the Yard by surprise when his lawyers produced in court the highly sensitive logbooks from the line room at NCIS – this is the secret phone-tapping section that provides transcripts of target criminals' conversations. The Yard called in the then chief constable of Northumbria, John Stevens, to conduct an inquiry into the security breach at NCIS. Leighton told us CIB always suspected the logbooks came from him. "I will always deny that," he said. But he admits knowing how Donald got them. He says someone in the Surbiton office, whom he refused to identify, knew he had stored the logbooks there and took them at Donald's request. Donald changed his plea to guilty during his trial. He was jailed on 28 June 1996 for 11 years.

7 Leighton was still suspended when the Donald and Guney trials were progressing in 1996. He had made a lengthy complaint against CIB officers conducting Operation Gallery, including its head, assistant chief constable Ian Blair, then of Thames Valley Police. The complaint – that CIB had leant on witnesses to give false evidence – was investigated internally and regarded by

NOTES

the Yard as an attempt to disrupt the prosecution of Donald. Statements, however, had to be taken from former colleagues of Leighton who had worked with him at SERCS. Two had gone on to work at NCIS on Operation Centurion. Detective inspector Mick Conner had been the liaison with MI5 and MI6 on the Turkish investigation. He left NCIS during the Gallery probe and transferred to Belgravia police station. Arthur Gilchrist, a customs officer, was the deputy at NCIS in charge of Operation Centurion. There is no suggestion either officer acted corruptly. Leighton's complaint was dismissed by CIB, although there was some corroboration. Conner made a statement claiming CIB effectively asked him to give perjured evidence about the whereabouts of a police car to corroborate Cressey. The statement was never used because Leighton wasn't charged. Instead he faced minor discipline for disobeying an order and had his wages docked. Leighton believes Cressey went to the BBC to set up Donald in the hope of ruining the prosecution against him for possessing 50 kilos of cannabis and to "dirty" Leighton on behalf of his associates, the Arifs. Leighton and detective constable Jim Tucker were part of the team that arrested Dogan Arif in 1989. The two officers' evidence was instrumental in his conviction. Tucker was working for NCIS when Leighton was suspended in 1993 over the Donald matter. He left the Met and is now a barrister. Leighton is a successful private investigator.
8 Stuart Sampson and Peter Moorhouse respectively.
9 This was the reason for giving Johnson "words of advice" after the trial. It didn't affect his career as he is now serving in a sensitive post.
10 Up until then, the Federation-funded lawyers, Russell Jones & Walker, had won 95 cases in the last 3 years, earning litigious cops a little over £1.5 million and themselves a lot more in fees.
11 Detectives Pat Melody and Kevin Harrison.

CHAPTER 22 SECRET JUSTICE
1 Sawnhney pleaded guilty to three counts of conspiracy to pervert the course of justice. He got five years in January 2001.
2 Carpenter had participated in the operation against corrupt ex-cops Martin King and Duncan Hanrahan. After a lengthy period of suspension, Carpenter, who denied the bribery allegations, was charged and committed for trial. But the crown withdrew the case against him, whilst still maintaining at court that he was "corrupt". A police spokesman explained: "Despite a rigorous three-year investigation the allegations have not been proved. Advice was sought from Treasury Counsel and the CPS, who advised there was insufficient evidence to warrant criminal proceedings. During the course of the investigation a number of potential disciplinary offences were disclosed. The officer involved resigned from the MPS in August 2002, and had recorded against him findings of guilt for procedural breaches of police regulations."
3 Other sentences were Patel (eighteen months); Tony Anthonakis, the courier in the corruption conspiracy (nine months); brothers Andy and Chris Nicolas (six and five years respectively); Michael Yiannakis, the accountant (seven years three months). Jimmy Karagozlu, the Nicolas brothers, Yiannakis and Attila Kansaran are at the time of writing fighting a £2.5 million confiscation order by Customs for the VAT fraud.
4 Two National Crime Squad detectives, Keith Clazie and Gary Wapplington, "fell into" the surveillance operation. They were on an operation in Scotland.

UNTOUCHABLES

Clazie, Morgan's friend, was reduced in rank following disciplinary proceedings over expenses and overtime claims. No further action was taken against Wapplington, said CIB3 detective Dave Pennant.

5 He pleaded to laundering £106,000 believed to belong to Kean. At Reading Crown Court on 11 September 2000 Sansom received 20 months. He was later kicked out of the supergrass system for not being totally truthful. CIB3 charged him with further money laundering, drugs and fraud offences.

6 Colourful Dublin gangster, Martin Cahill, aka the General, had thieved the paintings in 1986. The recovery of some of them involved a fall-out between the IRA and Protestant gangs, which may have also led to Cahill's murder in 1994.

7 Stephen Jory, 52, was serving eight years for a £50 million counterfeit operation of fake £10 and £20 notes after his arrest in 1998.

8 In 2004, Kean and Morgan had their sentences reduced to six years. The Appeal Court agreed they were "excessive" compared to other police corruption cases.

9 The charge of conspiracy to pervert the course of justice was left on file – until the disciplinary process concluded – which meant it could be resurrected in the event of fresh evidence. At the time of writing Paul Goscomb is still awaiting a disciplinary hearing.

10 Operation Jackpot had a statement from corrupt officer Roy Lewandowski alleging Le Blond had told him he was going to approach Morgan on behalf of a Greek Cypriot informant to help plant a shotgun on local black DJ Benny Wilson.

11 This was part of the covert inquiry into detective John Redgrave. He says he documented his friendship with Nico as a police officer to avoid compromise. Operation Cornwall, the CIB3 inquiry led by John Coles, interviewed Nico about his relationship with Redgrave and Morgan. Nico is believed to have listed all the police officers, including senior ones at Scotland Yard, he has had contact with over the years.

12 "He introduced me to Jimmy," recalls Kelly. Karagozlu also gave information on his competitors in the drugs trade, but Kelly says they couldn't get into his own organisation because they had "no leverage".

13 David Atkinson, Fred Davy, Jo Gunning, Steve Levy and Arthur Redbourne were arrested in June 1996 with 155 kilos of cannabis. The SERCS operation was codenamed Bank. According to Kelly, the man behind the parcel was hit man and police informer Kenneth Kenny, 55, aka Kenneth Beagle. He was in prison at the time. Kenny was shot dead in Romford on 1 November 2000.

14 R v Chic Matthews, Joey Pykett & Tommy Hole (27 November 1996, Court of Appeal); R v David Atkinson, Fred Davy, Jo Gunning, Steve Levy & Arthur Redbourne (3 June 1997, Snaresbrook Crown Court); R v Des Copeland & Roger and Benjamin Minall (27 June 1997, Lewes Crown Court); R v Daniel Downs & James Wooley (28 October 1997, Chelmsford Crown Court).

15 DC Geoff Curd.

16 Kelly went sick in June 1998 with a bad back and depression. He was disciplined for "a lack of supervision" of the surveillance logs in Operation Bank. DAC Townsend told him in November 1999 that after examining his involvement on Operations Nightshade and Bank and the Chic Matthews affair he had lost confidence in his integrity. Kelly took medical retirement.

17 McNamara was well connected with a senior figure in the Ghost Squad management, Bill Griffiths, who in turn was close friends with Roy Clark. McNamara and Griffiths along with other senior officers started the Malt

NOTES

Whisky Club at the Yard. Every month they'd meet to consume a bottle of scotch. Another member was commander Nial Mulvihill, the man who took over from Roy Clark at Stoke Newington. McNamara suffered a mental breakdown because it was never specified to him what those doubts were, although he subsequently heard informally that it concerned his perceived closeness to certain CIB targets in the Flying Squad and SERCS. He was medically retired in September 1998. Today he says he cannot recollect the conversation with Green about the alleged approach from Morgan and Gillan, but doesn't discount that it happened.

18 Robert Dellegrotti.

CHAPTER 23 A LURKING DOUBT

1 Court of Appeal ruling, 28 February 2002 R v Howell, May and Harris paragraphs 168–170.
2 Interestingly, in 2001 Scotland Yard's top fingerprint scientist used in the Lockerbie case, Allan Bayle, resigned in order to testify in the appeal case of businessman Alan McNamara because the police wouldn't let him give evidence against another force (Greater Manchester Police). He was quoted in the *Daily Telegraph* (26 August 2001) saying, "I realise there has been a slow degradation of standards within the force, and now men are being put into prison on less convincing forensic evidence."
3 The trial concluded on 23 March 1990. Ira Thomas was cleared of the first charge of attempted murder.
4 The case of Anson King, acquitted at Snaresbrook Crown Court on 22 November 1991. King's defence was that the crack cocaine had been planted on him. He made a complaint after his acquittal. McCulloch was one of the arresting officers. On 3 November 1994 HCDA announced King had been paid £70,000 by the Yard with no admission of liability. McCulloch was also involved in the case of Cyrus Baptiste, whose conviction was overturned by the Appeal Court on 25 May 1993. The prosecution said had they known about the King case and another (Thompson) they would not have proceeded in November 1991 with the prosecution. Operation Jackpot did not lead to any criminal proceedings against McCulloch. He was promoted to detective constable during the corruption probe.
5 R v Thomas, 13 February 1992 before Lord Justice Watkins and Justices Swinton Thomas and Garland.
6 Statement of Lee Pritchard, 23 March 1993.
7 One month after the Dando murder, home secretary Jack Straw rejected Fayed's passport application on the grounds he had made "improper and unethical" cash-for-questions payments to Tory MPs and because of his failure to report the deposit box break-ins to the police.
8 DC Robert McKenzie was required to resign on 12 February 2002, just before Barry George's appeal. McKenzie appealed to commissioner Stevens and was reinstated the following month with a fine of 13 days' pay. Another embarrassment was the affair between a key witness in the Dando trial, Charlotte de Rosnay, and DC Peter Bartlett. He was moved to another murder squad at Barnes, south-west London. De Rosnay then made allegations against Bartlett of harassment. He was charged but the CPS discontinued criminal proceedings on 18 February 2002.
9 Interview with Keeley, 8 November 2001.

UNTOUCHABLES

CHAPTER 24 W.O.G.S.
1 *Evening Standard*, 19 September 2002. *The Job*, 27 September 2002. We asked Moore to provide details of his arrest, just to ensure it wasn't one of those publicity stunts so favoured by the Yard's spin doctors. He declined.
2 When he was exposed in September 1988, Golder was working on an east London murder squad investigating a suspected Yardie-related killing in Stoke Newington. When he was acquitted of 13 corruption charges in December 1991 he told the press: "I was only pretending to be a bent copper to get information. I never took a penny off the lady."
3 Also in the photo is DS Jim Gillan.
4 DS John Bull's police car was bugged. He told us he was served a disciplinary notice concerning the incident on 17 October 1997.

CHAPTER 25 ... AND THE BEATING GOES ON AND ON
1 Germany defeated the Czech Republic 2–1.
2 MPA Minutes, 17 December 2001.
3 All three were found guilty in April 2003 of neglect of duty.
4 Scotland Yard Press release, 6 July 2002.
5 *The Independent*, "Met wasting millions with 'shambolic' cash control", 13 April 2001.
6 Stafford Solomon was awarded £45,000. His companion, Brian Douglas, was the first man to die after being hit with a long-handled police baton in 1995. The MPA was not told of the settlement, Lord Harris admitted to *The Independent*.
7 In April 2003 the Met agreed to pay 90% of the Wilsons' legal costs.

CHAPTER 26 IN-HOUSE
1 Employment Tribunal decision, 23 August 2000.
2 Michael Turner article, *Computers and Law*, February–March 2001.
3 DC Sarah Locker is an East End girl born to Turkish Cypriot parents. She joined the Met straight from school in 1980. Eleven years later she brought a racial and sexual discrimination case. Her problems occurred in the late eighties when she worked under John Grieve on the 2 Area Drug Squad. She was one of only two female detectives out of seventeen officers. She was the butt of sexually explicit and personally demeaning jokes. Her main persecutor was undercover cop DC Micky Barr, later involved in Operation Nightshade, and a friend of Grieve's. The Yard settled the claim in 1993 and paid Locker £32,000 plus legal costs. Barr gave a written apology and John Grieve publicly apologised at a special press conference, sealing his sincerity with an unwanted kiss. An agreement was drawn up for her return to work at SO11, run by Grieve and Roy Clark while they secretly oversaw the Ghost Squad. But the new job was a sham and the agreement was breached in other important respects. The pressure led to a breakdown. When she recovered, Locker sued in 1997, this time for breach of contract. The Yard eventually settled in June 2000 rather than submit Grieve and Clark plus others to potentially damaging public cross-examination. Locker left the force on an ill-health pension with a £215,000 payment. She still sees a psychiatrist and has genuine concerns about reprisals from the Yard.
4 Old Bailey, 25 February 2003.
5 Four of the other five were later named in court as Govarni Hussein (Bach),

NOTES

Jimmy Sanchez (Brahms), Irage Kiani (Elgar), Samual Salmassian (Verdi). The fifth man was not identified. The advance fee fraud was apparently under investigation by the Fraud Squad and Dutch police.

6 CIB sources say Iran has now released Mr Darougheh, who was working for MI6.
7 Under Norman were DCIs Buttivant and Jill McTigue and DI Mark Holmes. In CIBIC were DS Tim White and DI Stephen Wilkinson.
8 Law lecturer Ben Bowling, management consultant Andrea Cork, chair of the Lambeth community police consultative group, Jennifer Douglas and Kirpal Sahota, a consultant forensic psychiatrist.
9 Judge Hyam listed the intelligence areas that existed: cocaine; steroids; threats to an ex-girlfriend; concerns of connections to the Iranian Secret Service; assisting two sisters to remain in the UK for payment; £500 for assisting a woman's visa application; assisting people suspected of an advance fee fraud; assisting an Iranian who had once tried to deposit £2m in an account; interfering with police investigations into people Dizaei knew; receiving £800 from a man on bail for advice on a drink-drive charge; receiving 7 tickets for a concert he was responsible for policing.
10 Disciplinary report on DC Pudney, 14 October 1999.
11 Letter from Polaine to DI Paul Greenwood, 21 February 2002.
12 Dellegrotti statement, 11 June 2002.
13 *Daily Mirror*, 12 April 2003.
14 Letter to Martin Polaine, CPS, 5 August 2002.
15 Only 2.9% (3,915) of the total number of officers (136,386) are from ethnic minorities.
16 Chief inspector Logan's employment tribunal case went to conciliation. He later reportedly received £100,000. The Untouchables had investigated him for seven months over allegations he falsely claimed from the BPA a £80 hotel bill. The BPA hadn't complained. It was the Untouchables who brought the case after seizing BPA files as part of the Dizaei investigation. The case of WPC Joy Hendricks was also settled.

CHAPTER 27 "WE ARE SUBJECTS NOT CITIZENS"

1 *Mail on Sunday*, 1 June 1997 and 25 August 1997.
2 Smith letter to Straw, 5 June 1997.
3 Intelligence report, 5 August 1999.
4 Hampshire Police investigated Pedder's complaint to the PCA. There were 12 corruption and negligence allegations against CIB superintendent Ian Russell and inspectors Perry Spivey and Jeff Hayes, the director of intelligence, Alan Fry, and chief inspector Brian Battye of the Flying Squad. After almost three years, by which most of those complained of had retired, the PCA didn't uphold the complaint. Pedder says major evidence was ignored.
5 Intelligence reports, 2 and 11 February 1999.
6 Bhatt attendance note, 15 July 1999.
7 Clark letter to Alastair Morgan, 6 June 2000.
8 We have also established that the Yard lost a female witness who came forward after a 1987 *Crimewatch* saying she overheard two men in a pub planning a murder.
9 Hanrahan named to us a member of CIBIC who he claims was feeding information back to the targets around the Morgan case.

CHAPTER 28 WATCHDOGGED
1 Her Majesty's Inspectorate of Constabulary Report, June 1999.
2 Two of them were Martin Bridger and Chris Mahaffey. It was rumoured that disgruntled Flying Squad officers had tipped off their colleagues in the RUC of what to expect from the Untouchables. One Met detective claimed the RUC had sent a surveillance team to London to gather dirt on the Untouchables for later use.
3 Denham letter to Maude, 26 February 2003.

INDEX

Abbott, Diane, MP 180, 183–4, 188
Abbott, John 266
Abercrombie, Neil 525
ACPO 56, 186, 260, 266, 268, 355, 483–4, 506, 509, 525–6
Adams, Ray 78, 112–13, 116–18, 120, 122–5, 277–8, 302–6, 317, 519, 528
Adams crime family 76–8, 87, 173–4, 199, 202, 229–30, 237, 292, 368, 402, 419, 464, 528, 531
Al-Fayed, Mohammed 428, 532, 535
Angel, Jimmy 285, 297, 528
Anglin, Delroy 465
Apostolopoulos, Athanasis 401
Arif crime family 77, 79–80, 88, 128, 145, 197, 229, 288, 296, 389, 521–2, 528, 532–3
Arneil, Vincent 282
Ashdown, Paddy 275, 526
Atkins, Peter 91–8, 116, 290

Bailey, Dave 219–20, 222, 234–9, 241–2, 245, 253, 285, 299
Baker, Andre 471, 477
Baker, Maureen 298
Baldwin, Tom 310, 311, 316, 318
Barker, Brian, QC 372, 374, 376, 378
Barker, John 162, 163
Barker Review 162, 163, 187, 250, 262, 264, 271, 302, 313
Barkingside Police 178, 362
Barr, Micky 206, 207, 216, 522, 528, 536
Bassam, Lord 41, 515
Bate, David, QC 292, 293

Battye, Brian 537
Bazzoni, Stephen 408
Beer, Tim 133, 143, 144, 146
Bell, James 446, 452, 514
Benbow, Mark 473
Bennett, Paul 338
Berger, Bob 462
Berwick, Mark 530
Bhatt, Raju 186, 492, 537
Bird, Samantha 446, 471, 474
Blacketer, Peter 309, 529
Blair, Sir Ian 45, 189, 378, 379, 441, 449–50, 452, 454, 466, 481, 482, 514
Blair, Tony, MP 56, 311, 528
Blake, Laurel 225–6, 227, 228, 232, 244, 245, 529
Blanford, Diane 478
Bleksley, Peter 132, 133, 134, 135, 140–2, 144–6
Bluebell Hill robbery 77, 79, 80
Blunkett, David, MP 17, 45, 435, 481, 483
Boateng, Paul 162, 311
Border, Ron 515
Bott, Deborah 474
Bottomley, Peter, MP 162, 462, 467
Bowling, Ben 537
Bown, Bob 280, 281, 282, 283, 526
Boyce, Brian 77–82, 86 87, 89, 91, 93–4, 110, 118, 286, 287, 289, 290, 517
BPA 435, 462, 466–7, 481, 482, 483, 511, 537
Bradley, Tom 532
Brennan, Denise 196–7, 210, 213, 215, 221, 287, 289, 291, 373, 376, 527

Brennan, Geoffrey 193–234, 237, 251, 253, 284–96, 300–1, 303, 347, 357–8, 363, 370, 372–80, 467, 521, 528
Brennan, John 194–7, 288, 289, 521, 522
Brett, Freddy 417, 419, 421, 424, 426, 432
Bridger, Martin 265, 290, 321, 331, 339, 348, 538
Brightwell, Tony 83, 84, 197, 198
Brinklow, Sarah 338
Brinks Mat 51, 70, 71, 73, 74, 76–85, 86–98, 110, 111, 112, 114, 118, 122, 124, 128, 194 197, 198, 286, 287, 288, 289, 291, 296, 302, 304, 305, 368, 376, 386, 517, 522, 523
Brixton Robbery Squad 254, 290, 468
"Bromley" 471–2
Brooks, Duwayne 149, 153, 162
Brooks, Nigel 208
Brothers in Law 278
Brown, Bill 248
Brown, David 228–9
Brown, Harold 478
Brown, Ian 287, 288, 289, 290
Brown, Les 233, 234, 235, 244, 328, 329, 334–6, 337, 367, 420, 423, 427, 526, 531
de Brunner, Maxine 479–81
Buisson, Jackie 247, 249, 348, 353
Bull, John 92, 290, 343, 352, 527, 530, 536
Bunn, Fred 234
Bunyard, Roger 187
Burgess, Henry and Jean 111, 113, 114, 119, 120, 124

UNTOUCHABLES

Burgess, Jean 111, 113, 114, 119, 120, 124
Burnham, Andy, MP 45, 513
Burrell, Paul 478, 479, 480
Burstow, Paul, MP 480
Buttivant, Alan 537

Cahill, Debbie 296, 297, 298, 300, 301
CAIU 454
Cameron, Pearl 170, 171, 173, 175
Cammidge, Alan 338–40
Campbell, Alastair 108
Campbell, Douglas 108
Campbell, Hamish 428, 430, 447, 448
Capita 507
Carpenter, Paul 243, 401, 524, 533
Carroll, Gerry 70, 178, 179, 180, 516
Carroll, Mark 183
Carroll, Michael 353, 529
Carter, Chris 281, 282, 526–7
Cartwright, John 270, 285
CCRC 409–10, 530
Central Drug Squad 132, 133, 138
Charman, Michael 92, 112, 193–7, 199–205, 211, 214, 216, 217, 219–21, 223, 284–7, 289, 291–303, 359, 361, 372, 375, 377–9, 479
Cherry, Lisa 338–41, 530
Chiarini, Anne 421, 422, 424
Chitty, Terrence 183
Christian, Louise 168
Clark, Patrick 97, 197, 198
Clark, Robert 141, 142, 147, 306–8, 479, 528, 530
Clark, Roy 17, 33, 60–5, 68, 71, 72, 176–80, 183, 184, 188, 189, 219, 221, 222, 234, 248, 249, 251–6, 259–60, 265–6, 284–7, 289, 297, 320, 362, 370, 373–4, 399, 409, 414, 416, 421, 426–7, 439, 440, 441, 459–60, 462, 467, 469, 477, 486–93, 495, 501, 502, 507, 508, 510, 511–13, 516, 521, 534–5, 536, 537
Clarke, Alistair 135, 515
Clarke, Charles, MP 361
Clarke, Ken, MP 176, 182, 183
Clarke & Co. 526
Clazie, Keith 533
Clingham, Kevin 473
CO24 313, 316, 465, 466
Coles, Dave 157–9, 304, 476, 528
Coles, John 134, 137, 284, 285, 286, 290, 292, 293, 294, 297, 298, 300, 301, 303, 361, 372, 374, 377, 378, 511, 528, 531, 534
Condon, Lord Paul 28, 29, 55–7, 59, 60, 63–6, 68–70, 72, 80, 96, 160–4, 189, 210, 218, 250–1, 257–8, 260–4, 265, 302, 312–16, 321, 356, 456, 461, 465, 486, 501, 503
Connally, John 207, 522
Conner, Mick 533
Conway, Nicky 530
Cook, Dave 493, 495
Cook, Jimmy 282, 488, 493, 494
Cook, Robin, MP 276, 360, 528
Cook, Tom 304
Coomber, Chris 332, 529
Corbett, Phil 83, 86, 91–4, 116, 286, 287
Cork, Andrea 537
Costello, Declan 166, 179, 188, 403–5, 406, 413
Courtney, Dave 488, 493
Cousins, Simon 338, 509
Couzens, Geoff 366, 367, 531
Cox, Steve 524
CPS 52, 64, 186, 260, 294, 347, 436, 468, 481, 497, 510, 511, 514, 526, 527, 529, 530, 533
CRA 13, 257, 267–8
Crampton, Ian 135, 136, 138, 139, 140, 154, 155, 158, 163, 205, 317, 469, 519, 527
Crawford, Catherine 448
Cressey, Kevin 160, 520, 532, 533
Crimestoppers 272, 433
Crooks, Roger 206–9, 213, 215, 216, 295, 296, 359, 522, 523, 527
Cross, Dave 469–70, 475
Crush, Judge Harvey 343, 344
Cudworth, John 307
Cullen, Richard 457
Curd, Geoff 534
Curtis, Tony 92, 93
Customs and Excise 25, 172, 509, 524, 525, 532

Daly, Mark 440–1, 482
Dando, Jill 416, 428–30, 436, 447, 535
Darougheh, Mandy 463, 537
Das, Nathaniel 400, 402
Davidson, John 113, 308
Davies, Elmore 25, 26, 30–3, 40
Davies, Phillip 527
Day, James 367
DEA 199
Deighton, Jane 168
Dellegrotti, Robert 475–6, 535
Dellow, John 83
Demitriou, Andy 385, 388, 389, 400, 402
Denham, John, MP 462, 467, 513, 514, 538
Denktash, Rauf 387, 394
Dennison, Renwick 135–7, 147, 160
Denton, Delroy 239

Derbyshire, Sally 437
Dizaei, Ali 461–72, 478, 481–2, 483, 511, 537
Donald, John 71, 135, 159, 160, 187, 189, 253, 279, 290, 395–6, 520, 525, 526, 532, 533
Donavan, Steven 368, 371, 517
Douglas, Brian 536, 537
DPP 520
Driberg, Tom, MP 364–6
Drury, Chris 307, 309, 479, 528, 530
Duggal, Rohit 150
Dwyer, Kevin 233

Eady, Mr Justice 299
Edmonton Police Station 172
Edwards, Dave 420, 424, 432
Edwards, Jeff 268
Edwards, Maxine 397
Elcock, Peter 526
Elwen, Mr Justice 396–7
Evans, Anthony, QC 345
Evans, Colin 282, 427, 529

Farrant, Tommy 290
Farrer, David, QC 422, 423, 425
Fedorcio, Dick 379
Fillery, Sid 102–7, 273, 274, 278, 279, 486–95
Finucane, Pat 519
Fleckney, Evelyn 147, 306–8, 344, 347, 478, 528–9
Fleming, Gerald 242–3
Fleming, John 76, 83, 84, 194, 195, 198, 213, 287, 290, 517, 521, 523
Flood, Gary 474
Flying Squad 289, 290, 307, 323, 356, 358, 510, 523, 524, 538
see also Rigg Approach Flying Squad and Tower Bridge Flying Squad
Foot, Michael, MP 365
Fordham, John 51, 78, 80, 82, 83, 288
Foye, Danny 527
Francis, George 521
Frankel, Sidney 366
Fraser, David 229, 523
Fraser, Frank 93, 229, 517
French, Gary 156
Fry, Alan 530, 537
Fry, Mick 238, 329, 331
Fuller, Tony 36, 37, 45

Galbraith, Bruce 183
Garner, Kevin 246–9, 258, 260, 261–5, 268–70, 271–2, 320, 321, 324, 327–8, 329, 333, 335, 347–51, 353–7, 392, 410, 427, 502, 530
Garner, Roy 82, 83, 84
Gaspar, Roger 61–4, 68, 210–19, 222, 237, 245, 253, 266, 285,

540

INDEX

294, 296, 299, 370, 371, 373, 502, 523, 525, 531
George, Barry 416, 429–31, 535
Ghaffur, Tarique 437, 465
Gilchrist, Arthur 533
Gilchrist, Roger 527
Gillan, Jim 390, 395, 396–7, 399, 406, 408, 413–14, 535, 536
Gittings, Emma Blackburn 366
Gittings, John Blackburn 517
Glass, Tony, QC 330–1
Golder, Graham 438, 536
Goldsmith, James 109
Goodridge, Paul 103, 490–1
Goodwin, Jo-Ann 531
Goscomb, Paul 166, 183, 403–7, 534
Grant, Martin 291
Gray, Raymond 117–19, 123, 518
Grayston, Nigel 487, 526–7
Green, Eton 239–40, 524
Green, Keith 260, 261, 262, 269–70, 271, 272, 283, 352, 392–4, 395, 408, 409, 411, 413, 525, 532
Green, Mickey 402
Greene, Tim 384, 409, 410
Greenwood, Paul 537
Grieve, John 60, 61, 65, 68, 71, 72, 206, 228, 231, 234, 239–41, 251, 313, 314, 315, 332, 362, 422, 465, 497, 527, 536
Griffiths, Bill 61, 65, 147, 210, 219, 428, 471–2, 477, 485, 495, 535
Griffiths, Brian 86, 87
Grundy, Reg 525, 528
Guardian, The 16, 55, 257, 264, 301, 315, 397
Guerard, Len 526, 527
Guney, Erkin "Egg" 383–99, 408–11, 412, 414, 512, 532
Guney, Ramadan 387–8, 390, 391–2, 393–4, 395, 397, 399, 411, 532
Gunning, Jo 534
GX Impex 200, 202, 203, 214, 374, 522

Hacker-Hughes, Dr 354-55
Hackney Police Station 438
Hague, William, MP 434
Hain, Peter, MP 360, 531
Hamilton, David 432
Hamilton, Neil 109
Hampshire Police 490, 491, 492, 495, 496, 538
Hanrahan, Duncan 107, 108, 120, 276–83, 305, 352, 358, 369, 371, 485, 487, 494, 496, 497, 502, 526, 527, 533, 538
Hardwick, Nick 507, 508, 509, 512
Hare, Peter 531

Harper, Adrian 410, 411
Harris, Eamonn 233, 234, 239, 246, 249, 328, 329, 334, 347, 352, 353, 525–6, 535
Harris, Lord Toby 23, 24, 436, 448–9, 452–3, 467, 481
Harrison, Audley 185
Harrison, Kevin 533
Harrison, Ron 130
Hart, Christopher 183
Harvey, Hector 193, 224–49, 251, 253, 265, 281, 319–42, 347–8, 353, 357, 358, 509, 523,528, 531
Haslam, Derrick 109, 111, 113, 115, 117–24, 496, 518–19, 529
Hassan, Halil "Perry" 390–1, 394
Hassan, Tunay 168
Hayes, Brian 240, 248, 260, 284
Hayes, Jeff 538
Hayman, Andy 45, 301, 306, 338, 345, 359, 361, 378–9, 450, 463, 470, 474, 478–82, 493, 502, 508, 511, 516, 519, 520
Hazlebury 219
HCDA 167–9, 177, 180, 181, 184–6, 189, 520, 535
Hendricks, Joy 537
Henry, Dean 229, 230, 236
Hepburn, Gregory 228–33, 244, 245, 523, 524, 525
Herbert, Mark 531
Hester, Richard 28, 207, 208, 216, 522, 523
Hewitt, Commander 528
HMIC 525, 538
Hobbs, Clifford 524
Holman, Peter 28
Holmes, Alan "Taffy" 70, 109–25, 179, 273, 303, 304, 308, 495, 516
Holmes, Mark 537
Home Affairs select committee 35, 254, 256, 259, 399, 501, 505, 512, 513
Hooker, Kevin 524
Horam, John, MP 475
Horrocks, Ian 447–8
House, Steve 472–3, 475, 476–7, 479
Howard, Michael, MP 55, 66, 67, 96, 163, 172, 185, 249, 388, 434, 516
Howell, Dave 328, 329, 331, 334, 347, 525–6, 535
Howells, Malcolm 527
Hunt crime family 361, 362, 385, 530–1
Hutt, Steve 434, 440

IAG 459, 465
IDG 410, 493
Ilsley, Bill 154–6, 158, 161, 163, 205, 317, 527

Imbert, Peter 54, 55, 96, 114
Immigration Department 460, 509
Inland Revenue 509
INQUEST 169, 450
Intercell 385, 388, 389
IPCC 17, 414, 432, 441, 482, 483, 505–14
"Irish" Mick 248, 259, 261, 268, 271, 272, 327, 330
Ishmael, Jeannie 198
Ishmael, Micky 362, 365

Jackson, Mark 175–7, 181, 188, 511
James, Graham 41, 457, 460–1, 468, 516
James, Kim 488, 490, 493
James, Simon 488, 493
Jarratt, Chris 29, 30, 34, 44, 136, 138–9, 145, 147, 253–4, 258, 265, 268–9, 270, 271, 280, 281, 305, 324, 344, 348, 352, 353, 356, 399–402, 409, 468, 470–1, 472–4, 475–9, 483–4, 488, 489, 529
Jeffrey, Nick 151
Jennings, Andrew 83
Jeremy, David 397
Jhumat, Jasvir 354, 530
Johnson, Dave 386, 388–9, 396, 398
Johnston, Ian 61, 306, 461
Jones, Alan 108, 279
Jones, Alun, QC 530
Jones, Chris 26, 35, 38–9, 515
Jones, Phil 26, 30, 32, 37–40
Jones, Sylvia 107
Jones, Vernon "Butch" 200, 201–6, 215, 375
Jones, Wyn 388
Jory, Stephen 534

Kansaran, Attila 533
Karagozlu crime family 388–98, 400–3, 407, 411, 413, 534
Kararia, Sudesh 530
Kean, Bob 403–7
Keeley, Robin 425, 535
Keep, Shaun 414
Kelly, Jack 136
Kelly, Paul 147, 203, 213, 296, 407, 408
Kelly, Phil 372
Kennedy, Lord Justice 383, 411
Kenny, Kenneth 403, 534
Kent Police 55, 78, 258, 262, 270, 492
Khan, Imran 308, 497
Kiani, Irage, 537
King, Alex 367
King, Martin 90, 279, 281, 305, 372, 526, 533
Kingston, Tom 526, 528
Kiszko, Stefan 53–4
KPMG 506

541

Kray brothers 196, 247, 364
Kroll Associates 317
Kyriacou, Michael 171–5

Laidlaw, Jonathan, QC 354–5
Lake, Mark 325, 357, 379, 479–80, 295
Lander, Stephen 508
Lapite, Shiji 186
Latham, Richard, QC 298, 299, 374, 377
Law & Commercial 490, 494
Law Society, the 508
Lawes, Marcia 239–40
Lawrence family 149, 158, 161, 164, 250, 302, 433, 434, 520
Lawrence Inquiry, the 262, 265, 266, 283, 303–6, 308, 313, 361, 399, 428, 435, 440, 448, 456, 461, 471, 476, 485–8, 492, 493, 502, 503, 506, 508, 520, 528
Lawrence, Mick 439, 440
Lawrence, Stephen 15, 16, 35, 70, 71, 72, 148, 149–64, 187, 189, 254, 257, 258, 262, 312, 456, 467, 496, 494
Lawson, Peter 528
Lawyers' Liaison Group 181–2, 185
Le, Walter 206, 208, 295
Le Blond, Graham 171–5, 370, 534
Lee, Steven 281
Leighton, Alec 277–80, 135, 137, 159, 160, 349, 369, 487, 519, 526, 532–3
Lennon, Kevin 101, 105–7, 495, 518
Leppard, David 292
Lewandowski, Roy 170–4, 183, 186, 520, 534
Lewis, Darren 322, 529
Lewis, Ian 467–8
Liberty 446, 506, 509
Livesey, Richard, MP 486
Livingstone, Gordon 417, 419, 424, 427, 432, 529
Livingstone, Ken 435
Lloyd, Gary 74–5
Lloyd, John 76, 77, 79, 80, 105–8, 286, 288, 289, 291, 376, 522, 527
Lloyds 239, 522
Locker, Sarah 459, 471, 536–7
Loftus, Bob 429
Logan, Leroy 482, 537
Lundy, Tony 81–5, 91, 92, 94, 113, 516, 518
Lyons, Barry 183–4

Macdonald, Ken, QC 497
Mackinlay, Andrew, MP 359, 360, 361, 372, 512, 528
Maclean, Bill 410

Macpherson, Sir William 304, 312
McAleenan, Paul 472
McAvoy, Micky 76, 83, 88
McCormack, Chris 229, 230, 235, 236, 237, 242–3, 244, 319, 330, 515, 524, 528
McCreery, Thomas 135–7, 519
McCullagh, Mike 527
McCulloch, Peter 184, 420, 424, 432
McCunn, Bob 198, 522
McGuiness, Terry 259–60, 261–3, 264, 269–70, 320, 325–8, 335, 347–52, 357, 392, 412, 416–17, 419–20, 422, 427, 432, 502, 525, 529
McKenzie, David 528
McKenzie, Robert 536
McLagan, Graeme 267, 379
McNamara, Norman 245–6, 248, 254, 363, 409, 531, 534–5
McTigue, Jill 537
McVicar, John 428
Mahaffey, Chris 538
Mahmood, Mazher 274
Mail on Sunday 129, 278, 433, 435–7
Major, John 54, 55, 56, 66, 172, 187, 406
Mandela, Nelson 161
Mann, Simon 527
Mansfield, Michael, QC 154, 159, 163, 252, 302, 304, 305, 430–1, 462, 466, 467, 506
Mark, Sir Robert 75, 90, 260, 503
Marks, Howard 532
Marshall, Peter 457–8
Marunchak, Alex 113, 273, 278
Mates, Michael, MP 387–8
Maude, Francis, MP 513, 538
Maul, Kevin 205, 209, 210, 219, 220, 295, 378
May, Fred 328–9, 331, 334, 347, 526, 535
May, Jeff 478–81
Maybanks, Adrian 474
Mee, Michael 523
Mellins, Peter 286, 289, 527
Mellish, Lord 88
Melody, Pat 533
Mendy, Ambrose 173, 174
Merseyside Police 24, 30, 37, 515
MI5 67, 68, 114, 275, 317, 378, 508, 510, 525, 532, 533
MI6 67, 317, 525, 533
Michael, Michael 401–2, 524
Miller, Russell 169, 181, 186, 188, 263–4, 491
Miller, Sam 321
Mills, Barbara 520
Minton, Julia 473
Monerville, Trevor 165–8
Moore, Brian 36–7, 45, 265, 324, 332, 334, 336, 339, 416–17,
419–22, 424–5, 426–30, 432, 436–40, 473
Moore, John 427, 432
Moore, Peter 365
Moorhouse, Peter 270–1, 533
Moralee, Alan 285, 292, 293, 528
Morgan, Alastair 100–5, 278, 485, 486, 490–7, 512, 537
Morgan, Daniel 70–1, 99–109, 125, 273, 276, 279, 283, 486, 488, 489, 490, 491, 493–6, 512
Morgan, Dave 527
Morgan, Lorraine 299
Morgan, Martin 370, 395, 403–7, 408–11, 413, 414, 421, 430, 432
Morland, Mr Justice 447–8
Morris, Bill 511, 514
Mott, Spencer 285, 297, 528
Mounter, Julian 74
MPA 318, 436, 437, 448–9, 452–3, 459, 467, 514, 515, 536
Mullin, Chris, MP 256–7, 259, 262–3, 264
Mulvihill, Nial 183, 535
Murphy, Tony 431
Murray, Martin 470

Nadir, Asil 384, 387–8, 391, 392, 393, 398
Nahome, Solly 464
Nash, Barry 281–2, 494
National Front, the 455–456
NCIS 160, 187, 203, 249, 265, 266, 267, 314, 317, 318, 391, 392–4, 396, 466, 517, 525, 532–3
Nelson, Brian 519
New Labour 56, 71
Newell, Jeremy 233, 234, 325
Newman, Peter 204
News of the World 273–6, 278, 321
Newstead, Mick 529
Niccol, Dave 241–6, 249, 332, 524, 525
Nickell, Rachel 489
"Nico" 391, 394, 395, 407
Nicolas, Andy and Chris 533
Norman, Barry 146, 463–4, 465, 467, 481, 482, 537
Norris, Clifford 156–9, 304–6, 476, 528
Norris, David 70–1, 127–48, 150, 152, 154, 155, 156, 158, 159, 187, 205, 235, 254, 302–4, 306, 307, 309, 469, 489, 515, 519–20, 528
Norris, Debbie 129, 138–40, 143, 147, 202, 204, 205, 523
Norris, Tim 227, 231, 232, 233, 234, 235, 239, 244, 328–9, 330–1, 334–6, 337, 525–6
North, Peter 30, 34, 515

INDEX

Northamptonshire Police 451–2
Norton, Mark 138–40, 202, 204, 205, 375, 522, 523
Nott, Sir John 319
Nottinghamshire Police 461
Noye, Kenny 51, 71, 76–80, 86, 87, 89, 112–13, 116, 118, 123, 124, 132, 159, 160, 195, 198, 286, 290, 291, 304, 375, 396, 517, 522

O'Connell, Terry 344, 358, 528
O'Connor, John 317
O'Loan, Nuala 508
O'Mahoney, Maurice 95–8, 290, 519, 527
O'Neill, Mike 238–9
Oatley, Michael 317
Oderinde, Ida 172, 173, 177, 178, 183
Onstead, Martin 368
Operation
  Abelard 493, 495
  Admiral 26
  Ambleside 297, 300
  Athena 316, 465
  Bank 534
  Beryk 386
  Bitten 462–3
  Bohemian 135
  Brunei 258–9, 268
  Cancer 171
  Carter 360
  Centurion 393, 395, 396, 532, 533
  Cornwall 284, 286, 294, 297, 300, 534
  Countryman 75–6, 81, 90, 366
  Crayfish 24–5
  Crocus 531
  Ethiopia 267, 321, 323, 334, 338, 427
  Fairway 531
  Fantasy 531
  Florida 31, 33, 35, 37, 515
  Frantic 531
  Gallery 160, 189, 533
  Greyhound 403, 407
  Helios 463–4, 465–6, 467, 468, 484
  Jackpot 61, 175–8, 181–9, 253, 255, 370, 386, 395, 396–7, 406, 411–12, 426, 427, 534, 535
  Mamba 400
  Masterpiece 249
  Mongoose 400
  Naples 367–8, 370–1
  Nectarine 343, 344, 352
  Nigeria 486–8, 492
  Nightshade 196, 199, 204, 205, 210, 213, 216, 221, 294, 295, 296, 359, 360, 369, 371, 373, 375, 377, 528, 534, 536

Oxborough 428
Russia 147, 307
Sienna 29, 30
Spy 235, 237, 239, 241, 246, 248, 258, 319, 331–2, 524
Trident 511
Trinity 237, 243
Two Bridges 488
Wrabness 216, 217, 218, 300
Wrecker 521
Zorba 160
Orde, Hugh 508
Osbourne, Colin "the Duke" 196, 521
Osland, David 162, 163

Paddick, Brian 433, 435–7, 470–1
Paddle, Chris 438
Padgett, Bill 201, 204, 205, 209, 215, 216, 295, 375
Padon, Billy 200, 294, 295
Palmer, John 76, 386, 398, 517
Palmer, Maggie 284
Palumbo, Ronnie 177, 184, 185, 521
Panorama 56–7, 71, 109, 160, 525, 532
Parry, Gordon 97, 517–18
Patel, Gunsul 400, 533
Patrick, Albert 227, 228
Pattinson, Terry 130, 402
PCA 17, 53, 177, 182, 185–7, 240, 258, 262, 263–4, 270, 271, 283, 285, 292, 297, 299, 300, 301, 303, 352, 436, 451–2, 464, 468, 472, 480, 482, 483, 490, 491, 492, 503, 505, 506, 508, 511, 514, 520, 526, 528, 537
Peach, Blair 169
Pearce, Roger 528
Pedder, Keith 145, 489, 537
Penfold, Peter 527
Pennant, Dave 271, 321, 322, 407, 524, 534
Penrose, Roy 65, 205, 206, 209, 266, 527
Perry, Brian 76, 87, 88, 91, 93, 97, 198, 517–18, 522
Phillips, James 292
Pitman, Richard 31
Polaine, Martin 252–3, 340, 346–7, 412, 453, 475, 510, 516, 530, 537
Police Federation 49, 260, 380, 510, 532, 533
Pollock, Steven 135–7
Powell, Ray 482, 511
Pownall, Orlando, QC 346, 406, 430, 530
Price, Richard 343
Price, Tony 169
Proctor, Jason 281, 282
Protheroe, Alan 83
Pryce, Robert 423
Pudney, Mark 468, 537

Putnam, Neil 146, 307–9, 344, 345, 358, 502, 528

Quick, Bob 463, 468, 494, 511
Quinn, Ian 61, 488

Raison, George 240–5, 249, 329, 330, 331–3, 348, 524–5, 529
Ramis, Harry 385, 388, 389
Ramm, Roy 28, 35, 386, 398, 515
Raymond, Stephen 363–72, 531
Redbourne, Arthur 534
Redford, Judy 510
Redgrave, John 88–92, 193, 195, 196, 201–4, 208, 209, 211, 213, 214, 216–21, 223, 284, 285, 286, 287, 289, 291–302, 359, 360, 361, 363, 367, 368, 369, 370, 372, 375, 377, 378, 379, 395, 460, 471, 525, 531, 534
Rees, Jonathan 101–3, 105–8, 273, 274, 278, 279, 282, 486–9, 490–4, 526
Reeves, Steve 475–6, 519
Reeves, Terry 136, 137, 141
Reilly crime family 230
Relton, Michael 76, 87–97, 112, 122, 195, 279, 290, 517
Rexstrew, Paul 90, 517
Reynolds, Tom 526, 528
Rigg Approach Flying Squad 234, 238–41, 245–6, 249, 253, 258, 264–5, 266, 268, 270, 323–4, 326, 333, 349, 353, 356, 357, 394, 416, 438, 427, 505, 524
Roberts, Steve 514
Rolfe, Linda 474, 477, 484
Rose, Peter 56, 456, 516
de Rosnay, Charlotte 535
Ross, John 90, 97, 98, 518
Ross, Michael 90, 91, 93, 94, 95, 98
Rowell, Andy 430
RUC 508, 538
Rusbridger, Alan 16, 301
Russell, Ian 61, 171–3, 177, 182, 185, 186, 189, 255, 377, 508, 525
Russell, Jones & Walker 37, 39, 40, 458, 506, 533
Ryan, Roy 530

Sabini crime family 361–3, 531
Sahota, Kirpal 537
Sampson, Stuart 182, 294, 523, 533
Sanchez, Jimmy 464
Sansom, Ashley 403–4, 406
Saunders, Ian 353, 524
Savage, Jean 77, 97, 198
Sawhney, Kalaish 400–1, 533
Sawyer, Shaun 338, 340, 355, 468, 473, 475, 503

543

UNTOUCHABLES

Scarman Inquiry, the 52, 153, 263, 505
Scott, Robin 176
Scott Inquiry, the 329
Seaton, Steve 287, 288, 291, 376
Security Express robberies 228, 230, 236, 238, 239, 240, 242–3, 246, 247, 258, 265, 270, 347, 529, 530
Sedgemore, Brian, MP 179, 180, 183
Seed, Geoff 25, 67, 267
Sentamu, Bishop John 303, 304, 312, 314–16, 472
SERCS 63, 130–4, 138, 140, 142, 147–8, 155, 156, 159, 160, 204, 205, 216, 249, 306, 308, 344, 362, 367, 369, 378, 395, 403, 406–8, 426, 475, 478, 479, 526, 530, 532, 533, 534
Serious Fraud Office 387
Serpico 115, 117, 144
Service Confidence Policy 413, 475, 505
Shakes, Abraham 350
Sharples, James 25, 32, 38, 515
Shave, Alan 457
Shayler, David 317, 529
Short, Martin 292, 516
Sidhu, Kulwant 530
Sierra Leone 197, 206, 208, 216, 359, 527, 528
Simms, Joey 228–32, 235, 239, 240, 244–5, 247, 320, 324, 330, 525, 529
Simon, John 310
Simpson, Chris 130–2, 139–40, 309
Simpson, Vyv 83
Skully, Bob 386, 388–9, 390, 396, 398
Skully, Will 517
Smalls, Derek 212
Smith, Chris, MP 71, 84, 485, 537
Smith, Chris 195, 203–4, 210–11, 218–19, 221–3, 285–301, 374, 377, 522, 527, 531
Smith, Graham 167–8, 184, 186, 188
Smith, John 61, 172
Smith, Paul 231–4, 239, 328, 331, 526, 529
Southern Investigations 101, 109, 274–6, 282, 486–8, 490
Special Branch 114, 275, 463, 466, 514
Spivey, Perry 537
Sprouce, James 200, 295, 521
Staffordshire Police 472
Stern, Chester 129

Stevens, Sir John 13, 21–3, 36, 41, 44–5, 70, 146, 337, 356, 359, 379, 412, 435, 446, 449, 453, 456, 459–60, 472, 483, 488, 493, 502–3, 508, 514, 519, 525, 532, 535
Stewart, Janet 460
Stivrins, Yan 438–40
Stoke Newington Police 165–89, 415, 422, 426, 427, 431, 438, 440, 477, 492, 510–12, 521
Stone, Dr Richard 304
Straw, Jack, MP 23, 41, 256, 262–3, 276, 310, 317, 360, 434, 462, 467, 485, 526, 529, 530, 535, 537
Suckling, Bob 79, 80, 195, 286–9, 295
Sunday Telegraph 265, 267, 310, 316–18, 433
Sunday Times 292, 297
Sylvester, Roger 451, 536
Symonds, John 75

Tansey, Rock, QC 396–7
Tate, John 510
Taverner, Mike 247–9, 259, 261, 268, 271–2, 327, 330, 356
Taylor, Bill 478, 507–8
Taylor, Damilola 434, 471–2, 479
Taylor, Mike 178, 397
Thames Valley Police 532
Thatcher, Margaret 49, 50–5, 86, 87
This Week 257
Thomas, Ira 415–32, 437, 440, 512, 535
Thomas, Leslie 446
Thompson, Beverley 465
Thompson, Dave *353*
Times, The 74, 75, 310, 364
Timms, Stephen, MP 40, 515
Todd, Michael 441, 457, 464, 478, 511
Todner, Karen 39, 40, 515
Toombs, Barry 172, 525
Tower Bridge Flying Squad 136, 254, 265, 269, 475, 489
Townsend, John 408, 534
Townsend List 408, 413
Trollope, Anthony, QC 335, 372–7
Trotter, Andy 300, 301
Turner, Michael 458
Tweedie, June 105–8

Undercover 599 (Michael) 21–45, 265, 460, 469
Uppal, Kundan 530
Urquhart, Donald 246–7, 330

Vassell, Jacqueline 341
Veness, David 61, 131, 469

Vian, Glen 102, 104, 494
Virciglio, Ray 367, 370, 371, 531
Virdi, Gurpal and Sathat 455–63, 465–7, 471, 511

Wadham, John 509
Wagstaff, Thelma 116, 117, 119–123
Wang, Tom and Sam 200–4, 209, 211, 214, 219, 220, 284, 289, 374–5, 378, 380, 522
Wapplington, Gary 533
Ward, Gary 228–32, 235, 239–40, 244–5, 247, 320, 324, 330, 529
Ward, Steve 30–3, 37–40
Warne, Stuart 135, 136, 147, 160, 520
Warner, Steve 281, 282, 494
Warnes, Austin 488, 493
Warren, Curtis "Cocky" 24, 25, 30, 31, 33, 515
Waters, David 328, 329, 332
Watkins, Lord Justice 535
Watt, John 516
Webb, Chris 257
Wells, Stephen 311, 313–17
West, Graeme 247
West Midlands Serious Crime Squad 54, 176, 256
Whittaker, Ben 520
Wilkinson, Stephen 462, 537
Williams, Edward "Tall Ted" 194–9, 201, 203, 210–15, 284, 288–90, 374, 376–78, 521–2, 527
Williams, Nicola 414, 512
Wilson, Benny 173, 174, 534
Wilson, John and Susan 443–54, 471, 513, 536
Wilton, Peter 439
Wink, Sidney 516, 518
Winship, Peter 116, 122, 178, 179, 520
W.O.G.S. 433–41
Wood, Carl 404
Wood, David 29, 34, 304–6, 501, 508, 516, 253–54, 258, 268–9, 270–2, 280, 281, 468–9, 525
Woods, Dave 62, 251, 253, 254, 352, 362, 363, 531
Wright, Brian 368, 371, 531
Wright, Steve 456
Wright crime family 361
Wyatt, Oscar 207, 522
Wynter, Gilbert 173

Yates, John 307, 345, 346, 478–81, 508

Zinzan, David 493, 494